LIVINGSTONE

———◆———

TIM JEAL

D0062006

YALE UNIVERSITY PRESS
NEW HAVEN AND LONDON

This revised edition published 2013

First published in the United States as a Yale Nota Bene book in 2001.
Originally published by William Heinemann Ltd, 1973.
Published by Futura Publications 1975; Penguin Books 1985; Pimlico Press in 1993,
1994 and 1996.
Copyright © 1973, 1985 and 2013 by Tim Jeal.

For information about this and other Yale University Press publications,
please contact:
   U.S. office   sales.press@yale.edu
   Europe office   sales@yaleup.co.uk

Typeset in Adobe Caslon Pro by IDSUK (DataConnection) Ltd.
Printed in Great Britain by TJ International Ltd, Padstow, Cornwall

Library of Congress catalogue card number: 2001088764

Jeal, Tim.
   Livingstone / Tim Jeal.
     p. cm.
   Includes bibliographical references and index.
   ISBN 978-0-300-19100-4 (cloth: alk. paper)
1. Livingstone, David, 1813–1873. 2. Explorers—Great Britain—Biography. 3. Africa,
Sub-Saharan—Discovery and exploration. I. Title.
   DT1110.L58J43 2013
   916.70423—dc23

                                      2012042787

ISBN 978-0-300-19100-4 (pbk)

A catalogue record for this book is available from the British Library.

9 8 7 6 5 4 3 2 1

To the memory of my parents

Contents

Illustrations

Line Illustrations

Line illustrations nos 1, 2, and 3 are reproduced from D. Livingstone, *Missionary Travels and Researches in South Africa* (London, 1857); nos 4 and 7 from H.M. Stanley, *How I Found Livingstone* (London 1872); and nos 5, 6, 8 and 9 from H. Waller (ed.), *The Last Journals of David Livingstone in Central Africa* (London, 1874).

Maps

Plates

Preface

I am delighted that my publisher, Yale University Press, has decided to bring out a new and expanded edition of my life of David Livingstone to coincide with the bicentenary of the great missionary-explorer's birth. I wrote this biography in my mid to late twenties but it had had its origins ten years earlier when, aged eighteen, I hitched from Cairo to Cape Town during the nine months before going to Oxford University. My lifelong fascination with Africa's explorers sprang from this journey.

It is now forty years since my book was published in 1973, and it has never been out of print. Whatever its other merits may be, I think its longevity is mainly due to my having gained access to a wide variety of previously unpublished papers which enabled me to present a portrait of Livingstone strikingly different from the hagiographical depictions of my three biographical predecessors. Consequently, my account would remain unchallenged in its factual essentials by the biographers who published in the decades that followed. With this in mind, I certainly have no intention of amending the text except in some very specific areas.

In 2004, when I was researching my biography of Henry Morton Stanley, I gained admission to the hitherto closed Stanley family archive in the Royal Museum of Central Africa in Brussels and found material demonstrating to me that my brief summary of Stanley's life in my biography of Livingstone had been inaccurate and incomplete. I also saw that my account of the two men's relationship would have benefited if I had been able to see Stanley's original diaries back in the 1970s. I am now able to give a fuller and more intimate description of Livingstone in 1871–2, partly through Stanley's eyes.

Much earlier, in the 1980s, I had become aware that revealing material had been present in the proofs of Livingstone's late journals but had been omitted from the published work: *The Last Journals of David Livingstone in Central Africa*, 2 vols (1874), on which I had then relied. The American scholar Professor Dorothy Helly had first drawn scholarly attention to these omitted passages seven years after my *Livingstone*'s publication.

More recently, in 2011, Dr Adrian Wisnicki and his talented transatlantic team of scholars, imaging scientists and archivists produced a legible version of Livingstone's faded 1871 Field Diary, providing a clearer view than was available to me in the 1970s of Livingstone's life in the crucial year during which his Nile search received a decisive setback and in which he was 'found' by Stanley. Thanks to the documents highlighted by Helly and Wisnicki and to my own investigation of Livingstone's Unyanyembe diary for my book *Explorers of the Nile*, I have been able to add some new details about his relations with the Arab Swahili on his last journey and also about the violent behaviour of his African servants and porters at this time. I have also been able to address the recent claim that Livingstone's men may have participated as gunmen in the Nyangwe massacre.

While researching the final chapters of *Explorers of the Nile*, on the subject of the Nile explorers' legacy in Africa, I made discoveries, some of which contradicted arguments which I advanced in my biography of Livingstone in the chapter entitled 'Livingstone and the British Empire'. I have therefore amended this chapter, both adding new details, deleting others and I hope giving a clearer insight into the immense extent of Livingstone's posthumous influence on Africa's subsequent colonial history. But the new facts disclosed by me in 1973 had been quite sufficient to explode at that time the 'Livingstone myth' of earlier biographers, and within a few years had formed the basis for a new 'accepted' version of his life. This revised orthodoxy owed its existence to many ingredients in my book, including my contention that Livingstone (hitherto considered a great missionary) had failed in conventional missionary terms, making but a single convert, a chief, who subsequently lapsed; that the two missions that went to Africa, at his behest, ended in fiasco and heavy loss of life largely through his fault; that a series of geographical miscalculations destroyed his government-sponsored Zambesi expedition, and that another series of errors in basic mapping and calculating, on his last journey, made him suppose himself on the upper Nile when he was in fact on the upper Congo; that his wife became an alcoholic, after spending years alone, and that his eldest son distanced himself from his father to the extent of changing his surname.

But in the decade that followed my book's first publication, further claims were made which the facts did not support. I must mention the controversial claim made in the London *Sunday Telegraph* on 27 February 2000. In 1936, Thomas Fox Pitt—the British District Commissioner for the area of Zambia (then Northern Rhodesia) within which Livingstone had died sixty-three years earlier—was informed by the nephew of Chief Chitambo (in whose village Livingstone had died) that the explorer had during his last journey travelled with a half-African son, aged thirteen at the time of Livingstone's death. This would suggest that the 'son' had been conceived and born when Livingstone was leading the disastrous Zambesi Expedition, precisely the point at which he had had no privacy at all and was surrounded by numerous enemies, both expedition members (including his own brother Charles) and clerics attached to the Universities' Mission. Although these men alleged that Livingstone possessed almost every possible character defect, none ever suggested that he had been sexually involved with African women. And I myself found no evidence, anywhere in his papers, to suggest he ever was.

On Livingstone's last journey (1866–73), he set out from the coast with 46 Africans and 13 Indian sepoys, and although their number would drop briefly to 3, it would soon rise to 13, and for the last phase of his journey was stable at about 60. This would be the number with him at the time of his death. So it is a singular fact that not one of these men—not even the four who had first been engaged by him in the early 1860s—mentioned the 'son' either to any member of the relief expedition led by Lieutenant V.L. Cameron, R.N., when they met up en route to the coast, or to Captain W.F. Prideaux, the acting British Consul at Zanzibar, to whom the Africans delivered Livingstone's body when they reached Bagamoyo. Jacob Wainwright, the African follower chosen to accompany the coffin home aboard H.M.S. *Vulture*, had a reputation for indiscretion, so it is curious that no story about the boy was heard by the captain and crew of the *Vulture*. So what became of this 'son', and how could he have vanished so completely? And where had he been when Livingstone was with H.M. Stanley between November 1871 and March 1872? The absence of any convincing answers to these questions suggests that the stories had grown up over the years and had no foundation.

General probability militates against the boy's existence, as does the testimony given by Lupoko, the son of Chief Chitambo, to District Commissioner Fox Pitt in 1936. His claim was that Livingstone had entered the village the day before his death, riding a donkey, whereas according to his personal servants, Chuma and Susi, he had been carried in on a litter—which must be so since Livingstone had been too weak to write in his diary for four days. But the least likely statement made by Lupoko was that Livingstone's 'son' was himself carried on a litter. Even a cursory look at Livingstone's letters to his real sons makes it clear that none of them would ever have dared be carried in their father's presence, unless themselves too weak to walk. But Lupoko stated: 'He went in a *machila* (hammock/litter) because he was a chief's son, not because he was ill.'

Possibly, false rumours—which were spreading through the area north-east of Lake Nyassa during the early months of 1873, that Oswell

Livingstone was coming to relieve his father—may lie behind the tales of a mixed race son that would emerge six decades later.

A similar manifestation of the enduring newsworthiness of claims that 'saintly' Dr Livingstone had in fact had feet of clay appeared on 29 July 2010 in the *Daily Mail*. This was in a long article entitled 'The dark side of Dr Livingstone' in which it was asserted that a Livingstone letter, recently deciphered by Dr Wisnicki and his team, contained proof that: 'His [Livingstone's] Christian morals did not stop him sleeping with African women on a regular and prolific basis.' In fact, as Dr Wisnicki told me, the letter contained no hint of any such behaviour.

In 1996 I was invited by the National Portrait Gallery in London to contribute the introductory essay to the published catalogue of its exhibition, 'David Livingstone and the Victorian Experience of Africa'. This chance to revisit Livingstone's life served to confirm my earlier general view of him as a towering figure despite his flaws and misjudgements.

It had been apparent to me in 1973 that, despite his character defects and his failures, Livingstone remained a very great man whose overall achievement was unique—not simply because he was the first European to have made an authenticated crossing of the continent from coast to coast; nor even for the many geographical discoveries he made during thousands of miles of tramping with inadequate supplies and assistance. For, in addition, his contributions to ethnology, natural history, tropical medicine and linguistics were hugely influential, as were his roles as a crusader against the slave trade, and as a colonial theoretician and prophet. The events of the thirty years following his death would seem to bear out his claim that his journeys would one day open the way into Africa for others and change the continent's history.

Although the three full-length biographies written before mine—and published between Livingstone's death and the appearance of my life— were written from a religious standpoint and were almost entirely uncritical, I must emphasize that Livingstone had not, at that point, escaped all criticism. Sir Reginald Coupland's *Kirk on the Zambesi* (1928) and George Martelli's *Livingstone's River* (1970) had condemned his leadership of the Zambesi Expedition between 1858 and 1864. Again restricted to a single period of Livingstone's life, but again accurate and objective, were the analytical introductions to Professor Schapera's excellent editions of *Family Letters 1849–1856* (1959) and *Missionary Correspondence 1841–1856* (1961). But apart from a few brief but illuminating passages in H.A.C. Cairns's *Prelude to Imperialism* (1965), there had been no serious analysis of Livingstone's colonial thinking at the time I wrote my biography.

In the early 1970s, I would not have been able to attempt a thorough reappraisal of the man if I had not gained access to two large and vitally important manuscript collections (both previously unavailable to all but Livingstone's first and extremely circumspect biographer, Dr Blaikie). In 1963 Miss Diana Livingstone-Bruce (later Mrs Ray Harryhausen) presented eighty-five letters to the British Museum, and a few years later Livingstone's grandson, Dr Hubert Wilson, entrusted his large collection of letters and journals to the National Library of Scotland. The first collection contained many unguarded letters from Livingstone to his favourite child, Agnes (then a young woman), and enabled me to give a more detailed account of the later years than had hitherto been possible. The second collection—then owned by Livingstone's grandson Dr Hubert Wilson— was of broad assistance throughout my account of Livingstone's life.

Other major collections which had received little attention were those in the National Archives of Rhodesia (now Zimbabwe), and the Charles Livingstone Papers in the Livingstone Museum, Zambia. The first of these provided much of the material that enabled me to give a fuller account of Livingstone's colonial ambitions than had previously been attempted. The London Missionary Society Archives (now at S.O.A.S. in London) had been more exhaustively examined, but there was still much unpublished material to be found in the Moir, Helmore and Watt correspondence. The same applied to much of Livingstone's official government correspondence in the Public Record Office. Smaller and hitherto neglected collections were located in the Wellcome Institute Library, Mrs Harryhausen's private collection, and within a collection of letters in the possession of Mr A.B. Pyne. I was also most fortunate that an important journal of the crucial years 1861–3 had recently come to light at the Livingstone Memorial (now the David Livingstone Centre), Blantyre, Scotland.

My good fortune extended from manuscript sources to the field of published letters and journals. Professor Schapera's superbly edited volumes of family letters, mentioned above, were an immense help, as was his edition of the three volumes of Livingstone's journals written between 1851 and 1856. Another piece of luck was the then-recent publication of the journals of two members of the Zambesi Expedition and one member of the Universities' Mission.

I should like to show my appreciation of the late Dr Hubert Wilson's decision to allow me to quote from letters and other documents in his collection in the National Library of Scotland which had not been generally available to scholars at that time; I also wish to thank Mr W. Cunningham, then the Custodian of the Livingstone Memorial, Blantyre, for general assistance; the late Miss I. Fletcher of the London Missionary Society Archives for help with points of detail relating to Livingstone's missionary years; Mrs Harryhausen and Mr A.B. Pyne for granting me access to their private collections; Mr R. Dupuis for sharing his research into the transatlantic influence on Livingstone's early religious thought; the late Mr Quentin Keynes for showing me his collection of Livingstone letters and Africana; Mr G.L. Guy of Dullstroom, South Africa, for letting me read his unpublished articles on Mary and Robert Livingstone; Mr P. Emmerson of the National Archives of Zimbabwe for sending me microfilm of letters, and to Dr L. Holy of the Livingstone Museum, Zambia, for a similar kindness. I owe a great debt of gratitude to my brilliant original editor, the late Venetia Pollock, and to my editor at William Heinemann, the late Roland Gant, who ensured that the book reached a wide audience.

Finally, my thanks to Robert Baldock of Yale University Press for initiating this bicentenary edition.

Tim Jeal
London, July 2012

Note on Spelling

As a rule I have followed Livingstone's own spelling of African names. Only where clarity demands it, have I used modern spellings. I thought it right, when quoting direct, not to alter Livingstone's spelling of names; and since modern versions are very different, to avoid confusion I decided to use the same spellings in my text as in the quotations. To prove my point about these confusing differences, here is a list of some of Livingstone's spellings, followed by their modern equivalents:

Ajawa: Yao	Bechuana people: Ba Tswana
Bakhatla: BaKgatla	Makololo: Kololo
Bakwains: BaKwena	Mosilikatse: Mzilikazi
Bamangwato: BaNgwato	Sebitoane: Sebetwane
Bechuanaland: Botswana	Sichuana: Sechuana

With tribal names I have made one exception. Since Livingstone wrote Matebele and Matibele in almost equal proportion, I have used the more familiar spelling: Matabele. Today, Ndebele is the accepted spelling. With place-names, Livingstone's versions are usually immediately recognizable. There is little difference between Livingstone's Loanda and Luanda, and the same can be said of his Quilimane and the more usual Quelimane. Livingstone's Lake Bangweolo is very much like the more familiar Bangweulu. Two exceptions should be mentioned. Livingstone's Kebrabasa is the modern Cabora Bassa, and his Lake Moero is Lake Mweru. While I have stuck to Livingstone's Lake Nyassa, in line with my general policy, I have spelled Nyasaland with a single 's'. This is because Livingstone never wrote the word Nyasaland or Nyassaland; it was coined later and spelled from the beginning with a single 's'. It should perhaps be added that there is no overall consensus of agreement by many African scholars on the correct spellings of a wide range of names and places.

Livingstone spelled his own name without a final 'e' until the latter part of 1855. I have used the later form throughout the book. Livingstone was the usual spelling in Scotland, but Livingstone's father Neil had dropped the 'e' because, according to his daughter Janet, 'he thought his name long enough without it'.* For reasons best known to himself, he resumed it in the mid-1850s. Shortly after using the final 'e' in spelling his name on the title deeds of a new cottage in Hamilton, he wrote to his children asking them to revert to the old spelling.

* Note written by Janet Livingstone *c.* 1880 for Dr Blaikie, National Library of Scotland.

A Contradictory Hero

—————⋙•◆•⋘—————

On 18 April 1874 Dr Livingstone's body was buried in Westminster Abbey. The Prime Minister and the Prince of Wales attended, thick crowds lined Pall Mall and Whitehall, and many people wept, inside and outside the Abbey. The press agreed that there had been nothing like it since Lord Palmerston's funeral.

During his last wanderings in Africa no fewer than four search parties had been sent out in as many years, and the most expensive journalistic venture of all time had been instigated by the *New York Herald* when the proprietor sent Stanley to find him. Three years after their much publicized meeting, Livingstone's body, disguised as a bale of cloth, had been carried by his native followers from the heart of Africa to the coast: a journey of fifteen hundred miles which took over five months. This feat of devotion seemed the poignant but fitting finale to a saintly life. When Florence Nightingale called him 'the greatest man of his generation',[1] there would have been few discordant voices; to have questioned his greatness in 1874 would have seemed sheer perversity.

Yet today such excessive adulation and reverence are hard to understand, for Livingstone appears to have failed in all he most wished to achieve. He failed as a conventional missionary, making but one convert, who subsequently lapsed. He failed as the promoter of other men's missionary efforts (the two missions that went to Africa at his behest ended in fiasco and heavy loss of life). His first great journey across Africa from coast to coast was an outstanding achievement, but even this was partially marred by his discovery that Portuguese and Arab traders had already reached the centre of the continent. His subsequent return to the Zambesi, as the leader of a government-sponsored expedition, was disastrous. The abrupt ending of his optimistic dream that the Zambesi would prove a navigable river was not offset by the discovery of Lake Nyassa— a lake which, in all probability, had been reached by the Portuguese some years before. Other explorers, such as Burton, Speke and Baker, had travelled fewer miles but had made discoveries of equal importance. None of them enjoyed such fame or received such praise. Livingstone was considered by many to be the greatest geographer of his age, yet a series of miscalculations deceived him into believing that he had found the source of the Nile when he was in fact on the upper Congo. There were other failures too: failure as a husband and a father, failure to persuade the British Government to advance into Africa—yet, almost unbelievably, failures that did nothing to impair his influence, for Livingstone's ideas, both original and inherited, were to change the way Europeans viewed Africans and Africa itself.

His thinking would lead to a reassessment of the role of missions; his elevation of trade to the position of an equal and indispensable partner of the Gospel would prove the pattern for future advances. And within thirty years of his death these theories, coupled with his desire to undermine tribal institutions by introducing Western economics, and his ardent propagation of a new form of colonization, would have played a crucial part in precipitating the British Government into annexing vast areas of a previously ignored continent. By then the thoughts and actions of those who had gone to Africa, in direct response to his lead, would have altered the whole basis of Empire.

He was a failure in the aims he set himself, yet famous; successful only after his death through those who came after; a man remembered primarily as a missionary but completely neglected for his greater significance as a colonial theoretician and prophet. These are not the only contradictions that surround Livingstone. His thinking sprang from a bewildering range of paradoxical views: many of them contradictory, some naive, others prescient beyond his times.

Livingstone believed that the rising industrial society (which he knew at first hand through a childhood spent in the cotton mills) was pernicious and cruel, but he also maintained that it would bring great benefits to the African. He recognized that Scotland's cities were overcrowded and 'starved their inhabitants', so he begged his parents to emigrate; yet he thought this same industrialism would bring a golden age to the African. He considered that the inhabitants of workhouses enjoyed more numerous material benefits than did poor African chiefs. His glorification of trade, and his insistence that without commerce Christianity could make no headway, was in direct opposition to his feeling that individual traders were exploiting Africans scandalously. He felt that Africans were usually made worse by contact with Europeans, yet he wished to increase that contact. Unlike most of his contemporaries, he made considerable efforts to understand tribal customs and was annoyed by those who condemned polygamy as adultery and thought initiation rites a barbarous form of black magic; yet, while seeing many benefits in tribal life, he was also aware that no missionaries could make any progress till that life style had been disorganized and destroyed. Failing to convert even a few people, he advocated new methods to bring Christianity to whole tribes. His actions were often at variance with cherished personal beliefs.

Yet Livingstone's fame was due not so much to what he had done, or even to what he had been; the crucial factor was what he had come to represent. More than any of his contemporaries, he had become a myth in his own lifetime. It was not simply that he could be admired as exemplifying bravery, endurance, modesty and self-sacrifice—all the virtues Victorians wished to possess—or even that he had been a humanitarian and a Christian. It was more subtle. By praising him, the British public could feel pride without guilt, reconciling seemingly contradictory elements in a soothingly self-righteous combination of patriotism and Christianity, recalling for many the sense of moral superiority and national virtue experienced when Britain led the fight against slavery. The parallel was certainly there, since Livingstone had devoted the latter part of his life to the extermination of the East African slave trade. But, more than that, he had told his countrymen that they were the most philanthropic and freedom-loving in the world, and had emphasized this by saying that on them, above all others, was laid the sacred trust of bringing progress and liberty to the benighted.

Sources that had been made available in the decade before I wrote my biography showed Livingstone to have been far more extraordinary than any of the Victorian stereotypes of him. Just as it was in 1973, it is no less fascinating forty years later to look at Livingstone afresh, for now we can do so without either the fulsome praise lavished by his contemporaries or the self-denigrating collective guilt that marred so many examinations of colonial history during the decades that followed the end of Empire. The incorporation of Nyasaland, Uganda and Kenya into the British Empire owed much to Livingstone's posthumous influence. Now, with most of British Africa independent for sixty years, we can view that influence with greater detachment. British statesmen at the end of the nineteenth and the beginning of the twentieth centuries were convinced, regardless of the coercive force involved, that European colonial expansion in Africa was exclusively beneficial: a means of bringing peace, stability and progress. After the First World War the pendulum began to swing the other way. Nineteenth-century missionaries and traders in Africa were characterized as arrogant interferers wantonly enforcing alien and inappropriate values on innocent and ideal societies. Expansion was seen as exploitation and greed, thinly disguised as philanthropy. There were those who felt that if Africans had been left in peace they would have found their own way into the modern world with far less pain. Yet it is clear now that both approaches were inadequate. The motives were as mixed as the men themselves who went to Africa at the end of the nineteenth century.

Today we can acknowledge the full complexity of the situation, and, while granting that Livingstone and others like him were culturally arrogant and that the legacy of colonialism would not be benign, admit that Africa by the middle of the Victorian age had ceased to be an earthly paradise. By 1860 the slave trade and the search for ivory had already brought disintegration and death to the heart of the continent. The alien influence of the Portuguese and the Arabs had ended Africa's isolation long before Livingstone made his discoveries. By the time he died, an expanding gun frontier, and the willingness of many Africans to sell their own people into slavery, gave a strong basis to the case for European intervention on humanitarian grounds.

As with Africa, so too with Livingstone: there were many facets to his character. He was neither saint nor cultural wrecker, philanthropist nor advocate of trade. He was more than all these.

In this book I hope to resolve some of the contradictions inherent in this most strange and unusual of men, to explain how apparent failure was claimed as success, and to show, within the context of his time and against the background of nineteenth-century Africa, how his character and thinking altered as his personal circumstances changed and his knowledge of the African hinterland grew; to demonstrate how, even when he was forced into illogical action and contradictory aims, failure only reinforced his determination.

Ultimately, I hope to prove that Livingstone's direct influence on the next generation of nineteenth-century missionaries and politicians changed not only the way in which they viewed Africa and its peoples but also their vision of the Empire. Livingstone, with his missionary aims and his almost messianic passion for exporting British values and culture, seemed to his successors to have provided the moral basis for massive imperial expansion. The coupling of moral fervour with the right to power had been implicit in much of what he wrote and said. Twenty years after his death, his notion of Britain as a country with a unique mission was recognized, with many consequences that he had never envisaged.

PART ONE

ASPIRATION

Factory Boy
1813–1836

The harsh conditions which David Livingstone endured during his childhood wore down and destroyed all but a handful of those who experienced similar early hardships. Survivors won through by dint of a determination so forceful that it marked their characters for life. With Livingstone the legacy was to be a lasting sense of personal isolation and an inability to live with or tolerate less exceptional people.

Scotland, at the end of the eighteenth and the beginning of the nineteenth centuries, was going through a period of intense and drastic social change. At a time when landowners discovered that they could make more money from their estates by expelling their tenants and devoting the land to sheep-grazing, the dispossessed crofters poured in thousands into the already crowded and insanitary industrial cities. David Livingstone's grandfather, Neil, was one of these men. Formerly a tenant farmer on the small island of Ulva, off the west coast of Mull, he was evicted in 1792. Coming to Glasgow, he found work in a newly established cotton mill at Blantyre, eight miles south-east of the city. He was lucky; for the many thousands who did not find work, starvation or emigration were the only other choices.

Livingstone's father, also called Neil, was four when the family came to Blantyre. One of five sons in a poor family, he was put to work in the mills as a child, but his father, after several promotions, felt secure enough to apprentice him to a local tailor. Young Neil was not grateful for this new opportunity and disliked tailoring from the beginning, but he stuck to the job long enough to meet and subsequently marry the tailor's daughter, Mary Hunter. The couple moved to Glasgow itself for a while and Neil gave tailoring a last chance, but the wages were low, the rents in the city high, and he grew disgusted with the language and behaviour of his workmates.[1] So the Livingstones returned to Blantyre where Neil became a travelling tea-salesman, a job which paid little but gave his religious interests greater scope, enabling him to distribute tracts to his customers. It was in Blantyre on 19 March 1813 that David Livingstone was born, the second of seven children, two of whom died in infancy.

The tenement in which Livingstone was born and spent his childhood was owned by the company which ran Blantyre Mills. Built in 1775, it housed twenty-four families, eight on each of its three floors. Every family had a 'single kitchen apartment house' which consisted of a single room fourteen feet by ten, with two bed recesses: one for the parents and one for the children. Truckle beds were pulled out at night to cover the whole floorspace. Cooking, eating, reading, washing and mending all went on in the one room. There was no piped water, and slops and garbage were sloshed down crude sluice-holes cut into the sides of the communal circular staircases. The earth closets at the back of the building stank, and while regulations for refuse collection and a tenants' rota for cleaning stairs and passages were observed, recently dispossessed crofters found it hard to break rural habits and ignored the company's orders forbidding the keeping of poultry and other animals in their rooms. Shuttle Row, Blantyre, was not as bad as many tenement blocks in Glasgow, but that did not make it any more adequate for satisfactorily housing over a hundred people. Having suffered fourteen years of overcrowding, David and his brother John were eventually boarded out with their grandparents, who lived in a neighbouring cottage. The only wonder is how five children and two adults penned into a single room could have endured each other so long.

Although Neil Livingstone had a great admiration for learning and had devoted considerable energy to his own self-education, the size of his family and the small financial rewards of tea-selling forced him to put his three sons to work in the mills while still children. David started at the age of ten. Previous biographers have glossed over the conditions in which he worked and represented them as a suitably rigorous upbringing for a future explorer. The reality was very different. All employees at Blantyre Mills, both adults and children, worked from six in the morning till eight at night, with half an hour for breakfast and an hour for lunch: a working day of twelve and a half hours, six days a week. The management claimed that times were too hard to shorten working hours, and constantly referred to cotton shortages to back up their case; but James Monteith, the owner of the mills, in five bad years made a personal fortune of £80,000,[2] and his employees only had to gaze across the park adjoining the works and see the manager's large house to know just how hard times were.

Three-quarters of the work force at Blantyre were children, and most of these, like Livingstone, were employed as 'piecers', their job being to piece together threads on the spinning frames if they looked like breaking. Contemporary manuals on cotton-spinning stress how important this job was, for unless flaws were detected early on they were incorporated into the finished yarn. Piecers needed sharp eyes and an ability to concentrate for hours at a time if they were to avoid frequent beatings. They also had to be unusually agile since their work often involved climbing under the machinery or balancing over it. Piecers walked anything up to twenty miles a day in the mills and much of this distance was covered crawling or stooping. Long hours on their feet often resulted in bow legs and varicose veins.

Each adult spinner had three piecers attending to his machines and, since he was paid in proportion to what he produced, it was in his interests to force the children on. Often towards evening they started to fall asleep on their feet, but a beating with a leather strap or a dousing with a bucket of water generally renewed their energies. Evidence given to contemporary government commissions inquiring into factory conditions confirmed that many of these children ended up with 'limbs deformed and growth stunted'.[3] The mills were steam-heated to temperatures of between 80° and 90° Fahrenheit since this was thought ideal for the production of fine thread. So the workers inevitably caught colds on leaving work. Also these conditions encouraged promiscuity, for to make the heat and humidity endurable, most employees, male and female, would shed their clothes.

By the end of the working day most piecers were too tired to play, and certainly in no frame of mind to learn. David Livingstone and a handful of other children were made of sterner stuff. Defying aching limbs and tired minds, they made their way to the company school to spend two hours, from 8 to 10 p.m., learning to read and write. Less than 10 per cent of the child workers ever achieved any degree of literacy. Against this background, Livingstone's scholastic perseverance and success astounded his schoolmaster. Already taught to read and write by his father, Livingstone started Latin during his first year of evening school. During the next few years he spent what little money he did not give to his mother on classical textbooks. At night he often read till midnight, his mother frequently having to take his book away before he would go to sleep. Six hours later he would be in the mills again. There was no time for playing. David Livingstone had no childhood in any normally accepted sense of the word.

It would be surprising if the events of Livingstone's boyhood and adolescence had been minutely chronicled either by himself or by any other member of his family. They were busy enough trying to survive, and none of them had the slightest reason to feel that their daily lives might be of interest to their contemporaries or to posterity. There was small reason to expect anything except continued drudgery in the mills. Many of the stories about Livingstone's boyhood were therefore related after he became famous, and tend to be apocryphal rather than authentic, intended to illustrate the early development of saintliness and honesty. The picture that emerges from the few existing letters written by his father, and from his sister Janet's reminiscences,[4] is of an over-earnest boy, exceptional not for his intelligence but for his obsessive determination to learn. This got him a reputation for unsociability and remoteness, and did not gain him any sympathy or admiration. A man who had worked with him as a child, when interviewed in old age in the late 1880s, said that Livingstone 'was no thocht to be a by-ordinar [out of the ordinary] laddie; just a sulky, quiet, feckless sort o' boy'.[5] The charge of fecklessness was solely due to his constant reading; it got him into trouble with a local farmer who complained that he paid him to watch his cattle on Sundays and not to be 'aye lyin' on his belly readin' a book', and at work it made him a laughing stock. When he tried to balance textbooks on the frame of the spinning-jenny, the other children pitched bobbins to knock them off. His relationship with his fellow-workers was never easy, as he told his brother-in-law, J. S. Moffat, many years later. 'When I was a piecer,' he wrote, 'the fellows used to try to turn me off from the path I had chosen, and always began with "I think you ought etc.", till I snapped them up with a mild: "You think! I can think and act for myself; don't need anybody to think for me." '[6]

And nothing did turn him from his chosen path. From the age of thirteen he attended an extra class in Latin given by the village school-master; when all the others gave up, he was the only one to stay on. Only the abandonment of the class by the master forced him to stop.

On Sundays, in the time that was left to him after lengthy religious observance and occasional extra tasks like cattle-watching, he rarely indulged in ordinary childhood playing; Livingstone's recreations were usually more practical. In his early teens he would leave Blantyre when he could and roam the neighbouring countryside, studying rocks and trees, and bringing home plants and herbs to identify with the help of William Patrick's *The Indigenous Plants of Lanarkshire* and Culpeper's *Herbal*. He was an unusually hardy boy, and his sister Janet recalled only one instance when she had seen him in tears. That was when as a child of nine he had dropped his piece of oatcake into the burn at Hamilton Muir. Janet's only light-hearted story was of the occasion when he and his brother Charles had poached a salmon; to disguise it, David stuck it down Charles's trouser leg and got the boy to limp painfully to persuade anybody they might meet that the concealed fish was a monstrous swelling. Later Livingstone enthusiasts, unable to accept that their hero could have been a poacher, insisted that the fish was dead when he found it.

At home Mrs Livingstone had a hard job making ends meet, even with the children's earnings; but in spite of this she was a fastidious woman—as fastidious as was possible with seven people living in one small room. On

Sunday all her boys were dressed with frills and ribbons round their necks, which must have caused them considerable embarrassment with other local children. The wife of the manager of the works was most put out by their smart appearance and considered it altogether above their station. Mrs Livingstone could not afford to be generous with luxuries, but on special occasions she treated the children to barley sugar and indulged her own pleasure in tobacco by smoking a clay 'cutty' pipe.

The dominant figure in David's early life was his father Neil, a man who rarely did things by halves. His disapproval of alcohol was expressed by total abstinence, while he labelled all literature not of a religious nature as 'trashy novels'. About the use of bad language he was fanatical. No word could be spoken if there was any chance that it might have a religious connotation that could be sullied by casual use. David preferred reading travel books and scientific manuals to the religious tracts which his father pushed at him, and once he was thrashed for refusing to read Wilberforce's *Practical Christianity*, an experience that increased his dislike of what he was to call 'dry doctrinal reading'. But while he was ready to laugh at his sister for being afraid of divine punishment, he too was terrified by the possibility of his personal damnation. A child could have few defences to pit against a determined father's reiteration of impending doom. Worse still, all Calvinists believed that deeds and conscious effort were irrelevant and could not guarantee a man's salvation or place him with the Elect. Salvation or damnation lay in God's hands and his only. The Elect generally knew their good fortune for they felt that the Holy Spirit had touched them; Livingstone, however, had no such conviction, and from the age of twelve this began to distress him. He reproached himself for his sinfulness and prayed for peace of mind, but this was useless since the Holy Spirit could not be cajoled. Eventually he acknowledged that his only resort was 'to wait for the good pleasure of God'. During this time, as he later admitted: 'I found neither peace nor happiness, which caused me (never having revealed my state of mind to anyone) often to bewail my sad estate with tears in secret.'[7]

This religious fear was to last throughout Livingstone's boyhood and was only to be resolved when he was almost twenty. His distress increased with his father's frequent denunciations of his interest in science as ungodly. Relief from this worry only came in his nineteenth year when by chance he purchased a book by a Scottish nonconformist minister and amateur astronomer, Dr Thomas Dick. Dick's style is maddeningly profuse and his sentences often a page long, but they did not stop Livingstone reading *The Philosophy of a Future State* with avid enjoyment. Science, the elderly astronomer assured his readers, was in no way opposed to Christian beliefs and did not in any sense render God obsolete. Far from it; a greater awareness of the complexity and variety of creation only confirmed Christians in the necessity of there being a Maker. At last convinced that his botanical excursions had been innocent, Livingstone wrote to Dr Dick expressing his gratitude. Some months later he went to see Dick at his home in Broughty Ferry, near Dundee, eighty miles from Glasgow. Dick was an eccentric old man who had built his house on an enormous mound which was the result of eight thousand barrowfuls of earth that had taken him the best part of a year to heap up. The idea was to provide him with a suitable site for an observatory.[8] Whatever Livingstone made of him, it did nothing to weaken his new sense of well-being.

Once influenced away from orthodox Calvinism, he became ever more aware of the religious revival which was taking place in Scotland during these crucial years of his life. After 1830 there was increasing agitation for reform of abuses within the Scottish Church. The Established Kirk was felt by growing numbers to be conservative, restrictive and moribund. The link between Church and State was attacked as unscriptural, and the central authority of the Presbytery was challenged by local churches wanting more autonomy in matters of church government. There was indignation about the system of church patronage, whereby a minister could be foisted on a congregation whether they wanted him or not. A significant cause for dissatisfaction was the feeling that insufficient attention was given to foreign missions. Although most of the protests were about the autocratic discipline that the central Presbytery continued to enforce on distant churches, complaints about the form of church government also led to attacks on orthodox theology.

It may seem superfluous to record Livingstone's religious influences in detail, but since strong Christian beliefs dominated his life and much of his thinking, it is vital to understand the nature of his religious ideas at the time they crystallized in his mind; otherwise his later attitudes and behaviour may often seem incomprehensible. In 1832, the same year that Livingstone read Dick for the first time, his father was unexpectedly persuaded by some friends to go and listen to Henry Wilkes, a young Canadian preacher well known for his liberal theological views. Wilkes's withering attack on the Established Kirk and on orthodox Calvinist theology proved a turning-point in Neil Livingstone's life. He had heard this sermon in the independent church at Hamilton, near Blantyre, and shortly afterwards he applied for membership of that church. The independent churches had no unified approach to theology but reserved the right to govern their own affairs on the Congregational principle—the congregation electing their own elders and making their own decisions about church discipline. At this date the Congregational Union was only a voluntary fellowship of churches sharing the same autonomous form of church government; it implied no common theology although, in practice, beliefs were usually less rigid than orthodox Calvinism.

Neil Livingstone's change of heart brought him closer to David than he had ever been before and the old rifts were completely healed when at this time they went to hear the famous Glaswegian Congregationalist, Dr Wardlaw, lecturing on atonement. They were not the sort of lectures that would attract many today, but then, in the atmosphere of growing religious revival, people came in thousands. For those in fear of eternal damnation, it was worth coming a great many miles to listen to anybody who suggested that salvation might be universal. Strict Calvinists believed that atonement was limited to the Elect, and its benefits secured to them alone by the special influence of the Spirit, over which the individual had no control; now Wardlaw allowed that atonement was available to all if they were able to receive the Holy Spirit. The distinction may sound trivial now, but to Livingstone it was a real release from fear.

His father's membership of the Hamilton church was important to Livingstone in another way too. It brought him in touch with a far wider social circle. Several members of the congregation were relatively wealthy and well-educated men, like Henry Drummond, a lace-manufacturer, and Fergus Ferguson, a draper. These two corresponded with theologians in America, where a simultaneous religious revival was taking place. The new American theology was more liberal than anything Wardlaw had formulated. Livingstone read much of this literature and was greatly influenced by one particular American theologian, Charles Finney. The impact on the rest of the family was as great. David's younger brother, Charles, would shortly leave Scotland to attend Oberlin College where Finney taught. This was achieved with Drummond's help. Livingstone himself completely accepted Finney's proposition that 'the Holy Spirit is promised to all who ask it'.[9]

Previous biographers have described his religious beliefs as simple Calvinism, but this is far from the truth. He imbibed the new liberalism from both sides of the Atlantic and his beliefs were founded on this knowledge.

Today, with religion so often pronounced dying, if not entirely dead, it is hard to describe the intense pride that Livingstone and like-minded men felt in their more liberal faith. They believed themselves to be in the vanguard of contemporary thought, modern pioneers of a new and stronger truth. Moreover, to reject the tenets of the established Presbyterian Church seemed a more significant protest than any political defiance, for their passions were concerned not with mere worldly institutions but with the eternal state of man. There was nothing archaic about ardent belief at a time when Protestantism saw itself marching towards the conquest of the world. This great revival was closely linked with the anti-slavery movement, which in 1833 recorded its greatest triumph: in that year slavery was abolished throughout the British Empire by Act of Parliament. This victory against massive vested interests had been achieved by the concerted action of Protestants, both Anglican and nonconformist. Success also spurred on the missionary societies, whose members considered freeing the slaves to be the first step towards spiritual freedom; the heathen must next be given the Gospel. And 1832 had been the year of the Reform Bill, which stimulated rather than abated demands for social and educational reform. The Temperance, Bible and Tract societies joined with the purely secular and humanitarian reformers in demanding better conditions for the urban poor. It would not be enough to stamp out drunkenness and vice by moral preaching; the conditions that bred them would also have to be destroyed. The confident optimism of the 1830s was to stay with Livingstone long after he left Britain. Within ten years hopes of the glorious approaching dawn would have been blighted, but Livingstone would not be at home to see this. His optimism remained.

Optimist or not, at twenty-one Livingstone was still working in the mills. Two years earlier he had been promoted to spinner, but the increase in wages brought no real hope of freedom. Although he had expressed an interest in medicine, his father had made it clear that he would oppose any medical training unless his son was to put it to a specifically religious end. And so the matter rested for a while, and might have rested for ever had the same luck that once led him to read Dick not saved him again. This time, in the middle of 1834, he happened to read a pamphlet his father brought home from the Hamilton church; it had been issued in the previous year from Canton by Karl Gutzlaff of the Netherlands Missionary Society and was an appeal for missionaries to be sent from Britain and America to China. There was nothing very special about that, certainly nothing dramatic enough to change Livingstone's situation. It was the *sort* of missionary Gutzlaff wanted that convinced David that a turning-point had been reached. Medical missionaries were a comparatively new phenomenon and it is probable that Livingstone had heard little or nothing about them before. Gutzlaff argued that a medical training made the missionary far more effective in converting, for gratitude inevitably followed the relief of physical suffering. This idea was not in itself crucial for Livingstone, but he saw at once that if his father could be made to see how medicine could serve a religious purpose, he himself could leave the mills and train as a doctor. Fortunately Gutzlaff was highly respected in the missionary world and in the same year his account of *Three Journeys along the Coast of China* had been published with an introduction by the

Foreign Secretary of the well-known London Missionary Society. Neil Livingstone was duly convinced and his son seemed at last to have found a way in which science and religion could be combined in a practical manner. The idea of missionary work would have been impossible before his recent renewal of faith, but coming at the time it did, it seemed a real possibility, and revived his childhood interest in travel. He read more about Gutzlaff, who was represented in current missionary literature as a romantic figure, but practical with it, speaking Chinese and dressing in Chinese clothes. China, too, was a field hardly touched by Protestant missionaries, and the people themselves presented the greatest of all missionary challenges, comprising as they did the largest non-Christian population in the world. The goal of a missionary life in China soon became much more than an excuse to leave the mills.

A medical education still remained the first requirement and there were severe problems to be overcome before he could obtain it. For the vast majority of boys at the mills, the idea would have been unthinkable. But Livingstone knew enough Latin to be able to understand most medical terms and had read remarkably widely for a boy from his background. University entrance requirements at this time were hardly stringent and the main obstacle to becoming a student was financial. The fees for each session came to £12 and, since Livingstone for much of his working life had been earning less than four shillings a week, this was an enormous sum to find. But with his father's encouragement and his own determination, he saved most of the money during the next year and a half, and with a little help from his brother John the goal appeared attainable. He would, of course, have to work at the mills during his vacations to make a further year's study possible.

When Livingstone began his first session at Anderson's College, Glasgow, in the autumn of 1836, he had already achieved something that statistics alone made grotesquely improbable. Of all the children put to work in mills during the first three decades of the nineteenth century, less than 10 per cent learnt to read or write with any proficiency. Those who managed to do this and devote time to Latin, botany, theology and simple mathematics were virtually unheard of. The working stint from six in the morning to eight at night was alone enough to make any effort in the evening a severe trial, quite apart from the exhausting nature of the work, the heated workplaces, the noise of machines and the mockery of workfellows. At the age of twenty-three, Livingstone had already shown himself a rarity.

2

Medical Studies and Missionary Training

1836–1840

⟹⟶◆⟵⟸

On a day in the late autumn of 1836, David Livingstone and his father trudged the eight miles to Glasgow through thick snow to try to find a room. They took with them a list of likely lodgings provided by a friend from Hamilton, but this was not as useful as they had hoped, and as they grew colder and more tired, still no place was to be found at a rent they could afford. In the evening they at last came upon a room costing only two shillings a week. The name of the street was Rotten Row.

Although he came home at weekends Livingstone confessed to his sister Janet how lonely he was during these early days in Glasgow; his solitary digs could hardly have been less like the crowded single room at Blantyre. He was horrified to find that his landlady sneaked into her tenants' rooms when they were out, and helped herself to their tea and sugar. He decided to move, and after a few weeks found rooms in the High Street that were sixpence a week more but where his food was left alone. Loneliness was not his only hardship. During his first session at Anderson's College, he suffered badly from inflammation of the bowels that became bad enough for his father to have to hire a conveyance to get him back to Blantyre. But he recovered, and allowed nothing to interfere with his studies. He went home each weekend, and although Fergus Ferguson offered to take him to Glasgow each Monday morning in his gig, Livingstone refused, preferring a long walk through the snow to missing part of one of the morning's lectures. His refusal of the offer also meant that he had to get up before five in order to reach Glasgow by eight.[1]

The medical training Livingstone received so eagerly, between 1836 and 1838, was primitive. Surgical operations were performed at hazardous speed because of the lack of anaesthetics. Chloroform and ether were not introduced till seven years later and the discovery of antisepsis lay twenty-five years ahead. The study of chemistry was growing, but that of physics had hardly started and biochemistry and bacteriology were unknown.

Contemporary knowledge about the origins of diseases was extremely limited. Contradictory views were entertained, most of them mistaken. External stimuli, such as excessive heat, were believed by some medical men to cause chemical changes that affected the normal functions of the body; others put every disease down to inflammation of the veins or impurities in the gastro-intestinal tract. Livingstone himself later applied leeches to the abdomen to try to cure intestinal complaints. During Livingstone's training he would have learnt little about clinical heart disease or lung complaints.[2] Nothing was known about the tropical diseases he would soon encounter, such as malaria and blackwater fever; and the role played by insects in their transmission was unguessed at until almost the end of the century. The sale of bodies for dissection had only been legalized four years before Livingstone began his training, and so knowledge of anatomy was still rudimentary. Before that the body-snatchers had provided the medical profession with their only cadavers for dissection. The extent of Livingstone's medical education should not be exaggerated. He would be no more capable of dealing with serious illness than were the native witch-doctors he would soon be meeting. Nevertheless he later managed to cure some skin diseases and successfully treated scurvy: a complaint common in countries with a largely cereal diet. He read about innovations, and would, whenever possible, have *The Lancet* sent to him. Thus he learned about chloroform and helped his wife through several births with it. Wide reading also drew his attention to the benefits of quinine in the treatment and prevention of malaria. He did not, however, forsake bleeding for many years, and near the end of his own life was to remain convinced that inducing heavy loss of his own blood relieved his headaches and acted as a 'safety valve'.

During the next two years, as well as studying medicine, he went to Greek classes at Glasgow University and attended more theology lectures given by Dr Wardlaw. He also made a range of new contacts which would have been inconceivable at Blantyre. The most important of these was James Young, a chemist who was soon to invent a process for distilling oil from shale and was, as a result, appropriately dubbed 'Sir Paraffin' by Livingstone. Young was to be a lifelong friend and correspondent, and thirty years later his generosity would offset the Government's stinginess and enable Livingstone to depart on his final journey.

During his second year at Anderson's College, Livingstone began to think seriously about which missionary society he ought to approach, and on his visits home he discussed the matter with his father. In the end he chose the London Missionary Society, largely because of its sympathies for congregational church government and its acceptance of candidates from all Protestant denominations. Methodists, Baptists and Presbyterians were all able to apply. The Society, founded in 1795, had been the second of the score of missionary societies set up in Britain, Europe and America between 1790 and 1840. By the time Livingstone applied, towards the end of 1837, the Society's operations were world-wide and included missions in China, the South Seas, the West Indies, India, Sierra Leone and South Africa. In January 1838, after a delay of three months, Livingstone was sent a small booklet by the Directors of the Society. He was required to write in it his answers to seventeen questions, mainly concerned with his background and his reasons for wishing to be a missionary. Livingstone's replies were decisive to the point of brusqueness. His answer to a question relating to marriage being typical: 'Unmarried; under no engagement relating to marriage, never made proposals of marriage, nor conducted myself so to any woman as to cause her to suspect that I intended anything relating to marriage . . .'[3]

But decisive or not, he was kept waiting so long for a reply that his father felt impelled to write to the Directors, telling them a few facts about his son, which the young man in his modesty might not have divulged. David's refusal of Fergus Ferguson's lift into Glasgow was made much of, as was young Livingstone's early aptitude for Latin. The Directors were told that David had recently turned down a teaching job worth £150 a year because acceptance would have meant returning to the tyrannical Established Church. Neil Livingstone went on to point out why the refusal of this offer deserved especial praise: 'The manager of the factory who is frequently under the influence of whisky, told him yesterday that if he went to Glasgow any more, following after education, he must lose his work as he would not keep it for him.'[4]

Neil concluded by assuring the Directors that he had not told his son that he was writing and would rather he never knew, since he would certainly disapprove. This touching letter must have taken him a long time to plan and write and is an impressive achievement for a man who had had little or no formal education. Whether it tilted the balance in favour of his son is impossible to say, but David was eventually invited to appear in London for an interview with the Directors set for 13 August 1838. No decision was made at once and a further interview took place on the 20th, and after this second scrutiny the Directors decided to accept Livingstone on probation. He might never have got to London had Fergus Ferguson not given him the money for his fare.

The plan worked out was that Livingstone's probation should be spent under the tuition of the Rev. Richard Cecil at the small market town of Chipping Ongar in Essex. Then, if he proved competent in Latin, Greek and theology, he would go on to a theological college, such as Cheshunt, and after that complete his medical training in London. He must have impressed at his interviews, for this treatment was reserved only for the pick of London Missionary Society recruits. Many went out to their respective mission fields as artisan missionaries, trained only in basic theology and a craft such as carpentry or bricklaying—both indispensable skills in places where missionaries often had to build their own houses.

In Chipping Ongar, Livingstone lodged with six other students in a long, low building where they lived by themselves, doing their own cooking, washing and so on. His room was over a central arch that led to the Congregational Chapel. The teaching took place in Richard Cecil's large house a couple of hundred yards down the road. It would be hard to think up a worse training for aspiring missionaries than the rigid diet of Greek, Latin, Hebrew and theology meted out to the young men at Ongar with Livingstone. Their new knowledge would have been excellent had they been destined for work as ministers in British university towns or in affluent areas of major cities, but for practical assistance in converting Indians, Africans or Chinese it was worse than useless. But Richard Cecil, an elderly and pedantic man, took his job seriously and judged his charges by exacting standards. By January 1839 he had already formed a far from favourable opinion of Livingstone: 'His heaviness of manner, united as it is with a rusticity, not likely to be removed, still strikes me as having importance, but he has sense and quiet vigour; his temper is good and his character substantial, so that I do not like the thought of his being rejected.'[5]

But rejection was still a distinct possibility, in spite of quiet sense and vigour. Livingstone's twelve years in the mills had not made him refined, and his pronounced Scots accent jarred on southern ears. But Cecil was also disappointed with his academic progress. In February he wrote again to the Directors and regretfully told them that Livingstone was 'hardly ready in point of knowledge' to go to a theological college, whatever plans had been entertained for him. Cecil's judgement was more than a little harsh considering that Livingstone was almost entirely self-taught. The other students at Ongar, though none had come from privileged homes, had almost all enjoyed several years of continuous formal education. Cecil considered Livingstone plodding, 'worthy but remote from brilliant', and described his progress as 'steady but not rapid'. He ended his report wearily with the hope that his stodgy Scottish student 'might kindle a little'.[6]

Since Livingstone's primary interest was in medicine and not in the classics, there was little sign of 'kindling' in the next few months. Livingstone's attempts at preaching were equally unimpressive and on one occasion, when, as part of his training, he had to stand in for the minister of the chapel at a neighbouring village, he forgot everything he had intended to say and, having admitted as much, hurried out of the pulpit. Later, when he

had managed to complete a sermon, he himself confessed that his delivery
had been so bad that many members of the congregation had told him that
if they 'knew he was to preach again they would not enter the chapel'.[7]

Livingstone's awkward manner was not his only problem as a preacher.
His uvula, at the back of his throat, was too large and made his speaking
voice rather thick and indistinct. Eventually it troubled him so much that
he had it cut out.

Walter Inglis, one of his contemporaries, later wrote a description of
Livingstone which confirms the picture of him at twenty-six as an
awkward, sullen young man.

> I have to admit he was 'no bonny'. His face wore at all times the strongly
> marked lines of potent will. I never recollect of him relaxing into the
> abandon of youthful frolic or play . . . I only recollect of him playing one
> practical joke. A man came with a ripe boil that only required to be
> lanced. He gave the boil an honest skelp with a book. He had a grin for
> dry Scottish humour . . .[8]

What was so humorous about biffing a ripe boil is hard to say, but another
fellow-student, Joseph Moore, liked him in spite of 'all his rather ungainly
ways and by no means winning face'. Moore confessed himself at a loss to
know why he liked the young Scot but claimed that he possessed an 'inde-
scribable charm'.[9] It was evidently an elusive quality for it did not help
him in his courtship of a girl he knew at Ongar.

Catherine Ridley was the first middle-class girl he had ever met and his
background made him feel gauche and inept in her company. In a letter
to her he confessed sadly that he was 'not very well acquainted with the
feelings of those who have been ladies all their lives'.[10] But although they
met quite often and exchanged little gifts, she preferred Thomas Prentice,
another student at Ongar. Before that, Livingstone had sent her some
sentimental religious verses written by an elderly Scottish spinster called
Miss Sigourney. The poems were full of clichés and stock images of
'parting bosoms bleeding' and 'native shores receding' and were so sickly
that it would be comforting to feel that they reflected Miss Ridley's taste
rather than Livingstone's. But he evidently liked Miss Sigourney's work
since he later sent his sister Janet a copy of Lays from the West with a
covering note assuring her that the book contained 'some very good pieces
& all religious'.[11] After his rejection, Livingstone derided religious verse
and wrote poor Janet a stern reprimand for sending him the work of a pair
'of poetastresses who would have been far more usefully employed darning
their grannies' stockings than clinking words together, cruelly murdering
the English language in the attempt'.[12] Although there was undoubted

humour in the reproof, Catherine's decision to marry Prentice hurt Livingstone more than he cared to admit, and in a letter written to his son Thomas, thirty years later, he told him that *he* had broken with Catherine and not the other way round. Livingstone's claim was that she had been too much of a lady to make a good missionary's wife.[13] Long before that he told a friend that Prentice had got her on false pretences since he had never intended to be a missionary. In fact Prentice was prevented from going abroad by ill-health, which did not pre-empt Livingstone's bitter remark, made some five years later, that Catherine 'did not enjoy the married state' and was miserably unhappy. She consoled herself by joining the strict Plymouth Brotherhood, which, Livingstone argued, showed that it was lucky he had never married her.

In 1839 world events altered Livingstone's subsequent career in a manner far more decisive than Catherine Ridley's rejection. In September of that year Britain and China drifted into the inglorious Opium War that was to last until August 1842. The British claimed that the Chinese Emperor was trying to exclude all British trade from Canton; the Emperor, with more justification, argued that he had been forced into counter-measures to stem the vast illicit opium trade carried on openly with Chinese smugglers by members of the British East India Company. Right was on the Chinese side, might on the British, and the war finally ended with Britain wresting massive trading concessions and taking Hong Kong. The opium trade went on.

At the outset nobody knew how long the war would last and the Directors of the London Missionary Society were not prepared to speculate. They decided that no more missionaries ought to be risked in China till the war was over. Livingstone therefore had to think of somewhere else to begin his missionary life. The Society in fact made the first suggestion in July, when it was proposed that he should go to the West Indies. Although the British West Indies were then facing horrifying social and economic problems posed by the decay of many sugar plantations struggling with the after-effects of the abolition of slavery, Livingstone objected on the grounds that the islands had been settled so long that a post there would be too 'like the ministry at home'. Apart from that, as he pointed out, there were numerous medical men already there and the addition of another would only cause resentment. He wanted a more taxing field of labour and suggested South Africa.[14]

The Directors accepted his arguments later that month and told him that after Christmas he would continue his medical studies in London 'to fit himself for some station in South Africa or the South Seas'.

His move to London took place on 2 January 1840 and he stayed in a boarding-house for young missionaries in Aldersgate. It was there that he met the famous South African missionary, Robert Moffat, whose tales of 'the smoke of a thousand villages where no missionary had ever been' have previously been said to have made Livingstone decide to go to South Africa. In fact he had made his mind up six months before. Mr and Mrs Moffat did, however, worry him about his unmarried condition and distressed him considerably by suggesting a Miss Collier, a woman fully ten years his senior, as a suitable future wife.[15] Their warnings that he would be lonely and wretched in South Africa without a partner did nothing to help him find one and only left him feeling confused and, as he put it to a friend, 'as deep in the mud as any man was'.[16]

The pressure of work in London left him no time to make friends with likely ladies and within a few months the strain had made him take to his bed. His complaint he believed was congestion of liver and lungs, caused by 'too much effluvia of sick chambers, dissecting rooms etc.'[17] He had been attending numerous lectures at the British and Foreign Medical School, Charing Cross Hospital and Moorfields. The subjects ranged from medical practice to midwifery and botany. He also managed to fit in a course in comparative anatomy at the Hunterian Museum. After his illness, he returned to Scotland, and in November, after sitting the relevant exams, qualified as a doctor, having gained the licence of the Faculty of Physicians and Surgeons, Glasgow. The fees for sitting similar exams set by the Royal College of Surgeons in London were more than the Directors of the London Missionary Society were prepared to pay.

Unrelated to his medical studies, but of far greater importance for his subsequent thinking, was his attendance, on 1 June 1840, at the vast public meeting in Exeter Hall, in the Strand, mounted by the Society for the Extinction of the Slave Trade and for the Civilization of Africa. The Prince Consort was there, and Livingstone heard for the first time Thomas Fowell Buxton, Wilberforce's successor, put forward his panacea for the remedy of every African evil. Africans would only be saved from the slave trade if they were woken up to the possibilities of selling their own produce; otherwise chiefs would continue to sell their own people to pay for the European beads, cloth, guns and trinkets they coveted. Commerce and Christianity could achieve the miracle, not Christianity alone. Free trade, legitimate commerce, the end of protectionism would all help usher in the new era. These were ideas which Livingstone would one day publicize on a massive scale. With this meeting, Buxton set in motion the Niger Expedition that was to end with heavy loss of life and little or no achievement. Even when Livingstone later learned about the expedition's failure it did not make him doubt the practical value of Buxton's big idea. This meeting meant that before Livingstone even arrived in Africa he held views shared by very few missionaries. Most of those he would meet in South Africa considered trading a distinctly immoral business, quite unsuitable for missionaries to have anything to do with.

On 20 November 1840 Dr Livingstone had returned from Scotland and was ready for the culmination of his missionary training. On that day he went to Albion Chapel, Finsbury, to be ordained a minister. His exact standing after the ceremony needs further explanation. He had become a nonconformist minister, not affiliated to any Church or Establishment, but within the voluntary Congregational Union of England and Wales, of which the Albion Chapel was a member. Congregationalism, as will be recalled, was not an institutionalized Church, nor a body of theology; it was merely a word describing the system of church government shared by the members of the voluntary Union. Livingstone's purely academic preparation for ordination had not been very different from that of a contemporary Anglican, with the exception of some crucial points of theology, and the major difference of church organization and the relationship of Church and State. Livingstone's ordination would have been recognized by all nonconformists, but not by Anglicans or Catholics who would not have allowed him to preach in their churches. His full designation would have been 'a minister within the Congregational Union serving overseas under the London Missionary Society, with its fundamental principle of non-alliance'.[18]

Livingstone's date of sailing was now set for 8 December. Shortly before leaving, he sat down to compose a farewell letter to his mother. Previously unpublished, this cold and priggish letter deals with none of the topics a young man leaving his own country for a long time might have been expected to mention: moments of shared happiness, memories of shared suffering, personal love. Instead, Livingstone's tone was moral and admonitory. He began by reminding his mother that he had normally written to both parents and then went on:

> Now, however, as I am sorry to learn your health and strength are declining, and as we are separated for some time, who knows but it is forever . . . I now take this opportunity to draw your mind and direct my own to that subject which of all others, concerns us most, viz that of eternity . . . You have had many trials in passing through life, I believe it has been to you one continual long struggle with poverty for many years, perhaps this may still be your lot, this may have been temptation, you may have felt it was impossible you could bestow much attention on the concerns of the soul, but this just exactly is what you should certainly have felt . . .[19]

Later he would be able to show concern for his mother's soul with more humour and with precisely the personal touch that is lacking here. In fact in a letter to her, dated October 1859, he laughs to recall the story of a young minister in Aberdeen who 'visited an old woman in affliction and began to talk very fine to her on the duty of resignation, trusting—hoping and the rest of it—when the old woman looked up and said "Teer thing, ye ken naething aboot it." '[20]

But at twenty-seven, on the eve of his departure for South Africa, David Livingstone did not easily entertain thoughts that were not closely related to his calling. He was very conscious of what he had achieved, and at what cost: no real childhood or adolescence, little or no play or recreation, day after day in the mills, evening after evening working. At nine he had managed to repeat the 119th Psalm—the longest, with 176 verses—with only five errors on two successive evenings. At thirteen he had been the only boy at the mills prepared to go on with Latin. At twenty-one he had been ready to walk through a snowstorm rather than miss a single lecture. To achieve all this demanded qualities that left little room for any but serious sentiments. Sometimes it is hard not to be chilled by his resilience and almost inhuman perseverance. Yet he had been homesick in Glasgow and had cried when he dropped his oatcake in the burn at Hamilton. He was soon to begin writing numerous letters to friends, many of them affectionate and many spiced with a caustic wit. And yet the obstacles he had overcome and the suffering he had endured had permanently marked him. He was never to be able to judge others except by the standards he had set himself, and, as time passed, these standards would become less flexible; nor would he have much patience with views that ran counter to his own.

When Livingstone sailed from London on 8 December 1840 on the *George*, he would have known that many humanitarians disapproved of missionary work abroad, believing with Charles Dickens that 'the work at home must be completed thoroughly or there is no hope abroad',[21] but Livingstone would have brushed aside such arguments with scorn. All men had the right to hear God's word. No nation ought to hoard the Gospel like a miser. The social problems of Britain might take a generation to sort out and in the meantime the African could hardly be expected to wait for the blessing of true religion. Christianity was for all men at all times in all places. Besides, the needs of the heathen were great, the labourers few and the potential harvest immeasurably greater than any that could be imagined in a small island like Britain. Men like Livingstone were firmly convinced that interest in work abroad would stimulate religious life at home. Besides, there was the sin of the former British involvement in the slave trade to expiate. No anti-missionary arguments or any fears of the discomforts ahead would have troubled Livingstone as he watched the London docks fall astern.

The wide use of steamships by shipping companies did not get under way till the late 1850s, and before that the voyages in small, cramped and often rotting wooden sailing vessels were not pleasant experiences for the steerage passengers. Whole families were invariably crammed together, with all their luggage and possessions, in less than ten square feet. In this area they sometimes cooked their own food, vomited when the weather was rough and the hatches closed, and on occasion even died when cholera broke out aboard. Irritations included cockroaches and screaming children, and every storm brought a pandemonium of crashing packing cases and falling people.

In mid-voyage the *George* nearly foundered in a severe gale and one of the masts split, obliging the captain to make a detour to Rio de Janeiro to refit. Livingstone remembered Rio for the prevalence of drunkenness, particularly among British and American sailors. One evening, with more daring than good sense, he went to a notorious waterfront bar and started handing out temperance tracts. At one time, surrounded by twenty drunk and angry sailors, he was lucky to get away unscathed.[22] The incident proved his courage but underlined his priggishness. Ten years later he had learned a lot and was to say of drinking: 'We ought perhaps to judge acts more leniently to which we have no temptation ourselves.'[23] But at twenty-eight, Livingstone was intolerant, narrow and self-opinionated. He was also determined, courageous and resilient. Taken together, these characteristics did not make him likeable, but given his early life it would have been strange if he had emerged a polished, kindly and open-minded young man. Without his absolute self-confidence and belief in his own rectitude, he would never have left the mill, trained to be a doctor or voyaged to Africa.

On 15 March 1841, after a voyage of over three months, the *George* anchored in Simon's Bay, and Livingstone went ashore. A few days later he was in Cape Town.

3

Africa and South Africa
1841*

————⟫•◆•⟪————

When Livingstone landed at the Cape in 1841, the geography of
central Africa was still as much of a mystery to Europeans as it had
been to the Greeks and Romans two thousand years before. The existence
of the great lakes was not suspected, and the positions of the sources of
major rivers such as the Nile and Congo were matters only for wild and
unproductive speculation.

At first sight it seems unlikely, even improbable, that in the fourth
decade of the nineteenth century so little was known of a continent which,
over a thousand years before, had seen the establishment of Arab settlements along its eastern seaboard from Mombasa in the north to Sofala,
opposite Madagascar, in the south. But the Arabs, south of the Sahara at
least, had been happy merely to pursue a coastal trade, leaving the native
tribes to bring to their settlements slaves, ivory and gold dust from the
interior. When the first European invaders tried to push inland six
hundred years later their efforts were hampered and largely nullified by
problems not to be overcome for another four centuries.

These first European efforts had been made in the early sixteenth
century by the Portuguese. By 1450 Portuguese ships had sailed south
down the west coast of Africa past Sierra Leone, and just before 1500
Vasco da Gama had reached Mozambique and finally India via the Cape
of Good Hope. During the first decade of the sixteenth century Portuguese
forts were built along the East African coast from Mombasa to Sofala and
the Arabs were crushed or overawed. Still confident, and driven on by
rumours of inexhaustible silver and gold mines in the interior, the
Portuguese thrust their way inland into East Africa up the Zambesi. By
the middle of the century forts had been established at Tete and Sena, but
the dreams of swift progress and easily accessible wealth had ended; the
problems of tropical Africa were now understood.

The Zambesi had been hard enough to sail into at all, and it was soon
realized that that river's surf-beaten sand bars and complete lack of natural

harbours in their estuaries were defects common to most African water-
ways. Then there were the cataracts, the intense heat and the inexplicable
and sudden deaths. Malaria might carry off entire expeditions of three
or four hundred men with such effectiveness and speed that at first
the Portuguese believed that they had been poisoned by Africans or
coastal Arabs. The climate brought other problems: periodic rains could
turn flat, dry, easily traversable country into impassable swamp within a
matter of days. All supplies had to be brought from the coast, and in
a country where tropical forests obstructed wheeled transport and the
tsetse fly killed horses and oxen, human porterage provided the only
means of conveyance. Worst of all, it appeared that the black inhabitants
of the country possessed neither wealth nor an easily exploitable terrain.
A few Portuguese stayed on the lower Zambesi, but did not prosper. All
interest in Africa might have died away in the sixteenth century had not
events elsewhere suggested a use for one African commodity: the African
himself.

Six years before da Gama rounded the Cape, Christopher Columbus
had landed in the West Indies. By the time the Portuguese were struggling
up the Zambesi, their fellow-countrymen were settling in Brazil, and the
Spanish in the Caribbean, Mexico and Peru. The European discoverers
of the western New World soon found that its sparse population was insufficient for its development. More labourers would be needed for the mines,
sugar plantations and later for the cotton fields. At that very moment
thousands of strong, hardy black men were known to be living lives of
apparent idleness on the other side of the Atlantic. The transatlantic slave
trade was the inevitable result. Taken up at first by the Portuguese and
Spanish, the French, Dutch, English and Danes were not slow to join in.
The European settlement of North America during the seventeenth
century greatly increased the demand for slaves. By that time the Portuguese
had founded their colony of Angola on the West African coast, and most
of the other European nations had established coastal slaving forts further
north. The first English fort was set up at the mouth of the Gambia river
in 1618. Within a hundred years this commerce had become so essential a
part of the British system of trade, and apparently so vital to the economy
of the Caribbean and the Americas, that it would take the humanitarians
some fifty years of struggle to end British participation worldwide. That
was in 1833. For another thirty years after the triumphs of Wilberforce
and Buxton, the British naval blockade on the West African coast would
not be able to stop completely the flow of slaves to Brazil, Cuba and
the southern states of America. Meanwhile in East Africa the Arabs had
reasserted themselves after their earlier humiliation by the Portuguese,
and continued supplying Arabia, the Gulf states and Iran with many

thousands of African slaves annually. The extent and volume of this other slave trade was to remain largely unknown in Britain till the late 1850s.

The vigour of the anti-slavery movement of the late eighteenth and early nineteenth centuries had implications for Africa's future that went beyond curbing the trade itself. The humanitarians demanded a more positive policy in the 'Dark Continent'. In 1791 a British philanthropic association received a charter for the purpose of settling in their continent of origin African slaves freed in the New World. The result was the British colony of Sierra Leone. Liberia had similar beginnings. Running parallel with this humanitarian interest was a new fascination with African geographical problems. In 1788 the African Association was founded to promote exploration. Between 1795 and 1831, the British explorers Park, Clapperton, Lander and Laing had together traced the Niger from source to sea, and in East Africa, Bruce had reached the source of the Blue Nile. These journeys were not followed up, largely because the problems known to the Portuguese for centuries now confronted the unsuspecting British. Africa was still a continent of fringe coastal settlement in 1841.

Only in Africa south of the Zambesi had events been different; there, with a clement climate, no malaria and, in the Cape Colony at least, no tsetse fly, there was a real opening for a European colony to rival any in North America or Australia. But the British had not got there first; in 1652 the Dutch had made their first small settlement at the Cape. The Directors of the Dutch East India Company had had no intention of founding a colony, let alone a nation; all they wanted was a victualling port for their vessels en route for the spice markets of the east. But the port could only be supported by a permanent farming community, so Europeans received grants of land to enable them to produce grain, meat and wine to sell to the garrison and to passing Dutch East Indiamen. At first all went well, but since the Company would not sanction emigration from the Netherlands on any scale, the new settlement had to depend for labour on the services of the sparse aboriginal population: the Hottentots and Bushmen. The Bushmen were hunters, the Hottentots cattle farmers, and the habits of the former did not endear them to the latter. The Bushmen were diminutive and in the eyes of the colonists extremely primitive, while the Hottentots, although more familiar with European ways, were insufficiently numerous and too dispersed to supply the labour needs of the new settlement. Therefore the decision was made to import slaves. These did not come from a single source but were drawn from places as far apart as West Africa and Malaya. Slaves and Hottentots intermarried and a sizeable mixed race population brought worse social problems, which interbreeding with Europeans complicated further.

Although the settlement at the Cape grew, and Cape Town itself came to comprise over a thousand houses by the end of the eighteenth century, the little colony was not a happy or a prosperous one. The economic history of an isolated European community, based on slave labour and oppressed by a now failing monopolistic company, was inevitably uninspiring. The Company did not allow the colonists sufficient freedom in trade to dispose of their surplus produce and it cut the farmers' profits by buying their grain at a fixed price. The introduction of sheep failed, tobacco would not grow, nor would olives, while bad harvests and cattle disease, striking simultaneously, threatened to bring the entire population to the brink of starvation. The decline of the Dutch East India Company through bad management and increasing French and British competition added to the colonists' miseries. In 1750 only sixty-eight ships called at the Cape; the same number had anchored in Table Bay fifty years before.

However, world events were shaping a new future for the Cape Colony. The 1750s and 1760s saw an intensification of Franco-British rivalry in India and this in turn led both powers to view the Cape as a useful strategic base for future acquisition. But neither nation was prepared to fight the Dutch for it. Only with the advent of the war waged by Revolutionary France against Britain in the 1790s did the situation change, for the Netherlands was dragged in on the French side. Britain, to protect her shipping routes to India and the Far East, occupied the Cape in 1795. This first occupation did not last long and the Dutch were handed back their colony when peace came. But when war again broke out between Britain and Napoleonic France, the British returned to the Cape in 1806 and this time they stayed.

From the beginning the British Government saw the Cape Colony as a strategic gain and was not interested in its development as a territory. They wished to maintain the existing situation with as little extra expenditure as possible. The realities of the situation decreed otherwise.

Early on in the colony's history, the entirely Dutch society had been a divided one: there were the townsmen at the Cape, predominantly European in dress, manners and habits; and the farmers or Boers, who as early as the 1720s had started to trek east from the Cape beyond the Drakenstein Mountains into the plains of the Karoo. The further the Boers went, the more remote the Company's administration became for them and the more these frontiersmen liked it. They relished their new independence and made a virtue of their simple nomadic life. Their visits to Cape Town were infrequent and endured only because they had to sell their cattle and buy supplies such as gunpowder, tea and sugar. The Company tried to contain their dispersal but failed.

In 1776 the Boers made their first contact with a new African people, the Xhosa, at the Great Fish river, five hundred miles east of Cape Town. Soon it was realized that while the Boers were moving east and north-west, a vast Bantu tribal migration was sweeping towards them from the north. Confrontation was inevitable. The British Government inherited a border problem which it had no idea how to solve. It could control neither the Boers nor the Xhosa. In the land and cattle squabbles that took place between white and black during the following years it was impossible for the British to determine the guilty party. The Boers wanted the British to expand the borders of the colony and sweep back the Bantu, and the British administrators, seeing that this would create a wider and less accessible border, opted for a policy of containment. To implement the policy, troops had to be sent. To create a white buffer between the Cape Colony proper and the advancing Bantu, the administrators, acting with the British Government, launched a state-aided immigration scheme for British settlers to come out and farm just west of the Great Fish river. The Boers, checked in their east-ward expansion, viewed these new arrivals as competitors and interlopers. The British got on well enough with the Dutch in and around Cape Town, but with the more distant Boers their relations steadily worsened. An important additional cause for this deterioration came with the arrival of foreign missionaries.

In the late 1730s a German missionary, George Schmidt, had enraged the Boers by baptizing slaves and was compelled to leave by the ensuing outcry. Seventy years passed before the London Missionary Society sent their first member to the Cape to work among the slaves and Hottentots. By 1816 there were twenty men from the same Society working in the colony. By this time the anti-slavery movement was at its strongest in England and abolition of slavery throughout the British Empire seemed a real possibility. While the missionaries looked forward to the day of liberation with delight and did everything they could to hasten its advent, the slave-owning colonists viewed the future with apprehension and the missionaries with dislike. The missionaries, however, were not easily intimidated, and in 1811 two London Missionary Society men, Vanderkemp and Read, working near the eastern border, informed the Governor of the Cape about crimes committed by various farmers against Hottentots and slaves. As a result, a number of Boers were charged with brutal crimes and some were convicted. From that time onwards the Boers considered the members of the London Missionary Society to be dangerous enemies.

In 1819 the London Missionary Society sent out John Philip to super-vise their work within the colony. Philip quickly realized that the

Government wished to restrict missionary activities in the borderlands both to the north and to the east: nor was he slow to see why. The pressure of the advancing colonists in search of cheap labour and fresh land had led the authorities to turn a blind eye to crimes. This enabled the farmers to use forced labour and take land from Africans without government intervention, so long as no major border incident was provoked. Philip sent evidence home to England which was examined by Wilberforce and Buxton and led within months to the appointment of Crown Commissioners to come to South Africa 'to inquire into the state not only of the civil government and legal administration of the Cape, but into the general condition of the slave and Hottentot populations'. This was a slap in the face for the Cape Government and from now on the missionaries could add the colonial administrators to the list of those who mistrusted them. In 1828 Westminster, acting on the recommendations of the Crown Commissioners, passed a resolution desiring that 'directions be given for effectually securing to all the natives of South Africa the same freedom and protection as are enjoyed by other free persons residing at the Cape, whether they be English or Dutch'.

With the abolition of slavery throughout the British Empire in 1833, the colonists were faced with a situation they had long dreaded. Although abolition did not immediately bring equality or anything remotely resembling it, some seven thousand Boers decided, during the late 1830s and early to mid-1840s, to trek north-east beyond the borders of the colony. The Boers objected not so much to the emancipation but to the idea bred by the missionaries that Africans ought to be considered the equals of white Christians. Their trek was also inspired by land hunger and the Government's refusal to remove the Xhosa barrier to the east. The Boers were accustomed to moving their cattle on when a given acreage was exhausted, and were incensed when the Government informed them that in future land would not be granted freely but would be sold at auction. This combination of circumstances increased the numbers of those leaving the colony for the lands north of the Orange and Vaal rivers. The massive Boer exodus was welcome neither to the Government nor to the missionaries. The Government was now left with a depopulated eastern frontier at a time when Xhosa pressure was increasing, and the missionaries saw that away from the power of British officials, the Boers would be able to do as they wished with the natives in the areas they had removed to. From now on the same missionaries who had once been so strongly opposed to colonial expansion tried to persuade the Government to extend the colony to include the new Boer Republics. The missionaries would fail completely, for in 1852 the Government was to recognize the independence of the Orange Free State and the Transvaal.

The Government's new policy of laissez-faire towards the trekkers was to have serious repercussions for the missionaries long before the formal recognition of the Republics' independence occurred. As early as 1805 the first London Missionary Society station had been established north of the Orange river in Namaqualand, outside the borders of the colony. Since then, Kuruman and Griqua Town had become not only the London Missionary Society's remotest missions* but also their most cherished ones. With the arrival of the Boers just to the east in the adjacent Transvaal, the missionaries in Kuruman and Griqua Town were convinced that they would attempt to stop the expansion of all missionary activity to the north and to the east of their present situation. The Boers' known hostility towards missionaries made these fears realistic rather than alarmist. Trouble in Bechuanaland between missionary and Boer could not be far off. If and when that trouble came, the missionaries knew that they could expect little help from the Cape Government, which had originally tried to discourage missionary activities beyond the colonial borders.

Kuruman was used by the Directors of the London Missionary Society in all their propaganda at home to show what a mission station ought to be: neat, well laid out, well watered, houses made of stone with little gardens and orchards of fruit trees. To fit in with the ideal, the native Christians should also be neat and tidy; they should wash with European soap, and, so as not to offend European ideas about physical modesty, they should cover their bodies with European clothes. Tribal values and patterns of behaviour should be condemned and rooted out. There was an ideal missionary too, and he was also to be found at Kuruman. Robert Moffat had started his work there in 1821 as a young man in his early twenties. Through his labours the watercourses were dug, the houses built and the orchards planted. Through his patient and inflexible persuasion the first converts had been made, not after weeks or even months, but after eight years of disappointment and frustration. The Directors of the London Missionary Society did not, however, dwell on the length of time that had passed before conversions had been made. Moffat had spent decades translating the Bible into Sichuana, the language of the Bechuanas. He had set up a printing press to disseminate the newly translated Gospel and had run a school to teach the local Africans to read and write in their own language. His devotion to a single tribe and a single place for a lifetime epitomized what the Directors' considered the best type of missionary life: that led by the settled, patient missionary who did not aim

---

* Both were between 500 and 600 miles north-east of Cape Town.

at converting a whole nation but contented himself with the gradual 'civilization and Christianization' of a small tribal community. Of course the diligent efforts of hundreds of Moffats working in this way would never have made much of an impression on Africa as a whole, or even on Africa south of the Zambesi. But the Directors were happy, and pointed to Kuruman with its small population as the jewel in the South African missionary crown. Besides, they could remind the sceptic that there had been no foreign missionaries in southern Africa in 1800, but that, following their lead, several hundred had come out by 1841 and were at work on a total of eighty mission stations scattered throughout the colony, with a handful outside it. These men came from Europe as well as Britain, and missionaries from the Moravian, Rhenish and Paris societies worked alongside members of the London, Glasgow and Wesleyan societies. In 1835 six American missionaries had arrived. In the year that Livingstone came to Africa, the Directors of the London Missionary Society might have admitted privately that the speed and number of conversions had disappointed them, but they would have denied emphatically that any new missionary policy was needed or that the future would not see a massive acceleration in the number of conversions.

4

Early Disappointment: Kuruman
1841–1843

The plan was that Livingstone should spend a short period at the Cape, recovering from his sea voyage, before going on to Bechuanaland and Kuruman to begin his life's work. There was nothing specifically African that Livingstone could see in Cape Town as he wandered through the streets. The place was still very much the small Dutch port it had been fifty years before. The streets were largely unpaved and the vehicles most in evidence were not smart carriages but the lumbering ox waggons of the farmers. The buildings were pleasant gabled houses, mostly stuccoed, and either whitewashed or painted green. Avenues of oaks had been planted along many streets and most houses had gardens in front. It had been arranged for Livingstone to stay with the veteran campaigner Dr John Philip. The young missionary ought to have enjoyed his time in Cape Town staying with such a famous man, but from the beginning Livingstone felt uneasy.

When Livingstone had met Robert Moffat in London early the previous year, the venerable founder of Kuruman had launched into a scathing attack on Dr Philip, whom Livingstone had previously felt bound to consider the champion of the Hottentots and slaves. Moffat claimed that Philip had started to use his position as the London Missionary Society's financial agent at the Cape to exercise authority over the missions north of the Orange river. Furthermore, Moffat went on, Philip had become senile, autocratic and more interested in politics than in the conversion of the heathen. Livingstone had listened to all this and had believed it implicitly; it was hardly for him to doubt what the ideal missionary had to say.

At Cape Town, however, everything seemed rather different. Philip appeared to be a calm, reasonable and unambitious man with no desire to exercise authority over Moffat or anyone else. Livingstone wrote to a friend rather shamefacedly, acknowledging that he had come out expecting to find a monster and had instead discovered 'an amiable man . . . who claims no superiority over us'. Philip discovered from Livingstone that Moffat had been blackening his character in England, and decided to repay the compliment before Moffat could get back to Africa from his London fund-raising trip. The young missionary had soon sucked in Philip's stories about Moffat being a scandalmonger and trouble-maker, so much so that within weeks Livingstone was writing to friends telling them that 'Mr Moffat is not on speaking terms with the Griqua Town missionaries and takes another route when visiting the colony to avoid seeing them. They in their turn *hate* the bretheren in the colony and amongst the whole there exists a pretty respectable amount of floating scandal one against the other.'[1] Livingstone was next shocked to hear rumours that a number of missionaries outside the colony had taken African mistresses and he condemned the whole situation as 'most disgraceful'. Even if scandalous behaviour could not easily be proved, one thing Livingstone was sure of was the genuine hatred felt by Moffat and the missionaries beyond the colonial borders for the missionaries working on the older, more settled stations within the colony. Those at Kuruman and Griqua Town did not get on together, but they were united in their scorn for men who called themselves missionaries and worked in established communities within a few days of Cape Town. In the distant missionaries' view, that was not mission work, but a life like that of a provincial minister in England.

Livingstone might gasp with indignation at the squabbles and hatreds of his new colleagues, and make much of his own determination not to quarrel, but before he had even reached Cape Town he had already taken a lasting dislike to William Ross, a London Missionary Society artisan travelling out to South Africa on the same ship. Ross's wife had been constantly seasick and Livingstone had tried his medical skills to bring relief; all he brought was a husband's fury and accusations that he had designs on Mrs Ross. Livingstone told a friend indignantly that he would rather have flirted with his grandmother than with Ross's 'blooming bride of 34 or 5'.[2] From then on Livingstone wrote off Ross as a man with 'an exceedingly contracted mind', whose opinions should receive no more attention than an illiterate Hottentot child's. Ross repaid Livingstone by suggesting that he was unmarried because no girl would look at such a disagreeable young man. Livingstone, not to be bested, had countered by pointing to 'all the silly married people . . . as proof of how easy it is to get noosed'. For a while there was a chance that Ross might stay in Cape Town and Livingstone was delighted, especially since Ross might become the minister at Philip's old church, where the congregation had proved themselves unworthy of 'a good pastor' by forcing Philip to resign because of his championship of the slaves. But in the end Ross came on to Bechuanaland to remain, for many years to come, a constant subject for scorn and ridicule in Livingstone's letters.

Already depressed by Philip's gloomy picture of missionary arguing, Livingstone was made still more apprehensive when Philip told him that a local missionary committee was being planned to run the affairs of the missions north of the Orange river. Philip's claim that Moffat was behind it would prove unfounded, but whoever was responsible, the very idea shocked Livingstone and brought out all his independent fervour. After what he had heard about his future colleagues, Livingstone was already convinced that to have to do anything at their instructions would be agony. 'I shall yield cheerful obedience to the committee in London [the Directors of the Society],' he told a friend, 'but to a presbytery of missionaries I cannot; for take us as a body we are really a bad set.'³

On 16 April Livingstone and Ross once more boarded the *George*, this time bound for Algoa Bay, 450 miles to the east of the Cape. From there they were to collect their oxen and waggons for the journey north. On parting from them, Dr Philip told them that their most important task was to live in peace not with the natives so much as with fellow-missionaries. With a temperament like Livingstone's, and an inherent belief in the superiority of his mind over other people's, clearly this was going to be uphill work.

Kuruman, the most remote mission station in southern Africa, was between five and six hundred miles north of Algoa Bay. Travelling in South Africa was slow and expensive; standard transport was the lumbering ox waggon, costing £40 to £75, while the dozen oxen needed to pull it came to about £3 each. A day's progress was rarely more than ten miles and in sandy or very rocky country, sometimes less. Livingstone's journey to Kuruman took him the best part of two months; but provided there was enough water on the way for the oxen, and the roads were reasonably flat, travelling by waggon could be pleasant enough. The waggons themselves were miniature houses with large chests at the front and back for daily supplies such as tea, coffee, rice and so on, and smaller lockers down the sides for cutlery and china. In the middle of the waggon, boxes were stored, and over them a stretcher was placed with bedding laid on top of that. The traveller only pitched a tent if he was stopping for several days or if there were too many people in one waggon to make sleeping inside it comfortable. Other provisions, such as meal, would be hung suspended in large canvas sacks and still more could be roped under the waggon itself. The driving would be done by two or three Africans with long whips made of giraffe or rhinoceros skin.

From the very beginning of the journey, in spite of the unwelcome company of Mr and Mrs Ross, Livingstone was delighted by African travel. After the strict routine in Ongar and London, the complete freedom of stopping where and when he wanted, lighting a fire and

1 LIVINGSTONE'S JOURNEYS,
1841–1852

cooking when he was hungry, and looking across miles and miles of thinly populated country, seemed to mark a complete break with his cramped and regulated past existence. At times the roads were so bad that Livingstone feared the waggon might tip over and crush them all, and at others, steep hills alarmed him in case the oxen stumbled and let the waggon run forward out of control.

For several days Livingstone thought the scenery not unlike Scotland, only hotter, but as he came closer to Kuruman and Bechuanaland the country began to change and he saw for the first time the endless vistas of rock, sand and lifeless scrub that he was to become so well accustomed to. Cutting across the sun-baked table-land were broad, dried-out river beds filled with boulders, which posed terrible problems to the oxen; and the only relief on the horizon would be low, flat-topped ranges of hills with strange crumbling sides, like cake roughly cut with a blunt knife. The Dutch called them kopjes. Where trickles of water appeared in the river beds, acacias grew, and around them low scrub with villainous 'wait-a-bit' thorns. Near water there would also be a variety of grasses and aloes with fleshy, purple-blotched leaves and spikes of waxy red or yellow tube flowers. Occasionally near river beds were small fan-palms with sage-coloured spiky fronds, and huge gouty baobab trees with their broad, distended trunks and spindly branches, bare for all but two months of the year.

In the spring or after the rains, the river beds would fill again briefly and the grass grow green, while water-melons would rapidly ripen and straggling gourds revive. There would be lilies too, white and pink, and the mopane trees would put out new, tender, pinkish-blue shoots, but soon everything would return to the old parched greyness and the rocks and sand once more would dominate the landscape.

Throughout his time in Bechuanaland, Livingstone was amazed at the quantity of wild life capable of supporting itself in such apparently unpromising terrain. Spiders, scorpions, ants, lizards and frogs were all numerous, and herds of giraffe would scud across the plains to feed on the scarce foliage of the acacias. Antelope, wildebeest, blesboks, springboks and pallahs were to be seen in large numbers, and further north the lion and rhinoceros were still abundant and the distinctively marked zebra was often to be found.

When Livingstone arrived at Kuruman on the last day of July, the South African winter was nowhere near over and the country would remain parched and dreary for another three months.

All around is a dreary desert for a great part of the year, enough indeed, from its nakedness and sand, to give its people most of that opthalmia with which they are so often afflicted. There is not a tree near the station which has not been planted by the missionaries. Low stunted scraggy bushes, many of them armed with bent thorns villainously sharp and strong are the chief objects which present themselves to the eye.[4]

Livingstone had not expected Kuruman to be an aesthetic paradise but he *had* expected the place where Moffat had laboured for twenty years to be large, densely populated, entirely Christian and within reach of other heavily peopled areas. Moffat himself had spoken of the smoke rising from the fires of a thousand villages to the north. Livingstone was horrified to find that almost all his hopes had been false and the mental picture of the place which he had treasured for so long was a grossly distorted image. To start with, Moffat seemed to have misled people about Kuruman's size: it was no more than a small village. That in itself would not have mattered if there had been native villages clustered around, but there were no such settlements, and most estimates of the population for twenty miles around did not exceed a thousand. If most of these thousand people had been Christians, Livingstone might have felt his disappointment less keenly, but the vast majority, while often wearing crudely made European clothes, had never been baptized. Moffat's native congregation amounted to about 350, an impressive figure, but of these just under forty were communicants. Forty Christians made in twenty years by the most famous missionary in southern Africa—Livingstone was staggered. He wanted to write home to the Directors of the London Missionary Society to tell them that they had been duped, but as he told a friend, 'If I wrote home to the Directors they won't believe me for I am a nobody in their eyes.' But, novice or not, he could not endure saying nothing and wrote telling the Directors that Kuruman could never become populous and would probably lose people in the future, since the Bechuanas were cattle-farmers and would inevitably choose better-watered and more fertile places to graze their oxen and sheep.[5] Livingstone was telling the truth but the Directors were not alarmed; nobody could seriously expect them to believe that their most publicized African mission station was an arid, underpeopled village that might soon be deserted. Magnanimously they put down Livingstone's complaint to youthful enthusiasm.

When Livingstone had finished tormenting himself with the problems of cattle-grazing and population, his thoughts usually returned to the question of conversions. He concluded, logically enough, that there must be some explanation for the tiny number of converts. The missionaries could only have been going about things the wrong way. On his way to Kuruman he had passed through Griqua Town and had met the missionaries there. He had found out that the reason why the Kuruman missionaries disliked their neighbouring colleagues was the Griqua Town policy of using African teachers for effecting conversions. In Moffat's view, no Africans had been trained sufficiently to enable them to give a faithful and accurate version of the Gospel, or to make them more than purveyors of falsehood. Livingstone nevertheless was certain that the Griqua Town Mission had found the answer. It seemed obvious to him that Africans would resist Christianity less adamantly if it were offered to them by people with black skins. Then Christianity would not simply appear as one of the white man's customs.[6] In theory Livingstone was absolutely right, but in practice he would soon find that suitable African teachers were very hard to find.

Livingstone undoubtedly got a far worse impression of Kuruman than he would have done had Moffat already returned from England. The almost total paralysis in the place had a simple cause: Moffat was the driving force and Moffat was not there. The trouble was that the Directors had left no instructions for what ought to be done with Livingstone; he was expected patiently to await Moffat's return. Nobody had the faintest idea when that return might be: maybe the end of the year, maybe the end of the next. Livingstone very much resented the implication of the Directors' refusal to issue him with instructions. It seemed that the worthy men in London believed that nobody could do anything in Africa without Moffat's guidance. 'I did not come to be suspended on the tail of any one,' Livingstone wrote home bitterly. He also made up his mind that he would never stay at Kuruman, whatever he was told to do.[7]

Disappointed already, the waiting and sitting about increased Livingstone's bitterness and frustration. It was not long before he discovered that the tribes living roughly a hundred miles from Kuruman to the north had developed a dislike and scorn for the people of Christian-dominated Kuruman. The reason was that these more distant tribes had only been preached to a few times and their impression of Christianity was the usual distorted version: that the white man's religion was just a trick to get them to give up their wives. Livingstone became certain that this attitude would soon poison the minds of tribes living two and three hundred miles north of Kuruman. It therefore seemed imperative for a missionary to make contact with these untouched people before that happened. There was also a danger that if missionaries did not reach them soon, traders would get there first and give them quite the wrong impression of what white men wanted. Livingstone wrote telling the Directors this, but received no satisfactory reply. By now thoroughly disgusted, all Livingstone could do was try to cure minor ailments and learn Sichuana.

Livingstone's misery during his early days in Bechuanaland has not received much attention in the past, for in later published accounts of this period of his life he did not make much of his disappointment, largely out of respect for Moffat's feelings. But his initial disillusion was to be an important early determining factor in his life. If twenty years' hard work by Moffat had only produced Kuruman, Livingstone came to feel that he would have to spend the next twenty years of his life working in a different way. With the shock of disappointment still fresh, he was not yet sure how his own future would differ, but differ in some way he knew it would have to.

Had Livingstone been shown figures for conversions in other South African missions before he left England, he would have realized that Moffat had achieved as much at Kuruman as any other missionary else-where, inside or outside the colony. Ignorance of the problems that men like Moffat had faced, coupled with a previously uncritical acceptance of missionary propaganda at home, had left Livingstone incapable of making an objective judgment when faced with the real situation. The Hebrew, Greek and theology learned at Ongar had done nothing to offset the stories of African missionary successes which Livingstone had so eagerly read about in the *Missionary Magazine* and the *Evangelical Magazine*. Both these publications had been far more concerned with missionary fund-raising than with truthful reporting. Had it been admitted that most missionaries laboured for years before achieving anything at all, and that Africans only tolerated missionaries because they could mend guns and bring beads, the public would not have dipped their hands into their pockets. Instead there had to be reports of instant success or spectacular failure, accompanied if possible by martyrdom. When missionaries returned to harangue the faithful, the heads of their societies would not have thanked them if they had painted bleak pictures of failure and isola-tion. Accurate information about African conversions were not to be had from missionary sources in England. The only alternative source of infor-mation available to Livingstone in England had been the writings of travellers like Park, Clapperton and Lander. Unfortunately these books had been written for entertainment and, while they made the public gasp with stupefaction at the alleged absurdity, barbarity or pure nonsense of tribal customs, they had been worse than useless for any reader wanting to discover more about the African's way of life and the problems which it might pose to missionaries. Park and the rest of them used customs out of context simply as extravaganzas—vignettes of local colour to add spice to already spicy stories.

Nothing that Livingstone had been told or read had given him any idea of what Moffat had been through after his arrival at Kuruman in 1821. For a start Moffat had needed to gain the tribe's consent to settle with them, then he had to grapple with building houses for himself and his fellow-workers and with starting gardens and planting crops and vegetables. With no knowledge of the Sichuana language he had had to reduce it, write it down and finally work out its grammar. Completely cut off from the outside world, he had needed to return to Cape Town for supplies when they ran out, and this journey had each time taken six months there and back. Much of his time had to be devoted to daily agricultural tasks, mending waggons, making ploughs or attending to animals. No thought could be given to conversions till he was sure that he had mastered the language. His wife had lived an equally hard and difficult life; in addition to the usual tasks of cooking, washing and mending, she had been obliged to make clothes, and learn how to manufacture soap and candles. Making cheese and butter had also occupied her time. Frequent pregnancies and inadequate medical attention had weighed heavily on her. It is not hard to imagine what such isolation could do to people over long periods of time; cut off from their own society and usually facing total indifference on the part of the Africans they had come to 'save', it is a wonder that Moffat persevered for eight years to make his first converts. Livingstone had imagined converts being made after a short struggle and had never thought about the possibility of their backsliding. Moffat could have told him that it was almost impossible to tell whether a conversion was genuine or not. Conversions could simply be the result of gratitude for agricultural improvements or a desire to please the 'gun mender', which is the role the missionaries were often given. Add to these difficulties the low rainfall and frequent cattle disease, and Moffat's achievement can be seen in perspective. Livingstone would get that perspective later, but by that time his mind was moving in other directions.

Before Moffat returned to Africa, and before Livingstone made any independent moves of his own, the young missionary had written a confidential letter to his sisters in Scotland telling them: 'I would never build on another man's foundation. I shall preach the gospel beyond every other man's line of things.'[8] There is certainly nothing in this that suggests that he was already primarily interested in exploration, but it does pose a difficult question. If Livingstone chose a tribe that was *then* beyond other men's lines of operation, would he remain content to stay there if other missionaries started to outdistance him? Livingstone often repeated this phrase about working in more remote places than everybody else, so it is significant, and pointed to an ambition to excel personally: a very questionable motive for a young man ostensibly about to begin a grinding and largely frustrating life of humble service with a single tribe. There are other clues in letters of this date that again indicate thinking opposed to conventional missionary aims. Livingstone told a friend that he had heard that there was a large lake hundreds of miles to the north, which 'everyone would like to be the first to see'.[9] 'Everyone', Livingstone admitted in the same letter, included himself.

Livingstone had been at Kuruman only a month when to his amazement and delight he heard that Rogers Edwards, the missionary with whom he was temporarily lodging, had just gained permission from the Directors to make a journey of several hundred miles to the north of Kuruman with a view to selecting a site for a new mission station. Edwards asked Livingstone if he would like to come too, and understandably the younger man leapt at the offer. In contrast to his initial reaction to Ross, Livingstone had liked Edwards from the beginning, considering him 'an excellent friend'.[10] Edwards was in his late forties and had been at Kuruman almost as long as Moffat himself. Unlike Moffat, however, Edwards had been an artisan missionary all those years and had never been promoted to the post of full missionary. He had disliked being what he called 'Moffat's lackey' and saw the chance of forming a new mission as his last chance to gain promotion.

The journey that Edwards and Livingstone made between September and December 1841 was to lead Livingstone to undertake two more trips on his own between April 1842 and June 1843. The three journeys together paved the way for the selection of a site for the new mission and its inauguration by Livingstone and Edwards in August 1843. During this two-year period Moffat remained in England and the Directors did not send Livingstone any further instructions; neither did they give their permission for him to join with Edwards in starting the new station till July 1843, when Livingstone had already made definite plans to do so.

The three journeys were all to the north-east, and the furthest Livingstone travelled from Kuruman was five hundred miles as the crow flies. The main tribes he met were the Bakhatla, 250 miles north-east of Kuruman; the Bakwains, a tribe split under two rival chiefs, and situated 60 miles north-west of the Bakhatla; and the Bamangwato, 150 miles north of the Bakwains. The Bamangwato had already been visited by two travelling ivory and skin traders, Wilson and Hume, in the early 1830s. So, while Livingstone met many Africans who had never seen a white face before, he was not, strictly speaking, breaking into totally unexplored country. The main importance of the three trips to him, apart from the ultimate foundation of the new mission, was the knowledge they gave him of the difficulties he would face when he began his own work as a missionary. What he discovered was anything but encouraging and led him to view Kuruman with a less critical eye.

To begin with, Livingstone realized that travel in Bechuanaland could be a lot less comfortable than his journey up to Kuruman. Any journey undertaken between November and January—the hottest time of the year—was a physical ordeal in a country with very little water. The waggon oxen might have to go two days without water in temperatures well over 100° Fahrenheit, and the same would apply to human beings if a known water-hole turned out to be dry. On his first trip to the north, Livingstone described the heat as so great that 'the very flies sought the shade and the enormous centipedes coming out by mistake from their holes were roasted to death on the burning sand'.[11] The scenery, for the most part, was as uninspiring as that around Kuruman, and, as Livingstone mournfully acknowledged, Bechuanaland was no more populous further north. 'We travelled over hundreds of miles of dreary wilderness, not a soul appearing in sight.'[12] There were few compensations, but Livingstone did at least see his first elephants and marvelled at the digestive powers of an animal that could eat branches as thick as his thumb and 'covered with large strong thorns more than an inch in length'.[13]

At first, African reactions to the arrival of so strange a visitor as a white man amused Livingstone. He noted how his straight hair was a source of fascination and incredulity, and laughed when a woman touched his nose 'to make herself sure that it really was so far elevated from the level of my face as it appeared to be and was not like her own little flat thing'.[14] Livingstone was also entertained by African fascination with European technical gadgets like watches and cutlery. 'Show one a looking glass,' he told a friend, 'and he will almost go into convulsions at his own image.'[15] But while European strangeness led the locals to show Livingstone respect, their automatic assumption that he was 'a great wizard . . . possessed of supernatural power . . . capable of even raising the dead' did not please him at all.[16] He realized that while this kind of hold over the people was useful to persuade them to dig watercourses and build small dams, it was a terrible barrier to any form of religious teaching. Even at Kuruman he had seen people hiding under the benches in the chapel to avoid the preacher's eye and sometimes rushing out of the building screaming with fear.[17] He was often horrified to hear people calling him by the Sichuana word for God, a title frequently given to chiefs.

When he tried to get across to Africans the idea of praying to an unseen deity, and knelt down to show them the position in which Christians prayed, he was greeted with delighted laughter. Livingstone's head bowed to the earth convinced his audience that he was talking to a god who lived under the ground. His first attempts to explain to them in Sichuana about the coming of Christ and His great sacrifice made no impression at all. On his second journey, full of optimism, he had taken the two most reliable native Christians in Kuruman to preach to the northern tribes. The result had been no better, and although the preachers had managed to collect an audience, interruptions, sometimes ten minutes long, had quickly brought the instruction to a halt.

Livingstone did a little better when talking to individual chiefs in private. Sekhomi, chief of the Bamangwato, when told that Christianity could change people's hearts, immediately expressed interest. Sekhomi explained to Livingstone that for a long time he had been afflicted by violent and quite unpredictable fits of rage. Christianity, he felt, might cure him. Livingstone did his best to point out that the Gospel was not a medicine, but Sekhomi brushed this explanation aside. If Christianity would stop his rages, he would accept it straight away, if only his white visitor would stop making excuses and give him the magic drink. His heart troubled him, Sekhomi went on: 'I wish to have it changed by medicine, to drink and have it changed at once.'[18] Further attempts at reasoning got Livingstone nowhere.

With Sechele, chief of part of the divided Bakwain tribe, Livingstone at least managed to get over the idea of Christianity as something to be understood rather than eaten or drunk. Sechele in fact embarrassed him by asking some extremely difficult questions. Why was it, the chief enquired, that Europeans had not tried to convert Africans sooner, since they had known for centuries that Christianity brought great benefits? 'My ancestors are gone,' he continued, 'and none of them knew anything of what you tell me. How is this?'[19] Livingstone later remarked: 'I thought immediately of the guilt of the church, but did not confess.'[20] At the time he made excuses about Africa being a faraway country and very difficult to travel in. Sechele was not impressed.

Reactions to Livingstone ranged from superstitious dread to sceptical indifference, and made him decide that a new approach to Africans was called for: a far less humble way of dealing with them. Later he told friends that the results were gratifying: 'I make my presence with any of them a favour, and when they show any impudence I threaten to leave them, and if they don't amend I put my threat into execution. By a bold free course among them, I have not had the least difficulty in managing even the most fierce.'[21]

None of this brought him any closer to explaining the Christian faith although he did manage, by explanation of the practical benefits, to persuade several tribes to dig ditches from distant streams to irrigate their crops. At this early stage he began paying Africans for work and always tried to find a poor individual who would 'esteem employment a favour'.[22] Payment would be in tea, coffee, sugar or beads. By making himself useful as an agricultural adviser and general handyman, and by doling out rewards, Livingstone gained some popularity and standing, but this very popularity made him uncertain, when people listened to his preaching, whether they were simply doing so to encourage him to stay with them long enough to give more technical help. As time passed he became sure that in their eyes he was somebody to be exploited by a little politeness.

Nevertheless there were small compensations, as when the Bakhatla allowed him to see their iron-smelting process: a sight never before witnessed by a European. Before they would reveal these mysteries Livingstone was asked whether he had recently had sexual intercourse. Indignantly he told his questioners that he was unmarried, and when they were still unsatisfied, he tried to explain his views on fornication and adultery. At last they were convinced and he was taken to see the smelting; his hosts apologized for the questions but pointed out that the presence of anybody who had had intercourse within the past month would spoil the iron. The Bakhatla in fact showed Livingstone such friendliness that he felt safe to ask their chief, Moseealele, whether he would consent to have a missionary settle with him. Moseealele, recognizing that a missionary might attract traders and would certainly bring a knowledge of gun-mending, agreed at once. Livingstone, still uncertain of the Directors' intentions, was not able to say when he and Edwards would come, but at least the chief's consent had been given.

Back in Kuruman in June 1843, with these three preparatory journeys behind him, Livingstone was left to ponder the vast difficulties that lay ahead. In July he heard from the Directors, who at last agreed to his joining in the formation of a new mission station but suggested that the move should not be made till Moffat came back. Livingstone, having just experienced the heady freedom of travelling hundreds of miles with only three African attendants, was not pleased by this check. He was still more distressed when he read that the Directors intended Moffat to organize a local committee as soon as he returned. The committee would discuss whether the site Livingstone proposed was suitable. Feeling as he did about committees, and having, as he put it, 'not the least confidence in the wisdom either collective or individual of our South African bretheren',[23] Livingstone decided that to wait for Moffat's return would be to court endless delay and quibbling. Perhaps the committee might wreck the whole scheme. This possibility was more than Livingstone could endure. He imagined that unless he could get out of Kuruman before Moffat returned, he might have to spend years as Moffat's 'lackey' just as Edwards had done. He confided his fears to Edwards and reminded him that both their futures were bound up in the new venture. Edwards was frightened of doing anything that might give the Directors offence but eventually he confessed that Livingstone's reasoning was sound. Unless they left soon, both men knew that the weather would become too hot for them to build huts on their arrival at Moseealele's.

Livingstone and Edwards planned to leave Kuruman for the north-east in early August. As they were preparing to depart, three young Englishmen arrived; they were officers on leave from postings with British regiments stationed in India and had come to South Africa for some hunting. When they asked to come north too, the two missionaries raised no objections, so Livingstone got his first close view of members of the British upper class. Although he disapproved of the three men's pointless killing of game, he liked them as people and did not react like a man with a chip on his shoulder. He liked best Captain Steele, the current aide-de-camp to the Governor of Madras. Steele was apparently 'well versed in the classics & possessed of much general knowledge'.[24] Livingstone later corresponded with him. While Livingstone was never exactly a social climber, he had considerable respect for people who were 'well bred' and tended to keep in touch for longer than he did with humbler acquaintances of earlier years.

Once the party arrived among the Bakhatla, the three hunters went off together, and Livingstone and Edwards attended a meeting that Moseealele had called to inform his people of the missionaries' intended settlement and to gauge his subjects' feelings. After some discussion, Moseealele gave his formal consent. The *Missionary Chronicle*, true as ever to its unfailing standard of inaccuracy, depicted this event, in the April edition of 1844, with Livingstone and Edwards both wearing top hats and frock-coats.

The Bakhatla had independently made up their minds to move to the spot which Livingstone had selected for the new mission, so there was no argument on that score. The missionaries bought the land they intended to live on and cultivate. Although they could have had it for nothing, they felt that only by paying would they not be beholden to the chief. Moseealele did not mind either way. As far as he was concerned a man who asked for land became his vassal whether he gave gifts or not. Nevertheless Livingstone and Edwards drew up formal title deeds for their new property and got the chief to make his mark. The area bought was a mile and a half in width and two in length; it was purchased with a gun, some powder, lead and beads. The legal formalities over, the missionaries set to work to build a large hut: no less than fifty feet by eighteen. This would one day be the chapel, they hoped. Neither man, however, was under any illusions about why they were wanted. 'They wish the residence of white men,' declared Livingstone, 'not from any desire to know the Gospel, but merely, as some of them in conversation afterwards expressed it, "That by our presence and prayers they may get plenty of rain, beads, guns &c. &c."'[25]

The Bakhatla also rather optimistically believed that the missionaries might in some inexplicable way be able to help them if they were attacked by the Boers or the Matabele, who were then fighting each other for possession of the Transvaal just to the east. But whatever the reasons behind the Bakhatla's desire for missionaries, Livingstone was satisfied that Mabotsa, the site of the new mission, was a more fertile and well-watered place than Kuruman. The presence of wild fig trees even led him rashly to tell a friend that he believed 'all kinds of tropical fruits might be cultivated with ease'.[26]

So in August 1843, two years after his first arrival in Bechuanaland, Livingstone was about to embark on missionary work of his own. He had shown he was ambitious, and to date he had achieved his desire to live and work in a place 'beyond every other man's line of things'. In his ignorance he had scorned Moffat's achievement; now he would see whether he could do any better.

5

A False Start: Mabotsa
1844–1845

<hr>

B efore looking in detail at Livingstone's missionary work, it is necessary to have a picture of the people he was trying to convert: their
numbers, beliefs and tribal organization. To date, in explaining the
minute number of converts, I have concentrated on the physical difficulties that faced the early missionaries: their isolation, agricultural tasks and
problems ranging from the compilation of a language to the building of a
house. All these activities dissipated energies and contributed to their
failure, but the primary cause always lay with the Africans themselves.

Livingstone's estimate for the population of Bechuanaland was thirty
thousand, and although it was a conservative guess, he was probably not
more than ten thousand out. There were eight or so major tribes, all of
the same Bechuana or Tswana stock, and the numbers of each ranged
from two to seven thousand. Livingstone worked first with the Bakhatla
and then with the Bakwains (Kwena) and they accounted for 2,000 and
3,500 people, respectively.[1] The primary activity of these tribes was cattle-
farming, with agriculture coming a poor second, maize and sorghum
being the principal crops. The only agricultural implements were hoes and
primitive ploughs. A very low annual rainfall guaranteed disappointing
results. The Bechuana tribes lived in towns or villages and these centres
remained occupied for many years at a time. When Livingstone visited
Shoshong, the capital of the Bamangwato, he found over three thousand
people living there. Mabotsa was rather smaller with 400 huts and a population of about 1,500. The Bechuanas paid the price for keeping their
established villages; as the cattle-grazing around them diminished, they
had to move their cattle further away to distant cattle posts. Cattle might
be grazing over fifty miles away before the people would accept a move as
inevitable. Crops, too, were often grown many miles away. As a result
people were often travelling backwards and forwards between their
villages and the grazing pastures and gardens. These absences were naturally a hindrance to consecutive missionary teaching sessions. Dress was
fairly uniform: a leather or fur cloak or *kaross* worn over a leather apron.
Ivory or copper rings and ornaments were often worn, and most people

smeared their skins with a mixture of grease and a metallic powder called *sibilo*. Men and women divided their tasks: the men tending the all-important cattle—milking was a male job—as well as preparing leather, sewing clothes, and when necessary making war; while the women grew the crops, fetched water and fuel, cooked, looked after the children and built the houses.

Tribal chiefs were hereditary rulers and in Bechuanaland, at least, the succession passed to the first son of the chief's principal wife. The chief had religious as well as temporal duties. He was often the tribe's rain-maker: a much respected office in a country with very little rain. Rather surprisingly, constant failure did not make the people doubt their rain-maker's powers. Without his work they believed no rain at all would fall. The chief also performed the rituals connected with sowing and harvest, with moving a village and going to war. As head of the tribal government he had the last word on policy decisions; he acted as judge in all disputes and distributed the land for use by his subjects. Land was freely given on a basis of tenure rather than possession. The chief was also responsible for looking after his people's interests and safeguarding them, as much as he could, against famine. The poor turned to him for help and he always had to feed numerous relatives. His generosity was taken for granted and to maintain it he needed all the dues and privileges he received in exchange for his allocation of land. His powers were tempered by his being the representative of the people and the living embodiment of the tribal will. He usually consulted a circle of advisers before making vital decisions.

The heart of the missionaries' difficulties lay in the enormous differences between the social, moral and economic requirements of nineteenth-century industrial Britain and those of a small African tribal community. Victorian virtues such as work, punctuality, thrift, monogamous marriage and personal ambition were all vices which a good African tribesman wanted to avoid. In a tribal community men and women certainly worked, but they did not do so to grow rich or to build up a surplus of food. Work was limited to providing the necessities of life and setting aside a small communal store of food to protect the tribe against drought and famine. A man who attempted to keep for himself a surplus of food to sell at a profit would have been ostracized for an antisocial act. Each man depended on his neighbour; and in a society where no exchanges of goods were made on a money basis, it was advisable to be generous when your own crops were fruitful, for the next year they might fail and you would be dependent on another's generosity. The whole tribe was a closely knit, interdependent community based on a comprehensive set of mutual obligations. These obligations to be generous and to think more of the tribe's security than his own did not weigh heavily on a man, since he knew that by fulfilling them he was acting in a correct and moral way. Thrift and personal ambition would have run directly counter to all his beliefs about contributing to the collective benefit of the society of which he was a member. Besides, to become wealthy and to hoard grain was a dangerous course to pursue: such people were often accused of witchcraft.

Economic competition and other ideas associated with capitalism were quite alien to tribal societies. The small scale of the communities and the lack of external markets meant that each society operated as a self-sufficient unit. Competition would only have been possible with outsiders; but with vast distances separating tribes, and the lack of any means of carrying goods except on the backs of oxen or on the heads of men and women, external trade rarely developed. When the missionaries accused the Africans of being lazy and not helping themselves to gain the good things of life by working hard, there was complete incredulity. The missionaries talked about factories and steam engines, but to people who had never seen a house bigger than a hut or any form of transport more sophisticated than a waggon, these stories sounded too far-fetched to be taken seriously. Besides, the Africans were content with the beads, glass, guns and other oddments that the missionaries and traders brought with them. The missionary could give his pupils no better proof of the technical superiority of the European than his pocket watch and his magnifying glass. The tribesmen were impressed, but not enough to wish to change their culture. The missionary was isolated and therefore helpless.

Polygamy was a worse stumbling block than work. At least the missionary could claim some rewards for work and thrift, even if they were thought to be illusory. On the subject of polygamy, the African was convinced that the white man was mad. It was as clear as day that to be satisfied with only one wife was to court social and economic disaster. While economic competition was alien to a tribal community, competition among the various headmen for influence within the tribe was quite legitimate. Such influence could only be acquired by a man with many dependants, and the best way to obtain dependants was to beget them. One wife could only have a limited number of children; the implication was obvious: a man who wanted influence had to have many wives. These wives would also be able to grow more food than would be needed even by the enlarged family, and this would enable the head of the family to give feasts to gain prestige. With luck, if his feasts were impressive enough, he might be able to attract the dependants of other headmen. His generosity would not only advance his own position but would help his tribe. Generosity might not bring an individual short-term profit, but it would certainly bring long-term social benefit. A man would be unable to honour all his obligations if he had only one wife. The chief was always particularly conscious of this. In a technically primitive society he could not show his primacy by living in a house very different from those of his subjects, nor could he demonstrate his superiority by amassing an impressive range of possessions. His position depended solely on the extent of his largesse. Generosity was the basis of tribal security. It would have been completely undermined had nuclear families been substituted for large, interdependent kinship groups. Therefore the missionary who told Africans that polygamy was sinful was laughed at and ignored. In their circumstances the tribesmen knew that monogamy would have brought them disaster.

Obviously, with such different values, the missionaries were unable to get across the Christian idea of sin; nor, where men thought of their well-being in terms of their community, was it possible adequately to explain a concept like individual salvation. Even the notion of Christian equality was repugnant to most Africans; to the chiefs it sounded like open sedition. They might have viewed it with less alarm had they known that most European rulers were nominal Christians. The idea of the resurrection of the dead was almost as bad as the notion of equality. An African chief was not ready to be convinced that those he had killed in battle might rise again.

Grounds for misunderstandings between missionaries and their pupils were too numerous to be conveniently listed. Some, however, were marked. Africans gained a reputation for lying and boasting that was partly due to the fact that a man who had inherited rights from, say, his grandfather would tend to speak in the first person and use the present tense for things his grandfather had done. Again, myth and tribal history were closely interwoven, and in a society with no written records, discrepancies of dating events were inevitable. Africans also got a reputation for imprecise thinking because of failure to give reliable instructions to travellers. Sometimes the reason was that they had never travelled far from their home village, and anyway, as often as not, they failed to see the point of geographical discovery. A pond was water and so was a large lake. Who but a fool would risk life and limb to gaze at gallons of water? They also probably felt that it was unreasonable for strangers to expect from them a great deal of information about their locality before they had got to know them.

Then there were occasions when missionaries witnessed fights and protracted quarrels over apparently trivial incidents: a gift not given, a spear taken from its owner or an obligation waived. But it was on these courtesies that the whole society depended. A spear could symbolize the link between father and son, just as the giving of cattle formed a physical manifestation of the new status of a man and woman after marriage. Rituals, too, were deplored by missionaries, one reason being the obscenity of some of them. On most occasions rituals portrayed behaviour that was to be frowned on. Thus rebellion would be the theme of rituals of national unity, immorality the subject of rituals enjoining proper behaviour, and so on. This ritual licence was and is believed to bless the participants and those who allow the licence. Thus tensions could be released and the statement of conflicts render them harmless.

Europeans also found it almost impossible to grasp African attitudes to ownership and could not understand how matters could run smoothly without enforceable rules. Indeed, disputes over the ownership of cattle were often simply insoluble; two or more men might have different rights over the same beast, and still others rights over the offspring. Then there were different claims to succession to the chiefship and no easily apprehended hard and fast rule. It really is neither true nor fair to see these early missionaries as men successfully deluding helpless Africans with their more powerful culture. While the missionaries were alone and had no help from their own society, they had no hope at all. In their own terms they acknowledged that short of direct intervention by the Holy Spirit, their prospects were extremely bleak.

In this impossible situation it would have been strange if the missionaries had not worked out two main methods for comforting themselves. The first was to subscribe to an unquestioning faith in God's Providence. Death and failure could not be understood by mere mortals but God undoubtedly had a plan too large for any individual to understand. If failure came, it was obvious that God was holding things back for a good reason. Perhaps he was aiding other men's efforts elsewhere. They believed in 'sowing seed that would not bear fruit in their own lifetimes'. The ways of God might be slow but they were also sure and in the end Christianity would triumph everywhere. The second major source of comfort came from exaggerating the supposed depravity of Africans. The African was congenitally indolent, he lied, smelled, rarely attained intelligence greater than that of a fourteen-year-old white child. His nudity and tribal customs were barbarous and his use of women as labourers was disgraceful. Like a child, he displayed his anger and grief in sudden bursts, and even his good qualities usually went to extremes, so that obedience became servility, generosity indulgence and limited intellect deceit. Even those missionaries who retained their philanthropic love for the 'noble savage', and managed to some extent to continue to love the man while hating his habits, were inevitably patronizing. Phrases such as 'the poor African', 'the untaught child of nature' and the 'humble Negro', who might be 'raised' with God's help, were all designed to bolster the missionary's morale and persuade him that until the African grew from childhood to maturity he would not be able to appreciate the gift of true religion.

Robert Moffat exemplified the total condemnation school. Every missionary, he wrote, would have to get accustomed to the natives' 'ignorance, their degradation and their wallowing in wickedness'.[2] By the middle of 1842, Livingstone, taking his cue from his predecessors, was writing equally ringing denunciations: 'The population is sunk into the very lowest state of mental and moral degradation, so much so indeed it must be difficult or rather impossible for Christians at home to realise anything like an accurate notion of the grossness which shrouds their minds.'[3]

But by the middle of 1844, after only a year at Mabotsa, Livingstone was writing about Africans with a perception greater than that shown by any previous missionary observer. First of all he realized, accurately, that Christianity was a direct threat to tribal society on every level. Christianity, he wrote, 'appears to them as that which will reduce them & overturn their much loved "domestic institutions" '.[4] It was a crucial observation and, having made it, Livingstone came to other logical conclusions. He decided that missionaries had failed in the past by too readily condemning what they did not understand. The *boguera* or initiation rites had previously been treated as barbarous black magic and a perverted religious ceremony. Livingstone soon saw that the *boguera* was 'more a national civil rite than a religious observance'. 'Those who have gone to the circumcision together', he wrote, 'are bound into a cohort under one of the chief's sons or brothers for ever afterwards and have to render service, go wherever he is sent, do whatever he likes under pain of death.'[5]

In other words, tribal unity and survival depended on the continuation of the *boguera* and, having grasped this, Livingstone knew that former attacks on it 'had been a great hindrance to the spread of Christianity'. He went as far as to say that he did not consider that 'Christianity gives any licence for assaulting the civil institutions of man',[6] and included polygamy in this. Almost every other missionary working in Africa denounced polygamy, but Livingstone said, 'We cannot call it adultery,' and admitted that whenever he thought about the subject he felt confused and perplexed.[7] Whereas missionaries in the past had always believed that the marriage gift of cattle by the groom to his wife's family constituted 'bride-buying', Livingstone saw that it was more a pledge of good faith for the future, and the physical manifestation of a change in relationship. Although the system complicated cattle ownership, he was aware that the gift of cattle made for ties between families, and encouraged husbands not to desert their wives, since if they did they lost the cattle, which had not been given absolutely, but were on loan.

At Mabotsa Livingstone soon learned that the usual missionary sermons, based on common texts like 'God so loved the world' (John 3:16), were quite useless and equivalent to delivering an address in Greek.[8] Conventional Christian words and images had to be thought out afresh to be made intelligible. For a start the Sichuana word for love, he discovered, made no distinction between sexual and spiritual love, and Bechuanas always understood it in the sense of *eros* rather than *agape*. The Sichuana word usually employed by missionaries for 'holiness' was used by Bechuanas to describe 'a nice fat ox or cow. Beauty is nearest the word in our language but not that exactly'.[9] Similarly the missionary translation of 'sin' was in Sichuana equally applicable to cow dung. There was no Sichuana word that directly translated meant 'soul'; the nearest the missionaries could get was a word used to describe air or steam from a boiling pot.[10]

Livingstone's father used to drive his son into rages when he talked about useful sermons he had heard in Hamilton. 'We don't preach to Scotchmen,' Livingstone wrote back scathingly. The Bakhatla were not people to appreciate Scottish theological quibbles.

Moffat and his colleagues had always claimed that the Bechuanas had no idea of God or a supreme being. Livingstone soon felt convinced that ancestor worship precluded neither the idea of an overall deity nor belief in a future existence.[11] He did not, as many missionaries did, claim that the Africans refused the Gospel out of stupidity; in fact he believed that, in what they knew about from direct experience, they 'showed more intelligence than is to be met with in our own uneducated peasantry'.[12]

Livingstone had no training or background reading to make him so responsive and it is truly remarkable that even when he made no impression on the Bakhatla he retained his liberal beliefs. It would be seven or eight years before he became convinced that every tribal custom, good or bad, would have to give way to British values if Christianity was to make any headway. Only a society in disintegration would prove responsive to an alien religion. But in 1844, at Mabotsa, Livingstone was still a long way from these later beliefs. The Bakhatla's indifference to his teaching did, nevertheless, drive him to the borders of despair. For a time he found consolation in studying plants and animals, finding in them proof of God's 'wonderful intelligence and design'. Only this pursuit, in his view, saved him from callousness and melancholy.[13] But there were times when even he admitted that the habits of ants and scavenger beetles failed to make up for his isolation. While Edwards, his fellow-missionary, was married, he was not. He wrote to all his friends asking them to write as often as they could, but a letter could take from four to six months to reach England and as long again for the reply to come back. Often he implored his family to write more letters and, after one such request, he described his isolation hauntingly:

> Next month I expect to receive letters from home. What are you all doing? is a question that I sometimes ask myself, but no answer but the still deathlike quietness which you can almost hear in this wide wilderness land. Here in the evenings I hear the bleating of sheep & goats, the lowing of oxen & the jabber of the Natives mingling with the yell of the jackal & howling of the wolf. Occasionally the Natives dance & screech their own wild unearthly music the greater portion of the night ... I have written very often to you, but if I don't get letters from you I suppose I shall get tired by & by.[14]

Back in 1840, while still in London, he had written to a friend telling him that if he married it would be only to 'render me most useful, but whether', he went on, 'my usefulness will be augmented by getting a wife, I really don't know'.[15] Again, before leaving Kuruman for Mabotsa, he had written to another fellow-student from Ongar days, firmly repudiating any hints that he was thinking of marriage. 'You thought I should turn foolish at the Cape, what nonsense, man. Do you think I would take a thing in hand and not carry it through?'[16]

At Kuruman, with his journeys and inflated hopes to take the edge off his isolation, it had been easy to sneer at the settled comforts of marriage as weak-minded escapism, but at Mabotsa, with the daily indifference of the locals and no diversions in prospect, he was left far more time to contemplate his personal loneliness. In the few letters he received from home, he was asked about whether he intended to get married. Some friends even sent him some baby clothes to give him the right idea,[17] but even when he knew that he wanted a wife, it was by no means certain that he would find one. Apart from missionary daughters, there were no white women in Bechuanaland, and, knowing the privations of the missionary life, many of those were not prepared to spend their whole lives facing hardships. Anyway Livingstone was not keen to marry into a missionary family. In his view, as he told a friend, 'daughters of missionaries have miserably contracted minds, colonial ladies worse and worse. There's no outlet for me when I begin to think of getting married but that of sending home an advertisement to the Evang. Mag. And if I get very old it must be for some decent sort of widow.'[18]

The half-joking tone could not disguise his real distress. Missionaries often did advertise in missionary publications, and the unions that followed were hardly guaranteed success from the outset. A well-meaning missionary couple had sent their daughter to see Livingstone while he had been at Kuruman, and when nothing had happened, the honest people had started to make enquiries about his female correspondents in England; these efforts included opening some of his letters, and keeping those written to Mrs Sewell, the elderly woman who ran the boarding-house where he had lodged in London. Mrs Sewell was assumed to be some young widow.[19]

Three miserable months passed at Mabotsa, during which Livingstone and Edwards finished the large hut they had begun on their first visit, completed a ditch and watercourse and built one more hut besides. In late October news came from Kuruman that Moffat was at last on his way up from the coast. Livingstone and Edwards knew that they would have to go south to meet him and explain why they had not waited till his arrival before beginning their new mission. On his way to Kuruman, Livingstone felt apprehensive about the coming meeting; he remembered what Dr Philip had said about Moffat and had not entirely got over his own suspicion that the founder of Kuruman had deceived the Directors about the population of Bechuanaland. Rumour, of the usual bitter missionary sort, had it that Moffat had been spoilt by the praise lavished on him in England. It was also said that he was returning a rich man, having made a fortune out of his recently published book, *Missionary Labours and Scenes in Southern Africa*. This was untrue, as was the allegation that he had bought so much in England that his luggage weighed fifty tons.[20] Livingstone was nevertheless inclined to fear the worst. He had already written to his parents telling them to ignore Moffat's book as it was bound to be full of lies.

But just as he had been forced to admit that he was gullible to have believed all he had heard about Philip, Livingstone was soon admitting that he had been a credulous idiot to have misjudged Moffat too. The rapport between the two men was immediate and it marked the beginning of a long friendship. Moffat at forty-eight was still a visually impressive figure, with his long black beard streaked with grey and his commanding height of over six feet. He had a lot in common with Livingstone: both had come from poor Scottish families and both had educated themselves in the first place through their own efforts. Although Moffat's absolute conviction and his inflexible refusal to see anything good in African society must have distressed Livingstone, he had to concede that Moffat was respected by large numbers of local Africans, many of them not Christians. Moffat's most extraordinary success had been with the universally dreaded Mosilikatse (Mzilikazi), the king of the Matabele (Ndebele). Moffat had already visited Mosilikatse twice at his kraal, in what is now Zimbabwe. On each visit he had the courage to criticize an autocrat who normally killed people for saying much less. In fact, Mosilikatse had tears in his eyes on both occasions when Moffat left him. Livingstone felt the power of Moffat's presence at once and described how excited he had been on first seeing Moffat's waggon, and how the new arrival's horse had raced across a wide plain under the burning sun as if 'at Ascot or the Derby', and how once they had started talking, they had not stopped for many hours.[21]

Livingstone had ridden down south almost as far as the Vaal river to meet Moffat. It took them a week or so to return to Kuruman, where they arrived on 13 December.[22] Livingstone, to his great relief, very soon learned that Moffat was not so opposed to 'native teachers' as he had been led to believe, nor was he in favour of a committee. Apart from stimulating discussions there were other pleasures to be had at the Kuruman home of Mr and Mrs Moffat. The Moffats had two daughters of marriageable age, Ann and Mary. Livingstone only stayed at Kuruman for two weeks, but during that time he managed to make some headway with Mary, who, although by no stretch of the imagination beautiful, was attentive and good-tempered. Livingstone knew that a man in his position could not afford to be fussy and he soon made up his mind that Miss Moffat had better become Mrs Livingstone. But he decided to delay asking her formally until his next visit to Kuruman.

Shortly after Christmas, Livingstone was on his way back to Mabotsa, where he experienced far less pleasing embraces. As early as 1842 he had seen 'a woman actually devoured in her garden' by a lion, and had noticed that there was a plague of these animals at Mabotsa. Nevertheless he had never been worried by the thought of any threat to his own skin, and had assured friends in England that 'the sense of danger vanishes when you are in a country of lions'.[23] On 16 February 1844 Livingstone was working in the ditches of the watercourse when some people came screaming to him to help them kill a lion that had just dragged off some sheep. As Livingstone put it later: 'I very imprudently ventured across the valley in order to encourage them to destroy him.'[24] It was not Livingstone's only mistake; he went with only one gun and with no armed African at his side. He fired both barrels at the lion but only wounded him. As he vainly tried to reload, the lion leapt on him and, catching him by the arm, shook him 'as a terrier dog does a rat'. Livingstone's upper arm was splintered at once; the lion's teeth made a series of gashes like 'gun-shot wounds'. Livingstone was only saved by the sudden appearance of Mebalwe, an elderly convert whom Livingstone had brought from Kuruman as a 'native teacher'. Mebalwe, knowing that his master would be dead within moments unless he acted, snatched a gun from another African, loaded and fired both barrels. The gun misfired but the lion was diverted at this crucial moment and bounded off to attack his new assailant. Mebalwe was badly bitten on the thigh and another man who tried to help him was in turn bitten on the shoulder. At this stage, however, the lion suddenly dropped dead, killed at last by the wounds initially inflicted by Livingstone.

In letters written afterwards, Livingstone was extremely reticent about his terrible injuries; this was doubtless partly to avoid worrying people and partly so as not to advertise his own carelessness. In fact he was gravely ill for weeks and too enfeebled to move his limbs for a while. The wounds suppurated for several months. The long-term effects were not as bad as might have been expected and Livingstone was subsequently able to shoot, lift heavy weights and do everything that he had done before. His only limitation was an inability to lift his left arm higher than the shoulder. It is hard to imagine the agony he must have suffered without anaesthetic and without the help of another doctor. He had to supervise the setting of the badly splintered arm himself. Nevertheless he made an astoundingly fast recovery and within three months was working cautiously on the lighter tasks involved in building his house. Then in early July he left for Kuruman and a short period of convalescence. His stay lasted three weeks and during this time he proposed to Mary Moffat and was accepted.

Sophistication was certainly never one of Mary's qualities, and if her manners were unpolished that was to be expected. She had lived all but four of her twenty-three years in Africa. During all that time, apart from occasional visits to the Cape, there had been no social life worth the name; no balls, carriage rides or outings. But what she lacked in refinement, she made up for in other ways. She was literate and had been taught by her mother all the household tasks a missionary's wife ought to be able to manage, ranging from making clothes to making candles and soap. She would never be homesick for England, since Africa had always been her home, and that was a considerable advantage. Livingstone was also convinced that having a wife would help his missionary work; she would run an infants' school and would help allay the suspicions which Africans inevitably felt towards a bachelor missionary who questioned their women on subjects like fornication and adultery. Discussions of sexual ethics with African women would obviously be easier for Mary than for her husband. Mary's presence would also go some way towards cutting out any missionary gossip about him finding consolation with African women. All single missionaries were suspected by the married ones of carrying on in this way.

The marriage was one of convenience to start with, but would become more than that over the years. Livingstone knew that he would be better looked after than hitherto, and there were advantages for Mary too.

Her mother was a domineering woman and it was a relief for her daughter to escape from the house at Kuruman to a home of her own. Like Livingstone she had also had a meagre choice of partners; added to which she was overweight and homely and felt fortunate to be getting married. Moffat's other two daughters eventually married missionaries too.

Livingstone treated his impending marriage with a matter-of-factness that seemed to border on indifference. He could not have been more impersonal in announcing it to the Directors of the Society if he had tried:

> Various considerations connected with this new sphere of labour, and which to you need not be specified in detail, having led me to the conclusion that it was my duty to enter into the marriage relation. I have made the necessary arrangements for union with Mary, the eldest daughter of Mr Moffat, in the beginning of January 1845 ... and if I have not deceived myself I was in some measure guided by a desire that the Divine glory might be promoted in my increased usefulness.[25]

Writing to a friend shortly to begin a missionary career in India, Livingstone advised him to choose a wife before leaving, on the grounds that the missionary, with whom he would otherwise have to lodge, would think him inferior. Livingstone also suggested the best sort of woman for the job: 'a plain common sense woman, not a romantic. Mine is a matter of fact lady, a little thick black haired girl, sturdy and all I want.'[26] For some other friends, he compared his bride with the wife of a mutual acquaintance but added that Mrs Livingstone was 'a great deal stouter'. In later life Mary grew extremely fat but it is interesting that this should already have been a feature in her early twenties. A couple of years later Livingstone was writing to the same people asking them to send some dress material. He told them not to worry much about what they sent, and then described Mary: 'She is a good deal of an African in complexion, a stout stumpy body so you will have no difficulty in selecting the proper sort of thing.'[27] There are no photographs of Mary prior to 1857 and those after that date certainly show that Livingstone's descriptions were accurate; by then she was a stout, heavy-jowled woman with a large nose. Even so, Livingstone's mother might have expected her son to open his heart to her on the subject of his new bride. Livingstone, however, had no intention of gushing about Mary. All he felt able to say was: 'My wife is amiable & good tempered, and my new connections pious, which you know to be the best certificate of character.'[28]

Poor Mary Livingstone was not to have a happy married life. Had she known Livingstone's views on marriage before their wedding, she might have had second thoughts. ' I have never found two agreeing unless one were a cypher,' Livingstone later told his brother-in-law, J.S. Moffat.[29] Livingstone was not joking either; he believed without question that in all working relationships one person had to dominate the other person or persons absolutely, whether man, wife or fellow-missionary. It was a belief that would have much to do with his failure as a leader of Europeans, and to a large extent accounted for his later preference for travelling only with Africans. Livingstone felt that the one mistake he would never make in his marriage was to expect too much of his wife.[30] In the romantic sense he kept his word and certainly never gave her an idyllic role she could not live up to. In other ways he expected a great deal too much. As the old trader Aloysius Horn put it much later, 'dragging that poor Mary Moffat along until she was forced to a long rest in her grave'.[31] But Mary Livingstone's suffering was still in the future when she married David Livingstone on 2 January 1845.

Livingstone had become engaged to Mary in May 1844 and then returned to Mabotsa for five months to finish the house he and Mary would live in. This early separation was the first of many. The letters Livingstone wrote to Mary during it were pleasant, affectionate even, but they contained very little of his thinking on missionary topics. These he reserved for a couple of friends made at Ongar, and for his father-in-law. Later he would confine his serious thinking to letters written to more famous men, and Mary would never be told about his plans for commerce and colonization, when his mind started moving in those directions. Nor were his letters to his wife ever so light-hearted or amusing as those sent to male friends. The disparity in the respective intellectual gifts of husband and wife sometimes worried Livingstone. A lack of communication between Mary and himself is hinted at in a letter he wrote to a friend just a few months after the marriage. 'This is private. I reflect on no one, but there is guilt. I tell you my sorrows although I have a wife.'[32] This single enigmatic sentence stands in isolation, and is made no clearer by the context. The 'guilt' could have been over some wish that he could enjoy prettier women, but it is certain that Livingstone found it distressing to have to talk about problems and 'sorrows' to people other than his wife. There exist only a handful of letters written by Mary herself, and none of these are particularly revealing about the personal aspects of her marriage; they all deal with physical rather than mental hardships.

Livingstone's own feelings about marriage fluctuated. He told J.S. Moffat some ten years later that if he could begin again it would be on a mission station alone with his wife. But at other times he regretted the loss of independence and advocated an isolated, celibate missionary life. His reading about the work of the Jesuits in foreign mission fields made him confess that 'although quite happy and contented in the married state I should like to commence being more of a Jesuit . . . O that I could begin again.'[33] He did not, of course, mean that he would have preferred to have been a Roman Catholic missionary, but that he would rather have stayed celibate.

After their wedding the Livingstones spent January and February of 1845 in Kuruman. During this time Livingstone had a row with his father-in-law about the possible foundation of a seminary for African teachers. Moffat and his colleagues felt that there was insufficient zeal among existing converts to make such an institution viable. Livingstone countered that if they went on with the present system of Bible classes, there would never be enough zeal. He went on openly to criticize the set-up at Kuruman, and, as a result, made himself extremely unpopular. Later he realized that had he attempted to win over one or two of the older missionaries and suggested that one of them should run the new seminary, he might have got somewhere, but instead his own championship of the idea merely appeared as a challenge to the existing order and an implied criticism. Livingstone was also accused of having ambitions to run the seminary himself and thus attract the attention of the Directors. Before that, many of the other missionaries had come to dislike Livingstone because of his openly expressed hostility to the committee. They were not fools and could see that his real objection was to his fellow-workers themselves. The young man's journeys, and his setting up of the new mission before being finally authorized to do so by the committee, gained him a reputation for ambition and 'the wrong kind of ambition' at that.[34]

Livingstone's scathing attacks on William Ross, who had travelled out to Africa on the same ship, gave early indication of his tendency to judge harshly on little evidence. His ready acceptance of unfavourable reports of Philip and Moffat confirmed the feeling that eagerness to condemn others might be a serious defect in his character. This was further supported by events during 1844 and 1845.

On his return to Africa, Moffat was accompanied by a young missionary called Walter Inglis, who had been a fellow-student of Livingstone's at Ongar. Before Inglis arrived, Livingstone had written to the Directors telling them that he would prefer to work at Mabotsa with a young man like Inglis rather than with an older man like Edwards. Nevertheless Moffat told Livingstone that Inglis had many faults and would probably not make a good missionary. Livingstone immediately wrote to his parents telling them: 'Inglis I suspect won't do for Africa . . . he will be a curse.' In the same letter Livingstone denounced those who had lied about Moffat's character without evidence. He seems to have been unaware of his own hypocrisy. Livingstone had denounced Moffat as eagerly as anybody and was now maligning Inglis before he was even reunited with him in Africa. Ironically Livingstone's attack was due to Inglis's objections to the committee. The arguments which now struck Livingstone as examples of 'ridiculous intellectual pride' were almost identical to his own earlier complaints about the committee. Livingstone's attitude to Inglis showed a complete inability to detect faults in himself, even when guilty of failings he happily condemned in others.

But it was not to be Inglis who would provoke Livingstone to display all the worst aspects of his character, but Edwards. Within weeks of his return to Mabotsa at the end of March 1845 with his new bride, Livingstone was to show himself capable not only of hypocrisy and self-righteousness in his dealings with colleagues but also of lies and double-dealing.

Between August 1843 and December 1844, in the months when Livingstone and Edwards were at Mabotsa together, their relationship had steadily deteriorated but with few outward signs. On two occasions there had been rows over trivial incidents that led Edwards to claim that Livingstone was attempting to undermine his authority over the Bakhatla by taking the side of tribesmen whom Edwards had censured for various reasons. It was unfortunate for Edwards that he chose two minor incidents with which to challenge Livingstone; for it made it easy for the younger man to represent Edwards as a small-minded idiot who could work himself into a frenzy over trivial matters. This was precisely the line Livingstone took when he wrote a 9,000-word letter to the Directors, telling them about Edwards's unstable temperament. In this gigantic piece of self-justification, Livingstone cannily relegated to a secondary position the real cause for tension. Behind all Edwards's hostility lay an absolute conviction that Livingstone was attempting to claim all the credit for the foundation of the new mission.

Edwards had good grounds too. A letter written by Livingstone in 1843, for publication in the *Missionary Chronicle*,[35] had not included a single mention of Edwards as co-founder of Mabotsa. Edwards was not unaware that Livingstone had told several missionaries at Kuruman that the choice of site was entirely due to his own preparatory journeys. Edwards quite justifiably considered that if he had not taken Livingstone with him on his journey of 1841, Livingstone might never have made his subsequent trips. Also Livingstone had tried to persuade the Directors that on this first journey he and Edwards had not visited the Bakhatla at all. This was a lie designed to cut Edwards out altogether. The two men had gone to the Bakhatla together on that first occasion, and afterwards Edwards had written to the Directors proposing a mission among the Bakhatla near Mosega. Mabotsa was less than thirty miles from Mosega.

Soon Livingstone was even claiming that Edwards had never wanted to found another mission anyway. Edwards did not see Livingstone's letters to the Directors but he guessed what Livingstone was up to, partly through what he heard from other missionaries and partly from the accounts of the foundation of the station, which Livingstone had sent home for publication.

Livingstone's attempt to make the Directors see him as an innocent wounded by the sudden tantrums of a madman was by no means the result of naivety. He cannot have failed to realize how important Mabotsa was to Edwards: it represented his last chance to establish himself as an independent missionary, his final opportunity to escape from a life dominated by Moffat. Nor, knowing Edwards's feelings about Moffat, could Livingstone have been surprised that Edwards was distressed to see Mary Moffat at Mabotsa. It almost seemed as though Moffat had sent a spy to report back to Kuruman. Livingstone must surely have known that to avoid serious trouble with Edwards he would have needed to be especially forbearing. In the event, when Edwards first lost his temper, Livingstone made sure that the row boiled up into something serious enough to create a lasting rift.

The worst aspect of Livingstone's behaviour was his failure to tell Edwards that he intended leaving Mabotsa anyway. This decision had been made while Livingstone was at Kuruman just after his wedding. Before returning to the Bakhatla he had written to friends telling them that Mabotsa was too small to provide work for two missionaries. He went on to say that he did not fancy working with another man, for he wanted to be responsible for introducing the Gospel to a tribe 'wholly by my instrumentality'. He concluded with the statement that he would leave Mabotsa 'as soon as possible'.[36]

Had Livingstone told Edwards that he meant to leave anyway, all Edwards's suspicions and worries would have melted away. Livingstone must have known this too, and yet it was months before he finally got round to telling Edwards. When the older man then stated that he would never have quarrelled had he known, Livingstone used the admission as clinching proof that Edwards had never had a leg to stand on.[37]

Livingstone later argued that his long letter to the Directors vilifying Edwards was made necessary by a letter Edwards had written laying charges against him. Although Edwards wrote such a letter and Livingstone said he saw it, Edwards never actually sent it, and his next letter to the Directors, written a year after the quarrel, hardly mentioned Livingstone at all. Livingstone claimed that he felt degraded by the whole business, but later wrote dozens of letters to Moffat filled with bitter remarks about Edwards. The matter even seemed to give a spur to other animosities,

and led Livingstone to attack the Rosses again. Not even the death of
Mrs Ross made him relent. 'Mrs Ross is gone,' he wrote. 'No loss
certainly, not even to her own children.'[38] He went on telling tales to the
Directors too, until they finally had to tell him to learn the meaning of the
word 'charity' and to stop expecting them to take his word as gospel when
he himself was one of the parties concerned.[39] Yet not even this stinging
rebuke could stop him telling lies about Edwards. Soon Livingstone was
claiming that Edwards had never helped him with his house-building in
spite of the injuries to his arm caused by the lion. At the time he had told
Mary the truth: that Edwards was unable to assist because of an injury to
his hand.[40] Edwards said that he had done everything he could to nurse
Livingstone after the lion accident, going so far as to build an extra room
on to his own house especially for the invalid. Livingstone however told
Moffat that he had had difficulty in getting Edwards or his wife to dress
his arm 'even when crawling with maggots'.[41] On the whole Edwards's
version is easier to believe, since Livingstone did not complain about this
neglect till after the quarrel. It is quite inconceivable that a man with
Livingstone's temperament could have remained silent about such brutal
treatment for such a long time.

The accusations and spite were not all on Livingstone's side, however,
since Mrs Edwards took it upon herself to write to Mrs Moffat telling her
that her son-in-law was 'shabby, ungentlemanly and unchristian'.[42] On
Livingstone's side it can also be claimed that the long time-lag between
his first visit to the Bakhatla with Edwards and the establishment of the
mission three years later suggests that Edwards had really played a subsidiary role. But, whatever the facts, Livingstone's behaviour throughout the
whole affair brought him little credit. Past biographers have glossed over
the whole incident and have therefore not only distorted Livingstone's
character but in doing so have also ignored an important contributory
motive for his later decision to leave Bechuanaland: namely his complete
inability to live and cooperate with other missionaries.

After the row it was quite evident that the Livingstones and the
Edwardses could no longer remain on the same mission station. Since
Livingstone intended to leave anyway, it would have been grotesquely
inconsistent of him if he had suggested that Edwards ought to be the one
to clear out. Livingstone has been said to have left a well-established and
thriving mission to his disagreeable fellow-missionary, simply out of the
goodness of his heart.[43] Nothing could be further from the truth.
Livingstone was relieved to be going because the Bakhatla had already
shown definite signs of caring not a damn for Christianity. Livingstone
had met Sechele, chief of half the Bakwain tribe, on two of his early
excursions from Kuruman, and Sechele had impressed him as a more

likely candidate for conversion than the chief of the Bakhatla. Sechele had also recently moved to a place called Chonuane, only forty miles north of Mabotsa. Having asked Sechele if he would have him as his missionary, and having received a positive invitation, Livingstone began making preparations for his move. He ought to have asked the Directors' permission first, but since their reply would take anything up to a year to come back, Livingstone decided to move first and explain later.

6

Livingstone and the Boers: Chonuane
1845–1847

—⟫•◆•⟪—

The rapidity of Livingstone's move to Chonuane was understandable, given the state of his relations with Edwards, but the choice of site could not have been worse. Sechele had already discovered this but had not wanted to discourage such potentially useful visitors as the Livingstones by telling them about his difficulties. Of course Sechele was no keener to become a Christian than the chief of the Bakhatla had been; he merely wanted a gun mender and technical adviser.

Shortly after his arrival at Chonuane, Livingstone wrote proudly to friends, telling them that he was now the most remotely situated missionary in southern Africa, living at a place which was 'a blank on the map'. His excitement was nevertheless short-lived. The water supply was bad at the best of times and for most of the year dried up entirely. The year 1845 had also seen a severe drought and most of the corn had been ruined. Sechele had been compelled to plant crops forty miles away from his village, and had recently heard that these new plantings had been wrecked by a herd of buffalo. It was not many months before Livingstone had to resort to bringing corn from Kuruman: a humiliating experience since many African women in Kuruman suggested that Mary had been starved by her new husband.[1]

Food and water shortages were bad enough in themselves, but the Livingstones also had to foot their removals bill and pay expenses connected with building a new house, a chapel and a school. Mrs Livingstone was by now expecting her first child and her husband was £30 in debt: an unhappy situation for a man earning only £100 a year. In spite of the hard labour that he had to put in on the new buildings, Livingstone appeared determined to put a brave face on what seemed to be a hopeless situation. The Bakwains, he assured Robert Moffat, were altogether a superior tribe to the Bakhatla and the prospect for conversions was infinitely brighter. Sechele was in every way a most superior African, with hardly a barbarous habit to his name. Nonetheless, Livingstone had to admit that Sechele had shown no interest in Christianity. Other signs were a little better and Livingstone clutched at them. Sechele's desire to possess various types of European goods sent Livingstone into rhapsodies. 'That he is desirous of civilization I think we may conclude since he sent out goods with us [on a journey to Kuruman] to purchase a mattress—4 lanterns—6 candle boxes—a baking pot, a smoothing iron, a table, & soap.'[2]

Since cleanliness was next to godliness in the view of many missionaries, a desire for it might well be an indication of better things to come. Its application also had beneficial practical results since the Bechuanas used grease in lieu of clothing, meaning that ticks and fleas bred on them prodigiously unless they washed with soap. Many of these parasites found their way on to the missionaries as well. Sechele had already deserted grease for the sartorial pleasures of European clothing, and had already managed to get hold of a few old coats, one of them red. At Livingstone's request, the Moffats sent up a red cap to match and some shirts and handkerchiefs. Livingstone also sent some hartebeest skin to Kuruman, to have it made up into a suit for the chief. Henry Methuen, an English traveller, was to see Sechele at about this time, and his description did not say much for Mrs Moffat's skills as a suitmaker. Sechele's trousers, Methuen wrote, were 'too short, his coat too tight, and his stockings the colour of the soil around. He walked amongst his admiring subjects with conscious superiority, but, despite his efforts to conceal it, looked ill at ease in the tramels of civilized dress.'[3]

Other hunters and traders remarked on Sechele's bizarre collection of clothes. One day he was to be seen in 'moleskin trousers, a duffel jacket, a wide-awake hat, and military boots',[4] the next 'in a suit of tiger-skin clothes made in European fashion'.[5] Nor did he see anything incongruous in wearing an 'immense Mackintosh overcoat with huge water-boots' on a boiling hot day. Yet, in spite of the amusement he sometimes afforded, almost all paid tribute to his good looks, bearing and intelligence. Livingstone was well aware of the comedy in all this.

> You would be amused [he told a friend] to see his royal highness . . . a king standing up to his knees in water and two persons scrubbing his royal person all over. As a preliminary to his washing his wardrobe himself. It takes a whole day to wash an old red coat and a few other duds the which if sold to a Jew in London would not realise 5/-. His wives too are fond of European clothing.[6]

But Livingstone soon had good cause for rejoicing. Sechele had an astounding aptitude for learning, and made such rapid progress in learning to read that he 'acquired a perfect knowledge of the alphabet, large small and mixed, in two days'.[7] Within a month he was spelling words of two syllables and asking questions about England. Soon he was compiling his own spelling books and persuading his five wives to read with him. In time three of them became Livingstone's best pupils; but for pure eagerness Sechele knew no rival. It did not take him long to get through all the Moffat translations Livingstone had brought with him, and so he then started to read the same material over again.[8]

Not only did Sechele enjoy reading; he wanted to possess books, and Livingstone was asked to write for 'a Testament of the imitation Russia, [in] a brownish colour' and for selected translations by Moffat. Yet in spite of Sechele's keenness, he did not give up his wives and gave no indication that he might wish to be converted. He often told Livingstone that he could not understand 'why I should persist, as he says, with tears in my eyes, to entreat his people to believe, seeing they don't want to hear about futurity'. Livingstone's only answer was to 'point to my works and ask if I am a fool'.[9] Sechele also helpfully suggested a more effective way to get converts: 'If you like, I shall call my head men, and with our whips we will soon make them all believe together.'[10]

The offer was rejected. Sechele himself continued in most of his old beliefs, still considering it 'highly meritorious to put all suspected witches to death'. On one occasion he asked Livingstone whether he would be saved if he 'acted justly, fairly avoided fighting, treated both his own people and strangers kindly, killed witches, & prayed to God'.[11] It was a fair question too, since he believed that killing witches was a necessary social duty. Witches could kill people or cause them serious inconvenience, so they were clearly better out of the way.

Livingstone did, however, secure one early success by persuading Sechele to give up rain-making for a while. But it was a success which he later regretted for the whole Bakwain tribe blamed Livingstone for the prolonged drought which followed Sechele's decision. In the end Sechele was obliged to make rain again.

Just when Sechele was progressing so well with his religious reading, Livingstone's hopes received a severe setback. For twenty years Sechele had ruled over only half the Bakwain tribe. The split had taken place during Sechele's childhood and had come about as a result of his father's murder. After a period of chaos Sechele found himself an exile, and two of the conspirators who had planned his father's murder divided the tribe and became chiefs of the two respective sections: Bubi took one and Molese the other. Eventually in 1829, at the age of nineteen, Sechele managed to oust Molese, but Bubi retained his hold over his part of the tribe. This was still the situation when Livingstone arrived at Chonuane in 1845. In August that year, Sechele sent Bubi a gift of gunpowder. Bubi, suspecting that this unexpected present was enchanted, set about dissolving the charm. The method he chose was to pass hot embers over the gunpowder. The result was an explosion that killed him. After his death many of his subjects went over to Sechele but many stayed with Bubi's successor, Khake. Livingstone managed to dissuade Sechele from attacking Khake till very near the end of 1845. He argued that Sechele might lose some of the cattle he had spent so long rearing and might even come off worse in the fight. Besides, many people might be killed on both sides. Out of respect for Livingstone, Sechele tried diplomacy. This merely led Khake to accuse him of cowardice. Then one day Livingstone saw Sechele's warriors arming for what he was told was an elephant hunt. Towards evening Livingstone emerged from his house to see 'the wounded carried past to the town' and this was 'soon, followed by the sounds of heathenish joy mingled with the loud wailing of those who had lost their friends'.[12] Probably not many more than fifty were killed but that was still a very significant loss for a tribe numbering less than four thousand in all.

Livingstone's prestige suffered greatly, for it was widely known that the chief had ignored his missionary's advice. In the eyes of most of the Bakwains their chief had been right, for by fighting he had united his tribe. Although Sechele remained affable towards Livingstone and went on with his reading, the numbers attending public worship fell off dramatically. Since people had only ever come to hear Livingstone preach because Sechele had told them to, Livingstone was left to draw his own conclusions. Sechele in fact started making rain again soon after his victory over Khake. There were few people in the village anyway, for most of them were walking backwards and forwards between their homes and their distant crops and cattle. A mere trickle came to hear Livingstone preach and most of these were women who had been threatened by the man who called them together. His usual method was to yell out that he would knock down any woman failing to come to the meeting place.[13] Those who did hear Livingstone's exhortations delivered 'again and again in the plainest language' were quite indifferent. 'They seem dry bones indeed,' Livingstone wrote despondently.[14]

His repeated failure seemed to point more and more to the necessity for giving 'native teachers' a proper trial. Livingstone had also been stung by a letter from the Directors, sent in December 1845, alluding to his 'former' interest in 'native agency' and suggesting that he should think about it sufficiently to put it into action.[15] This reproach angered him when he thought of his efforts to get an African seminary started at Kuruman. But it was quite true that what with his two moves and the quarrel with Edwards, he had had little time to think about settling either of his two African teachers with another tribe. Livingstone brought both men from Kuruman to Mabotsa and thence to Chonuane. Of the two, only Mebalwe has already been mentioned; the other was called Paul. Neither had received any real training as Christian teachers but in view of their white colleagues' lack of success, it is doubtful whether more instruction would have improved their chances. Both men had been among Moffat's early converts. Mebalwe had not only saved Livingstone's life but had since then made himself invaluable as a general handyman. Livingstone was therefore very reluctant to think of settling him with some distant tribe; instead he decided that Paul ought to begin independent missionary work first. With this end in view, Paul and Livingstone set out in July 1846 on the first of two journeys which together would occupy the best part of eight months. They did not go without some trepidation, for a couple of months earlier the commandant of the Boers settled in the neighbouring Transvaal had sent Livingstone a note informing him that any future missionary expansion should not take place without prior permission.[16] Livingstone had sent a civil reply telling the commandant that his intentions were entirely innocent and could only meet with the approval of all good Christians. The Boers, with their allegiance to the Dutch Reformed Church, were, after all, nominal Christians. Their Church did not, however, acknowledge the equality of black and white.

The Boers were not primarily worried about missionary expansion as such. Missionaries had so few successes that the Boers often used to suggest they would do better trying to convert baboons.[17] Nevertheless the Transvaal Boers had other reasons to feel concerned, for they remembered the days before they had trekked out of the colony; then the political pressure exerted by the missionaries had compelled the Cape Government to condemn the Boers' use of forced labour and their indiscriminate seizure of African land. In the mid-1840s the Boers saw Livingstone's plans to introduce 'native teachers' into the Transvaal as a political rather than a religious move. The 'native teachers' would report back to Livingstone on the Boers' treatment of Africans, and Livingstone would then publish the reports and do his best to force the British Governor at the Cape to end his policy of laissez-faire towards the Boers beyond the borders of the colony. If Livingstone was successful, some Boers even believed that Britain might attempt to incorporate the Transvaal and Orange Sovereignty into the Cape Colony. If that happened there would be all the old difficulties caused by blacks being the equal of whites before the law; there would also be restrictions placed on the confiscation of native land, and in general a return to the bad old days.

Since Livingstone knew that making converts was nigh impossible even in favourable circumstances, it might well be asked why he decided to try and settle African teachers to the east of Chonuane in the Transvaal, adding Boer opposition to all the usual problems. The Boers thought they knew the answer: Livingstone was a political trouble-maker. Livingstone himself saw things differently. He could not settle 'native teachers' to the west of Chonuane because of the Kalahari Desert; to the north the Bamangwato were too far away and were in any case an isolated tribe; to the south the Bakhatla already had a mission at Mabotsa. The east, Livingstone argued, was the only option left to him. One further question remains, and that is how Livingstone could have been naive enough to suppose that the tribes in the Transvaal would listen to 'native teachers' when these same teachers had been ignored by the residents of Mabotsa and Chonuane. In fact Livingstone was far from confident of success, but with personal failure as a missionary staring him in the face, the settle-ment of African teachers in the densely populated Transvaal seemed the last positive move he could make. He comforted himself by thinking that Paul and Mebalwe would do better on their own, away from any white missionaries—his idea being that only when Africans saw 'native teachers' as Christians in their own right, and not as the puppets of a resident European, would they make progress.

The two journeys Livingstone made in the second half of 1846 were not encouraging. He found that between a hundred and two hundred miles east of Chonuane there were certainly lots of people, many more than in Bechuanaland, but the Boers had already started to set tribe against tribe and had themselves raided tribes, taking vast numbers of sheep and several hundred captives at a time. Livingstone concluded that neither Paul nor Mebalwe would be able to make headway under such circumstances; they might even be killed.

Livingstone soon discovered to his disgust that the captives taken by the Boers on their raids were usually young children, who then became 'apprentices'. The barest legal formalities were gone through to declare the children orphans and once done, the child worked for his master for nothing for the next twenty years; and the younger the children were when captured, the better. Older ones might remember their homes and try to run away. What made this look even more like slavery was the common practice of exchanging 'orphans' for a transfer fee of about two guineas. The original cost of registering the child as an 'orphan apprentice' on the *landrost* did not come to more than 1s 6d, so the profits to be made were substantial. As late as 1865 three children could be bought for 'two white blankets',[18] and then be made to work for fifty years for nothing. Livingstone admitted that physical maltreatment of 'apprentices' was not the rule and that many of the emigrants regretted what was going on, but there was still a prevailing feeling that labour was merely in exchange for the Africans remaining in the country where they were settled.

The Boers knew very well that the less the Cape Government found out about their system of 'apprenticeship' the better. Therefore they made up their minds to keep Livingstone out. With this end in view they accused him of providing the Bakwains and the Bakhatla with guns and thus creating a dangerous situation on the western border of the Transvaal. When the charge was made public, Livingstone denied it emphatically and wrote to a Cape Town newspaper challenging the Boers to publish their evidence: 'If you can prove that I either *lent* or *sold*, or *gave* a gun to Sechele', he told the Boers, 'I shall willingly leave the country.'[19]

The Boers claimed that Livingstone had supplied the Bakwains with five hundred guns and a cannon: a ridiculous exaggeration. But Livingstone was also being less than truthful when he suggested that the Bakwains could not muster more than five guns between them. He himself had supplied them with many more than that, as his letters to his father-in-law bear out. As early as February 1846 Livingstone was writing to Robert Moffat telling him that Sechele 'is greatly in love with your rifles'.[20] A month later Moffat was told that a Scottish big-game hunter, Gordon Cumming, had left a 'good deal of powder' under Livingstone's care 'with liberty to assist any of the people with it'.[21] Letters from Livingstone to Moffat in March and November 1848 refer to guns sent from Kuruman to Sechele's people.[22] Livingstone later wrote to Joseph Sturge, a leading Quaker and pacifist, justifying arming Africans and saying that he loved peace so much that he would be quite prepared to fight for it.[23] He was certain that if the Boers knew that the Bakwains were armed they would not come and take captives from Sechele. It was a balance-of-power theory that was later proved mistaken.

By early 1847 Livingstone knew that the Boers would never tolerate any 'native teachers' in the Transvaal; he was therefore thrown back on Chonuane again with no better prospects of success than he had had in 1845. Livingstone now had to face the idea of spending the rest of his life with the Bakwains, making thirty or so converts if he was lucky. It was not a pleasing prospect for an ambitious man in his early thirties, and Livingstone squirmed and wriggled to try and find a let-out. As in his early days at Kuruman, he once more began to doubt whether he could endure the conventional static missionary life with its scant and ill-recognized rewards. With the settlement of 'native teachers' temporarily out of the reckoning, it was hard to think of any way to exercise his ambitions for working beyond every other man's lines. Gradually he began to persuade himself that the abandonment of a tribe *before* making conversions might be a positive and not a negative step. Could a missionary, he asked himself, be reasonably expected to stay with a single tribe for more than ten years if that tribe showed no interest? Moffat would have pointed out that there would only be progress *after* ten years, but Livingstone preferred to ignore such inconvenient thoughts. He decided that if a decade passed and the Bakwains were still resistant, he would 'move on to the regions beyond'. In ten years he would have told them all he could, so it would be their fault if they had not listened: 'Now is their opportunity, and if they do not learn, the guilt will be on their heads'.[24] Having thus easily salved his conscience, Livingstone adapted the old missionary formula of 'sowing seed not to bear fruit in a single lifetime' for his own ends. He suggested that seed could be sown just as effectively in years as it could be in lifetimes. The missionary ought not to waste seed on barren ground but should eventually leave a tribe which consistently refused to listen and move on to another tribe whose people might be more deserving and receptive. These were convenient views to hold for a man who had once wanted to discover the lake to the north and who had anticipated such pleasures in travelling. That this thinking contained a stinging irony either did not occur to Livingstone or, if it did, did not bother him. His new ideas were tantamount to the suggestion that a missionary who might otherwise fail to convert one tribe in a lifetime should somehow, by some mysterious process, succeed in converting many tribes by briefly saying his piece and passing on to 'the regions beyond'.

At any rate in 1847, after less than two years with the Bakwains, Livingstone knew that he would have to stay a little longer if he wished to avoid the derision of all his colleagues. Whether Livingstone or Sechele liked it, the Bakwains were to have one last chance; but the continued drought and the drying up of all springs within reach of Chonuane meant that this chance would have to be given somewhere else. Another move had to be made. This time it was to a place called Kolobeng, forty miles to the north-west. The Directors of the London Missionary Society had only just written accepting Livingstone's move to Chonuane. When they heard about the next move, they wrote with weary tolerance: 'We hope we may now regard you as permanently settled, knowing well the disadvantages attending frequent changes of this nature.'[25] They would not have been so polite had they known that Livingstone's thinking was gradually leading him to consider 'permanent settlement' unacceptable.

7

The Only Convert: Kolobeng
1847–1849

———◆———

Although Kolobeng had a better water supply than Chonuane, in other ways it was hardly more comfortable or more attractive: perched, as an English hunter later put it, 'in naked deformity on the side of and under a ridge of red ironstone'.[1] There were woods several miles away but most of the surrounding country was as bleak and arid as any in Bechuanaland. Wild animals were numerous but this was no great advantage, for quite often a buffalo or rhinoceros would charge through the new settlement terrifying the women and children.

Moving had become almost second nature to the Livingstones, but it was no less exhausting for all that. In fact, for Mrs Livingstone, now the mother of two children, it was far worse. Robert had been born early in 1846 and Agnes was just three months old when the Livingstones' waggon rumbled out of Chonuane for the last time. Mary Livingstone's life had been hard even before the arrival of children, and she had needed all the skills her mother had taught her. In addition, she had had to run an infants' school with numbers sometimes rising to eighty. Local mothers used the school as a child-minding facility, and of course it was never much more than that. Mrs Livingstone was hard put to keep order, let alone teach anything. In less than a year after their arrival at Kolobeng, Mary was pregnant again. Livingstone called her frequent pregnancies 'the great Irish manufactory',[2] a description which probably amused him more than his wife. Another son, Thomas, was born in March 1849; a daughter, Elizabeth, who survived only a month, in August 1850; and a further son, William, in September 1851. To have five children in six years is an ordeal today, but for Mrs Livingstone, constantly on the move and always overworked, it was nearly fatal. Livingstone told Robert Moffat that Mary was often in pain and usually tired, but that, he remarked complacently, 'is hardly to be wondered at, for she has much work on her hands'.

Mary had other problems too. Her family lived in a crudely made hut for a year after their arrival at Kolobeng; it took that long for Livingstone to build a stone house, nor did he find the work easy. Once he nearly broke his bad arm, when he slipped and found himself dangling by it from a beam. Then he fell off the roof while thatching. Next he cut himself badly with an axe; and all the time he was working, the incessant rays of the sun split his lips and burned his face so much that it became cracked and pitted with scabs.[3] And all the while the small hut they lived in was purgatory: too hot in summer and painfully cold in winter. Livingstone, even when being humorous about a very distressing period, could not disguise the discomfort: 'A year in a hut through which the wind blew our candles into glorious icicles (as a poet would say) by night, and in which crowds of flies continually settled on the eyes of our poor little brats by day.'[4]

Livingstone never wrote much about the arrival of the 'brats' and usually greeted Mrs Livingstone's deliveries with a bare record of the date and the intended name of the child. His parents, if they hoped for more information, never got it. Livingstone did, however, make a concession to his father, Neil, when he told the old man that his first grandchild might have been called Neil 'if it were not such an ugly name'.[5] Livingstone did grudgingly consent to call his eldest daughter Agnes after his mother but could not help adding that it was 'not a pretty name'.[6] As the children grew, their father was still sparing with descriptions, and so Janet, his sister, wrote begging him to say more about them. Her reward was one sentence about Robert 'singing at the top of his voice' and Agnes trying to bite his leg. Livingstone, evidently pleased with such expansiveness, added a sentence to let his sister know how lucky she was: 'You see I am making an effort to please you.'[7] Usually when Livingstone wrote anything more about his family, it was to bemoan their sad state. 'One does not know how our children may turn out,' he told his parents ominously. 'Ours are surrounded by heathenism. It is very difficult to keep them from contact with it.' The children still managed to treat their spiritual danger lightly. Robert had seen Livingstone baptize Mrs Livingstone's latest arrival and promptly 'went out and came in again with some water on his face and said: "Papa, I have baptised myself"!'[8]

The Livingstones' children had few toys, and those they did have came from the Livingstone seniors in Scotland. Since Neil Livingstone now earned rather less than he had done when his son had been in England, the flow of toys was like the Kolobeng river: erratic. A lack of toys was not all the children had to put up with. Often they cried with hunger and on one occasion, when all the corn failed, Mary had to take them three hundred miles south to Kuruman. After their departure Livingstone dug up some tiny potatoes and ate them. When he had enjoyed these tiny vegetables, which he had previously described as being the size of marbles, he regretted not digging them up before the children had left. 'They would have enjoyed them so much.'[9] The Livingstones' diet was at the best of times bizarre; often the whole family would sit down to a feast of locusts, which, Livingstone assured friends in England, were not unlike shrimps and excellent with wild honey. The Baptist's food, he added, maintained a delicate alimentary balance: 'the former is excessively constipating, and the latter has quite the opposite tendency'.[10] The children particularly relished a species of caterpillar and a large frog called *matlametlo*. Livingstone enjoyed the frog too and thought it looked and tasted just like chicken. Diet was not all that marked off the Livingstone children from their contemporaries in Britain. They grew up bilingual, and, to their father's alarm, their Sichuana was soon better than their English.

When the outer walls of the house had been built and the roof was at last in place, Livingstone started to think of possible improvements. He placed antlers on the walls and rather shamefacedly ordered a sofa from Cape Town. Mrs Livingstone was soon proudly playing her part in making the house habitable. To outsiders her methods might have seemed strange, especially when she came to clean the floor. Her proceedings were the same her mother had boasted about twenty years before. 'We smear all our rooms with cow dung once a week at least . . . It lays the dust better than anything, kills the fleas which would otherwise breed abundantly, and is a fine clear green.'[11] The fleas often made Livingstone wish that he had a bath and he wrote to his sisters asking if they knew of any way whereby one might be sent from Scotland in pieces, to be soldered up on arrival. But no bath ever arrived and perhaps it was just as well for they would have felt guilty about wasting valuable water. The last improvements Livingstone made for the house were the doors and window frames. Strangely, he left the outside door to the very end. Before it was in place Mrs Livingstone showed she was equal to any emergency, as her husband recorded: 'A big wolf came . . . & took away a buffalo's skin from the door. Mary wanted me to go and see whether the room door were fastened, but . . . I advised her to take a fork in her hand and go herself, as I was too comfortably situated to go myself.'[12]

Mary's tasks were all-embracing. At Chonuane she had learned something of dentistry, and Livingstone amusingly described her successful efforts at pulling out one of his teeth with a pair of 'shoemaker's nippers'.

Every pull was like a haul at my entrails . . . Another wrench and I roared out 'murder'. It came a little farther, but was still sticking doggedly. Another trial of the nippers, forceps, &c . . . . completed the first attempt at dentistry. We were a pretty sight in our ghostly dresses, I on the floor & Mary standing over me. It was dreadful.

'Teeth drawn at Chonuane 1/- each.' Mouth rinsed out afterwards
with dirty water *gratis*.[13]

The Livingstones usually got up at dawn, had family prayers, breakfast
and then school for anybody prepared to come. The rest of the morning
Livingstone devoted to manual work—sawing, ploughing, smithy work
and anything else that needed doing. Mary would spend her morning
cooking, sewing and looking after the children. Lunch would be followed
by a short rest, and after that Mary went to her infants' school and
Livingstone continued his manual tasks till about five o'clock. After that
he generally went into the town to talk to anybody who felt like it, milked
the cows, and finally visited the chief's house to pray and give him special
instruction. He would arrive home at 8.30, worn out. In letters to friends
he bemoaned the fact that so much of his day was given to agriculture and
so little to real missionary work. 'As I write now my hands have the same
aching sensation I had when spinning. My mind is often so exhausted by
sympathy with the body I cannot write in the evenings, and this is the only
time I have.'[14]

The help given by a local couple made matters a bit better, but not
much. Livingstone's ten cows were quite inadequate to give them milk all
the year round, and even when seven were simultaneously in milk he
claimed they produced no more than one back in Scotland. The reason
was that the local grazing was bad because of the same drought that had
afflicted them at Chonuane. The situation was so serious that trees started
to die and the corn failed completely. Potatoes withered and so did all the
other vegetables. Worse still, the Kolobeng river had 'dwindled down to a
dribbling rill' and was therefore useless for irrigation. A year later it had
dried up altogether, and in the meantime the fish had started to die and
'the hyenas from the whole country round collected to the feast, and were
unable to finish the putrid masses'.[15] Livingstone measured the temperature three inches under the soil and found that it was 132° at midday. Less
than two inches of rain had fallen in two years. An increasing number of
people believed that Livingstone's presence was responsible. Sechele kept
the Livingstone family going by sending them what food he could spare.
Livingstone got used to the drought, the fleas, the chirr of the crickets,
the endless zebra meat that Sechele sent, and he even became hardened to
his children's emaciated faces. But he could never get used to the
Bakwains' indifference to the Gospel. Every evening he wrote in his
journal, and practised every form of self-deception to keep up his spirits.
'It seems very unfair', he wrote, 'to judge of the success of these [missions]
by the number of conversions which have followed.' That was how he had
judged Moffat, but now it was another story. Conversions themselves

were not what really mattered, Livingstone went on; the real significance
of missionary work lay in the fact that missionaries 'are diffusing a knowledge of Christianity throughout the world'. Livingstone concluded the
passage almost in a pleading tone: 'No mission which has His approbation
is entirely unsuccessful. His purposes have been fulfilled if we have been
faithful.'[16]

At other times Livingstone was anything but sure that remaining
faithful was enough; on those occasions he comforted himself with
reading about failures in the Bible. Noah and Isaiah, he was thankful to
record, had both considered their achievements negligible, so too had
Jeremiah and Ezekiel. Paul had spoken the truth when he had written:
'All seek their own, not the things of Jesus Christ.' But in the end no
comparisons or comforting arguments helped Livingstone in his unhap-
piness. Yet strangely, at this very moment when almost the whole
Bakwain tribe were showing complete indifference, Sechele, their chief,
sent his brother to see Livingstone with the request that Livingstone
should establish an evening prayer-meeting in Sechele's house for the
whole of the chief's family. Livingstone could hardly believe it when
Sechele told him that he 'knew he was living in sin, but though he had not
given up those with whom he sinned [his wives], he wished to pray in his
family'.[17] The chief's conversion now seemed a distinct possibility and
Livingstone watched him eagerly for signs. Glistening eyes were, he felt
sure, excellent external evidence of a change of heart, and, as Livingstone
told Moffat, Sechele's eyes had often glistened after his request for an
evening prayer-meeting.

But glistening eyes did not remove Sechele's problems. A Bechuana
chief who opposed his people's wishes ran a real danger of deposition, and
Sechele, who had endured a childhood and adolescence in exile, knew
what that meant. He was well aware that all his headmen and advisers
hated the idea of Christianity. Under normal circumstances polygamy
presented any chief wishing to be a Christian with impossible problems,
but for Sechele they were worse than usual. Two of his five wives were the
daughters of under-chiefs who had been directly responsible for rein-
stating him after his exile. Rejection of these wives would therefore make
enemies of several of the leading families in the tribe. This dilemma led
Sechele to ask Livingstone whether it might not be a good idea for him
to go to England for a period of several years, ostensibly to study but really
to give his wives a chance to forget him and remarry. Livingstone saw the
sense in this suggestion, but knew that it would be too expensive to be
practicable.[18] In fact he sympathized deeply with Sechele and considered
his superfluous wives to be his best pupils. More perplexing still was the
thought that if Sechele rejected them he would be left with his principal

wife, who was one of the tribe's most staunch opponents of Christianity. Livingstone described her as 'about the most unlikely subject in the tribe ever to become anything else than an out-and-out greasy disciple of the old school'. Sechele was frequently compelled to ask her to leave prayer-meetings because she had come without a gown and was therefore inde-cently dressed. Then, 'away she would go with her lips shot out, the very picture of unutterable disgust'.[19]

Livingstone had never been certain whether missionaries could condemn a custom that was socially approved by the tribal society, and was now even less sure what course Sechele should follow. He was even doubtful whether he ought to refuse Sechele baptism if the chief asked to be baptized before he had disowned his wives. In August 1848 Sechele came and asked for advice. Livingstone did not feel able to give it and merely pushed the responsibility back on to the chief by telling him to look in the Bible for guidance. When Livingstone learned that Sechele had decided on rejection, he told the chief to treat his wives gently 'for they had sinned in ignorance'. Sechele announced his intention to become a Christian and give up his wives on Monday, 7 August 1848. It was not, as Livingstone confessed in his journal, a happy day for the Bakwains.

> Great commotion in the town. All seemed to be in perplexity. Complete cessation of work. Women all remained at home, although on every other lawful day they are seen going to the gardens in crowds. The men seemed downcast and dismayed. A large meeting in the khotla [meeting place]. Many spoke fiercely, so much so as to surprise the chief himself. Next morning he resolved to call the people together generally to explain his conduct, and say if they wished to kill him to do so immediately.

Sechele's bravery must remove all doubts about the genuineness of his conversion. What had tilted the balance for him in favour of Christianity will never be known, but in view of the danger and inconvenience he caused himself, to say nothing of the suffering inflicted on his wives, it was little short of miraculous that he decided to take the plunge. Livingstone, without doubt feeling guilty about the rejected wives, went to see them all to try and soften the blow. He started with Makhari. 'Poor thing, she was melted in tears, could not speak but with a choking voice. Offered me back her book, "as she must now go where there is no word of God". Wished that they could have remained in the town that they too might be saved, but Makhari has no relations. She was much loved and worthy of it.'[20]

His meeting with Mokokon was equally distressing and she told him, 'while the tears chased each other down her cheeks . . . she could not leave us and her child'. The other two wives showed their grief with violent anger.

On 10 August Makhari left, leaving her Bible behind. That night a large *picho* (meeting) was held to intimidate Sechele and it was proposed that he should at least allow his wives to remain in their old homes. He compromised and allowed them all the possessions from their former homes and gave them new clothing, but they were still to go to their parents or families. Mokokon stayed at Kolobeng because she had no parents to go to.

Throughout September the opposition to Sechele's impending baptism went on unabated. Livingstone shared this unpopularity. Many suggested that it was a pity the lion had not killed him at Mabotsa, but the main onslaught was aimed at the chief who had to endure 'very bitter curses' that would formerly have been punished by death.[21] Hostility increased as the day of the baptism grew closer and in the end what ought to have been the most joyful and triumphant day in Livingstone's missionary life turned out to be an ordeal. Two religious ladies in Birmingham had sent out two chairs for Sechele and these were used in the ceremony. So too was a long cloak that had been ordered from Scotland. But the details of the ceremony paled before the large crowd of spectators, most of them in tears. Afterwards Livingstone tried to find humour in what had been at the time a depressing experience. 'The old stereotyped case-hardened characters were weeping to see him "so far left to himself"—After the meeting we heard of an old man wiping off the stream from his cheek saying—"this beats the putting away of wives hollow. What shall we do?" Another old gentleman said to me, "You might have delayed till we got rain." '[22]

The belief that Sechele had become the white man's creature was common and the rumour, or, as Livingstone put it, the 'satanic suggestion', was widespread that baptism meant 'being caused to drink men's brains'.[23]

Three months after his baptism, Sechele was still standing up to his people's taunts and appeared to be making good progress. To Livingstone's delight he began learning English. He had already been introduced to English books in translation when Moffat had sent his Sichuana version of *The Pilgrim's Progress*. Sechele had enjoyed it, for, as Livingstone noted, 'some parts of the Pilgrim's experience and his are exactly alike, and make him extol the wisdom of Johane Bunyana'.[24] His interest in European merchandise also continued, and a jug, representing the Duke of Wellington's head, became one of his most precious possessions. It was not till five months after the baptism that Livingstone noticed that Mokokon, Sechele's rejected wife who had been allowed to remain, was showing symptoms that looked unpleasantly like pregnancy. Livingstone made a terse note in his journal for 7 March 1849: 'Symptoms of pregnancy discovered in Mokokon. Enquired of Sechele. Confessed he had been twice with her . . . about the beginning of January 1849.'[25]

The blow to Livingstone was devastating. Sechele made no excuses and gave him an honest account of what had happened. Writing to Moffat, Livingstone admitted how deeply hurt he was. 'The confession loosened all my bones. I felt as if I should sink to the earth or run away . . . no one except yourselves can imagine the lancinating pangs. They fell on the soul like drops of aqua fortis on an ulcerated surface.' Sechele said he was deeply sorry and asked how he could obtain forgiveness. Although Livingstone cut him off from fellowship, the Congregationalists' name for church membership, he could not help acknowledging that Sechele's lapse 'had required no effort such as going to another man's wife . . . He had become so accustomed to their customs it was like his ordinary food.'[26] Sechele's fall from grace was not the only one at this time. Livingstone had always looked on the families of Paul and Mebalwe as irreproachable. Now he discovered that one of Paul's sons, Isak, had been regularly committing adultery and had got another man's wife pregnant. Paul had hidden this from Livingstone, and Mebalwe, who had also known, had remained equally silent. Livingstone subsequently found out that many of the Bakwains had shared Isak's guilty secret and had laughed at the missionary for not having guessed. Livingstone sent Sechele a note: 'My heart is broken. First Isak, then you. I can no longer be a teacher here.'[27]

Livingstone's attempt to make Sechele believe that the lapses were entirely responsible for his determination to leave the Bakwains was convenient rather than truthful. Livingstone's first mention of plans not to stay with the tribe for longer than a given period had been made at Chonuane two years before, in March 1847. Later in that same year he had written to Robert Moffat suggesting that the two of them should attempt a journey to the unknown lake to the north. This plan had fallen through, owing partly to lack of funds and partly to Moffat's determination to press on with his translation of the Bible. Nevertheless Livingstone was not beaten; in June 1845, while still at Mabotsa, he had met an English hunter and traveller, William Cotton Oswell: a man with a bent for exploring and money to indulge it. So late in 1847 Livingstone wrote to Oswell in an attempt to persuade him to come to the lake. At first there had been no response because Oswell had been in England and India during 1847 and 1848; but in early 1849, the time of Sechele's lapse, Livingstone received a letter from Oswell saying that he and a companion, Mungo Murray, would arrive at Kolobeng at the end of May that year, and that the three of them would then attempt to reach the lake.

Nevertheless, Livingstone's determination to reach the lake—called Ngami by the natives—was a symptom rather than a direct cause of his now clearly formed conviction that he would very soon end his stay with the Bakwains, and with it his own static missionary life. So how clearly defined were Livingstone's ideas and plans for the future by the middle of 1849?

In 1847 he had been toying with the idea of itinerant missionaries 'diffusing a knowledge of Christianity'. But, as I have already suggested, the vagueness of the terms emphasized rather than disguised the fact that Livingstone was looking for some comforting formula to help him through a difficult and depressing period. In the same way, when Livingstone wrote to the Directors of the London Missionary Society in May 1849, on the eve of his departure for Ngami, his suggestions for a new kind of missionary work were uncertain and confused. He explained the difficulties he had been having with the drought and argued that, since the Boers had prevented him settling African teachers to the east, the only direction for future expansion was the north. He briefly mentioned Sechele's lapse but gave it no weight. Instead he suggested that the real reason for a series of journeys to the north was the fact that the Bakwains would not be persuaded to believe 'precipitously' and that in the meantime thousands of precious souls to the north were perishing. 'It is therefore', Livingstone went on, 'imperatively necessary to endeavour to extend the *gospel to all* the surrounding tribes. This . . . is the only way which permits the rational hope that when people do turn to the Lord it will be by groups.'[28] The hope was anything but rational and was based on self-deception. There was no evidence at all to support the belief that occasional visits to distant tribes would make them 'turn to the Lord by groups'. Flying visits could never be more successful than long years with a single tribe. Livingstone was inventing excuses partly to deceive himself and partly to fool the Directors into thinking that he had hit on a viable new missionary policy. His allusion to the 'perishing thousands' fitted in nicely with his previous complaints about the size of Bechuanaland's population, but it was also a blind, for he had already suggested that the *diffusion* of a knowledge of Christianity was almost as valuable as conversion itself. Having thus relegated conversion to a position of reduced importance, he could hardly logically claim to be so alarmed about the spiritual future of the unconverted, or reasonably suggest that thousands were perishing. This argument led him into other contradictions for he had moved away from strict Calvinism in his late teens and early twenties, and when he shortly came to write about his initial missionary impulse, he was to ascribe it to a desire to work for the 'alleviation of human misery', rather than to any longing to save perishing souls.[29] In fact, when he set out for Lake Ngami in June 1849, Livingstone was thankful for a long journey in which to try and clarify his thoughts.

The contradictions I have pointed out are glaring, but it would be wrong not to acknowledge that Livingstone was less certain than his colleagues about the ideal form of missionary work, because, ironically, he possessed a far greater insight into the basic causes of tribal rejection of Christianity. Unlike his colleagues, he had understood the role of the *boguera* or initiation rites; unlike them, he had not been happy about voicing an outright condemnation of polygamy. He had never considered tribal marriage to be 'bride-buying'. This more liberal approach laid him open to uncertainties unguessed at by the type of missionary who automatically castigated every African custom and belief. Livingstone often repeated the phrase 'Jesus came not to judge', and insisted that missionaries ought 'to follow His example, neither insist upon their rights'.[30] Yet unless the missionary did judge and condemn, his own position became untenable, for his very presence implied a criticism—he had a message for the 'benighted', to tell them about the one true faith in Jesus Christ. In addition that faith was antithetical to almost every tribal custom and belief.

Livingstone realized this and cast about for a way out of the impasse: a method of changing tribal society without compulsion. He came to believe that if only he could make the Bechuanas understand the technological superiority of Europeans, he might be able to persuade them that a change in their own society would be to their advantage. He tried to explain the benefits of wider trade and better communications and to convince them that selling skins and ivory to Europeans and to distant tribes would bring them greater wealth, and in the end enable them to increase their range of production. He soon realized that it was easier to have the idea than to explain it.

> It is extremely difficult to explain to the people of this country the use of money or machinery, or of any of the sciences as sources of pure intellectual pleasure. If they can count as many as serve in all their simple transactions, which can almost always be effected on the fingers, what need is there for the rules of proportion &c.? The art of writing is very curious, but of what use is it to those who can send all their messages viva voce and who have all their family and connections within five minutes walk of their own residence, and will have so little news to communicate.[31]

When Livingstone tried to explain the workings of steam-engines and cotton mills, he was met with blank incomprehension. People who had never even seen two-storey houses were not going to be taken in by far-fetched stories about things called steamships and trains. The unpleasant truth soon became apparent to Livingstone that the Bakwains were content with what they had and were not going to put themselves out to facilitate changes they thought unnecessary. They obtained guns, beads and brass wire from missionaries and traders, and that was good enough. As Livingstone observed, 'As there is no pressing necessity apparent to those whose wants are few, they take the world easy.'[32]

So Livingstone's dilemma grew worse. While Africans were satisfied with their existing society and contrived to survive and be happy, it was hard to claim that occasional tribal wars and regrettable customs like witch-craft and infanticide gave anybody the right to contemplate undermining the whole system. Livingstone even had moments when he doubted whether Africans derived any benefit from contact with Europeans. While maintaining that the presence of missionaries was beneficial, he criticized the Cape Government and the Boers for their treatment of Africans. 'If natives are not elevated by contact with Europeans,' he wrote, 'they are sure to be deteriorated. It is with pain I have observed that all the tribes I have seen lately* are undergoing the latter process.'[33] This was an especially unwelcome observation for Livingstone to have to make, given his feeling that only with a greater knowledge of European economics and customs were Africans likely to take more kindly to Christianity. In fact Livingstone's conclusions had forced him into a position in which the logical response would have been to argue in favour of leaving the Africans to their own devices. This, however, was a course he found quite unacceptable, for, believing that he had a divine mission to spread Christianity, he could not allow himself to be dissuaded by mundane facts and problems. His own Christian faith was of supreme importance to him and he wanted others to be able to share it. In 1849 he was uncertain how this could be brought about, but he knew he must go on trying.

In the meantime, if a journey to the unknown lake did not solve anything, it might provide him with hints for a new approach. He would also be able to review his situation and his ideas away from the depressing indifference of the Bakwains.

* He was referring particularly to the tribes in the Transvaal.

PART TWO

ACHIEVEMENT

8

North to the Zambesi
1849–1851

B etween 1849 and 1851 Livingstone made three long journeys north of Kolobeng, and these, especially the third, irrevocably altered the direction of his life and gave a definite form to his hitherto incoherent ideas. Between June and October 1849, he travelled over three hundred miles north-west of Kolobeng to Lake Ngami in the extreme north of modern Botswana—formerly Bechuanaland. His second trip, also to Ngami, took place between April and August 1850 and achieved no more than the first. On the third crucial journey, Livingstone reached the upper Zambesi, at the very heart of south-central Africa, in the area of the Barotse valley. This was two hundred miles north-east of Ngami and at a place where the modern Caprivi Strip—part of Namibia—divides the northern boundary of Botswana from the south-western border of Zambia.

Before describing these journeys, it is important, in view of Livingstone's reputation for being the first European to penetrate south-central Africa, to record what, if anything, was already known about the area he was to visit. Lake Ngami itself had often been visited by Africans from the south, but Livingstone's journey of 1849 is the first recorded visit by any European. Two attempts had been made in the 1830s, and on both occasions the Kalahari Desert had defeated the explorers. Ngami, however, was a minor affair compared with Livingstone's arrival on the upper Zambesi in 1851, and there he had definitely been anticipated by other Europeans—the Portuguese.

The Portuguese colonies of Angola on the West African coast and Mozambique on the eastern side of the continent had been established during the sixteenth century and were, of course, well known to Livingstone and his contemporaries. Nevertheless, the extent to which individual Portuguese explorers had penetrated the interior was far less widely appreciated. Their efforts inland from Mozambique were better known than similar attempts made from Angola. While, for instance, it was known that in 1798 Lacerda had travelled six hundred miles north-west of Tete in Mozambique to Lake Moero, very close to the southern end of the then 'undiscovered' Lake Tanganyika, it was almost entirely unknown in Britain that in 1846 Rodrigues Graça had reached south-western Katanga from Angola. While Graça's journey had been north of the area Livingstone was to reach in 1851, another Portuguese trader, Silva Porto, had reached the upper Zambesi between 1847 and 1848, at almost the very spot where Livingstone first saw that river. Therefore Livingstone's generally accepted claim that the Portuguese never imagined the Zambesi to flow from so far to the west was false. When Livingstone later met Porto and other Portuguese traders on the upper Zambesi in 1853, he would inaccurately pronounce them Portuguese half-castes in order to defend his position as the only true European to have been in the area. By the late 1840s the Portuguese realized that the large river which Porto had reached from Angola was without doubt the upper reaches of the Zambesi they knew in Mozambique. For three hundred years the Portuguese had possessed detailed knowledge of the Zambesi up to six hundred miles inland from the east coast. They had merely never filled in the 400-mile gap between Porto's discoveries and their furthest progress up the river from Mozambique.

The Portuguese, while being the only Europeans to precede Livingstone, were not alone in their prior penetration of south-central Africa. During the first decade of the nineteenth century, two African traders had travelled from Angola to Tete in Mozambique. Since the only records of these journeys were to be found in Portuguese periodicals and archives, the general public in Britain and other European countries outside Portugal knew nothing of them. British geographers who did read the relevant papers were often sceptical because the journeys had been so badly documented. But, as will be seen, they had other reasons also for acclaiming Livingstone as the only European to have made important discoveries in south-central Africa.

Livingstone, on his £100 a year salary, would never have been able to make his three journeys between 1849 and 1851 had it not been for the generosity of William Cotton Oswell, who accompanied him on the first and third trips. At first sight it would seem most improbable that a man with Livingstone's vocation and background should have taken a liking to somebody from the upper class, whose life had been mainly devoted to pig-sticking, boxing, racquets and cricket. Educated at Rugby and Haileybury, Oswell had entered the Indian Civil Service, but had retired after ten years for a life of leisure and the delights of African travel and big-game hunting. Oswell, however, was no mindless young man with a private fortune and little else. He was exceptionally generous, modest and completely lacking in personal ambition. These last two qualities provide the key to the success of his relationship with Livingstone, who had already proved himself incapable of suffering any European whose views conflicted with his own. Livingstone liked to get his full measure of praise for what he did, and Oswell conveniently never saw fit to press his own claims. Oswell's companion, Mungo Murray, who also came on the 1849 journey to Lake Ngami, was a man of similar character, who preferred doing things to talking about them afterwards.

The importance of Oswell's contribution to the first trip to Ngami can be gauged from the fact that he brought to Kolobeng, for the journey, twenty horses, eighty oxen, two waggons and enough supplies to keep three Europeans and eight Africans in gunpowder, bullets, tea, coffee and sugar for a year. The party that left Kolobeng for Ngami on 1 June 1849 was a large one, for it included not only Oswell, Livingstone and Murray, with their dozen African drivers and attendants, but also thirty Bakwains sent by Sechele to bring back any ivory they might find near the lake. J.H. Wilson, a trader centred on Kuruman, had asked to come too and had been accepted as one of the party. Wilson, like Sechele, wanted to get his hands on some of the copious stocks of ivory supposed to exist in Ngamiland.

Previous travellers had failed to reach Ngami because of the Kalahari Desert, which started to the west of Kolobeng and extended two hundred miles to the north. These early expeditions had, however, been made at the wrong time of year, for the Kalahari is not a desert in the strict sense of the word, because during the rainy season water is retained in the sun-baked hollows and does not dry up till several months afterwards. At this time water-melons and red cucumbers are an added source of moisture. The Bushmen managed to find water-holes and extract enough liquid to survive by sucking it up from under the ground with the help of long, hollow reeds; some antelopes, notably the eland, lived there too without apparent ill-effects. But all this said, the Kalahari was a nightmarish place to cross, even at its outermost extremities, and the oxen which drew the party's waggons on several occasions had to travel seventy miles without water, a distance that could take three days or more, in areas where the soft sand bogged down the axles. When the oxen seemed in danger of dying there was no alternative but to send them back as much as twenty miles to the last wells, leaving the waggons where they were till the beasts returned refreshed.

There were other problems besides water shortage. On a flat plain, which stretched as far as the eye could see, and where the only landmarks were occasional stunted trees or bushes, it was easy to alter course without noticing it. Even Bushmen guides often lost the track they were attempting to follow. Throughout their time in the Kalahari the travellers were deceived by mirages caused by large, dried-out pools covered with a thick salt deposit. The heat was so intense that the oxen could only travel in the evening and very early morning.

Five weeks after leaving Kolobeng, they reached the river Zouga and enthused about the large trees and thick vegetation on its banks. The Zouga was flowing from a west-north-westerly direction and the travellers had no doubt but that its source lay in Lake Ngami. Their sole remaining task was to trace it there. This was to prove a straightforward journey of three hundred miles. Before they arrived at the lake, they discovered that another river flowed into the Zouga from the north.* Livingstone was now firmly convinced that the area to the north of the Zouga would contain a major river network. In his view this completely eclipsed the impending discovery of the lake itself. So when Livingstone stood on the shores of Ngami he was unimpressed and made no plans to walk round it or to ask the natives more than a few questions about its depth and extent. It was in fact shallow and, including the surrounding marshes, was about seventy miles long. While Oswell made detailed enquiries, Livingstone, still in a state of great excitement, thought about the river system to the north. He had not read about Graça or Porto and therefore genuinely believed he had hit on important new information concerning the geography of south-central Africa. Never having read any Portuguese periodicals, or having met any well-informed British geographers, Livingstone was sure that he was on the verge of proving that central Africa was a well-watered, fertile land instead of being, as popular fancy had it, a desert as large as the Sahara.

So while Livingstone ignored Ngami he asked a great many questions about the area to the north, and the answers he received confirmed what he already firmly believed. He therefore decided to set out at once for the area to the north-east. Unfortunately, the Zouga had to be crossed first, and the chief of the principal tribe round Ngami gave orders that the white men should not cross. The chief knew the direction Livingstone was planning to go in and knew that if this white man and his friends went about two hundred miles north-east, they would reach Sebitoane, chief of the far from pacific Makololo. The chief of the Ngami people not only feared an attack by Sebitoane but also believed that the white men would make matters worse by selling guns to the Makololo. Livingstone and Oswell tried to argue, but in vain—no canoes were forthcoming. Livingstone started to build a raft but the wood was too heavy and sank by its own weight. He then tried a lighter wood but this turned out to be worm-eaten and absorbed the water like a sponge. The river at this point

---

* The Thamalakane, a tributary of the Okavango.

was about fifty yards across. 'I could easily have swam across, and fain would have done it, but landing stark naked and bullying the Bakoba for the loan of a boat would scarcely be the thing for a messenger of peace, even though no alligator met me in the passage.'[1] So when Oswell offered to return to the Cape and bring up a collapsible boat on his next trip in slightly under a year's time, Livingstone agreed to give up for the present. Their journey to date had taken much longer than Livingstone had anticipated and he was worried about his wife and children, who had gone to stay with his father-in-law at Kuruman but would soon be returning to Kolobeng.

The return journey was uneventful and Kolobeng was reached on 9 October. Livingstone lost no time in sitting down to write letters to the Directors of the London Missionary Society, to his parents and to Robert Moffat, informing them of his discovery. Before leaving he had told his brother Charles that Oswell might well get the credit for the journey, and now after his return, while conceding that the finance had been Oswell's, Livingstone vehemently insisted that the motive power behind the whole trip had been his own original suggestion. Even so, Livingstone warned his parents that 'others less closely connected may be more highly favoured', and suggested that Oswell and Murray 'could never have reached this point without my assistance'. But Livingstone felt that the people he really had to impress were the Directors of the London Missionary Society; he had not asked their permission to leave his post at Kolobeng and was uncertain what their reaction might be. Livingstone decided the best approach was going to be to play down the purely exploratory goal of reaching Lake Ngami and concentrate on the river system to the north, the revelation of which, in any case, he considered the most important result of his journey. This network of rivers, he went on, 'opens out the prospect of a highway capable of being quickly traversed by boats to a large section of well-peopled territory . . . I do not wish to convey hopes of speedily effecting any great works through my poor instrumentality. I hope to be permitted to work as long as I live beyond other men's line of things and plant the seed of the gospel where others have not planted.'[2]

Working beyond everybody else and disseminating the word in some general and unspecified way were old ideas. What was new in Livingstone's thinking was the idea of using rivers as highways to open up the continent. Once this notion had gripped his imagination, he would never get free of it. Rivers would bring him spectacular success and bitter failure.

In fact Livingstone need not have worried greatly about the attitude of the Directors. Arthur Tidman, the Foreign Secretary of the Society, realized at once that if the discovery of Ngami was given publicity it would encourage public generosity. He published Livingstone's account of the discovery in the March 1850 edition of the *Missionary Magazine*, and when the Royal Geographical Society decided to award Livingstone one half of the year's Royal Premium—the far from regal sum of £25—Tidman went along to collect it on behalf of the intrepid Dr Livingstone. The prize would be good for quite a few donations to the missionary cause. The Royal Geographical Society had also seen the advantage of publicizing the discovery of the lake. Founded in 1830, this body had been incompetently run for some years by a group of naval officers and was only just becoming what it had been intended to be: a society for the promotion of geographical discovery and for providing those interested in geography with published accounts of new discoveries. In recent years the Royal Geographical Society's financial fortunes had been so bad that, to the horror of many members, the Board had decided to allow women to attend some lectures and had started organizing social entertainments to attract more members. The Society's new president, the well-known geologist Sir Roderick Murchison, knew, like Tidman, that subscriptions to any sort of society were the result of advantageous publicity. Making the work of individual explorers as widely known as possible was therefore one of Murchison's aims. Tidman, for his own financial reasons, had no objection to Sir Roderick publicizing Dr Livingstone's work, although the Directors of the London Missionary Society had no intention of starting new and costly ventures in central Africa. They were, in spite of all their talk of success, none too impressed by the state of the mission stations in Bechuanaland.* But if Livingstone wanted to go off travelling they were prepared to let him, especially since he had found a rich man to pay for most of it.

In spite of Livingstone's fears that Oswell might get all the credit, neither Oswell nor Murray wrote home for some months after reaching Ngami and in the meantime Livingstone gained most of the recognition. He alone caught Murchison's eye. Livingstone would remain unaware of this eminent man's interest until seven years later, when Murchison intervened decisively in the missionary explorer's life. By that time, under Murchison's guidance, the R.G.S. had become an influential body, with close links with the Government and the Admiralty developed for the one purpose of sponsoring specific exploratory expeditions.

From the moment Livingstone returned to Kolobeng from his first journey to Ngami, his one thought was to get back to examine the country further north. The hottest season of the year was upon him, however, and

---

* In late 1849 and early 1850 J.V. Freeman, a Director of the L.M.S., visited Bechuanaland and was dismayed by the lack of missionary progress.

he knew that it would be madness to attempt a crossing of the Kalahari till the spring of the following year, 1850. The results of this second journey north were nil, and this was because Livingstone in the first place decided not to wait for Oswell to join him, and in the second decided to travel with his family. This trip between April and August 1850 is interesting only because it sheds light on Livingstone's character.

The reason why Livingstone decided not to wait for Oswell is simple: he could not bear the thought of anybody else getting the credit for penetrating further north than Ngami—he was not yet aware of the complete success of his attempt to gain all the praise for the first journey. Livingstone later tried to excuse his behaviour in leaving Kolobeng before Oswell got there by saying that there had never been any prior arrangement between them. He told his father-in-law, Moffat, that Oswell had asked to come but that he had refused to let him.[3] This was clearly a lie, since when Oswell did reach Kolobeng, shortly after the Livingstones had left, he had brought the promised boat with him. He would hardly have gone to the trouble if there had been no previous agreement. Besides, Livingstone had recently accepted £40 from Oswell to defray expenses. Not only does Livingstone's action look ungrateful, it seems foolish too. He must have realized that if the recalcitrant chief at Ngami did not change his mind about a crossing of the Zouga, no further progress would be possible without Oswell's boat.

If Livingstone's behaviour towards Oswell is confusing, his attitude to his family is more extraordinary still. For a start, the children were very young: Robert was four, Agnes three, and Thomas only one. Apart from that, in April 1850 Mrs Livingstone was five months pregnant, and it could not have taxed her husband's medical knowledge to work out that she would probably give birth on the journey home, very likely in the desert. Mrs Livingstone was used to Africa and had a strong constitution but, even so, Oswell's description of Livingstone's decision to take her as 'rather unwise' was a remarkably charitable understatement.

The Livingstones managed to get to the Zouga without mishap, but there for the first time Livingstone encountered the tsetse fly. As soon as the oxen had been bitten, they began to sicken and die. The tsetse were unknown south of the Kalahari but had long been known to the tribes of central and eastern Africa as a menace which made long journeys with animals a hazardous business. But Livingstone soon gained experience of a far more serious problem. Earlier travellers, such as Park and Lander, had suffered a great deal from 'fever' during their travels in West Africa near the Niger. Livingstone had read about malaria in medical periodicals and therefore knew that quinine was then the only effective remedy. Mercifully he had had the foresight to bring some with him in 1850, for within days of their arrival at Ngami, his children had contracted fever. Livingstone's attitude to their suffering was remarkably clinical. 'It is an interesting fever,' he told Robert Moffat. 'I should like to have an hospital here to study it. In Morukanelo [a driver] it was continued fever. Thomas had it in the remittent form & Agnes in the intermittent. In some it was simple bilious fever. In others it chiefly affected the vascular system of the abdomen . . . The source is no doubt marshy miasmata.'[4]*

This scientific detachment must have amazed Robert Moffat; nor, in view of his daughter's advanced state of pregnancy, could he have been amused by Livingstone's light-hearted mention of another incident. The tribes round Ngami snared game with deep pitfalls. One day Livingstone and Mary were travelling in the waggon when it 'turned clean over in a pitfall'. Mary, Livingstone went on, had often feared being crushed in this sort of accident, 'but when it came could not help saying to herself, "Is this all?"'[5] Livingstone told his own parents that the mosquitoes were so bad that 'I could not touch a square half-inch on the bodies of the children unbitten after a single night's exposure'. Added to that, the children had no vegetables for over four months.[6] The children soon became so weak that Livingstone knew that any thought of going on north from Ngami would have to be abandoned. Ironically, though, just before the children had contracted fever, the Ngami chief had agreed to let Livingstone cross the Zouga in exchange for his best gun.

After recrossing the Kalahari, where on one occasion they went without water for two days, the Livingstones arrived back at Kolobeng. It was mid-August. Mary's baby was already overdue. A week later she had a daughter. It is hard to imagine the strain of going through the last months of pregnancy in a jolting waggon, eating an unbalanced diet, drinking too little water, experiencing terrible heat. Mrs Livingstone had not been able to think only of herself, for Thomas and Agnes had had to be nursed constantly since both were too weak to stand unassisted. Already enfeebled, the Livingstone children soon caught a bronchial infection that was widespread among the Bakwains at the time. In turn the new baby succumbed to it and very soon died screaming. The final scream haunted Livingstone for a long time afterwards but he still managed to clear his conscience with chilling ease. 'It was the first death in our family,' he wrote, 'but just as likely to have happened if we had remained at home, and we now have one of our number in heaven.'[7] Naturally he had not paused to ask himself whether the other children would have caught the infection and passed it on to the baby if they had been in good health. It

* Malaria was not known to be connected with the anopheles mosquito till the end of the nineteenth century.

is doubtful whether Mrs Livingstone viewed with such apparent equanimity the loss of a child that she had carried at such cost to herself. That cost was not just weariness. She became ill with shivering and earache, which Livingstone put down to a rotten tooth. But soon the right half of Mary's face was paralysed. 'The affection', Livingstone confessed, 'causes considerable deformity, especially in smiling.'[8] What Mrs Livingstone had to smile about is hard to imagine, but happily the paralysis had eased within a couple of months.

At Mary's mother's insistence the whole family went down to Kuruman to convalesce from November 1850 to February 1851. The children enjoyed their first fresh fruit in months, but for the adults it was a tense and disagreeable time. The Moffats had discovered that Livingstone was planning yet another journey to the north, and once again intended taking his family. Mary's mother was violently opposed to this. She was unimpressed by her son-in-law's argument that if Mary stayed at Kolobeng while he went off again, the Bakwains might move to a better-watered spot in his absence. Mrs Moffat easily countered this by suggesting that the obvious course would be for Mary and the children to stay on at Kuruman. To this Livingstone had two unconvincing replies: in the first place, if he left Mary behind other missionaries would say that he could not stand her company, and in the second, she would be better off with him since he was her doctor. While missionary gossip seems a quite inadequate excuse for risking four lives, his idea that his wife and family would be better off with him in a fever-ridden region was laughable. Then, in early April, Mrs Moffat discovered that her daughter was pregnant yet again, and this time she wrote to Livingstone telling him precisely how she felt about his endangering Mary's life.

My dear Livingstone

Before you left the Kuruman I did all I dared to do to broach the subject of your intended journey, and thus bring on a candid discussion, more especially with regard to Mary's accompanying you with those dear children. But seeing how averse both you and Father* were to speak about it, and the hope that you would never be guilty of such temerity (after the dangers they escaped last year), I too timidly shrank from what I ought to have had courage to do. Mary had told me all along that should she be pregnant you would not take her, but let her come out here after you were fairly off. Though I suspected at the end that

* Robert Moffat.

she began to falter in this resolution, still I hoped it would never take place, i.e. *her going with you*, and looked and longed for things transpiring to prevent it. But to my dismay I now get a letter, in which she writes, 'I must again wend my way to the far Interior, perhaps to be confined in the field.' O Livingstone, what do you mean? Was it not enough that you lost one lovely babe, and scarcely saved the other, while the mother came home threatened with Paralysis? And will you again expose her & them in those sickly regions on an exploring expedition? All the world will condemn the *cruelty* of the thing to say nothing of the indecorousness of it. A pregnant woman with three little children trailing about with a company of the other sex, through the wilds of Africa, among savage men and beasts! Had you *found a place* to which you wished to go and commence missionary operations, the case would be altered. Not one word would I say, were it to the mountains of the moon. But to go with an exploring party, the thing is preposterous. I remain yours in great perturbation.

M. Moffat.[9]

This letter increased rather than lessened Livingstone's determination to take Mary. He had been at great pains to try to explain to the Moffats that what seemed to be 'an exploring expedition' was nothing of the sort: it was opening the way to get to thousands of Africans waiting to become Christians. He had also tried to put across his idea that finding a place from which to commence 'missionary operations' had to take second place till he had discovered more about the network of rivers. The idea of hundreds of missionaries punting their way up malarial rivers and bringing the Gospel to a land lying on the wrong side of a sizeable desert seemed unrealistic to the Moffats, who had worked hard to make their thirty converts and had found little time to experiment with 'navigable highways' or 'introducing the gospel into a new land'. It should be added that although Moffat had made two long journeys to the Matabele in the area of modern Zimbabwe, these had been his only major excursions from Kuruman in twenty years. In the past, Livingstone admirers have tried to represent the Moffats as conservative die-hards, who could not see the worth of a new and far-sighted approach even when it was pushed in their faces.

In the meantime, to get over what Livingstone regarded as an unjustified personal attack by Mrs Moffat, he began reflecting on the worth of sacrifice as proof of a true Christian vocation. 'It is a venture to take wife & children into a country where fever, African fever, prevails. But who that believes in Jesus would refuse to make a venture for such a Captain?'[10]

Livingstone often thought of missionaries as members of an army with Christ as their captain or general. Sometimes he developed the argument that if soldiers died for the Queen, missionaries ought to be prepared to die for Christ. The parallel was nonetheless misleading, for not even the most bellicose soldier would have thought of sending his small children into the firing line.

By April 1851, with his pregnant wife and his scarcely recovered children, Livingstone was once more ready to set out on his third and, as it turned out, his most important journey from Kolobeng. This time he had had the sense to wait for the ever-forgiving Oswell, who had gone on a few days ahead to dig out the wells in the Kalahari. This service undoubtedly reduced the children's sufferings at the beginning of the journey. On the way, however, Livingstone learned that three other Europeans were attempting to reach the area he was aiming at— this trio consisted of J.H. Wilson, the same who had gone to Ngami on Livingstone's first visit, Sam Edwards, the son of Livingstone's former missionary colleague, and J. Leyland, an English naturalist. At once Livingstone was determined that at all costs these men should not beat him to his goal. He discovered at the Zouga that it was possible to reach the country of the Makololo, his intended destination, by striking due north instead of going west to Ngami and then north-east after that. There was, however, a difficulty: there would be very few wells on the direct route and many of these might be dried up after an unusually hot summer.

Livingstone was prepared to take the risk. As usual it would be his family who suffered for it. Not long afterwards they had to go five days without water, and as Livingstone, with his gift for being humorous after the event, put it, 'the less there was of water, the more thirsty the little rogues became'. He did, however, concede that the possibility of the children 'perishing before our eyes was terrible'.[11]

When they did finally reach water, it was stagnant and full of rhinoceros dung. But people with swollen lips and blackened tongues were not inclined to be fussy. As Livingstone wrote with typical stoicism: 'No one knows the value of water till he is deprived of it . . . I have drunk water swarming with insects, thick with mud and putrid with rhinoceros urine and buffaloes' dung, and no stinted draughts of it either.'[12]

By mid-June the party had travelled 170 miles from the river Zouga and had now reached the river Chobe, which Livingstone would later learn was a major tributary of the Zambesi. Across the Chobe, Livingstone knew from the reports of the people near Ngami, lived Sebitoane, the chief of the Makololo. Since Sebitoane's tribe occupied the area north of the Chobe, Livingstone knew that he had all but achieved his object.

Since the waggons were too large to transport across the river on canoes, Mrs Livingstone and the children were left while Livingstone and Oswell went some twenty miles upstream to the place where locals assured them Sebitoane was temporarily settled.

Sebitoane received his two white visitors with visible emotion, but his pleasure at their arrival had nothing to do with Livingstone's statement of the aims of his visit: 'the preaching of the Gospel' and the Makololo's 'elevation in the scale of humanity'. In fact the chief of the Makololo wanted guns; he had been fighting almost constantly for the last thirty years, so his desire was understandable. White men were usually reputed to bring guns, so they were welcome. As Livingstone admitted: 'He had the idea that our teaching was chiefly the art of shooting.'[13]

Since the Makololo featured prominently in Livingstone's life during the following ten years, it is necessary to say more about them. A tribe of the southern Sotho group, they had been driven from their home, in what was to become the Orange Free State, during the great Zulu emigration that took place in the first three decades of the nineteenth century. In the early 1820s the Makololo had been forced east into Bechuanaland but had then been driven north by the better-armed Griquas after a battle near Kuruman in 1824. They had continued northwards and had finally reached the Chobe. During the next ten years they established themselves as overlords of the Barotse valley and the Batoka Plateau further along the Zambesi to the east. Their position, however, was still not secure, for they were threatened by the Matabele, one of the Zulu tribes which had originally forced them out of their true home. The Matabele, under their chief Mosilikatse, had themselves been forced north out of the Transvaal by the Boers into a region which today lies near the town of Bulawayo in Zimbabwe. This was three hundred miles to the south-east of the Makololo, but still too close for comfort, since the Matabele had sent a number of raiding parties in recent years. To protect themselves, the Makololo had withdrawn to the area between the Chobe and the Zambesi, for the two rivers afforded excellent protection. Unfortunately, the surrounding swamps left the Makololo in the worst kind of country for malaria. They were in fact in a death-trap and knew it. Apart from guns, they saw another way of returning to the more healthy territory which they had been compelled to leave: diplomacy.

Sebitoane had heard about the extraordinary affection Mosilikatse, the Matabele chief, had developed for Robert Moffat, who had already twice made the 600-mile journey from Kuruman to Mosilikatse's kraal. The Makololo chief had also learned, through messengers sent down to Sechele, that Livingstone was Moffat's son-in-law. Sebitoane therefore reasoned that if Livingstone came to live with him as his missionary,

Moffat would use his influence on Mosilikatse to stop him attacking the Makololo. There is no evidence that Livingstone fully appreciated this reason for the Makololos' helpfulness before 1853.

Although the Makololo were full of wounded indignation at the Matabele's attitude towards them, they were none too pacific themselves; their standard tactic with their enemies was to entice them on to islands in the Chobe or Zambesi and kill them all when they had nearly starved. During his visit Livingstone heard that one of Sebitoane's wives had eloped, taking nine attendants with her. The wife and eight servants were stabbed to death when caught and the ninth servant was only spared because Livingstone begged for her life. The Makololo also smoked cannabis and ate half-cooked meat, both unpleasant habits in Livingstone's eyes.

Although he had been delighted by Sebitoane's extraordinary eagerness to keep him and Mary as his missionary teachers, Livingstone's principal aim was to get to the great river which he had heard lay a hundred miles to the north. In the event, his plans to get there were suddenly disrupted when Sebitoane unexpectedly died of pneumonia. It was not therefore till the end of July that Livingstone and Oswell were able to set out for their objective. Livingstone's arrival on the banks of the Zambesi near the town of Sesheke, on 4 August 1851, was to prove a turning-point in his life. Both he and Oswell were stunned by the size of the great river; neither had seen anything like it before. The river was between three and five hundred yards across and was flowing fast, although it had been an unusually dry year. The two men persuaded an old African to take them out on to the river in his canoe. Livingstone, ignorant of Silva Porto's discoveries, was so moved by the thought that he and Oswell were the first white men ever to have seen this mighty river that he felt close to tears. Only 'the fear that the old man who was conducting us across might ask, "What are you blubbering at? ain't afraid of these alligators, are you?" made me hold my tears for some other occasion.'[14] It is quite clear that if the two men did not at once connect their river with the Zambesi that flowed into the sea in Mozambique, they made the deduction soon afterwards, having questioned the Makololo closely. Oswell sent home a sketch map with the river flowing downstream past the Portuguese settlement of Tete on the lower Zambesi. Although Livingstone had heard that there was a massive waterfall eighty miles to the east, he soon resumed his reverie of a navigable *highway*. If this river, as seemed clear beyond doubt, really did flow on for a thousand miles to the east coast of Africa, would it not be possible for traders and missionaries to come up it as far as the great falls? There might, of course, be other lesser falls, but Livingstone preferred not to think about them. His dream of the Zambesi as a God-given highway into the interior had already begun to take solid shape in his mind.

This idea would never have had such a momentous impact on Livingstone's thinking had he not made a further discovery on his return to the Makololo's town of Linyanti on the river Chobe. Livingstone's attention was drawn to the clothing worn by some of the Makololo: many were dressed in cloaks made of European cloth, either cotton or baize. One or two proudly sported dressing-gowns. Livingstone lost no time in making enquiries about the suppliers of these items, and soon discovered that they were a tribe known to the Makololo as the Mambari. From what he learned, the Mambari came from a place far to the west: actually the area around Bie in central Angola, six hundred miles north-west of Linyanti. Livingstone next made the disquieting discovery that the Mambari acted as middlemen and agents for Portuguese and mixed race traders living in Angola. Worse still, these traders —'either true Portuguese or bastards'—had themselves come to the Makololo's country to deal in slaves. The slave trade had therefore already penetrated into the interior far further than anybody in Britain had previously believed.

The abolition of slavery throughout the British Empire in 1833 had cut by a half the number of slaves crossing the Atlantic, bound mainly for the West Indies. But just under twenty years later, when Livingstone first reached the heart of south-central Africa, some sixty thousand slaves were still crossing annually from West Africa to Brazil, Cuba and the southern states of America. This was in spite of the presence of a British blockading squadron on the West African coast which accounted for no less than a sixth of the Royal Navy's total strength. Although nations such as Portugal, Spain and France had officially outlawed the trade, in practice they turned a blind eye to its continuation, neither imposing stiff enough penalties nor making any efforts to apprehend slave traders.

Livingstone's realization that the slave-trade had reached the upper Zambesi did not lead him to hold back from his rapidly growing conviction that the area dominated by the Makololo could become a thriving new mission field. In fact the presence of slave traders made him still more determined that the region should be occupied by missionaries without delay. Even when he conceded to himself that missionaries on their own would be unable to cope with the usual problems of African indifference and the slave trade as well, he was not downcast; he felt sure that a straightforward way to defeat the slave trade had already been devised.

In 1840, while studying in London, Livingstone had visited Exeter Hall to hear the famous Thomas Fowell Buxton speak about the benefits 'legitimate commerce' could bring to West Africa. The central idea had been that the African would no longer sell his fellow-men to slave traders if he had an alternative means of acquiring European cloth, guns and trinkets. If 'legitimate' traders pressed into the interior and offered to exchange cloth and guns for wax, palm oil and ivory, chiefs would have this alternative and the slave trader would therefore be 'cut out'. The problem had always been how traders could be persuaded to penetrate hundreds of miles into an unknown continent where the tsetse fly ruled out carriage by waggon and oxen, and where malaria frequently killed those foolish enough to hack their way through tropical rain-forests. The difficulties posed by the environment would also cut profits. Buxton's great idea of Christianity and commerce forging into the 'Dark Continent', and together bringing civilization and the end of the slave trade, had not therefore been taken up. Livingstone felt that his magnificent Zambesi would solve the communication problem that had bedevilled all trading efforts in West Africa.

Unfortunately the situation on the upper Zambesi was more disturbing than Livingstone at first realized. Soon he discovered that the Makololo themselves were eager slave traders, and sold members of their subject tribes to the Mambari without compunction. Recently Sebitoane had gone on a slave raid with the Mambari and had handed over two hundred captives in exchange for the cattle taken on the foray. So Livingstone had to acknowledge that the Makololo were not averse to slavery because they operated a system that 'cannot be called slavery, though akin to it'.[15] Livingstone's previous assumption that the Makololo were a simple and untouched people, without any of the vices of the already contaminated Bechuanas, now had to be dropped. To soften the blow, Livingstone tried to convince himself that the Portuguese and the Mambari had only arrived the year before and had therefore not had time completely to corrupt the Makololo. He was wrong. Silva Porto had reached Barotseland in the mid-1840s and the Mambari probably ten years before that. It was not long before Livingstone admitted his mistake and wrote of the 'perpetual capturing and sale of children' from subject tribes as a crime which made the external slave trade 'appear a small evil in comparison'.[16]

Had Livingstone not already committed himself mentally to a mission station in Makololo country, he might have acknowledged that the Makololo themselves would be unlikely to abandon their old and deeply ingrained habits for the sake of a few traders and missionaries. But Livingstone had made up his mind: traders and missionaries would come up the Zambesi in boats from the east coast to a point as far west as the great falls. Of course, if the missionaries were going to have any hope of success, the operations of the traders would have to be substantial. One or two men buying ivory in exchange for cloth were not going to be able to dissuade the Makololo from selling slaves to the Portuguese and the Mambari. Only widespread European intrusion would have any effect at all.

Livingstone's position was painfully ironic; he had come hoping to find an untouched people, and having found that they had already been corrupted by external influences, was now advocating far more contact with outsiders. In the past he had usually felt that individual traders were interested only in profits and did not care in the least if the Africans were robbed and exploited. He had also noted that as often as not Africans were made worse rather than better by contact with Europeans. Now he was arguing in a very different way and one that made nonsense of much of his earlier tolerance of local customs and institutions. But in his determination that the new area he had discovered should become his own mission field, Livingstone was prepared to forget his old strictures on traders. By using calming phrases like 'legitimate commerce' and 'Christian traders', he managed for a while to square his conscience.

But in the long term Livingstone wanted better justification for his new thinking than a few catchphrases. If traders were going to come and undermine tribal society in central Africa, Livingstone had to persuade himself that he had formerly been wrong to see any merits in African culture. The central problem which any Christian critic of tribal organization faced was the fact that the whole system was based on collective generosity rather than on private ownership and personal wealth: a far more 'Christian' society in that respect than capitalist nineteenth-century Britain. The trade which Livingstone would be recommending would be based on capitalist economics: the sale of surplus goods at a profit to outsiders rather than distribution of the surplus among the producers. This was hardly consistent with the Christian teaching of the vanity of all worldly wealth and goods. To counteract unpleasant thoughts like these, Livingstone set about convincing himself that tribal generosity was not generosity at all. He began by asking himself whether Western concepts like individual freedom and personal choice could mean anything in a tribal society. Since tribal organization was conservative and the social structure static, he decided they could not. Having satisfied himself on that score by pointing to the permanent social inferiority of the Makololo's subject tribes, he went on to draw his next conclusion. If freedom of choice did not exist, then tribal generosity could not spring from any real or freely made decision; instead it was simply a reflex action dictated by custom, the need to survive and the hope of future benefits. 'Every action and all public movements', he concluded, 'are made under stern compulsion . . . the entire system is one of selfishness.'[17] Livingstone added further condemnations of tribalism. All the members of tribes were so busy fulfilling their mutual obligations that they had no time to devote to any kind of advances, either collective or personal. Only private ownership of land, Livingstone argued, would free people from their dues and services to the chief, which he expected in return for the allocation of land. If feudalism had survived in England there could never have been any progress because the major part of the population would have remained tied to the land.

So, ignoring the fact that tribal society served the needs of the people and enabled them to survive famines and to operate in a country where trade with distant tribes was made impossible by the nature of the terrain, Livingstone went on to contrast African poverty with British industrial wealth. His object was to persuade himself that Africans could only benefit from wide-scale European intrusion. Thus he unthinkingly endorsed the common mid-Victorian equation of industrialism with progress and 'civilization'. There was no mention now of contact with Europeans making Africans worse, instead he wrote confidently that Africans would only become civilized 'by a long-continued discipline and contact with superior races by commerce'.[18] Conveniently setting on one side his own miserable childhood, Livingstone enthused about the great advantages enjoyed by the inmates of British workhouses, who had 'glass windows and chimneys', not to mention 'soap and clean linen', all usually way beyond the reach of African chiefs. In Britain, Livingstone went on rhapsodically: 'Surgical operations are performed without pain, fire is obtained instantaneously, and travellers are conveyed on the ocean and on the land with a celerity which our forefathers could not comprehend and which Africans now consider fabulous.' In short: 'The world is rolling on to the Golden Age.'[19] Livingstone was not unusually gullible to have had thoughts like these; many of his contemporaries were convinced that through reforms and representative institutions the injustices which rapid industrialization had brought about would soon be swept away. Because Livingstone had left England in the early 1840s he would not see the continuance of the old poverty and exploitation which he himself had suffered.

This optimism helped Livingstone to justify his new determination that European commerce should invade Africa, not merely as a weapon against the slave trade but as a means of undermining tribal society. The theory was that when the Africans' tribal collectivism had been weakened by Western trading methods, they would be in a more receptive state of mind to appreciate the alien Christian faith. Yet Livingstone could not entirely escape the implications of his new philosophy, as he admitted when he wrote about 'the advance of ruthless colonists' as a 'terrible necessity'.[20]

Livingstone had abandoned much of his earlier thinking largely because of his passionate desire to make the area between the Chobe and the Zambesi a viable field for missionary work. He had felt that God had directed him north from Kolobeng to this region, and his discovery of the upper Zambesi had strengthened this belief. The fact that the Makololo spoke Sichuana was an added reason for his feeling that a mission with them could succeed. His conviction was so fixed that he would ignore or underestimate all the problems associated with his chosen field. Apart from the difficulties posed by the slave trade and the Makololo's involvement in it, there was malaria. Livingstone told the Directors of the London Missionary Society that traders, if they came up the Zambesi during June, July and August, would not get fever. However, Livingstone's son, Thomas, had had fever throughout June and July. In any case, Livingstone's plans for the region depended on traders and missionaries being able to live there all the year round. That would only be possible if a healthier and preferably higher adjacent area were to be found.

Then the Makololo would have to be persuaded to move, and that of course would depend on the attitude of the Matabele. The greatest imponderable of all was whether the Zambesi would be navigable from the coast. If the river should prove impassable because of rapids or sandbanks, then few traders would come to the area, for they would never be prepared, in sufficient numbers, to endure the long and perilous overland journey from the Cape to the upper Zambesi. Livingstone had suggested that a brisk trade could be done in ivory, but indiscriminate slaughter of elephants would soon put an end to it. Apart from ostrich feathers and wax, he had few ideas for the establishment of longer-term trade. Instead, with typical optimism, he had suggested that since gold had recently been discovered in South Africa (albeit not yet in vast quantities), it might be found further north. God, he claimed, would do for central Africa something 'just as wonderful and unexpected as the discovery of gold'.[21] This prophecy would not be fulfilled.

Livingstone's determination to leave Bechuanaland and to gain the distinction of being the man who, hundreds of miles beyond every other man's lines, began successful missionary operations in Makololo country led him to turn his thinking upside-down and encouraged him to see circumstances not as they were, but as he wanted them to be. This trait would enable him to press on where others more logically minded would have given up, but it would also pinpoint many inconsistencies in his ideas and pave the way for future disappointments. At a later date it would also lay him open to charges of deliberate misrepresentation.

Before Livingstone started south again in August 1851, he had nonetheless made two realistic decisions. He would return as soon as possible to the Zambesi, in the first place to see whether he could find a healthy spot for a mission and trading centre, and in the second to reach the coast either to the east or west, to see whether the Zambesi was a realistic *highway*.

By September, Livingstone and his family had reached the river Zouga and there they had to wait a month while Mrs Livingstone gave birth to her

long-awaited child. The Livingstones called their new son William Oswell*
after their friend and benefactor. During this inevitable period of delay
Livingstone wasted no time in writing numerous letters which would be
ready for despatch when he got further south. The most important was to
the Directors. In it he outlined his new plan for sending his wife and family
back to England while he took a closer look at central Africa and tried
to open a direct way to the coast which would be far shorter than the
1,300-mile trek from the Cape to Makololo country. Livingstone told
the Directors flatly that if they would not support Mrs Livingstone and the
children in England, he would still go north 'no matter who opposes'.[22]
When Livingstone finally put his wife and family on to a ship bound for
England in April 1852, he had still had no reply from the Directors and so
could not have been sure whether they would help Mary or not. By now
Livingstone knew it would be folly to take his family back to the Zambesi
and thus endanger their health and lives by a prolonged stay—but his failure
to wait and hear what provision the Directors would make was typical of his
attitude to his wife and children. When they became a hindrance to his
cherished plans, his family, and not the plans, would be sacrificed.

Livingstone arrived at Kolobeng on 27 November 1851 and found that
the Bakwains had moved on in search of a better-watered place. The sight
of the deserted village neither surprised nor distressed him; in fact, if
anything, it pleased him. The Bakwains' move could be added to the list
of excuses he had already worked out for leaving Sechele and Bechuanaland
for good. So he told the Directors that since Sechele had deserted
Kolobeng and would probably have to move on from the new site he had
chosen higher up the Kolobeng stream, there could be no justification for
trying to build up a new settlement with the Bakwains. Livingstone argued
that all the houses he would be expected to erect would be wasted labour.

He made other excuses too: the Boers and the drought had prevented
the Bakwains accepting the Word, and would continue to do so. The tiny
population of Bechuanaland gave no scope for settling 'native agents' in
any numbers, while the area near the Zambesi was populous and fertile
and offered far better prospects. All the reasons Livingstone had given for
leaving Bechuanaland had been false except the last. Had he wished to
stay with the Bakwains, nothing would have stopped a man of his determination from moving with them many more times and building new
houses on each occasion. Nor would he have given in on account of the
drought if he had wished to remain with them. The Boers had not yet
directly threatened the existence of Kolobeng, and at their closest were

* Livingstone sometimes called him Bill or William but more often Oswell.

living between three and five days' journey to the east. Besides, if Livingstone had really expected the Boers to attack Sechele he ought to have stayed with him to act as his ambassador and diplomatist. Nor could Livingstone truthfully claim that the size of Bechuanaland's population gave him a good reason to leave. He had failed to convert even a small part of that population and his claim that there were insufficient tribes to send 'native teachers' to was equally misleading. He would have been more honest if he had admitted that there were too few 'native teachers' to send to any tribes. Mebalwe and Paul had been thought by Moffat to be the best 'native teachers' in Bechuanaland and Livingstone had lost faith in both of them.

It is significant that at this stage Livingstone did not include the Bakwains' failure to be converted as a reason for leaving them. He realized that if he did, the other missionaries would accuse him of quitting because of failure. Only three years later would he confess to a friend that of all his reasons for leaving the Bakwains 'the principal one was determined hostility to the requirements of the gospel'.[23] But in 1851, precisely because he wished to create the impression that he was not leaving the Bakwains because of their lack of faith, Livingstone assured the Directors: 'I by no means give up the hope that they will be converted.'[24]

There can be no doubt, however, that although missionary failure had originally driven Livingstone north, his principal motive in 1851 for leaving Bechuanaland was his feeling that there was more exciting work to be done among the Makololo. Bechuanaland could never offer the thrilling prospect of traders sailing hundreds of miles along a navigable river, nor could it give scope to Livingstone's abiding ambition to 'preach the Gospel beyond every other man's line of things'. He sensed that his ideas on commerce and Christianity might have a revolutionary impact on Africa, far greater than anything that an individual missionary working with one tribe could ever hope to achieve. Missionary work in the conventional sense was often dull, usually disappointing and never very successful. Livingstone had now chosen a far more attractive role, that of a man who opened the way for others, who would then follow and establish missionary and trading settlements. Then Livingstone would go on and open up more territory, and so on. The important thing was that he should lead and others follow. It was the ideal formula for the personally ambitious missionary.

Livingstone was not the first religiously motivated man to see his own wishes and personal preferences in terms of the dictates of Providence, and to justify them accordingly. In his situation it seemed crystal clear that unless a new conception of missionary work in Africa was formulated, no significant number of Africans would ever be converted. Therefore any moves that he could make which might radically alter the situation throughout the continent would surely find favour with God. That they were also in Livingstone's best interests was more than coincidental, for when Livingstone had claimed, after Lake Ngami had brought him a measure of recognition, that he had been 'regardless of the fame of discovery',[25] he had been less than truthful. His efforts to claim as much of the praise as he could for that discovery hardly accord with self-effacing modesty. Livingstone himself was uneasy about being ambitious, and although he often denied that he was, sometimes admitted his obsession with doing things and getting to places first. 'Perhaps it arises from ambition,' he told the Directors, 'but it is not of an ignoble sort.'[26] At other times he was a great deal less certain and although suggesting that all his actions were ultimately intended 'for the benefit of Him to whom I have dedicated my all', he admitted that there was 'much impurity in my motives' and confessed that he mistrusted his ambition.[27] If he mistrusted it, his fellow-missionaries were open in their condemnations. They did not, as Livingstone put it, 'hesitate to tell the natives that my object is to obtain the applause of men'. They also suggested that Livingstone had stopped being a missionary and was now simply a traveller. This last jibe really hit home. 'A few as I understand in Africa, in writing home have styled my efforts as *wanderings*', he complained. 'The very word contains a lie coiled like a serpent in its bosom. It means travelling without an object, or uselessly . . .'[28]

For somebody who had thought about bringing social change to Africa as thoroughly as Livingstone had done, the charge was clearly maddening. But the other missionaries can hardly be blamed. Moffat never really forgave Livingstone for abandoning Sechele 'at the time he required the most watchful eye and encouraging voice of his missionary'. All this, Moffat went on, was 'notwithstanding the importance of Mr Livingstone's discoveries'.[29]

By 1852 Livingstone had certainly ceased being a missionary in any sense that the members of the London Missionary Society could accept, but that still did not make him purely a traveller. Quite what he was is impossible to define; he had become part social theorist, part explorer, part missionary propagandist, part trading expansionist, part anti-slavery proponent. Many of his aims appeared to outsiders to be inconsistent. But force of circumstance and his own experiences, since his arrival in Africa eleven years before, had slowly combined together in Livingstone's mind to form a strange mixture of ideas both contradictory and complementary. How such unlikely components would hold together, only the future would tell, but in 1852, as Livingstone stood poised to set out on what would prove to be his greatest feat of exploration, he had persuaded himself, albeit by some fairly startling mental gymnastics, that hold together they would.

9

Return to Linyanti
1852–1853

On 16 March 1852 the Livingstone family arrived in Cape Town, having come directly from Linyanti. The journey of roughly fifteen hundred miles had taken six months, including stops at the river Zouga, at Kolobeng and Kuruman. Livingstone had not seen a town for twelve years, and at first he found stairs so strange that he had to come down them backwards. He also had difficulty expressing himself in English; at Kolobeng he had spoken Sichuana almost the whole time. The family made a bizarre spectacle entering Cape Town in their waggon, with the children's clothes in rags and the parents hardly better dressed. Only through Oswell's generosity was Mrs Livingstone saved having to take her children home looking like paupers. He gave Livingstone £200 to buy his whole family an entire new wardrobe. Livingstone, who had always thought the missionaries in the Colony pampered, was enraged to see them and their children wearing smart and expensive clothing, and fumed about 'the utter respectability' of the citizens of Cape Town for ever 'exchanging their how-d'ye-do's, their noddings, curtsyings and ministerial breakfasts'.[1] There is no record of what the would-be socialites of the town thought of this weird-looking man with his deeply tanned face and uncouth manners.

From the moment he arrived at the Cape Livingstone's one thought was to get a passage for his wife and children as quickly as possible, so that he could head north again. To his irritation he had to wait till late April before they could be got on to a ship bound for England. Livingstone was grieved at parting, but he could reflect with pride that the unique work he was about to begin more than compensated for his personal sorrow. His advice to his children was to consider Jesus, rather than himself, as their father from now on. 'I have given you back to Him and you are in His care.' Privately Livingstone admitted 'my children are become absolutely vagabonds', beggars dependent on the charity of the Directors of the London Missionary Society: a body of men more used to receiving money than handing it out. Although he must have hated leaving them behind, and said that parting with his children was 'like tearing out my entrails', *they* would be the ones to suffer four years of poverty and helplessness. To Mary he wrote: 'How I miss you and the dear children . . . I feel as if I would treat you all much more lovingly than ever . . . You attended to my comfort in many ways . . . May God bless you for all your kindnesses.'[2] But in future Livingstone's most frequently repeated worry would be that his wife and children might forget him.

When Mr and Mrs Moffat had asked Livingstone what plans had been made for their daughter and grandchildren in England, their son-in-law had had to confess that he did not know, but he added with more bravado than realism 'that if they [the Directors] crimp my wife and family they will hear thunder'.[3] The Directors in fact heard nothing from Livingstone for several years and in the meantime Mrs Livingstone had begun a miserable four and a half years of poverty and homelessness.

She began by staying with her husband's parents, and his two spinster sisters, in Scotland. In the early 1840s the Livingstone seniors had moved into a tiny house in Hamilton. It is not hard to imagine the impact of the arrival of a strange daughter-in-law and four children, none of them older than seven, on a religious and meticulously ordered Scottish household. The children had been allowed to play in the open air most of the day with few restrictions, and much of their young lives had been spent with their mother and father travelling hundreds of miles by waggon. The contrast with their new environment could not have been more startling. Mary Livingstone, too, was ill-suited for her new role; and her strait-laced parents-in-law's constant meddling with the children soon drove her into rages. Within six months the situation had become unbearable. Mary left the house and told the Livingstone seniors that they were not to enquire after her and not to try and contact the children. Neil Livingstone told the Directors of the London Missionary Society that owing to his daughter-in-law's 'remarkably strange conduct', he 'had resolved to have no more intercourse with her until there is evidence she is a changed person'.[4]

After leaving Hamilton, Mary and the children lived a wretched nomadic existence. Sometimes they stayed a few months in rented rooms, sometimes with friends her father had made during his last visit to England between 1839 and 1843. Mrs Livingstone moved from Hamilton to Hackney, from Hackney to Manchester and from Manchester to Kendal where the kindness of a Quaker family, the Braithwaites, preserved her sanity. Finally she spent some months at Epsom. To start with, she was sustained by the hope that her husband would return after two years, but as three and then four years passed she began to despair, until she scandalized people by making bitter remarks about missionaries. The Directors never gave her enough money and she was for ever writing grovelling and apologetic letters begging for more. 'I would beg of you to be lenient with me, I don't attempt to justify myself. I may not have been so discreet in the use of my money.'[5] She had not been discreet either. Mrs Livingstone had begun to drink. It was a habit she would not break till her death ten years later. Innocent observers often wondered why she so often had to borrow money. Had those same observers known what sort of a life she had to lead, with her four children whose father was to become a total stranger to them, they would have been neither surprised nor censorious about her drinking. Poor woman, she became seriously ill in 1854 and could not afford to pay for medical attention. Only a doctor's offer of free treatment saved her. In her misery she wrote to her husband begging him to return. It was two years before his refusal came back and by then he was on the way home. She did receive a few letters from him, sent when he was in the Portuguese colonies of Mozambique and Angola, but they could not have comforted her much. The tone was usually harsh. 'Hope you give much of your time to the children,' he wrote self-righteously on one occasion. 'You will be sorry for it if you don't . . . I have nothing worth writing, having no news. I write only because you will be anxious to hear from me.'[6]

Four years later, on his way back to England his ship was delayed by a storm, and so Mrs Livingstone had to wait still longer for him. Her husband did not write a consoling letter, but instead told her that 'patience is a great virtue', and added that the captain of the ship bringing him home had 'been six years away from his family, I only four and a half'.[7] During his time in central Africa, Livingstone had been concerned that his children should not be spoiled, and in case they should think themselves hard done by, he told them stories of worse suffering. 'I saw a poor woman in a chain with many others, up at the Barotse . . . See how kind Jesus was to you.' But they should not, he warned, presume on that kindness by doing 'bad things', for then 'Satan will have you in the chains of sin, and you will be hurried on in his bad ways till you are put into the dreadful place which God hath prepared for him and all like him'.[8] One can hardly imagine Livingstone's children eagerly awaiting such letters. Sometimes he gave them advice which would have meant something to adolescents in their late teens. But for children between six and nine it could not have been cheering to read letters containing information like the following: 'I have no money to leave you. Each of you must work for himself in the world . . . the sooner you learn the better.'[9]

With his wife and children out of the way, Livingstone began getting his supplies together. He also learned how to take accurate geographical observations using a chronometer watch and a sextant. His tutor was the Astronomer Royal at the Cape, Sir Thomas Maclear. The two men became friends, and for the rest of his life, Livingstone would send Maclear observations and maps to check, and would give him details of his new schemes and ambitions. Livingstone also arranged to have his photograph taken for the first time. He sent his brother Charles two prints and added a note saying, 'the ugliest is most like the original . . . a little pedantic looking'.[10] It is sad that Livingstone so rarely joked like this in his letters to Mary and the children.

The thought of leaving Bechuanaland filled Livingstone with joy. One of the advantages that pleased him most was that he would be leaving all his old missionary colleagues behind, escaping 'their envy and back-biting'.[11] On 24 May he heard from the Directors of the London Missionary Society, who suggested that he ought to perform his exploration with another missionary. One of the men they suggested was William Ross. Livingstone wrote back telling them that in twelve years Ross had learned no Sichuana and was so bad-tempered that his presence would be disastrous. William Ashton, one of Moffat's colleagues at Kuruman, had also been suggested as a possible companion. 'You might as well recommend the Lieutenant-Governor as Mr Ashton,' Livingstone assured the Directors. 'He will not go unless forced to it by some agency more potent that moral suasion.' Ashton, he added, had been frightened of travelling further than eighty miles from Kuruman.[12] In short Livingstone had no intention of letting any other missionary share in the glory of what he felt sure would be his greatest achievement. In fact the Directors' motives for suggesting that Livingstone travelled with a companion had been impeccable; they had simply considered that two men would have a safer journey than one, on the general principle that, unless both got malaria simultaneously, one would be able to look after the other. The dangers Livingstone faced were, after all, very real. Of the early explorers, Park, Clapperton and Lander had all died in Africa, while the death rate on the four expeditions sent from Britain between 1816 and 1841 to examine the rivers Congo, Zambesi and Niger had been over 60 per cent. All these expeditions had been total failures due to malaria. Yet the Directors of the London Missionary Society had never tried to dissuade Livingstone from setting out. If he died on his journey he would become a martyr and that would be useful for gaining subscriptions; if he succeeded, that too would stimulate public generosity. The Directors, unknown to Livingstone, had no intention of carrying ambitious operations into tropical Africa. Their policy had always been one of cautious advances into the interior along a linked chain of mission stations. In 1849 John Freeman, one of the Directors, had come out to Bechuanaland and had not been impressed by what he had seen. His view had been that until the position there had been improved, no further plans could be considered for southern, let alone central, Africa. Of course the Directors realized that if Livingstone came home safe and successful, he might attempt to force the Society into premature advances into unsuitable territory. But Tidman and Freeman felt that they would be able to face that problem if and when it came. In the meantime, whatever happened, they felt confident that Livingstone's travels would provide financial benefits. They had therefore been happy to tell Livingstone that his wife would be supported till his return.

Livingstone finally left Cape Town on 8 June, and, after a series of minor accidents to his waggon, arrived at Kuruman on 29 August. He wanted to head north as soon as possible, but he had only been at Kuruman a few days when news came in that the Transvaal Boers had attacked Sechele near Kolobeng, killing sixty Bakwains and losing thirty-six of their own number. The Boers gave several reasons for the attack. They claimed that Sechele had harboured the chief of the neighbouring Bakhatla, who had refused the Boers free labour, and they also used Sechele's refusal to surrender his fire-arms as an excuse. The attack had really been a punishment for Sechele's rejection of a Boer demand to stop British hunters and ivory traders passing through his territory on their way to the north. The Transvaal Boers believed that unless they stopped these men getting through, there was a real danger that the British might in the end encircle them and begin settlements to the north, in the area of modern Zimbabwe.

In the attack Sechele lost three thousand cattle, eleven horses, forty-eight guns and two hundred women and children as captives. Livingstone's house at Kolobeng was sacked. It might be thought that Livingstone's automatic reaction would have been sympathy for Sechele; he had after all risked universal unpopularity by his acceptance of Christianity. But Livingstone was unmoved. The Boer attack, he wrote in his journal, was not in the least mysterious, it was simply the result of the Bakwains' refusal of the Gospel. 'God had dealt graciously with them for years and now suffers them to feel the rod of his anger.'[13] The other missionaries suggested that if Livingstone had still been with Sechele, he would have been able to negotiate with the Boers on the chief's behalf.

Livingstone saw matters differently. Had he been with Sechele, he argued, he would probably have been killed. God had clearly not intended him to die till he had achieved more important goals. It was this idea of the Providential role he had to play that kept Livingstone in Kuruman for another three months. Normally far from cautious, Livingstone consid-ered it would be foolish to move north until the Boers had returned to their homes. Otherwise they might teach him a lesson for having sold guns to Sechele.

Livingstone's three months at Kuruman were unhappy for more reasons than the attack on Kolobeng. During this time he stayed with his parents-in-law, neither of whom approved his plans. Livingstone had earlier written to Robert Moffat asking him to stop Mrs Moffat giving 'soft-headed' advice, but she went on referring to her son-in-law's intended journeys as 'wanderings' and suggested that his going north again was a tempting of Providence rather than a true response to God's wishes. Mrs Moffat felt convinced that Livingstone was going to his death and naturally she was alarmed about the prospects for Mary and the children if this happened. Her continuing complaints led to ugly scenes, with Livingstone saying that people who confined their actions to a narrow field were showing their lack of faith. 'Commit thy way unto the Lord, and He shall direct thy steps. Is this all gammon?'[14] he asked angrily. Both Livingstone and the Moffats were thankful when he finally left Kuruman on 14 December.

Livingstone had not gone far when he met an angry Sechele heading south, determined to take his complaint to the Governor at the Cape, and if need be to the Queen herself. Livingstone told him he 'might as well have remained at home'.[15] By the Sand River Convention of 1852, the Governor of the Cape had relinquished all pretence to any authority north of the river Vaal. Sechele, however, went on his way, but only as far as the borders of the Colony, where he was compelled to turn back because his resources were exhausted. Two years later Moffat visited the Bakwains. Their feelings were bitter and Sechele's younger brother said scornfully: 'The teachers prayed, and where are they now? Look where we are and what we are by taking such advice.'[16] Livingstone never saw Sechele or the Bakwains again. For the next seven years the Makololo would be the focal point of his hopes.

As Livingstone pressed on to the north, he thought of the two main purposes of his current endeavour: to find a suitably healthy place in Makololo country for the establishment of a mission and trading centre, and to open a viable route to the east or west coast along the Zambesi. The essential preliminary to both operations was the trip to Linyanti, for from there he would begin his real work. The journey from Kuruman to Linyanti was a dull necessity for Livingstone, since he had covered the same ground in 1851; nevertheless it needs mentioning, for on it he displayed for the first time a number of the characteristics which were to make him such an unusual explorer.

He set out with three African drivers and a travelling companion, George Fleming. While Livingstone had refused European company, Fleming he considered suitable since he was black, being in fact of West Indian mixed race who had been sponsored by a Cape Town merchant to start an ivory trade with the Makololo. Any European companion might have annoyed Livingstone by expecting to have his opinions considered, but, from the beginning, George knew that his role was distinctly that of a subordinate. Nor was George going to come further than Linyanti.

By the second week of March 1854 the party had crossed the river Zouga and were soon travelling into country where malaria was common. Although to most observers it would have been quite obvious that the illness was serious, since it had soon smitten down every member of the party except Livingstone and one African boy, Livingstone maintained that their sickness resembled 'bilious attacks more than fever'.[17] When he at last had to recognize that perspiring, fainting, violent pains in the head, neck and stomach, coupled with frequent vomiting, was not the same as a bilious attack, he still complained that his attendants kept 'on pretending to great illness when weakness alone remains'.[18] When George suggested that they were all going to die, Livingstone could 'scarcely avoid a guffaw' at such spineless sentiments and finally did break out laughing at George's 'utterly mock cadaveric face'.[19]

This inability to appreciate or sympathize with other people's physical sufferings owed a lot to Livingstone's tough and gruesome childhood in the mills. There was, however, nothing hypocritical about his heartlessness; he would be irritated and ashamed by his own incapacity when laid low by fever, talking about his lack of pluck and being unmanned by the disease. Yet he would force himself to keep going, even when suffering repeated intermittent attacks. His great will-power was to save him from death many times. A man without such reserves would have given up and died. In his early days in Bechuanaland the locals had laughed at Livingstone and suggested that the heat and the lack of water would soon 'knock him up'. 'This', wrote Livingstone, 'caused my Highland blood to rise, and made me despise the fatigue of keeping them all at the top of their speed for days together, and until I heard them expressing proper opinions of my pedestrian powers.'[20] This determination was a key both to his own personal prowess as an explorer, and also to his later failure to travel happily with other Europeans; he expected them to be capable of his own exceptional endurance and despised them when they were not. Few men possessed Livingstone's greatest personal advantage. 'If God has accepted my service,' he wrote confidently, 'then my life is charmed till my work is done.'[21] Already the belief was forming that he was God's chosen instrument for opening up Africa to the healing light of the Gospel. Unless God's desire for the whole world to become Christian changed radically, Livingstone could feel certain that he would not be allowed to die until he had achieved something significant. Given the heavy mortality of previous explorers, this was a comforting belief to hold.

On the journey to Linyanti Livingstone also began to make up for his previous inattention to detailed natural observation. From now on his notebooks and diaries would be full of longitudes and latitudes, altitudes and figures for rainfall. The reason for this change in Livingstone's approach to accurate recording of his travels is in part due to a rebuke he received from the Directors for not having made more notes about Lake Ngami, and also to the influence of Thomas Maclear, the Astronomer Royal at the Cape. But Livingstone's powers of description were not confined to scientific figures and cartography. He even described the arid country of Bechuanaland with a love and wealth of detail that owed much to his belief that all creation was an expression of the Creator's purpose.

The noon tide quiet of nature—the herds retire to sleep in the thickest shade, but amid the apparent silence there is a stifled sound—murmurs— a continual hum of insects which fills the lower strata of air . . . myriads of insects crawl on the ground & flutter round the plants scorched by the heat of the sun. A confused noise issues from every bush, from the decayed trunks of the trees, the fissures of the rocks & from the ground . . . it is a voice that proclaims to us that all nature breathes—that in a thousand forms life is diffused in the dry & dusty soil, as in the bosom of the waters and the air that circulates around us.[22]

Nothing was too small to escape his attention and he gave many hours to studying the behaviour of the white ant. His main preoccupation was to find out how they communicated. 'At some of their operations,' he wrote, 'they beat time in a curious manner. Hundreds of them are engaged in building a large tube, and they wish to beat it smooth. At a signal they all give three or four energetic beats on the plaster in unison . . .' He then went on to describe how the white ant broke down wood and thus helped to enrich the soil. During the journey north to Linyanti, Livingstone noted down hundreds of facts, ranging from the strange attraction the camp-fire at night had for toads, to similarities in the diets of elephants and Bushmen: they both enjoyed eating the bole of young palmyra trees. The extent and detail of Livingstone's scientific and descriptive observations made him unique among contemporary explorers.

By 23 April the party was within striking distance of the Chobe, which they soon discovered had burst its banks, flooding most of the adjacent low-lying country. This forced them to travel for hours at a time through waist-deep water. Soon Livingstone's guides deserted, and his people refused to go any further. For the first time he proved his exceptional powers of endurance when he and one other man set off alone to try to find a way through the swamps. The reeds were so high that it was impossible to see more than a few feet ahead and progress could only be effected by 'putting a staff against the reeds & pressing against it with all our might; when it reached the water we mounted on it & bent it down further'. Nor were reeds the only difficulty: 'bramble papyrus, nearly as thick as the wrist, vines and sedgy grass bound together by a kind of creeper'[23] all had to be flattened or hacked through. Soon Livingstone's canvas trousers were in ribbons and his knees and hands were bleeding and lacerated. Hippopotami posed yet another threat in the flooded valleys. It took Livingstone and his companion two days to force their way through the swamps to the river Chobe itself. For some time afterwards the African who had accompanied Livingstone had to walk with a stick, so badly had his legs been injured.

The Makololo themselves were incredulous. They had assumed the swamps to be impenetrable at the point where Livingstone had come through. The Matabele had certainly never managed to get past them. Livingstone was told that it was as though he had 'dropped from a cloud'.[24] The Makololo soon suggested a better way in which the waggons could be brought to the river without going through the swamps, and on 3 May the whole party crossed the river, waggons and all, on dozens of canoes lashed together into vast floating platforms. On 23 May Livingstone entered Linyanti in his waggon, watched by the entire population of the town: six thousand people. The first phase had ended and the real work was about to begin.

10

From Coast to Coast
1853–1856

To avoid confusion I am beginning this chapter with a brief summary of Livingstone's movements between May 1853, when he arrived at Linyanti, and May 1856, when he embarked for England from the East African coast near Quilimane in Mozambique.

There are three distinct phases. The first, beginning in June 1853, was taken up with Livingstone's search for a malaria-free site for a trading centre and mission on the upper Zambesi. This quest was in the Barotse valley, due north of Linyanti, and took Livingstone three hundred miles north-west up the Zambesi. Having failed to find a suitable site, Livingstone returned to Linyanti in September 1853, ready for the second phase. This was his attempt to open a viable path for traders to follow into the interior from the West African coast. Livingstone set out west from Linyanti in November 1853 and, after a journey of over a thousand miles, reached the Atlantic port of Loanda, in Portuguese Angola. Dissatisfied with this route, the indomitable man prepared for phase three. Leaving Loanda in September 1854, Livingstone retraced his steps to Linyanti and from there set out, downstream along the Zambesi, for the East African coast, which he reached near Quilimane in Portuguese Mozambique in May 1856. His journey from Loanda to Quilimane had been little short of 2,500 miles, and was the first authenticated crossing of the continent from coast to coast by a European. From Quilimane, Livingstone sailed for England, where he arrived on 9 December 1856. From the day he had left the Cape in 1852 to the day he sailed from Quilimane in 1856 he had travelled almost six thousand miles.

In the spring of 1853 Livingstone found that the Makololo had a new chief, a young man of nineteen called Sekeletu. Sebitoane had been initially succeeded by the oldest daughter of his principal wife, but she had voluntarily abdicated in favour of Sekeletu, who was her brother. Livingstone found the new chief just as friendly as Sebitoane had been. Sekeletu's reasons were the same as his father's: namely that Livingstone, being Moffat's son-in-law, might prove useful for improving the Makololo's relations with the Matabele. It is not clear from Livingstone's

Lake Nyassa

Lake Tanganyika

Indian Ocean

QUILLIMANE

Zambesi

TETE

Kebrabasa Rapids

ZUMBO

Batoka Plateau

Victoria Falls

Kabompo

SHINTE'S

Zambesi

Barotse Valley

SESHEKE

LINYANTI

Chobe

Okavango Delta

Lake Ngami

Quango

CASSANGE

BIE O

BENGUELA

LOANDA

Atlantic Ocean

2 LIVINGSTONE'S
TRANS-CONTINENTAL JOURNEY,
NOVEMBER 1853–MAY 1856

miles   500

km   800

0

0

journals and correspondence precisely when he realized this primary reason for Makololo friendliness, but since the Makololo were Sichuana-speaking—having originally come from far to the south, in the area of the Orange Free State—Livingstone probably tumbled to it during 1853. Later he was to write that the Makololo had plans for Mrs Livingstone, as Moffat's daughter, 'to be a shield against Mosilikatse',[1] the chief of the Matabele. Mosilikatse, it will be remembered, had developed a unique affection for Moffat. It was probably because Livingstone had grasped the strength of Sekeletu's desire to persuade him and Mrs Livingstone to settle with the Makololo that he promised the chief that both Mary and he would eventually begin work as missionaries in the area.[2] In the end, as will be seen, Livingstone did not stay with the Makololo. But in 1853 it seems likely that he meant it when he told Sekeletu that after achieving his other objectives he intended to spend some years as a missionary in Makololo country.

Although Sekeletu's main motive for being helpful to Livingstone was the Matabele problem, the young chief had other reasons too. Like his father he wanted guns, cloth and other European goods. So when Livingstone offered to take ivory to the coast and return with these items, Sekeletu eagerly accepted. Of course the white man might trick him, but since there was little demand for ivory among the Makololo, it would not much matter if some tusks were lost.

Since Livingstone completely depended on Makololo porters for his journey to the coast, it is not surprising that he gave Sekeletu an inflated idea of the benefits which trade would bring. His plan was to promise Sekeletu considerable future rewards and thus induce the chief to give him the free labour of a number of men for a couple of years. He was entirely successful, for the Makololo came to believe that he had unique commercial abilities. Their immense faith in Livingstone was clearly evident in their treatment of James Chapman, an ivory trader, who managed to reach Makololo country from the Cape in the summer of 1853. Chapman was told bluntly that the Makololo would do no trade with him, since Livingstone had 'promised them all the good things of the earth, rain, corn, cattle &c . . . and that they would have nothing to do with anyone but Nake (as they called Dr Livingstone)—he was their trader—who would give them two barrels of powder, a large heap of lead, and sundry other articles, for a small tusk of ivory'.[3] Chapman argued bitterly that if Livingstone really wanted the Makololo not to trade with the Mambari and the Portuguese, he should not have given them such high hopes of treasure to be acquired in Loanda. Their rejection of southern traders, Chapman went on, would merely leave the tribe more dependent on the slave trade than ever. Although this was partly sour grapes, there was much truth in Chapman's argument. Livingstone himself had to admit that there were some disadvantages in a close alliance between commerce and Christianity, for the Makololo soon believed that simply by listening to the words of the Bible they would quickly acquire everything they wanted materially. But he still reckoned that this was the price he had to pay for Sekeletu's cooperation.

At the end of June, Livingstone, accompanied by Sekeletu and two hundred men, set out on the hundred-mile trip north from Linyanti to the Zambesi. There they all embarked in a fleet of thirty-three canoes and headed north-west up the river, bound for the Barotse valley. Livingstone eventually went three hundred miles upstream from the point of embarkation. His aim on this journey, which lasted till mid-September, was to find a suitable site for a mission and trading post. He failed in his objective, but other factors contributed to the acute depression he felt on his return to Linyanti.

On his visit to Linyanti in 1851, Livingstone had been shocked to find that the Makololo sold members of their subject tribes to the Mambari, but he had considered this their solitary fault. Largely through wishful thinking, he had built up a mental picture of them as unspoiled noble savages ripe to receive the Gospel. His first shock on his journey up the Zambesi in 1853 was that they seemed very much more bloodthirsty than any tribe in despicable Bechuanaland. Conversation as a rule took the form of boasting about the number of men an individual had killed. Livingstone was often told about battles, and the Makololo, to make the story live, would usually 'imitate the death cry of the victim, a fine joke apparently from the hearty laugh, exhibiting immense mouths, white teeth and glistening eyes'.[4] Sekeletu himself often behaved badly. One day Livingstone was about to preach when the chief and forty of his subjects started 'dancing and roaring at the top of their voices'.[5] Services were treated with derision, and were usually punctuated by the coughings and sneezings of those smoking wild hemp. As soon as Livingstone finished speaking, the chief would generally call for a sheep, which would then be roasted and eaten within half an hour. Then, less than an hour after Livingstone had been talking about God's infinite goodness in sending His only son to redeem their sins, the Makololo would be dancing to the music of the court musicians, whose antics Livingstone considered 'the most ungraceful I have ever seen. I was sorry to see any of our human family so degraded.'[6]

Worse was to come. Livingstone had only been travelling with Sekeletu for a couple of days when a cousin of the chief, a man called Mpepe, attempted to assassinate Sekeletu. Mpepe was foiled because, at the very moment planned for the attack, Livingstone unwittingly sat down between the chief and his would-be murderer. Afterwards nobody was quite sure why Mpepe had not cut down Livingstone first and then killed the chief. Mpepe's aim had been to usurp the chiefship, and the plot seemed even more sinister to Livingstone when he heard that Mpepe had been in league with the Mambari. The incident therefore worried him not only because he had been in such personal danger but also because it proved that the Makololo were politically unstable. Livingstone felt that he might labour to open up a trade with the coast, only to find while he was away that Sekeletu had been deposed. Meantime his successor might (as Mpepe had planned) have formed an exclusive trading arrangement with the Mambari.

After the abortive assassination attempt Mpepe was summarily stabbed to death and members of his family rounded up and killed. Livingstone was a reluctant witness to the murder of Mpepe's father and uncle. 'The men, both upwards of fifty were paralysed with terror . . . the two were led forth with a man on each side and one behind each with a battle axe in hand, to execution. They were led slowly to the river, there hewn down and their bodies deposited by means of a canoe in the middle of the river to be the food of alligators.'[7] 'I am forced to witness, and protest almost in vain,' Livingstone wrote in anguish.

In the Barotse valley, where the Makololo were the overlords of a number of subject tribes, Livingstone noticed that the people dreaded their oppressors. The Makololo, Livingstone soon confessed, 'never visit anywhere but for the purpose of plunder and oppression. They never go anywhere without a club or spear in hand.'[8] 'Nine weeks,' he told a friend, 'hearing their quarrelling, roaring, dancing, singing and murdering, have imparted a greater disgust at heathenism than I ever had before.'[9]

In early July, to add to Livingstone's depression, he met Silva Porto, the famous Portuguese trader who had reached the upper Zambesi before him. Early in the same year Porto had been appointed by the Angolan Government to attempt a trans-continental journey from Angola to Mozambique, but had been prevented getting beyond Barotseland by illness and tribal disturbances.* When Livingstone met him, he had been trading in slaves and ivory. Livingstone hated the idea that he had been outdone by another European, so he conveniently classified Porto as 'half-caste'. This would be his usual method of dealing with other Portuguese when he met them deep in the interior. In this way he protected his own claim to have been the first true European to reach the upper Zambesi.

---

* Two of Porto's African attendants did complete the trans-continental journey; after passing the southern end of Lake Nyassa they reached the East African coast at Kilwa.

Although Livingstone detested the slave trade, he was aware that Porto could give him useful information about the best route to Loanda in Angola. So the two men dined together, Porto 'swilling' Livingstone's wine as well as his own. Livingstone departed with some geographical tips, two Dutch cheeses, some preserved pears and a cauliflower: all gifts. Porto had erected a stockade nearby to contain several hundred slaves. Livingstone had seen a line of chained captives led inside.

In late August, Livingstone met two Arabs who had made an epic journey from the island of Zanzibar, fifteen hundred miles to the north-east. They were assessing the slave and ivory potential of Barotseland. These men later went on to Angola and then recrossed the continent to Mozambique: a journey even more formidable than the one Livingstone was about to undertake. Livingstone's depression deepened. He was now in no doubt that far from having reached a virgin land, he had arrived at a place where 'the slave trade seems pushed into the very centre of the continent from both sides'.[10] In fact Arab slaving operations would remain confined to the area hundreds of miles to the north-east, around Lake Nyassa, and to the regions immediately north of that. For the next ten years, as will be seen, Livingstone was to be far more distressed by Portuguese slaving than by Arab activities. Only when he started exploring around Lake Nyassa in 1863 did he realize the extent of the East African slave trade. Since the British had never participated in the centuries-old Arab slave trade, it was not a subject that preoccupied them overmuch till Livingstone's revelations in the 1860s.

Livingstone's last disappointment on his journey through Barotseland was due to his complete failure to find any place free of malaria. He himself had never contracted malaria before late May 1853, and his first experience of the disease did much more to persuade him that it was serious than his previous observations of other people's sufferings. Between May and September, Livingstone suffered eight attacks of fever. His tongue had been painful, his face had come out in boils, he had constantly wanted to urinate and his head and stomach felt as though they were exploding. Worse than that, 'the fever frequently affects the bowels, producing bloody stools and great pain ... The people report the whole country as excessively sickly, and the appearance of the Makololo as contrasted with the aboriginal inhabitants fully confirms this assertion.'[11] As Livingstone acknowledged in his journal, 'The prospects for these dark regions are not bright.'[12] In 1851 he had confidently told the Directors that traders would be able to come to Barotseland between June and September in perfect safety. During these months he had had fever once every couple of weeks. He was extremely alarmed at the thought that if traders came they might die and 'then others might esteem it a tempting of Providence to follow'. Of course he could have made a clean breast of it by telling the Directors the real state of affairs, but that would certainly have prevented any future efforts being made in the area. He could also have told them that the Makololo were more savage than any of the tribes to the south, but this too would have made his earlier pronouncements look like foolish over-optimism. Instead he decided to play down all the difficulties, including the firm foothold the Mambari and the Portuguese had established. So while Livingstone admitted to the Directors that he had not yet found a healthy locality for a mission, he informed them that he would 'not give up the case as hopeless'; instead, he went on: 'I have decided to try and fulfil the second part of my enterprise, viz. to open up a way to the coast.'[13] Realizing that he would have to say a little more about fever, he assured the Directors that none of his party had died of it, and 'if I had been able to regulate my diet, &c, I should not have been subjected to so many attacks'. The frequent wettings he had endured while travelling by canoe he added as another reason for the frequency of his own bouts of fever.[14] He concluded his letter by suggesting that he might well find a healthy spot east of Linyanti at a later stage. In his journal he told the truth: 'We must submit to malaria and trust in God for the rest.'[15]

So when Livingstone returned from Barotseland and the Zambesi to Linyanti in September 1853, he faced an insoluble dilemma. Having failed to find a suitable place for missionaries or traders to settle in, even if he did then manage to open a suitable route from the sea, it would still not justify him in recommending widespread European penetration of the interior. This was a crucial setback, for all his plans had hinged on the establishment of European trade in south-central Africa. Without commerce there could be no curbing of the slave trade and no economic subversion of tribal society. Missionary success, Livingstone was certain, depended on those two preconditions. Otherwise missionaries would risk their lives to achieve less than they had in Bechuanaland. With good reason Livingstone wrote miserably: 'I am at a loss what to do.'[16]

Yet there was one thing he could not do, and that was to give up. He had given all his energies to convincing the Directors, his wife, his parents-in-law and his missionary colleagues that the only real hope of missionary expansion lay in the north. If he backed down he would be accused of loss of faith and held up to universal ridicule. There was nothing else for it but to try to open a path to the coast, regardless of whether anybody would want to follow it once they knew the dangers they would face in Barotseland and the adjacent country. It would have helped Livingstone if he had not known that Porto had travelled from Loanda to Linyanti several years before. His own trip to Loanda would not even be unique. But unique or not, he knew that he would be praised for it and that in itself would do something to take the edge off his sense of failure.

Of course Livingstone could have chosen to go to the east coast first, instead of deciding, as he did, to go west to Loanda. In many ways his choice was surprising. Had he gone east to start with, he could have followed the Zambesi all the way to the coast, and would thus have been able to pioneer a route that offered water transport for traders throughout its length. He gave various reasons for preferring the west. In the first place, he said, it was nearer—in fact the difference in distance was marginal, and in any case, since he would be going up the Zambesi against the current, the time involved would be greater. Another reason he gave was that there were 'Englishmen' in Loanda. As he would soon discover, there was only one Englishman there.[17] It is probable that he was also influenced by the fact that Porto had already successfully made the journey. Livingstone's choice of Loanda itself is rather confusing. It was far further north than the port of Benguela on the same coast and was therefore much further from Linyanti—Loanda was north-west, Benguela west. Livingstone argued that Benguela lay on the main slave route to the coast and that, if he followed that path, he would encounter suspicion and hostility from the tribes on the way. He must, however, have known that Loanda received as many slaves as Benguela.[18] Although he did not say so, he was probably influenced in favour of Loanda because the Zambesi flowed from north-west instead of west. This would place Loanda closer than Benguela to the highest navigable section of the river.

As Livingstone sat in Linyanti planning his journey during September and October 1853, he must have reflected that the signs were not propitious. His attacks of fever had left him thin and weak and he also suffered badly from a common concomitant of malaria: giddiness. 'Everything', he wrote, 'seemed to rush to the left, and if I did not catch hold of some object I fell heavily on the ground.'[19] Meanwhile, as he waited for his health to improve sufficiently for him to depart, he failed to persuade Sekeletu to take lessons in reading. The chief's only concession was to appoint some of his subjects as guinea pigs. If reading had no terrible effect on them he might try it himself later, but if they decided to abandon their wives, as Sechele had done, he was not going to look at a book. Livingstone could only accept this, for he depended on Sekeletu completely for the goods and men he would need on his journey. The chief finally decided to loan Livingstone the free services of twenty-seven men, only two of whom were true Makololo, the rest being drawn from subject tribes like the Barotse, Batoka and Ambonda. Sekeletu was also prepared to lend his own canoe. He gave Livingstone several riding oxen and as much food as could be carried. Livingstone also received some ivory as a gift and took some more to sell in Loanda for Sekeletu. The amount of ivory that could be taken was nonetheless minimal, for twenty-seven men could barely carry all the supplies and trade goods needed to accomplish such a long journey. And in spite of this, Livingstone was still dangerously underprovisioned. His beads, cloth and wire would not be enough to pay for food on the way, let alone sufficient to meet demands for payment for granting passage. There could be no guarantee that, even if food was available and themselves able to pay, the villagers would part with it; then all twenty-seven men and Livingstone himself would have to rely on his shooting skill, which, giddiness and fever apart, had not been improved by the lion's gnashing of his arm. Nor could he allow the Makololo to help him, since they were notoriously bad shots and his ammunition and powder supplies were small.

When it is remembered that later explorers, such as Stanley, rarely travelled with fewer than two hundred porters, carrying enormous quantities of food and trade goods, the size of Livingstone's following is seen in proper perspective. Later Livingstone was to make a virtue of necessity by suggesting that 'the art of successful travel consisted in taking as few "impedimenta" as possible'.[20] The fact remains that had he been able to afford it, he would have taken more trade goods, more ammunition, more food and, to carry these, more men. He would also have provided himself with a watertight tent rather than the small and leaky one he was obliged to take. When he was on the point of departure he noticed that somebody had stolen all the medicines he had prepared. Even the traveller who claimed to believe that travelling light was the best way admitted: 'This loss cripples me sadly.'[21] It is a striking token of Livingstone's bravery or foolhardiness that, with most of his quinine gone, he was still prepared to continue. Loanda was a thousand miles to the north-west, and once the twists and turns of the Zambesi and dozens of other diversions had been taken into account, that distance was likely to increase by a half. In modern terms, the journey ahead of Livingstone would take him a quarter of the way along the Zambesi through south-western Zambia. Then near the borders of modern Angola—nineteenth-century Angola was far smaller—he would have to leave the Zambesi and strike out overland for the remaining three-quarters of the way. This part of the journey was to prove the hardest.

When Livingstone left Linyanti on 11 November 1853, he took little, but still everything he possessed. An inventory included a rifle and double-barrelled smooth-bore gun, a small collection of spare shirts and trousers, his Nautical Almanac, Thomson's Logarithm Tables and his Bible. He had a tiny tent, a sheepskin blanket, a rug and no ' "nick-nacks" advertised as indispensable for travellers'. All this, including ammunition, beads and a little sugar, coffee and tea, fitted into four tin chests. His more precious possessions were carried separately: a sextant made by Troughton and Sims of Fleet Street, a chronometer watch with a stop second hand made by Dent's of the Strand, an artificial horizon, a pair of compasses, a thermometer and a magic lantern. Most of these had been bought with his prize money awarded by the Royal Geographical Society.

On 19 November he and his men embarked on the Zambesi at Sesheke, and from then on, while he was travelling by water, a routine was established. The party would rise at five in the morning and while Livingstone dressed, coffee would be made. After coffee and the loading of the canoes, all would embark. 'The next two hours are the most pleasant part of the day's sail. The men paddle away most vigorously . . . they often engage in loud scolding of each other, in order to relieve the tedium of their work. About eleven we land, and eat any meat which may have remained from the previous meal, or a biscuit with honey, and drink water. After an hour's rest we again embark and cower under an umbrella. The heat is oppressive.'[22]

Two hours before sunset they would stop for the night, have coffee again and, if no animal had been shot, eat a piece of coarse bread made of maize meal. After this sparse supper, a routine worthy of a far larger expedition would begin. First of all, wrote Livingstone:

> . . . some of the men cut a little grass for my bed, while Mashauana [the head man] plants the poles of the little tent. These are used by day for carrying burdens . . . The bed is made and boxes ranged on each side of it, and then the tent pitched over all. Four or five feet in front of my tent is placed the principal or kotla fire . . . Each person knows the station he is to occupy, in reference to the post of honour at the fire in front of the door of the tent. The two Makololo occupy my right and left, both in eating and sleeping, as long as the journey lasts. But Mashauana, my head boatman, makes his bed at the door of the tent as soon as I retire. The rest, divided into small companies, according to their tribes, make sheds all round the fire, leaving a horse-shoe shaped space in front sufficient for the cattle to stand in . . . The sheds are formed by planting two stout forked poles in an inclined direction, and placing another over these in a horizontal position. A number of branches are then stuck in the ground in the direction to which the poles are inclined, the twigs drawn down to the horizontal pole and tied with strips of bark, long grass is then laid over the branches in sufficient quantity to draw off the rain, and we have sheds open to the fire in front and secure from beasts behind. In less than an hour we were usually under cover.[23]

Free at last from the chatter of his now sleeping men, Livingstone would sit up for an hour or more writing in his journal by the light of the fire. Around him was the silence of the forest, only broken by the occasional howl of a hyena and the croaking of frogs. By day, although the Barotse valley was unbearably hot and humid, Livingstone took pleasure in making notes about plants, flowers and birds. Fishes also received attention, but one variety was most unwelcome: 'a striped fellow having a most formidable row of teeth outside his lips sometimes leaps into the canoe'.[24] But the Zambesi itself impressed Livingstone most.

> The river is indeed a magnificent one, often more than a mile broad, and adorned with many islands of from three to five miles in length. Both islands and banks are covered with forest, and most of the trees on the brink of the water send down roots from their branches like the banian . . . The beauty of the scenery of some of the islands is greatly increased by the date palm, with its gracefully curved fronds and refreshing light green colour, near the bottom of the picture, and the lofty palmyra towering far above, and casting its feathery foliage against a cloudless sky.[25]

The river was low and progress through the occasional rapids was difficult. Sometimes the rocks produced steep falls, but generally they merely caused the water to race and boil through narrow gaps. The rocks themselves interested him, some being covered with a small, hard aquatic plant, and others coated with a shining black glaze. During his attacks of fever the rapids were formidable obstacles. 'The people have often to jump out and drag the canoe, and the fall is so much the stern goes under, the water above filling the canoe before they can bring up the after part to the higher level.'[26]

If the canoe was allowed to come broadside to the stream, approaching rapids, there was great danger of capsizing. Navigation would have been easier in the middle of the river where there was deeper water, but Livingstone's men were too wary of hippopotami to risk this. They knew very well that in a river full of crocodiles, it was as well not to end up in the water.

Throughout the second half of December, Livingstone was ill with fever, but he forced himself to go on travelling. The narrow canoe became a nightmare for a man whose heart raced uncomfortably all the time and who was constantly having to be sick. Livingstone was either shivering or sweating, and his vomiting was accompanied by painful diarrhoea. In these circumstances the endless singing and chatting of his attendants nearly drove him mad. 'I was so much pained by the obscene talk of our people I often wished to remove myself beyond hearing.'[27] In a canoe, that was hardly feasible.

By the end of 1853, Livingstone had reached the point where he had turned back after his first examination of the Barotse valley earlier in the year. Here the Kabompo river flowed into the Zambesi from the east. Livingstone mistook the Kabompo for the upper reaches of the Zambesi and assumed as he continued north-west that he had left the main Zambesi and was following a new river, called the Leeba by locals. In a sense this mistake was unimportant, for since Livingstone was still on the Zambesi, which he now called the Leeba, he went on mapping its course. Livingstone was soon delighted by a sudden change of scenery, when the forests gave way to country more like 'a carefully tended gentleman's park' than anything he had previously seen in Africa.

By the end of the first week of January 1854, Livingstone had travelled sixty miles upstream from the junction with the Kabompo. The Zambesi was now much narrower and Livingstone could see that it could not be long before he would have to leave the canoe and go on overland. They were now passing through the territory of a tribe called the Balonda. Many of the Balonda under-chiefs were women, and it was at the village of one such lady that Livingstone spent the night of 6 January. The chief's name was Nyamoana, and this formidable female decided to detain Livingstone longer than he wanted to stay. She also told him not to go any further by canoe, for if a dangerous cataract did not stop him after a few miles, an aggressive tribe called the Balobale certainly would. Livingstone told her he was not worried by aggressive tribes and insisted that he wanted to follow the river as far as he could before travelling by land. Nyamoana listened politely and told him she would not give him permission to go further. What she wanted was to get Livingstone to make a small diversion to the north-east to visit her brother Shinte, the paramount chief of the Balonda. The argument went on and Nyamoana was soon backed up by her twenty-year-old daughter, Manenko, who arrived from her village while discussions were in progress. The two women, having failed to convince Livingstone that he ought to abandon the river, set to work on his followers instead and soon had them thoroughly scared of being butchered by the fierce tribe ahead. Livingstone, however, would not give in and the issue was finally resolved by Manenko resorting to force. When Livingstone gave orders to load the canoes, she instructed her people to stop this operation. Since Livingstone was hopelessly outnumbered he had to submit, to the relief of his men. Manenko was amused by Livingstone's irritation, and, putting a hand on his shoulder, 'put on a motherly look, saying, "Now my little man, just do as the rest have done." '[28]

This was one of the very few occasions when Africans managed to change Livingstone's plans. He never took kindly to being thwarted, and the irony of having to do the bidding of a young woman smeared with fat and red ochre, and covered only by a profusion of ornaments and charms, did not escape him. He described her condition as one of 'frightful nudity' and deplored the thin strip of leather, less than three inches across, that was all that hid her genitals. His Makololo had in the meantime started to have dreams that told them not to go on, but they still proved amenable to a firm scolding. When all was ready for departure, Manenko's period started and another delay had to be endured. At last on 11 January the whole party set off. 'Manenko was accompanied by her husband and her drummer; the latter continued to thump most vigorously, until a heavy drizzling mist set in and compelled him to desist . . . On our Amazon went, in the very lightest marching order, at a pace that few of the men could keep up with.'[29] Although Livingstone did not know it, he could not profitably have gone more than another sixty or seventy miles by river, for then the Zambesi turns north-eastwards towards its source 150 miles in that direction. He had therefore all but reached the river's most westerly point. Nor would the diversion to Shinte's town be a severe inconvenience, for it was more north than east and lay only twelve miles east of the Zambesi. At Shinte's, Livingstone would be roughly eight hundred miles from Loanda, which lay in a west-north-westerly direction.

As Livingstone and Manenko trudged the thirty or so miles to Shinte's the full fury of the rainy season set in, and Livingstone was happy to ride an ox rather than trudge through the mud. Not so Manenko, who strode ahead on foot. The country had now become dense jungle and progress was reduced to a crawl as the men worked with axes to cut through the thickly entwined creepers and undergrowth. Paths seemed to have been obliterated by climbing plants that had wound themselves round 'gigantic trees like boa-constrictors'. The light was dim and the damp gloominess of this shut-in green world did nothing for the morale of Livingstone's men. He himself was suffering from fever again: a condition which constant rain and a diet of manioc roots or tapioca did not help.

On 15 January they arrived outside Shinte's town, and, to Livingstone's annoyance, Manenko waited there till she could exchange messages with her uncle. But neither the pouring rain nor anything that he could say would make her consider altering the normal procedure for entering the town. Only at midday on the 16th were they able to move on.

Livingstone heard that: 'Shinte had been employed during the night in passing from the court of one wife to another till the morning dawned . . . Solomon,' he concluded, 'must have been in a similar predicament with his outrageous female establishment.'[30]

Shinte was the most substantial ruler Livingstone had come across since leaving Sekeletu, and the size of the welcoming ceremony was an

1 Livingstone's reception at Shinte's

indication of this. A thousand men in all were present, including a number of musicians, several Mambari and two Portuguese, whom Livingstone as usual described as 'half-castes'. One of the Portuguese was dressed in a blue frock-coat with epaulettes and had brought, to add to the general noise, 'his drummer and a key bugler making as much music as they could out of very old instruments'. 'The space allotted for Kotla* was at least one hundred yards apart, and two evergreens stood gracefully in the centre. Under these sat Shinte, clothed in a large kilt, the principal colours of which were scarlet and blue edging; he had a checked jacket on and a profusion of iron and copper leglets, his head covered with a helmet of beads and goose feathers.'[31]

Livingstone sat under a tree forty yards from Shinte, while the purposes of his visit were explained by a spokesman of Nyamoana. The connection of trade and the word of God were usually mixed up, and Jesus turned into a kind of medicine for acquiring cloth, rifles and beads. But Livingstone, who could not speak the Balonda's language, could do little about this. His declared desire for peace was treated with scepticism on account of his travelling with two Makololo. Nevertheless, Shinte was glad that he had come, and in the middle of the night of the 18th he had his guest woken

* The meeting place.

up and asked to come to see him. Livingstone, who was in the sweating agonies of an intermittent fever, refused and the meeting took place the following day at ten o'clock in the morning. This formal meeting was less significant than one that took place during the night of the 19th. Shinte wanted to present Livingstone with a small girl, and when he refused, had a second larger one fetched, thinking his visitor had been dissatisfied because of the first one's size. One night Shinte came to Livingstone's tent and looked with astonishment at his hairbrush, thermometer and matches:

> Then, closing the tent, so that none of his own people might see the extravagance of which he was about to be guilty, he drew out from his clothing a string of beads, and the end of a conical shell which is considered, in regions far from the sea, of as great value as the Lord Mayor's badge is in London. He hung it round my neck and said, 'There, now you *have* a proof of my friendship.'[32]

Livingstone was touched by this generosity but was still depressed to note the readiness with which Shinte and his under-chiefs sold men to the Mambari or the Portuguese. He estimated that the slave trade had been actively prosecuted in the region for fifty years. He saw further evidence of this in the extreme subservience of the Balonda to those in authority: a habit cultivated, he supposed, so that they might avoid being sold. 'The inferiors in meeting their superiors in the street at once go down on their knees and rub dust on the upper part of their arms, clapping their hands till the great ones have passed.'[33]

He was too ill during his stay at Shinte's to do much preaching but he did try his magic lantern on a large audience. The result was not happy. The first picture was of Abraham about to slaughter Isaac.

> The Balonda men remarked that the picture was more like a god than the things of wood or clay they worshipped. I explained that this man was the first of a race to whom God had given the Bible we now hold . . . The ladies listened with silent awe; but when I moved the slide, the up lifted dagger moving towards them, they thought it was to be sheathed in their bodies instead of Isaac's. 'Mother! Mother!' all shouted at once, and off they rushed helter-skelter, tumbling pell-mell over each other, and over the little idol huts and tobacco bushes; we could not get one of them back again.[34]

The task of explaining that the lantern itself was not supernatural proved too difficult. The Balonda had already been told by the Mambari that

English cloth came out of the sea and that the white men did too. Since they only had a dim idea of what the sea might be, these stories made their ideas of white people still more fantastic. Therefore in producing his matches, hairbrush and lantern, Livingstone inevitably appeared as a magician—an impression that his constant mention of the Son of God coming down to earth and dying for everybody did nothing to dispel. The idea too that 'words' could be contained in writing seemed almost more extraordinary than the lantern itself. When Livingstone wrote up his journal crowds often collected around him to watch the strange process.

His own followers were no more receptive to his religious instruction than the Balonda, and the Barotse contingent stuck unflinchingly to their belief of metamorphosis into animals, regardless of anything he could say. They also seemed confused by their present instructions not to molest anybody. 'Going in a peaceful manner is so strange they are disposed to follow the dictation of every one we meet.'

By the end of January he was on the move again, once more in pouring rain. His guns and surgical instruments were soon rusty and everything from his tent to his clothing became damp and mildewed. By 14 February he was seventy miles north-west of Shinte's and had reached the next town, named after its chief, Katema. Here the slave trade's influence was still more marked and he learned with horror that potential slaves were often acquired by chiefs selecting a family or village with few or no connections elsewhere, and after killing the headmen, selling all the women and children. He was also told that when a local chief died, 'a great number of people are slaughtered to accompany him'.[35] His attempts to tell them about Christian charity were useless and largely incomprehensible because of bad interpreters. After one sermon, he discovered to his disgust 'that my "words of God" meant "words of rain"'. Katema himself would only listen to compliments anyway, so a few mistakes of translation in Livingstone's preaching hardly mattered to him.

By late February most of the party were ill and thoroughly fed up with the dark rainforests. They had other difficulties too. Only by accepting guides from each village was Livingstone able to allay the suspicions of the people he was now passing, and these guides often took them to villages they did not want to visit, and deliberately detained them. Livingstone was still six hundred miles from the coast and was alarmed that already the slave trade had completely undermined the usual tribal hospitality. Food was no longer given as a gift but had to be paid for. Since Livingstone's party had little to exchange, they often went hungry. Livingstone seemed unaware of the irony that the Africans' insistence on payment was one of the commercial habits he had hoped would break down the tribal structure. His complaint about their meanness in withholding food was a good example of his ability to adopt a double standard when it suited him. Nevertheless the commercial habits of these tribes were not of the 'legitimate' or Christian kind he had envisaged. The Africans frequentiy asked for *hongo*, or payment, for the right to pass through their territory. The demand was usually for a slave. The slave trade had also undermined usual standards of honesty and fair play. Fines were often extorted by tricks. On one occasion a knife was planted on one of his men and cloth demanded as recompense. Soon all the beads and cloth had gone and Livingstone was reduced to parting with his shirts.

As they travelled west, the forests became slightly less dense but the rains had flooded the valleys they were crossing, forcing them to wade and swim across the worst streams and gullies. In such circumstances Livingstone and the men held on to the tails of their surviving oxen. Once, Livingstone lost his grasp, and his men, who had already reached dry land, leapt in again to save him. He was amused that they were surprised he could swim and also touched by their loyalty. It was the only pleasing incident for many weeks.

The people they were now among were the Chiboque, whose manners, in Livingstone's view, matched their appearance: their teeth were filed into points and many had straws thrust through the cartilage of their noses. The Chiboque were the first people seriously to threaten the lives of Livingstone and his followers. In spite of his weakness and fever Livingstone responded with the same courage he so often showed. Ill-feeling had been provoked on both sides by failure to give presents of a suitable size. The demands being made on Livingstone were far more than he could meet and he was determined, at whatever cost, never to sell any of his own people.

> We heard some of the Chiboque remark, 'They have only five guns;' and about midday, Njambi* collected all his people and surrounded our encampment. Their object was evidently to plunder us of everything. My men seized their javelins, and stood on the defensive, while the young Chiboque had drawn their swords and brandished them with great fury. Some even pointed their guns at me, and nodded to each other, as much as to say, 'This is the way we shall do with him.' I sat on my camp stool, with my double-barrelled gun across my knees and invited the chief to be seated also.

The Chiboque were claiming that one of Livingstone's men had spat at one of them. After this incident had been explained as an accident, the old

---

* A Chiboque chief.

demands for a man or an ox were made. Finally these were changed to demands for guns. Livingstone was told this was what they usually got from the Mambari and they were going to get the same from him. His followers, whose nerve was now starting to crack, begged him to give some shirts and they offered to give some of their own beads. But this attempt to come to a settlement only made the Chiboque demand more and more. 'A shout was raised by the armed party, and a rush made around us with brandishing of arms. One young man made a charge at my head from behind, but I quickly brought round the muzzle of my gun to his mouth, and he retreated.'

In the meantime some of Livingstone's men had crept round behind the chief and his headmen and were now able to threaten them with their spears. In this more advantageous position, Livingstone asked once again why they wanted to shed blood when all he wished was to pass on his way peacefully. All the time he was acutely conscious that if the Chiboque used their guns, he would be their first target. 'But I was careful not to appear flurried, and, having four barrels ready for instant action, looked quietly at the savage scene around.'[36]

Eventually the demands for guns and slaves were dropped, and an ox was asked for instead, with the added promise that if this gift was made, they would provide anything asked for. Livingstone decided to lower the tension by giving in and parting with an ox. The Chiboque broke their part of the bargain by giving very little in return, but at least no lives were lost. Very few later travellers displayed the same restraint in similar circumstances. But although Livingstone was not angry with the Chiboque personally, his depression increased. This would be the treatment that European traders would have to cope with if they came into central Africa from the west coast. He had no doubt at all that the Chiboque's behaviour was entirely due to the slave trade. A single chief, provided he had a few guns, could give asylum to slaves and thus beggar an individual slave trader. The slave traders knew this and therefore yielded to the demands of every chief for cloth, beads and guns. The Mambari could content themselves with the thought that whatever they paid out, they would still make a decent profit in Angola. This new African rapacity was likely to discourage the introduction of missions and trading centres more than any of the old tribal habits he had so much deplored. This was not a pleasant thought to entertain when immediate difficulties were so great. Demands for oxen, slaves or ivory went on, and Livingstone soon feared that the trip might have to be abandoned. One resort was to travel by night, but this was not easy in swampy forests. Livingstone was now emaciated and very weak. On average he fell off his ox three or four times a day and his bottom was covered with sores caused by constant riding. His men had now given up all hope of reaching the sea and started accusing Livingstone of having invented it. In order to quell a mutiny he had to threaten to shoot several of his followers. Immediately after this they were lured to a nearby village and robbed. To crown it all, they were then accused of stealing from a couple of slave traders working in the area. The injustice and wearisome inevitability of the demands for recompense took Livingstone to the brink of despair. 'We came here against our will, the traders were called here without our knowledge or wish, yet all was laid gravely to our charge. After talking nearly the whole day we gave the chief an ox, but he would not take it but another.'[37]

On 2 April they were at last on the edge of the Portuguese settlements and on that day the party slaughtered their last spare ox. Livingstone had now parted with all his clothes, save those he stood up in; his razors, spoons, beads and cloth had gone some weeks before, but at long last the forests were thinning out and they stepped out of the darkness on to a wide plain: the valley of the river Quango. This river had to be crossed, and once more the demands for *hongo* started, backed up by a few inaccurate volleys of rifle fire. But deliverance was at hand in the shape of a young Portuguese sergeant of militia. Angola had been reached. Loanda was four hundred miles to the west.

Ever since its foundation in the early sixteenth century, the prosperity of this Portuguese colony had depended on the continuance of the transatlantic slave trade. Most slaves leaving Angola were ferried straight across to another Portuguese colony: Brazil. In 1815 the Portuguese had yielded to British pressure and agreed to limit their shipments of slaves, from their possessions in Africa, solely to Brazil. The agreement was broken, and when in 1839 the British Government decided to use force to stop all exportation of slaves from Africa, whether to Brazil or anywhere else, Portuguese Angolans realized that the days of their prosperity were numbered. Nevertheless they still managed to smuggle out twenty thousand slaves a year—a quarter of their previous total. In 1850 the British Government authorized the Royal Navy to seize and search suspected vessels within Brazilian territorial waters. This was the death-blow for the Angolan slave traders. By 1854, the year Livingstone arrived in Angola, the number of slaves exported numbered less than a couple of hundred.

The effect on the Angolan economy was disastrous. Britain had been able to abandon the slave trade with negligible financial consequences, largely due to her rapidly expanding industries, but the Angolans had not even developed their agriculture let alone started on ambitious projects like cotton-spinning. Most of the Portuguese Angolans lived on the coast in Ambriz, Loanda or Benguela, where they were vainly striving to start cotton-growing and other activities to replace the slave trade. All trade in the Portuguese African colonies was hampered by the metropolitan country's refusal to allow in foreign capital and by a protectionist policy. Portugal would not promote emigration schemes to bolster the tiny European population in Angola, nor would it invest capital. The result was a general sense of demoralization. Most of the white inhabitants had originally come out with the one intention of making some quick money and then returning home. Their hopes had gone very sour on them. In the interior Portuguese occupation was nominal rather than real. Livingstone reached his first Portuguese settlement fifty miles west of the river Quango, three hundred miles from the coast. This was the military and trading post of Cassange, with a total white population of fifty. Cassange was linked with the coast by a line of a dozen similar fortified trading posts. Life in these remote outposts was harsher than at the coast. Fever, tribal raids, an almost total absence of roads and the indifference of the Angolan Government left these distant settlers without hope or incentives. Their most profitable activities were journeys into the interior to buy ivory and slaves, who would be sold not for export but for domestic use in one of the coastal towns. The central Government had recently decided to curtail this one lucrative pursuit on the grounds that such expeditions into the interior might provoke incidents with distant tribes and thus create a border problem. In fact the traders knew that there was no real border; and since the central Government could not enforce the law even on the coast, it could do nothing at all to remedy the situation four hundred miles inland.

It took Livingstone no time to point out the colony's failings and his scorn increased when he heard that many of the white inhabitants had been transported there as convicts. He deplored the lack of European women but was impressed that the Portuguese who had mixed race children treated them with the same consideration as their white offspring. There was in fact, as Livingstone noted, far less racial prejudice in this former stronghold of the slave trade than there was in the Cape Colony. But this liberality was in his view more than offset by the apparent apathy of most settlers. He wrote confidently that had Britain originally colonized Angola, it would now be producing as much cotton as the southern states of America. Nevertheless, there was one Portuguese virtue he could not deny and that was their hospitality.

It is miraculous that Livingstone was welcomed so warmly at Cassange and at all the other Portuguese settlements where he stayed on the way from the Quango river to Loanda. The British Navy had wrecked the economy of the colony, and here was a Briton, who called himself a missionary but probably was an agent of the British Government, snooping around, taking longitudes and latitudes, and making numerous notes about everything he saw. The Portuguese never did really believe that Livingstone was a missionary but they still fed him, gave him new clothes, took him into their houses and treated him as a friend. Livingstone gratefully acknowledged each individual act of kindness, but did not change his broader views about Angola being a corrupt and unprogressive place.

Livingstone stayed at Cassange from 12 to 21 April. Cassange, he soon discovered, was typical of most inland trading posts which he passed through on his way to Loanda. Of the fifty Europeans there, most were officers in the Angolan militia. Since they were hardly ever paid, these men also worked as traders, employing 'native agents' and middlemen, like the Mambari, to make journeys into the interior to buy slaves and ivory. Sometimes the Portuguese took time off to go into the interior themselves. The soldiery at Cassange mainly consisted of native levies, whose loyalty was questionable and whose discipline was non-existent. The soldiers were there largely to give credibility to Portugal's claim to have established authority over an area extending three hundred miles into the interior. They were also supposed to be guarding against incursions by hostile tribes. None of the officers were married to European wives and therefore all the children were of mixed race. Nevertheless, life at Cassange was not without some compensations; the gardens around the town were full of many different kinds of fruit and the lush grass suited cattle. Ivory trading also brought some of the inhabitants a decent profit. Had they not been so prone to regular bouts of malaria, the residents of Cassange would not have found too many reasons to bemoan their lot, unprogressive and corrupt though they were.

Strengthened by cheese, milk and meat, Livingstone made good progress from Cassange and by the end of the first week of May had travelled another two hundred miles to Ambaca, the next Portuguese settlement of any size. His host there was a man called Arsenio de Carpo, whom Livingstone found exceptionally kind and pleasant. Later he changed his mind when he heard that Carpo had killed his father some years before and had also been convicted of fraud. Shortly after leaving Ambaca on the final 150 miles of his journey, Livingstone's health cracked up and he was prostrated by almost continuous attacks of fever. His followers were also becoming more and more apprehensive. Perhaps, after all, Livingstone would turn out to be a particularly plausible slaver who would sell them all as soon as they reached the coast. But Livingstone managed to reassure them. Twenty miles outside Loanda, Livingstone's condition worsened and he began to wonder whether he was going to live. His fever was so bad that he could not summon enough strength to stay on his ox for more than ten minutes at a time. He was also suffering from chronic dysentery. When Livingstone was carried into Loanda on 1 May 1854, he seemed very close to death.

He had heard at the Cape that there were a number of Englishmen in Loanda but his men soon found that there was only one: a Mr Edmund Gabriel, whose impressive official title was Her Majesty's Commissioner for the Suppression of the Slave Trade in Loanda. From Livingstone's later letters, nobody would have guessed how ill he had been on his arrival. Certainly none of his correspondents would have thought he had been all but given up for dead by Gabriel. Livingstone was a prolific letter-writer and was extremely regular in making entries in his journal. He would keep up his journal till a few days before his death in 1873. But from 24 May to 14 June he was evidently too weak to write anything. As long after his arrival in Loanda as 4 July, he was unable to write a full-length letter and had to dictate one to Edmund Gabriel so that the Directors would know that he was alive. Only in early August, two months after his arrival in the town, was he able to write a letter unaided.

As usual Livingstone's motives for playing down his sickness had little to do with a desire to save his friends and family unnecessary worry. It was his old device for making conditions appear less malignant than they really were. Soon he was telling the Directors that had his party travelled in the dry, as opposed to the rainy, season he would not have suffered nearly so much. Then if he had been able to take more food and changes of clothing,

2   Loanda, from a sketch by Captain Henry Need

things might have been different. Even so, he could hardly deny that his journey had been hard. The problems, even when understated, seemed formidable: dense rain-forests, swamps, hostile tribes, slave traders and fever were difficulties which even in watered-down language were not likely to encourage traders to believe that an ideal route into the interior had been found. Livingstone told the Directors that he intended to retrace his steps to Linyanti and then attempt to reach the east coast. The reason for this new journey, he assured them, was not that the route he had 'opened' was impossible but that a way to 'the Eastern coast may be less difficult'. 'If I succeed,' he went on, 'we shall at least have a choice.'[38] A little later Livingstone was telling a friend: 'The path we have already opened has many advantages.' When listed they were not impressive. The principal one was that the Portuguese coastal towns were in regular communication with Cassange and that this gave traders a good start. He did not go on to emphasize that Cassange was still almost a thousand miles from Linyanti. Later on in the same letter, Livingstone's enthusiasm was even greater. 'The only fault of the new path is it admits of conveyance by human labour alone. The forests and boggy rivers present insurmountable obstacles to waggons.'[39] Having stressed over and over again that he had not set out as a mere traveller, in order to justify himself Livingstone had to pretend that his trip had had some practical result. He might try and fool others, but he could not fool himself; his journey, he knew very well, had established beyond doubt that commercial operations in the interior could never be begun on any scale from the west coast. Unless he was to content himself with the glory of being the first British explorer to have reached the west coast from Barotseland, he was going to have to return to Linyanti and find a better route to the east coast along the Zambesi. Providence, he had told everybody, had favoured missionary and commercial operations in Makololo country. An east coast route was the only chance he had left to prevent others suggesting that he had been deluded and that his interest had always been primarily in exploring. His position would have been happier if Porto, and another Portuguese trader Caetano Ferra, had not previously made the journey from the coast to Barotseland. There is no denying that Livingstone's success in reaching Loanda, under-provisioned, ill-equipped and completely dependent on the voluntary labour of twenty-seven Africans, had been a magnificent achievement. But since it had disproved almost everything Livingstone had wished to demonstrate, it was not simply self-effacing modesty that made him feel he would have to do better. His decision to try to reach the other side of the continent is nonetheless remarkable for that. The journey from Linyanti to Loanda had nearly killed him; now he was going to attempt not only to repeat that journey but also to go on for another thousand miles east of Linyanti.

While he was at Loanda, Livingstone refused a passage home to England in a British warship. Later this was seen as a mark of his true heroism, and more than that it proved, according to most of his biographers, that rather than abandon his faithful Makololo porters he was prepared to undergo the horrors of the 'Dark Continent' once more. The fate of the Makololo who had come with him was in fact a very low priority. He would take them back to Linyanti because he needed them. When he arrived at the Indian Ocean in 1856, he was happy enough to sail for England, leaving his 'faithful' Makololo at Tete for four years. He had promised to return for them within a single year.

Livingstone's four months in Loanda were marred by repeated attacks of fever. He was lucky that three British warships of the blockading squadron were in harbour, for without the attentions of the doctor on H.M.S. *Polyphemus* he might have died. Mr Cockin, however, prescribed and made up pills of opium, opium suppositories, calomel and quinine. The treatment was successful, for by August Livingstone was able to take the Makololo aboard another British warship, the *Pluto*. Since the Makololo had never seen any ship larger than a canoe, they were amazed. The ship's cannons were fired in their honour, and when they had understood the destructive potential of such weapons they begged Livingstone to let them take one back to Linyanti to fire at the Matabele. Livingstone had never before managed to get across the idea of European technological superiority. These warships did more to support what he had said than months of explanation. From then on, wrote Livingstone, 'I rose rapidly in their estimation . . . and always afterwards they treated me with the greatest deference'.[40] The *Pluto*'s captain was a Commander Norman Bedingfeld, whom Livingstone took a liking to. Three years later he was to regret he had ever met the man.

Even when Livingstone was well, there were problems that weighed on his mind and gave him no peace. Once he got back to Linyanti, there was no knowing whether Sekeletu would allow him to take men with him for his proposed journey to the east coast. The thought of travelling 1,300 miles over Africa only to be told that further progress was impossible was a terrifying prospect. Livingstone would have felt more secure had he made a profit with Sekeletu's ivory but he had had to sell most of it on the way to buy food and to pay *hongo*. There was another disturbing possibility: even if Sekeletu ordered men to accompany him, they might desert after being told about the hardships their companions had endured on the way to the west coast. It is possible that thoughts like these made Livingstone wonder whether he had made the right decision in refusing a passage home in one of the warships. The majority of Englishmen would, in all likelihood, never have heard of Silva Porto and Caetano Ferra, nor would they probably understand that, in Livingstone's terms, his journey had been a failure. The Directors of the London Missionary Society would have been sure to announce his return as a triumphant occasion. He would have lectured all over the country and raised thousands of pounds for the Society. If the Royal Geographical Society had awarded him half the annual Royal Premium for reaching Lake Ngami, they too could have been expected to do even more this time. Since Livingstone liked praise and must have known that he would have received plenty had he returned, his sense of personal failure and disappointment must have been very great to have stopped him. In fact, he had become completely obsessed with the idea of opening a *highway* into the interior. Without that highway there would be no commerce, without commerce there would be no social change and without that there would be no diffusion of Christianity. If the highway was found, Livingstone was convinced that not only African history but the future of Christianity itself would benefit from his discovery. If he could hold out that prospect on his return to England, that would be something immeasurably greater than anything he had so far achieved. He might die in the attempt, but though it was a gamble, the stakes were unusually high and Livingstone felt that he had an advantage which few gamblers possessed: his life was 'charmed' till his work was done. God must want Christianity to come to central Africa, so Livingstone would live. Such was his conviction. It did not, however, stop him relishing the drama of his situation. 'I will open a way to the interior or perish,' he told his brother.

Before he left for the interior again, the Board of Works in Loanda donated a colonel's dress uniform and a horse for Sekeletu and clothing for all Livingstone's men. In addition they were all bought muskets, which meant that, in one respect at least, the expedition was better supplied now than when it had started. Official generosity did not, however, impress Livingstone. He reckoned that if he had not unexpectedly approached Angola from the east, but had instead come by sea, matters would have been very different. Livingstone felt that because the Portuguese would know that Gabriel had informed the British Government of his arrival in Angola, 'they could not for shame refuse me a passage back. But it is ten to one if they would allow me to land a box of bibles at Loanda.'[41]

Livingstone left Loanda on 20 September 1854 and within a month was a hundred miles inland. He had had the offer of European company but had as usual turned it down. His proposed companion had been an Austrian botanist, Dr Walweitch, currently working for the Angolan Government. But, wrote Livingstone, 'as it appeared evident to me this plan would afford Dr Walweitch an opportunity of availing himself of all my previous labours . . . without acknowledging his obligations to me in Europe, I considered it would not be prudent to put such a strong temptation in his way'.[42] If Livingstone finally found his precious *highway*, nobody else was going to be in on the act.

Livingstone made very poor progress during the first months of his trip back to Linyanti. Numerous officers at the various militia posts detained him to give them treatment for fever, and then in mid-December, still only two hundred miles from the coast, he heard that the ship carrying the letters he had written in Loanda had been wrecked. This detained him for a further two weeks while he rewrote everything, and he was not on his way again till New Year's Day 1855. While he was doing this rewriting, letters from Gabriel reached Pungo Adongo, where he was staying. Enclosed was a copy of a letter from Lord Clarendon, in which the Foreign Secretary, expressed pleasure at Livingstone's safe arrival, and a cutting from *The Times*, dated 8 August 1854, describing Livingstone's journey as 'one of the greatest geographical explorations of the age'. Livingstone transcribed the cutting into his journal but made no comment.

By 2 February he had reached Cassange. A distance of just over three hundred miles had taken him four months. He had completed the entire journey from Linyanti to Loanda in six. It was probably this prolonged stay in the decaying Portuguese settlements that temporarily made Livingstone revert to his old liberal attitudes towards the Africans. If Angola was an example of what white settlers had achieved in the course of three hundred years, could elaborate claims really be made for European civilization? It was an embarrassing question, made more acute by Livingstone's conviction that the nearer the Portuguese borders he had travelled on his journey out, the worse the Africans had become morally and the more extortionate in their demands. This was hardly an example of Africans being 'elevated' by a 'superior race'.

It is a peculiar paradox that, at the beginning of a journey intended as the first stage in the break-up of tribal society, Livingstone should once again have been writing about Africans with sympathy and understanding.

> With a general opinion they are wiser than their white neighbours. I think this good opinion of ourselves is very general in the world. Each tribe has a considerable consciousness of goodness, or following its own interests in the best ways. Austria would find its own counterpart in every dirty little village in Africa. In Africa, however, they have less of what the Germans call philosophy to uphold their views; less diplomacy, protocols, & notes. They go direct to the point, and in so doing shew a more philosophic spirit than the Germans. They have few theories but many

ideas . . . There is no search after the supreme good, such as we are to believe the ancient philosophers engaged in, but which were perhaps rather a search for what words more could flow from the pen to produce the impression among his contemporaries, who might read his endless rhapsodies as unfathomable and pronounce their author to be a profound remarkable man . . . But the African cares not at all for these utterly inane speculations. The pleasures of animal life are ever present to his mind as the supreme good, and but for his innumerable phantoms he would enjoy his luscious climate as well as it is possible for man to do.[43]

Yet he was to go even further than this, in what appeared to be a flat contradiction of much of what he had written between 1851 and 1853. Then he had compared the state of the inmates of workhouses and the lot of African chiefs and had confidently stated that in every respect the British poor were better off. Now he made a very different comparison in which the Africans came off best. 'To one who has observed the hard toil of the poor in old civilized countries, the state in which the inhabitants [of Africa] live is one of glorious ease . . . Food abounds and very little effort is needed for its cultivation; the soil is so rich that no manure is required.'[44]

In other ways, too, he decided that Africans could learn nothing from Europeans: 'Africans are not by any means unreasonable. I think unreasonableness is more a hereditary disease in Europe than in this land.'[45] It was almost as though Livingstone could divide all his thoughts into different and unconnected compartments. Sometimes he would emphasize only Europe's technological prowess, sometimes he would see only the social problems. Africans were either miserable savages capable of selling their own women and children to heartless slavers, or they were unspoiled and innocent people living in a worldly paradise. His judgement, inevitably, was often influenced by the conditions of travel and the state of his health. At the beginning of his journey back to Linyanti his health was good, and in the dry season the going was firm. The quality of the light, the gentle warmth of the air and the sense of freedom that travelling gave combined to lead Livingstone into writing passages of lyrical description that owed more to his aesthetic feelings than to moral or economic judgements.

How often have I beheld, in still mornings, scenes the very essence of beauty, and all bathed in a quiet air of delicious warmth! Yet the occasional slight motion imparted a pleasing sensation of coolness as of a fan. Green grassy meadows, the cattle feeding, the goats browsing, the kids skipping, the groups of herdboys with miniature bows, arrows and spears; the women wending their way to the river with watering pots poised jauntily on their heads; men sewing under the shady banians; and old grey-headed fathers sitting on the ground, with staff in hand, listening to the morning gossip.[46]

Yet within weeks it is hard to believe that Livingstone had ever written such words. As the plains gave way to the forests, and his health again began to deteriorate, the old condemnatory tone once more took over. After being attacked again by the Chiboque, and having discovered that most of the forest tribes were idolaters, Livingstone used the scenic beauty of Africa, not to show the happiness of the African's life but as a contrast to point out his spiritual degradation. 'How painful is the contrast between the inward gloom and the brightness of the outer world, between the undefined terrors of the spirit and the peace and beauty that pervades the scene around.'[47]

A little later Livingstone was transcribing into his journal, under the heading 'Prospects of the Negro', his belief in progress and the coming of the 'Golden Age' through the works of inventors, reformers and missionaries. Everything, he repeated, was hopeless for Africa unless there was 'contact with superior races by commerce'.[48] The Africans, he went on, are 'inured to bloodshed and murder, and care for no god except being bewitched'. They were cowardly and through their constant use of cannabis could not form 'any clear thought on any subject'.

By mid-March, Livingstone's fever had become more serious and the rate of travel had sunk to below seven miles a day. The countryside was so badly flooded that at times they had to dig trenches around the spot where they proposed to sleep so that some of the water would drain off. Three months later, Livingstone was in the Balonda country. He had partially lost the sight of one eye through walking into a jutting out branch and his hearing was failing due to repeated doses of quinine. To add to his misery, he was vomiting blood. At this time Livingstone had to put down another mutiny among his followers. He did so by hitting the leading trouble-maker on the head with his revolver. Given his weakness it was quite a feat. Livingstone did not see it in a positive light. The infliction of any corporal punishment, whether premeditated or not, always disgusted him. These were awkward views to hold when passing the Balonda, who, Livingstone felt, would strip harmless travellers of everything they possessed unless they showed a willingness to fight.

By late July, Livingstone had reached the northern end of the Barotse valley. Linyanti lay three hundred miles to the south-east. Many of his men came from Barotseland, and as they came closer to their homes, many heard that their wives had remarried in their absence. To Livingstone's dismay few seemed depressed, even when some former wives arrived with tiny infants fathered by other men. Their reaction was that there were lots of women about and that they would soon have more wives than they had had before they set out. Clearly Livingstone had not managed to persuade them that monogamy was the ideal form of marriage. In fact none of his religious teaching had had any effect on his men, even though he had been with them almost two years. They had admired the large houses in Loanda and had been impressed by the British warships but, contrary to Livingstone's theories, this had not made them any more interested in Christianity. James Chapman, the trader who visited the Makololo in 1853 and then again in 1862, said that one of the tribe's favourite pastimes was imitating Livingstone singing psalms. This would always be accompanied by howls of derisive laughter. The Makololo's word for psalm-singing, *bokolella*, meant to bellow like a bull.[49] During the whole of Livingstone's association with the Makololo he made no converts.

The party reached Linyanti on 13 September 1855, having been away for two months short of two years. The men who had come with Livingstone were soon boasting shamelessly about their experiences, talking about the large ships which had eaten 'black stones'—there was no coal in Barotseland—and showing off their new clothes. Dressed in red caps and red and white jackets, 'they tried to walk like the soldiers they had seen in Loanda ... and excited the unbounded admiration of the women and children'.[50] Sekeletu was also pleased with his colonel's uniform, and from then on wore it continuously until it fell to bits. Livingstone was immensely relieved that Sekeletu did not seem annoyed or surprised that he had not brought back more cloth and guns. In fact, the chief was delighted that his white man had returned at all. When Livingstone explained to him that he intended to go down to the east coast, Sekeletu seemed as eager as ever to help him. This time, he said, he would lend Livingstone over a hundred men and would send much more ivory to be sold at the coast. In exchange, Livingstone undertook to bring back a long list of goods that included guns, bullets, revolvers, shirts, blankets, soldiers' uniforms, cutlery, an iron rocking-chair and a pair of spectacles with green glass lenses.[51] The agreement was that Livingstone should bring back the men and the goods within two years. After that Sekeletu believed that Livingstone and his wife, the all-important daughter of Moffat, would come to live on the Zambesi. This would enable the Makololo to move away from the swamps without fear of the Matabele. It was this thought above all that persuaded Sekeletu that Livingstone was worth helping. Sadly for Sekeletu, time would show that Livingstone had used him and not the other way round. It would be five years before the two men met again and by that time Livingstone's interests would have shifted yet again. The Makololo would no longer be God's chosen tribe. Livingstone gained fame and recognition for the journeys he made between 1853 and 1856. Without the help of the Makololo he could not have made them. Sekeletu and his tribe gained nothing; in fact in the end they lost by their association with Livingstone. Already cut off behind the Chobe river in an unhealthy place, and with little security, their reliance on Livingstone led them to reject the few traders who fought their way to the Zambesi from the south. When no trade came up the Zambesi from the coast, as Livingstone had promised it would, they were more isolated than before. Unable to leave their swamps for fear of the Matabele, the true Makololo were dying out through fever, bringing the day closer when their numbers would prove insufficient to keep down their vassals. Livingstone was their last chance for getting out of an impossible situation. They did everything they could for him and in the end he let them down. When Livingstone left Linyanti for the east coast in November 1855, the Makololo were eight years from extinction. Sekeletu died in 1863 and the Makololo's Barotse vassals seized the opportunity of a disputed succession to overthrow their overlords and butcher them all. It would be too much to suggest that Livingstone was responsible. But Sekeletu was probably right in thinking that Livingstone could have helped them to return to a healthier area without danger and could thus have saved them and their tribe.

Back at Linyanti, as well as planning the next stage in his journey, Livingstone wrote letters home. He was still worried in case his illness at Loanda had given the Directors the idea that missionaries ought not to work in central Africa. During three years Livingstone had had twenty-seven attacks of fever, but he still told the Directors jauntily: 'I apprehend no great mortality among missionaries, men of education and prudence who can, if they will, adopt proper hygienic precautions.'[52] Within a few years such dangerous false optimism would lead to tragedy.

On 3 November Livingstone and his 114 porters set out for the Zambesi. His plan was to follow the river right down to its mouth on the east coast, just south of the Portuguese town of Quilimane. This intended journey was roughly a thousand miles, three or four hundred less than his journey to Loanda. In modern terms, for half the way he would be travelling along the Zambesi where it divides Zambia and Zimbabwe; for the rest, he would be following the river through Portuguese Mozambique to the sea. Theoretically Livingstone could have followed another route to the coast: that used by the Arabs he had met in 1853. This would have meant following a more northerly route taking him to the east coast via Lake Nyassa. His navigable highway fixation inevitably ruled out this second option.

In late November, five years after he had first heard about the great falls east of Sesheke, Livingstone reached the falls of Mosioatunya or 'the smoke that thunders'. Livingstone was impressed, but a waterfall, even the most spectacular in the world, did not thrill him to the extent that the Zambesi itself had done in 1851. It was very fine to look at, but beyond that it had no useful function. Livingstone's description, on reaching what is still considered one of the great scenic wonders of the world, is so miraculously precise and flat that it is worth quoting. The lack of adjectives is an outstanding feature.

The falls are singularly formed. They are simply the whole mass of the Zambesi waters rushing into a fissure or rent made right across the bed of the river. In other falls we have usually a great change of level both in the bed of the river and adjacent country, and after the leap the river is not much different from what it was above the falls; but here the river, flowing rapidly among numerous islands and from 800 to 1,000 yards wide, meets a rent in its bed at least 100 feet deep and at right angles with its course, or nearly due east and west, leaps into it, and becomes a boiling white mass at the bottom ten or twelve yards broad.[53]

An indication of how little Livingstone cared about his 'discovery' was his complete underestimation of both the height and the width of the falls. The actual width is 1,900 yards, double his figure, and the height varies from two to three hundred feet, again double his estimate. Livingstone only wrote his famous set pieces about the falls on his return to England, when his publisher John Murray suggested it would be a good idea. And so various famous phrases were written such as: 'scenes so lovely must have been gazed upon by angels in their flight'. He would not sketch the falls in watercolour until he returned briefly in 1860 (see plate 12). Nevertheless, Livingstone could see that although the falls would not help him in any practical way, they might still serve a purpose. He would call them the Victoria Falls, which might help interest the British public in the area where they were situated. For some time he had been thinking of calling some geographical feature after Her Majesty and this one was eminently suitable.

Immediately east of the falls the Zambesi loops to the south before flowing on east and then north-east. This arc was roughly 250 miles in length. Livingstone decided to travel on north of the river, cutting out the loop altogether. His decision owed nothing to a desire to reach the coast speedily. He had heard that the area north of the Zambesi and just east of the falls was high, fertile and healthy. It might be the place he had so long hoped to find for missionary and trading settlements. As Livingstone pressed on eastwards across the Batoka Plateau, he became more and more convinced that he had made a crucial discovery. The plateau was relatively high and, although it was well watered by streams, it was not swampy. Because of the height, the temperature was cooler than in the river valley. The area seemed suitable for cattle and supported sizeable trees. In a state of euphoria Livingstone tramped on, making detailed notes of all the favourable characteristics he could find. Of course he knew that the Matabele lived due south, across the Zambesi, but he was not going to let this worry him yet. Nor was his faith in the area shaken by the Batoka themselves, whom he considered even 'more degraded than the Barotse', and the Barotse had never impressed him much. The Batoka, he fumed, are lacking in 'all self-respect, savage and cruel under success, but easily cowed and devoid of all moral courage'.[54] Almost everything they did he found repellent, but he singled out their mode of greeting strangers for special disparagement.

> They throw themselves on their backs on the ground, and rolling from side to side, slap the outside of their thighs as expression of thankfulness and welcome, uttering the words, 'Kina bomba.' This method of salutation was to me very disagreeable, and I never could get reconciled to it. I called out 'Stop, stop! I don't want that;' but they, imagining I was dissatisfied, only tumbled about more furiously, and slapped their thighs with greater vigour. The men being totally unclothed, this performance imparted to my mind a painful sense of their extreme degradation.[55]

Yet no habit or custom was sufficiently distasteful to discourage Livingstone from believing that he had found an area where Europeans could live in central Africa. Not even an attack by a frenzied African with an axe shook his faith. The Batoka Plateau was the place: the centre from which trade and Christianity would together send out cleansing waves in wider and wider circles till the whole area had been purged of the slave trade and tribal barbarism. There was, however, one more drawback. The Batoka Plateau at its most easterly point was eight hundred miles from the mouth of the Zambesi. For traders to come, the Zambesi would have to be navigable for almost a thousand miles. It was therefore to the Zambesi that Livingstone now gave his undivided attention.

At the beginning of the year 1856 he had crossed the Batoka Plateau and rejoined the Zambesi on the eastern side of the loop, at a point a hundred miles from the Mozambique border, where the river begins to flow due east. Just as when he had been approaching Angola, African hostility had suddenly increased, now, as Livingstone came closer to the deserted Portuguese settlement of Zumbo, the same pattern began to repeat itself. Just outside Zumbo the river Loango flows into the Zambesi from the north. Livingstone realized at once that without the help of local tribes and the loan of canoes he would be unable to cross. It was a most unfortunate moment to be so dependent. Recently the people had been behaving very suspiciously, 'collecting from all sides and keeping at a distance from us though professing friendship'.[56] Livingstone knew that when his men forded the river they would be split up and therefore at the mercy of the locals. He was also alarmed when these people refused to tell him why the Portuguese had left Zumbo. After prolonged discussions with the chief, Livingstone was offered two canoes for the crossing. This would mean making numerous trips to transport his 114 men. It now seemed certain that an attack would be made when they began crossing. It was now evening and so no move could be made till the following day. In such circumstances Livingstone derived inner strength from comparisons which many of his former missionary colleagues would have thought blasphemous: 'See, O Lord,' he wrote, 'how the heathen rise up against me as they did to Thy Son.'[57] For a time he toyed with the idea of evading his enemies by crossing during the night, but at last he rejected this plan. Was that the way any Instrument of God's Providence should behave? 'I will not cross furtively by night as intended. It would appear as flight, and should such a man as I flee? Nay, verily. I shall take observations for lat. & long, tonight, though they may be the last. I feel quite calm now, thank God.'[58]

This mixture of bravery, pride, faith and truculent obstinacy was typical of the man. But Livingstone's decision owed a lot to another cause; by risking his life he was showing his absolute faith in Providence. If God wanted him to live, then God's will would be done. 'But if I am cut off . . . my efforts are no longer needed by Him who knows what is best.'[59] A belief that God controlled every event might seem to provide an insurance strong enough to exclude all fear. In a sense this may explain some of Livingstone's outstandingly brave actions; but it should also be kept in mind that when setbacks occurred, the man who believed he had a providential role to play, was faced with something far worse than physical fear: a sense that God might not after all have intended him to follow the course he was pursuing and that He had rejected him.

The following morning the signs were as ominous as before. The women had been sent away and large numbers of armed men appeared. Although two canoes had been promised, only one was provided and this seemed more alarming because two further canoes were tied to the bank near by. Getting all the goods, cattle and men across in a single canoe was a lengthy and nerve-wracking experience. Livingstone decided that he should be the last to cross. Surrounded as he was by tribesmen with their spears at the ready, he showed no fear and started to talk to them, showing his watch, lens and compass 'to keep them amused until there remained only those who were to enter the canoe with me'. Afterwards he bore them no malice for having behaved so threateningly, suggesting that they had probably been afraid he might play them some trick.

It was late January when Livingstone passed Zumbo. He was now about five hundred miles from the mouth of the Zambesi. The reason why the Portuguese had left this area was obvious: the local Africans had forced them out. Twenty miles beyond Zumbo at a place called Pangura, Livingstone made a decision which would later bring him more grief than any he had yet made. He heard from a local chief called Mpende that the Zambesi flowed on due east for seventy miles and then turned sharply south-east. That being the case, if Livingstone headed south-east at once he would be able to cut off a corner and reach the Portuguese settlement of Tete much more quickly. Mpende's direct route to Tete was fifty miles shorter than the bending course of the Zambesi. Livingstone would not have been influenced by distance alone; for somebody who had travelled thousands of miles, 200 as opposed to 250 miles was not a significant difference. Mpende also told him that if he tried to follow the Zambesi he would have to cope with a hilly and rocky path. Livingstone, who was not feeling strong, considered this last piece of information and decided to cross the Zambesi and do as Mpende suggested. On the southern bank Livingstone expressed himself 'most sincerely thankful' that matters had turned out as they had. The irony of these words would only become apparent two years later.

By leaving the Zambesi at this point, Livingstone failed to discover the Kebrabasa Rapids, which were finally to wreck his hopes of the Zambesi becoming a navigable highway. Had he seen these cataracts in 1856, he would have been saved the ignominy of building up false hopes, only later to have to admit to the public and the British Government that he had been deceived.

When he arrived at Tete, Livingstone made enquiries about the section of the Zambesi he had not seen. 'I was informed of the existence of a small rapid in the river near Chicova; had I known of this previously, I certainly would not have left the river without examining it. It is called Kebrabasa and is described as a number of rocks which jut out across the stream.'[60] It is most puzzling that Livingstone managed to leave Tete with the impression that Kebrabasa posed so slight a threat to future navigation of the river. A number of Portuguese living in the town had seen the devastating series of cataracts that extended along the river for thirty miles. Perhaps Livingstone never spoke to these men, or if he did, he heard what he wanted to hear rather than what he was told. He was determined that the Zambesi was going to provide a navigable highway to the Batoka Plateau and nobody was going to persuade him otherwise.

His own scientific calculations about the Zambesi certainly show a marked propensity for wishful thinking. He must have felt slightly uneasy at Tete, for he wrote down a list of figures in his journal designed to prove by the speed of the river's flow that there were no steep drops between the Victoria Falls and Tete. Unfortunately all his deductions were based on the false assumption that the speed of the river was the same for nearly a thousand miles. He also ignored the vast differences in heights that he had previously noted: 3,702 feet at Linyanti and 1,537 feet a hundred miles west of Zumbo. Livingstone had also made a crucial omission. Normally at significant points he estimated the height of a place by measuring the boiling point of water with a special thermometer. When he left the Zambesi at Pangura he had not done this. If he had, he would have discovered on his arrival at Tete that he was six hundred feet lower than he had been at Pangura. The only conclusion he could have drawn from such a figure would have been that the rapid at Chicova could not be small.[61] But oblivious of this, he wrote to the Directors with his usual confidence, telling them that 'the only impediment' to navigation of the Zambesi was 'one or two rapids, not cataracts'.[62]

After the abandonment of Zumbo, Tete had become the most westerly Portuguese settlement in Mozambique. Out of a total population of 4,000, only 350 of the inhabitants of Tete were not slaves. Of these 350, only thirty were true Portuguese. The town had been established in the early sixteenth century, mainly on the false assumption that large quantities of gold and silver could easily be extracted from the neighbouring countryside. When this hope proved an illusion, the residents had been left totally dependent on the slave trade and various subsidiary pursuits like the sale of gold dust, ivory and coffee. Angola had always been far better placed for participation in the slave trade. Closer to Brazil and Portugal than Mozambique, the Angolans had soon cornered most of the lucrative trade in men. Economic decline in Mozambique had therefore been more gradual, but because there had never been the wealth that Angola had once enjoyed, Livingstone was far more disturbed to see the decay and stagnation. The Angolan Portuguese had had comparatively little trouble with African tribes, but the Portuguese in Mozambique were often forced to buy off tribes whom they could not militarily defeat. Then there was another separate problem; over the years the Portuguese Government had made grants of land to individual families living in Mozambique. In order to defend their interests these landowners had raised private armies. Within a hundred years the original Portuguese families had intermarried with Africans, and their descendants had become mixed race, often adopting African names. When the Portuguese authorities had attempted to curb the power of their former subjects they were beaten back and defeated by them. One of these landowners, Antonio Vincente da Cruz, more commonly known by his African name Bonga, had sacked Tete three years before Livingstone's arrival; and, until 1870, when the authorities were forced to come to terms with him, he was to remain a constant thorn in their sides.

Livingstone's remarks about the Portuguese in Angola had been scathing; in Mozambique, they were to be openly hostile. The reason for his former relative tolerance had been his knowledge that penetration of the interior from Angola was impossible. On his arrival at Tete he was convinced that the Zambesi would be navigable, and thus he came to believe that British traders and missionaries would only be prevented from sailing up the river if the Portuguese Government raised objections. Since the Portuguese were notorious protectionists, Livingstone's serious doubts as to whether they would ever allow the Zambesi to become an international waterway were understandable. It was also unlikely that a Catholic nation would willingly bend over backwards to be helpful to Protestant missionaries. Livingstone must have realized at the outset that Portuguese recalcitrance might defeat all his plans, but, as with almost every other problem, he would refuse to face it until forced to do so.

The condition of the inhabitants at Tete also posed an awkward question which some thoughtless people might decide to put to Livingstone on his return to England. How was it, if the Zambesi was such an ideal commercial waterway, and if the potential of central Africa was really so attractive, that the Portuguese had not made anything of it in their three hundred years of residence? The only answer that Livingstone would be able to give was that the Portuguese had failed because they were a decadent, lazy, spineless lot, who were rotting with venereal disease and drink. One Briton was worth dozens of them. Rather surprisingly, he would get away with this argument when he returned home.

Livingstone gave no credence to the possibility that the Portuguese might have been defeated by factors like the climate, malaria and the nature of the terrain. Nor did he ask whether the Zambesi itself was everything that it appeared to be. The Portuguese could have told him that the sand bars at the mouth were a death-trap and that shifting sand and mudbanks in the river made navigation a hazardous business for much of the year. But instead Livingstone concentrated on Portuguese shortcomings to explain every failure. The reasons why they had not progressed were simple: there were not enough white women, the authorities were corrupt and the population had neglected natural assets such as coal, iron and gold. This neglect, he went on, had nothing to do with their physical circumstances, but was due to their criminal addiction to slavery. Of course in many respects Livingstone was right. The colony needed more colonists with their wives and families. But the Portuguese at Tete knew that these settlers would not come until conditions improved. They also knew that conditions would not improve till new settlers came. Their situation was impossible. Knowing, as they did, that colonists would not come to Africa, they viewed as insanity suggestions that they should abandon their only source of labour: their slaves.

Livingstone had arrived in Tete during the first week of March 1856. He stayed till the end of April and during that time was entertained as hospitably as he had been anywhere in Angola. The commandant of the garrison, Major Sicard, was particularly kind. Livingstone did not willingly spend nearly two months as Sicard's guest but was ill on his arrival at Tete and then had a further relapse during his stay.

From Tete, Livingstone intended to go on down the Zambesi by canoe; this would clearly be impossible with all his Makololo attendants. Considering that he had characterized Tete as a moral sink, it may seem surprising that Livingstone decided to leave his followers there. There was, however, very little else he could have done. The expense of bringing over a hundred Africans to London would obviously have been prohibitive, so the Makololo had to remain in Mozambique. Sicard had promised to allocate them land and see they did not starve, so Tete was probably as good a place as any. Having promised the Makololo that he would return to take them home within a year, Livingstone set off downstream in a canoe with eight of his original followers. The remaining 270 miles to the sea were easier than any previous part of his journey. But for much of the way Livingstone was very ill with fever, so ill that when, on 25 May, he arrived at Quilimane, within a few miles of the coast, he gave instructions for the sale of Sekeletu's ivory in the event of his death. Rather surprisingly, he recovered within a few days and was soon contemplating the satisfying news that warships had been calling at the mouth of the Zambesi every few months to enquire whether anything had been heard of him. These calls had been made as the result of a letter written by Gabriel to the Foreign Secretary giving him approximate dates between which Livingstone might be expected to arrive on the East African coast. The visits of these ships were a sure sign, if Livingstone needed any after reading what *The Times* had had to say in 1854, that when he returned home it would be to a hero's welcome. But before that there were to be more trials.

At Quilimane, Livingstone heard that H.M.S. *Frolic* had recently sent a brig over the bar at the mouth of the river to enquire about him. This

vessel had capsized in the surf that always pounded the bar and all eight
crew members were drowned. This was distressing news. Livingstone did
not, however, equate this tragedy with the unsuitability of the mouth of
the Zambesi for shipping. He preferred to see it as a chance accident.
Before Livingstone reached England the sea was to claim another
victim. He had only intended to take one African home with him and had
chosen for this honour his right-hand man and interpreter, Sekwebu.
Unfortunately the same rough seas that had drowned the sailors were still
raging when Livingstone and his companion were ferried out to the *Frolic*
on 12 July. Sekwebu, who had never seen the sea before and whose only
experience of boats had been canoes on the Zambesi, was terrified by the
large waves that broke over the pinnace and seemed about to swamp her.
Sekwebu's next ordeal was being hoisted aboard the *Frolic* in a bosun's
chair. Not many days later, Sekwebu's mind broke under the strain of such
novel circumstances. When the *Frolic* anchored off Mauritius, Sekwebu
leapt down into a boat that had been launched. When Livingstone
clambered down after him, Sekwebu backed towards the stern, screaming:
'No, no! It is enough that I die alone.' After a great deal of persuasion
Livingstone managed to get him back on board. The officers annoyed
Livingstone by saying that mad savages ought to be put in chains. He
argued that Sekwebu would immediately assume he had been made a
slave and that probably would make him mad for life. The officers gave
way. That evening Sekwebu tried to stab one of the sailors and then
leapt overboard. The last Livingstone saw of his interpreter was his head
and arms, as he gripped the anchor cable and 'pulled himself down hand
under hand'.

   More bad news was to come. At Cairo, Livingstone would learn that
his father had died. But this was nothing compared with the blow that
he sustained at Quilimane. The Directors of the London Missionary
Society had sent a letter to await him there that seemed to negate everything he had been attempting to achieve.

> The Directors, while yielding to none in their appreciation of the objects
> upon which, for some years past, your energies have been concentrated
> . . . are nevertheless restricted in their power of aiding plans connected
> only remotely with the spread of the Gospel . . . Your reports make it
> sufficiently obvious that the nature of the country, the insalubrity of the
> climate, the prevalence of poisonous insects, and other adverse influ-
> ences, constitute a very serious array of obstacles to missionary effort;
> and even were there a reasonable prospect of these being surmounted—
> and we by no means assume they are insurmountable—yet, in that event,
> the financial circumstances of the Society are not such as to afford any

ground of hope that it would be in a position, within any definite period, to venture upon untried, remote, and difficult fields of labour.[63]

Livingstone was bitterly angry that the Directors had declared themselves in favour of the journey when he had set out and yet now were telling him that it was out of the question for his explorations to be followed up. The Society must have known before he left that central Africa would remain one of the 'untried, remote and difficult fields of labour', whatever he managed to achieve. Distance alone made that certain. While his colleagues had accused him of being a traveller rather than a missionary, Livingstone had always derived comfort from his belief that at least the Directors understood his aims. But now it seemed that they had been as blind as everybody else. It must have been especially galling for Livingstone that although he had played down every difficulty, he had still not prevented the Directors taking alarm. The truth seemed to be that the London Missionary Society had encouraged his journeys as a fund-raising stunt and nothing else. This was a painful discovery, and Livingstone's sense of disappointment was almost too great for his fame to appease. He had argued that he had never been concerned with geographical discovery as an end in itself, and now, by their attitude, the Directors had made it appear to everyone that his work from the beginning had been simple exploration without practical application.

When Livingstone landed in England on 9 December 1856 he was famous, but he was also angry and sick at heart.

Before describing Livingstone's hero's reception in England, it is important briefly to summarize his achievement to date. His work between 1853 and 1856, as I said at the beginning of the chapter, can be seen in three distinct phases. The first phase, during 1853, had been taken up with Livingstone's search for a healthy place from which to begin trading and missionary operations in Makololo country. In all respects this phase was a failure. Livingstone not only found no suitable location but also discovered that the Mambari and Portuguese were well established and that the Makololo themselves were far from pacific and unspoiled individuals. The second phase of his work, which lasted from late 1853 to mid-1854, had thus started in unfortunate circumstances. Livingstone had had to face the probability that even if he opened a way to the interior from the west coast, traders and missionaries would not be able to stay with any safety in central Africa. His route to the west coast seemed to him quite impracticable, and this added to his feeling of failure. The next phase had been the most important. Between 1854 and 1856, Livingstone had crossed the continent from Loanda to Quilimane. This journey, he believed, had led to the discovery of an ideal place for the

3 'Boat Capsized by a Hippopotamus Robbed of her Young'

settlement of missionaries and traders: the Batoka Plateau east of the Victoria Falls. Livingstone had reached the east coast firmly convinced that the Zambesi would turn out to be a navigable highway to the plateau. During this period he had come to the conclusion that the existence of coal and iron in western Mozambique indicated that south-central Africa could be developed on 'European lines' and that traders would not in the end have to depend on a transitory commerce in ivory, wax and ostrich feathers. He was also certain that cotton, coffee and sugar could be grown in vast quantities on the Batoka Plateau. Of course the success of any such enterprises would depend on the viability of the Zambesi, but Livingstone, who had narrowly missed discovering the impassable Kebrabasa Rapids, considered the river's navigability to be a foregone conclusion. In his own estimation a worse problem was posed by possible Portuguese objections to the opening of the Zambesi as an international waterway. Nevertheless Livingstone did not see this as a permanent obstacle. He supposed that if he could prove what a rich field south-central Africa could become for industry and commerce, the British Government might lean on Portugal to persuade her to abandon her protectionist policies. An objective judge might have reckoned that the Zambesi, until properly charted, and the attitude of Portugal, were alone enough to place sizeable question marks over Livingstone's ultimate plans.

In fact it could well have been that Livingstone would never have become a national hero if the public had chosen to assess his achievements between 1853 and 1856 in the light in which he saw them: as a means to an end.

In 1854 Livingstone's trip to Loanda had been hailed by Sir Roderick Murchison of the Royal Geographical Society as 'the greatest triumph in geographical research which has been effected in our times'.[64] A number of British papers, including *The Times*, had reiterated this view. Ironically, Livingstone had seen this journey as a failure. When he arrived at Quilimane, the first European to have crossed the continent from coast to coast, he knew that his journey had been a great geographical feat, but his main preoccupation was with far wider objectives. Once again, when he was hailed as the greatest British explorer since the Elizabethans, his own most cherished aims were not being put under scrutiny. His fame was entirely due to his exploration and not to any prospects it might hold out for Africa. Livingstone realized this on his arrival in England and, in his attempt to stress his own estimate of his achievement, greatly exaggerated the potential and accessibility of the areas he had 'opened up'. As will be seen, many of his future difficulties and failures would stem from this.

Finally, if one views Livingstone's great journey in the light in which most of his contemporaries saw it, as an amazing feat of exploration, there can be no doubt that he deserved all the praise he got. He had suffered over thirty attacks of fever during three years, had repeatedly risked his life and had continued when everything appeared hopeless. He had achieved the trans-continental crossing of Africa with the slenderest of resources, and with no more than his salary of £100 a year had relied on the assistance of an African chief. His observations and cartography were infinitely superior to anything produced by the Portuguese, who had preceded him in south-central Africa but had never crossed the continent. Certainly, the fact that Arabs had crossed from Zanzibar to Benguela between 1853 and 1854, and that two African traders had travelled from Angola to Mozambique during the first decade of the century, had not been taken into account by many of Livingstone's public admirers in 1856, but even if these previous journeys had been known about and acknowledged, it seems unlikely that Livingstone's fame would have been much affected.

PART THREE

FAME

National Hero: the First Visit Home
1856–1858

———⟫◆⟪———

During the time Livingstone spent in England, between December 1856 and March 1858, he received a measure of praise and adulation which, even in view of his impressive geographical achievement, strikes one today as excessive. The Royal Geographical Society gave him its gold medal, as did most similar European organizations, he was granted the freedoms of half a dozen major cities, became an honorary Doctor of Civil Law (D.C.L.) of Oxford University and finally had a private audience with Queen Victoria. His book, *Missionary Travels and Researches in South Africa*, published in November 1857, sold seventy thousand copies, earning £9,000 and making its author rich as well as famous. A further two thousand guineas came his way through public subscription funds raised on his behalf in Glasgow and London. After a few months he was so well known in London that he had to be careful where he went in case he was mobbed. On one occasion he narrowly escaped being crushed by a large crowd in Regent Street. In church, if he was recognized, the service would break up in chaos, with people clambering over the pews to try and shake his hand.[1]

There is no one reason that accounts for Livingstone's sudden emergence as a national hero. On one level his trans-continental journey seemed to his contemporaries to be a feat comparable in modern terms with a landing on Mars. Few people in Britain knew about previous Portuguese discoveries, largely because the Portuguese had never wished to interest other European nations in Africa. Their own decaying colonies could hardly cope with competitors, so most of the records of earlier exploration remained in libraries and archives in Lisbon. In 1856 the commonly held British view of south-central Africa, outside professional geographical circles, was of a dry and useless area not unlike the Sahara. Nor did geographers see fit to disillusion the public. Their own calling would become much more significant if British explorers were praised to the skies. Livingstone's description of rivers and forests in central Africa therefore struck most newspaper readers as an incredible 'discovery'. As one journalist put it: 'Europe had always heard that the central regions of southern Africa were burning solitudes, bleak, and barren, heated by poisonous winds, infested by snakes and only roamed over by a few scattered tribes of untameable barbarians ... But Dr. Livingstone found himself in a high country, full of fruit trees, abounding in shade, watered by a perfect network of rivers.'[2]

But Livingstone was not simply praised as an explorer. The Livingstone myth was in the making. He became for many a great missionary too. One paper's description of him was typical. Having portrayed him as 'this truly apostolic preacher of Christian truth', the editorial went on: 'Seldom have savage nations met with the representative of English Civilization in such a shape. He came not for conquest or for gold, but for the love of his fellow men.'[3] Most papers called him a 'devoted' or 'humble missionary', not for a moment trying to establish what form his missionary work had taken. The rapidly expanding penny press therefore carried to the public the vague but unchallenged assertion that Livingstone had been a great missionary. It was an image of himself which, for all its inaccuracy, Livingstone did not see fit to contradict; nor did the Directors of the London Missionary Society breathe a word about his solitary convert who had lapsed. The more it was assumed that 'this truly apostolic preacher' had converted thousands, the more donations could be expected from the public.

So Livingstone was not merely seen as a kind of Victorian astronaut but also as a saintly and successful missionary. Since the missionary societies had never made it their business to tell people that conversions took decades of hard work with a single tribe, most people found perfectly acceptable the idea of Livingstone making conversions after a single sermon.

Much of Livingstone's initial publicity sprang from the determination of various interested parties to make him famous. Sir Roderick Murchison, the President of the Royal Geographical Society, had hailed the discovery of Lake Ngami in 1849 as part of a conscious drive to interest the public in exploration and explorers. A famous Livingstone could be a great financial asset to the R.G.S., attracting subscriptions from hundreds of new members. The London Missionary Society, with a current overdraft of £13,000, also had high hopes of what could be done with massive publicity. Murchison, however, had beaten them with the first move, by arranging an official reception for Livingstone at the R.G.S. headquarters in Savile Row on 15 December. He had invited as many eminent people as could be squeezed into the building and the press had naturally been informed. The Directors of the London Missionary Society held a similar gathering the following day, with no less a figure than Lord Shaftesbury in the chair. Next a series of public lectures was arranged for Livingstone throughout the country. With his weathered face, and his strange, almost foreign, manner of speaking, Livingstone was sure to be a success.

In 1856 the religious fervour that had gripped the nation during the fight against slavery was no longer so marked. But the expanding middle class, whose money had been made in the still growing industries, kept up religious appearances. It had been quickly discovered that Christian virtues could easily be exchanged for business virtues; abstinence, diligence, an exemplary home life and a weekly confrontation with one's Maker could produce rewards in this life as well as the next. Meanwhile guilt could easily be assuaged by occasional acts of charity. Strangely this decline in pure religious standards and the coupling of divine and economic virtues made Livingstone still more popular. His life itself was a comforting justification of the status quo. The boy from the mills, who had made good by self-help, thrift and determination, could be seen as a living proof that exceptional men could overcome their origins, however disadvantageous. But Livingstone's real balm to the consciences of godly industrialists was his argument that Christianity could only make headway in Africa with the help of commerce. Commerce and Christianity, he told numerous audiences, together became civilization. There could have been no more comforting thought for the Christian mill-owner, as he watched his workpeople toil, than the idea that they, under his guidance, were working for civilization and Christ. Livingstone's projection of the image of industrial Britain as the universal ideal flattered many of his fellow-countrymen so much that they never stopped to examine the equation too carefully. They did not, however, leap at the opportunity of investing in a remote and so far untried market. Livingstone's appeal for traders to risk their lives and capital fell on suddenly deaf ears. Even philanthropy expected its guaranteed five per cent.

Livingstone, as befitting his modesty and reticence—both virtues attributed to him by the press—acted his role well and wrote letters to friends telling them what a bore 'this lionising is',[4] and claiming that he would far rather be having quiet meals with a few acquaintances than be feasting with the Lord Mayor.[5] Be that as it may, he went out almost every evening to dine with members of 'the best society' and had 'invitations every day'.[6] He had taken the pledge at Ongar as a student but now that he was famous, he proved that he could drink with anybody; and as his brother, Charles, remarked of one evening: 'We had wines, claret, port, champagne, porter &c. which were most excellent & so did David.' Livingstone's feeling was that there was no harm in private drinking with the well-to-do; public abstinence was only useful as an example to the poorer classes.[7] Livingstone thoroughly enjoyed his new life, and his much-vaunted claim that he disliked publicity comes strangely from a man who insisted on wearing his distinctive peaked cap wherever he went.

With all this frenzied activity it is not surprising that Livingstone's wife and children, who had spent four and a half miserable years of separation, saw little of the national hero. Livingstone, however, felt able to joke about it. When he went to lecture in Dublin, he wrote home to his wife jocosely: 'I am just admiring what a good husband you have got. No sooner does he land in Ireland than he sits down & writes to his wife. Well he is a good fellow after all.'[8] Good fellow or not, when he left for Africa again he wrote to his eldest son Robert, admitting: 'While I was in England I was so busy that I could not enjoy much the company of my children.' There was a brief period when the family was safely hidden away from the attention of 'the best society' in the village of Hadley Green just to the north of London, but this was after much moving about and socializing. In Africa Mary's practical skills and her stoicism had made her an ideal missionary's wife, but in London, with her old-fashioned 1840s straw bonnet and lack of polite small talk, she cut a ludicrous figure in the eyes of the great and good. Certainly she was no social asset to her famous husband.[9]

Without doubt, most can be learned about Livingstone's character at this time through a close examination of the manner in which he left the London Missionary Society and entered government employment. In the past it has always been assumed that Livingstone parted cordially with the Society, having magnanimously forgiven the Directors their thought-less letter which he had received at Quilimane. The facts do not support this interpretation. Livingstone, it has previously been acknowledged, lied on occasions during the Zambesi Expedition between 1858 and 1863, but the strain and the climate and dozens of other problems can be named as mitigating factors. It has not, however, been suggested that before then he was prepared to falsify and distort in order to get his own way. Duplicity and ruthlessness are by no means uncommon in exceptional men, but when they occur in the personality of a man usually considered to have been honest to a fault and gentle in his dealings, it does call for remark. In order to begin a full explanation of the negotiations on which Livingstone embarked with the London Missionary Society and with the British Government and Sir Roderick Murchison during his time in England, the far from happy situation of his missionary employers needs to be mentioned.

Dr Tidman, the Foreign Secretary of the London Missionary Society, had thought a great deal before sending the letter that had so much offended Livingstone. Tidman's motives had been straightforward. Having seen the way the press reacted to Livingstone's arrival in Loanda in 1854, he and his fellow-Directors had realized that if Livingstone ever returned home alive, it would be as an extremely famous man. While this would be excellent from the point of view of fund-raising there were other dangers. For a start, Livingstone might try to put pressure on the Society to send missionaries to the areas he had travelled through. The public might support Livingstone in such rash expansionist ideas and the whole thing might get out of control.

It therefore seemed obvious to Tidman that he had to tell Livingstone that he should not think that forward moves in Africa could be made on any scale in the near future. The Society's £13,000 overdraft was a compelling reason for squashing ambitious schemes at the outset. But having discouraged Livingstone, Tidman then had to try and hang on to him. If Livingstone left the Society before his name could be used for fund-raising, a unique opportunity would be lost. Unfortunately for Tidman, he had forgotten that Livingstone had already shown a paranoid hatred of criticism after the minor trouble with his colleague Rogers Edwards twelve years before. Nor had any of the Directors supposed that Livingstone had entertained, prior to the offending letter, any ill-feeling towards the Society. Had they known how wrong they were, Tidman would have played his cards very differently.

While at Tete in early 1856, Livingstone had written to Edmund Gabriel complaining about the dismal prospect that lay before him on his return to England. The Directors, Livingstone told his friend, would force him 'to go through the country . . . lecturing and imparting informa-tion as a means of exciting more liberality. Now I cannot speak English in public, nor am I willing to be a public beggar . . . The most disagreeable thing I anticipate is haggling about money.' 'My wife,' he went on, 'thinking to leave in 1854 for the Cape, asked something to furnish an outfit for the voyage, she had been visiting some rich Quaker friends and the paltry £30 was refused because some of these *financiers* believed she must have got presents during her visits. Expect me to go begging after that.'[10] Livingstone's feelings towards the Society had been ambiguous as early as 1853, for in September that year he had told his family that 'if the Society should object [to his plans] I would consider it my duty to with-draw from it'.[11] Tidman's letter had not therefore suddenly suggested a novel idea.

But Tidman's real gamble had been that Livingstone would remain financially dependent on the Society for some time after his arrival in England. None of the Directors had any idea that Livingstone had already opened a confidential correspondence with Sir Roderick Murchison. A letter from Sir Roderick had reached Livingstone at Quilimane in the same batch as Tidman's. Murchison's praise was so rapturous that

Livingstone had at once begun a long reply. Having gone over all his reasons for supposing that Africa would turn out to be a trader's paradise, he told him about his position with the London Missionary Society.

> I suspect I am to be sent somewhere else, but will prefer dissolving my connection with the Society and follow out my own plans as a private Christian. This is rather trying, for, the salary being professedly only a bare subsistence (£100 per annum), we have in addition the certainty of education for our family and some provision for our widows . . . Should I be unable to return I hope you will direct the attention of travellers to developing the rich resources of the country.[12]

This was a direct appeal for help and an open intimation that if Murchison found alternative employment, Livingstone would probably take it. From the moment he received this letter Murchison did everything in his power to see that Livingstone became financially independent. On 5 January 1857 Murchison had arranged a meeting, at the Mansion House, to inaugurate a testimonial fund for Livingstone. And that evening, deciding still more could be done, Murchison wrote to Lord Clarendon, the British Foreign Secretary, on his protégé's behalf. Sir Roderick referred to the speech he had made at the meeting earlier in the day and asked, tongue in cheek, to be forgiven for having said that Clarendon was a whole-hearted Livingstone supporter. 'I ventured to say that I hoped that you might make good use of the man who knows more African languages than any other European and who seemed to have such a happy way of carrying on an intercourse with the natives along our frontiers.'[13]

The Directors of the London Missionary Society would not have got wind of these overtures to the Government, but they must have known that with mounting public interest they could not remain inactive much longer. They were also extremely worried about the Mansion House subscription fund. In their view, the Society ought to be getting the money, and not Livingstone himself.[14] But the fact that Livingstone was getting it gave them proof that he would not be financially dependent on them for as long as they had hoped. According to Livingstone, they actually tried to stop him getting any more donations.[15] But whatever clandestine efforts the Society made, if any, on 12 January the Directors held a special meeting with Livingstone as their honoured guest. Tidman had already told Livingstone that with the Society's funds in such a state of imbalance, he could not contemplate new missions, but Livingstone was unmoved. At the meeting he told the Directors that they ought to send a mission to the Batoka Plateau and claimed that the Makololo would willingly move to that area as soon as such a mission was established. Livingstone went on to explain that a mission should also be started just to the south, with the Matabele, so that the Makololo mission would not be threatened. Livingstone had evidently explained about the influence Moffat had with the Matabele, for the board minutes for the meeting stated: 'That in his [Livingstone's] judgment the result would be promoted by the residence of himself and Mrs Livingstone amongst the Makololo and with God's blessing almost certainly secured were Mr Moffat to commence a Mission at the town of Moselekatsee, the chief of the Matebele.'[16]

So at this stage, a day after Murchison had written a second letter to Clarendon suggesting a meeting with Livingstone, the Directors of the London Missionary Society had been led to believe that if any mission to the Makololo went ahead, Livingstone would lead it. Livingstone had also acknowledged the reasons why it was crucial that members of his or Moffat's family should be attached to each of the two missions. Yet Livingstone must have known about Murchison's efforts to interest the Foreign Secretary, Lord Clarendon, in employing him. Oblivious to all this, the Directors, assuming Livingstone had meant what he said, submitted his proposals to the Southern Committee of the Society, which duly reported on 22 January. The committee advised the Society to go ahead with the two missions, on condition that Moffat, or a member of his family, should head the Matabele Mission, and they went on to propose that 'A missionary be appointed *to assist Dr. Livingstone in the organisation of the intended mission** among the Makololo'.[17]

The words in italics have in the past been taken to mean that the committee understood that Livingstone's role was now simply to be one of organization and not participation.[18] Yet since it had been stressed as recently as 12 January how important Dr and Mrs Livingstone's personal presence would be, it is inconceivable that this single weakly phrased sentence would have been the only mention of such a momentous alteration of plans. The minutes would certainly have included any refusal by Livingstone to fulfil his earlier promise. The obvious meaning of the wording is that Livingstone was to have a missionary helper to assist with organization of the mission prior to his actual departure. In view of Livingstone's other engagements, there was nothing surprising in such an arrangement.

The Directors believed this was the position anyway. At the Society's General Meeting on 14 May, they included a resolution adopted at a meeting of the Town and Country Directors on 10 February. The resolution begins: 'That two new Mission Stations should be opened—the one among the Makololo, north of the Zambese, *under the charge of*

* Author's italics.

*Dr. Livingstone** assisted by another missionary; and the other among the Matebele . . .'[19]

A mission over a thousand miles in the interior of Africa could hardly have been under the charge of anybody if he was not physically present. Livingstone attended the meeting on 10 February, so he could well have objected to the form of words if he had chosen to. In fact he 'expressed his entire concurrence'. Nor at the General Meeting in May did he deny that his wife and he would be joining the Makololo Mission. His lack of objections taken with his previous assurances, written from Africa, that should a mission ever be set up among the Makololo, he and his wife would go, 'whoever remains behind', must have left the Directors firmly convinced by May that even if the mission was a risky one, at least Livingstone would be there.

The amazing fact is that by May, when Livingstone had given firm assurances to the Directors, Murchison's clandestine efforts with the British Government had entered a crucial phase, and Livingstone knew very well that he would be offered employment of some sort. It might be argued that his double-dealing with the Directors served them right for having failed initially to see the long-term possibilities opened up by his journey. Or the whole confusion might be put down to a strange and inexplicable mental block on his part or on that of the Directors. The matter cannot, however, be dismissed lightly, since the implications do more than touch on Livingstone's truthfulness. When the Makololo Mission finally arrived at Linyanti without him, three adults and three children died of fever out of the five children and two married couples who had originally gone out. Furthermore, afterwards Livingstone denied any responsibility for the tragedy. Since so much is at stake, it is necessary to examine Livingstone's approaches, through Murchison, to the Government more closely, taking careful note of dates. Only in this way can it be seen whether he deliberately misled the Directors.

From the moment Livingstone realized his popularity, he had encouraged all Murchison's approaches to the Government and had expressed wry amusement at the Directors' hasty moves to change the impression they had made before. Two weeks after his arrival in England he had written to Sir Roderick from the Ship Hotel, Charing Cross, stating magnanimously:

I have no wish to take any public advantage of their mistake, for such I now suppose they feel it to be . . . But you will perceive the reason why

* Author's italics.

I said I should be willing to adopt the plan you suggested of a roving commission ... I have not the slightest wish or intention of giving up working for the amelioration of Africa. I have devoted my life to that and, if I could be put into a position where I could be more effective and at the same time benefit my children by giving them a good education, I should think it my duty to accept it.[20]

So five months before the London Missionary Society General Meeting in May Livingstone had determined to leave it if a good enough offer was made. But it was not simply because he did not wish to 'take advantage' of the Society that he remained silent for so long, even after he was almost certain Clarendon would employ him. In fact, on 15 April, a month before the General Meeting, he had written to Murchison, and this letter goes some way to explain why he wanted to say nothing to the Directors till later. He told Sir Roderick that he wanted to delay putting in a formal application for government employment till nearer the time of his departure, not because he intended to refuse it and not because the suggestions Clarendon had already made were unacceptable. 'I fear if I got it [a government job] now, my friends of the Mission House will make use of the fact to damage my character in the public estimation by saying I have forsaken the Mission for higher pay. I have refused to take any more from them, and wish to do my future work in as unostentatious a way as possible.' He went on to say that he had suggested, and Clarendon had approved, 'a consulship to the Makololo and other central African tribes' which 'would enable me to do all I wish for both them and English Commerce'.[21]

Livingstone therefore appeared to be deceiving the Directors deliberately to safeguard his reputation. It might be claimed that his 'consulship' would not conflict with his position on the Makololo Mission, but this argument does not stand up to close examination. In the first place he would inevitably be away from the mission for long periods of time, charting the Zambesi and making commercial treaties with numerous tribes along it; and, second, he had already told Murchison in a letter, intended to be sent on to Clarendon, and dated 26 January, that roving government employment would enable him 'to effect a much greater amount of good than I could do by settling down for the remaining portion of my life with any one of the small tribes which are dotted over the country'.[22] Again in this same letter he referred to his fear that he would be accused of leaving the Society 'for the sake of filthy lucre'.

There was one other important motive for leading the Directors up the garden path, as he explained to Maclear in May: 'I am not yet fairly on with the Government but am nearly quite off with the Society.'[23]

But really, as his letter to Murchison of 15 April (quoted above) showed, he was as sure about the Government as he could be and had, at his own wish, postponed an official announcement of his appointment. Two letters prove beyond doubt that an appointment had been decided on by Clarendon by the first week in May; the first was written by Livingstone's brother, Charles, who told his wife that Livingstone had already 'concluded to accept Lord C's offer and has accordingly written him and the matter will be decided soon'.[24] This letter was dated 5 May, and the following day Murchison wrote to Clarendon suggesting a salary of £500 per annum for Livingstone; so by then the only questions left to be answered were practical: what sort of expedition should Livingstone lead and how much money should be laid out? Already Livingstone had told Clarendon what he intended to do: to open the Zambesi for commerce, to start cotton-growing and to try and work with the Portuguese to establish 'legitimate commerce' strong enough to drive out the slave trade. He was not being unconsciously naive in suggesting that the Portuguese would cooperate, but was eager to avoid mentioning difficulties to Clarendon at such an early stage.[25]

Meanwhile Tidman and his colleagues proceeded cautiously. Their appeal for funds for the two missions had only been started in March and the target of £5,000 would not be reached for some months. This, combined with Tidman's desire to make sure that Livingstone was going to stick to his word, accounts for his putting off writing to Robert Moffat till 4 April. Moffat was sent a copy of the Board Minutes for the meetings attended by Livingstone on 12 and 22 January, which, as will be remembered, set out the importance of Livingstone and Mrs Livingstone being with the Makololo Mission and stressed the need for a simultaneous mission to the Matabele. Moffat was now to visit the chief of the Matabele and to 'devote about a twelvemonth' to preparing the ground for the mission. 'No step to be actually taken.'[26] Tidman's motive for delaying everything was not just natural prudence. He had never been in favour of any mission to the Makololo without the prior establishment of a chain of missions to connect it with the coast, and he probably hoped that, as time passed and the funds came in, Livingstone would grow impatient and go back alone, either with or without the backing of the Society. If that happened, a lot of money would already have been raised, the missions could be shelved and the Society would no longer be in danger of having to run its operations at the dictation of Dr Livingstone or public pressure. In this way it might appear that Livingstone had left the Society because he was too impatient to wait for reasonable preparations to be made. Thus the Directors would be able to part with him without their reputation suffering. This is hypothetical, but without such motivation it is very hard to explain Tidman's delay of over two months before writing to Moffat. Of course it is just possible that Livingstone told Tidman about his government appointment in May and colluded with him to keep the matter secret so that Tidman's fund-raising would not be impeded and his own reputation would not be damaged by remarks to the effect that he was leaving the Society hastily without giving the proposed missions a chance. But this last seems doubtful since neither man could risk this kind of deception ever becoming public.

From May to October, Livingstone had no dealings with Tidman, and Tidman did not contact Livingstone. Tidman's reasons would have been that the fund had not yet reached the target and that nothing could be done until Moffat reported on the attitude of the Matabele. Livingstone in the meantime was working night and day on his book, *Missionary Travels*, for John Murray.

There is no evidence that Livingstone told the Society of his real intentions till October, five months after Clarendon had made his offer of government employment. But on 27 October there was a meeting at the Mission House and Dr Tidman read to a stunned board of Directors a letter from Livingstone, stating that 'although he declined to receive pecuniary support from the Society, and would probably in future sustain some relation to the British Government, he would, there was every reason to believe, render the Directors his best assistance in the establishment of a Mission north of the Zambesi'.[27] Regrettably, Livingstone's letter is not in the London Missionary Society archives. Although many of the Directors were distressed, Tidman probably did not share their feelings. He had never been in favour of the proposed missions and now it seemed to him that after a decent pause he would be able to scrap the whole scheme. After all, acceptance of Livingstone's proposals had depended on his leadership, and clearly this could no longer be counted on. And so it was that in February 1858, over a year after the proposals had been accepted by the Society's Southern Committee, Tidman had still not selected candidates for either mission. By this time Tidman obviously felt that since Livingstone had let the Society down, he would not have the gall to tell the Directors that it was their duty to proceed with the missions. But Livingstone did have the gall. On 22 February an astonished Tidman read a letter from Livingstone, asking when the missionaries for the Makololo and Matabele were leaving Britain. Livingstone's tone was threatening. 'Abundant funds having been furnished* for all that is needed on the case . . . I should be glad to be assured that the intentions of the friends in subscribing so liberally are likely soon to be realised.'[28]

---

* £6,400 had been raised by the end of 1857—£1,400 more than the target.

The implicit blackmail was clear: if the money were used to clear the Society's overdraft and not for the purpose for which it had been ostensibly raised, there might be some awkward questions asked in public. Tidman was trapped and knew it. On 27 February he wrote to Livingstone claiming that a party would leave in May. He added that there had never been any intention of shelving the project. Subsidiary evidence for doubting Tidman's word is strong. John Moffat, Livingstone's brother-in-law, had understood, as early as the middle of 1857, that he was to go to either the Matabele or the Makololo, but the delays and changes of plans that he was still being subjected to in early 1858 hardly indicated a determination to proceed on Tidman's part. Robert Moffat himself, after his return from the Matabele, was also chafing at the total lack of information from the Directors.

On 6 March Livingstone wrote to Tidman, at last telling him what his true position was in relation to the Makololo Mission.

> Should they [the missionaries] come through Mosilikatse's country to the Zambesi to a point below the Victoria Falls where our steam launch will be of any service to them, my companions will readily lend their aid in crossing the river . . . It might be better to go by Lake Ngami, as that is the only known opening Northwards; on every other point Mr. Helmore* can be trusted in implicitly.[29]

It is not difficult to imagine Tidman's feelings on reading this. He had not wanted to embark on any mission to the Makololo and had been pushed into it against his will, on condition that Livingstone was leader. Livingstone had kept him in the dark about his other plans for five months after those plans had produced results. Now, a year after the mission had been approved, Livingstone had pressured the Society into going ahead, while blandly informing them that the most they could expect him to do would be to help the missionaries cross the Zambesi, if by chance he happened to be at the right place at the right time. How much this 'assistance' was worth could be seen at a glance. He had suggested that the missionaries should go to Makolololand via Lake Ngami. This route would mean that they would cross the river above the Victoria Falls and not below them. Thus Livingstone would not be able to help even if his steamer ever got to the Falls.

Livingstone's part in the planning of the Makololo Mission has not previously been adequately dealt with, because it has always been assumed

---

* Holloway Helmore (1815–60), missionary at Likatlong in South Africa since 1839. In 1858 he was appointed leader of the Makololo Mission.

1 Shuttle Row, Blantyre, *c.* 1870.

2 The room where Livingstone was born and lived as a child. Seven people slept here.

3 The Old Mill, Blantyre.

4 Miniature of David Livingstone shortly
before he left for Africa in 1841.

5 View of Kuruman.

6 Livingstone's wife, Mary, in her late thirties.

7 Livingstone in 1852, on the eve of his trans-continental journey.

8 Chief Sechele.

9 Livingstone's prismastic compass.

10 David and Mary Livingstone with their children at Lake Ngami.

11 Livingstone and the Lion: Magic lantern slide published by the London Missionary Society *c*. 1900.

Image of a water colour and pencil diagram-sketch with handwritten annotations including "trees", "400 paces", "covered with trees", "covered with trees", "covered with trees", "filled in Metres", "Dry", "150 paces", "400 feet deep", "sides perpendicular neck so marrow", "one can see across from + down to the water", "Victoria Falls - 1860 yards wide - 310 feet deep - Garden island in middle - blue line shews water flowing from both ends to the escape -"

12 Water colour and pencil diagram-sketch by Livingstone of the Victoria Falls, drawn on his second visit in 1860.

13 Gold Medal presented to Livingstone by the Royal Geographical Society on his return from his trans-Africa journey of 1853–6.

14 Arthur Tidman, Foreign Secretary of the London Missionary Society.

15 Livingstone and his family, 1857.

16 Painting by Thomas Baines of the *Ma-Robert*, Livingstone's much-reviled steam launch.

17 Commander Norman Bedingfeld, R.N.

18 Dr John Kirk.

19 Thomas Baines in 1868.

20 Richard Thornton, aged nineteen.

21 Rapids above the main Kebrabasa falls, painted by Thomas Baines in 1859.

22 Zambesi Expedition; trading from the *Ma-Robert*, painted by Thomas Baines.

23 Bishop Mackenzie.

24 James Stewart.

25 Missionaries buying food at Magomero: pencil and watercolour wash by
Charles Mellor.

26 Livingstone in 1864 on his last visit home.

27 The Royal Geographical Society outing during the meeting of the British Association in Bath, 1864. Livingstone is standing left of centre, wearing his distinctive cap. Further right is Sir Roderick Murchison in a white suit.

28 Livingstone on his last visit home (1864–5) photographed with his youngest child, Anna Mary, who had only just met him. She had been conceived in 1858, just before the Zambesi Expedition began.

29 Robert Livingstone.

30 Livingstone's sketch map of the central African watershed.

31 Medicine chest used by Livingstone on his last journeys.

32 Chuma (left) and Susi.

33 James Gordon Bennett, owner of the
New York Herald.

34 Henry Morton Stanley and Kalulu, his young African servant; a studio portrait, after
Stanley's return from successfully locating Livingstone.

35 Carrying the Body to the Coast: a magic lantern slide published by the London Missionary Society *c.* 1900.

36 Chuma (left) and Susi with Livingstone's relics, on their visit to England after his death.

THE ILLUSTRATED LONDON NEWS

REGISTERED AT THE GENERAL POST-OFFICE FOR TRANSMISSION ABROAD.

No. 1809 — VOL. LXIV.   SATURDAY, APRIL 25, 1874.   WITH EXTRA SUPPLEMENT   SIXPENCE
BY POST, 6½D.

37 'Dr Livingstone's remains at Southampton; procession to the railway station'.

that the Directors were quickly disabused of the idea that Livingstone would have personal charge of the mission. The evidence quoted above proves this to have been false.

Before resuming a strict chronology and completing the record of Livingstone's negotiations with the Government, it is best to continue with the Makololo Mission and try to determine how much responsibility Livingstone must bear for the tragic outcome of that project. Because the disaster occurred in 1860, two years after Livingstone left England as leader of the Government-financed Zambesi Expedition, it has usually been dealt with briefly *en passant*, during a description of the events of the expedition. But this placing inevitably tends to isolate the mission from its conception in London during 1857, and therefore tends to blur the part Livingstone played in forcing the mission on, even after he had dissociated himself from it.

12

The Price of Optimism: the Makololo Mission

1857–1860

⇒◈⇐

The Makololo Mission was dogged from the very beginning by false expectations. In *Missionary Travels* Livingstone had deliberately written about the Makololo in a much more favourable light than he had in his private correspondence. The cruel treatment meted out to their vassals was glossed over and the constant raids on neighbouring tribes made light of. He had also played down his own sufferings from fever, partly through modesty, and partly to avoid the implication that he considered missionary work to be a sacrifice. Nevertheless his predominant motive for appearing optimistic about the conditions in south-central Africa had been the fear that if he did not, the area would be abandoned as hopeless.

The Directors, however, had plenty of evidence from his letters to show that any mission would be fraught with dangers; indeed, it had been these very dangers that had initially put them off. It is therefore all the more remarkable that they allowed a mission consisting of two missionaries, their wives and five young children to go ahead. It is true that Livingstone had written: 'I apprehend no great mortality among missionaries, men of education and prudence who can, if they will, adopt proper hygienic precautions.'[1]

But in the same letter he had talked of his own attacks of fever and the constant vomiting of blood. This was hardly the only reference to the severity of the fever. The Directors had been told that the Makololo themselves were dying out because of it. The unhealthiness of Linyanti had led him to suggest that a move to the Batoka Plateau was indispensable. The Makololo would nevertheless have to be persuaded to move, and, as Livingstone himself had told the Directors in 1853, this would be hard: 'Because the vicinity of Mosilikatse renders it impossible for Makololo or any other tribe to reside there. A change may yet be effected among the Matibele which would change the present aspect of affairs.'[2]

It could be claimed that the problem had been solved by the proposed mission to the Matabele, but it would *still* take a year or two, after the start of that mission, for the Makololo to judge whether the Matabele had reformed. Therefore if a party went to the Makololo at the same time as the party to the Matabele, it might still be several years before the move to the Batoka Plateau could be effected. During that time the missionaries would be constantly exposed to fever. Even though Livingstone was confident that he himself could persuade them to move, he had still told the Directors late in 1855: 'I feel a difficulty as to taking my children there, without their own intelligent self-dedication. I can speak for my wife and myself only.'[3]

It is therefore puzzling that the Directors ever allowed the missionaries to set out for Linyanti with their wives and children. They could well have insisted that the men went on alone first, till the move to healthier ground could take place. The truth seems to have been that they trusted the missionaries to judge for themselves. They should have confided in Robert Moffat more and trusted in his judgement.

Regrettably, Moffat had been told little and believed himself responsible only for the Matabele Mission. Tidman had not seen fit to tell him that Livingstone had opted out of the Makololo Mission till two months before the missionaries were due to leave England. On 19 April 1858 Moffat wrote acidly to the Directors: 'Of course I had not the slightest idea of being of use to the missies [missionaries] for the Makololo who it was taken for granted would go with Livingstone himself.'[4]

Moffat had heard, only a couple of weeks before writing this letter, that Livingstone had left the Society and was to lead an expedition up the Zambesi. His immediate thought, he told the Directors bluntly, was that it was madness for the missionaries to go overland, especially after what Livingstone had told them about fever, the tsetse and the lack of water crossing the Kalahari. The obvious course was for them to go with Livingstone and to approach Linyanti via the Zambesi. Livingstone could have told him that the Portuguese would not allow more than the basic personnel of the expedition to pass through their territory, but Moffat could hardly have known this without being told. Between April and July 1858 Moffat wrote repeatedly to the Directors, trying to get them to abandon the Makololo Mission for the time being. 'I have my fears, and feel my mind beset with difficulties connected with the Mission to the Makololo which I cannot overcome.' Moffat went on that unless he or Livingstone visited the Makololo in person the tribe could not be expected to move from the malarial area around Linyanti to the healthier Batoka Plateau. Either Moffat or Livingstone would have to come to convince them they were safe from the Matabele. 'All this', Moffat continued, 'makes it a serious matter to recommend three missionaries and their wives to proceed at once to Linyanti', where fever might in a few months 'prove fatal to some if not all'. Moffat ended his letter by begging the Directors to put off the mission until Livingstone had first arrived at Linyanti and persuaded the Makololo to move.[5]

The Directors could hardly accede to this since the last letter they had had from Livingstone had given them no idea when he might be at Linyanti or anywhere near it. The Directors had never wanted the mission to get under way, but now that it had, they had to think of the effect on public opinion if they pulled out at the eleventh hour. But one aspect of their behaviour remains a complete mystery. They had been given definite information in Livingstone's letter of 6 March 1858 that he would help the Makololo missionaries only if he happened to be at the Victoria Falls at the right time. It is therefore completely confounding that in 1859 all the Makololo party, and Moffat himself, still believed that Livingstone would meet them at Linyanti. It was this misapprehension, which at this stage was not Livingstone's fault, that contributed so much to the deaths of so many of the party. A single example will be enough to show that the missionaries really did indeed believe Livingstone would meet them at Linyanti.

One of the party, John Mackenzie, who, luckily for him, did not go with the rest because his wife was due to have a child and was ill as well, was later to claim with absolute certainty that the leader of the party, Helmore, was sure Livingstone would meet them.

> Above all his [Helmore's] great thought was to be at Linyanti in time to meet Dr. Livingstone there. He knew enough of the natives to be aware that a stranger would not be likely suddenly to acquire such influence with the chief and people as would be necessary to induce them to change their residence. Hence the importance of being introduced to the tribe by Dr. Livingstone as his friend. On no account must the Doctor reach Linyanti, and find that Helmore had not arrived.[6]

So Helmore, who knew that to be safe he should wait another nine months or so, set out at the worst possible time of year and arrived at Linyanti in February, a month notorious for fever. This would never have happened had he not been terrified of missing Livingstone. Within two months of their arrival, Helmore and Mrs Helmore were dead. So too was the other missionary wife, Mrs Price, and three out of a total of five children. Roger Price and two of Helmore's children were the sole survivors.

The deaths themselves need not be gone into except to say that, although Price thought they had died from poison, he was almost certainly wrong. Fever accounted for all the symptoms mentioned. But the missionaries had some reason to suspect foul play. From the time of their arrival, the Makololo did not disguise their bitter disappointment that neither Livingstone nor Moffat had come. From their point of view these strangers were no earthly use to them as protection against the Matabele. They had not even brought guns to trade.

Sekeletu had expected his relationship with Livingstone to make him rich, and now it seemed all it had brought was a sickly group of people who only wanted to talk of God. As Price said later, Sekeletu was angry that Livingstone had not brought his men back; he had promised to do so within a year and now four had passed, and these missionaries could not even tell him when the Doctor was likely to come. The Makololo had repeatedly turned away traders from the south in order to wait for the traders who, Livingstone had promised, would soon come paddling up the Zambesi. Had Livingstone thought about Sekeletu's feelings earlier, he would have warned the missionaries that they might encounter hostility. But shortly before leaving for Africa he had told Tidman that there was no point in his meeting Helmore as he had nothing to tell him.[7]

The Makololo had reason to be bitter, but nothing can excuse the way they treated Price when he, his dying wife and the Helmore children tried to leave Linyanti. Sekeletu took away Helmore's waggon and refused to allow them to cross the Chobe till they had parted with most of their supplies and clothing. They were all ill and now had to attempt a journey of over a thousand miles with hardly any food or provisions. Had Mackenzie not met them on the way, all might have died like the rest. The Makololo provided guides who deliberately led the party into the tsetse fly area, so most of the oxen were lost. The last straw was that after Mrs Price's burial, the Makololo exhumed her body, cut off her head and took it to Sekeletu. At the time of her death, Mrs Price had been so thin that she had had to put plaster over her joints to stop the bones breaking the skin. The suffering they all endured can hardly be exaggerated. One child died begging for water that was never fetched, another died unnoticed by his father, who was also near death. The last letter Mrs Helmore ever wrote was to her daughter Olive in England, telling her that she would soon be with them all in Africa. 'Lizzie says I am to tell you to bring some comfits, little baskets &c that we may have a Christmas Tree the first Christmas you are all at home.'[8] By the time Olive read the letter her mother was dead.

The Makololo Mission had already ended when Livingstone decided to take Sekeletu's men back to Barotseland in April 1860. He had only been prompted to take them back then because he could do no more on the lower Zambesi until a second steamer came from Britain, so it was chance that dictated the exact time he chose. To be fair, had he not encountered the horrifying obstacle of the Kebrabasa Rapids he might well have arrived very much earlier.

He did not hurry once he set out, and again he cannot be blamed. He felt that his last letter to Tidman, the one written on 6 March 1858, had made it clear that he could guarantee nothing. On 9 August he reached the Victoria Falls and stopped for several days to reassess his previous measurements. Several weeks later he reached Sesheke, where he heard what had happened at Linyanti. When the initial shock had passed, Livingstone was tormented by the thought that people were going to accuse him of being partially responsible for the disaster. He set to work at once to try and forestall any such criticism. His letter to Tidman could hardly have been more irritating to the recipient had he deliberately written it to annoy him. Tidman, too, was aware that he himself would probably be blamed, and was as sensitive as Livingstone to possible criticism. The letter opened with conventional expressions of sorrow and then went on: 'The poignancy of my unavailing regret is not diminished by remembering that at the very time when our friends were helplessly perishing we were at a lower and much more unhealthy part of the river, and curing the complaint so quickly that in very severe cases the patient was able to resume his march on foot a day or so after the operation of the remedy.'

As though to rub in the irony of this, Livingstone went on to tell him that he had first tried quinine as a remedy as early as 1850 and that it 'has been successful in every case of African fever met with since'. Tidman might well have been wondering why Livingstone had not told him more about the remedy while he was in London. Livingstone's answer was that he had included a sentence about it in *Missionary Travels* 'towards the end' and that he had kept quiet about it because it was bad medical etiquette to publicize anything till a proper trial had been given it. Worse was to come. 'From all I could learn the Makololo took most cordially to Mr. Helmore—they wished to become acquainted with him, a very natural desire, before removing to the Highlands, and hence the delay which ended so fatally . . . The Makololo are quite ready to remove, they are perishing themselves . . .'

This claim that the Makololo had met the missionaries with friendship and had agreed to remove once they got to know them was in direct conflict with all Price's evidence. He had claimed that the Makololo had absolutely refused to move, and had ordered the party to stay when they asked permission to leave for the healthier highlands to wait there for Dr Livingstone. Tidman was more enraged still that Livingstone had not mentioned the fact that Sekeletu had robbed Price of almost all he possessed. Livingstone's final thrust had been aimed at the Directors themselves. He stated that he hoped the Society would not now be cowardly and leave this field because of an initial setback.[9] Livingstone's praise of Helmore may have been due to genuine admiration, but Tidman would have had no doubt that Livingstone was commending him because he was dead and would therefore be unable to say anything unpleasant about the Makololo. Price, on the other hand, who had survived and was doing his utmost to discredit Livingstone's 'faithful' tribe, was soon to be abused at every possible opportunity.

On 5 July, Tidman replied to Livingstone's letter, pointing out that the Makololo had not been prepared to leave, and expressing anger that he had been told nothing of 'an antidote of known efficacy' for fever. He also suggested that Sekeletu had misrepresented the case to avoid Livingstone's displeasure. This letter and its implications were, Livingstone thundered in his reply, 'perfectly astonishing'. Sekeletu had treated him just as well as ever, although he was suffering from a serious skin disease. Furthermore, nobody, not even a member of a subject tribe, had ever suggested that Helmore had been disliked. The real trouble, he went on, was that Price had been unpopular and with reason. On one occasion he had kicked a man, on another tied a Makololo to the wheel of his waggon and had even threatened people with his revolver. If Price had been robbed, how was it, he asked, that his own waggon and its contents had not been pilfered although he had been away four years? The truth was clearly that Price had provoked them. Livingstone ended by again asking the Directors not to give up. 'I still feel convinced that a flourishing mission might be established by a judicious missionary.'[10]

Price himself was horrified that Livingstone had accepted Sekeletu's story rather than his own and wrote to the Directors on 20 July 1861 suggesting that the final proof of whether the Makololo had intended to move would be their actual removal. Livingstone, however, would have claimed that even if they did not move (and they did not) it would be because the missionaries had given them up.

There is no evidence that Price bound a man to a waggon wheel or that he kicked anybody. The revolver incident, he explained to Tidman, in a letter written on 4 November 1861, had occurred after he had first been threatened. In any case, had Price been suffering from fever at the time, he might well have been delirious. It should be remembered that Livingstone himself had had to threaten to shoot some of his men on his journey to Loanda. Livingstone's anger with Price was not really concerned with any actions of his, but was due in the first place to the failure of the mission. Price, as the only adult survivor, bore the brunt of his displeasure.

Livingstone's vilification of the Makololo missionaries was not only due to his fear that unless he could prove them responsible for their own deaths, he might be blamed. He was really trying to excuse his own failures by condemning Price and his colleagues. By 1860 Livingstone had discovered the impassable Kebrabasa Rapids and therefore knew that the Batoka Plateau and the Makololo could never be linked with the coast via the Zambesi. That was the real drawback to any future missionary or trading efforts in south-central Africa. Now Livingstone took the deaths of the missionaries as an excuse. He claimed that the Makololo and the surrounding tribes would be abandoned, not because of Kebrabasa but because no traders or missionaries would dare go to them after a handful of stupid and culpably negligent men had allowed themselves to die. Furthermore, Price's *lies* about the Makololo being robbers would alone be enough to discourage potential traders. Livingstone argued that he had laboured for years to open the interior, and now a group of incompetents had wrecked it all. Livingstone's agonizing time on the lower Zambesi during 1858 and 1859 may partially explain his callousness, but it cannot justify his deliberate distortions. Another cause for his violent reaction was his by now bitter hatred of the Directors of the London Missionary Society. A few months before learning about the Linyanti tragedy, Livingstone had written to his brother-in-law, John Moffat, telling him how the Directors had tried to defraud him out of the money raised for him in London by Murchison, and how they had even made efforts to get a bookseller to sue him for a £40 debt. 'Were I disposed I could tell a tale,' he had ended darkly. A year later Livingstone's disgust with the Society had increased still more; he had heard that one of their agents, a Mr Farebrother, was going 'about the country telling at public meetings that I am morally responsible for the loss of the missionaries at Linyanti'. The missionaries, Livingstone went on, were entirely to blame for what had happened to them. 'Helmore did not write to me even. I think they wanted to do it all themselves and have it to say they did not require any aid from me. A precious mull they made of it.'[11] As will be remembered, Helmore's most cherished desire had been to meet Livingstone at Linyanti.

When anybody suggested that he had had anything to do with the deaths, Livingstone denied it furiously. His sister Janet was bold enough to ask him why he had not kept in touch with the Society. His answer, as usual, was that neither Helmore nor Tidman had ever seen fit to write to him. In fact, as will be remembered, just before leaving for Africa, Livingstone had written to Tidman telling him that there was no point in him meeting Helmore because he had nothing to tell him.

Janet had also reproached her brother for giving the missionaries a false picture of the problems they would face. This, too, Livingstone vigorously denied. 'I gave information according to the varying phases of my experience. If life was in danger I committed it as I always do to the Divine keeping. If reputation and usefulness among the heathen were endangered by false bretheren* I spoke of it even as St Paul did long before me.'[12]

When Livingstone wrote his own official account of the disaster in his book *Narrative of an Expedition to the Zambesi* he took only two pages to do so. These pages are full of inaccuracies and false implications. Livingstone could not bring himself to name Price, except as 'the missionary associate of Helmore', even though Price had now married Mrs Livingstone's sister Bessie. He referred to the party as nine Europeans which, although accurate numerically, is not the same as two missionaries and their families. The deaths of children would have been seen as a tragedy but the deaths of 'five Europeans' gave the impression that all were adults, and their extinction would thus only have excited from the public a slightly contemptuous pity for human weakness. As it was, he cut the number of European dead down from six to five. He also claimed, quite incorrectly, that the whole party had been on the point of leaving for the Batoka Plateau and had only been prevented by fever. The missionaries had not been at death's door when they arrived, and yet Livingstone laboured to make it appear that the journey was almost as much responsible for their demise as the fever. In his account he made no mention of his own part in getting the mission set up, and at no point did he admit that at one time he had been appointed to lead the mission. The theft of the missionaries' goods was omitted and Livingstone even implied that Price had *given* Helmore's waggon to Sekeletu, with no consideration for the interests of Helmore's two orphaned children. Some of these slips may be thought to be due to faulty African information, but Livingstone's final criticism of the party leaves little doubt that the distortions were deliberate: 'Had it been possible for one with the wisdom, experience and conciliating manners of Mr Moffat to have visited the Makololo, he would have found them easily influenced to fairness, and not at all the unreasonable savages they were represented to be.'[13]

In a sense this statement was true, but not quite in the way that Livingstone intended. The Makololo wanted a member of the Moffat family to live with them, so naturally they would have behaved better had Moffat himself come among them. Livingstone's real fault in the matter was not that he did not turn up in time to cure the missionaries—he could well have arrived at Linyanti before their arrival and been no use—but that he encouraged the Makololo Mission to go ahead when the original

---

* By this he meant Price.

guarantee of success had been withdrawn. The success of the Matabele and Makololo Missions had always hinged on there being a member of the Moffat family in each party. When he and Mrs Livingstone withdrew, the grounds on which the missions had been accepted by the London Missionary Society had been nullified. Livingstone admitted as much to his sister Agnes. 'I was sadly blamed for not bringing Mrs L. as all believe that the presence of one of Mr Moffat's family would secure them from attack by Mosilikatze.'[14]

To Janet he also admitted that the Makololo were 'naturally dissatisfied with their men being so long away'. This makes his scathing remarks about the missionaries even less pardonable. But this said, it must again be stressed that he was not directly responsible for the loss of life. He had told Tidman he would probably not be any help to the party, and yet this information was not passed on; both Price and Helmore believed that Livingstone would be at Linyanti to meet them. Tidman had also been warned several times by Moffat about the idiocy of sending the party before the tribe had removed, and yet he had weakly yielded to possible public disapprobation and had let the mission go on.

After the disaster Livingstone asked why no doctor had gone with them. In the first place, Tidman had thought the mission would have a doctor in the shape of Livingstone himself, but, after he had finally made his intentions clear, no second doctor was appointed. Maybe if Livingstone had given more time to the planning of a scheme he had forced into being, Tidman would have made sure a doctor was sent; but he still ought to have realized the necessity for one, even without any outside advice. Although Livingstone's letters to him had played down the severity of fever, the picture that emerged had still been alarming. As it was, the supplies provided for the missionaries were inadequate, as Mackenzie told the Directors in a letter written in October 1859 several months before the missionaries died. 'It was the opinion of Messrs Helmore, Price & myself that in the *supply of medicines* there was a deficiency.'[15]

So Livingstone, the Directors and the Makololo were all to blame in various ways, but Livingstone comes out of the affair worst of all. He unleashed all the fury of his own already frustrated hopes on to men and women who had given their lives in an attempt to bring Christianity to an area he had now given up. He knew that no mission in Barotseland could survive without river communication with the coast, and by 1860 he knew such communication was impossible, but when Price said all this in Cape Town, Livingstone did his best to discredit him with accusations of lying and cowardice. It was the old story: Livingstone had been wrong and could not bring himself to say so. Instead he argued that if better men were sent, they would succeed where Price and Helmore had failed. To prove his point he cited examples of success following over forty deaths in the west coast mission stations in Gabon. But a coastal mission was of course a completely misleading comparison.

His refusal to acknowledge the truth of a word Price was saying was nothing less than a calculated attempt to cover up for his own miscalculations about the Makololo. On his trip to Linyanti in 1860 he had found that the Makololo were dying out at an astounding rate and that Sekeletu had effectively lost his grip over his subject tribes. He did not mention this in any of his letters, but those written by his brother Charles, who was with him, put the matter beyond doubt. Charles told a friend:

> I have no doubt he [Sekeletu] treated the mission body badly ... I suspected at the time that he stole from Mr Price ... Mr Price was no doubt very much frightened, and they seeing this, took advantage and plundered him. I believe they would have treated us the same way had we been afraid of them ... There were not more than fifty men alive of the true Makololo; soon they will all be dead. I presume that the kingdom of Sebitoane is all in pieces now.[16]

Charles wrote this letter in 1862, and at that date the Makololo had three years left before their total extermination during an uprising of their Barotse vassals. What was obvious to Charles ought to have been obvious to his brother and should alone have stopped him vilifying Price and suggesting that other men ought to go to Linyanti to try again. Livingstone's readiness to believe that Europeans were more often at fault than Africans was often admirable, but on this occasion it cannot disguise one of the worst blots on his reputation. He had deliberately maligned innocent people for whose deaths he had been partially responsible, in order to escape the slur of having misrepresented the true situation in Barotseland. He never showed regret for this behaviour nor did he ever exhibit any trace of remorse for having maliciously maligned and slandered Roger Price, a man who had just suffered the horrifying personal tragedy of losing his wife and only child—a tiny baby. There are other blots on Livingstone's reputation, but because none would be greater than his response to the Makololo disaster, I have dealt at length with this previously neglected episode.

Now it is possible to return to 1857 and the culmination of Livingstone's negotiations with the British Government.

13

Her Majesty's Consul

———⟩◆⟨———

In this chapter I will try to explain how Livingstone, still a missionary in name if not in fact, became the leader of a government-sponsored expedition to Africa, and I will also attempt to show what he hoped to achieve in his new position. But before doing so it is essential to note the radically new direction Livingstone's thinking had taken since he had returned home at the end of 1856. Unfortunately for Livingstone's hopes, his new ideas were completely at variance with contemporary Government thinking on colonial affairs.

During his trans-continental journey, Livingstone's plans for south-central Africa had rested on a loosely thought-out voluntary scheme whereby European traders penetrated the area west of Portuguese Mozambique and began commercial operations there. The idea had been that these traders would 'cut out' the slave trader and undermine tribal organization, thus leaving individual Africans in a suitably confused frame of mind to listen to alien Christian teaching, which they would otherwise have rejected. Livingstone had never thought about the need for a coordinating central authority for these random international trading efforts. He had envisaged the work being done by the individual enterprise of numerous philanthropic businessmen with unlimited time and capital to invest. Nevertheless, by early 1856, while he was at Tete, Livingstone had started thinking more realistically. He had realized that the whole project depended on Portuguese willingness to allow the Zambesi to become an international waterway. The more he had thought about it, the more certain he became that there was little chance of the Portuguese giving permission without some firm prodding. In fact, he thought it might be necessary to boot the Portuguese out altogether. The booting would of course have to be done by the British Government. Since Portugal, spent force though she might be, was still Britain's 'oldest ally', there were clearly going to be diplomatic problems. But Livingstone talked the matter over with Sir Roderick Murchison, and having persuaded him that the Batoka Plateau could produce crops of cotton larger than the southern states of America, and having impressed upon him the enormous profits

that English businessmen could make if the Government led the way,
Livingstone suggested that Murchison should sound out Lord Clarendon
cautiously. Sir Roderick took the bull by the horns and in May 1857 wrote
a letter to the Foreign Secretary. Clarendon was told about the amazing
prospects that central Africa held out for every sort of commercial oper-
ator, and Murchison went on to restate the arguments about legitimate
commerce defeating the slave trade. Everything, Clarendon was informed,
depended on Britain's determination. Then Sir Roderick spelled it out:
'Either England and her ally Portugal may be made one for this great
object, or the latter country might readily part with her Colony of
Quilimane and Tete, etc., useless to her, but which in our hands might be
rendered a paradise of wealth.'[1]

Lord Clarendon, however, doubted whether Portugal would 'readily
part' with her 'useless' colony, and politely ignored the suggestion that he
should try a little persuasion. Meanwhile rebuffs did not stop Livingstone
developing his ideas.

> That you may have a clear idea of my objects [he told a friend], I may
> state that they have something more in them than meets the eye. They
> are not merely exploratory, for I go with the intention of benefitting the
> African and my own countrymen . . . All this ostensible machinery [the
> planned expedition and its members] has for its ostensible object the
> development of African trade and the promotion of civilization, but I
> hope it may result in an English colony in the healthy highlands of
> central Africa. (I have told it only to the Duke of Argyll) . . .[2]

Since Britain had plenty of overseas colonies by the middle of the nineteenth century, Livingstone's reticence about his colonial ambitions will
seem theatrical and absurd unless more is said about the attitudes of politicians and public to the British Empire at that time. The Empire
certainly existed, and had done for decades, but in general it had not come
into being as the result of any unified or planned government policy.
Britain's West Indian possessions owed their existence to the initial
efforts of individual British planters and slave traders. Australia, until the
1840s, had meant no more to Britain than a suitably remote location for
convict dumping. The North American colonies and Canada had been
started by the arrival of English emigrants who had left their homes to
escape religious discrimination and persecution in the seventeenth century.
The Cape Colony again demonstrates the random nature of the causes for
the Empire; it had been taken from the Dutch because of the tactical
advantage it offered Britain during the Napoleonic Wars. India had
become 'British' because the London-based East India Company had

started trading operations there in the seventeenth century, and had later successfully defeated Dutch and French rivals. In short, there had never been a deliberate policy of annexation by superior might with the object of increasing Britain's power and influence. Coaling bases here and there, the odd island like Mauritius, were taken to provide ports for the Royal Navy, but in 1856 no politician and few members of the public would have been prepared to express any feelings except horror towards those who advocated large colonial advances. The reasons for this were practical rather than moral.

Mid-Victorian Britain did not need wider possessions to increase her wealth or power. Since she had a wider share of world shipping than any other nation and could out-manufacture and out-export all potential rivals, free trade and a policy of colonial laissez-faire suited her interests better than any more overtly assertive policies. Livingstone had seen this in South Africa. In 1852 the British Government had given independence to the Boers north of the Vaal and Orange rivers, rather than embark on expensive and probably unremunerative advances.

But one other crucial consideration militated against Livingstone's hopes for a British colony, or colonies, in central Africa. His contemporaries, when they heard the words 'The British Empire', did not think of multi-racial subject nations bowing to a central imperial power. Their pride in Empire was not the late-Victorian love of prestige and power, but more a pride in the idea that British men and women had settled in distant and previously thinly populated parts of the world, and were there reproducing all that was best in the British way of life—a free press, trial by jury and government by representative institutions. Most of Livingstone's fellow-countrymen during the 1850s saw Empire as the link of common nationality that bound together, more by voluntary union than by power, a mother country and her white settled, and soon to be self-governing, colonies overseas. In this family, the West Indies and, above all, India were seen as strange anomalies simply because they, unlike for example Canada, Australia and New Zealand, had large 'native' populations and were not predominantly 'British' and white. The problems encountered in India, where a handful of whites were vastly outnumbered by the indigenous coloured population, had taught British governments to think twice before contemplating committing themselves to any new colonies where the whites could only ever be a minority. The Indian Mutiny would shortly appear to justify this caution. In fact, until Disraeli's long period in office in the 1870s, the British Empire and the Indian Empire were often spoken of as two separate entities. So in 1857 the prospects for new colonies were bad everywhere, but in a black continent like Africa they seemed hopeless.

'Imperialism' is often loosely used almost as a synonym for Victorian, but in fact its use as a laudatory description of indiscriminate colonial annexation did not gain general acceptance till the late 1870s and early 1880s; and by then Livingstone had been dead the best part of a decade. But though he did not live to see the European partition of Africa, Livingstone was one of imperialism's earliest prophets and advocates. From the mid-1850s he began writing about the British as a 'superior race' with a divine mission 'to elevate the more degraded portions of the human family'.[3] British businessmen, he averred, were 'the most upright and benevolent in the world',[4] and it was upon such men, he claimed, 'that the hopes of the world for liberty and freedom rest'.[5] The British colonist in Africa would elevate and civilize by his very presence. This idea of 'superior' moral values bringing the right to govern alien races would be a common imperial theme in the 1880s and 1890s, but in 1857 Livingstone was voicing ideas that even the morally fervent found embarrassing. Livingstone was not oblivious to the public mood or to the Government's attitude on these matters; for that reason he had not risked writing to Clarendon himself about ousting the Portuguese, but had got Murchison to do it for him. Livingstone knew that if he were to gain a Foreign Office appointment and Treasury money to support any new African venture, he would have to tread gingerly. He would certainly not be able to mention his colonial ambitions for the time being.

Past Livingstone biographers have usually accepted Livingstone's own assessment of his reasons for becoming a government employee. He claimed that the Directors of the London Missionary Society had attempted to confine missionary operations within too narrow limits and had therefore forced him to choose another employer. In fact the Directors, as has been recorded, had granted, reluctantly it is true, all that Livingstone asked. As representatives of a missionary society they could have done no more than give their permission for the inauguration of two new missions in south-central Africa. Yet Livingstone turned it all down. It is hard not to believe that once again his missionary disappointments with the Bakwains played an important part in his decision, and his letters to Murchison make it plain that the minimal salary paid to missionaries was another important consideration. But the principal reason was that his thinking had taken him so far from 'missionary work', even in the widest possible interpretation of the words, that a settled life with the Makololo no longer satisfied his new ambitions. Convinced, as he now was, that individual traders could not, unassisted, undermine tribal society, he wanted organized colonization to do this work, which he saw as an essential prelude to Christian success. If he settled with the Makololo, he would not be able to do much to hurry along such grandiose schemes. Colonists would only come if they and their sponsors were convinced that central Africa would prove profitable and relatively accessible. Livingstone would therefore have to prove that the area was commercially viable and that steamers could sail up the Zambesi without hindrance. When all this had been established, the British Government might then exert pressure on the Portuguese to make the Zambesi international, and they might eventually oust the Portuguese altogether.

Commercial prospects could only be assessed by means of expert judgements on the Batoka Plateau's real potential for growing sugar, wheat, coffee and cotton. The quality and quantity of the coal and iron-ore in western Mozambique would also have to be estimated. Livingstone would not be able to perform this work alone, so he would need an expedition, and that could not be mounted without government aid. The Government could not, however, be told of the ultimate end Livingstone had in view. Instead he represented his ostensible objects to Clarendon as a desire to promote international trade and to increase scientific and geographical knowledge—an understandable subterfuge, given the circumstances.

In May 1857, Sir Roderick had managed to persuade the Foreign Secretary to offer Livingstone employment as a British consul with a roving commission extending throughout Mozambique to the areas west of it. A salary of £500 per annum was agreed in the same month. No detailed plans had been made and Livingstone's demands to date had been cautious to the point of cowardice. He had not made any mention of an expedition with a steamer and other European members, but had confined his requests to two simple cotton gins, two or three iron ploughs and two small rollers for extracting the juice from sugar cane. Knowing his objects, it is hard to believe that he was being sincere in telling Clarendon that he wanted 'a small beginning with a view of making greater efforts as the prospects open out'.[6] Livingstone clearly had wanted to secure a definite offer of employment before stepping up his demands. Even later he preferred to gain concessions from Clarendon by the representation of third parties. For example, when he lectured before the British Association at Dublin that August, he gave his listeners such an alluring description of the commercial prospects of the Batoka Plateau, and represented the Zambesi as such an ideal waterway for shipping, that General Edward Sabine, soon to be the President of the Royal Society, asked him whether he would object to an official petition from the British Association to the Foreign Secretary on the subject of providing Dr Livingstone with a steamer for his next venture. Livingstone of course did not discourage him. Later he spoke to the Manchester Chamber of Commerce and so impressed the businessmen in his audience with the possibilities of African cotton, that they too decided to ask the Government to assist Dr Livingstone to the full. Clarendon inevitably took note of these men's opinions.

After the offer of employment in May 1857, no more official moves were made till the following October. This long gap can be explained partly by Clarendon's preoccupation with the Indian Mutiny and by Livingstone's commitment to the writing of his book *Missionary Travels*, which was not finished till October. Publication in a blaze of publicity may have stimulated government activity on Dr Livingstone's behalf at that time. At any rate in that month Clarendon began a correspondence with Livingstone and the British Ambassador in Lisbon over the role of the Portuguese in any future expedition. Livingstone could sense that the Foreign Secretary was worried by thoughts of possible diplomatic complications and wrote to him proposing a combined effort by Britain and Portugal 'to establish new stations on the higher portions of the Zambesi for the purpose of developing the rich revenues of the country'.[7] Of course he knew very well that such an overture would be rejected out of hand by Lisbon. The suggestion was aimed more at Clarendon than the Portuguese. Livingstone was eager to make his plans seem entirely innocent. Perhaps Clarendon was satisfied by this ploy, for on 11 December 1857 the Chancellor of the Exchequer announced to the House of Commons that the Treasury intended to vote £5,000 for Dr Livingstone 'to embark on a voyage of discovery upon the Zambesi'. The commercial prospects were made much of and almost every statement made by the Chancellor was greeted with cheers. The following day Livingstone attended a reception at 10 Downing Street, and was told by the Prime Minister, Lord Palmerston, that preparations for a full-scale expedition would be set in motion at once.

Neither Palmerston nor Clarendon hoped for a great deal from the expedition they had sanctioned. They did not want new colonies and they did not want any diplomatic wrangling with the Portuguese. But Livingstone was a national hero and they could only gain in popularity by supporting him: £5,000 was not a heavy price to pay. Besides, it was just possible that there might be some commercial advantages in it, even though the Portuguese themselves had never benefited much. With luck the expedition might make some new discoveries, and that would bring the Government a little reflected glory. Logically Clarendon could not really have refused Livingstone backing, since in 1856 he had contributed funds to assist two young army officers, Richard Burton and John Speke, to strike inland from Zanzibar to find a large lake rumoured by missionaries to lie hundreds of miles due west, in the interior. The two men would discover Lake Tanganyika in February 1858. Livingstone, by the way, would not learn about this achievement until several years later. In

1857 he did, however, know that Burton and Speke were in Africa and he was eager to get back to forestall them in case they started operations further south.

Clarendon's first move towards the creation of the Zambesi Expedition was a letter of instructions to Captain Washington, an influential Admiralty official, asking him to draw up plans. Washington lost no time in doing so and by the end of December there were two suggested schemes on the Foreign Secretary's desk. Both of these were for ambitious projects, not unlike the 1841 Niger Expedition that had involved a number of ships and two hundred men. This was not at all what Livingstone had in mind and he immediately rejected both plans on the grounds that such large parties would be unwieldy and unmanageable. A week later, on 7 January, he put forward his own more modest scheme, which Clarendon at once accepted. In the past it has generally been argued that Livingstone had never wanted to go to Africa with any sort of expedition, but had been swept into it against his will as a result of his popularity. This does not accord with the facts. Had he wished to go out alone rather than with an expedition, he would never have made deliberate attempts in his speeches in Dublin and Manchester to get his audiences to put pressure on Clarendon, nor, once the expedition was in being, would he have written telling a friend that he had set up everything primarily to encourage future colonization.[8] The fact that he was able within a week to tell Lord Clarendon how many people he wanted, and to name all but one of them, is hardly good supporting evidence for a claim that he was hustled into a scheme he had never really wanted.

The expedition Livingstone outlined was to consist of seven Europeans including himself, ten Africans, a paddle-steamer of shallow draught and an iron house in sections. Livingstone indicated what he wanted the six other Europeans to do in the way of agricultural and mineral experiments and in charting the Zambesi; these men were to include an economic botanist, a geologist and a naval officer. Since Clarendon had been told what Livingstone's ostensible aims were, Livingstone did not bother to repeat them in detail; instead he gave a brief itinerary, which would be accomplished, he hoped, within two years.

He intended to reach Tete as quickly as possible and then to proceed to the Kebrabasa Rapids 'to discover whether the launch would be able to steam up there when the river is high'. Having proved the Zambesi to be navigable, the next step would be to steam on upstream to the Batoka Plateau, erect the iron house as a centre for stores, and begin agricultural experiments aimed at proving that enough sugar and cotton could be grown to make the area a commercial proposition. Meanwhile some expedition members would go on to explore the upper reaches of the Zambesi.

This was a breathtakingly simple schedule of operations that impressed Clarendon by its cheapness. There was, however, one imponderable: Livingstone had never seen the rapids he hoped so confidently to ascend 'when the river is high'. Since the area below the rapids was notorious for malaria, the success of the expedition depended on getting beyond them to his much-vaunted Batoka Plateau. The steamer could clearly not be taken to pieces and carried without wheeled transport, pulleys and a large number of mules or oxen. When he had first visited Tete, Livingstone had made some enquiries about the rapids, but they had not been exhaustive. It was well known in Mozambique that the cataracts were impassable, for the Portuguese Minister of Marine and Colonies told the British Ambassador in Lisbon, towards the end of 1858, that African canoes always had to be carried overland at Kebrabasa.[9] But if Livingstone worried about the crucial gamble he was taking he did not show it. In any case the matter was now in the hands of Captain Washington, who had approved plans for a steamer before Livingstone had told him how many men he wanted. In spite of this the steamer was no liner: 75 feet in length and 8 feet in beam. She was built by the Macgregor Laird yard at Birkenhead in little over a month.

Once stores and equipment had been dealt with, there were only a few loose ends left. These, however, included the thorny matter of the attitude of the Portuguese to the expedition. Ministers in Lisbon had not been amused by transcriptions of Livingstone's English speeches. It was obviously vexing to read thousands of words about all the marvellous economic possibilities of their African colonies, which they had failed to realize because of addiction to the slave trade, official corruption and general ineptitude. The Portuguese Government was inevitably suspicious of a British Government-sponsored expedition that claimed only to be seeking new geographical and scientific information. They were not fools and foresaw that the commercial part of the expedition's programme would eventually lead to requests for the Zambesi to be opened to international shipping. That might even lead to other European nations staking territorial claims in Mozambique. So the Portuguese disliked the new expedition from the outset. They did not want foreigners poking about in their decaying colony, nor did they want to stir up the philanthropic British fervour that had destroyed their lucrative transatlantic slave trade. Nevertheless it would, they feared, be unwise to forbid the expedition altogether. Britain was a powerful nation. So the Portuguese accepted the inevitable and did their best to be gracious. But, while promising Livingstone all the help they could give him, the Government in Lisbon took steps to try and preclude later territorial claims. On 4 February a royal decree came from Lisbon, stating that: 'The name of Zambesia shall be given in all official documents to all the territories to which the Crown of Portugal has a right in the valley of the Zambezi from the mouth of that river to beyond the fortress of Zumbo.'[10]

This was rather better than might have been expected. After all, a western limit had been set to Portuguese territorial ambitions and the boundary was not beyond Zumbo,* which the Portuguese, as Livingstone knew, had once occupied. The Portuguese, however, followed up this moderate statement of their position with the outright refusal of a Foreign Office request. Clarendon had wanted Livingstone's consular appointment to be for the whole of Mozambique, including Sena and Tete. The Portuguese, however, would only give their *exequatur* for Livingstone for Quilimane—their reason being, they said, that Quilimane was open to foreign trade but that Sena and Tete were not.[11]

Livingstone wrote angrily to Clarendon, telling him that this must be challenged since it implied that the Portuguese had authority over the independent tribes along the river and the right to exclude international trade from the Zambesi. Clarendon remonstrated but was not prepared to make an issue out of the Portuguese attitude. In 1855, as the Foreign Secretary remembered well, Anglo-Portuguese relations had been severely strained and he did not wish to open old wounds. In that year the British Government had asked Portugal to act against all ships taking slaves to the French islands in the Indian Ocean, particularly to the island of Reunion. The Portuguese had responded by seizing a French ship, the *Charles et Georges*. The French Government had immediately despatched gunboats to Mozambique. The Portuguese had appealed to Britain, only to be told they must submit to the French demand, since the British Government was not prepared to go to war over such a small issue. It was his guilty conscience over this that led Clarendon not to press the Portuguese too hard about the freedom of the Zambesi and the precise extent of Dr Livingstone's consular authority. Livingstone felt that to leave matters like this was politically unwise but he could not persuade Clarendon to protest any further.

But the state of Anglo-Portuguese relations was only one problem which Livingstone faced in March 1858 as he prepared to sail for Africa. He himself had created more formidable difficulties. All these centred on his own exaggerated accounts of what might be expected from the regions he was going to. Sir Roderick Murchison, normally a calculating and

* Two hundred miles west of Tete.

sober individual, had spoken of the Batoka Plateau becoming 'a paradise of wealth'. Similar assurances had been made by Livingstone to businessmen up and down the country. He was already pledged to brush aside trivial obstacles that had held up the spineless Portuguese for three centuries. Naturally the public took note of these fair words. Livingstone had got his expedition together by painting glowing pictures of vast cotton fields and huge mineral resources. Now he was saddled with enormous public expectations. He had promised miracles and he would have to perform them if he wished to remain a national hero.

PART FOUR

REVERSAL

14

The Zambesi Expedition Sets Sail

The Zambesi Expedition set sail from Liverpool in the Colonial Office steamship *Pearl* on 10 March 1858. Flurries of snow stung the faces of the more intrepid members of the party who had stayed on deck to see the coast of England disappear from sight. Within an hour or so the ship was pitching violently and most of them were below, being sick. Among those afflicted in this way were Mrs Livingstone and her youngest son, six-year-old Oswell, who had been so named after William Cotton Oswell, Livingstone's former companion and benefactor. Already Livingstone had been heavily criticized for letting his wife and young son come out to face possible death from fever, but after her previous experiences of life alone in Britain, Mary Livingstone was ready to endure whatever the Zambesi might do to her. The other children had been left to the tender mercies of their devout grandparents and a succession of guardians. Livingstone had set aside £5,100 of his earnings from *Missionary Travels* to provide for them.[1]

By the time the ship was off West Africa and heading south for the Cape, everybody had stopped being sick except Mrs Livingstone. Livingstone soon knew why. Mary was pregnant again. This news stunned her husband, but not because it would grieve her so deeply to be left at the Cape in order to have the baby at Kuruman. Livingstone was more concerned with the inconvenience to himself. 'This is a great trial to me,' he confided to his journal, 'for had she come with us, she might have proved of essential service to the expedition in cases of sickness and otherwise.'[2] Another consideration worried Livingstone too: people would think him a fool for having got her pregnant at such an awkward time. So in most of his letters he referred to her condition as an 'illness'.

Several of Livingstone's colleagues guessed what was wrong with Mary and were not sorry that she would have to stay behind. Africa, they felt, was no place for a woman. One of these was Livingstone's second-in-command, Commander Norman Bedingfeld, R.N. Bedingfeld had impressed Livingstone when he had met him briefly in Loanda in 1854, but at that time Livingstone had not made enquiries about him. Later

Livingstone discovered that he had been twice court-martialled and once dismissed from his ship for 'contempt and quarrelsome conduct towards a superior officer'. When Captain Washington of the Admiralty warned Livingstone about Bedingfeld's record and advised him not to take him, Livingstone brushed this well-meant warning aside as a piece of interference.[3] He would regret it later.

Dr John Kirk, who at twenty-five was ten years younger than Bedingfeld and twenty years Livingstone's junior, was to be the only person to leave the expedition with an enhanced reputation. Kirk, a Scot, had done medical work in the Crimea and was an experienced botanist and a doctor of medicine. He had been recommended by the Director of Kew and two Edinburgh professors. Unlike all his colleagues, Kirk would prove consistently reliable and hardworking. He also had the good sense to confine his complaints to his journal. His official designation was economic botanist, although he was expected to help Livingstone with medical duties.

Richard Thornton, the geologist, was even younger than Kirk; in fact he was not yet twenty when the expedition sailed. Sir Roderick Murchison had described him as one of the most brilliant students ever to pass through the Royal College of Mines, but Livingstone would make little use of him. Thornton, like Bedingfeld and Thomas Baines, the artist and storekeeper, would be dismissed. Baines, with the exception of Livingstone, was the oldest member of the party. At thirty-eight he was an experienced man too. He had left England for South Africa as a young man and, after working in Cape Town for a while as an ornamental sign-painter, he had been employed by the army as an official war artist during the 1850–3 Kaffir War. From 1855 to 1857 he went, again as an official artist, on a government-sponsored expedition to northern Australia. His work had been highly praised and in 1857 he was made a Fellow of the Royal Geographical Society. He was easygoing, modest, and willing to work hard when the occasion demanded it. But, although all the others liked him, he would fall foul of Livingstone.

George Rae, the engineer, like Kirk managed to stay the course. Perhaps it helped that he had been born at Blantyre like Livingstone. He was to prove competent at his job, and the dourness which most of his colleagues disliked did not distress Livingstone, who hated idle social chatter. Rae shared another characteristic with Livingstone: he took to heart gossip that reflected badly on colleagues and tended to use it to his own advantage.

Livingstone's most startling appointment had been his choice of his younger brother Charles. David Livingstone had not seen him since 1840, when Charles had sailed for America to get an education there. Quite by chance, Charles had returned, as he thought for a brief trip to England in

1857 and had been offered a job as the Zambesi Expedition's 'moral agent'. This post had been created for him by Livingstone, who wanted him mainly as a personal assistant to support him in any troubles that might erupt with other members of the party. Charles's qualification to be a 'moral agent'—Livingstone never described what the job involved—was his theological education at Oberlin College, Ohio, and his subsequent ordination as a nonconformist minister. Livingstone justified his appointment to the Foreign Office on the grounds that Charles knew about the relatively new pursuit of photography and also claimed that life in America had taught him all about cotton. In fact he knew little about either. Nevertheless he had roughed it in America and had worked hard to pay for his education. Livingstone's letters to Charles before 1857 had been almost paternal, and he had helped his younger brother with money from time to time. Nothing in their past relationship gave any hint of the ascendancy which Charles was soon to establish over his older brother with such distressing consequences. Livingstone ought, however, to have known that since Charles had married only a few years before and had three children aged five, four and one, he might have personal problems to face which would make him a difficult companion. Later Charles would write miserable letters to his wife, begging her to write more about the children, and repeatedly asking for more photographs of them all.[4] Livingstone's later reliance on Charles would be due to his own inability to lead Europeans.

Livingstone himself would in many ways prove to be the weakest link in the party. Needless to say, his weakness would not be physical. He would simply prove a disastrous leader. Had the British Government thought about it, a man who had just passed four years entirely without European company was hardly an ideal person to lead, live and work with six other men in claustrophobic proximity. No previous experience had prepared him for it. The nearest he had been to living and cooperating with a fellow-countryman in the past had been during his time with Edwards at Mabotsa. That was hardly an encouraging precedent. With the exception of his wife and family, whom he had seen little enough of, Livingstone had done his best to avoid Europeans when there was any chance of doing so. His success with William Cotton Oswell was due to Oswell's exceptional tolerance and his ability, as he put it, to 'agree to differ'. Agreeing to differ would not be enough to keep together an expedition where success would depend on agreement and close cooperation. Livingstone's iron will and incredible powers of endurance were paradoxically to prove counter-productive, since they set him apart; a leader needs to be able to identify with his men and share their experience. Livingstone underestimated his own uniqueness and expected the same physical and mental dedication from the others. He had always been limitlessly patient with Africans but had never missed an opportunity to condemn weakness or stupidity in Europeans.

His years alone had made him self-sufficient and disinclined to talk unless he had something specific to say. To men unused to his long silences, they seemed to indicate aloofness and a lack of warmth. He had not lost the 'rusticity' of manner that his tutor Richard Cecil had noticed twenty years before, and while this had not mattered during his previous journeys, it was to be a severe handicap now. He could not make jokes when things went wrong or encourage his party by showing that he appreciated what they were doing, nor could he laugh at himself. The wit so often displayed in his letters and journal was confined to paper and formed a contrast with his brusque and inarticulate manner of speaking. He felt criticism more keenly than most men and knew that as leader he was more exposed to it than anybody else, and this added to his self-consciousness. His moods seemed unpredictable, since he would often keep a grievance to himself for weeks and then blurt it out when the others had forgotten the circumstances. The same attributes that had made him successful as a lone traveller were often those that made him a failure when journeying with others. He had always hated any kind of restriction and had never been constrained on his epic journey; he had rested when he decreed and set out when he was ready. Now there would be countless checks and delays: the steamer had to get steam up; the others had to pack up their gear and finish what they were doing; and for any smoothness of operation each member had to know what the others were up to. Tragically, Livingstone believed that men worked best when left mostly to themselves. This policy was laudable in many ways but inevitably led to confusion and misunderstanding when time was limited and aims changing. Perhaps his most crucial mistake was not to realize that since the leader would get most of the credit if the expedition was a success, he could not expect his men to push themselves to the limits of their endurance as he pushed himself. Of course if the expedition failed he would be blamed and get no credit for having exerted himself more than everybody else.

Five days out from Liverpool the whole party was assembled to hear Livingstone read out the Foreign Office Instructions to the Expedition. Livingstone had drafted them himself and they certainly did not read like most government documents of the day. Full of exhortations to the party to use their 'moral influence' on the Africans to show them how 'a superior race' behaved, the instructions stressed the importance of 'a well regulated and orderly household of Europeans setting an example of consistent moral conduct'.[5] The terrible arguments and squabbles that soon broke out would make every word ring with irony. Having outlined the scientific and geographical aspects of the work ahead—he kept his colonial ambitions to himself—Livingstone went on to advocate a deliberate policy of paying Africans for any work done, thus helping to break down the chiefs' expectations of free labour from their people.[6] Thus individual Africans might learn to see their prospects as individual rather than collective. With his usual habit for wanting the best of both worlds, Livingstone told his colleagues that they should not pay for gifts of food since it would be 'impolitic to allow the ancient custom of feeding strangers to go into disuse'.

On a more personal note, Livingstone turned to personal hygiene and admonished his companions to defecate with faultless regularity. Constipation, he warned them, should be avoided, if necessary by regular use of laxatives. Livingstone's own bowel problems, the result of numerous attacks of dysentery on his trans-continental journey, made him almost obsessive on the subject. His companions would notice that the state of his bowels affected his moods considerably. Livingstone ended by warning everybody that he had powers of instant dismissal and could change the aims of the expedition if he thought it expedient. Each individual member of the party was issued with personal instructions about his duties, and these were often very precise. Kirk's duties covered seventeen densely written paragraphs and contained a vast number of matters to be attended to in the fields of botany and zoology.

As the *Pearl* steamed south, Livingstone had no inkling of what lay ahead. He was pleased with his colleagues and wrote telling a friend that all 'seem to me to be of the right stamp'.[7] This was still his view when they sailed into Table Bay on 21 April.

While it was gratifying to Livingstone to find many of those who had once laughed at him for his uncouthness and poverty falling over themselves to be agreeable, his meeting with Robert Moffat, then in Cape Town waiting for the Makololo missionaries, was far from happy. Moffat was angry that Livingstone was not going with the new missionaries and felt that he had deceived the London Missionary Society. Worse than that, Livingstone, during his time in England, had persuaded Moffat's son John to leave the Society and set up as an independent missionary. To get him to do so, Livingstone had promised him a salary and a lump sum of £500. John had accepted. Moffat felt that John had also betrayed the Society, and taken the education and training they had given him only to ditch them when he reached maturity. Then there was the general sadness about Mary Livingstone. When she watched the *Pearl* sail from Cape Town, it would be four more years before she saw her husband again. Ahead of her lay a year in Kuruman and nearly three in Scotland with her disagreeable in-laws.

The *Pearl* sailed for the mouth of the Zambesi on 1 May 1858.

15

The Rocks in God's Highway
1858

On 14 May the *Pearl* anchored off the maze of sandbanks and arid mudflats that formed the mouth of the Zambesi. The night before, there had been a storm which had come at a very bad time for Livingstone: during a severe attack of dysentery. 'Nothing can exceed the discomfort and pain', he wrote in his journal, 'when one is obliged to hold on with all his might to prevent being pitched off the closet.'[1] It was a bad beginning.

Most of the party were surprised to see a far from inviting coastline: monotonous mudflats and mangrove swamps stretched as far as the eye could see, and the river mouths were obstructed by dangerous sandbars, pounded by heavy surf and tall breakers. Livingstone believed there were four channels but all the charts were inaccurate and there were no local pilots to offer advice. During the next two weeks two separate attempts were made to enter the Zambesi proper, and both failed. Tempers became frayed and the Kongone mouth, discovered at the end of the first week of June, was found only just in time to prevent serious quarrelling.

Livingstone's plan was to get everybody up to Tete in one trip in the *Pearl*. This would mean that the party would not need to split up and it would also cut out dozens of separate journeys in the expedition's small steamer in order to get stores upriver. From Tete, Livingstone proposed to sail on in the smaller vessel, past the Kebrabasa Rapids to the Batoka Plateau, where the agricultural experiments were to begin. For a short time all went according to plan. The metal parts of the steamer were soon taken off the *Pearl* and bolted together by George Rae, the engineer. Livingstone called the vessel the *Ma-Robert*, because that had been the Makololo's name for Mrs Livingstone, and literally meant 'mother of Robert'. Robert was the name of Mary's eldest son.

Within a week, navigation had become slow and hazardous and by 16 June it was clear to everybody that the *Pearl*, a steamer 160 feet long, was not going to be able to go further. Livingstone's much-vaunted river was shallow with channels that shifted from month to month. The *Pearl* had been loaned to the expedition by the Colonial Office and therefore no risk could be taken with her. The river was falling and if she went further she

0   miles   100

0   km   100

Lake Nyassa

KOTA KOTA

Lake Malombe

*Kebrabasa
Rapids*

Lake Shirwa

*Murchison
Cataracts*

MAGOMERO

TETE

Shire

Ruo

Z a m b e s i

SENA

▲ *Mount Morambala*

QUILIMANE

SHUPANGA

*Expedition
Island*

East Luabo

Kongone

West Luabo

Indian Ocean

ROUTES TO SESHEKE
AND THE ROVUMA

Rovuma

*Lake
Nyassa*

Johanna I.

MOZAMBIQUE

SESKEKE

Zambesi

Victoria Falls

QUILIMANE

*Indian
Ocean*

might be stuck for six months or more. The blow was stunning to Livingstone's hopes of getting the party through the malarial lower reaches of the river quickly. He did not confess to anybody how completely he had depended on this quick beginning. Now the iron house for stores would have to be set up barely fifty miles from the sea and all the stores brought up to Tete in the small *Ma-Robert*; the job, Livingstone knew, could take months, during which time no scientific work could be done. In the meantime morale and health would suffer.

The conditions faced by the party during the first few months of the expedition were entirely new to most of them and far worse than anything they had expected. All had read *Missionary Travels*, and because Livingstone had omitted almost every unpleasant feature of African travel, they had come out expecting adventure, even danger, but certainly not the continual debilitating hardships they were soon enduring. After the departure of the *Pearl*, the *Ma-Robert* was always overcrowded due to the greatly increased quantity of stores she had to carry. Consequently everybody was squeezed into close proximity, at a time when many were experiencing fever for the first time. The temperature was usually more than 100°F and the only place to escape the sun was the tiny cabin of the steamer, which, although in the shade, still heated up like an oven. Tropical rain was almost as bad as the sun, and in severe storms water would pour through the decking of the *Ma-Robert*, soaking men, stores and food. Because the river itself was much shallower than expected, and the steamer considerably overloaded, the vessel was perpetually grounding on sandbanks. Hours of almost every day were spent dragging the boat along with ropes and winches: back-breaking work under the blazing sun. Mosquitoes, ticks, tropical ulcers and an unfamiliar diet were other causes for irritation and distress. If serious arguments had not broken out it would have been a miracle.

Barely two months after entering the Zambesi, Livingstone faced the first real test of his leadership. The *Pearl* had to go, there was no doubt about that, but immediately before this decision was made, certain incidents produced an ugly situation. Commander Bedingfeld justly felt that, in view of his instructions, he had overall command of navigation and he believed that this also made him responsible for the *Pearl*. The master of the *Pearl*, a mere officer in the Merchant Navy, Captain Duncan, had challenged Bedingfeld's authority and had ignored his piloting instructions. Eventually a violent row broke out between Bedingfeld and Duncan, with both men shouting at each other in front of Livingstone. Livingstone did the worst thing he could have done: he took sides. Livingstone's lower-class origins made him more sympathetic to Duncan, a man with a similar background. Bedingfeld sensed this and became more rather than less arrogant. The upshot was that Livingstone rebuked Bedingfeld in front of everybody.[2] The same evening the enraged naval officer wrote Livingstone an angry letter of complaint. Bedingfeld suggested that Livingstone's public rebuke had undermined his standing with the other members of the expedition and pointed out that private consultation was the normal procedure adopted by senior officers when differences arose. The letter went further: 'I trust', Bedingfeld told Livingstone, 'if your confidence in me is shaken, as it appears to be, you will allow me to return to England as soon as it can be done without inconvenience to the Public Service.'[3]

Livingstone's first reaction was that he should take this as a resignation and send Bedingfeld back to England as soon as possible. But he decided against this since he knew that without Bedingfeld he would have to navigate the river himself. Later he made a virtue out of this forbearance. The truce did not last long. Earlier Livingstone had promised, without a word to Bedingfeld, that the *Ma-Robert* would pilot the departing *Pearl* out of the river. When Duncan came to see Bedingfeld and told him this, the naval officer was bitterly angry that he had not previously been warned. He had made plans for painting the *Ma-Robert*'s rivet heads and for doing a number of minor repairs to fit out the vessel for the series of journeys to Tete which she would soon be making, carrying heavy loads. Since the expedition at the time had a naval pinnace, Bedingfeld argued that this could be used to pilot Duncan to the mouth. When Duncan heard these arguments he simply told Bedingfeld that he should do what Dr Livingstone said. Again shouting began, and again Livingstone had to intervene. Ironically Livingstone did not want to have to keep his rash promise, but he was prepared to do anything rather than admit that Bedingfeld had been right.

Bedingfeld wrote to Livingstone with all his arguments against the *Ma-Robert*'s intended journey, only to hear from his leader that Duncan had decided to go down with the pinnace after all. Had Livingstone acknowledged that he ought to have told Bedingfeld his plans in advance, and had he decided to have a quiet chat with him, everything could have been patched up, for a time at least. But Livingstone's next letter to his naval officer was the last straw. Knowing Livingstone's gift for sarcasm, it seems quite impossible that he did not intend to annoy Bedingfeld with the gratuitous addition of some personal advice, offered by way of a parting shot.

A pretty extensive acquaintance with African Expeditions enables me to offer a hint which, if you take it in the same frank and friendly spirit in which it is offered, you will on some future day thank me and smile at the puerilities which now afflict you. With the change of climate there is often a peculiar condition of the bowels which makes the individual imagine all manner of things in others. Now I earnestly and most respectfully recommend you try a little aperient medicine occasionally and you will find it much more soothing than writing official letters.[4]

Bedingfeld described this letter as 'the most insulting I ever received' and suggested it would have 'been better addressed to a child'. He wrote back telling Livingstone once again that he would 'gladly return to England', as soon as Livingstone could replace him. 'In the meantime,' he added, 'I will do my best to carry out your wishes as far as I know them.' Bedingfeld, like most officers in the services at that time, was a snob and, as he told Livingstone, he had never been so hurt as when the opinions of Duncan, 'who was behind a counter and a steward's boy, long after I obtained my first commission', had been preferred to his own.[5] Livingstone could only have been wilfully blind not to recognize these feelings. Bedingfeld had just abandoned the command of a large warship with several hundred men under him to take up the command of a tiny vessel like the *Ma-Robert*, and Livingstone had not even consulted him about what that vessel ought and ought not to do. Livingstone appeared almost deliberately to have made Bedingfeld's position untenable. He might, however, have delayed dismissing the man if the *Ma-Robert* had performed as expected during the next few weeks.

It was soon apparent that the *Ma-Robert* was a very dubious vessel. Her consumption of wood was outrageous, being several tons a day, and, to make matters worse, steam could only be raised satisfactorily on very hard woods like ebony and *lignum vitae*, both of which took a long time to chop up. Fuel was sometimes consumed at such a rate that a day and a half's wood cutting would not be enough to keep the boilers going for one day's steaming. There were other faults too: the ship's feed pipes often became choked and the cylinders and boilers were always giving trouble. Livingstone was soon describing the *Ma-Robert* as 'a wretched sham vessel' with an engine 'evidently made to grind coffee in a shop window'.[6] Mr Laird the builder had of course had no idea that his steamer would have to carry loads in excess of ten tons several hundred miles up a shallow river against the current, but that did not stop Livingstone accusing him of greed, deceit and incompetence.[7] Laird had used a new kind of steel in thin sheets to build the hull of the steamship, and here all Livingstone's criticisms were sound, for this steel sheeting had not been properly tested and soon started to rust through in a honeycomb of holes that had to be plugged with clay. In short, the *Ma-Robert* was a disaster. But Livingstone did not only blame the builder; he blamed Bedingfeld too, for he had been the only member of the expedition present at the vessel's trials. Livingstone accused Bedingfeld of having been duped by Laird into believing that steam raised on coal had actually been raised on wood. Bedingfeld retorted that he had seen wood put in with his own eyes. Bedingfeld did not make Livingstone's temper any sweeter by suggesting that he ought to have insisted that the engineer go on the trials too. The row over the *Ma-Robert* finally made Livingstone decide to get rid of his naval officer.

There was a problem, however. Bedingfeld had not resigned; he had merely said that he would continue serving until replaced. The onus was therefore on Livingstone to dismiss him. This he did not wish to do in case there was a full Admiralty investigation. He got round this difficulty by claiming that Bedingfeld's letter of a month before—it was now late July—had been the equivalent of a resignation. Bedingfeld, when he learned what Livingstone intended doing, went round the other members of the expedition asking them to let him have written confirmation of the fact that he had offered to serve until replaced. Only Thomas Baines obliged him and for that perfectly honest service Baines became the next object of Livingstone's hatred.[8] Meanwhile Livingstone obliged Bedingfeld to proceed overland to Quilimane to await a passage on the next ship that called.

It is undeniable that Livingstone's treatment of Bedingfeld was colossally inept. But few members of the party were sad to see him go. Kirk usually summed things up correctly, and his opinion goes some way towards justifying Livingstone's apparently irrational behaviour. Bedingfeld, wrote Kirk, 'seems to have expected to live the life of a Man of War Commander and no idea of being a subordinate. He also feels that he has done nothing but act sailing master of the launch; but I do not see much desire for scientific observations and of surveying. He has no more knowledge than any other one with a little common sense.'[9] Yet Kirk's words also point up a lack of foresight in Livingstone's planning of the expedition. Bedingfeld never really did have any role except acting as 'sailing master of the launch'. Once, Livingstone had imagined him making charts of the river, but since it had been discovered that shifting sandbanks altered all the channels dozens of times within a single year, such charts would have been useless. It should be added that Bedingfeld went on to become an Admiral, retiring at his own request in 1877; so he could not have been the idiot Livingstone claimed he was. The Bedingfeld affair did great harm to the morale of the party at a time when unity would have helped them surmount a series of initial disappointments.

Throughout July, August and September the *Ma-Robert* chugged up and down the Zambesi in a painfully slow series of five separate trips to drop off supplies upstream at Shupanga, Sena and Tete. Only in November had all the supplies been removed from the temporary base near the river mouth. It was six months after the *Pearl* had first anchored off the Zambesi before the whole party were reunited at Tete. By then morale was low and early eagerness had gone for good. Most members of the expedition felt that Livingstone had deliberately deceived the Government about the Zambesi. Miles below Tete they had spent days aground on sandbanks while all of them sweated with winches and cables to get the *Ma-Robert* off. Sometimes 150 miles from the sea the river had been less than two feet in depth at its deepest point. The *Ma-Robert* drew three feet. Livingstone had often driven his companions into a frenzy with the contradictory instructions he gave them for refloating the vessel; in fact 'the Doctor', as Kirk put it, was 'nothing more than a landsman out of his element'.[10] Three days aground was not uncommon, nor was it unusual for the vessel to have to be dragged two hundred yards across mud and sand. To add to the miseries of the party, many of them were suffering from malaria for the first time. As usual Livingstone was distant and unsympathetic. In his despatches he described delirium, giddiness and vomiting as an illness no worse than the common cold. In view of his problems with Bedingfeld, the *Ma-Robert* and the Zambesi, he had not felt inclined to worry about 'trivial' ailments.

In Tete, during the first week of November 1858, there was one thought which above all others occupied Livingstone's mind: the 'small rapid' he had missed on his way to the coast in 1856. All Livingstone's plans, both immediate and distant, depended on the steamer being able to sail past the Kebrabasa Rapids on to the Batoka Plateau. In the short term, if the *Ma-Robert* failed to get through, the basic aim of the expedition to examine the agricultural and mineral potential of the plateau would be vitiated. But, worse than that, all plans for traders to reach the Makololo and the new missions from the coast would have to be abandoned. That in turn would rule out his long-term dream of the Batoka Plateau becoming a British colony. Quite apart from these terrifying possibilities, the effect on Livingstone's reputation, should the rapids prove impassable, would be disastrous. All his optimistic forecasts for south-central Africa had hinged on his claim that the Zambesi would be navigable as far as the Batoka Plateau. During their first few days at Tete, Kirk noticed his leader's preoccupied state and was worried to hear Livingstone talking about blasting a way through if need be.[11] None of the party knew much about explosives, and Kirk found it strange that, although Livingstone had made light of the rapids in England, he now spoke about the possibility of getting army sappers sent out.

In spite of his troubles, Livingstone could at least enjoy his reunion with the Makololo whom he had left at Tete in 1856. They were genuinely delighted to see him and showed no irritation that he had returned a year later than he had promised. Yet even this reunion brought Livingstone new heartache. The Makololo seemed to enjoy living with the decadent Portuguese, and some of them even suggested that they did not want to go back to Sekeletu.

On 8 November Livingstone, Kirk and Rae set out for Kebrabasa in the *Ma-Robert*, leaving Charles, Thornton and Baines in Tete recuperating from fever. After a day and a half's steaming, the Zambesi began to narrow rapidly until it was soon only thirty yards across. The current soon became much faster and the *Ma-Robert's* progress against it was reduced to a crawl. On each side of the stream, sheer black rocks rose up to form cliffs several hundred feet high. The steamer managed to pass the first small rapid she came to, but at the second, the force of the current swung her bows round on to a rock, holing her above the water line. It was a depressingly bad start.

The next day Livingstone and Kirk set off on foot over rough, rocky country to see what happened further upstream. By mid-afternoon they came to a point where the river split into several channels and the two men separated to examine a channel each. A little later Kirk was looking down at the water pouring over a ledge 'at a considerable angle and becoming a mass of broken water at the bottom'.[12] Livingstone's cataract was as bad, with a fall of eight feet within twenty yards. Towards evening they came to two more rapids which were rather worse. Kirk's view was that when the river was in flood, the speed of the current would be so great, and the pull of the eddies so strong that no steamer could hope to pass up or down in any safety. Livingstone disagreed. 'I believe', he wrote in his journal, 'when the water rises about six feet, the cascades may be safely passed. If not, then at flood, when the water is spread over all the dell.'[13] Livingstone's optimism rested on the assumption that the river would rise enough after the rains to burst its rocky banks and thus reduce the speed of the current. Kirk's opinion, which would prove correct, was that the banks were quite steep and high enough to contain an enormous amount more water; enough perhaps to rule out flooding altogether. That being the case, the water would come down at a speed too great for any steamer to combat. With so much depending on getting past these obstacles, Livingstone would not yet admit defeat. Already he began thinking up excuses to use at a later date. One useful one that came to mind was the power of the *Ma-Robert*. He would argue that a more powerful vessel could do what Mr Laird's 'sham vessel' could not. Since locals said that there were other rapids many miles further on, Livingstone decided to return to Tete again to collect the other members of the party, before coming back to Kebrabasa for a thorough survey. On 13 November, five days after setting out, the *Ma-Robert* dropped anchor off Tete.

No sooner was he back than Livingstone began making feverish enquiries about Kebrabasa, and the answers he got soon established that his efforts in 1856 to get hard information about the rapids had been far from exhaustive. One man arrived saying that he had seen the rapids beyond the minor falls Livingstone had just examined. This Portuguese trader, José St Anna, confirmed Kirk's view that Kebrabasa was far worse when the Zambesi was in flood. Africans, he said, tried to get down from time to time in canoes, and never lived to tell the tale. Even an empty canoe had failed to make it, being smashed to matchwood after a few miles. Livingstone did not say a word about his fears to anybody, but confessed in his journal: 'Things look dark for our enterprise. This Kebrabasa is what I never expected. No hint of its nature ever reached my ears.'[14] He also began looking for ways to justify his earlier optimism. The thought that he had gained such popularity because of exaggerated claims tortured him, and he now tried to delude himself and others into believing that he had written his book and given his lectures against his will. 'The honours heaped upon me were not of my own seeking,' he wrote hopelessly. 'They came unbidden.'[15] Recently he had heard from Thomas Maclear, at the Cape, that Bedingfeld was doing his best to blacken his name. Livingstone did not have to rack his brains to see what men like Bedingfeld could do with a piece of ammunition as damning as failure to pass the rapids. Livingstone therefore tried to prepare himself for future criticism. 'I expected snarling after I was gone,' he told his brother-in-law, John Moffat; 'I did not seek their praise, nor do I much care for their frowns. All came unsought. I have had abuse before.'[16] And when he had had abuse he had overreacted like a wounded child.

Before the end of November the whole party left Tete for a thorough survey of the rapids, and although Thornton and Baines were still ill, they too were forced to come. Clambering over large boulders was not ideal treatment to mete out to convalescents and soon the sick men were holding up the party. Charles Livingstone was the main offender. According to Kirk, 'more than half the time is occupied allowing Mr L. to have a little snooze every half hour'.[17] While Livingstone criticized Baines and Thornton, he ignored the constant delays caused by his brother. It was the beginning of a favouritism that was to shatter the last remnants of the expedition's unity. Baines became Livingstone's whipping-boy for every failure and soon Livingstone was claiming that he had failed to issue the Makololo with proper rations. In fact he himself had given Baines no instructions on the matter, but Livingstone was not swayed by such facts. Baines, he felt, had betrayed him in giving Bedingfeld written confirmation of his agreement to serve till replaced. Kirk was angry that Baines was being picked on, especially since Baines was so much harder-working than Charles Livingstone.

Soon the going was so hard that Charles and Thornton had to stay behind. The banks of the river were formed from a mass of rocks and boulders heaped one on top of the other in a crazy jumble of stone. Some boulders were thirty feet high and all were smooth and covered with a black glaze that made them slippery. The sun was so hot—Livingstone's thermometer gave readings up to 130°F—that if anybody left his hand on a rock for more than a few seconds, the skin was badly burned. This of course made climbing even more hazardous. On 30 November the Makololo, who were acting as porters, refused to go on. Their feet were a mass of burns and blisters. Yet, incredibly, after some hours of arguing, Livingstone managed to persuade them to make one last effort.

They had now travelled for four days without seeing any worse rapids than Livingstone and Kirk had encountered on their first visit, and every hour Livingstone's hopes began to rise. It *might* be possible to get rid of the rocks he had seen already by blasting. A powerful steamer *might* then be able to get through. Before long Livingstone decided that the worst rapids had already been passed and that they might as well return to the steamer. Everybody with him was thankful for the decision. His spirits were much higher than they had been for weeks.

They had been clambering homewards for a couple of hours when one of the Makololo casually mentioned that he had heard something from some locals near the place where they turned back. Livingstone said that any detail was interesting, and so in a matter-of-fact way the man told him that some miles further upstream there was supposed to be a fearful waterfall as high as a tree and so dangerous that anybody, even a man 'perishing with thirst . . . would retire in fear from it'.[18]

Livingstone listened in stunned silence, furious that at the very time when his spirits were rising, this man had known something that would destroy all his hopes with a few words. After yelling at the offending Makololo for having kept such crucial information to himself, he rounded on the rest of the party. They could all stay where they were, he did not care what they did, but he would go on alone to finish the job. Now that defeat seemed a foregone conclusion, Livingstone found the sight and company of his companions unendurable. They would complain about fever and the heat and the rough going while what was really at stake was the future of south-central Africa. After a pause Kirk said that he was quite able to go on, and asked Livingstone whether he could reasonably expect everybody to sit idly 'smoking their pipes' while their leader went 'off alone on difficult service'.[19] Livingstone took Kirk's point and agreed to accept him if he volunteered. Kirk did so at once.

During the next couple of days the two men experienced worse conditions than ever and Livingstone described keeping going as 'the hardest work he had ever had in his whole life'. The boulders were just as bad, and in addition they were soon coping with thick scrub. Then the hills got higher, and in order to proceed a quarter of a mile, they often had to cross valleys with a drop of several thousand feet in the middle. On 2 December they reached two more rapids, but these were clearly not what they had set out to find. Later that day, after clambering up an almost perpendicular cliff, the two men were rewarded with a sight that made Livingstone's blood run cold. Below them was a waterfall thirty feet high with the water thundering over it at less than 30°. Kirk concluded that even to think of getting past such an obstruction was lunacy. For a while Livingstone was unable to say anything, but then to Kirk's amazement he suggested that if the water rose eighty feet after the rains, even this waterfall might not prove an insuperable barrier. But Livingstone must have known in his heart that such claims were futile. He did not admit as much publicly for a very good reason: if he did, the news would get back to England and thence to the Foreign Office. The Foreign Secretary might then feel impelled to consider whether it was right for an expedition to continue when its ostensible aims had become impracticable. It was for this reason that Livingstone wrote to the new Foreign Secretary, Lord Malmesbury, on 17 December, telling him: 'We are all of the opinion that a steamer of light draught would pass the rapids without difficulty when the river is in full flood.'[20] When Kirk saw this despatch he could not believe his eyes. Since Livingstone knew that within a year or so the already rusting *Ma-Robert* would be finished, he decided that it would be an ideal time to ask the Foreign Office for a replacement. Thus he would be able to persuade them with his criticisms of the *Ma-Robert* that only his 'tin kettle of a steamer' had prevented the party reaching the Batoka Plateau as planned. Of course he did not tell Lord Malmesbury that when the new steamer came, whatever else he might use it for, it would not be to get past Kebrabasa. Now Livingstone knew he would have to play for time in the hope of making face-saving and prestigious new discoveries before eventually being forced to admit to a crushing initial failure. Just to make sure that those in touch with the Foreign Secretary would back up his version of events, Livingstone wrote them confident letters. In one to Maclear he said: 'I have not the smallest doubt but a steamer of good power could pass up easily in flood.'[21] In the long term, however, these optimistic lies were not going to solve anything. If Livingstone hoped to justify his request for a new steamer at some future date, he would have to prove that there was work for the steamer to do. In fact Livingstone had made up his mind before getting back to Tete that from now on his energies must be devoted to a different area altogether. The Zambesi and the Batoka Plateau were to be deserted for another river: the Shire.

The Shire flowed into the Zambesi from the north at a point roughly one hundred miles from the coast. Livingstone was not sure that it was navigable, but he knew that if it was not, he might as well cancel the order for the new steamer and disband the expedition. The Shire offered the only possible alternative open to him. The whole venture was a gamble but Livingstone was comforted by the memory of what he had been told in 1856 by a Tete trader, Candido José da Costa Cardoso. Candido claimed that the Shire was fed by a vast lake which could be reached directly from Tete in forty-five days' march. At the time Livingstone had been sufficiently impressed to draw a map based on Candido's information.[22] Livingstone now decided that he would not take the overland route from Tete but would try, if he could, to reach the lake via the river Shire. If the lake really was a large one he would be able to keep quiet about Candido's previous discovery and claim it for the expedition and himself. A major geographical find would do a lot to make up for Kebrabasa.

Of course Livingstone's new decision to abandon the upper Zambesi was a volte-face more extreme than any he had contrived in the past. By turning to the Shire he was abandoning the Makololo, abandoning the Batoka Plateau and abandoning God's Highway: the Zambesi itself. The new direction he was taking was tantamount to an admission that all but the very last part of his trans-continental journey and his previous trip to Linyanti had been fruitless. He was now preparing to devote himself to an area which was at no point further than four hundred miles from the east coast.

Many men would have been unable to adjust to such a sudden and fundamental change, but Livingstone was made of sterner stuff. If everything he had said and done in the past seemed to be contradicted by the plans he had now started to lay, he would still go on. But he would do much more than that; Livingstone would even manage to persuade himself that the hundreds of thousands of tons of rock, blocking the river he had once thought the answer to every African problem, had been placed there by God for an excellent reason. God had obviously intended him to turn his attention to the areas from which the Shire flowed. God's plan had evidently never included the Makololo, or the Batoka Plateau, or the Zambesi. There was, however, an alternative theory to explain the existence of Kebrabasa: that God had rejected the services of his chosen instrument, David Livingstone. Not unnaturally Livingstone preferred the other interpretation. He sustained himself with the thought that although a lot had changed, he might well be able to find a new area just as suitable for a British colony as the Batoka Plateau. There would be another promised land.

16

Colonial Dreams: the Shire and Lake Nyassa

1859–1860

━━━►◆◄━━━

Between December 1858 and November 1859, the Zambesi Expedition would record its only positive achievements, and yet, ironically, Livingstone's notorious over-optimism and ambitious new schemes would nullify these successes and sow the seeds of future disintegration and collapse.

On 20 December 1858 Livingstone, Kirk and Rae left Tete in the *Ma-Robert* on the beginning of the 200-mile trip downriver to the point where the Shire flowed into the Zambesi from the north. The Shire joins the Zambesi roughly a hundred miles from the sea, having flowed three hundred miles south from its source in Lake Nyassa. On New Year's Day Livingstone entered the Shire and was delighted to find the river broad and deep. The only problem was posed by a thick aquatic weed which tended to clog the paddle-wheels. As they steamed north, it was not long before Livingstone began to imagine rice, cotton and sugar-cane growing on the flat plains that extended for miles on both sides of the river. Soon he had even persuaded himself that the Shire's potential might be as great as the Nile's. But since the country was flat and had a tendency to flood, Livingstone had to admit that there was a fair chance that it would be unhealthy. Other more obvious drawbacks soon became apparent.

On the Zambesi itself, people had often come running to the steamer simply to gaze at such a strange-looking boat, but on the Shire many Africans ran away and those who came near were clearly hostile. On several occasions arrows were fired at the steamer and Livingstone had to ask Kirk to fire warning shots at the aggressors. It became quite usual to see large crowds of tribesmen running along the banks shouting to the steamer to stop and pay them dues for passage. Livingstone refused these requests and preferred to run the risk of being showered with poisoned arrows to setting a precedent that might convince the tribesmen that they could prevent people passing if they wished.

In spite of the hostility of the inhabitants of this new region, Livingstone was still enthusiastic about the river Shire. By the end of the first week of January 1859 they had steamed over a hundred miles without grounding once. Of course the *Ma-Robert* was not heavily laden and the river was high after the rains, but Livingstone was not one to let considerations like that qualify his optimism. On 9 January, however, they encountered an obstacle that no wishful thinking could remove: the first rapid in a chain of cataracts extending for thirty miles. Livingstone named these rapids the Murchison Cataracts.* After several days' depression his spirits began to rise again with the thought that a smaller vessel, made in portable sections, might be carried past the rapids at a later date. For the present the only way to make further progress was on foot. For the time being, however, Livingstone decided to postpone further exploration in the hope that after a few months the Africans would have become accustomed to the steamer, and would therefore be less hostile. Before steaming south again Livingstone made enquiries about the area to the north and heard that it was a high, fertile country with hills and a great lake. As soon as he heard about these fertile hills Livingstone convinced himself that he had found a substitute for the Batoka Plateau. Once he had come to this conclusion nothing would change his mind.

Livingstone's next visit to the Shire was in mid-March. His companion was Kirk. Because Rae the engineer had pronounced the *Ma-Robert* unsafe for further service, due to thousands of leaks, the Doctor had left him behind. As they steamed closer to the Murchison Cataracts, Kirk noticed how preoccupied Livingstone was and wondered why, but as usual the leader of the Zambesi Expedition kept his thoughts to himself. In fact he was beginning to believe that the area they were going to would be the ideal location for a British colony. They had not seen the region which Livingstone would call the Shire Highlands but already he was building up grandiose dreams for the future. On the banks tribesmen screamed and fired off occasional arrows as they had done the previous January, but Livingstone took little notice. Even when someone on the bank was seized and eaten by a crocodile, the Doctor remained impassive, as his journal shows: '21st. March 1859. A woman was taken off by an alligator [*sic*] near to where we anchored, and we saw him dragging her up to a quiet spot to eat her. A relative, probably her mother, stood wailing on the bank. Started at 8½ A.M. Cut wood.'[1]

At the Murchison Cataracts, Livingstone and Kirk set off on foot. They had heard that before reaching the great lake, they would discover a smaller

---

* Not to be confused with the Murchison Falls in Uganda.

one, forty miles north of the cataracts. They were now entering country dominated by a tribe called the Ajawa (Yao), who acted as middlemen for Arab slave traders operating further north. Soon Livingstone had no doubts about why the Manganja people on the banks of the Shire had been either frightened or aggressive: the slave trade had reached the upper Shire. The Ajawa were no more friendly to Livingstone than the Manganja had been, but instead of firing arrows at him they gave him guides who turned out to be local lunatics.

On 18 April, after three weeks' walking round in circles, they reached Lake Shirwa and looked out across its blue waters to the mountains beyond. When they paddled in the cool water they were attacked by thousands of leeches. Shirwa was seventy miles long and thirty wide but the locals assured the white men that the great lake to the north was many times larger. Since Livingstone reckoned that the 'discovery' of this lake would be a major achievement for the expedition, he decided that he ought to try to map the lake and stay there for some time. This would mean a return to Tete for the other members of the party and for more supplies. It would therefore be late August when he set out north once more from the Murchison Cataracts.

The first hundred miles of the 200-mile journey to Lake Nyassa took all of three weeks, and by the time the expedition members started to climb into the Shire Highlands they were already exhausted and irritable. Livingstone was in a terrible mood, largely because it was dawning on him for the first time that the slave trade was already firmly established in the area. When they passed through villages, the people ran into their huts, 'the children screamed in terror, and even the hens would fly away and leave their chickens'.[2] Soon by the side of the path Livingstone saw piles of slave-taming sticks, with forked ends for securing the captive's neck. A little later he met a large slaving party led by Arabs. Evidently one of the main Arab slave routes passed just south of Nyassa. It was hardly a good omen for Livingstone's hopes for the area. He knew it as well; so much so that when he reached the southern shore of Lake Nyassa—the second largest lake in Africa—it was a distinct anticlimax. He recorded the moment in ten words: '17th. Sept. Reached Lake Nyassa from which the Shire emerges.'[3]

In fact as Livingstone gazed out over the waters of the vast lake, he felt no elation or sense of triumph. The mountains rising high above the blue water were very fine, and there could be no doubt that the locals were right in asserting that Nyassa extended several hundred miles to the north, but still Livingstone felt no pleasure. The embarrassing fact, as he very well knew, was that he was not the first European to have reached Nyassa. The Tete trader, Candido José da Costa Cardoso, had told Livingstone in 1856 that he had reached a very large lake, about three hundred miles from Tete, on a trading expedition some years before. The lake, according to Candido, was the source of the Shire. Livingstone had written this information into his journal, with a map.[4] After his arrival at Nyassa, Livingstone did his best to make it appear, from certain inconsistencies in Candido's descriptions, that the trader had been to a different lake altogether. But try as he would, Livingstone could not suggest what other lake he could possibly have seen. All Candido's information ruled out Lake Shirwa. But Livingstone was successful in getting himself accepted as the 'discoverer' of Nyassa and not one of his previous biographers has refuted it.[5]

But the fact that Livingstone had been beaten to Lake Nyassa was not his worst worry. Ever since he had first heard about the Shire Highlands and the region around Nyassa, he had been determined that this would be the new area for traders, settlers and missionaries, which he had once thought lay in the Batoka Plateau. But the problems in this region were immense.

In 1840 the Sultan of Muscat had moved his court from Muscat and Oman to Zanzibar, the administrative centre of his East African coastal possessions. By the end of the decade his Arab Swahili subjects, in eager pursuit of slaves and ivory, had penetrated inland beyond Lake Nyassa as far west as Katanga. Nyassa itself soon lay directly on the slave route from Katanga to the coastal town of Kilwa, and slave parties were either ferried across the lake in dhows or marched just south of it. In the Shire Highlands the Arabs acquired their slaves through African middlemen, the Ajawa, who had recently moved south from their original home just east of Nyassa. Livingstone had first realized the role played by the Ajawa at the time of his visit to Lake Shirwa. But he had not fully appreciated that the Ajawa were not merely selling members of the more numerous Manganja tribe to the Arabs, but were attempting to establish their own tribal dominance throughout the Shire Highlands. Thus tribal war was added to the disruption caused by the slave raids. But Livingstone was alive to another problem: he had heard on arrival at Nyassa in September 1859 that the area to the north was being devastated by a marauding tribe called the Mazitu, a part of the Ngoni people.*

As if these problems were not enough, there was one further serious threat to any future exploitation of the Shire Highlands: the area could only be reached via the river Shire, which in turn could only be entered from the Zambesi. The future of the Shire Highlands therefore rested on

---

* One of the Zulu tribal groups that had left Natal in the early nineteenth century, in the same mass emigration that had forced the Makololo northwards; the Ngoni had gone as far north as Lake Victoria, but by the 1850s had headed south again.

Portuguese goodwill, since the Zambesi could be closed to foreigners by orders from Lisbon at any time. By the middle of 1859, as Livingstone was well aware, there was very little goodwill left. As Kirk observed in January that year, 'There is some undercurrent of opinion among the Portuguese which has no love to the Doctor.'[6] There were many reasons for this. From the beginning, officials in Lisbon and Mozambique had found Livingstone's motives suspect. They had read copies of the speeches he had made in England during 1857 and could not see how his encouragement of British trade in Africa could work without British territorial claims being made. The Portuguese were also stung by criticisms of the administration of Angola and Mozambique made by Livingstone in his book *Missionary Travels*. A further cause for irritation had been Livingstone's suggestion that prior to his own discoveries very little effort had gone into the exploration of the interior. During 1859 Livingstone heard that the official Portuguese *Boletim* and the *Almanaque de Mozambique* had included essays and maps claiming that most of his discoveries had been anticipated by Portuguese explorers.[7] The truth of much of what the Portuguese claimed did not make Livingstone any more favourably disposed towards them. The Portuguese meanwhile went on suspecting that Livingstone had territorial ambitions and had been sent as a colonial agent of the British Government.

The Portuguese, to forestall any future British advances, decided to make their position plain by building a customs post at the junction of the Shire and the Zambesi and a fort at the Zambesi's Kongone mouth. Livingstone interpreted these defensive measures as a deliberate attempt to obstruct him. It underlined for him the deplorable fact that Portugal had the whip hand as regards the Shire Highlands. The best policy Livingstone could have adopted would have been one of diplomatic conciliation, but instead he made no secret of his now bitter feelings towards Portugal, and his letters and journals gave constant proof of a passionate dislike verging on obsessive hatred. He described Portuguese morality as 'worse than Sodom and utterly bad and abominable' and suggested to friends that the Portuguese only hated him for his 'standing protests against vice and uncleanness'.[8] But that, as he told another correspondent, was hardly surprising since the Portuguese were nothing more than 'an utterly effete worn out used up syphilitic race'.[9] Portuguese morality in Mozambique was certainly far from exemplary and venereal diseases troubled most of the whites in the country, but their dislike of Livingstone and the expedition, as Kirk noted, had nothing to do with Livingstone's moral censure. The cause was more fundamental. The members of the expedition were intruders in a foreign country. The Portuguese, Kirk felt, had been remarkably tolerant to allow the expedition to come to Mozambique in the first place. The British would never have contemplated allowing a German or French party into one of their overseas colonies.[10] Apart from this major conflict of interest, there was another significant cause for mutual friction: the Portuguese in Mozambique were beginning to expand rather than contract their external slave trade.

By the early 1850s the British Royal Navy's activities had virtually destroyed participation in the transatlantic slave trade by Angola and Mozambique. In the late 1850s and early 1860s, however, demands for slaves by the plantation owners on the French islands in the Indian Ocean once more stimulated the Portuguese in Mozambique to renew their old pursuit. Since domestic slavery had never been abolished in the colony, old habits were resumed with few pangs of conscience. The Portuguese Government in Lisbon condemned all external slave trading, but officials in poverty-stricken Mozambique, who remembered how Britain had yielded to France over the seizure of the *Charles et Georges*, were determined to turn a blind eye to the new traffic. In fact, as Livingstone soon discovered, the Governors of Tete and Quilimane were soon playing a leading part in the trade. These gentlemen made it quite clear to Livingstone that, while it was true that there was an official ban on the export of slaves, this was virtually unenforceable since the laws of the colony allowed parties of slaves to be moved by land without hindrance. In fact anybody who hindered them was breaking the law.[11] Livingstone was not slow to realize that since he had just pioneered a new route up the Shire, the Portuguese might soon start slaving operations on the lower reaches of that river. When that happened, as Livingstone feared it would, the Shire Highlands would suffer from Portuguese raids from the south, Arab raids from the north and general Ajawa disruption in the middle.

By the end of 1859 Livingstone needed few prophetic gifts to be able to see that, whatever the agricultural and climatic advantages of the Shire Highlands, no future occupants, whether traders, colonists or missionaries, were going to have an easy time. Past biographers have claimed that the difficulties in the Shire Highlands which destroyed the Zambesi Expedition in 1862 and 1863 could not have been foreseen in 1859. That is untrue. Livingstone was aware of all the problems from September 1859, but played them down because he felt that if the Shire Highlands had no future, all the work he had so far done from 1853 onwards in south-central Africa would have been wasted.

Had Livingstone believed that there was another less ravaged area within reach, he would undoubtedly have explored it before attempting to press a case for occupation of the Shire Highlands, but he was certain that there would never be any alternative in south-central or south-eastern

Africa. River transport was essential to success since the tsetse fly ruled out land transport by oxen. Livingstone dismissed areas to the north for a number of reasons. To start with, he knew that the Arab slave traders operating from Zanzibar and Kilwa would pose far greater problems than the small-time Portuguese slavers of Tete and Quilimane. Then, Speke and Burton were travelling in the area due west of Zanzibar, and Livingstone had no wish to work in any place where he had been preceded. Finally, Livingstone was still bent on proving that rivers could be highways from the coast into the interior; further north there was no suitable river.

So, having made up his mind that the Shire Highlands was the only place for future exploitation, both Christian and colonial, Livingstone had to think of ways in which action could be taken quickly enough to anticipate further deterioration. He decided that, in these circumstances, he could no longer keep his colonial plans a secret and in March 1859 he had started a correspondence with the Foreign Secretary, in which he proposed a scheme for government-sponsored emigration and the creation of a new colony. Livingstone knew that these proposals cut across the declared objects of current British foreign policy. He was therefore painfully aware of the need to put forward strong arguments to justify his suggestions. Unfortunately he was faced with an impossible dilemma. If he asked for colonists, simply on the grounds that the Shire Highlands was an ideal location, in terms of both climate and agriculture, he would be rejected out of hand. The Foreign Secretary would point out that there were many similar areas in the world, which by the same argument ought also to be occupied. If such a policy were followed to its logical conclusion Britain would find herself embarked on a massive series of annexations. If, on the other hand, Livingstone tried to persuade the Government to send colonists to prevent the area being engulfed by Portuguese and Arab slave raids, and to avert the annihilation of the Manganja by the Ajawa, the Foreign Secretary would probably argue that however morally impeccable were the aims of such a venture, it would still be madness to expose a handful of settlers to anarchic conditions which they would be unable to control without the help of troops.

So Livingstone had to try to have his cake and eat it. The area would have to be represented as ideal and peaceful at present, but menaced by certain threats which would bring disaster unless colonists arrived soon. This was all right as far as it went, but Livingstone's situation was not quite that straightforward. He wanted the Foreign Office to grant an additional request, which would involve him in admitting that the Arab slave trade was already a serious menace. Livingstone could see that until the Arab slave routes across Lake Nyassa and just to the south of it were blocked, there could be no real stability in the Shire Highlands. The only way, it seemed to Livingstone, to sever these routes was to employ an armed steamer on the upper Shire and Lake Nyassa itself. This vessel could then patrol the crossing places, capturing dhows and freeing slaves. Since Livingstone did not wish to pay for such a vessel out of the profits of his book, he could only ask the Foreign Office to ask the Treasury to vote the necessary funds. But the matter did not stop there, for this steamer would have to be built in portable sections which could be carried thirty miles overland, past the Murchison Cataracts. That in turn might involve the Government in the added expense of sending out a company of sappers to build a road so that the parts of the steamer could be conveyed on carts. The whole business would clearly be expensive. But in any case Livingstone's arguments fell between two stools. The extent and severity of the East African slave trade in one sense offered Livingstone his only realistic weapon for enlisting government assistance. But if he used it too much, and admitted how bad conditions were already, he would have no hope of trying to persuade potential colonists to risk their lives. In trying to have it both ways, Livingstone could neither present the slave trade as sufficiently horrific to justify direct government action, nor could he depict the Shire Highlands as a safe and stable area where colonists would have a real opportunity to prosper.

Since Livingstone either had to take his despatches to the mouth of the Zambesi, to leave them at an agreed place where Royal Naval warships could collect them every three months, or had to trust Portuguese traders to convey them to the same spot, the Foreign Secretary did not receive any of the despatches penned by Livingstone in 1859 till early the following year. In April 1860, Lord John Russell, the new Foreign Secretary, sent the Prime Minister, Lord Palmerston, copies of Livingstone's proposals.[12] Palmerston returned them with a note: 'I am very unwilling to embark on new schemes of British possessions. Dr L's information is valuable, but he must not be allowed to tempt us to form colonies only to be reached by forcing steamers up cataracts.'[13] Russell therefore wrote to Livingstone, suggesting that his colonization scheme was 'premature', and telling him that he would be unwise to be optimistic over his chances of persuading the Treasury to pay for a portable steamer. Livingstone's request for sappers was rejected outright on financial grounds. Russell also suggested that Livingstone would do well to tone down his criticisms of the Portuguese since the British Government had no desire to become embroiled in a diplomatic crisis with Lisbon.[14] Livingstone would not receive this dismissive despatch until early 1861. In the meantime his conviction that colonization would prove the answer to every evil grew stronger month by month.

Between February and November 1859, Livingstone wrote a series of letters to his friends Sir Thomas Maclear and Sir Roderick Murchison repeating again and again that there was one 'subject which becomes every day more impressed upon my mind ... It is that the interior of this country ought to be colonised by our countrymen ... I see more in that for the benefit of England & Africa than in any other plan.'[15] Six months, later it was the same story: 'I am becoming every day more convinced that we must have an English colony in the cotton-producing districts of Africa.'[16] He stressed how Britain would thus be spared the guilt of using the slave-produced cotton of the southern states of America for her textiles industry, and listed other commodities which could be produced cheaply: coffee, sugar, indigo and fibrous tissues such as sisal. There would be, he claimed, 'immense commercial benefits for England'. He did not admit that his desire to found a colony had been stimulated by the real fear that without one the Shire Highlands would descend into a state of anarchy and chaos. But he had this in mind when he begged Sir Roderick to do all he could to persuade the Foreign Secretary to back the venture.

At first Livingstone's plan was to have a small colony, but as the months passed his ideas became more and more ambitious. 'The soil is so rich,' he told his son Thomas, 'that it could support millions of people where now there are just thousands or hundreds'. Livingstone soon felt that he had discovered a remedy for England's problems as well as Africa's. If large numbers of the British urban poor emigrated to Africa they could begin new lives, no longer 'crowded together in cities ... in close ill-ventilated narrow lanes'.[17] He had evidently forgotten his old ideas about the inhabitants of poor-houses having more benefits than African chiefs and, now that necessity demanded it, he also conveniently mislaid his former fears about the African character suffering from 'intercourse with the lower ranks of our own population'.[18] These new settlers would consist of 'Christian families' and would be members of the 'honest' and not the 'blackguard' poor.[19] Before long Livingstone would realize that this sort of mass emigration would not work in Africa and he came to abandon his idea of new lives for the poor. The 'lower ranks' would, after all, not be able to elevate the Africans, and it would be detrimental for white men to compete in manual labour of 'any kind' with the Africans: 'But they [English colonists] can take a leading part in managing the land, improving the quality, increasing the quantity and extending the varieties of the production of the soil; and by taking a lead too in trade and in all public matters, the Englishman would be an unmixed advantage to every one below and around him, for he would fill a place which is now practically vacant.'[20]

This sort of colonization, with the whites simply as leaders, could be effected with far fewer colonists, and therefore seemed more practicable.

But even though Livingstone was sometimes confused about what British colonies in Africa ought to be like, he was convinced that without them there would be none of the massive social changes that were needed to make Africans susceptible to Christianity. In the short term he also knew that unless colonists came to the Shire Highlands quickly, all hopes for the area would have to be abandoned.

Throughout 1859 and 1860 Livingstone prayed that the Government would back his proposals. But during this time of waiting he was not inactive, for he set in motion a definite chain of events which he would later bitterly regret having started. During 1857 he had made speeches at Oxford and Cambridge, appealing for young men to dedicate themselves to a life of service in Africa. He had ended his address delivered in the Cambridge Senate House with a dramatic plea: 'I beg to attract your attention to Africa;—I know that in a few years I shall be cut off again in that country, which is now open, do not let it be shut again! I go back to Africa to make an open path for commerce and Christianity; do you carry out the work which I have begun. I leave it with you!'

During the first months of 1859 he had heard that, due to his appeal, a combined Oxford and Cambridge Universities Mission had been formed, with Durham and Dublin also joining the venture. In March 1859 Robert Gray, the Bishop of Cape Town, had written to Livingstone telling him about the determination of the Universities Mission to begin work in central Africa. Gray went on to ask what area Dr Livingstone would recommend as a suitable field for these men.[21] The decision was a difficult one for Livingstone. In his view the Shire Highlands needed colonists and not just an isolated group of missionaries, who would be able to do little about the serious problems which would face them there. On the other hand if Livingstone told the Bishop of Cape Town that the Shire Highlands was not a suitable area for missionaries, this news would get back to London and the Foreign Office, and would probably put paid to any plans for a colony. So on 31 October 1859 Livingstone wrote to the Bishop telling him that the Shire Highlands would prove an ideal location for a mission.[22] Livingstone knew that he was taking a risk, but could not see any way out. If the Government agreed to send colonists, there would be no risk at all; if not, then the missionaries might have a hard time. How hard, Livingstone did not dare think. Had he done so he might have spared himself the disasters of 1862 and 1863.

The arrival of the Universities Mission in early 1861 would mark the beginning of a new and crucial phase in the history of the Zambesi Expedition, but, before going on to deal with this period, it is important to describe the complete disintegration of the morale of the expedition itself during 1859 and 1860.

In 1858, Bedingfeld's dismissal, the inadequacy of the *Ma-Robert*, the depth of the Zambesi and the obstructions at Kebrabasa had dealt morale some heavy blows. The discovery of the Shire Highlands and Lake Nyassa, in the following year, ought to have improved matters, but in fact the situation worsened. The principal reason for this was Livingstone's inability to share his feelings and his hopes with his colleagues. Kirk noticed that as soon as Livingstone's health suffered he became impossible, and even his normally excellent relationship with Africans deteriorated. 'He knows how to come round niggers very well, but if his digestive system don't go all right, he loses his diplomatic power wonderfully.'[23] Livingstone himself knew that he was prone to moods of manic depression, when 'cheerfulness vanishes and the whole mental horizon is overcast with black clouds of gloom and sadness'. In such a state, he acknowledged, 'the liveliest joke cannot even provoke the semblance of a smile'.[24] In this state Livingstone would say nothing for days, even weeks at a time, but would stare in front of him with a fixed expression, sometimes humming to himself. For his companions, such behaviour was strange and alarming. Kirk could not bear being on deck with his leader when he was in a depressed mood and would be forced to go down to the cabin to escape him, but that was as bad, if not worse. Kirk wrote miserably about 'being alone in the cabin for four months with millions of cockroaches and not a single companion to speak to'.[25] The cockroaches were a nightmare and no trivial cause for complaint. They bred, as Kirk said, in millions in the warm dark hold of the *Ma-Robert* and ate into botanical specimens, food, candles and anything they could find. They bit humans too, 'nibbling at the legs by night and making sores'. Livingstone trapped two in a bottle on one occasion to see how fast they reproduced and discovered to his horror that from two of the female's egg cases, seventy-eight young ones appeared. Livingstone adopted a tame mongoose as a counter-measure and introduced several species of spider, but all to no effect. But he usually made light of mere physical discomfort. He noticed that the mongoose was losing weight, although eating thousands of cockroaches. 'This would be invaluable to fat young ladies,' he wrote in his journal. It was a pity he never joked with his colleagues but kept his humour confined to his writing. Yet Livingstone did sometimes worry about the state of his mind. He realized that only constant physical activity was any use against his depression, and yet, as he confessed, when he was inactive his powers of sympathy diminished and his 'heart became cold and dead'.[26] Ironically at this time, when all communication with his staff broke down completely, he wrote advising his eldest son, Robert, to 'be natural in everything. Let your smile be pleasant and easy. Seldom show that you are displeased for very often the cause of displeasure may be a mistake you have made yourself.'[27] Yet being 'natural' and smiling pleasantly were skills Livingstone himself never mastered. All through 1859 he was troubled by unpleasant forebodings. If chaos did come to the Shire Highlands, might it not be a judgement on his usefulness to God? The Kebrabasa Rapids had been a severe shock, and Livingstone did not like to imagine whether he would be able to remain sane if more setbacks hit him. 'This heart is sometimes fearfully guilty of mistrust', he confided to his journal. 'I am ashamed to think of it.'[28]

Meanwhile his colleagues, cut off from their leader, struggled with repeated attacks of fever and laboured to keep the *Ma-Robert* afloat. Livingstone never praised their efforts nor gave encouragement; in his heart of hearts he wanted to get rid of all of them and would have done so if he could have managed it without the Foreign Office knowing. 'All the exploration effected would have been better done alone, or with my brother.'[29]

His undiminished faith in his brother soon led him into direct conflict with other members of the party. The troubles that eventually led to the dismissal of Baines and Thornton dated back to the time the two men spent at Tete with Charles Livingstone in late 1858. Unfortunately this trio spent many months together in 1859 too; most of the exploration up the Shire was done by Livingstone, Rae and Kirk on their own.

Charles Livingstone was far more religiously narrow-minded than his brother, and tended to dislike anyone who did not share his theological interests. Neither Baines nor Thornton had any interest in religion; both were sociable, outgoing men with more interest in present enjoyment than future salvation. Charles shared his brother's hysterical hatred of the Portuguese and was horrified to see that Baines and Thornton got on well with these 'degenerate' companions. When they went to drink wine with individual residents of Tete, Charles considered that they were doing something almost as sinful as participating in an orgy. Baines and Thornton soon actively disliked Charles for his attitude to men like the Commandant of Tete, Major Sicard, who had consistently shown members of the expedition kindness and courtesy. Both men found Charles's habits infuriating. The younger Livingstone paid a great deal of attention to his appearance and rarely ventured out of doors without a felt hat or umbrella.[30] They were also irritated by Charles's constant complaints about the food, and his employment of a washerwoman to launder his own clothes with especial care.[31] But worst of all was Charles's assumption that since he was officially ranked higher in the expedition's chain of command, he could expect Baines and Thornton to run around doing whatever he asked them to. Baines was particularly annoyed by this since he was ten years older than Charles. Eventually he told Charles 'that he had not come as his servant but as an officer that had duties of his own to attend to'.[32] After this incident Charles wrote telling his wife that Baines was disagreeable and 'exceedingly stupid'.[33] Then relations became so strained that Charles moved to a room at the other end of the expedition's house in Tete. Soon he regretted this action, since when callers came they went to see Thornton and Baines and always left him alone. The other two men often received gifts of fruit, meat and poultry from the Portuguese, and Charles of course got nothing. This made him feel vindictive and jealous. Soon he was bribing Africans to spy on his two colleagues and to report back anything discreditable that they might see.[34] Gradually Charles became convinced that Baines and Thornton were hard drinkers who attended Portuguese 'orgies'. His spies were ready to tell him anything he wanted to hear, since the more damning their stories, the more cloth they were paid.

Since the Portuguese were always friendly and often came with presents, Baines, as storekeeper, felt that it was only right that he should occasionally give them small gifts like a little sugar or a tin of sardines in return. Baines considered that it was essential to be sociable to ensure that the Portuguese continued to look favourably on the expedition. When Charles heard about these presents and also discovered that Baines had painted the portraits of several Portuguese friends, using the expedition's artist's materials, the younger Livingstone felt that he had grounds to accuse Baines of giving away supplies that did not belong to him. Charles was soon convinced that a lot of sugar had been stolen. Since Baines had been given no place to lock up stores, it was hardly surprising that some pilfering took place. But there was no shred of evidence to accuse Baines of theft; and yet that was the accusation Charles made publicly in front of his brother in June 1859.

As usual, Livingstone believed what his brother told him but, while condemning Baines behind his back, he did not order an investigation. Kirk thought that some stores probably had been squandered but blamed Charles Livingstone whose 'own utter want of method in these matters would completely confound anyone in keeping exact lists'.[35] Charles Livingstone decided that it suited his own interests best to claim that Baines had 'made away with expedition goods' while suffering from brain fever.[36] David Livingstone did not much care about a few pounds of sugar, but he still remembered that Baines had taken Bedingfeld's side, and was eager to suggest to the Foreign Office that Baines's testimony was worthless since he was mentally ill. Of course Baines suffered from fever like all the others, but there was never any suggestion by anybody except Livingstone that he might be liable to occasional bouts of insanity.

While Charles had done his best to turn his brother against Baines, he had also worked hard to discredit Thornton. Thornton's sin in Charles's eyes was that he 'sneered at Scotchmen' and laughed at religiously minded men for their seriousness.[37] Livingstone did not care for being laughed at, but he hated indolence much more than insolence. Thornton had been asked to excavate a shaft into a coal seam near Tete, to a depth of thirty feet. In six months the young geologist had only achieved fifteen feet. Thornton had often been deserted by his African attendants, whose language he could not speak, and he had suffered so much from mosquito bites that his legs had become a mass of festering sores. He had also suffered constant attacks of malaria and some painful boils on his feet. In spite of all this he had extracted five tons of coal for the *Ma-Robert*'s boilers. This was much less than Livingstone had hoped for and he soon pronounced Thornton 'insufferably lazy'.[38] The young man excused himself on the grounds of his illnesses, but Livingstone still decided to dismiss him, having, as he put it, made 'every allowance for your suffering from prickly heat and other little illnesses'. After his dismissal Thornton decided to stay on and pay for his own keep. Within a few months Livingstone noticed to his annoyance that Thornton was working much better and making good progress. Thornton was only twenty-one and Livingstone had left him entirely to his own devices from the moment the expedition had arrived in Africa. Had he taken more interest in the young man, there can be no doubt that he would have got some good work out of him. Livingstone was forced to admit his mistake when he accepted Thornton back as a member of the expedition two years later. The precise part Charles Livingstone played in Thornton's dismissal is not entirely clear, but it is certain that Thornton himself felt Charles had been responsible. Thornton's sisters, Helen and Octavia, both referred to 'Mr Charles Livingstone's brutality' and suggested that their brother had been 'foolish and imprudent to irritate Mr C.L.'[39]

Thornton was sacked on 25 June 1859, and, after this success, Charles Livingstone once more turned his attention to Baines; by July he had managed to persuade his brother to dismiss his artist and storekeeper. No new evidence had been produced, and when Kirk, much against his will and on Livingstone's orders, searched through Baines's boxes in late October and went through his storekeeping books, Charles's claim that Baines had stolen a quarter of the expedition's total sugar stocks was proved false.[40] Kirk discovered that butter had been badly accounted for and that one cask of sugar could not be traced. There was one piece of canvas in Baines's personal luggage which he could not explain how he came to possess. But since this article was not worth more than a few shillings, it did not strike Kirk as very important. At the end of his search, Kirk wrote that there was 'no expedition property which I can claim at once'.[41] All the Portuguese at Tete firmly asserted that Baines was innocent of all charges of theft.

Livingstone was acutely embarrassed by Kirk's lack of condemning evidence. He had already sacked Baines and felt that he could not retract now. Instead he suggested that Kirk had been deceived and that Baines 'had cooked the book of store expenditure, making it appear as if 4 lbs of sugar had been consumed per day'. Livingstone rejected the sworn statements of the Portuguese on the grounds that all the residents of Tete were too degenerate to know the difference between truth and falsehood.

Baines was given a hearing of sorts by Livingstone and Charles, but since both his accusers refused to accept his denials of the charges made and would not return to Tete for a proper re-examination of the evidence, the artist was condemned without any chance of proving his innocence. When Livingstone was later accused of having refused a proper trial, he replied that there had been no judge and jury within a thousand miles and that he had spared Baines the ignominy of additional publicity by refusing a full enquiry.[42] Although Livingstone made much of his desire not to blacken Baines's character, he wrote to numerous friends in England telling them about Baines's stealing, 'drinking & debauchery'.[43] When he wrote his official *Narrative* of the expedition, Livingstone did not once mention Baines by name and refused to acknowledge that Baines had drawn most of the pictures which appeared in the *Narrative* as illustrations. During the time that remained to Baines on the Zambesi, Livingstone isolated him from the rest of the party so that he could not contaminate anybody. Livingstone evidently saw nothing inhuman in this for he wrote almost with pride: 'I do not allow Baines to our table but send him a good share of all we eat ourselves. He lives in a whaler, with a sail as an awning over him.'[44]

When Baines was put on to a warship bound for England on 7 December 1859, all his possessions were still at Tete. He never saw most of his paintings again, and had Kirk and Rae not given him money and clothing, he would have left with nothing but the clothes he stood up in.

At the end of 1859 Livingstone may have congratulated himself on purging the expedition of evil-doers, but in all respects his position was unenviable. He had lost half of the six European colleagues he had come out with, the *Ma-Robert* was leaking like a colander and could not be expected to float more than a few months, no letters had been received from the Foreign Secretary in response to Livingstone's request for a new steamer to replace the *Ma-Robert* and it seemed unlikely that the Foreign Office would send their reaction to his plans for the Shire Highlands for another six months or a year. Meanwhile George Rae, the engineer, was talking about resigning, and Livingstone was losing all control over his African crew. After Kirk had been attacked by a member of the crew with an iron bar, Livingstone lost his temper and, in an undignified fit of rage, jumped into the water to beat the offending man with a cook's ladle. Shortly afterwards Livingstone had to quell another near-mutiny by hitting the ringleader with a stout piece of wood. Kirk was horrified when his leader, normally so restrained and tolerant where Africans were concerned, told him 'to break their heads if they did not do as I told them'.[45]

All these troubles were at their worst in mid-December 1859 when Livingstone and the remnants of his party came down for supplies to the Kongone mouth of the Zambesi after their journey to Lake Nyassa. For a week or so Livingstone remained in a state of complete indecision. There seemed little or nothing he could do. Until a new steamer came he was helpless, and even then there would be little to be done until the Foreign Office either sanctioned or refused his other plans. The Universities Mission would not be arriving for another year and so that project offered no immediate hope for profitable work. Yet Livingstone's great strength was his ability to ignore present difficulties even when they seemed overwhelming. In late December he told his colleagues that instead of sitting around for most of the coming year, they would use 1860 to take the Makololo back to their chief. He had promised Sekeletu that his men would be back by 1858, and now that there was nothing else to do, Livingstone felt able to honour his promise. He also made a more important decision. George Rae was told by him that he was to embark on the next warship for England and that on his arrival he should supervise the designing and building of a portable steamer for the upper Shire and Lake Nyassa. If the Foreign Office would not pay, Livingstone said that he would spend all the rest of the profits from *Missionary Travels*, up to £6,000, on the vessel. There is no denying that this was a brave and magnificent gesture, once more proving Livingstone's total commitment to the Shire Highlands. But Livingstone had now set himself an almost impossible task for the future. The parts of this portable steamer would have to be carried past the Murchison Cataracts for thirty miles, and that would only be possible if a road were built first. In any case, vast numbers of men would be needed, not only as labourers on the road but also as porters to manhandle the parts of the steamer past the cataracts. Carts would be needed too. In view of events that followed in 1863, it is hard to believe that Livingstone could ever have given serious thought to the practical details of such an ambitious operation. But in his desperation to create circumstances in the Shire Highlands suitable for the establishment of a colony, Livingstone was prepared to defy odds which appeared, to a rational observer, to be hopelessly against him.

Rae was sent back to England according to plan, and in early 1860 Livingstone, Charles and Kirk set off for Tete from the mouth of the

Zambesi. The idea of taking the Makololo home was excellent from Livingstone's point of view, since it conveniently filled in time that would otherwise have been wasted, but the Makololo themselves had settled in well at Tete and many elected not to return. When Livingstone left for Makololo country, in May 1860, he did so with roughly sixty of the original 114. According to Charles Livingstone, thirty of these had deserted to return to Tete before Livingstone had got them as far as Kebrabasa. Livingstone blamed their behaviour on the Portuguese who had 'perverted' them. Charles thought this ridiculous and said that they 'could hardly have learned anything bad which they did not know and practice before they left their own country'.[46]

Livingstone would not return to Tete from Makololo country till the end of November 1860. The importance of this trip was not the home-coming of some thirty Makololo, but Livingstone's discovery of the deaths of six of the nine Europeans associated with the London Missionary Society mission to the Makololo, which he himself had set in hand in 1857. Since I have dealt fully with this episode in Chapter 12, little more need be said about it now but two points are important. The discovery of the deaths, and Livingstone's realization that the Makololo were disinte-grating as a tribe, confirmed his conviction that all hopes for the future lay in the Shire Highlands. Second, the actual journey to Sekeletu's town was important, since it was then that a series of rows broke out between Charles and David Livingstone. These disagreements ended their close relationship, leaving the latter completely isolated.

The trouble had really started when Charles made it perfectly clear to his brother, before leaving Tete, that the trip was a waste of time and energy. Livingstone never liked his plans to be challenged and could sense that Kirk agreed with Charles. Only two of the men being taken back to Sekeletu were true Makololo; all the rest were members of subject tribes. The Makololo never treated their vassals well and it seemed to Kirk folly to risk a great deal of hardship and fatigue simply to take thirty Africans back to central Africa when twenty-eight of them probably did not want to go. Kirk, however, had the sense not to argue. Charles showed less self-control and on 13 May Livingstone found himself transcribing some hurtful things his brother had said to him. 'My brother informs me that the members of the Expedition did not get orders what to do, and were always at a loss how to act . . . All were willing and anxious to help if I only could have told them. He never told me before.'[47]

Livingstone was completely confounded by this since Charles had taken such a leading role in the dismissal of Baines and Thornton. In the past Livingstone had believed that whoever else might fail him, Charles would not. Thus, in spite of a mass of evidence to the contrary, Livingstone had suggested that Charles was the only ideal travelling companion in the party. When he found that Charles was repaying such loyalty with criticism, Livingstone was astounded. Without his famous brother's recommendation, Charles would never have gained a job on the expedition in the first place. Livingstone at once accused him of ingratitude and treachery. Not satisfied with this, Livingstone sat down to write an assessment of Charles in his journal. 'As an assistant he has been of no value. Photography very unsatisfactory. Magnetism still more so. Meteorological observations not creditable, and writing in the journal in arrears. In going up with us now he is useless, as he knows nothing of Portuguese or the native language. He often expected me to be his assistant instead of acting as mine.'[48]

Kirk claimed that the first violent row between the brothers broke out over 'an old pillow which had rotted in the ship, like many other things'.[49] The triviality of this *casus belli* is a good indication of the state of mind the two men were in. Livingstone had accused Charles of deliberately destroying the pillow without considering to whom it belonged. The result had been a long argument with 'Mr C.L. using most improper expressions to a superior officer, and Dr L. saying that he had been a failure from the beginning and that the only mistake made was in bringing him out'.[50] Worse was to come.

For several weeks Charles sulked and occasionally muttered about his brother being 'no Christian gentleman' and being employed 'in the service of the Devil'. Then one day Charles, who had recently fallen six feet into an elephant pitfall, lost his temper with the headman of the Makololo and kicked him with all his strength. Since they were now within days of reaching Sekeletu's town, this was a crazy thing to do. Sekeletu would not be pleased to hear that his men had been beaten up on their way home. Livingstone flew into an uncontrollable rage and Kirk confessed that he then listened to 'the most abusive filthy language ever heard in that class of society'. During this scene the headman had nearly murdered Charles, and the two brothers had come to blows. Kirk wrote coolly in his journal:

I trust that if I am sent on an overland trip, I may not have C.L. for a companion, for if he can break out and abuse, tearing with nails so as to draw blood and tear clothes, saying his brother was serving the Devil, indulge in epithets such as 'the cursing consul of Quillimane', repeated over and over again, acting before the men in such a way as to make them look on him as mad, which if I could only say that I thought he was, would be the most charitable thing I could do. But under one who loses his temper so suddenly so as to change from joking to kicking with iron nailed boots the chief man sent by a proud powerful savage chief . . .

is one on whom no reliance can be placed. Nothing but the high personal regard for Dr L. averted bloodshed in that case. The spear was poised and needed only a stroke of the arm to send it to the heart. I never expected so much moderation from savages.[51]

From the time of this incident all order and discipline broke down and it was with the greatest difficulty that Livingstone prevented the whole party disbanding en route. That evening Livingstone wrote down sadly some of the insults his brother had thrown at him: 'Manners of a cotton spinner, of the Boers', 'that I had cursed him, that I had set the devil into him . . . and repeated again and again that I had cursed him', 'seemed intent on a row. Would be but a short time in the Expedition: regretted that he was on this journey. Would rejoice when he could leave it.'[52] At last, too late to remedy things, Livingstone realized that Charles had probably slandered other members of the party without grounds. In the meantime, Livingstone knew that he could not dismiss Charles without appearing a fool. From July 1860 till the middle of 1863, when Charles returned to England, Livingstone saw him and talked to him only when he could not avoid doing so. From now on Livingstone felt entirely alone.

The trouble with his brother evidently did little for Livingstone's judgement, for on the way back to Tete he decided to try and shoot the first rapids at Kebrabasa. Charles and Kirk were too tired and disenchanted to argue. During the attempt Kirk's canoe was upset and he himself nearly drowned. Livingstone emerged on the other side of this first section of the Kebrabasa Rapids wet but unharmed. In his journal Livingstone dismissed in a few sentences this incident, which had nearly cost his botanist's life.

The three men were back at Tete by the end of November, and there Livingstone was handed a mail-bag containing the Foreign Secretary's answer to his suggestions for the development of the Shire Highlands. While Livingstone was dismayed that his colonial plans had been rejected out of hand, he could comfort himself with the news that Lord Russell had agreed to prolong the expedition for a further three years. The steamer to replace the *Ma-Robert*, he was told, had started from England earlier the same year, which meant that she should already be at the mouth of the Zambesi. The Foreign Secretary had refused an additional vessel for Lake Nyassa, and so Livingstone realized that the ship Rae had gone to order would have to be paid for with the remains of his book money. He had known that this was a distinct possibility from the beginning.

The most important news Livingstone received was from the organizers of the Universities Mission, who wrote telling him that the first members of the mission could be expected at the Zambesi mouth during January of the New Year. After the Foreign Secretary's flat rejection of plans for a colony in the Shire Highlands, Livingstone could not help being alarmed about the prospects of the new mission; none of its members had been prepared in any way for the problems they would shortly have to face. Livingstone had recommended the mission to come to the Shire Highlands because, had he done otherwise, his earlier optimism about the area's glorious future would have seemed grotesquely inconsistent, and all future efforts in the region would have been blighted. But without the help of colonists from the beginning, Livingstone realized that life for the missionaries would be far from simple. This was a Church of England mission that had been inaugurated with a great deal of publicity. If a disaster like that at Linyanti happened to these members of the Established Church, it was going to be a lot harder to explain away than the deaths of a few nonconformists and their children. Livingstone could see that his future reputation to a large extent depended on what would happen to these men whom he had been obliged to summon to the Shire Highlands.

With the Portuguese and Arab slave raids, and the inter-tribal conflict between the Ajawa and the Manganja very much in mind, Livingstone decided at once to try and qualify some of his earlier unrestrained enthusiasm, just in case anything went wrong at a later date. He wrote to the Secretaries of the Mission telling them that the country was healthy and fertile, but that the missionaries should expect some hostility and suspicion from the locals on account of the slave trade.[53] He wrote in similar terms to the Bishop of Oxford, informing him that, although the area held out 'glorious prospects', 'there are difficulties, no doubt—an unreduced language, and people quite ignorant of the motives of missionaries, with all the evils of its being in the slave market. But your university men are believed to possess genuine English pluck, and will no doubt rejoice to preach Christ's Gospel beyond other men's line of things.'[54] Having gone some way towards redressing his formerly unblemished picture of the Shire Highlands, Livingstone went on to assure the Bishop of Oxford that the missionaries would have nothing to fear from malaria, which, if treated correctly, was no worse than a common cold.

Even after this spate of letter-writing, Livingstone still felt uneasy. But he felt elated as well as fearful. He had heard that the Universities Mission was to be headed by a bishop, and Livingstone realized that the creation of a bishopric in an area that was not a British possession was equivalent to a quasi-claim over that territory.[55] For this reason the British Government had been against the appointment of a bishop as leader of the new mission; in the eyes of the Foreign Secretary it had set a dangerous precedent.

Livingstone was delighted for the very reason that distressed Lord John Russell so much: namely that if the Bishop was hindered by Portuguese or Arab slave traders, there might be a massive upsurge of public feeling in favour of annexing the area. Yet Livingstone could see that if harm befell the Bishop, public anger might turn on the man who had sent him to so difficult a region. Missionary failures could lead to a revulsion against sending more men to an area which had proved fatal to others. As Livingstone left Tete in early December and headed downriver towards the mouth of the Zambesi to meet the newcomers, he knew that a great deal hung on the success or failure of the new Bishop and his colleagues: not just the fate of the Zambesi Expedition and the Shire Highlands, but the kind of attitude the British Goverment and public would entertain towards colonial expansion in Africa for maybe the next twenty or thirty years.

17

Death of a Fighting Bishop

The first members of the Universities Mission arrived at the Kongone mouth of the Zambesi at the end of January 1861 in two ships of the blockading squadron: H.M.S. *Sidon* and H.M.S. *Lyra*. Livingstone, Charles and Kirk had spent a wet and gloomy month in a group of damp, mosquito-infested huts, waiting for the new arrivals. A few days before reaching the mouth, the *Ma-Robert* had done what she had promised to do for some months: she had gone to the bottom. Fortunately the crew had enough warning to get out most of the supplies and goods. Before leaving Tete, Livingstone had selected a fresh crew to man the new steamer that was expected to arrive at the same time as the missionaries. This crew had been chosen from among those Makololo who had preferred to remain in Mozambique rather than return to Linyanti. The sight of the *Sidon* with the *Pioneer*—the *Ma-Robert*'s replacement vessel— in tow did much to raise the spirits of the small reception party after their miserable month of waiting.

The missionaries' first impressions of the Zambesi delta were nonetheless far from favourable. They were surprised to see the *Pioneer* almost capsize while crossing the bar, especially since they had heard that the Zambesi was such an excellent waterway. The naval officers on both the warships found their confusion entertaining and told them with lugubrious relish that eight or nine men had already lost their lives on the bar coming and going on Dr Livingstone's business. One of the missionaries was soon writing bitterly in his journal that 'nothing could be more impracticable for ordinary commercial purposes' than the Kongone mouth.[1]

Yet Livingstone, on his affable best behaviour, soon reassured the newcomers. Kirk was equally friendly and even Charles, who had already decided on theological grounds to despise the Church of England men, managed to conceal his true feelings. Bishop Mackenzie was an energetic and hearty man in the best traditions of muscular Christianity. He had had a brilliant career at Cambridge, where he had taught theology and mathematics. He had then gone to work among the Zulus as a missionary, soon rising to the rank of Archdeacon of Natal. He had recently been consecrated Bishop in Cape Town. Kirk at once dubbed this prematurely bald prelate, with his luxuriant sideboards and easy manner, 'a trump of a fellow' and Livingstone, with rare generosity, pronounced him 'A1'. Livingstone was also delighted with the other members of the party and wrote to the Foreign Secretary telling him so: 'I hail their arrival with very great satisfaction for they seem to have sound practical views of the work before them, and during our short intercourse have shown that they have no nonsense about them.'[2]

At this stage Livingstone had not become acquainted with the extremely High Church views of the Bishop and his Deacon, Henry Rowley. But he had genuinely taken to an Anglican priest, H.C. Scudamore, and to a young man designated as 'lay superintendent', Horace Waller. His judgement was later shown to be sound; Waller became one of his greatest friends, and Scudamore, while he lived, worked with tireless unselfishness. Both men were Low Church, unlike Mackenzie and Rowley. Another member of the party, Lovell Procter, made no marked impression on either Kirk, Charles or Livingstone. In addition to these men, the mission included a carpenter called Gamble, and Adams, a cockney labourer, whose official title was 'agriculturalist'. A doctor, John Dickinson, and another young clergyman, Henry Burrup, were expected to come out shortly.

In spite of all the initial goodwill, discord was not long in coming. Mackenzie had expected to be taken to his new mission field without delay. He was therefore more than surprised when Livingstone told him that he would have to wait three months. Livingstone wanted to explore an alternative route into the Shire Highlands before taking the missionaries anywhere. The Doctor had never been entirely satisfied with the river Shire, partly because the upper reaches became very shallow in the dry season, but mainly because the Portuguese could prevent entrance via the Zambesi if and when they might wish to do so. Recently Livingstone had made up his mind that the river Rovuma, which flowed into the Indian Ocean some six hundred miles north of Quilimane, had its source in Lake Nyassa and would therefore prove an ideal highway into the Shire Highlands. The Rovuma's main advantage was its situation outside the northern limits of Portuguese Mozambique.

Mackenzie was not impressed when Livingstone claimed that the Portuguese would become obstructive unless another way into the Highlands were found. The Bishop had previously been promised that there would be no interference; in fact he had letters of recommendation from the Portuguese Government and had been assured of complete cooperation. Apart from that, Mackenzie had always understood that the Shire was an ideal river with no navigation problems at any time of year.

Livingstone did not want to admit that he had deceived anybody in the past, and instead suggested that it would be best for the Bishop to wait a few months while the Rovuma was explored, since the Mission as yet had no doctor. Again Mackenzie was puzzled. Since Livingstone would be with his party till they were settled, Livingstone and Kirk would be their doctors. Besides, Livingstone had suggested that fever was easy to treat and no more serious than the common cold. Livingstone eventually had to admit that another important reason for wishing to avoid the Shire was the existence of widespread fighting on its lower reaches. He blamed the Portuguese slave raids for this and conveniently omitted mentioning the primary cause: the Ajawa.

Eventually Mackenzie reluctantly gave in and agreed to wait three months. He knew very well that if any misfortune did befall his men, and it was subsequently discovered that he had rejected Dr Livingstone's advice, there would be recrimination in Britain. This did not stop him telling Livingstone that in his view the delay would mean a loss of morale and possibly the cooling of public enthusiasm for the venture at home. The Mission had been launched with official fanfares by Brougham, Gladstone and Dr Wilberforce, and Mackenzie was terrified by the possibility of failure. 'I am afraid of this,' he wrote; 'most works of this kind have been carried on by one or two men in a quieter way, and have had a quieter beginning.'[3]

The missionaries had been surprised in the first place that Livingstone was putting so much faith in the Rovuma. They had heard from their naval friends that the river had been surveyed by a Commander Owen, and found to be navigable by steamer for only forty-five miles.[4] Captain Crawford of the *Sidon* told Mackenzie that when the river was low, as it was in the first quarter of the year, Livingstone could not expect to get more than thirty miles upstream. Crawford was right. When Livingstone met the missionaries again in April, they had ceased to think of him as the man of sound judgement they had been led to believe he was.

The party steamed into the Zambesi on board the *Pioneer* on 1 May 1861 and the bonhomie of January was very much a thing of the past. Livingstone had offered to do all he could for the missionaries, and now he had been landed with the job of transporting them around with all their gear. He had been quite firm with their organizers when he had suggested that they bring their own vessel but, although the appeal for the venture had reached £20,000, no steamer had been ordered. He had been surprised and irritated that they should have tried to thwart him in his plan to explore the Rovuma, and felt that they had no right to try to dictate what he did when he was doing so much for them. In the meantime he had been having nautical troubles. The *Pioneer* had arrived with a master, Mr May, who thought that he was to succeed Bedingfeld as overall naval commander on the river. When Livingstone assured him that he was mistaken, he resigned. So now Livingstone was in charge of the *Pioneer*, plus his own expedition, plus, for the time being, the missionaries. Morale among his own men was no better than usual, and Kirk was currently depressed by a typical piece of his leader's thoughtlessness. Livingstone had not told him that he had asked for another medical officer and botanist to come out with the *Pioneer*, but now, without any warning, a Dr Meller had arrived. Kirk immediately liked Meller but still felt that his appointment was a slap in the face. Meanwhile Charles was doing his best to try to set the Low Church section of the mission against the High Church section. Worse still, all the missionaries, except the irritable Rowley, had now suffered from fever and had discovered it to be a far worse affliction than a 'common cold'. Rowley described this part of their venture well: 'Fever still prevailed among us, and from the foul and crowded state of the little ship, this was not to be wondered at. At most there was but healthy accommodation for twenty people on board the *Pioneer*, and there were forty-eight . . . The deck was blocked up with boxes, bales, and sacks of coal. The saloon and after-cabin were offensive with the odour from the mass of stuff stored in them.'[5]

On 8 May, when they were steaming through the delta, Mackenzie wrote telling his sister that they would all be at the Murchison Cataracts within seventeen days.[6] This estimate was far too optimistic. A week later the *Pioneer* went aground, and for the next two months it was a rare day when she was not being dragged along by anchors and ropes. Livingstone had asked the Foreign Office to see that his new vessel should draw no more than three feet, but it was hardly surprising that, overloaded way beyond any limit that had been envisaged, she should draw over five feet. At the end of June, when all the ship's capstans had been ripped out of their mountings by the strain put on them in pulling the *Pioneer* across sandbanks, Livingstone was soon landing surplus stores in an attempt to lighten the ship and get the draught down to three feet. After this process was completed, progress became a little faster, and by 8 July they were a few miles below the Murchison Cataracts.

It says a lot for the characters of the missionaries that after their disappointment over the initial delay due to the Rovuma, they did not criticize Livingstone for misinforming them about the navigability of the Shire, or for suggesting that the Shire valley was well populated when it was not. Although most of them suffered badly from fever, Procter particularly, they pulled hard at the ropes and rarely became irritable or depressed. Much of the credit must go to Mackenzie, who, unlike Livingstone, was a born mixer who combined an almost feminine gentleness with masculine heartiness. Even Charles Livingstone liked him. Mackenzie never minded seeming ridiculous and was quite happy to take a bath in full view of everybody in the space under one of the paddle-boxes. On one occasion the paddle-wheel started to turn suddenly, and he was 'like a squirrel in a cage'. As his clothes were flipped into the air, he rushed out naked 'crying to the seamen to save the cassock'.[7] Only Rowley had serious misgivings about the future. The state of the river Shire told him that communication with the sea was going to be very difficult in future and, in his view, virtually ruled out any traders following in their footsteps. But the rest, like Waller and the Bishop, still trusted Livingstone, if not as a miracle-worker, at least as a man who would guide them to a safe and peaceful place from which to begin missionary operations.

The mood on 15 July was one of almost unalloyed optimism as the whole party, led by Livingstone, set off on foot from a village just below the Murchison Cataracts. Mackenzie summed it up in a light-hearted description of them all:

> You would like to see our picturesque appearance on the march . . . Livingstone in his jacket and trousers of blue serge and his blue cloth cap. His brother, a taller man, in something of the same dress. I with trousers of Oxford grey and a coat like a shooting coat, a broad-brimmed wide awake hat with white cover, which Livingstone laughs at, but which all the same keeps the sun off. *He* is a salamander.[8]

However, after a few hours of the seventy-mile march towards Magomero —the village chosen by Livingstone as the new mission site—the good spirits started to decline. The porters were soon slacking, and Mackenzie, who was unused to this normal hazard of African travel, made matters worse by prodding dawdlers with his crozier. Real trouble was not far off.

Livingstone and the Bishop had already argued about whether missionaries should carry arms, and although Livingstone had managed to win over all the other members of the University party to the view that arms were the best means of deterring attack, Mackenzie had only reluctantly given in. Thus, as he marched, he was painfully aware of the incongruity of carrying a double-barrelled gun in one hand and his bishop's crozier in the other. But the events of 16 July were to banish his pacifist leanings for good; on that day he and his companions saw their first slaving party.

There were eighty-four slaves, many of them women and children, with their hands tied and their necks secured to forked wooden taming-sticks. The missionaries were euphoric as they watched most of the slave drivers run away at the appearance of the combined Christian party. Clearly the hand of God was behind it. Livingstone remained less rapturous. He put down the flight of the slavers to the warlike gestures of his Makololo crew, who were now accompanying him as porters. Waller at once started to cut through the ropes that bound the captives and Mackenzie listened in horror to the interpreted story of one woman whose baby's brains had been dashed out before her eyes. No shots had been fired, but the Bishop had already made up his mind that 'in such cases it is right to use force, and even fire if necessary to rescue captives'.[9] Livingstone was not so concerned with the rights or wrongs of firing or not firing. He had just seen among the slavers a couple of former slaves from Tete. Portuguese slaving operations had already reached the heart of the Shire Highlands. The implications were grim for the future of the Mission. Livingstone had been warned by the Governor of Tete that it was illegal to interfere with slave caravans. The Bishop's letters of recommendation from the Portuguese Government were not going to be any use from now on. Livingstone could also see that if Mackenzie went on freeing slaves, he would have to feed them. Already he had made himself responsible for eighty-four people before he had even planted any crops. Yet the issue, as Livingstone could see, was not a simple one. If the slavers were allowed to continue operations with impunity, there would be no peace in the area in future. News soon reached the combined party that there were other slave caravans in the area, and so, on Livingstone's instructions, his men split up to search these other slavers out. Soon a further fifty-seven people had been freed.

On arrival at Magomero it soon became apparent that the Portuguese slavers constituted a relatively small problem when set beside the raids being carried out by the Ajawa. It was said that more raids were planned. While Livingstone had told Mackenzie about the Portuguese slavers, he had not warned him about the role the Ajawa played as Arab middlemen. Nor had he admitted that the Ajawa were at war with the Manganja. But there was no time for retrospective explanations or calm deliberation. By 22 July the rumours of imminent Ajawa attacks had hardened to certainty. A raid was expected soon on a village some ten miles away. Livingstone and Mackenzie set out in that direction with most of their party, including a group of armed Makololo and some of the local Manganja people. Soon they were passing through burned-out villages and could see in the distance another village still burning. As they marched closer they could hear shouting and the noise of women wailing for their dead menfolk. The Bishop suggested that the whole party pray, and so they did. When they got up from their knees, it was to see a long line of Ajawa warriors and their captives coming round the hillside to their right. The Ajawa headman stood up on a conveniently placed anthill to get a good view of the opposition, and decided that it was negligible. When Livingstone attempted to talk peacefully, this was taken as confirmation that the strangers were too cowardly to fight. Soon Livingstone and Mackenzie found themselves ducking poisoned arrows, fired with uncomfortable accuracy—in fact one fell right between them.

The aggressors now advanced to a distance of fifty yards and seemed to be preparing to charge. A Manganja near Livingstone doubled up with an arrow through his arm. Livingstone gave the order to fire, and the Bishop, not wishing to fire himself, handed his weapon to the Doctor, who promptly started to blaze away. In later accounts of the engagement Livingstone did not mention the number of Ajawa killed, but Kirk reckoned it to have been six. None of Livingstone's party was hit, although one Manganja was killed and several others wounded. Livingstone estimated that the Ajawa had had four guns, and that their use of them had been far from expert. The Doctor finally led his party into the Ajawa's town and set fire to it.[10] As he was later to tell his son Robert, it was the end of 'a hungry, fatiguing and most unpleasant day'.

Livingstone now realized that the Mission's position was an extremely dangerous one. He cursed himself for having got mixed up in a situation where he had been obliged, for the first time in his life, to shoot Africans. The whole incident would probably be used by the Bishop as a precedent for future counter-attacks. That the Ajawa would want revenge Livingstone had no doubt. The missionaries might have secured the lasting friendship of the Manganja but they would never make any headway with the Ajawa, who seemed destined to become the dominant people in the area before long. Livingstone did not see fit to warn Mackenzie that no one side in any African tribal conflict ever had a monopoly of right, and that the Manganja would probably sell Ajawa into slavery if they ever got the chance.

Mackenzie was at first inclined to move to a more peaceful region further south, but Livingstone was against this for two reasons: in the first place, Magomero was in an ideal defensive position, being on a peninsula formed by a stream, and in the second the Ajawa would soon take their revenge on the local Manganja, who would be without a place of refuge when the missionaries had moved away. But Magomero was not without its problems. It lay in a hollow, and water drained into it rather than out. This would pose health problems since the excrement of 150 people could not be carried away by the stream. But Livingstone ignored this difficulty, and having promised to leave the Bishop two sailors, who had come out with the *Pioneer* as helpers, he advised them to build a defensive stockade and prepared to leave. He wanted to make a thorough survey of Lake Nyassa to see whether the Rovuma really did flow out of it.

On 25 July Livingstone invited the local Manganja chiefs to meet him at Magomero. He then made a formal speech. Mackenzie was certain that

in it he pledged himself and the Mission to assist the Manganja against
the Ajawa. Livingstone later denied this, and Waller, the only other
European witness to the speech besides Mackenzie, thought that this help
was to be purely defensive.[11]

Before Livingstone left Magomero for Nyassa, Mackenzie asked him in
some perplexity what he meant by defence. When they had killed six
Ajawa they had been defending themselves, and yet they had put themselves in a position where they had had no alternative other than a
counter-attack. Livingstone admitted that it was a thorny question, but
advised the missionaries that whatever the circumstances they should on
no account become involved in a tribal war. He warned Mackenzie that
Manganja chiefs would ask for help. 'You will be oppressed with requests,
but don't go.' This was good general advice but useless in their present
situation. The missionaries had already been committed to the Manganja
cause by the events of 22 July. If they gave refuge to the Manganja, the
Ajawa would automatically view the missionaries as their enemies. Since
Livingstone had suggested that Mackenzie ought to provide refuge,
it was futile his telling the Bishop to avoid taking sides. Had Livingstone
discussed the issue in greater depth before he left, he would have realized
that the missionaries would lose even the slender hold they now had
over the Manganja if they stood aside while the Ajawa destroyed
village after village. Neutrality would win them no converts. The missionaries could see that there was no great difference between releasing
slaves and preventing their capture. Both actions constituted active intervention. So the Universities Mission was a confused and worried body of
men when Livingstone set out north at the end of July 1861. None of
them could speak any African language, they had 150 people to feed
and no crops sown, and on top of all this they faced being sucked into a
tribal war.

Livingstone was away at Lake Nyassa till mid-November, and during
that time he achieved little he wanted to. He mapped, with remarkable
accuracy, two hundred miles of the west side of the lake, but on the east
side he did not find any outlet that could have been the Rovuma. In fact
the Rovuma's source was some forty miles to the east of Nyassa.
Livingstone had hoped to reach the northern end of the lake, but he was
forced back by famine and tribal disturbances before reaching his goal. All
in all, this trip consisted of three and a half very depressing months. From
the number of dhows they had seen crossing Nyassa, Livingstone and his
companions had little reason to doubt that the lake lay in the path of a
major Arab slave route. They were equally distressed at the havoc caused
by the aggressive Ngoni at the northern end of the lake and further south
they had passed through villages littered with 'skeletons and the putrid

bodies of the slain'.[12] When Livingstone reached the *Pioneer* below the Murchison Cataracts in early November, he desperately wanted to hear good news. Instead he learned to his horror that Bishop Mackenzie had made two separate attacks on the Ajawa, driving them away without waiting to be attacked. Instead of wondering whether Mackenzie had had any alternative, and without blaming himself for having brought the mission to such a chaotic place, Livingstone at once concluded that the missionaries had deliberately flouted his advice. Livingstone's immediate concern was not for the welfare of the Bishop and his men but for his own reputation at home. His journal makes this very plain. 'People', he wrote, 'will not approve of men coming out to convert people shooting them. I am sorry that I am mixed up with it, as they will not care what view of my character is given at home.'[13]

Livingstone's assessment of public feeling would be proved correct. As soon as he heard about the attacks, he felt he must see Mackenzie as soon as possible to stop him sending home information about recent events. So when the Bishop arrived at the *Pioneer* on 14 November, Livingstone lost no time in telling him that 'it would be as well if they agreed to say as little as possible about it at home'. Mackenzie then told him that letters about the fighting had already been despatched to the coast. These letters did not just contain casual references to the recent brushes but gave full and detailed accounts.[14] Worse still, Livingstone heard that Rowley had sent an article to a Cape Town newspaper claiming that the attacks had been in response to Dr Livingstone's first fight with the Ajawa. This information ended any chance there might ever have been of Livingstone showing the missionaries understanding and sympathy. Now his only priority was to see that people in England knew that he dissociated himself from the Universities Mission.

During the next few days Livingstone wrote numerous letters putting all the blame on Mackenzie and stressing over and over again that his own earlier fight had been forced upon him and had therefore set no precedent. He made a special point of telling the Foreign Secretary that he would 'keep carefully aloof from the policy adopted by this new mission'. It did not seem to have occurred to Livingstone that by damaging the Mission he was also damaging his own hopes for the Shire Highlands. His best course would have been to sit down with Mackenzie and work out some very convincing justifications. Instead, his condemnations of the Mission virtually brought to an end public subscriptions in England, and therefore crucially endangered the party's further existence. When, some time later, Livingstone realized that he had been lumped in with the missionaries whether he liked it or not, his defence of Mackenzie came too late to mend the earlier damage he had caused. In November 1861 he had felt able to treat the missionaries badly because he had recently heard that the Free Church of Scotland had arranged for one of their members to come out to pave the way for another mission.

Of course Mackenzie *had* gone against Livingstone's advice, but because he had seen no alternative. While he had realized that Christian missionaries damaged their peaceful image by fighting, at the same time he had seen that no successful mission could be established in an area where anarchy prevailed. Since there was nobody else to establish order, Mackenzie had taken the task upon himself. Livingstone refused to listen to this justification and told the Bishop bluntly that he could no longer expect much help from the members of the Zambesi Expedition, who had more important jobs to do than getting reckless missionaries out of scrapes. This was bad enough, but Livingstone added that Mackenzie ought to have come out with a steamer for the mission, since the *Pioneer* would no longer be able to act as their private 'passenger ship'.[15] It was true that Livingstone had suggested to the organizers of the mission that a steamer ought to be sent out, but since one had never arrived, his threat to leave the missionaries to their own devices made them fear they would soon have no contact with the outside world.

Livingstone had further reasons to be uneasy. Before he had realized quite how gruesome conditions were in the Shire Highlands, he had agreed to the idea of Mackenzie's elderly spinster sister coming out to help at Magomero. At the same time, Livingstone had sent word to his own wife in Britain telling her that when George Rae returned to Africa with the new portable steamer, she could come too. Mrs Livingstone, it will be remembered, had been forced by her pregnancy in 1858 to stay in South Africa for a year, and had then had to return to Scotland to stay with her husband's parents for a further three years. Earlier in 1861, Livingstone had also approved Mackenzie's decision to let the young bride of Henry Burrup, a new recruit to the Mission, come out at the same time as Mrs Livingstone and the Bishop's sister. All these females were expected within a month or two. After the fighting with the Ajawa, Livingstone was understandably anxious about the fate of Mrs Burrup and Miss Mackenzie. If these women died at Magomero, that really would spell the end of everything.

Although Livingstone had sanctioned the plan earlier, he now tried to push the full responsibility on to the missionaries by suggesting that they were too feeble to go on without feminine encouragement. 'Most high church people lean on wives or sisters . . . I would as soon lean on a policeman.'[16] But whatever his feelings, Livingstone knew that he was going to have to cooperate with Mackenzie to get these new arrivals to Magomero. In fact he did not expect this task to inconvenience him a great deal, since his next plan was to take the new portable steamer up past the Murchison Cataracts to Lake Nyassa. But, since the ladies would probably arrive early in the following month, when the Shire was low, the *Pioneer* would not be able to get up very far. With this in mind, Livingstone told Mackenzie that he would have to meet the steamer on New Year's Day 1862 at the point where the river Ruo flowed into the Shire: this was 130 miles south-east of Magomero. Livingstone also suggested to Mackenzie that he would have to open up a route overland from Magomero to this point so that the ladies and several tons of supplies, expected by the missionaries, could be safely conveyed to the mission from the mouth of the Ruo. To start with, the Bishop had wanted to come down to the mouth of the Zambesi to welcome his sister, but Livingstone had eventually persuaded him that to leave Magomero leaderless at such a dangerous time would be madness.

When the *Pioneer* left for the sea on 15 November, Mackenzie no longer entertained any illusions about Livingstone's sanctity. The Bishop felt sad and apprehensive. As Rowley remarked, from that time Mackenzie seemed 'to lose much of that bright hopefulness which had distinguished him above all other men'.[17] He would never regain it.

During the next two months, fate would deal both Bishop Mackenzie and Dr Livingstone a series of blows as swift and gratuitous as any sequence of disasters in a Hardy novel.

As soon as the *Pioneer* left, the Bishop hurried back to Magomero, where he immediately gave instructions to two of his colleagues, Procter and Scudamore, to go south to open a suitable path to the Ruo. The two men had only been travelling for a couple of days when they were attacked by hostile villagers and narrowly escaped with their lives. Most of their African attendants were taken captive. The missionaries were therefore faced with another moral and practical dilemma. If they rescued the captives and chastened the aggressors, they might unleash a host of new troubles. On the other hand if they left things as they were, the route to the Ruo would remain blocked. Again Mackenzie had little choice. Within a couple of days he was setting out south at the head of a hastily assembled punitive expedition. There was no fighting when they reached the village, for the inhabitants fled at the appearance of the Christians, but Mackenzie's followers still plundered the place and set fire to all the huts. Nevertheless, an hour or so later the villagers rallied and counter-attacked, and one of the Bishop's Manganja followers was killed in the fighting that ensued. The attack had solved nothing, for now all the surrounding people would be hostile. The Bishop could not wait to find out since he was obliged to return to Magomero before trying to follow the Ruo down to the Shire. By now Mackenzie was hopelessly behindhand in his plans to reach the agreed meeting place by New Year's Day. In fact it was already 2 January when he got back to Magomero. There he decided that he and Burrup, who had recently joined the Mission, should leave at once for the Shire and then go downstream in a canoe.

Unfortunately neither man was in good health, and both were suffering from diarrhoea when they began their journey in teeming rain. The other missionaries had begged the bishop to wait before starting, but he had not listened. He had been badly shaken by Livingstone's attitude in November and he was scared that if he failed to reach the Ruo within a few days, he might forfeit for ever any further assistance from the unpredictable explorer. By 9 January, after a week's travelling through non-stop rain, the two men procured canoes for their journey downstream. As the days passed, Mackenzie became totally obsessed by the idea that Livingstone might not wait for him.

By the merest of coincidences Livingstone had actually been at the place where he had arranged to meet Mackenzie on the appointed day. But he had neither had Miss Mackenzie with him, nor Burrup's young bride, who had been expected to arrive at the same time. In fact the Doctor had not been down to the sea at all. He had spent the month and a half since he had said goodbye to the Bishop dragging the *Pioneer* through mud and sand. Things had been so bad that it had taken three weeks to get the vessel over one bank. While he had cursed the Shire and the *Pioneer* and his crew, he had had little time to think of the Bishop, whose thoughts were at that time exclusively directed towards him. Livingstone's main worry was not that Mackenzie might have to wait for weeks at the Ruo's confluence with the Shire but that the ship bringing Mrs Livingstone and the other women might arrive at the Kongone mouth of the Zambesi and leave before he could get there. He was also horrified by the thought that his precious portable steamer, which Rae had gone to collect two years before, might be taken away for a further two months while the ship that had brought her as yet unassembled parts went north to Zanzibar to take on more coal and supplies.

When he finally arrived at the Kongone mouth on 10 January, a month later than planned, it was to hear that the brig *Hetty Ellen* with the steamer and his wife on board had called three weeks earlier and had been forced by heavy seas to sail again. 'Always too late,' Livingstone lamented in his journal.[18] In a state of abject depression the party prepared for a long wait till the ship returned.

On 11 January, the day after Livingstone had arrived at the Zambesi's mouth, Bishop Mackenzie and Henry Burrup came to the point where the clear waters of the Ruo joined the muddy currents of the Shire. The two missionaries had endured the most appalling journey. Several days earlier their canoe had filled with water and they had lost all their medicines. They had also suffered terribly from dense clouds of mosquitoes; but both men were elated to have arrived at the rendezvous alive. At once they started making enquiries about Dr Livingstone. To their horror, they discovered that the *Pioneer* had last been seen steaming *downstream*. Their immediate assumption was that he had come and not waited for them. Further questions seemed to establish that the steamer had not come up the Shire but had only gone down. The two men knew about the sandbanks and came to the right conclusion. In one way this was comforting: at least they had not been too late and could not be blamed on that account. In another respect the situation was potentially calamitous: they would have to wait in a notoriously unhealthy low-lying area for as long as it took Livingstone to return. Nevertheless, they were certain that Livingstone would by now have met the ladies and would be back within the next ten days. Mackenzie was in a dilemma about whether he ought to return to his post or whether he ought to wait. But his certainty that Livingstone would soon be back decided him. Medicine or no medicine, they would stay. Their only misgiving was due to their discovery that the Doctor had not left any letter for them. But he would be with them soon; the lack of a letter could not mean that he was not thinking about them.

The local chief of the area gave them a bare and damp hut on a small island off the Ruo mouth, and there the two men lived, and it was there that Mackenzie wrote his last letter: pathetically, an appeal to the boat clubs of Oxford and Cambridge for funds for a steamer.[19] As the days passed his remaining optimism started to drain away. He began to feel that he would never see his sister, never see a steamer belonging to the Mission, never return to Magomero. Twice every day Mackenzie went to the southern tip of the island and strained his eyes to catch sight of the *Pioneer*. But the scene was always the same: the tall reeds and the basking crocodiles, and no steamer. Burrup and the Bishop passed the time translating into Greek St Paul's letter to the Romans: 'O wretched man that I am! Who shall deliver me from the body of this death?'[20] The days passed very slowly.

By 18 January, Burrup's diarrhoea had worsened and the Bishop was also suffering from the same complaint. Soon fever came too. After this neither man could communicate with the other. The Bishop imagined that he was back at Magomero with his sister and that new stores had arrived. Meanwhile, the three Africans who had accompanied them treated them with great kindness. On 24 January, Mackenzie's condition worsened and he began to bleed profusely at the nose and mouth; soon he was in a coma and was breathing with difficulty. By the 31st he was very close to death but Burrup had not quite given up. To his horror, that same day the chief came and told him that the Bishop must be moved, because if he died in the hut there would be a taboo on it afterwards. In the end, after vain protests that taxed his declining strength to the utmost, Burrup agreed that Mackenzie should be moved to a less important hut. The movement caused fresh bleeding and by noon the end seemed close.[21]

On this same day, 31 January, Dr Livingstone sighted two ships off the East Luabo and experienced the most intense relief that he had felt for a long time. The vessels had not gone off for two months but only for three weeks. Through a telescope he could see that the larger of the two vessels was a man-of-war and that she was running up a signal: ' "I have—steamboat—in the brig—" to which we replied, "Welcome news" Then "Wife—aboard". With "accept my best thanks" concluded this conversation.'[22]

On board too was Burrup's bride of less than a year and Miss Mackenzie, both desperately eager to get to Magomero to be united with their men. Kirk described Mrs Burrup as 'full of life' and a young lady who delighted 'to talk nautical and jump about'. Miss Mackenzie, he saw, as 'an old invalid who had followed him [the Bishop] through some sort of fanatical infatuation'.[23] The women were attended by a couple of maids: Jessie Lennox and Sarah, whose surname nobody ever mentioned. On the voyage Mrs Livingstone had written a jocular letter to a friend in England describing 'the regular cargo of ladies' going out to the Zambesi. 'We shall take Livingstone by storm. I just fancy his surprise when he sees what a lot of women have come upon him.'[24] But the number of ladies was not to be his only surprise during the next two months.

At roughly the time Livingstone was exchanging signals with H.M.S. *Gorgon*, Bishop Mackenzie's laboured breathing stopped. Burrup was soon surrounded by local Africans who implored him to bury the body at once to avoid enchantment. He was hardly able to stand but he and his African followers wrapped the body in cloth and having placed it in a canoe, took it to the mainland; there among the tall reeds they cleared the ground beneath a mimosa tree and dug a grave. When they had finished it was almost dark. The first Bishop of the Central African Mission had been dead three hours. Burrup had his prayer-book with him but he could not see to read. Instead he repeated what he could remember of the burial service. The grave was left unmarked.

Burrup's supply of cloth was now all but exhausted and the sick man realized that soon he would not be able to buy food. There was therefore no question of remaining to wait for Livingstone. He would leave a letter and return to the mission. On 14 February, Burrup was carried into Magomero, a dying man. Three months before, he had been strong, athletic and confident. Now the young missionary was little more than a skeleton. He died on 22 February of a combination of dysentery and fever.

After Burrup's burial, Rowley wrote with understatement worthy of Livingstone: "The probable arrival of the ladies was now a great anxiety to us."[25]

While these tragic events were unfolding, Livingstone had no time to give much thought to the two men, who for all he knew were still waiting for him. Ever since the *Hetty Ellen*, escorted by the warship H.M.S. *Gorgon*, had anchored off the mouth of the Zambesi on 31 January 1862, Livingstone's life had been a nightmare. His object was to transport his new portable steamer as quickly as possible to the Murchison Cataracts and thence to Lake Nyassa. First, the steamer would have to be assembled for the trip up the Shire; then she would have to be dismantled for the overland journey past the Cataracts, and finally she would have to be reassembled again on the other side. In ideal circumstances such an ambitious project would have been difficult to achieve in a year, but now Livingstone's circumstances were far from ideal, and speed was all important to him. Unless he could get his steamer into the Shire within a couple of months, the river would be low again and the attempt would have to be abandoned till early the following year, and that in turn would mean that the steamer would not be floating on Lake Nyassa till the end of 1863. By then the extended time limit which the Foreign Office had granted the Zambesi Expedition would have been exceeded. The thought of being recalled before being able to use his steamer to cut the Arab slave routes across Nyassa and to the south of it into the Shire Highlands, after spending so much time and money in the attempt, caused Livingstone acute anxiety. What he now needed above all else was a calm atmosphere and a united, well-organized band of helpers. At this crucial time he was in fact surrounded by disunity and confusion.

In addition to her normal complement of expedition members, the *Pioneer* was now going to have to carry upstream five women and their luggage, another missionary and his possessions, the numerous metal plates of the unassembled steamer and thirty tons of stores for the Mission. Livingstone was clearly never going to be able to load everything on to the *Pioneer* without the help of sailors from H.M.S. *Gorgon*, and even then the operation would have to be well planned and executed. The man chosen as Livingstone's principal helper was Assistant Paymaster W.C. Devereux of the *Gorgon*. Devereux had an exceptionally orderly mind and almost everything he saw offended him: the heaps of baggage without inventories, the lack of discipline and the general disorder. He considered Livingstone and the organizers of the Universities Mission to be criminally irresponsible men who, 'not content to push part of their people blindfold and almost purposeless into the wilds of South Africa, add to their distressing position by allowing a lot of helpless females in their blind devotion to accompany them'.[26] Devereux was even more sceptical about Livingstone's chances of getting his portable steamer on to Lake Nyassa. 'If the Engineer [Rae]', wrote Devereux, 'carries all safely to its destination and floats the "*Lady Nyassa*", as his piecemeal steamer is called, on the lake, he will deserve a monument in the Institute of Civil Engineers; but I am afraid the obstacles will even overcome his energy, and that pieces of the steamer will be left here and there—small memorials, monuments of a great but wild endeavour.'[27]

Devereux was soon saying even more critical things. He claimed that he had 'never seen such constant vacillations, blunders, delays, and want of common thought and foresight as is displayed on the *Pioneer* . . . I have rarely, if ever, seen a man so easily led as Dr Livingstone.'[28] But although he probably had plenty of justification for such remarks, the parts of the *Lady Nyassa* were loaded on to the *Pioneer* within a week, with as much of the Mission's stores as could safely be stowed aboard. On 8 February the *Pioneer*, listing dangerously to port, with one paddle-wheel all but submerged, and the other hardly touching the water, started upriver.

As might have been predicted, the considerably overloaded vessel made slow progress, and her increased draught caused her to ground frequently. The seventy-mile trip upstream to Shupanga, where it was planned to assemble the *Lady Nyassa* for the first time, took from 8 February to the end of the month, and during that time Livingstone had to endure more than the agonizing delay itself.

For a start, Mrs Livingstone was no longer the placid and tranquil lady he remembered from Kolobeng days, the last time they had been together for any length of time. In the intervening decade little had happened to Mary to make her sweet-tempered and optimistic. She had had to shoulder the responsibility for bringing up a large family completely without her husband's assistance, and had suffered a great deal from the behaviour of Robert, her eldest son, who had become unmanageable. In order to rejoin her husband she had had to leave her little daughter, Anna Mary, who was not yet four, with Livingstone's family in Scotland. The other children also had to be left behind, either with relatives or at boarding schools. Mary felt that her husband's conception of his divine duty had destroyed any happiness which she and the children might ever have had. Now in 1862 she had few kind words to say for missionaries or mission work. In Livingstone's eyes this was a terrible state of affairs, but worst of all was his growing feeling that Mary had lost her faith. It was not long too before Livingstone heard some unsavoury rumours about his wife.

Expedition gossip had it that James Stewart, the good-looking young representative of the Free Church of Scotland, sent out to plan another mission for the Shire Highlands, had had an affair with Mrs Livingstone. The idea on the face of it was preposterous, for Stewart was a sensitive and handsome man of thirty, while Mary, at forty, was, in Kirk's eyes at least, 'a coarse vulgar woman' and extremely fat as well.[29] Nevertheless, Rae's claims that Stewart had visited Mrs Livingstone's cabin at night on the boat coming out were true. Stewart, however, had never been summoned for the purposes Rae imagined. Mary in fact was a heavy drinker, who, Stewart later acknowledged, often drank enough 'so as to be utterly besotted at times'.[30] During these bouts of drinking Mrs Livingstone sometimes became hysterical and on such occasions Stewart had been summoned by Mary's maid to go and calm her mistress down. Stewart, who had some medical knowledge, usually administered laudanum and then went back to bed. He certainly never enjoyed these nocturnal visits and normally returned to his cabin 'with feelings', as he put it, 'which I am not disposed to chronicle'.[31] Mary had distressed Stewart in other ways too. Her need to drink led her to borrow money from him; and when Stewart finally refused any more, she treated him to a stream of angry abuse. Afterwards Stewart often noticed her proneness to 'queer and disagreeable moods; dull, dumpy and discontented'.[32]

While Livingstone never believed that anything improper had taken place with Stewart, his wife's drinking was a fact that he could not deny even to himself. It was an added burden to him at a very difficult time. His peace of mind was further disturbed by the internal bickerings and hatreds within his greatly enlarged party. The Bishop's sister, Miss Mackenzie, had taken a dislike to Mrs Livingstone, since she considered Mary's criticisms of missionaries to be an implied attack on her brother and his colleagues. Charles Livingstone was also in an intractable mood and hated Stewart, whom he considered an impostor. 'What is this Mr Stewart?' he wrote home to a friend. 'None of us like him. Is he a humbug, or does he really intend to be a missionary? . . . We have no room for these missionaries. They eat up all our nice things and we can't get them replaced. They take care of their own boxes as this Stewart tried to do by turning our boxes out into the rain.'[33] Charles became so enraged by the loss of delicacies like jam and dates that he thought of placing rat-traps in the galley to discourage 'pilfering parsons'.[34] Conditions on board the *Pioneer* were bad enough without personal animosities.

The Doctor and Mrs Livingstone occupied the after-cabin, but the portholes could not be opened because the steamer was so low in the water; instead a hole had to be made in the deck to let in air, but even then, as Charles noted with relish, 'the unfortunate couple are nearly melted'.[35] Miss Mackenzie, Mrs Burrup and the two maids lived in an improvised tent on the deck and had little privacy from curious sailors. Neither Livingstone, nor even Captain Wilson of the *Gorgon*, who had agreed to come to Shupanga with fifty men in three boats to help offload the sections of the *Lady Nyassa*, seemed able to discipline the sailors. The bluejackets were soon drinking large quantities of a powerful Portuguese brew, *agua ardente*, which they nicknamed 'hoggydent'—Livingstone called it 'vile spirit secretly sold'. The men also went out on numerous sexual sorties, to the horror of James Stewart, who noted in his journal that 'one woman was abused five times'. Livingstone's stoker on the *Pioneer* had already fathered several mixed-race children. Drinking became such a problem that eventually Livingstone and Wilson had to agree to put anybody found drunk on half pay.[36]

Meanwhile the delay, the disorder and the quarrelling wore down Livingstone's patience and made him snap at everybody, including Miss Mackenzie, who described him as 'abrupt and ungracious'.[37] James Stewart, who had hero-worshipped Livingstone ever since reading *Missionary Travels*, was shocked at the Doctor's sudden explosions of bad temper. Soon Stewart was writing in dismay, after hearing Livingstone abusing his crew: 'I could hardly have credited that Dr L. would have said "Go forward, you useless trash!"'[38]

Everybody was heartily relieved when Shupanga was reached and some of the stores could be temporarily put ashore; work could also begin on the *Lady Nyassa*. Shupanga was reached at the end of February. Two weeks before that, Captain Wilson and Kirk had volunteered to take Miss Mackenzie and Mrs Burrup on ahead in an open boat to meet their men-folk at the mouth of the Ruo. It was not to be a pleasant journey. Miss Mackenzie was ill with fever and took up most of the stern of the small boat. Kirk soon loathed the sight of her. 'If she decided to shift her position, she had to get assistance and have herself supported with pillows.'[39] Before the elderly invalid could be persuaded to wash or change her clothes, a special 'bower or shelter had to be constructed'.

When they reached the Ruo there was no sign of anybody, and the locals denied ever having seen Burrup or the Bishop. On 3 March, just below the Murchison Cataracts, Kirk and Wilson heard that the Bishop was dead; poor Mrs Burrup had to wait another week before hearing that her husband had also perished. There was no question of the two women going to Magomero.

Kirk, Wilson and the two ladies, who were now prostrated with grief and exhaustion, arrived at Shupanga on 14 March. When Livingstone heard the news that the Bishop was dead, he sat in the small, dimly lit cabin of the *Pioneer* with his head in his hands and murmured: 'This will hurt us all.'[40] After Mackenzie's attack on the Ajawa, Livingstone's first reaction had been to work out how he might dissociate himself from any blame. The present situation seemed to call for similar tactics. Livingstone had no illusions about the reaction there would be in Britain to this double tragedy. A great many people were going to say that Dr Livingstone had lured a group of godly men to their deaths by duping them into believing that central Africa was a healthy and idyllic area. In the storm of indignation, the fact that the two men had died in notorious low-lying marshy country, and not in the Shire Highlands, was likely to be overlooked, and if that happened, all chances of trade or colonization, either with or without the Government's aid, would disappear for good. With this in mind, as well as his reputation, Livingstone sat down to blame the dead men for what had happened to them. Early the following day he was writing a despatch to the Foreign Secretary telling him that 'coarse living and rash exposure have ended in the sad loss of life'. Livingstone wrote to most of his friends telling them the same: if Mackenzie had taken reasonable care of his health he would not have died. His attacks on the dead Bishop almost outdid the calumnies he had penned after the Linyanti missionaries had died. With characteristic callousness he told his brother-in-law, John Moffat, that 'the effect will be better men will come to the work'.[41] When James Stewart offered his condolences, Livingstone informed him that in future no missionary would feel inclined 'to come for a lark or to make a good thing of playing the missionary for a few years and then reaping laurels'.[42] This attack, on the man whom he had once called 'the best of the bunch' and 'A1', cannot be excused by Livingstone's misery about the future. Mackenzie had been sincere and selfless; nor would he ever have taken the risks he had done if Livingstone had not threatened to stop helping the Mission in November 1861. Even when Livingstone wrote to a cousin of the Bishop, General Hay, he implied that Mackenzie had died because he had been late at the meeting place and because he had stayed there rather than return to Magomero or push on downstream after the *Pioneer*, once he knew that she had been detained.[43]

The missionaries still left at Magomero might have expected some sympathy from the man who had led them to the Shire Highlands, but Livingstone, to make sure the survivors did not use Mackenzie's death as an excuse to leave the country, wrote them a stern letter: 'Remember pray, that the eyes of the most influential people in England are upon you, and should anything prevent you doing your duty manfully you will be set down as a parcel of canting hypocrites that ought never to have been entrusted with anything.'[44]

Livingstone did not, of course, care what the most influential people in England thought of the missionaries, but he knew that they would not think much of his judgement if the members of the Universities Mission had to leave their 'ideal and fertile' location in order to save their lives. Livingstone concluded his savage letter by suggesting that he had told Mackenzie not to 'go down to the Ruo and explore upwards' on account of the rains at that time of year. Since he had also told the Bishop that the route would have to be pioneered by 1 January, it is hard to see how he could have avoided doing so outside the rainy season. Despite this, it had not been Livingstone's fault that the two men died, for the swamping of their canoe and the loss of their medicines had seen to that. But his many letters of self-justification and recrimination, all devoid of real grief at the loss of a man whom even Charles Livingstone had liked, point once more to that central defect in Livingstone's character: his virtual inability to respond to the suffering of others.

Livingstone could argue that he was thinking of the future of Christianity in the area for centuries to come, and could therefore not sympathize with men who, by their deaths, had done harm to the Christian prospects of a large region. But that was hardly enough. In 1859 he had known that missionaries who came to the Shire Highlands, as an isolated group of men, would face the most fearful problems posed by the Ajawa and the Arab and Portuguese slavers. But now he turned even these problems to his advantage by employing that argument in which he firmly believed: that settled African tribal communities were confident and rejected Christianity out of hand. In the Shire Highlands where all was anarchy, the Manganja ought to have been in an ideal psychological state to receive the Gospel. Christianity could have given them something to cling to when all else fell apart around them. Livingstone argued that the missionary prospects had been excellent because many of the freed slaves had been orphans and would not therefore have been taught tribal traditions by their parents. It was only Mackenzie's idiotic attacks on the Ajawa, and his needless death, that had prevented thousands of conversions. With more justification Livingstone claimed that if Mackenzie and Burrup, once they had found out what had delayed the *Pioneer*, had not stayed so long at the Ruo mouth, but had instead returned at once to Magomero, they would not have died. The Shire Highlands was, unlike the river Shire itself, a relatively healthy area. Livingstone's conviction that the Highlands would now be represented as a malarial death-trap increased his bitterness towards the dead men.

Only when Livingstone heard early in 1863 of a packed meeting that had taken place during the previous summer at the Sheldonian Theatre in Oxford did he begin belatedly to defend the missionaries. At that meeting, Dr Pusey, and other eminent High Churchmen, had attacked Dr Livingstone and the missionaries for using firearms, even in self-defence, for by doing so they had denied themselves that most prestigious of Christ's rewards: a martyr's death. This inanity at last forced Livingstone to admit to Horace Waller, one of the missionaries who by now had become a personal friend: 'I thought you wrong in attacking the Ajawa . . . because I thought you had shut yourselves up to one tribe, but I think differently now and only wish they would send out Dr Pusey here.'[45] Livingstone also paid glowing tribute to 'the good and noble bishop Mackenzie', but this change of heart came over a year too late. By then Livingstone's earlier attacks on the Mission had turned too many people against the missionaries for the mood to be reversible. Already, influential men like Murchison and Admiral Washington of the Admiralty had resigned from the Universities Mission Committee. When Livingstone saw that there was a danger of the Mission being withdrawn, he fought against it, for at last he had grasped the fact that such a move would destroy all his hopes for traders, colonists or missionaries to come to the Shire Highlands. As will be seen, he failed to undo the earlier damage he had done.

18

Disaster and Collapse: the End of the Zambesi Expedition

1862–1864

———⟫◆⟪———

B ishop Mackenzie's death did not change any of Livingstone's plans. In March 1862 he was still determined to get the *Lady Nyassa* up past the Murchison Cataracts to the lake after which she had been named. At Shupanga, Livingstone was three hundred miles from his objective and by the end of March the river had started to fall. There was no question of getting the steamer up to the cataracts in pieces on the *Pioneer*, that would mean weeks, maybe months, aground in the Shire. The new steamer would have to be towed up by the *Pioneer*, having been partially assembled at Shupanga. The engineer, George Rae, estimated that it would take him at least two months to bolt the hull together, and by then the *Pioneer*, even without any kind of load, would be unable to get up the Shire beyond the Ruo. Livingstone was forced to admit that the *Lady Nyassa* would not reach the Murchison Cataracts till early the following year. It was worrying enough for him that by then the extended period granted to the expedition by the Foreign Office would almost be ended, but equally distressing was the fact that the delay would force him to spend months on the lower Zambesi in far greater danger of malaria than he would have been in the Shire Highlands. He had never been personally afraid of fever—he was rarely afraid of anything—but he was badly scared to think that his wife would be exposed to fever for a long period. Partly for this reason, and partly because he hated inactivity, Livingstone decided that he would remain at Shupanga only until the hull of the *Lady Nyassa* had been put together; then, with Mrs Livingstone and the rest of the party, he would sail to the island of Johanna, six hundred miles north-east of Quilimane, to get fresh supplies to last into 1863. Then, after leaving his wife safely on Johanna, Livingstone intended to spend a couple of months making one more effort to get up the river Rovuma. By the time he returned to the Zambesi, the river would be high again and he would be able to tow the *Lady Nyassa* up the Shire to the Cataracts without difficulty. This then was the long-term plan.

When Livingstone knew that the Bishop was dead he decided to take the bereaved women down to the mouth of the river himself, to put them on to the *Gorgon* for the return voyage to England. This trip should have been accomplished in a couple of weeks, but when the *Pioneer* reached the Kongone mouth it was discovered that the *Gorgon* had been forced by dwindling stocks of coal to sail for the port of Mozambique. This meant that for the next two and a half weeks Livingstone and his wife were forced to remain in the notoriously malarial Zambesi delta, awaiting the *Gorgon*'s return. Even then there was yet another delay caused by the inefficiency of the *Pioneer*'s engineer, Hardesty, who had allowed the feed pipes to become blocked. Thus it was not until 14 April that the steamer was back at Shupanga. Livingstone dismissed Hardesty, but the damage had been done. For over a month the whole party had been exposed to malaria in the worst part of the river.

Mrs Livingstone had been worried and out of sorts ever since James Stewart had foolishly told her what people were saying about them both. On 21 April, less than a week after her return from the Zambesi delta to Shupanga, she fell ill with fever. From the beginning Livingstone took her complaint seriously but he was not seriously worried till the 24th. Stewart had seen her the day before and had thought drink was the root of the trouble. But by the 25th there was no doubt that her condition was grave; soon she was tormented by terrible spasms of nausea every quarter of an hour. The following day there was still no improvement and she was moved from the *Pioneer* to the one stone house in Shupanga. Kirk and Livingstone used every method they had learned to try and reduce the fever, but even the most massive doses of quinine seemed to have no effect. By now her mind was wandering; her thoughts were filled with her distant children. Robert, her eldest son, had rejected any efforts made by his teachers and had become a problem child. Often she mentioned him. Then she wept about her baby daughter, who had been left in Scotland. Later she burst out: 'See, see Agnes is falling down a precipice.'[1]

Livingstone stayed by her bed day and night, vainly trying to feed her. She could not even keep down slices of melon. Early on the morning of the 27th, she started moaning uncontrollably and could barely drink water from a spoon. At 3 a.m. Livingstone got Kirk out of bed and he arrived to find her in a half-comatose state. She could no longer swallow and so medicine could only be injected. By dawn the coma had deepened and her face and skin were becoming tinged with yellow. Kirk was distressed but not in any way emotionally involved. He wrote coolly in his journal: 'The state of her mind has been such as to predispose her to any disease while her indiscretions in eating and drinking previously have been such as to undermine her health.'[2] He was sure that she would have been more likely to rally had Stewart not told her about the rumours going around. It seemed unlikely that she would live beyond midday, but she did. Livingstone had remained hopeful until she lost the power to swallow. After that, his self-control cracked and he started to weep. At 6 p.m., scandal or no scandal, he summoned James Stewart from the *Pioneer*. The man had been his wife's friend and she had been fond of him. When Stewart arrived he saw Livingstone 'sitting by the side of a rude bed formed of boxes, but covered with a soft mattress, on which lay his dying wife . . . The man who had faced so many deaths, and braved so many dangers, was now utterly broken down and weeping like a child.'[3] Stewart found his own eyes filling. Livingstone asked him to say a prayer, while he and Kirk knelt. Afterwards her breathing became laboured and irregular. Livingstone once more broke down and, taking his wife in his arms, choked: 'My dearie, my dearie you are going to leave me . . . Are you resting on Jesus?' He was uncertain whether she had heard what he said because the quinine had deafened her. But she had looked upwards when he had spoken and he took this to mean that she had understood. Later he very much regretted not using writing to communicate with her during these last few hours. He knew quite well that she 'had fallen into a gloomy desponding state' and it haunted him to think that she might have died without faith. Just after seven he kissed her and she did not respond: 'lying with her mouth a little open she gently shut it and breathed her last'.[4]

During the night Rae made a coffin and Kirk and Stewart washed the body and wound it in cloth. The local Portuguese begged to be allowed to fire a salute at the funeral the following day, but Livingstone refused. Although he was dropping with tiredness, he spent much of the night going through her things. The thought of her dying without believing in God was agonizing to him. He gained some consolation on finding a short prayer among her papers: 'Accept me Lord as I am, and make me such as thou wouldst have me to be.'[5] Surely, Livingstone argued, there were plenty of examples in the lives of saints and other pious people when a time 'of religious gloom or paroxysms of opposition & fierce rebellion against God found vent in terrible expressions—these were followed by great elevations of faith'. But his doubts persisted. A few days before, she had said gloomily 'that she would never have a house in this country'.[6] At the time he had thought she was just being despondent and had joked about it. Now he wondered whether she had felt that she would soon die and had been using a religious metaphor. All the hardships she had endured in Britain, the journeys across the Kalahari, the long separation at the beginning of the expedition, seemed real to Livingstone for the first time. Providence might have led him but that did not redress her suffering. He wrote to his mother telling her: 'There are many regrets

which will follow me to my dying day. If I had done so and so &c. &c.
. . .'[7] In his journal he reproached himself as bitterly: 'My heart smites me
that I did not talk seriously on that [her doubts] and many things
besides.'[8] One of the 'many things' was the fact that Mary had had no
home for the last ten years of her life and had had no settled environment
in which to bring up the children. In the depths of his grief Livingstone
at last seemed to understand what his children had lived through. His
wife's death left him a more understanding father, and from then on the
tone of his letters to his children became more personal and less homiletic.
He told each one of their mother's death and in none of these letters did
he attempt to cloak his grief with conventional phrases of religious consolation. He started his letter to Oswell:

> With many tears running down my cheeks I have to tell you that poor
> dearly beloved Mama died last night about seven o' clock . . . She loved
> you dearly and often spoke of you and all the family, especially little
> Baby . . . She gave me the comb and toothbrush you kindly sent me. She
> was collecting some curiosities for you. There are two ostrich eggshells
> and other shells she brought from Mozambique . . . You must all love
> each other more than ever now.[9]

In his journal he wrote: 'For first time in my life I feel willing to die
D.L.'[10] James Stewart noticed a distinct change in the Doctor's manner
during the next few weeks. 'Dr L. peculiarly communicative and
agreeable. His recent loss seems to have had some effect of a softening
kind on him.'[11]

The day after her death Mary Livingstone was buried at noon under the
shadow of a massive baobab tree. She was only forty-one years old. The
day was misty and the sky heavy and leaden. Livingstone asked Stewart to
conduct the service and he was proud to do so. Four sailors carried the
coffin to the grave and afterwards mounted guard over it to protect the
body from wild animals till a stone cairn could be built.

That afternoon Rae went on working on the *Lady Nyassa* and Kirk
attended to three members of the *Pioneer*'s crew, who were all dangerously
ill with fever. Ironically, one of them was Hardesty, the engineer, whom
Livingstone blamed for delaying their progress. But, unlike Mrs
Livingstone, Hardesty recovered, as did the other two sick men. To the
accompaniment of the banging of bolts, the screaming of delirious men
and the distant howling of hyenas, Livingstone went on sorting his wife's
papers and clothes. He felt overcome with doubts and regrets. Perhaps she
ought never to have come. Perhaps once he had known that there would
be so many delays before the Highlands could be reached, he ought to

have sent her home. But, as he told his mother, 'it would have broken Mary's heart to have sent her away then'. He had known, too, that, while at Kuruman in 1859, she had often been taunted by other missionaries' wives with words like: 'O she is not good—she is here because her husband cannot live with her.'[12]

For the first time he began to have doubts about what God intended him to do. 'There is something I have to do or be; such I take to be the meaning of this dispensation. I wish I could find out.'[13] In his despondency, he remembered saying to her, after they had shared a joke just before she became ill: 'We old bodies ought now to be more sober.' She had replied: 'Oh no, you must always be as playful . . . I would not like you to be as grave as some folks I have seen.'[14] To Livingstone that conversation seemed a very long time ago.

When, months later, Livingstone started to receive letters of condolence, he was not blamed for encouraging his wife to join him. Dr Tidman, alone, could not deny his true feelings; the deaths at Linyanti were too recent: 'As it is easy to be wise after the event, the thought might occur to some persons that, if your dear wife had remained in England, her life might yet have been spared to her family and friends.'[15]

After his wife's death, Livingstone was eager to get away from Shupanga, but knew that he would not be able to do so till the *Lady Nyassa* was launched. Although Rae was working hard, this event would not take place for a further two months. During this time Livingstone made a couple of trips down to the mouth for mail and supplies but otherwise had to remain inactive, a situation which always depressed him.

At last, on 23 June, the *Lady Nyassa* was ready for launching. The operation was a shambles and the steamer nearly sank stern first during it, but before sunset, after twelve hours of constant heaving and shoving, she was forced down into the water over rollers made from the trunks of palm trees. Livingstone felt that there should be some sort of celebration, so he fired off a couple of rockets, one of which disappointingly sped along the ground into the river. A bottle of wine was opened and glasses raised to a future in which only Livingstone claimed to have any confidence. Most of the party doubted whether the new steamer would ever reach the Murchison Cataracts, let alone the lake. Nor was the *Lady Nyassa* anywhere near completion; a lot of fitting out would have to be done before she could be towed.

Mrs Livingstone's death had not altered her husband's determination to go to Johanna for stores and then to take a final look at the Rovuma. The previous survey had been enough to convince Charles and Kirk that any further effort in that direction would be futile. But both said nothing. Kirk badly wanted to object, but felt that if he did 'all former services would be lost sight of by Livingstone'.[16] Logic supported the view that the Rovuma could not be navigable for more than a hundred miles at most. Quite apart from previous surveys, the height of Lake Nyassa, 1,200 feet above sea level, and the distance of the lake from the sea, three hundred miles, made it a foregone conclusion that there would be cataracts somewhere along the course of the river. But after his loss Livingstone was less concerned with inconvenient facts than with remaining active during the months that remained before he would be able to get the steamer up the Shire. Whenever circumstances had threatened to crush Livingstone in the past he had fought back by forcing himself to go through with some physically gruelling exploring. Now in his personal misery he would try the same remedy on the Rovuma. His companions had noticed that since Mary's death, Livingstone's manner had softened a little, but they had also observed that his previously inflexible determination had hardened into an obsessive, almost masochistic desire to push himself to the limits of human endurance. The journey up the Rovuma during September and November 1862 would highlight this trait which was to become central during the remaining years of Livingstone's life.

There was so little water in the Rovuma that, from the beginning, it was obvious that Livingstone and his companions would have to go up in two open boats. They got off to a bad start when Rae flatly refused to travel in the same whaler as Charles Livingstone. After a reorganization Livingstone and Charles were put in one boat and Rae and Kirk in the other.

After five days it was crystal clear to Kirk that there was no point in going any further; the river was already a maze of shoals, and the main channels never more than a foot deep. But Livingstone seemed oblivious to this. When the water dwindled to a few inches he was quite undeterred and began hiring Africans to carry the boats over distances of anything up to half a mile. Kirk was soon writing in his journal: 'I can come to no other conclusion than that Dr L. is out of his mind.'[17] Had Kirk been able to see the sort of letters his leader was writing at this time, he would have been even more worried. Livingstone was now in a strange fatalistic frame of mind, as he confessed to Robert and Mary Moffat. 'It is probable', he told them, 'that I may fall in establishing a new system on that great centre of slaving, Lake Nyassa.'[18] Over and over again the thought of impending death appears in his journal at this time. 'Am I to be a martyr to my own cause?' he was soon asking himself. 'I begin to think that I may not live to see success. Am I to experience that this cause is to be founded on my sacrifice and cemented by my suffering? Every covenant was ratified with sacrifice . . . I hope this may be compensated if I die by my death.'[19]

As another week passed and Livingstone forced the boats on over the sand, Kirk wondered whether the Doctor had any idea of the dangerous situation they would all be in if the water fell too low for them to get back to the coast. They had already been fired on by locals and had had to return fire, killing two men in the process. A return to the sea on foot would now be extremely hazardous. 'Dr L. is a most unsafe leader,' Kirk noted in his journal, and added, 'It is useless making any remark to him.'[20]

During the evening of 26 September they at last came to a cataract and there, to the amazement of Livingstone's companions, he began making arrangements for the boats to be carried up over the rocks. But to everybody's intense relief, the following day he changed his mind and gave the order to turn back. The safety of his followers had not influenced his decision. His only reason for returning was his fear that if they got stuck, he might miss the next flood season in the Shire and Zambesi and thus fail to get the *Lady Nyassa* up to the Murchison Cataracts.

The journey up the Rovuma had not increased Livingstone's knowledge. At best, the continual labour of struggling up a useless and shallow river had kept his despair at bay. Unfortunately, it had determined the rest of the party to leave Africa as soon as they could decently do so.

Before they reached Shupanga again, in mid-December, George Rae had told his leader that he would resign as soon as the *Lady Nyassa*'s engines were installed. If he did so, Livingstone knew that there would be no hope of getting the steamer past the Murchison Cataracts. He had no choice but to swallow his pride and allow Rae to be as abusive and insubordinate as he wished. Soon Rae was writing the sort of letters to Livingstone which would have led to instant dismissal in the days of Bedingfeld and Baines. 'I have decided', the engineer told his leader in early January, 'not to go on board the *Pioneer* again unless duty calls me. Therefore I wish you to give me my provisions on board the *Lady Nyassa* and a boat for the use of the *Lady Nyassa*.'[21]

Livingstone objected, but Rae got his way and ate all his meals away from the rest of the party. In other ways discipline had reached a new nadir. On the way back from the Rovuma, Livingstone had been obliged to issue a Public Order prohibiting his officers from striking African crew members without permission.[22] Charles had already started writing to friends telling them that in his view the Government ought to recall the expedition before it fell to bits of its own accord.[23] When the *Pioneer* left Shupanga on 11 January 1863, with the *Lady Nyassa* in tow, only Livingstone himself felt that there was any point in continuing. The Zambesi Expedition was entering its final phase.

To start with, Livingstone and his party made excellent progress; after ten days steaming up the Shire they had reached the junction with the

Ruo. But a few days later, in early February, the *Pioneer* and the *Lady Nyassa* became firmly embedded in the mud and sand of the river bottom. The next few months were to be the worst any member of the party had ever known.

The previous year there had been a terrible drought in the Shire Highlands and on the lower Shire, and the low rainfall, besides ensuring that there was much less water in the river than usual for the time of year, had also caused all the crops to fail. The whole area was gripped by the worst famine any of the locals could remember. Upriver, the missionaries, themselves without adequate stockpiles of food, had looked on helplessly for many months as men and women scrabbled for roots to eat. All the Africans whom Livingstone and his colleagues now saw had swollen bellies, skeletal limbs and dull, dead eyes. The famine had been made far worse by the continuing aggression of the Ajawa, whose raids had diverted the people's attention from agriculture at a time when they had a chance to save a small percentage of their corn and crops. The dead soon littered paths and fields and nobody had the energy to bury them.

As February dragged on, and Livingstone and his unwilling companions forced their steamers upstream at the pitiful rate of a mile a week, they soon saw very real evidence of the severity of the famine. Bodies began to float past them downstream. The Africans knew that it was easier to dump a dead relative in the river than to dig a grave. Livingstone counted thirty-four corpses in three days. It was not an edifying sight to see crocodiles tearing at bloated stomachs and fighting each other to get more of an arm or leg. Soon fever added to the misery of those aboard the *Pioneer* and the *Lady Nyassa*. Livingstone's orders were disobeyed by everybody. Several members of the Mission, which had now moved out of the Highlands down to the river, came to see if they could help the *Pioneer*'s crew; they went away disgusted. As Waller put it, 'the discontent and murmurs are sickening: it is a ship divided against itself, plank by plank'.[24] Rowley was even more depressed by what he saw: 'The officers are all but in rebellion, and the Dr daily becomes more incapable of self-control. A catastrophe, or tragedy I fear is not far off.'[25] But tragedy, when it came, struck the missionaries and not the expedition men. Within a month Scudamore, who, with the exception of Mackenzie, had always been the most popular of all the missionaries, died in agony from ulcers on the neck and chest. Shortly afterwards, the doctor to the Mission, Dickenson, died of fever. Livingstone with characteristic brevity summed up his life in a sentence: 'A very weakly subject but very religious and resolved to brave out the fever which he had perpetually'. Livingstone was genuinely grieved at the loss of Scudamore, but his final observation on both deaths was predictable: 'This will be another blow to our work.'[26]

Nor could he help telling the three survivors of the once seven-strong mission that nobody would have died if they had remained in the Highlands. Poor Rowley had tried to explain that they had been driven out of Magomero by famine and the Ajawa.[27]

On 10 April the two steamers at last lay at anchor below the Murchison Cataracts. The last sixty miles had taken them ten weeks. Before Livingstone could make any preparations for the next stage of the work, the dismantling of the *Lady Nyassa*, another death occurred. In the summer of the year before, Richard Thornton had agreed to rejoin the expedition on condition that he was allowed to continue working independently. Livingstone, who wanted to add Thornton's geological notes to the expedition's scientific data, had agreed to this. Since his dismissal in 1859, Thornton had taken part in an expedition to Mount Kilimanjaro, led by the German explorer, Baron von der Decken. The young man had also worked hard on his own account and had filled dozens of notebooks with scientific observations. He had been working near the mission in early 1863 and, on discovering how little food they had there, offered to travel overland to Tete to bring back goats and sheep. He kept his word and returned to the mission on 13 April, but the journey had over-taxed his strength and he died five days later of fever and dysentery. Livingstone had witnessed so many deaths that another was no matter for unusual concern; just one more regrettable event that might be placed to his account at a later date. Once again he showed little sorrow, just a puzzled contempt for human weakness. 'Thornton was a fool and went off to Tete to buy goats for the lazies though he had my written orders to geologise in a healthy quarter ... Folly killed him.'[28] This was a pretty bleak, uncharitable obituary for a young man of twenty-five who died trying to help three men who had just suffered the loss of four companions. But Livingstone, who considered that the fallibility of his colleagues had played a major part in the expedition's failure, was in no mood to be charitable. *He* had not died, *he* had not stopped working or asked to go home. After Kebrabasa he had redoubled his efforts rather than admit defeat. He had met the death of his wife with the same determination to go on, whatever the cost. Why, he asked, should others be pitied when they succumbed to a disease that he had lived through and fought off so often? Only the weight of so many failures and disasters can explain Livingstone's contempt for those who died. To view death as a voluntary act of surrender is never the sign of a healthy mind, and when Kirk, on the journey up the Rovuma, had described Livingstone's head as 'not of the ordinary construction but what is termed cracked',[29] he had not been exaggerating. The disappointment at Kebrabasa, the disaster at Linyanti, the chaos in the Shire Highlands, the death of the Bishop and the loss of his own wife had in the end numbed Livingstone to all normal human emotions except one: the dull anger of despair.

Livingstone would later recover his power to feel emotions, but in the spring and summer of 1863, drained by the loss of Mary, and recognizing for the first time that complete failure was now inevitable, the sight of other human beings only sickened him. When Charles and Kirk asked permission to leave, a week after Thornton's death, Livingstone did not withhold consent. 'It would be well to get rid of them all and have no more,' he wrote, and added that all his white colleagues had never been more than 'a complete nuisance'.[30] When Kirk left, after six years of loyal service in hellish conditions, Livingstone did not thank him, and when he did finally sit down to write a brief note of thanks, Kirk had gone and the moment had passed. Kirk wrote bitterly to a friend:

> I find that in an underhand way Dr L. has given me no cause to thank him . . . He is about as ungrateful and slippery a mortal as I ever came in contact with, and, although he would be grievously offended to think that anyone doubted his honesty, I am sorry to say that I do. I think the explanation to be that he is one of those sanguine enthusiasts wrapped up in their own schemes whose reason and better judgment is blinded by headstrong passion.[31]

When Charles and Kirk left for the coast, George Rae was the only original member of the party still with Livingstone. There was one other officer, Lieutenant E.D. Young, who had been in charge of gunnery on the *Gorgon*, and had stayed on with the expedition after the other sailors had left in April the previous year. In Young's opinion the thirty-mile road which would have to be built before the pieces of the *Lady Nyassa* could be transported past the Cataracts would take a year to construct and would require the uninterrupted labour of a hundred Africans during that time. There were barely twenty Africans who could be relied upon to work for a week, let alone a year. The famine had left all the people too weak to devote any of their time to anything other than the search for food. Cloth could not buy the services of starving men. Livingstone by now realized that his own food supplies would not last more than two months, at the end of which he would be forced to go to Tete or the coast for more supplies. Once down the Shire, he would never get up again. Failure, he could see, was certain. On 17 April he wrote in his journal: 'If the Government looks on this as I do we may expect to be withdrawn.'[32]

But Livingstone would not publicly admit that he had given up. He wanted it to appear that when the order of recall came, it alone had stopped him achieving the successful launching of the steamer on the lake.* So, to the amazement of Rae and Young, Livingstone gave orders for the *Lady Nyassa* to be taken apart for the land journey past the Cataracts. Livingstone himself, with the handful of Africans he could persuade to work for him, started on the road, felling trees and rolling large rocks out of the way. At the same time he wrote a despatch to the Foreign Secretary claiming that he was still determined to get the steamer up to Nyassa, but painting such a bleak picture that Lord John Russell would have no alternative but to recall the expedition at once. In the past Livingstone had always minimized problems; now he laid them on thick, going so far as to admit that the Shire Highlands, that ideal place for a British colony, had become 'a desert strewed with human bones'.[33] Livingstone explained about the famine and suggested that he would soon have to abandon his work for several months to go down to the coast for supplies. Livingstone would not have felt happy if he had not excused himself for failing to predict the present situation in the Shire Highlands. He therefore suggested that, although the famine and the Ajawa had both been severe problems, the major part of the blame for the chaos and death should rest with the Portuguese. In fact the Portuguese slave raids had depopulated the lower Shire, but were not a crucial factor in the Highlands. The missionaries, when Livingstone tried this argument on them, were not impressed, and replied that the famine and the Ajawa had done all the damage. Livingstone merely repeated his argument: 'They [the Portuguese] have cleared this valley of people—I put it on them because famine from drought never utterly exterminates.'[34] Writing to his daughter Agnes, Livingstone used the same excuse. 'Half of the labour and toil I have undergone would have left an indelible mark on any part of Africa not subject to the Portuguese.'[35] Livingstone now knew that people in Britain would say that the Zambesi Expedition had been a failure from beginning to end, and he badly needed a public scapegoat. The Portuguese would serve very well. His only regret was that he had not abused them rather more often in his letters to the Government written during 1860 and 1861.

In fact, Lord John Russell did not in the end need Livingstone's despatches to convince himself that the expedition ought to be withdrawn. The deaths and dismissals had already persuaded him that nothing more would be achieved, and on 2 February he had issued the order of recall. The despatch did not reach Livingstone at the Murchison Cataracts till 2 July, when Adams, the cockney labourer from the mission, appeared

---

* His last biographer (at the time my biography was first published) George Seaver accepted that, given a month longer, Livingstone could have launched the *Lady Nyassa*. But Seaver did not see Livingstone's journal for 1863.

on the shore and yelled: 'Hallo you *Pioneer* chaps—no more pay for you after December. I brings the letter as says it.'[36] It was hardly the sort of dignified announcement of the termination of six years' work which Livingstone would have wished.

The reason Adams had known the contents of the despatch was simple. It had been brought up from the coast by the new Bishop who had been sent to replace Mackenzie. Bishop Tozer had felt little compunction in reading Livingstone's official papers, since the future of the expedition would crucially affect the future of the Mission. For a start, once the expedition had left, the Mission would have no link with the coast, and the naval warships that had called regularly at the Kongone mouth to collect official despatches would no longer come. From the beginning Tozer was convinced that the Mission would have to be withdrawn. He had not discovered that Scudamore and Procter had died until he arrived on the Shire, but when he did so his determination to pull out became total. To avoid accusations of cowardice he decided to give the Mission a final trial further south, on a mountain near the junction of the Shire and the Zambesi. This effort was to be a brief prelude to later withdrawal.

It was unfortunate that Livingstone so quickly got wind of Tozer's intentions, for with the collapse of the expedition the Doctor had decided that the Mission offered the 'one ray of hope' in an otherwise hopeless area.[37] Livingstone did not seem for a moment to be aware of the incongruity of his new love for the Mission. The truth was that he wanted the missionaries to stay on, not because he thought they could achieve anything, but because he felt that their continued presence in Africa would help him to claim, on his return to England, that he had left behind a stable and flourishing Christian community in the Shire Highlands. His vitriolic response to Tozer's plans was therefore no objective judgement but the last flashes of anger and disappointment at the loss of all his earlier hopes. If Tozer was going to leave, then Livingstone would add him to the other excuses for his own failure.

Livingstone in 1859 had described Mount Morambala, where Tozer re-established the Mission, as an ideal 'sanatorium', which the Portuguese had been mad not to utilize.[38] As soon as the new Bishop went there, the mountain changed its character and became 'a mountain 4,000 feet high, where clouds rest perpetually at some seasons and the condensed vapour drips constantly through the roofs of huts'.[39] In the past Livingstone had not noticed that Morambala had a thin and scattered population, but now he blamed Tozer for not having come to that conclusion after a single inspection. Tozer had actually asked Livingstone whether he considered the mountain to be a suitable spot for resettling the Mission, and had been told that, although not as good as the Shire Highlands, it was not a bad choice. It was, as it turned out, a terrible choice since, as Livingstone had observed with after-the-event wisdom, the clouds *did* rest 'perpetually at some seasons' and the water did drip through the roofs.

Tozer was soon writing angrily to the Bishop of Cape Town, telling him what he thought of Dr Livingstone. 'The idea of making a Portuguese sanatorium here, is a good specimen of the way in which Livingstone leaps to any conclusion he may wish to see adopted.' The criticism was a just one. Once Livingstone decided he wanted to achieve a particular aim, he would at once throw all his hopes and energies into the venture without pausing to consider at the outset whether it was practicable. This trait, Tozer went on, made the Doctor 'a very dangerous man'.[40] But, as Baines, Thornton or Bedingfeld could have told Tozer, to criticize Dr Livingstone was a hazardous undertaking. When Livingstone knew Tozer had set a date for leaving Africa, he wrote to the new Bishop telling him that he, Livingstone, would make him regret this decision 'till his dying day'.[41] Livingstone at once embarked on a campaign of character assassination worthy of any of his previous efforts.

While claiming that he would 'not say a word in public to injure them [the missionaries]',[42] Livingstone roundly condemned Tozer in his published account of the expedition, *A Narrative of an Expedition to the Zambesi*. The fact that Tozer intended to withdraw the Mission to Zanzibar suggested a suitably invidious comparison. 'The mission in fleeing from Morambala to an island in the Indian Ocean', thundered Livingstone, 'was acting as St Augustine would have done, had he located himself on one of the Channel Islands, when sent to Christianise the inhabitants of central England.'[43]

Not content with blackening Tozer in the eyes of the public, Livingstone next informed the Foreign Secretary that the new Bishop had been lacking in mental and physical courage and had been a classic case of a man whose 'zeal had collapsed'.[44] Members of Livingstone's family were told that Tozer had been a weak-minded, two-faced creature, fit for 'nothing but walking about in slippers made by admiring young ladies'.[45] The Zambesi Expedition ended as it had begun, with bitterness and recrimination.

Livingstone would have been happier if he could have pulled out at once, having received his recall orders, but he could not get down the Shire till the end of the year when the waters rose again. To pass the time and to show that while others might die or go home he at least still had plenty of energy left, he spent September and part of October in walking seven hundred miles along the western shores of Lake Nyassa and back again to the Murchison Cataracts. It was a remarkable feat, for by then Livingstone was ill and emaciated, so unwell in fact that, a month before,

Lieutenant Young had written that 'he could never remember having seen a man fail in health and appearance in so short a time as the Dr'.[46] But Livingstone was to provide still more remarkable proof of his tenacity and endurance before he returned to England.

At the mouth of the Zambesi in early February 1864, Livingstone handed over the *Pioneer* to Lieutenant Young to sail her to the Cape. He himself wanted to sell the *Lady Nyassa* at the nearest port where buyers might be found. Zanzibar, nearly a thousand miles to the north, was the closest possible market. A long sea voyage would be a dangerous under-taking in a small steamer that had been designed for lake and river use rather than as a sea-going vessel. But, in spite of his crew being untrained and too small, Livingstone made up his mind to risk it. When he arrived at Zanzibar in April and found no buyer, he made an even more remarkable decision: he would sail his tiny forty-foot ship two and a half thousand miles across the Indian Ocean to Bombay, where he had been told he would have a better chance of selling her. Not even the desertion of his long-suffering engineer, George Rae, could change his mind. Nor was he daunted by the information that the monsoons would break in roughly three weeks. But although he had only been able to carry enough coal for five days' steaming, Livingstone made it to Bombay, mainly under sail, in forty-five days. As his insignificant vessel entered the harbour, the first monsoon rains started to fall and the gales broke the following day. When Livingstone stepped ashore and walked slowly through the busy docks, nobody took any notice of him. It was not surprising; only madmen crossed the Indian Ocean from Africa in small ships at that time of year. At the Customs House, Livingstone asked if the Governor was in town. On being told that he was not, the leader of the Zambesi Expedition wandered into the Court House to listen to a few cases while he waited till the city magistrate could see him. It was a strangely banal ending to six horrifying years.

Livingstone embarked for England on 24 June and was back in London by the end of July.

On 20 January 1863, the editor of *The Times* had assessed the results of the Zambesi Expedition as follows: 'We were promised cotton, sugar and indigo . . . and of course we got none. We were promised trade; and there is no trade . . . We were promised converts and not one has been made. In a word, the thousands subscribed by the Universities and contributed by the Government have been productive only of the most fatal results.'

All this was perfectly correct. In 1858 Livingstone had promised that the Zambesi would prove navigable as far as the Victoria Falls, and that a brisk trade would soon be developed with the Makololo and the tribes living on the Batoka Plateau. He had suggested that traders and missionaries would be able to live in perfect safety in central Africa and would have no difficulty in communicating with the coast. Livingstone had argued that the real importance of his great trans-continental journey was that it had drawn his attention to the enormous Christian and commercial potential of the Batoka Plateau. With the discovery of the Kebrabasa Rapids in the first year of the expedition, all his optimistic plans lay in ruins.* In 1859 he thought that he had found in the Shire Highlands a suitable alternative for Christian and commercial exploitation, and since this region seemed to offer Livingstone his last chance to justify earlier rash promises, he committed himself to it totally. His almost simultaneous discovery of serious problems—Arab slave raids and the tribal war between the Ajawa and the Manganja—did not lead him to qualify his new optimism. As a result, when the Universities Mission came out, they faced a situation with which they were unable to cope. The complete anarchy in the Shire Highlands in 1863, and the missionaries' decision to withdraw, set the seal on the Zambesi Expedition's failure.

Given the vast distances travelled and the enormous amount of energy expended, this judgement inevitably seems harsh, especially since the Zambesi Expedition had made important discoveries. For a start, it had proved beyond doubt that the Zambesi was useless for navigation beyond Tete. The Shire Highlands had been found to be accessible only via the river Shire, which was shallow and treacherous for six months of the year above the junction with the Ruo. Important new facts about the Arab slave routes across Nyassa had also been brought to light. And although the lake itself had previously been reached by Candido, the Tete trader, Livingstone had fixed its position accurately for the first time, and had produced a reliable map of its southern and western shores. In fact, had Livingstone set out with the limited, but still significant, aim of finding out with scientific objectivity about the geographical problems of south-central and south-eastern Africa, with related facts on the number and disposition of tribes and their relations with the Arabs and the Portuguese, he would have returned home disappointed but satisfied that he had brought back the information he had set out to provide. As it was, Livingstone came back to England unable to claim any credit for the expedition's only achievement: its negative discoveries. Yet by promising too much too soon, he had in the end denied himself this one chance to

---

* In the early 1970s, 100 years after Livingstone's death, the Portuguese built a vast dam across the rapids. Its power, besides supplying a large area of southern Africa, is facilitating exploitation of the vast mineral assets found in the Tete area, where Livingstone set his geologist to work. Thornton's notes, written in a bizarre personal shorthand, have not yet been deciphered.

salvage a little glory from the ruins. Instead he was left with the feeble and untrue excuse that the malice of the Portuguese and the cowardice of the missionaries had robbed him of success. Nor would this be enough to convince many people that the expenditure of £50,000 of government money and the loss of a dozen lives had been satisfactorily justified or explained by Dr Livingstone.

And yet the restatement of obvious failure is not enough. The disconcerting fact remains that without his over-optimism, and without the determination that his work should have more far-reaching effects than the increase of geographical knowledge, Livingstone would never have crossed Africa, and would certainly never have been able to summon up the superhuman tenacity and endurance which had alone kept his deeply divided and disillusioned expedition in being. Livingstone had often treated his subordinates abysmally, had lied and shown unbelievable insensitivity, but his indestructible strength of will, which Kirk had at times felt to be not far from insanity, had kept the party pressing on after crippling disasters and setbacks. And there is a still more important consideration regarding Livingstone's false expectations: unless he had formulated plans for the colonial occupation of Africa at a time when the prospects for such moves were negligible, his later influence on the course of African history would have been no greater than that of any other explorer. But in 1863, after all his earlier overtures to the Government had been rejected, and when he had been bluntly told that it was out of the question for him to take possession of discoveries in the Queen's name,[47] he predicted that whatever the present administration said, there would one day be British colonies in central and eastern Africa. Then he proceeded to describe the colonial system which would become the pattern for the British African Empire fifteen years after his death. On the ship going home he developed his idea of a small minority of whites, not vying with the Africans in manual labour, but taking 'a leading part in managing the land . . . taking a lead too in trade and all public matters', and filling an organizing role 'which is now practically vacant'.[48] He also wrote, early in 1864, with an apparently, insane disregard for the facts that had ruined all immediate hope of the Shire Highlands being occupied: 'Viewing calmly all the circumstances . . . I could not conceive of a sphere in which the missionary prospects would be more inviting than that which has now been abandoned . . . I have no doubt that it will be done though I may not be alive to hear of it . . . the future will justify my words & hopes.'[49]

Had history disproved this boast, it would be possible to condemn Livingstone for another piece of characteristic over-optimism and leave the matter there. But incredibly, history did vindicate Livingstone's claim. Less than twenty years after his death, Nyasaland became a British Protectorate, and, as will be seen, this would be the result of Livingstone's posthumous influence. But in 1864 it would be misleading to believe that Livingstone was entirely confident in his predictions; not even he possessed that degree of self-confidence. At the time that he was writing optimistic letters about his certainty that the future would prove him right, his journal tells a different story: 'I shall have nothing to do at home,' he wrote miserably on the crossing to Bombay. 'By the failure of the Universities Mission my work seems vain. Am I to be cut off before I can do anything to affect permanent improvement in Africa? I have been unprofitable enough . . .'[50]

Certainly Livingstone had good reason to be alarmed about his immediate personal prospects. All his work from 1851, when he had seen the upper Zambesi for the first time, to early 1864, when he sailed from Zanzibar, had been undertaken on the assumption that his explorations would produce practical and tangible results. Yet his experiences during the Zambesi Expedition had made it impossible to think realistically of traders, missionaries or colonists settling in the foreseeable future in any of the areas he had 'opened up'. From 1859 onwards, because he knew that isolated groups of men would face problems too formidable for them to overcome, Livingstone had put all his faith for future progress in Africa on colonization; that alone in his view would break up tribal societies and leave Africans responsive to Christian teaching and European commercial habits. But in 1864, with the Government still adamantly opposed to any colonial expansion anywhere in the world, it was going to be impossible for Livingstone to go on suggesting that he was 'opening the way for others'. Colonists were not going to come without government aid, and no missionary or trader was going to catch the next boat for Africa after reading about the fighting, the deaths and the terrible communications. Livingstone had to face the fact that, unless he thought up a brand-new justification, if ever he went back to Africa it would be as an explorer, no more, no less.

Nor did his difficulties end there. If he returned, it could obviously be neither to Mozambique nor to any adjoining area. The Portuguese, after what he had said about them, were most unlikely to let him in again, and anyway, since Livingstone had claimed that the Portuguese presence by itself made all constructive moves impossible, he could not logically give either the Shire Highlands or the Zambesi another chance. This was a very serious state of affairs, for it cut him off from all the areas he had previously explored. If he returned to Africa, he was going to have to start in a new area and abandon any idea of utilizing any of the work he had done in the last ten years. It was a daunting prospect, and even more so now that he had spent the remainder of his money from *Missionary*

Travels on the *Lady Nyassa*. Nor would he be able to count on the Foreign Office or the Treasury to back him again. On the way back to England he wrote to Waller, of the Universities Mission, saying: 'I don't know whether I am to go on the shelf or not. If I do, I make Africa the shelf.'[51] But defiant statements were easier to write than to act out. Charles Livingstone thought that his brother's situation would be best remedied by marrying a rich, religious widow and living a life of prosperous retirement augmented by the profits of another book.[52] But Livingstone, although he had no definite plans, did not intend getting another wife. He had told a number of friends after Mary's death that he had abandoned all thoughts of a permanent home, more than ever now that three of his children were nearly grown up. Livingstone had spent over twenty years in Africa, most of them travelling, and this nomadic existence had left him with little taste for settling down. His experiences of the company of his fellow-countrymen on the Zambesi Expedition had not increased his desire to live a close domestic life in Britain. He longed to be able to recapture the happiness and freedom of his journey across Africa, and that could only be done in the company of Africans. *They* would not question his decisions or ask for their opinions to be considered. With them, acting as the well-behaved children of a benign if paternalistic leader, Livingstone felt he might begin achieving things again in Africa. Precisely where in Africa, he was uncertain, and when he would return and how were equally vexing questions, but the most puzzling question of all was what he would do when he got there.

PART FIVE

REJECTION

19

The Last Visit Home
1864–1865

W hen Livingstone reached London in July 1864, there were no banquets and official receptions as there had been in 1856; and although one evening he was invited to dine with the Prime Minister, Lord Palmerston, and on another occasion took tea with Mr Gladstone, Livingstone could soon sense that these invitations had been prompted by dutiful courtesy rather than by any real enthusiasm. At eighty, Lord Palmerston was struggling with failing sight and hearing, and had insufficient energy to interest himself in concerns other than vital policy decisions. At the time of Livingstone's return the Prime Minister was facing a serious European crisis provoked by the Prussian invasion of Schleswig-Holstein. Not surprisingly, Lord John Russell, the Foreign Secretary, was also preoccupied by events in Europe and could scarcely find time to see or discuss the future of a man who had just returned from leading an inglorious African expedition.

Lord John had never struck even his friends as the possessor of a warm personality, and Livingstone, when he met him on 26 July, was badly shaken by Russell's 'very cold manner'. There was really no reason why the Foreign Secretary should have been affable. Lord John had not been annoyed merely by criticisms of the Zambesi Expedition in the press and by the complaints of High Churchmen who blamed Dr Livingstone for the failure of the Universities Mission; the Foreign Secretary had been far more acutely embarrassed by Livingstone's constant outbursts against the Portuguese. Not only was Russell opposed to unnecessary diplomatic entanglements, but he resented Livingstone's attitude to the nation which had, after all, given permission for the expedition to enter the Zambesi. Apart from that, Prince Albert had been enraged by criticisms of his cousin the King of Portugal; and Russell, who did not get on with Victoria, had no desire to add more fuel to the Queen's hostility. By refusing to become Patron of the Universities Mission the Prince Consort had already made plain his views on Dr Livingstone. There were other reasons for the Foreign Secretary's 'very cold manner'. The Admiralty had reported adversely on the Zambesi Expedition and had claimed that all naval support had been carried out at a cost in cash and lives far too high to justify the negligible results. The Treasury too had censured Livingstone for costing the nation an extra £3,000 by failing to evacuate by the end of 1863.[1]

Nevertheless, Russell did not wish to turn away with nothing a man who had suffered a great deal of personal hardship. He told Livingstone that if he intended to return to Africa, the Government would pay £500 towards the cost of his supplies, provided he did not go near any territory where the Portuguese claimed direct or indirect authority. The Foreign Secretary then made it clear that there was no question of any regular salary; the £500 was all that he could offer. Livingstone left Russell's office trembling with anger and wounded pride. No expedition lasting two years could possibly be mounted with less than £2,000 and the Government was only going to provide a quarter. His anger was the more intense because he was well aware that Russell knew that after the Government's refusal to contribute towards the cost of the *Lady Nyassa*, he, Livingstone, had had to find the money himself. Livingstone had also taken deep offence when the Foreign Secretary had told him to moderate any remarks he might make in public about the Portuguese, and not to tell anybody about the £500 grant 'because so many people will bother the Foreign Office'.[2] In fact Russell had one person in mind: the Portuguese Ambassador. After his interview with Lord John, Livingstone thought only of how hurtfully he had been snubbed. He never acknowledged that Russell could have dismissed him with no offer of any sort and would have been able to justify such an action.

Since there were no banquets and few requests for lectures, there was nothing to keep Livingstone in London for more than a few days. In the street he was occasionally recognized, but generally by 'imbecile old ladies'.[3] In early August, Livingstone left for Scotland where he was relieved to discover that popular support had not diminished as much as in the south. The main purpose of his journey north was not the pursuit of cheering crowds, but to spend some time with his neglected family. He had seen none of his children for nearly seven years and the youngest, five-year-old Anna Mary, who had been born in Kuruman in November 1858, he had never seen. Agnes, the eldest daughter, had only been with her father for six of her eighteen years. How pathetically out of touch he had become can be seen from what he wrote to her just before his arrival in Scotland. 'I have some "sweeties" for you . . . I did not know what else to buy,'[4] he told his daughter, who was no longer a child but a young woman. Livingstone's time in his parents' small house in Hamilton was not happy. His mother was evidently dying and suffered from dementia. She did not recognize her son but talked to him as though he was one of his own children. Often she would ask him what had happened to his brother, meaning his eldest son Robert. The old woman could hardly have asked a more painful question.

Robert's life is really the story of Livingstone's tragic failure as a parent. Born in Bechuanaland in 1845, Robert had shown signs of rebellion at the tender age of four, when what had probably been no more than healthy independence had been called by Livingstone 'excessive obstinacy'. As his father had done before him, Livingstone tried to beat his son into submission, but the remedy increased rather than diminished the complaint. Robert had been seven when he and the rest of the family were sent back to England in 1852, while Livingstone tramped his way across Africa. Until his father's return in 1856, Robert had shared his mother's wretchedly poor existence, moving from room to room, from town to town. When Livingstone had set off on the Zambesi Expedition, the care of his children was shared by a board of trustees and Livingstone's spinster sisters in Hamilton. The aunts were narrow-minded, and their constant resort to the strict discipline enjoined by the elders of their Church was hopelessly inappropriate treatment for a strong-willed boy brought up on an African mission station, where, away from his father's eye, he had enjoyed a great deal of freedom. From the age of twelve he was sent to a series of boarding schools in Scotland and the north of England, but he would not work and often ran away, provoking stern letters from his father, commanding him to end his 'vagabond ways'. But such homilies did not give Robert the sense of love and security he needed. With his mother dead, and never really knowing his father, it was not surprising that Robert was considered difficult by his schoolteachers. At the age of eighteen he announced that he had finished with education. In the same year, 1863, Livingstone reluctantly agreed to his coming out to the Zambesi to discuss his future with a view to some sort of apprenticeship. Unfortunately the trustees knew nothing about Africa and made no arrangement for Robert to get any further than Natal. His father had believed that plans would be made for him to come up with Bishop Tozer, but nothing of the sort had been envisaged, and Robert arrived in Natal penniless and with no better prospect of getting to the Zambesi than he would have had thousands of miles away in London. When Robert's grandmother, Mary Moffat, heard about his situation she was beside herself with worry. Not so Livingstone, who had told Kirk, when he had left the expedition, that if he saw Robert and found out that no passage would be possible, Kirk was to tell the young man 'he must make his own way in Natal'.[5] Livingstone felt that by refusing an education, Robert had condemned himself to a life of manual labour.[6] In a letter to a friend written in November 1863, Livingstone admitted, 'often conscience accused me of being deficient in my duty to my children'.[7] It was sad that he never told Robert as much; more often he accused his son of deliberate laziness and a liking for 'bad company and drink'. From the end of 1863, till he returned to England in the summer of 1864, Livingstone heard no more about Robert.

But by 28 July, he had had more news of his son, for on that day he wrote to Kirk, telling him: 'My heart is rather sore—that bad boy has got into the American army and will be made manure of for those bloody fields.'* How Robert had entered the Northern forces against the Confederates Livingstone had no idea, until he received a letter from his son in October. This was a striking and moving letter, not simply because Robert addressed his father as 'My dear Sir' and ended 'your quondam son Robert', but because the young man emerges not as the delinquent his father considered him, but as gentle, honourable and brave. After explaining how he had been kidnapped in Natal and later impressed into the American army, Robert went on to describe two skirmishes and one battle which he had been in; another battle, he went on, was imminent: 'I have never hurt anyone knowingly in battle, have always fired high, and in that furious madness which always accompanies a bayonet charge and which seems to possess every soldier, I controlled my passion and took the man who surrendered prisoner.'

Robert admitted that he regretted throwing away his chance of an education and wished that a 'craving to travelling' had not led him astray. He concluded: 'I have changed my name for I am convinced that to bear your name here would lead to further dishonours to it.' Then, almost as an afterthought, he added that he was at present in a military field hospital suffering from exposure.[8]

Only a few months before, Livingstone had written to his son Thomas, telling him that Robert was only interested in making capital out of having a famous father, 'but when they see he has nothing in him he will be despised and be fit only to drive a "cuddy and a cart"'.[9] Robert was wounded in a skirmish at Laurel Hill, Virginia, and taken prisoner. He died in a prison camp in Salisbury, North Carolina, on 5 December 1864; a few days later he would have been nineteen. He had, as Livingstone had so indelicately suggested, been 'made manure of for those bloody fields'. The lesson, however, was not lost on Livingstone, for he never pressed Thomas or Oswell to take up any particular career unless they wanted to do so.

But Livingstone's real efforts to make up for his past failures as a parent were directed at his eldest daughter, Agnes, who was to have everything which had been denied the others. Nothing was to be too good for her.

---

* The American Civil War lasted from April 1861 to May 1865.

Livingstone thought of sending her to a £150-a-year finishing school in London and finally chose a still more expensive option. She could go to Paris to improve her piano-playing and her French. There, she could also take lessons in riding and drawing if she wished. Only 'injurious' French novels were to be forbidden her. It is more than ironic that while Livingstone was making such lavish plans for his eldest daughter, his eldest son lay dying, but even if Livingstone was sentimental about young girls, his real affection for Agnes cannot be denied. The large number of letters he wrote to her until his death are proof of that.

From September 1864 to April 1865, Livingstone and Agnes stayed at Newstead Abbey, the Nottinghamshire country home of William Webb, a former big game enthusiast, whom Livingstone had met in Bechuanaland through William Cotton Oswell, his first travelling companion. Livingstone's days at Newstead were among the happiest in his life and, while there, he was affectionate, unassertive and kind. Nobody who met him then could have believed him capable of callousness or lying. Dr Livingstone was always ready for a joke and delighted Mr and Mrs Webb by his constant attentions to their children. Ethel, their youngest, was a particular favourite, and Livingstone was always bringing down the wrath of her nanny for handing the child illicit scones and jam. He often went for walks with the children and one day got so involved in a game of blindman's buff that he blundered into the edge of a stone mantelpiece and cut his forehead. It was at this time that he confided more regrets to his friends over his inattention to his own children. 'Oh why did I not play more with my children in the Kolobeng days? Why was I so busy that I had so little time for my bairns?'[10] He tried hard with little Anna Mary, but his youngest daughter did not like being kissed by this strange man with a moustache who seemed to spend so many hours writing. Livingstone gave her a black doll, but she would have preferred a white one, as she admitted later.

Her memory of Livingstone endlessly writing was correct. At Newstead her father set about his second book, *A Narrative of an Expedition to the Zambezi and its Tributaries*. The *Narrative* was entirely for public consumption and glossed over all the problems and troubles which Livingstone had faced. But there was one obstacle to success which the author did write about at length. In spite of Lord John Russell's warning, Livingstone savagely attacked the Portuguese and once more suggested that every failure could be pinned on them.

In September 1864 Livingstone broke off his writing to go to Bath for the annual meeting of the British Association. He had been invited to address the members on his favourite subject: the Portuguese slave trade. It was an opportunity too good to be missed; and yet other aspects of the

Bath meeting did not please him. In 1856, at the Association's meeting in Dublin, he had been the only explorer of note, the undisputed star of the show, but now there were others with a title quite as good as his. The main attraction at Bath was not to be his vitriolic attack on the Portuguese, but what was expected to be a violently heated debate between Richard Burton and John Speke on the probable location of the source of the Nile. Before Livingstone came to Bath he was hoping to return to Africa, if he could raise enough money to do so through his new book and the generosity of public or private patrons, but he had not come to any conclusions about what he would do on arrival, or where he would head for. Although Livingstone did not acknowledge it at the time or afterwards, the Speke-versus-Burton Nile controversy marked the beginning of his own passionate interest in that river, and consequently changed the course of his life.

In 1856, with the backing of the Foreign Office and the Royal Geographical Society, Speke and Burton had set out into the interior from Zanzibar in an attempt to reach a large inland lake which numerous Arab and African traders had visited. The two men stood on the shores of Lake Tanganyika in February 1858, over a year before Livingstone reached the more southerly Lake Nyassa. On the way back to Zanzibar Speke had made a detour north on his own and had arrived at the southern shore of a vast lake which he named Victoria Nyanza.* From the great height (3,700 feet above sea level) and apparently gigantic size of this lake, Speke at once decided that he had found the source of the Nile. Burton, who was irritated beyond measure not to have accompanied Speke, dismissed contemptuously his companion's excited claims to have solved the world's greatest geographical mystery. Undismayed by Burton's hostile response, Speke in an epic journey had travelled to the northern side of his lake in the summer of 1862 and had found an outlet, which he called the Ripon Falls. This discovery he was certain clinched the matter. It did not. In March 1864, Samuel White Baker, who had met Speke and his new travelling companion, James Grant, in 1863, north of the Victoria Nyanza, discovered another large lake, 150 miles north-west of Speke's. Baker now claimed that this lake, which he called Lake Albert, was larger than Victoria and the *primary* source. He had also found a spectacular waterfall on the eastern side of the lake, which he was to name the Murchison Falls. Whether this waterfall was fed by the same river that began at Speke's Ripon Falls, Baker did not know, nor could he prove that the large body of water that flowed out of Lake Albert at its northern end was the Nile. That claim could only be substantiated by tracing the river

* See Map 5a on page 327.

north and seeing where it went. It was also impossible for Speke to make absolute claims for his lake until he had filled in the gaps in the map of the river which he and Grant had made when travelling north from the Ripon Falls towards the known lower Nile.

Thirteen years later it would be discovered by Stanley that Speke had been right and that the waters leaving the Victoria Nyanza at the Ripon Falls flowed on to join Lake Albert via the Murchison Falls, and then left the northern end of Albert as the Nile proper. Lake Albert is therefore at best a major reservoir of the Nile.

In September 1864 the extent of Baker's discovery was not yet known, and, in any case, when it was the following year, there was still no certainty that Baker's Albert or Speke's Victoria were responsible, either individually or jointly, for the lower Nile. Even before Lake Albert was found there were other very plausible alternatives to Speke's lake being the source, and Burton was prepared to put forward all of them in September 1864 at Bath.

For a start Burton would be able to argue that since Speke had not circumnavigated his lake, he could not even reliably claim that the water he had seen in 1858 was part of the same lake which contained the Ripon Falls. But, more tellingly, Burton could suggest quite plausibly that Lake Tanganyika might be the source of the Nile. A river might well flow out of the northern end of Tanganyika, and then, following a course to the west of Speke's lake, it could join the Nile several hundred miles north of the Victoria Nyanza. If that was so, any connection of Speke's or Baker's lakes with the Nile would become irrelevant, since Lake Tanganyika was so much further south.

Livingstone was briefed by Sir Roderick Murchison on all the arguments likely to be employed during the great debate, and Livingstone's interest was soon keenly aroused, not simply because it was common knowledge that the two men hated one another. Livingstone was beginning to form his own ideas, and once that happened he always wanted to act them out. The day set for the eagerly anticipated geographical slanging match was 16 September. But the ticket-holders would never have their fun. At 4 p.m. on the day before, John Speke, out shooting on his uncle's estate just outside Bath, clambered over a low wall. Before he reached the other side his gun went off, blasting a gaping wound in his chest. Speke died shortly afterwards. Although there was talk of suicide, the evidence pointed to an accident. Earlier in the day Speke had appeared as keen as ever to defend his claims against Burton. This tragedy increased rather than diminished public speculation about the Nile's source.

It is more than likely that Sir Roderick Murchison asked Livingstone, while he was in Bath, whether he would like to be sponsored by the Royal

Geographical Society to solve the riddle of the central African lakes once and for all. But in September 1864 Livingstone was not ready to commit himself. He feared that a straightforward search for the source of a river, albeit the longest in the world, would not be enough to persuade the public that he was returning to Africa as a missionary. Besides, if an announcement was made so soon after the Bath meeting, it might appear that Dr Livingstone was a little over-keen to compete with others for the greatest of all geographical prizes. There was no doubt that Livingstone already wanted to compete, none at all, but he was not quite ready to announce the fact. He had never liked the idea of other men making great discoveries and the thought of outsmarting them all gave him great pleasure.

In the past, Livingstone's determination to secure the credit for geographical discoveries had been underlined repeatedly by his bitter attacks on those claiming that others had preceded him. Speke himself had suggested that Dr Livingstone had never given Portuguese explorers enough praise, and for this insolence Livingstone declared that his young critic had 'such slender mental abilities that silence in this & other matters would have better become him'. After Speke's death, Livingstone wrote patronizingly of him as 'a poor misguided thing with such an intense desire to please that I always pity him'.[11] Had Livingstone been indifferent to Speke and Burton as men, it is possible that the source of the Nile might not have become so important to him, but from the time of the Bath meeting he became personally as well as scientifically involved. Soon he was writing with derision about Speke's theories.

> Speke gave the best example I know of the eager pursuit of a foregone conclusion. When he discovered Victoria Nyanza . . . here were the headwaters of the river of Egypt and no mistake. Though he saw that the little river that issues thence would not account for the Nile, he would not let it be doubted even in his own mind . . . and invented a 'backwater' to eke out his little river.[12]

When Livingstone heard about Baker's Lake Albert in 1865, he decided that the Nile source probably lay south-west of Lake Tanganyika. His theory was that this source or sources drained into Tanganyika and that a river, issuing from the northern end of Lake Tanganyika, joined the southern end of Lake Albert and flowed on north as the Nile proper. If this were so, Speke, Burton and Baker had all been working several hundred miles too far north; it was an idea that gave Livingstone grim satisfaction. With all the available knowledge in 1864 and 1865, Livingstone's theory seemed rather more likely than Speke's. After all, on the face of it, it seemed most unlikely that the Nile, which flowed for thousands of miles, much of the way through the largest and driest desert in the world, could primarily be supplied through the comparatively small Ripon Falls.

But derision of Speke and geographical interest were not enough to make Livingstone obsessively determined to outsmart his rivals. His bitter hatred of Burton was what swayed the balance. Almost everything about Burton distressed him: his view of travel in Africa as an entertainment rather than a mission, his undisguised contempt for conventional morality and conventional people, his admiration for Arabs, his scorn for Africans and his frequently expressed conviction that it was useless to try and change them. The last of these failings was in Livingstone's eyes the most serious. To suggest that Africans were 'un-progressive and unfit for change' was bad enough, but to Livingstone even this seemed trivial in comparison with Burton's further claim that religion was the 'mental expression of a race'. From this premise Burton had gone on to argue that it was crass wishful thinking to believe that the 'Bible *made* England, or the Koran Stambul'; the truth, he asserted, was that the higher or lower state of a race predetermined its religion.[13] Thus to attempt to force upon Africans a creed belonging to a different race was about as sensible as trying to graft a cat's head on to a dog's body. Christianity, Burton had claimed, could not achieve in decades what could only come about through generations of social change.[14]

This sort of thinking undercut every argument that Livingstone had ever uttered and he hated Burton for it. Burton had also attacked missionaries, largely because he considered, for the reasons given above, that their work was based on a completely false assumption. In 1860 Burton had accepted a Foreign Office consular appointment in West Africa, and there he became convinced that missionaries were badly selected, meddlesome and ignorant. Certainly it would have been strange if Burton, an intellectual snob who prized only the bizarre, had taken to worthy Christians from the lower middle class. In September 1864 Burton had been in England on leave but he had not confined his attentions to the Nile question. In the spring of the following year he had appeared as a witness before a House of Commons Select Committee on West African Settlements. The Committee's job had been to recommend the Government either to devote more money to bolster up existing private British enterprises in the area or to pull out altogether. The Committee in the end opted for the latter course. The Government in fact just left matters as they were. Livingstone felt that Burton's evidence had set back for years any hopes of a more positive British policy towards colonization. Burton had derided the economic potential of West Africa and had claimed that the missionaries there were doing more harm than good.

Livingstone was angry enough to write a sympathetic letter to Dr Tidman with condolences for the 'lies' and 'aspersions of that beastly fellow Burton against the missionaries on the West Coast'. 'Burton', Livingstone had gone on, 'seems to be a moral idiot. His conduct in Africa was so bad that it cannot be spoken of without disgust—systematically wicked, impure and untruthful.'[15] Livingstone was referring to the rumours that Burton had often failed to pay porters and had travelled with a harem of African women to serve his sexual needs. Burton, who liked shocking people, did little to dispel these rumours. Later Livingstone wrote: 'I don't like to face people who were witnesses of his [Burton's] bestial immorality.'[16]

I have described Livingstone's personal dislike of Speke and Burton in some detail since no previous biographer has devoted any space at all to what in my view seems to be an important motivating factor for Livingstone's search for the Nile source. His idea was that if he could prove the geographical theories of both men to have been wrong, thus making their discoveries seem insignificant, it would be a victory for his own views, on the benefits of trade and Christianity, over Burton's pessimistic assumption that Africans were immutably 'unprogressive and unfit for social change'. If there were ever to be British colonies in Africa it was vital that men with views like Burton's should be silenced.

Yet Livingstone was aware that his personal feelings could hardly be used publicly to justify his eternal claim that he was more than an explorer. To persuade anybody that he was still a missionary would take more than that, but until he had worked out supporting arguments, Livingstone was not going to risk admitting that he was planning to return to Africa to find the source of the Nile. For a start, as Livingstone told Sir Roderick Murchison, a purely geographical task would mean moving swiftly across country with no time to appear to be planting the seed of the Gospel in African minds. Unless he stayed for several months at a time in individual places, not even the most gullible of his supporters would believe that he was converting anybody. This problem appeared to be insurmountable, but there was another factor which saved Livingstone: the Arab Swahili slave trade.

Before 1865, Livingstone had concentrated most of his vitriol on the Portuguese trade, but from the autumn of 1861, after his first extensive survey of Lake Nyassa, he had realized that the Arab trade was a far more serious problem. There were two reasons why Livingstone had not given it more attention; in the first place, since Arab slave raids had been concentrated in the area north and west of Nyassa, they could not be used as an excuse to explain the chaos in the Shire Highlands. The Portuguese made better scapegoats. Livingstone's second reason for reticence on Arab slaving was the fact that he could hardly speak about it without reference to his own failure to launch his steamer on Lake Nyassa; his purpose, it will be remembered, had been to cut the main southern Arab Swahili slave routes. But now, in early 1865, Livingstone realized that if he went to the area just south of Lake Tanganyika to search for the source of the Nile, he would find himself in the heart of Arab slave-trading activities. This then provided him with the twin objectives he found acceptable. He would not only be looking for a river but would be reporting back on the slave trade too. Perhaps his information might even prove horrific enough to persuade the Government to intervene directly in central Africa and create colonies. Livingstone went on to argue that a search for the Nile's source, if successful, would greatly strengthen his anti-slavery campaign. 'The Nile sources', he told a friend, 'are valuable only as a means of enabling me to open my mouth with power among men. It is this power which I hope to apply to remedy an enormous evil [the slave trade]. Men may think I covet fame, but I make it a rule not to read aught written in my praise.'[17]

Although in 1865 the exposure of the Arab Swahili slave trade provided a reassuring justification for a journey to find the Nile's source, during Livingstone's last journey it became much more than that, and in time it would be hard to judge whether the search for the source or his desire to end the slave trade, and bring change to Africa, was his dominant motive.

When Sir Roderick wrote to Livingstone on 5 January 1865, formally inviting him on behalf of the Royal Geographical Society to return to Africa to clear up the mystery of the source of the Nile, he felt able to accept. With his justification now in place, Livingstone applauded the decision of the Council of the R.G.S. to send him out, and suggested that the Society had chosen 'the true scientific way of settling the matter'.[18] Had they selected Burton or Baker for the same task, Livingstone would have thought the decision anything but the 'true scientific way'. Nevertheless the R.G.S. only offered £500, which Livingstone thought mean, and he did not take kindly to some written instructions ordering him to make regular observations for longitude and latitude. He felt that for £500 he could hardly be expected to sit for weeks at a time in given positions to wait for cloud conditions to allow him to make accurate astronomical observations. But this was a mild irritant compared with the Council's request to be shown all his personal notes on his return. It was a pity that he did not have it out with them at the time, but as usual he kept his resentment to himself and harboured a grudge that would become obsessive within a couple of years.

With £500 from the R.G.S., Livingstone knew that he would need £1,500 more. If he took the money Russell had offered, he would have to raise only an extra £1,000 to have enough to last him two years in Africa. But this money still had to be found; it is therefore astounding that when, in early 1865, Lord Palmerston (who had always been more sympathetic to Livingstone than had Lord John Russell) sent his unofficial political agent, Mr Lionel Hayward Q.C., to visit the Doctor at Newstead, Livingstone failed to take advantage of it. Alas, Mr Hayward's discreet approaches were too discreet for Livingstone to understand. Hayward asked whether Lord Palmerston could be of any assistance. Livingstone was puzzled. The Foreign Secretary had told him with painful precision what the Government would and would not do for him. Rather than risk a second rebuff, Livingstone told Hayward coldly that he could ask Lord Palmerston to persuade the Portuguese to open the Zambesi to international shipping. Naturally enough, Palmerston let the matter drop. Since the Zambesi was unsuitable for navigation, the Prime Minister could not understand why Dr Livingstone had asked for such an impractical favour. A few hundred pounds or a K.C.B. would have been a different matter. It took Palmerston's death in October that year to wake Livingstone up to the opportunity he had missed, not through pride or altruism but through naivety. Unhappily he confessed the truth to a friend: 'Lord Palmerston sent Mr Hayward, a Queen's Council, to ask "how he could aid me for he was most anxious to be of service to me." Most unaccountably it never once glanced across my mind that he meant anything for me or my children.'[19]

Having missed this opportunity, Livingstone had to avail himself of Russell's £500. He therefore wrote to the Foreign Secretary and on 11 March was invited to meet Austen Layard, the Permanent Under-Secretary at the Foreign Office. Layard was friendly and courteous. He confirmed that Livingstone could have his £500 and would be given the honorary rank of Consul with certain exemptions from normal duties. As a rule British consuls had to be settled in one country, where they were meant to look after the interests of British subjects and to report back to the Foreign Office in London on developments both domestic and external that might be of interest to the British Government. After chatting to Layard for a while, Livingstone left in a far better mood than he had been in after his interview with Russell. It was therefore a sickening shock, when he received his Consul's commission and instructions dated 28 March 1865, to read a separate enclosure signed by Russell: 'Whilst I have been willing to obtain the grant of £500 from the public funds . . . I wish you distinctly to understand that you are not to receive additional consular salary for the service in which you are now engaged, and that your consular appointment gives you no future claim on Her Majesty's Government for a consular pension.'[20]

Livingstone had not expected either a salary or a pension, but he was mortally offended that the refusal had been put in writing and in such dismissive terms. Quite apart from this, Livingstone felt that if his appointment were renewed beyond the two years, a situation might arise when he ought to get a pension. Thus a definite rejection in 1865 might later be taken as final, even if circumstances changed. But the general tone of the instructions seemed to Livingstone to be brusque and aggressive. 'You will distinctly understand' was a phrase used on several occasions, and he was warned not to 'make any promise to, or to enter into any arrangement with, chiefs, which might form an embarrassment to Her Majesty's Government'. He was ordered not to allow himself to be made a prisoner, since, if the Government was unable to punish the offenders, the safety of other explorers might be put in jeopardy. Altogether it was a chilling document.

These instructions, drawn up by a Foreign Office official, Mr Murray, and signed by Russell, Livingstone was later to describe as 'the most exuberant impertinence that ever issued from the Foreign Office'.[21] Whenever Livingstone felt depressed or ill on his last journeys, he remembered this communication and it cut him to the heart. Over and over again he referred to it in the letters written between 1870 and 1872, five to seven years after it had been sent. Livingstone tried to soften the blow by believing that Murray had been solely responsible and that Russell had signed it without being aware of the contents.

On receiving his commission, Livingstone wrote to Sir Roderick Murchison, who in turn wrote to Lord Clarendon, who had been Foreign Secretary at the beginning of the Zambesi Expedition, and who would hold the same post again when Russell succeeded Palmerston as Prime Minister. Both men thought the Foreign Office's attitude had been 'ungracious and unjust',[22] but their thoughts did not change the matter or increase by a single pound the size of the grant. Ironically Russell, on first reading the despatch Murray had composed, suggested to Layard that it ought to be shown to Murchison before being sent. Unfortunately, for some reason Layard did not take this advice.[23] Murchison, on hearing from Livingstone, wrote to Russell telling him how upset Livingstone was, and on 26 April the Foreign Secretary sent a note to Murray. 'Dr Livingstone is much distressed at a letter he has got from me saying his present consular appointment is not to count towards a pension—I never intended this and I wish the letter to be withdrawn, as he is a regular Consul, only to fifty black chiefs instead of to one white one.'[24]

But, strangely, nothing was done about the pension. In fact Livingstone was not granted a Civil List pension till 19 June 1873. He had by then been dead nearly two months. The amount the Government decided on was £300. It is now impossible to discover why Russell's note was never acted on, although it seems extraordinary that nothing was done. On 23

May Livingstone even wrote to the Foreign Secretary returning the despatch and asking him to change the last clauses, since Sir Roderick Murchison and Lord Clarendon had assured him they no longer 'express your Lordship's view'.[25]

In mid-August 1865, just after Livingstone had left the country for Africa, Lord John belatedly sent the deeply wounded man a letter which made matters worse rather than better. Livingstone wanted an apology more than anything else and an assurance that the present refusal of a salary and pension would not be binding on future administrations. Livingstone described the contents of the Foreign Secretary's letter to a friend: 'Lord Russell says that he intended to give me £500 a year if I settled anywhere. My position he said was somewhat anomalous in not being stationary.'[26] This seemed to Livingstone to be nothing more than a macabre joke on Russell's part. The Foreign Secretary knew that Livingstone had agreed to search for the source of the Nile for the R.G.S. and had received £500 for that purpose. Russell must therefore also have realized that Livingstone could not settle down without abandoning the work he had gone out to do.

Livingstone's memory of Russell's 'very cold manner' and the 'impertinence' of Mr Murray were to be major factors in his later decision not to return to England while he still could, in 1872. He was determined never to return until he had finished his work and found the source of the Nile. Then Russell and the rest of them would be sorry for treating him so badly.

One person who treated Livingstone well in 1865 was James Young, the inventor of paraffin, whom Livingstone had first met as a student in Glasgow. Young gave Livingstone the extra £1,000 which enabled him to set out. During March, April and May 1865, when Livingstone was obsessed with money and his relations with the Government, it is hardly surprising that he neglected other important matters. He was not with his mother when she died in May, nor did he find time to have an operation for the severe piles that had plagued him on the Zambesi, causing loss of blood and constant diarrhoea. It is a sad irony that Livingstone, who had never lost an opportunity to tell others how to look after their bowels, should have failed to look after his own. The operation was not considered dangerous and yet a hatred of inactivity, coupled with a terror of possible statements in the press that he was too old and ill to return to Africa, made him decide against it. It was to prove a fatal mistake.

PART SIX

ATONEMENT

20

Nyassa to Tanganyika
1866–1869

L ivingstone's life as he prepared to leave England for the last time had already been shot through with many ironies: the missionary who made but one convert who lapsed, the expedition leader who hoped to navigate a river blocked by impassable cataracts, the guide who led two missions to disaster, the father who never knew his children. But the greatest irony of all was yet to come, for in the end the image of Livingstone which his contemporaries would retain and cherish owed nothing to these failures. The Livingstone myth rested entirely on the last eight years of his life, and its power was such that to this day, if Livingstone has a popular image, it is of an old and saintly man wandering meekly through the wilds of central Africa, cut off from the outside world for years at a time, pursuing an almost mystical quest in which a search for the Nile's source is somehow merged with the nobler but apparently hopeless objective of ending the slave trade with prayer and gentle persuasion. Livingstone's isolation and ill-health, his setbacks and disappointments, his refusal to come home while life remained, and finally his lonely death, earned him more posthumous praise than he had ever known during his lifetime. For the public at large, a lifelong pilgrimage had ended in glorious martyrdom.

More recently the verdict has been suicide brought about by a fatalistic obsession with the pursuit of an unattainable visionary goal.[1] But Livingstone was neither a mystic nor a visionary;[2] his thought had always been very much of the world—commerce, trade, economics, practical, if currently impracticable, measures for breaking down tribal structures and finally introducing Christianity. Certainly he had seen and still saw himself as an instrument of God's Providence, but it was a Providence that he interpreted in easily explicable terms—the Zambesi had been a highway for trade, the Shire Highlands a place for a British colony. When Livingstone had crossed Africa, and, later when he had struggled on the Zambesi and the Shire, circumstances had thwarted him, but he had known precisely what he had wanted to achieve. The trouble with his last journey was that circumstances had robbed him of a definite set of aims, and old ideas did not fit the new situation he would face in East Africa.

In the past, Livingstone had always been able to suggest that he was opening the way for others, and even in the dying days of the Zambesi Expedition, when he realized that nobody would follow his lead, he had comforted himself by claiming that 'better men' would succeed where amateurs and bunglers had failed. Now that he was planning to go to the centre of Arab slaving activities, he no longer felt that he could claim that anybody ought to follow until the trade itself had been crushed. In 1865 he knew, for example, that over 20,000 slaves were exported annually from Zanzibar; this was surely the tip of an iceberg which would sink any efforts by colonists or missionaries, however determined. As Livingstone admitted to Kirk at the end of March 1865: 'The slave trade must be suppressed as the first great step to any mission—*that* baffles every good effort.'[3]

So, now that he no longer felt able to recommend traders, missionaries or colonists to follow his lead, Livingstone had to face the fact that unless he could really hope to defeat the slave trade single-handed, he was returning to Africa simply as an explorer. And of course he knew that only whole-hearted and determined government action could make any impression on the East African slave trade. So the question was whether any information he could obtain would push the Government into such action. Livingstone had always been an incurable optimist, but on this subject he saw no reason to be hopeful.

British government thinking on the slave trade in Africa was founded on a dogmatic distinction between the west and east coast trades. The west coast slave trade, so ran the official argument, had been a special case of moral obligation, an atonement for the guilt of heavy British involvement, but the east coast trade had always been an Arab, and never a British, affair. There was therefore no similar moral obligation for any British Government to take upon itself sole responsibility for East African anti-slavery measures. Nor had the Government any desire to alter the status quo in East Africa. It had an excellent relationship with the Sultan of Zanzibar and felt that France or Germany would be the only beneficiaries if this friendship were ended as a result of Britain leaning too hard on the Sultan. In fact, the Government argued, the slave trade in East Africa had already been limited by treaties with the Sultan. In 1845 one had been signed restricting all movement of slaves to the area within the Sultan's East African possessions. And this, in theory if not in fact, had stopped the export of slaves to Saudi Arabia and the Persian Gulf. In 1864 a further treaty had banned the movement of all slaves by water during certain months of the year. The fact that thousands slipped through the blockading net was known to the Government, but it was still not prepared to act. This being the case, Livingstone realized that it was most unlikely that any new information on the slave trade, relayed by him to the Foreign Office, would have any effect on government policy.

It is only against this background that the apparent indecisiveness of Livingstone's plans and motives on his last journey can be understood. Believing, as he did, that colonization alone could bring about conditions in Africa suitable for the spread of Christianity, and knowing that colonists could not prosper till the slave trade was suppressed, Livingstone's realization that the Government intended no further anti-slavery moves in East Africa during the foreseeable future gave him a terrible feeling of impotence even before he left England. He wanted to believe himself more than an explorer, but if his efforts to bring social change by encouraging others to act seemed doomed to automatic failure, he would soon be unable to claim, even to himself, that he was anything else. Only once this central dilemma has been appreciated can it be seen how easy it was for him to use the search for the Nile's source as a compensation for all other problems. Eventually, to persuade himself that his task was not simply geographical, he would see the Nile as more than a river, its source as more than a physical lake or spring. His search had to be dignified as a divine mission, which could alone, if he was successful, give him the necessary fame and influence to persuade the press and politicians that European intervention in Africa was their moral duty. But on 13 August 1865, the day Livingstone left England for the last time, the simple thought of going back to Africa was alone enough to lift his depression. He felt the same excitement that had driven him to the north from Kuruman twenty-five years before. In Africa he could regain his old sense of freedom, the knowledge that he was going beyond other men's line of things. This time there would be no white companions to delay or irritate him. Alone once more with a band of Africans, he believed that he stood on the threshold of new achievements that would dwarf his transcontinental journey. His feelings at this time are best expressed by a long eulogy upon African travel:

The mere animal pleasure of travelling in a wild unexplored country is very great. When on lands of a couple of thousand feet elevation, brisk exercise imparts elasticity to the muscles, fresh and healthy blood circulates through the brain, the mind works well, the eye is clear, the step is firm . . . the mind is made more self reliant: it becomes more confident of its own resources—there is greater presence of mind. The body is soon well-knit; the muscles of the limbs grow as hard as a board, and seem to have no fat; the countenance is bronzed, and there is no dyspepsia. Africa is a wonderful country for appetite . . . No one can truly experience the charm of repose unless he has undergone severe exertion.[4]

In view of the terrible suffering and disappointment that lay ahead, this passage must rank as one of the most ironic Livingstone ever wrote. But, as with the best tragic irony, here too the tragic hero was utterly unsuspecting of his fate.

Livingstone planned to return to Africa via Bombay, since the *Lady Nyassa* had still not been sold and he hoped finally to dispose of her. He also wanted to re-employ the Africans he had taken over to India at the end of the Zambesi Expedition. It was a wise decision. Four of these men would be with Livingstone eight years later when he died. Two, Chuma and Wikatani, had been among the slaves freed by the missionaries back in 1861. Then they had been boys, and on his arrival in Bombay in 1864 Livingstone had found them places in the Free Church of Scotland Mission School. The other two, Susi and Amoda, had first been employed by Livingstone at Shupanga to fit together the pieces of the *Lady Nyassa*. Both men were too old to go to school and so Livingstone had found them work in the Bombay docks.[5]

In Bombay Livingstone stayed with Sir Bartle Frere, the Governor, a determined opponent of the East African slave trade, which he knew a great deal about, since many Anglo-Indians from Bombay traded with the Zanzibar Arabs. Frere recommended Livingstone to choose some of his party from the government-run school for freed slaves at Nassick, where the pupils were given an elementary education and were also taught music and handicrafts. Livingstone did not then know that most of the school's pupils had ambitions that went beyond acting as porters on African expeditions. So he selected eight. Frere next suggested that Livingstone take a dozen Sepoys from the Bombay Marine Battalion, with an Indian *havildar* or corporal in charge of them. This choice of men was almost as unwise as the selection of Nassick 'boys'. Livingstone knew nothing about Indian customs, habits or temperament. Before leaving England, he had written to the British Consul at Johanna for ten Johanna men to be sent to Zanzibar to await his arrival. Although Livingstone gave careful instructions for the selection of these men, it was another strange decision, since the natives of Johanna had a reputation for being deceitful and lazy. In view of the problems Livingstone had experienced with his European staff on the Zambesi Expedition, it is surprising that he did not take greater pains in selecting his African and Indian followers for his last journey.

Livingstone intended to travel with a small party of sixty men—he already had thirty-five and intended to hire twenty-five more either at Zanzibar or on landing in Africa itself. Even if he could get his full sixty, this would be a party of less than half the strength usually employed by African explorers. Speke and Burton, for example, had never travelled with less than 130. Livingstone's decision to travel with few followers was due partly to his meagre funds, but owed a lot to his absolute confidence in his ability to handle Africans. He also believed that to go in 'grande array' merely aroused hostility and caused greater demands for *hongo* or dues for passage. Apart from this he was convinced that the more men taken, the more there were to fall sick, and thus the more frequent the stoppages. Larger parties had to take more cloth and beads to pay for food. Nevertheless, the disadvantages of travelling with few followers outweighed the advantages. The fewer the porters, the fewer the trade goods that could be taken, and therefore the shorter the time till the caravan had to return to the coast to replenish its supplies. A white man without trade goods was virtually helpless in central Africa, and unless he could rely on his followers to go on carrying these precious items without deserting, his very life was threatened. The loss of forty porters might not be too much of a blow for a man with over a hundred followers, but for a man with only sixty the same loss could prove catastrophic. This meant that unless Livingstone could guarantee his men's loyalty, he would soon be in serious trouble. In

4 'A View of Zanzibar'

retrospect it seems amazing that Livingstone was not frightened to be setting out with such a small party, containing only four men he could be sure of. The truth is that his confidence stemmed from a false comparison. He was still thinking of his trans-continental journey. But then the Makololo had been with him under orders from their chief, and they themselves had believed that they were working not just for their leader but for the benefit of their entire tribe. Even then, with Livingstone's unique ability with Africans, he had at times nearly failed to keep his party together.

In late January 1866 Livingstone was at last in Zanzibar, poised to begin his work. During the next month and a half he was to gain a far more accurate and comprehensive picture of the slave trade and Arab slavery. For a start, Livingstone could see that the Sultan, who derived £20,000 of his annual revenue from the trade, was not going to give up such privileges without forcible encouragement; nor were his most important subjects. All the main firms in Zanzibar benefited from the trade in some way or other, and at a later date Livingstone was to discover to his horror that the firm of Jairam Sewji, where he went for his trade goods, employed a man, Ludha Damji, who also acted as the Sultan's Customs Master. Thus dues from the slave trade were often diverted into Sewji's firm.[6] In truth there were no caravan suppliers who did not have a vested interest in the slave trade. Their best customers were the leaders of slave caravans. But disgusted as Livingstone was by the slave market, he could not afford to offend the Sultan, since his Arab subjects had penetrated deep into the interior where they had established large trading posts as far away as Ujiji on the shores of Lake Tanganyika. So Livingstone politely sipped sherbet with the Sultan and listened to a brass band playing tunes suitable for a British visitor: the 'British Grenadiers' and the National Anthem.[7]

One of the great puzzles about Livingstone's behaviour on his last journey would be the way he travelled with, and became friendly towards, a number of Arabs whom he knew to be slavers. There is no completely satisfactory explanation, but it is important to realize that while he was at Zanzibar, Livingstone learned to make a distinction between Arab slavery as an institution—the possession and treatment of domestic slaves—and the process by which Africans were torn from their homes and subjected to terrible suffering on their land and sea journey to Zanzibar and more distant places in the Persian Gulf and Arabia. Once the slaves arrived at their destinations, they were treated without cruelty—better in fact than many employees of British industrialists. The reason, as Livingstone could see, was that Arabs were not thoroughly dominated by the profit motive, as were for example the plantation owners in the southern states of America, where slavery coexisted with European commercial habits. Livingstone expressed this well: 'When society advances,' he wrote, 'wants multiply; and to supply these the slaves' lot becomes harder. The distance between master and man increases as the lust of gain is developed.'[8] Livingstone realized how ironic it was that Arab slavery would become far worse if Western economics were adopted by Arabs and Africans. While this realization made Livingstone less antagonistic to individual Arab slave traders, it increased his certainty that no European 'progress' could come to Africa until total abolition had been achieved. Thus he would often express a greater hatred of domestic slavery than the system warranted.

In his early days in Africa, Livingstone had tried for a while to judge African customs objectively. Now, judging Arab behaviour in the same way, he could see that it was about as useful to accuse an Arab slaver of immorality as it was to accuse a British capitalist of deliberate exploitation. It is also important to recall that since the early 1850s Livingstone had known that Africans cooperated with slavers. Now he saw that Europeans too, by buying pianos with ivory keys and knives with ivory handles, were bolstering up the trade. The slave and ivory trades were closely related. Since the Arabs used slaves captured in the interior to carry their ivory, and since both tusks and porters were sold at the coast, an increase in the demand for ivory meant that more slaves were needed as porters, and thus more slaves were sold for export at the coast. These considerations, when taken together, undoubtedly made Livingstone less hostile towards individual Arabs, but this cannot explain how he managed to justify to himself travelling with men who, even if they treated their slaves well at home, subjected African men, women and children captured in the interior to horrifying hardships on the journey to the coast.

Before Livingstone left Zanzibar in March 1866, he heard that Colonel Playfair, the British Consul and Political Agent at Zanzibar, was resigning. Since Livingstone knew that Zanzibar was going to be his only lifeline with the outside world, he was keen to try and get somebody he knew appointed for the job. He had resumed reasonably friendly relations with John Kirk in England, and tried to use his influence to get him appointed. He failed, but finally succeeded in getting Kirk the job of Surgeon to the British Agency in Zanzibar, a stepping-stone to the consulship.

Livingstone sailed from Zanzibar for the mainland on 19 March. The officers of H.M.S. *Penguin* could hardly have guessed that after they lost sight of Livingstone, as he marched inland from Rovuma Bay, only one white man would see him alive again.

Livingstone began his last journey with a disastrous tactical mistake, which he could have avoided had he taken Sir Roderick Murchison's advice. Both Livingstone and Murchison now believed, mistakenly as it happened, that a river flowed out of the northern end of Lake Tanganyika and ultimately joined Baker's newly discovered Lake Albert. According to this theory, a river flowing into Lake Tanganyika, from the south, would provide the key to the Nile's source. Since this theory cut out Speke, Burton and Baker, Livingstone was determined to believe it. Sir Roderick, however, sensibly suggested that it was imperative for Livingstone to check the connection of lakes Tanganyika and Albert before searching for sources south of Tanganyika. But Livingstone had other ideas, as he told Murchison:

> Supposing that, as I almost fully believe, Tanganyika goes into Baker's lake, the discovery of this would leave the matter very much as it was before. The source would have to be sought for still . . . and I should be obliged to come away back to it in order to give a feasible account of the ultimate origin of the Nile. Much more time would be required for this than by my plan of going at once to the headwaters.[9]

This decision would account for many of Livingstone's future geographical misconceptions. By 1871 when he eventually discovered that there was no connection between lakes Tanganyika and Albert, his health had been severely undermined and his judgement had likewise been impaired.

Livingstone had landed just north of the Rovuma at a small port called Mikidani. His party consisted of thirty-five men—he had not yet managed to hire any more porters—and a bizarre assortment of baggage animals: three buffaloes and a calf, six camels, four donkeys and two mules. Livingstone's reason for bringing so many different kinds of animal was that he wished to find out if any one should prove immune to the tsetse fly. The immediate aim of the party was to head due west to Lake Nyassa, cross the lake in canoes and then head north-west for a lake called Bemba or Bangweolo, which Livingstone had first heard about during his second survey of Nyassa in 1863. Since then he had become convinced that Bangweolo would prove to be the source of the Nile. What Livingstone hoped to do was reach Bangweolo, trace a river north-east out of it into Lake Tanganyika and then proceed north triumphantly to Lake Albert and the Nile. Even if Livingstone's geographical assumptions had been correct, his task would still have been a terrifyingly difficult one.

As in the past, initial false optimism accounted for much of Livingstone's misery once things started to go wrong. From the day he landed, disappointments came in quick succession. He had hoped to add another twenty or thirty porters to his party at the coast, but he was assured by all those he asked that no local tribesmen would come with him for fear of

Lake Turkana

Nile

Lake Albert

Lomani

Lualaba

Lake Victoria
Nyanza

NYANGWE
BAMBARRE
UJIJI
UNYANYEMBE
TABORA
Zanzibar

Lukuga
Lake
Tanganyika
MPWAPWE
SIMBAWENNI
BAGAMOYO

Lake
Moero
Chambesi

CASEMBE
Luapula
Lake
Nyassa
Rovuma

Lake
Bangweolo
CHITAMBO

Kafue

ZUMBO
TETE
Shire

Zambesi
SESHEKE
Zambesi
Save

LINYANTI
Victoria
Falls
Okavango
Delta

QUILIMANE

Indian
Ocean

4 LIVINGSTONE'S LAST JOURNEYS

– – – Mar. 1866–Mar. 1869

········· July 1869–Oct. 1871

–·–·– Nov. 1871–Feb. 1872, with Stanley

——— Aug. 1872–Apr. 1873

——— Stanley's journey, 1871–2

(Livingstone's death occurred some distance
S.S.E. of Lake Bangweolo)

miles   500

0   km   800

being captured in the interior and sold into slavery. This was a damaging blow and meant that he had to leave behind stores that he could ill afford to lose. The first few weeks of travel were fraught with difficulties.

He had landed, it appeared, at one of the few points on the coast where there was thick jungle. This had to be hacked through with axes, and the size of the camels meant that a much wider path had to be cut. The air seemed heavy and smothering and the constant work with the axes soon began to sap the morale of his polyglot following.

Ten days after leaving the coast he noticed that his sepoys were maltreating the baggage animals. Yet, although several animals had been overloaded so cruelly that they often stumbled and fell, Livingstone did not assert his authority firmly on this crucial first occasion. He noted in his journal: 'They assure me with so much positiveness that they are not overloaded, that I have to be silent, or only, as I have done several times before express the opinion that they will kill these animals.'[10]

The matter was far more serious than the simple fact of cruelty. If the animals died from maltreatment, the experiment to judge their resistance to the tsetse fly would be vitiated; worse still, since the party was short of porters, if the animals were lost more stores might have to be abandoned. Overloading the camels and mules was therefore sabotage, but Livingstone had reacted with a mild rebuke. It seems barely credible that this was the same man who had disciplined Baines and Bedingfeld so severely seven years before. Yet whereas he had always been prepared to blame Europeans on the slightest pretext, he let Indians and Africans get away with far more serious sins with little or no remonstrance. The lack of authority he showed early on was to plague him severely as the months passed. By the end of April the camels were covered with bruises and festering wounds where they had been kicked and beaten. Several of the sepoys had by then also stolen some of Livingstone's clothing. Even when large gashes and deep wounds were inflicted on the animals, he still did not act but wrote wretchedly in his journal: 'I cannot always be near to prevent it.'[11] On his crossing of Africa he had once quelled a mutiny among his followers by felling the leader with the butt of his revolver, but that had been before the suffering of the Zambesi Expedition had taken its toll. Now in 1866 Livingstone had lost all authority, even over Africans. Personal determination was not enough to keep his followers in order.

Throughout May the sepoys continued to be a source of misery to their leader. They stole from villages, they dawdled, and they did not treat the animals any better. Four miles became the average daily progress and the camels now started to die one after another. By then they had been bitten by tsetse fly, and Livingstone was uncertain whether brutality or the fly had caused their deaths. In early May he managed to hire twenty-four porters at a village, and was delighted to be able to go on ahead and leave the sepoys dawdling several miles back in the company of the Nassick boys, who were also beginning to complain. One Nassick boy was in fact seriously ill and would die in a few weeks. In the past Livingstone had always had difficulty in telling when illness was feigned or genuine. Not surprisingly, a man who was dangerously ill resented being told he was shirking, and this lack of discernment was to prove yet another cause for ill-will.

Two hundred miles inland there was a great shortage of food, due in part to a severe drought, but made worse by Ngoni raids. Many people were starving and Livingstone could not help but recall the gruesome days in 1863 when the Zambesi Expedition was dragging to a close. Hunger made the men still more· mutinous and in early June the twenty-four porters refused to go on. In order to save his party from starvation, Livingstone had to make a series of forced marches to get out of this famine-stricken country. At this time he wrote a reassuring letter to Agnes: 'I am very well but have lost some of that beastly fatness that threatened to swallow me up.'[12] He might have lost his authority over his men but he had not lost his powers of understatement.

On 2 June the Nassick boys and the sepoys offered money and cloth to the party's Somali guide, Ben Ali, to misdirect them all so that they could get back to the coast. Livingstone heard of the conspiracy but did nothing until at last, on 4 June, he had to issue a long overdue ultimatum to the Nassick boys: either work or return to the coast. The incident that forced Livingstone to this step had been the adoption by the mission boys of a habit learned from the sepoys: the engaging of local Africans to carry their loads for them on the understanding that the white man would pay for it.

The shortage of food was still serious when Livingstone began to see the first signs of Arab penetration. Many people had guns; and occasion-ally piles of slave-taming sticks could be seen on either side of the path. The knowledge that he was entering a slaving country did something to revive the Doctor's firmness, and the next sepoy insurrection was met with a promise to flog any future offender. He kept his word and the next Indian to delay the party was given 'some smart cuts with a cane'. Livingstone always hated corporal punishment and noted in his journal: 'I felt that I was degrading myself, and resolved not to do the punishment myself again.'[13] Considering the disciplinary excesses of which almost every other explorer was guilty, Livingstone's forbearance was almost miraculous. Although he was all but certain that the sepoys were bent on turning both the Nassick boys and the Johanna men against him, he could still write patiently: 'I shall try to feel as charitably as I can in spite of it all, for the mind has a strong tendency to brood over the ills of travel.'[14]

During the period when internal tensions within the party were at their most acute, Livingstone saw evidence of far greater inhumanity than he had ever witnessed in the Shire Highlands. On 19 June he wrote: 'We passed a woman tied by the neck to a tree and dead, the people of the country explained that she had been unable to keep up with the other slaves in a gang, and her master had determined that she should not become the property of anybody else if she recovered after resting for a time.'[15]

Other groups of corpses were found with remorseless regularity. Some had been stabbed to death, others shot and many had simply been left tied together to die slowly of starvation. Over and over again Livingstone was told that the Arabs often grew so enraged with slaves who became too weak to walk that they murdered them because their investment had not come up to expectation. When slaves were left alive, the local people often came and rescued them, fed them up and then sold them again. In fact it could be a profitable business to follow a slave caravan in the hope of taking over the rejects. Livingstone deduced this at a very early stage from the number of taming sticks he saw on the path without bodies near them. His knowledge that Africans were as much responsible for the system as the Arabs had always horrified him. He spent many hours explaining to chiefs that 'if they sell their fellows, they are like the man who holds the victim while the Arab performs the murder'.[16] Livingstone pointed out repeatedly that they were under no compulsion to sell their people to a handful of alien intruders. He made little impression. The answers he got were predictable enough: "If so and so gives up selling so will we. He is the greatest offender in the country." "It is the fault of the Arabs who tempt us with fine clothes, powder and guns." "I would fain keep all my people to cultivate more land, but my next neighbour allows his people to kidnap mine and I must have ammunition to defend them."'[17]

Sickened though he was by African indifference to the fate of people, quite often of the same tribe, Livingstone did not for a moment turn against them. In 1851 he had discovered that the Makololo sold slaves to the Mambari, but he had gone on defending them long afterwards.

In June and July 1866 he might have tried to send out sensational reports to the coast of what he had seen, but he did not. Instead he wrote two cool and lucid despatches to the Foreign Secretary, setting out his arguments as to why the British restriction treaties, which legalized slavery within specified limits, could never work. When evasion of the blockade was so regular, he asked how the Foreign Office and Admiralty could countenance such vast expenditure to so little effect. He argued that the prohibition of all slave movements by sea would not create anarchy in Zanzibar because slavery on the island need not be abolished as an institution. Once the supply was cut, it would die slowly and peacefully. Domestic slavery

5 Slaves abandoned

was mild; only the export of slaves had to be ended. He had often heard the official government view expressed that if all sea-going movement of slaves was stopped to and from Zanzibar, many more markets would spring up on the coast, and thus the destruction of one big slave market would only produce a crop of little ones far more difficult to control. Livingstone's reply was simple. Slaves were only contained in Zanzibar because it was an island and they could not therefore run away. Any huge slaving emporium on the mainland would be untenable because it would be impossible to contain the slaves. Finally he made a number of suggestions about building depots for freed slaves along the coast, so that ships in the blockading squadron would not have to return to a distant port every time a slaving dhow was captured. He also suggested that it was imperative for British warships to be in Zanzibar harbour when the prevailing winds allowed the northern Arabs to come south.[18] Livingstone's proposals were workable and sound. When the slave market in Zanzibar was closed in June 1873, a month after his death, there was no anarchy in the island and no attempt was made by the coastal Arabs to set up large coastal markets. There is something enormously impressive about these despatches and the completely unemotional and logical way in which he marshalled his facts at the very time when he was personally so deeply involved in the far from abstract misery of the slaves themselves. Livingstone had decided to tackle the Foreign Office in their own impersonal terms. There is little overt anger, even against the Arabs, although at the time he was finding it very nearly impossible to buy food in exchange for cloth, since the Arabs had all but saturated the market.

By early July, Livingstone was within a hundred miles of Lake Nyassa and was leaving behind the famine-stricken, depopulated country. Now, instead of travelling across dried-up country with burned grass and stunted trees and shrubs, he was entering green undulating hills. This new terrain, although more pleasing to the eye, was not easy to cross. His weary followers found themselves endlessly climbing up to the tops of steep ridges and then descending to valleys with streams running down the middle. On one day they clambered into and out of fifteen such valleys.

Livingstone knew that his route into the interior was for much of the way identical with the southern Arab slave route from Lake Nyassa to the port of Kilwa on the coast. He had very much hoped to meet slave caravans returning from the interior, so that he could get an idea of their size, the areas the slaves had come from, the amount of ivory carried and any other information that might prove suitable for sending back to the Foreign Office. The Arabs, however, usually heard that he was approaching and took their caravan off in another direction for a day or two. The Arabs were certainly not frightened of a man with a small following, but since they knew from contacts at the coast that Livingstone was British, they had no desire to meet him. Although the Sultan of Zanzibar was well aware of the benefits of British protection—he had twice been saved by the intervention of the Royal Navy from *coups d'état* planned by his relatives—his subjects resented the existing British anti-slave trading treaties. Most caravan leaders, as soon as they heard that Livingstone was British, felt convinced that he had come as a spy of the British Government. Nevertheless the fact that the Sultan valued British friendship ensured that none of his subjects, however distant, were likely to murder Livingstone. He was, after all, a potential nuisance rather than an immediate threat.

On 14 July Livingstone came upon the first caravan that had not taken deliberate evasive action. The leader was an Arab called Seph Rubea, who on hearing that Livingstone was short of food, had actually made a detour to meet him and, as Livingstone put it, 'came forward like a man and brother with an ox and big bag of flour'.[19] After seeing the corpses of so many murdered slaves, it might be thought that Livingstone would have refused the gift, however altruistic the motives of the donor, but the hungry traveller took what was offered gratefully. He managed to square his conscience easily enough: if he starved, he would not be able to report on the slave trade and these reports were his only hope of getting the system stopped. Besides, if he offended the Arabs by rejecting their hospitality, he would never be able to elicit information from them. If the Arab slavers helped him it was because God was making them the agents of their own ultimate destruction. Even so, Livingstone realized the ambiguity of his position, and later, when he actually travelled with Arabs, he would find it necessary to make a distinction between the southern slave traders on the Nyassa–Kilwa route and the northern traders operating directly from Zanzibar in the Lake Tanganyika region. 'If one wanted to see the slave trade in its best phases,' he wrote the following year, 'he would accompany the gentlemen subjects of the Sultan of Zanzibar. If he wished to describe its worst form he would go with the Kilwa traders.'[20] It was true that in general the Kilwa traders were more brutal, largely because the Sultan of Zanzibar had less influence over them than he did over traders operating from Zanzibar itself. Nevertheless it must have occurred to Livingstone that no Arab was likely to murder slaves in front of him.

Yet for a Kilwa trader, Livingstone thought Seph Rubea an excellent man, and managed to learn a great deal from him: namely, that most of the slaves taken across Nyassa came from the area south-west of Lake Tanganyika where Livingstone hoped to find the Nile source. Seph also told Livingstone something that impressed him greatly: one hundred Arabs had died on the Kilwa route during the past year. Maybe, Livingstone reflected, similar European sacrifices might be necessary before philanthropists managed to get the trade stopped. Since Seph seemed friendly, Livingstone handed him the letters he had recently written, including his despatches to the Foreign Office, and asked him to see that they reached Zanzibar. Seph kept his word.

A few days later, the sepoys, in line with their previous behaviour, killed and ate the buffalo calf and then concocted a story about it being eaten by a tiger. Livingstone asked whether they had seen the tiger's stripes. They eagerly assented. Since there are no striped tigers in Africa, Livingstone was unimpressed. The following day a sepoy threatened to shoot a Nassick boy and another stole a large number of cartridges and some cloth from the stores. At last Livingstone had come to the end of his patience, and discharged them. They were given eighteen yards of cloth and left at a village to wait for the next caravan to the coast. The *havildar* begged to be allowed to stay on, and Livingstone reluctantly agreed. He deserted some weeks later.

At the beginning of August, Livingstone's party—now reduced to twenty-three—started to climb into the tall mountains that flank Nyassa. On 6 August he could see the blue water of the lake, ten or so miles away. Two days later he was on the shore itself. 'The roar of the waves and a dash in the breakers was quite exhilarating.'[21] Less exhilarating was the failure of all his efforts to get a dhow to take him across the lake, so that he could head straight for Lake Bangweolo without having to skirt Nyassa to the north or south. But all the Arabs were convinced that if he got hold of a boat he would burn it on the other side. In vain he showed them a letter of commendation from the Sultan of Zanzibar. Unfortunately nobody was able to read it, or that was what they said. In fact these Arabs on the lake knew more about Livingstone than those at the coast. Reports of his freeing slaves in the Shire Highlands had long since reached them. Unable to cross the lake, Livingstone rejected the shorter route round it to the north because it was rumoured that the Mazitu or Ngoni were ravaging the area. Instead he chose to go south and cross at the most southerly point of the lake, where the Shire ran out from it. He reached the Shire in mid-September and it brought back bitter memories of past failure. 'Many hopes have been disappointed here,' he wrote. 'Far down on the right bank of the Zambesi lies the dust of her whose death changed all my future prospects; and now, instead of a check being given to the slave trade by lawful commerce on the Lake, slave dhows prosper.'[22]

At this time one of the boys who had been with Livingstone since 1863 decided to rejoin his family in the Shire Highlands. Wikatani had been one of Mackenzie's favourites and had been rescued by Livingstone from the Ajawa. His loss was a sentimental rather than a practical blow. Although Amoda, Susi and Chuma would one day be the backbone of Livingstone's following, in 1866 they, like Wikatani, were still too young and unreliable to be much use. Already he had had to stop employing them as his personal servants because all his spoons and forks had been mislaid and he always had to repeat everything he told them, and rarely got breakfast when he asked for it. But despite this he was fonder of them than of any of the others, and although all were inclined to sing and giggle more than he liked, Chuma was learning to read and began to show other hopeful signs that he would soon be useful.

A few days after Wikatani left the party, the Johanna men made up their minds to do the same. The reason they gave for refusing to go on was the news they received from an Arab that the country ahead was being pillaged by the Mazitu. The leader of the Johanna men, Musa, had been a constant trouble-maker aboard the *Lady Nyassa*. Even when Livingstone forced him to listen to a local chief, Musa would not accept that the Arabs had exaggerated the severity of the Mazitu raids in order to stop Livingstone's party going on. Musa would have none of it and remained determined to quit. Although the sepoys had been without doubt the worse bane to date, and the Nassick boys a close second, the Johanna men had not been much better. They had stolen repeatedly from their loads and had recently started to dawdle. To do them justice, there were persistent rumours at the time that the Mazitu were in the neighbour-hood, and while Livingstone knew why he was risking his neck, it is extremely unlikely that the Johanna men understood the purpose of the fight against slavery or the search for the source of the Nile. As Musa said:

'I want to see my father, my mother, and my child at Johanna. I no want to be killed by Mazitu'.[23] Short of threatening to shoot Musa if he deserted, there was nothing Livingstone could do to retain the ten Johanna men. In the end he had to accept their desertion, although he knew that this made his party dangerously small—eleven men in all.

Incredibly, although Livingstone faced a host of terrible problems due to the loss of so many porters, he was still able to write serene passages of natural description.

> The morning was lovely, the whole country bathed in bright sunlight, and not a breath of air disturbed the smoke as it slowly curled up from the burning weeds . . . The people were generally busy hoeing in the cool of the day. One old man was carefully paring a stick for stirring the porridge, and others were enjoying the cool shade of the wild fig trees . . . I like to see the men weaving or spinning, or reclining under these glorious canopies, as much as I love to see our more civilised people lolling on their sofas or ottomans.[24]

This passage evokes all the pleasure he had felt in his early travels and is the more poignant since the same day a series of thunder storms shattered the rural calm and turned paradise into a muddy hell, where paths disappeared under water and small streams became rivers. The rains would last for two months. Soon the old problem of food shortage was added to the 'excessively adhesive mud' and the waterlogged paths. Because of the Mazitu raids, people were frightened of Livingstone and his small party and were therefore even less willing to part with any precious food. Agriculture had been neglected due to the raids and in many places the villagers were living on wild fruits. The air was muggy and the clouds too thick for any accurate observations to be made.

On 6 December the only entry in Livingstone's journal was: 'Too ill to march.' The night before, the whole party had been badly wetted by a storm and had slept in soaking clothes. Bad health was now to be a recurrent problem. December passed miserably. The only food to be got was the indigestible native porridge that brought back Livingstone's old enemy, dysentery. He managed to buy four goats, but on Christmas Day they were stolen. Nevertheless he pressed on north-west and by the end of the year had crossed the Loangwa river, midway between Bangweolo and Nyassa.

On New Year's Eve he wrote: 'We now end 1866. It has not been so fruitful or useful as I intended. Will try to do better in 1867, and be better—more gentle and loving; and may the Almighty, to whom I commit my way, bring my desires to pass and prosper me! Let all the sins of '66 be blotted out for Jesus' sake.'[25]

On 6 January the first serious mishap of the year occurred. They were clambering down the steep slopes of a ravine and the path was so slippery that two of the porters fell; one of these men was carrying the precious chronometers, without which no accurate longitudes could be taken. Livingstone reacted calmly, writing: 'This was a misfortune as it altered the rates, as was seen by the first comparison of them together this evening.'[26] Because the weather was so bad, and the clouds very rarely lifted, it was doubly important that the few longitudes he was able to take should be accurate. Unfortunately, for the next eighteen months they would all be some twenty miles to the eastward in error, due to the damage to the chronometers.[27] These mistakes did not have any immediate effect, but errors of this nature usually built up, and could, over a long period of time, dangerously mislead the traveller who relied on his observations being accurate. Two weeks after this incident, the man carrying the party's medicine chest deserted. Livingstone thought this a far worse disaster than the damage to the chronometers; in fact he called it 'the sentence of death'. He was wrong; the real death sentence came when he returned to this same general area six years later, and relied on his previous observations to guide him.

In the short term, however, the loss of the medicines was a devastating blow. Precisely at the time when everybody's health was deteriorating, the drugs, which alone could check malaria and dysentery, had gone. In similar circumstances many travellers would have abandoned their immediate work and returned to the coast to get more quinine. But Livingstone would not even retrace his steps to Nyassa to send to Kilwa for more medicines. He may have felt that he could not rely on the Arabs to transmit the message and then return with the drugs, but more likely he could not face the prospect of retracing his steps even for a mile. The thousand miles he had now travelled since leaving the coast had already taken him months more than he had expected. To struggle back for many days through the mud and the rain, feeling faint with hunger all the time, was psychologically out of the question. Soon Livingstone hoped to reach Lake Bangweolo, where he was certain he would find a large river flowing north to Lake Tanganyika. He would go on.

But the nearer they got to where Livingstone supposed Bangweolo to be, the harder the going became. The country was now an enormous swamp. On the evening of 16 January 1867 Livingstone recorded a typical day's march: 'The rain as usual made us halt early ... We roast a little grain and boil it, to make believe it is coffee ... Ground all sloppy; oozes full and overflowing—feet constantly wet. Rivulets rush strongly with clear water ... Rivulets can only be crossed by felling a tree on the bank and letting it fall across ... Nothing but famine and famine prices, the people living on mushrooms and leaves. We get some elephants' meat from the people, but high is no name for its condition. It is very bitter, but it prevents the heartburn.'[28]

In mid-January, Chitane, a little poodle Livingstone had bought in Zanzibar, was drowned. He had developed the greatest admiration for his dog and had often praised him for chasing off much larger curs in the villages they passed through. When all else had failed, Chitane had raised Livingstone's spirits by rushing tirelessly up and down the straggling line of porters. Fording a mile-wide marsh, waist-deep, nobody had noticed the little dog vainly struggling to keep up. In the weeks to come Livingstone often thought about his dead pet.

At the end of January, Livingstone crossed the Chambesi river, but did not realize that it flowed south-west into Lake Bangweolo. He had not been able to establish the precise position of the lake, and now, pressing on north, he had passed 120 miles to the east of it. By the time Livingstone realized his mistake a few weeks later, the lake lay one hundred miles to the south-west. Instead of retracing his steps, Livingstone made up his mind to continue his northward march, in the hope of finding the point where the river, which he assumed flowed north from Bangweolo, entered Lake Tanganyika. Livingstone would not now reach Bangweolo till July 1868, over a year later. Apart from the flooded state of the country, there was another reason why Livingstone decided not to retrace his steps to Bangweolo: by now he was seriously ill with what he suspected was rheumatic fever: 'Every step I take jars in the chest, and I am very weak; I can scarcely keep up the march, though formerly I was always first ... I have a constant singing in my ears, and can scarcely hear the loud tick of the chronometer.'[29]

February 3 brought the first gleam of hope he had known for months. He met a party of Arabs who were going to Bagamoyo on the mainland opposite Zanzibar. At last here was a chance to get letters to the outside world. Although he was not certain that the Arabs could be trusted, his packet did reach Zanzibar; one letter was to the Consul, Mr Seward. Livingstone asked for goods to be sent to Ujiji on Lake Tanganyika, where he hoped to be within a couple of months. Among other things he wanted coffee, candles, soap, sealing-wax, preserved meat, six bottles of port wine and, of course, medicines. He described his almost constantly gnawing hunger and ended: 'Don't think, please, that I make a moan over nothing but a little sharpness of appetite. I am a mere ruckle of bones, did all the hunting myself, and wet, hunger, and fatigue took away the flesh.'[30] Livingstone could of course have painted a far grimmer picture. He could hardly travel at all at this time, and although in early February he was only 150 miles from the southern end of Lake Tanganyika, he did not reach it till 1 April.

Once at Tanganyika, Livingstone was eager to head north along the western shore of the lake, where he was convinced there would be an inlet. He was preparing to set out when he heard that war had broken out north and west of his position, between local tribes and several large parties of Arab traders. There was nothing else Livingstone could do but head south again, in the hope that he would soon be able to make a looping detour round the trouble spot. But he did not get far, for soon he was laid out by the worst attack of fever he could ever remember. It came suddenly: 'I found myself floundering outside my hut and unable to get in; I tried to lift myself from my back by laying hold of two posts at the entrance, but when I got nearly upright I let them go, and fell back heavily on my head on a box . . . some hours elapsed before I could recognise where I was.'[31]

Chuma and Susi cared for Livingstone during his illness, and hung a blanket across the door of the hut so that no inquisitive strangers could see his helplessness. His condition was extremely precarious for a full month, so bad that he was unable to make a single entry for April in his journal. Just before he fell ill, Livingstone had heard of a large lake a hundred miles to the west, called Lake Moero, which he felt certain must be linked in some way with Lake Bangweolo. Now that he could no longer entertain the idea of finding an inlet on the western side of Tanganyika, Livingstone's new plan was to reach Lake Moero as soon as possible. But until he had found out more about the extent of the fighting between the Arabs and the local tribes, he did not feel able, with his tiny following, to risk travelling far to the west. Instead, as soon as he was strong enough, he set out south for the nearest Arab settlement, where he hoped to discover how serious the war was.

Livingstone joined the Arabs on 20 May and remained with them till August, waiting for the war to end. Although he was keen to get to Moero, he was happy to convalesce for a couple of months, with his well-supplied hosts, who raised no objection to his presence. It is worth noting that during July there was an earth tremor, which played further havoc with Livingstone's chronometers. The first accident to these instruments had made his observations for longitude twenty miles too far to the east. After the tremor, when he reset them, a further error crept in, and from this time his longitudes erred in the opposite direction, being fifty miles out to the west. Now Livingstone would have seventy miles more of space on his map than was in fact there.[32] If the maps he had previously drawn were inaccurate, those he would shortly make would be far worse.

With peace finally agreed by the Arabs and their African adversaries, in mid-September Livingstone was at last able to set out for Lake Moero. Since a party of Arabs was going in that direction, he decided to take advantage of their supplies by travelling with them. The leader of this particular caravan was Tippu Tip, an ivory and slave trader, who would soon establish political and commercial control of the whole area through which they 'were now passing on their journey west from the southern end of Lake Tanganyika. Progress was very slow because Tippu was always stopping to make enquiries about ivory. The hundred miles to Lake Moero took well over a month. So Livingstone did not stand on the banks of the lake until 8 November.

He was not particularly elated after his 'discovery'. He knew that the Portuguese explorer Francisco José de Lacerda had died just south of Moero in 1799, and that since then three other Portuguese expeditions had reached the area from Tete. Livingstone's only real interest in Moero—itself a mere puddle by African standards, being seventy miles long and twenty wide—was its relationship to lakes Bangweolo and Tanganyika.

Within a few days, with the help of local reports, Livingstone had made some important and entirely accurate deductions about the lake. He was convinced that a large river, the Lualaba, flowed out from the north-western corner of Lake Moero in a northerly direction. He also concluded that, to the south, Moero was linked with Lake Bangweolo by another river, the Luapula. Thus the ultimate source of the Lualaba, which was a colossal river, lay 150 miles south in Lake Bangweolo. All this informa-tion was correct, but Livingstone rather surprisingly did not immediately claim in letters or despatches that the Lualaba was the Nile and Bangweolo its source. When he did so the following April (1868) he was not in possession of very much more knowledge; in the meantime he had only verified that the river Luapula did indeed connect lakes Moero and Bangweolo. From the moment Livingstone first heard about the Lualaba, he knew that his major task would be to find out where it went. Believing secretly, as he did, even in November 1867, that it was the Nile, he would now have to sort out whether the Lualaba continued its northern journey from Moero into Tanganyika, and then, through that lake and via a river at its northern end, to Lake Albert, or whether instead it joined Albert direct without touching Lake Tanganyika.

At the end of 1867 Livingstone was aware that there were two impor-tant tasks ahead of him. The first was to go south to Lake Bangweolo to verify that it was, as the Africans claimed, the most southerly source of the Lualaba. The second was to follow the Lualaba north from Lake Bangweolo as far as might be necessary to prove that it was the Nile. But unfortunately matters were not quite so simple. Livingstone's supplies were dangerously low, he had only nine followers left and he could not hope to take on more until he could promise payment with trade goods.

As it was, he had insufficient cloth to buy food for the few men with him. He also needed medicines. Before leaving Zanzibar in 1866, Livingstone had wisely made arrangements for supplies to be sent to the Arab town of Ujiji, on the eastern side of Lake Tanganyika, for him to collect at a later date.

In December 1867, Livingstone could certainly not risk setting out on a long journey northwards down the Lualaba until he had first picked up his stores from Ujiji, 250 miles north-east of Lake Moero. So much was clear. It still remained for Livingstone to make up his mind whether he should travel the 150 miles south to Bangweolo and 'discover' the Lualaba's source, before making his long detour to Ujiji. In the end Livingstone made no real decision, but came to the stop-gap conclusion that, in view of his low supplies, he ought to stay with Tippu Tip and his party for as long as possible. Tippu planned to go twenty miles south to the town of Chief Casembe, the principal trading centre of the area; after that, the Arab assured Livingstone, he would head back for Ujiji and, when he did, Livingstone would be welcome to come with him. Livingstone intended to defer a final decision about his intentions until he reached Casembe's. There he meant to decide once and for all whether he would return north with Tippu or go on south to Lake Bangweolo. Livingstone wasted a month at Casembe's and then discovered that Tippu was going on west to Katanga and not back to Ujiji. After yet another bout of indecision Livingstone decided to abandon Bangweolo for the time being and to head north with an Arab called Muhammad bin Salim, who intended to go straight to Ujiji. Unfortunately, by the time Salim and Livingstone left Casembe's the winter rains had set in, and by the end of March 1868, after three months' travelling, the two men and their followers had only progressed fifty miles to the north. Ahead of them the rains had turned the entire region between the point they had reached and Lake Tanganyika into an enormous and impassable swamp. Livingstone's failure to act positively after reaching Lake Moero had cost him five months. Now it appeared that his only course was to find a village and sit out the rains with Salim for another two months. Livingstone estimated that, as things were, he would not reach Ujiji before June and would therefore be unable to get back to the Lualaba until October or November; since he had only counted on being away from England for two years in all, and had already been in Africa a year and eleven months, this was an extremely depressing time.

Right through the losses, delays and desertions of 1866 and 1867, Livingstone had displayed a patience and tolerance which, if told about, any member of the Zambesi Expedition would have considered too unlikely to be credible. But although Livingstone's character had softened a great deal in the past three or four years, the despair he felt during the first three months of 1868 brought back many old traits. Fearing that both time and money were running out, Livingstone wrote bitterly to Sir Roderick Murchison, attacking the Government for meanness and dishonesty. He went over his treatment by Russell in minute detail, telling Murchison that the 'impudent letter' from the Foreign Office still 'gnaws at my heart on every touch of illness or despondency'. Earlier grievances were aired again and Livingstone argued that Prince Albert and his cousin, the Portuguese king, had worked together to destroy the Zambesi Expedition. Once Livingstone had started pouring out a stream of bitterness, he could not stop, and now he went on to attack the Council of the Royal Geographical Society as well. They had given him a pittance, he claimed, and afterwards expected all his notes. This was just a plot to cheat him out of making money from any book on his return. He reserved his most biting criticism for the cartographer, John Arrowsmith, and the Society's secretary, Francis Galton, who had both instructed him to make regular observations. In view of the dense cloud conditions Livingstone had faced during the past few months, these orders seemed like a very bad joke. 'Put Arrowsmith & Galton into a hogshead,' Livingstone told Murchison, 'and ask them to take bearings out of the bunghole. I came for discovery and not for survey, and if I don't give a clear account of the countries traversed, I shall return the money.'[33]

At precisely the time when Livingstone appeared to be hopelessly lost in past grievances and quarrels, he suddenly cast aside all previous indecision and told the astonished Salim that he would not wait for the rains to stop but would head south at once for Lake Bangweolo and return north to Ujiji only when he had made sure of the Lualaba's source. With the country inundated, and food almost impossible to obtain, this was a decision brave to the point of foolhardiness.

On 13 April Livingstone told his nine followers to prepare to march. Salim argued with Livingstone and told him that to attempt the 200-mile journey south before the end of the rains would kill him and all his men. Livingstone was unmoved by this warning and did not change his mind when five of his followers refused to come with him. The party of thirty-five was now finally reduced to four. When Livingstone set out, Salim sent a messenger after him to make one last attempt to dissuade him from such a suicidal venture. Livingstone told this man 'to say to Mohamad [Salim] that I would on no account go to Ujiji, till I had done all in my power to reach the Lake I sought'.

And now the man who had written so bitterly to Murchison such a short time before forgave the five deserters completely. 'I did not blame them very severely in my own mind for absconding; they were tired of tramping, and so verily am I . . . Consciousness of my own defects makes me lenient.'[34]

During the previous year, Livingstone had felt it was unsafe to leave the shelter of Arab caravans. Then he had been able to count on nearly a dozen followers; now, with only four men, a few fathoms of cloth and no medicines, he was prepared to risk travelling two hundred miles through waterlogged country, in the worst of the rains, to an area said to be particularly unhealthy at this time of year. A little while before, he had written, 'It is needless to hide that I never travelled with less spirit.'[35] His recovery was little short of superhuman.

In the month that it took Livingstone and his four men to retrace their steps to Casembe's, en route for Bangweolo, they were often up to their waists in water for stretches up to four hours at a time; and, even when the water was shallower, 'black tenacious mud' clung to their feet, making walking a terrible effort. Unexpected areas of soft mud could suddenly plunge them up to their armpits in slime. Each step was usually followed 'by a rush of bubbles on the surface, which, bursting, discharged foul air of frightful faecal odour'.[36] Apart from midges and mosquitoes, they had to contend with leeches, which 'needed no coaxing to bite, but flew at the skin like furies'; with hands and fingers numbed by the water, these parasites were extremely hard to pull off.

But in spite of such dreadful conditions, Livingstone and his followers reached Casembe's after twenty-seven days' travelling. They had done well to average two miles a day. Livingstone left Casembe's and headed south on 11 June. This time he went with Muhammad Bogharib, an Arab trader, going to the Bangweolo district in search of ivory and copper. In spite of the fact that Bogharib also dealt in slaves, Livingstone soon grew to like him and during the next year grew so attached to him that later he would regret not having a photograph of the Arab as a memento. Bogharib proved more than a friend, for he shared his own food with Livingstone and personally nursed him when he was sick. As with all Livingstone's friendships with Arabs, it is hard to establish whether hypocrisy or a remarkably clear-sighted understanding of an alien culture played the more important part. Whatever the truth, Livingstone clearly made a distinction between the Arabs' acceptance of the slave trade as a legitimate and normal form of commerce and their personalities as men. Nor did Livingstone feel uneasy about this, for he often praised Bogharib in letters, even when they were addressed to the Foreign Secretary.

By the beginning of July, Livingstone and Bogharib were within thirty miles of Lake Bangweolo, and local reports had soon absolutely confirmed Livingstone's opinion, formed seven months before at Lake Moero, that

Bangweolo was the source of the Lualaba. Now that he knew that he would be at the Lualaba's source within a few days, Livingstone decided that before that historic moment, he should abandon his secrecy and tell the world that the Lualaba was the upper Nile. Of course Livingstone could not communicate with the coast unless he happened to encounter a caravan bound for Kilwa or Zanzibar, but this did not stop him writing letters and despatches to be ready for sending when an opportunity might occur. Although Livingstone had not followed the Lualaba north, his assumption that it was the Nile was not as rash as later events made it appear. His confidence would have surprised no geographer possessed of the same information at the same date.

Livingstone had located a very large river, flowing due north out of Lake Moero. Clearly this river's direction and size made it certain that it would enter the sea several thousand miles away. Even by the end of the sixteenth century the whole African coastline had been mapped with tolerable accuracy, and by 1868 Livingstone had no difficulty at all in concluding that, apart from the Nile, only one other African river could account for the Lualaba: the Congo. Livingstone felt able to reject the idea of it being the Congo on several counts. For a start, the two hundred miles of the Congo which had been navigated from the Atlantic had taken explorers not east or south-east, but *north-east*; so unless the Congo completely changed direction and described an enormous south-easterly loop (as indeed it does), it could have no possible connection with the Lualaba. Another simple fact, which Livingstone thought was evidence against the Congo being the Lualaba, was that Lake Moero was 1,100 miles from the west coast and only 700 from the east. In 1868 the Congo was not known to extend further east than a couple of hundred miles, at which point it was flowing *north-east*, a direction which made any connection with lakes Bangweolo and Moero—both over a thousand miles to the *south-east*—seem extremely unlikely.

On 8 July, still a few miles short of Bangweolo, Livingstone began a despatch, which he was certain would be the most important he had ever written. It was addressed to the Foreign Secretary, Lord Clarendon:*

I may safely assert [wrote an elated Livingstone] that the chief sources of the Nile, arise between 10° and 12° south latitude, or nearly in the

---

* Clarendon had once more become Foreign Secretary when Russell succeeded Palmerston as Prime Minister in October 1865.

position assigned to them by Ptolemy . . . If your Lordship will read the following short sketch of my discoveries, you will perceive that the springs of the Nile have hitherto been searched for very much too far to the north. They rise some 400 miles south of the most southerly portion of the Victoria Nyanza, and indeed south of all the lakes except Bangweolo.[37]

In a letter to Kirk written the same day, Livingstone gave him the same information about the Lualaba being the Nile and then added, almost as an afterthought: 'I have still to follow down the Lualaba, and see whether, as the natives assert, it passes Tanganyika to the west, or enters it and finds an exit into Baker's lake [Lake Albert].'[38] In his journal at this time, Livingstone played down the immensity of the task that still lay ahead of him. 'I have no doubts on the subject [of the Lualaba being the Nile], for I receive the reports of natives of intelligence at first hand, and they have no motive for deceiving me. The best maps are formed from the same sort of reports at third or fourth hand.'[39] Even though Livingstone could back up his suppositions with plausible arguments, this new admission, that he was prepared to base geographical theories partly on the testimony of third parties, marked a definitive move away from rigidly scientific deduction to something a great deal less precise. It was hardly a good augury for the future.

On 18 July, Livingstone at last arrived at Lake Bangweolo. It is important in view of events that happened to Livingstone there five years later, to describe in some detail not only his conclusions about Bangweolo's connection with the Lualaba but also his estimate of the lake's shape and extent. After a couple of days Livingstone persuaded some locals to take him out on to the lake in a canoe. The vessel, however, had been stolen and to his anger Livingstone had to be content with two days instead of four on the lake as agreed. In the short term this was no disaster. It merely meant that he mapped the lake wrongly. Livingstone had been taken out from the northern shore of the lake to one of four islands. Gazing south and east from this low island, he had looked across what appeared to be an uninterrupted stretch of water as far as the eye could see. Unfortunately his line of vision was restricted by the fact that the highest point on the island was only forty feet. He thus failed to see the beginning of a line of swamps just over the horizon. Had he seen them, he would have realized that Bangweolo proper was a small lake and not the vast expanse of water he imagined it to be. His final calculation was that it was 150 miles long from east to west. Had the natives, who had stolen the canoe, been prepared to paddle on south-east for two hours more, he would have discovered how large his error was. Bangweolo was only twenty-five miles long, and most of the area Livingstone thought was water was, in fact, marsh and swamp. The high level of the water was partly responsible for his misunderstanding; in the dry season he would undoubtedly have recognized that two of the 'islands' were not true islands at all, but higher ground surrounded by marsh, and that the two others were larger than he had thought, and different shapes.[40]

The fact that he saw Bangweolo at the end of the rainy season was not his only reason for exaggerating its size. For his estimate, he had also relied on the longitudes he had taken in 1867 and in the summer of 1868. One set, it will be remembered, had been twenty miles out to the east, the other fifty to the west. He thus added seventy miles more to the lake's length than he would otherwise have done. These errors did not affect his most important deductions about Bangweolo: that it was fed by the Chambesi, which he had crossed on his way to Lake Tanganyika in 1867, and that the Luapula left it for Lake Moero, after which it became the Lualaba. All this was perfectly correct. The only trouble would come if Livingstone should ever choose to return to the lake from a different direction and at a different time of year. Then he would not recognize any of the landmarks he had seen on his first visit, and his incorrect longitudes would lead him hopelessly astray into the swamps. But in late July 1868 Livingstone was unaware of his miscalculations and did not have any intention of coming back.

Two days later, on 1 August, Livingstone rejoined Bogharib at his encampment ten miles north of the lake. Livingstone realized that until he had collected his supplies from Ujiji he would be dependent for everything on his Arab friends, and would therefore have to fit in with their plans; but when Bogharib told him that he was planning to visit Manyuema, the area west and north-west of Lake Tanganyika, the very region through which, according to local reports, the Lualaba flowed on its journey north, Livingstone at once made up his mind to abandon Ujiji for the time being.

By 22 October Livingstone and his Arab escort had arrived at the point, a few miles west of Lake Moero, where he had left Muhammad Salim five months before. Salim was still there and another group of Arabs had recently joined him; with the addition of Bogharib's men, a vast caravan had been formed. Livingstone's five deserters who had stayed with Salim now begged to be taken back and Livingstone agreed without hesitation. 'More enlightened people often take advantage of men in similar circumstances,' he wrote in his journal. 'I have faults myself.'[41]

There was a delay of almost a month before the large caravan set off for Manyuema, but at last in late November a start was made. Two weeks later a group of Arabs in Bogharib's party took prisoners from a village in reprisal for the loss of some runaway slaves who had been sheltered by the villagers. This small matter soon led to more serious trouble and the Arabs shortly realized that if they wished to continue north to Manyuema they would have to fight their way past several hundred angry tribesmen. Since there were over a thousand slaves and a large amount of ivory at stake, the caravan leaders decided against such rashness and proposed instead to dispose of their precious merchandise at Ujiji on Lake Tanganyika and return to Manyuema for more ivory later. Livingstone was bitterly disappointed as the caravan altered course from north to north-east, but there was nothing he could do. Without supplies of his own he was helpless.

In early January 1869 the caravan was still sixty miles south-west of the point where the Arabs intended to cross Lake Tanganyika for Ujiji. Now the first of the rains began and after his exploits of the year before Livingstone's resistance to cold and damp was very low. Soon he was seriously ill. The entry in his journal for 7 January reads:

> Cannot walk: Pneumonia of right lung, and I cough all day and all night: sputa rust of iron and bloody: distressing weakness. Ideas flow through my mind with great rapidity and vividness, in groups of twos and threes: if I look at any piece of wood, the bark seems covered with figures and faces of men, and they remain, though I look away and turn to the same place again. I saw myself lying dead in the way to Ujiji, and all the letters I expected there useless. When I think of my children and friends, the lines ring through my head perpetually:
>
> > I shall look into your faces,
> > And listen to what you say,
> > And be often very near you
> > When you think I'm far away.[42]

But, in his delirium, lines from Tennyson could not comfort him when his thoughts turned to Robert's fate; and his son Tom would now be approaching a vital stage in his career. Livingstone was tormented by the thought that he would be unable to help him. He did not even know whether Tom had got through the course he had started at Glasgow University a few years earlier. No letters from his family had reached Livingstone since he had left Zanzibar in 1866. Minor family problems distressed him. Perhaps Tom would be refused jobs because of his appearance. 'He must get that front tooth out if it holds his lips apart, for that does not look smart & will be a drawback in any situation.'[43] So many people had told Livingstone that they would help his children in his absence, but they had probably done nothing. 'Again and again I have been left in the lurch,' he told a friend bitterly.[44]

Soon he was too ill to write or even think coherently. When he was conscious, one thought above all others gave him heart: at Ujiji there would be letters for him. During the long periods of delirium which he suffered throughout January and February, only Bogharib's devoted care and nursing kept Livingstone alive. Bogharib had a wooden litter made for Livingstone, and gave strict instructions that the sick man should be carried with the utmost care; but, even so, when the ground was rough, Livingstone was inevitably jolted from side to side, causing him, while conscious, terrible pain. Because he was too weak to move unassisted, when the sun shone, as it did when the rains temporarily let up, his face got badly burned; he found it too tiring to hold up a spray of leaves to shade himself.

At last in mid-February the caravan arrived at the western shore of Lake Tanganyika, but it was another month before the crossing would be made and Livingstone carried ashore on the other side at Ujiji. Here at last he believed he would find stores, food and, most important of all, medicines and letters. An hour later he knew that three-quarters of his supplies had been pillaged. There was no food, no medicine and no letters. After three years' travelling, he was ill, weary and destitute. The only provisions waiting for him could have been packed into one chest: a little sugar, tea and coffee, some low-quality beads and a quarter of the cloth he had ordered in Zanzibar.

21

Fantasy in Manyuema

1869–1871

Ujiji, situated seven hundred miles due west of Zanzibar, since the early 1840s had been a thriving Arab trading centre. From Ujiji's small harbour a procession of dhows crossed Lake Tanganyika, transporting caravans to the slave and ivory fields west and south-west of the lake. In Ujiji itself the streets were rarely empty and as a rule groups of Arabs in white flowing robes, strings of slaves laden with grain and ivory, and flocks of sheep and goats on their way to market, all gave the place an air of activity and bustle. There were probably no more than thirty or forty Arabs living in the town, but whenever caravans passed through, their numbers rose to two or three times that many. Arab houses, called *tembes*, were built of mud but appeared substantial, with their central courtyards and separate rooms for the domestic slaves and the harem. Around these flat-roofed buildings was a jumble of huts, some square but most beehive-shaped. There were at least two thousand Africans living in Ujiji in 1869.

Livingstone, to start with, took in little of his new surroundings; the terrible loss of his supplies, coming on top of his severe illness, left him feeling helpless and broken. The fact that his own men had pilfered from their loads in front of him during his travels should have prepared him for losses from supplies that had been at Ujiji for two years. Many of the Arabs who had helped themselves to Livingstone's cloth and beads had imagined that since the owner of the stores had not come for so long, he must have died some time before.

As soon as Livingstone was well enough to be up and about, he could see that he had two choices. He could either go to Zanzibar and return with new supplies, or he could try to get a letter to the coast asking Kirk, who was at present standing in for the Consul at Zanzibar, to send stores with the next caravan. There was really no certainty that this second method would be successful, since the goods might be stolen en route, and in any case there was a war raging between the Africans and the Arabs east of Ujiji on the Zanzibar caravan route. Livingstone also decided against going to Zanzibar in person for a number of reasons.

First of all, the journey there and back would be fourteen hundred miles, and in his present state of health Livingstone believed that he ought to conserve all his strength for his geographical work. In addition, he knew that once at Zanzibar, pressure might be put on him to abandon his work in view of his failing health. Another consideration was his determination that when he returned, it would be as the man who had once and for all proved that the source of the Nile lay not in the Victoria Nyanza, nor in Lake Albert, but in the area south-west of Lake Tanganyika. Then he would be able to show the Council of the R.G.S. and the officials at the Foreign Office that they had insulted and stinted the man who had single-handedly solved the world's greatest geographical mystery.

Having decided not to go to Zanzibar himself, Livingstone made arrangements to travel to Manyuema with Bogharib in the late summer. Since Bogharib would provide all the supplies needed for that journey, Livingstone felt that he could afford to leave Ujiji for a time and return there late in 1869, by which time Kirk would have sent more supplies from the coast. Nevertheless getting letters out of Ujiji was not easy, since Livingstone had unwisely let the Arab residents know that he thought them all thieves and parasites—in his journal he called them 'the vilest of the vile'.[1] Livingstone wrote forty-four letters while he was at Ujiji, but only one reached the coast—fortunately it was the letter addressed to Kirk. The Ujiji Arabs had evidently believed that unless they destroyed Livingstone's letters, news of his losses would reach the Sultan of Zanzibar and lead to some unpleasant recriminations.

While waiting to leave for Manyuema with Bogharib, Livingstone remained at Ujiji convalescing during the spring and early summer of 1869. This gave him plenty of time to think about his theories concerning the central African lake and river system. Many of the Arab traders he spoke to at this time horrified him by suggesting that the Lualaba flowed north-west and not north-east and was therefore more likely to be the Congo.[2] Livingstone sidestepped this unwelcome idea by arguing with typical optimism that the amount of water leaving the northern end of Lake Moero suggested that the Lualaba was large enough to be able to divide further north and supply both the Nile and Congo.[3] Livingstone made a great many enquiries about the area west and south-west of Lake Tanganyika, and, piecing together all the information, came to the conclusion that there were three main interconnecting 'lines of drainage' in central Africa, running roughly parallel with each other from south to north. The western line originated, according to the theory, due west of Bangweolo and joined the central line of drainage somewhere north of Lake Moero. The central line itself ran from Lake Bangweolo through Moero and then on north as the Lualaba. The eastern line, Livingstone believed, began at a point just north of Lake Moero where the Lualaba split in two, sending the main body of its water due north to continue as the central line, and the rest of its water north-east into the western side of Lake Tanganyika. Thus Lake Tanganyika and Lake Albert formed the eastern line of drainage. Livingstone thought that the two lakes were connected by a river flowing from the northern end of Tanganyika to the southern end of Albert.

Although fundamentally mistaken, in some respects Livingstone's theories were correct. A modern map of Africa shows that lakes Albert and Tanganyika do lie at opposite ends of a chain of lakes, but this chain is not connected. The Lualaba does flow northwards from Lake Moero for six hundred miles between the chain of lakes to the east and the river Lomani—a major tributary of the Lualaba—to the west. The fatal flaw in Livingstone's thinking was his conviction that the Lualaba was the Nile. It is in fact the upper Congo. Yet Livingstone's claims for Lake Bangweolo being the Nile's source did not depend solely on the ultimate destination of the Lualaba; he still had the eastern line of drainage up his sleeve. It was most unfortunate that he had not done what Sir Roderick Murchison told him to do in 1866 and gone straightaway to the northern end of Lake Tanganyika to check whether the river there flowed into or out of the lake. If it flowed in, the eastern line of drainage could have no possible connection with the Nile, since it would have been proved that lakes Albert and Tanganyika were not linked.

During his convalescence in the summer of 1869, Livingstone tried to determine which way the water in Lake Tanganyika flowed, but the results of his experiments were inconclusive. The only real test would have been to go to the northern end of Lake Tanganyika to see whether the water flowed into or out of it, but, while at Ujiji, Livingstone allowed himself to be discouraged by reports of tribal disturbances in the area. Thus when he set out for Manyuema in July to try to determine whither the Lualaba flowed, and whether it fed the Nile or the Congo, he felt that even if he came to no definite conclusion, he would still be able to return to Lake Tanganyika to find a river flowing out of that lake's northern end and running on north to Lake Albert; thus he would still be able to claim, if he also found that the Lualaba did send a tributary into the western side of Lake Tanganyika, that he had discovered a source of the Nile in Bangweolo, hundreds of miles south of the discoveries of Speke and Baker. This claim would not of course depend on the Lualaba itself being the Nile.

By the end of July 1869, Livingstone and Bogharib had crossed Lake Tanganyika and set out on their journey to Manyuema. By a typical piece of misfortune, Livingstone had landed less than twenty miles north of a

5b The watershed as
LIVINGSTONE BELIEVED IT TO BE
From deductions made between May 1869
and April 1871. See page 404 for sources.

5a The Central
AFRICAN WATERSHED AS IT IS

→ direction of flow

small river—the river Lukuga—flowing *out* of the western side of Lake Tanganyika. If Livingstone had known the direction in which this river flowed, he would have realized that the river at the northern end of Tanganyika would almost beyond doubt flow into the lake and not out of it; and if he had made this discovery Livingstone would also have realized in 1869 that the eastern line of drainage had nothing to do with the Nile and that everything depended on the Lualaba.

Livingstone's aim in July 1869 was to pass through Manyuema as quickly as possible and, on reaching the Lualaba at a point roughly three hundred miles west of Ujiji, to trace the Lualaba north to establish whether it was the Nile or the Congo. Livingstone believed that he would be able to achieve this within six months, at the end of which he could return to Ujiji. In fact a year later he was still only 150 miles west of Tanganyika and had failed to reach the Lualaba. His health had been a major reason for failure. He had thought that after his rest at Ujiji he was his old self again, but pneumonia had affected his lungs and he found that even three hours' walking over dry and level country left him exhausted. When the rains came and the mud clung to his feet, he had to rest every few minutes. But apart from his lungs, his resistance to fever had also lessened and soon he was also suffering from dysentery, accompanied by heavy anal bleeding. Then in July 1870 Livingstone was unable to move at all for three months. This time his complaint was ulcers on the feet. These terrible sores were probably due to the damp. The ulcers tended to spread and 'eat through everything—muscle, tendon, and bone, and often lame permanently if they do not kill'. 'If the foot were put to the ground, a discharge of bloody ichor flowed, and the same discharge happened every night with considerable pain, that prevented sleep.'[4]

Apart from ill-health and his old enemy the rainy season, other factors had contributed to Livingstone's slow progress. Manyuema had become an ivory boom area and hundreds of Arabs had flooded in to take advantage of it. Many of these newcomers were far more ruthless than Bogharib or the Arabs with whom Livingstone had travelled in the past. If villagers tried to get a decent price for their ivory they were often murdered and their villages fired. Soon there was widespread fighting throughout Manyuema between Arab Swahili and Africans. As a result Livingstone found it very hard to travel. He could not buy food, or gain permission to pass through the territory of chiefs who had been attacked by Arabs. Without medicines and supplies, Livingstone was helpless when Bogharib went off trading on his own. By the middle of 1870 six of Livingstone's nine followers had deserted and he was down to three: Chuma, Susi and a Nassick boy, Gardner.

The ulcers on his feet kept Livingstone a virtual prisoner at the town of Bambarre, midway between Lake Tanganyika and the Lualaba, from July

1870 to February 1871. Inactivity had always depressed him and now he even began to wonder whether he was too old to complete his work. He knew that he looked ten years older than his fifty-seven years. 'I shall not hide it from you', he told Agnes, 'that I am made very old & shaky—My cheeks fallen in—space round the eyes—the mouth almost toothless . . . a smile is that of a hippopotamus—a dreadful old Fogie.'[5] Livingstone also worried about his children, especially Tom and Agnes who might well be thinking of getting married. Livingstone had always professed himself completely uninterested where money was concerned but his advice to his children was chillingly practical and mercenary. Tom was told: 'On no account ought you to look to a girl however beautiful and loving if she or her parents have nothing.'[6] Agnes was warned about men who pretended to have money when really they were paupers: 'Wise people use the utmost precautions not to be taken in. Lawyers dig to the bottom of a man's affairs before they will allow a young lady to listen to the soft nothings of lovers or shams.'[7] This view of most suitors as parasites may have been influenced by Livingstone's personal feeling that he had been jilted by the Government and deceived by the R.G.S.

During his time at Bambarre, Livingstone realized that many tribes in Manyuema were cannibals and this depressed him still more, especially since one of his deserters, James, a Nassick boy, was killed and eaten. Yet Livingstone did not turn against the Manyuema, though he reluctantly admitted: 'They are cannibals, but not ostentatiously so'. He saw many of them captured and taken away as slaves and his response was to write the most haunting of all his indictments against the slave trade: 'The strangest disease I have seen in this country seems really to be broken-heartedness, and it attacks free men who have been captured and made slaves.'[8]

Many recently captured men seemed to waste away and die within weeks from no obvious physical cause. Livingstone talked to many of those in the first stages of this inexplicable disease, and wrote: 'They ascribed their only pain to the heart, and placed the hand correctly on the spot, though many think that the organ stands high up under the breast bone.'

As the months passed at Bambarre, Livingstone became an object of great curiosity to the local tribesmen, who would often try to steal into his hut for their first view of the white man. Eventually Livingstone had to eat in public to appease African curiosity. Then, seated at a solitary table in the centre of a roped-off enclosure, he would amaze everybody by eating elephant meat with a knife and fork. Crowds would also gather to see him write in his journal, but the greatest interest was aroused by the use of soap for washing his hair. The villagers watched with horrified fascination as the lather formed while he rubbed his scalp. There was no doubt about it: the white man was washing his brain. But moments of occasional humour were too few to stop Livingstone entering a strange, almost dream-like state of mind. Pain, isolation and inactivity soon seriously affected his judgement and patterns of thought.

During his seven months at Bambarre, Livingstone read the Bible through four times, giving special attention to the Old Testament, with Exodus getting a minute examination. In the summer of 1869, he had asserted as geographical facts theories which he could not substantiate, but from July 1870 Livingstone's ideas passed into the realms of pure fantasy. He himself soon began to describe his thoughts about the Nile as 'waking dreams'. The horrifying pain Livingstone suffered with the ulcers on his feet, coupled with periodic attacks of fever and loss of blood, help explain the strangeness of his new thinking. As Livingstone read and reread Exodus he became mesmerized by the figure of Moses. On 25 August he wrote: 'One of my waking dreams is that the legendary tales about Moses coming up into Inner Ethiopia with Merr his foster-mother, and founding a city which he called, in her honour "Meroe", may have a substratum of fact.'[9]

Reading this single entry the statement does not look too extreme, especially since it is qualified: 'may have a substratum of fact'. But during the next few months his journal is studded with references to Moses, like this one, written two months later:

I had a strong presentiment during the first three years that I should never live through the enterprise, but it weakened as I came near to the end of the journey, and an eager desire to discover any evidence of the great Moses having visited these parts bound me, spell bound me, I may say, for if I could bring to light anything to confirm the Sacred Oracles, I should not grudge one whit all the labour expended.[10]

Ten days later he was writing a similar passage. A desire 'to confirm the Sacred Oracles' was a new strand and added a new obsession to existing ones. Ever since reading, at the age of nineteen, the works of Thomas Dick, Livingstone had abandoned a strict fundamentalist's approach to the Bible. He had not disapproved of Darwin's *Origin of Species by Means of Natural Selection*, after that work was published in 1859, only taking issue over minor points rather than attacking the major thesis.[11] In 1864 and 1865 he had deliberately avoided becoming involved in current arguments about the historical accuracy of the Pentateuch, evidently not feeling strongly on the subject. His knowledge of geology had alone been enough to tell him that the dates given in the Old Testament for the age of the world were hopelessly wrong. But now in 1870 and 1871, after four years in Africa, he had stopped thinking logically. His search for the

source of the Nile had become no simple geographical task but a reaffirmation of faith, a quest which, if successfully accomplished, would
'confirm the Sacred Oracles'. Sick, destitute and helpless, Livingstone
could not have continued unless he gave to his work a dignity which no
geographical search could ever have possessed.

Almost every waking moment Livingstone thought about the Nile and
all the men, long since dead, who had tried to fathom the mystery of its
source. 'More than sixteen hundred years have elapsed since Ptolemy put
down the results of early explorers; and Emperors, Kings, Philosophers—
all the great men of antiquity longed to know whence flowed the famous
river and long in vain.'[12]

The ancients of the classical world, as well as those of the Bible, became
important figures in Livingstone's fantasy from the middle of August
1870. In that month two Arab traders came to Bambarre after a long
journey that had taken them to Katanga and beyond. Their names were
Josut and Moenepembé, and what they told Livingstone was to dominate
his thinking in the few years that remained to him. Their information was
that Lake Bangweolo was not the primary source of the Lualaba. While
still at Ujiji, in 1869, Livingstone himself had come to the conclusion that
the Lualaba was supplied not just by Bangweolo but by a western line of
drainage as well; now, in the summer of 1870, these two Arabs confirmed
this view. But they did much more than that. They told Livingstone that
some miles south-west of Bangweolo were two sources which supplied an
unnamed river—Livingstone soon called it the Lualaba west—which
flowed north through an unvisited lake and joined Livingstone's Lualaba
several hundred miles north of Lake Moero. Just south of the two sources,
the Arabs went on, were another two sources, whose waters flowed south
to become the upper Zambesi and its tributary, the Kafue river. In fact,
broadly speaking, this information was correct. The sources of the
Zambesi and Kafue rivers were within a hundred miles of two sources
whose waters flowed north to join Livingstone's Lualaba several hundred
miles above Lake Moero. So Livingstone was not gullible in believing the
Arabs; it was the use he made of their information that was alarming.

Before leaving England in 1865 he had read all the classical allusions to
the Nile's source, and in particular a key reference in Book Two of
Herodotus' *History*. When Herodotus visited Egypt in the fifth century
BC he made enquiries about the source of the Nile, and on his return home
he wrote: 'Not one writer of the Egyptians or of the Libyans or of the
Hellenes, who came to speech with me, professed to know anything,
except the scribe of the sacred treasury of Athene at the city of Saïs
in Egypt.'[13] But the scribe made up for all the others: he said most
specifically that at a point midway between two hills with conical tops 'are

the fountains of the Nile, fountains which it is impossible to fathom: half the water runs northward into Egypt; half to the south'.[14] This detail, about half of the water flowing south and half north, immediately led Livingstone to the conclusion that the scribe of the sacred treasury had been right. The two Arabs had spoken about a hill between the four sources, and one hill was not so very different from two hills with conical tops. Herodotus had only quoted the story because it was all he could discover about the source of the Nile, not because he had believed it. But, once Livingstone had listened to the two Arabs, he was convinced that the scribe had had access to definite information which had since been lost. In November, Livingstone told a friend: 'I feel so certain on the matter, that I have given English names to the fountains [sources] by anticipation.'[15] The four names he chose were those of Palmerston, William Cotton Oswell, James 'Paraffin' Young and Bartle Frere, the Governor of Bombay. The unvisited lake he called Lake Lincoln.* The only reason why Livingstone felt so sure that the Arabs had been right was the similarity between what they said and the story recounted by Herodotus. But soon Livingstone went even further in his reverence for classical accounts.

Livingstone had read Ptolemy's *Geography* and had carefully scrutinized his map of Africa. Ptolemy suggested that the source of the Nile consisted of two springs situated in a range of hills which he called the Mountains of the Moon. Once more the mention of twin sources left Livingstone still more convinced. Of course it was sad that Ptolemy had not known about the two sources flowing south, but Livingstone easily explained this away. 'He [Ptolemy] probably got information from his predecessors who inquired of men who had visited this very region, and mistakes were natural in oral information.'[16] But whatever his mistakes, Livingstone decided that Ptolemy's Lake Coloe 'is probably a more correct view of the Victoria Nyanza than that given by Grant and Speke'.[17]

Ptolemy, who lived in Alexandria during the second century AD, had been a remarkable man, and his astronomical theories were accepted till the time of Copernicus and Kepler; but to take his maps of Africa seriously was unwise. In fact by the end of 1870 the whole patchwork of Livingstone's thinking had become an impossibly intertwined web of fantasy and reality. The Arabs had not invented the sources west of Bangweolo, but of course they had nothing at all to do with the Nile, and nothing to do with the real Mountains of the Moon (the Ruwenzoris) 800 miles to the north. Livingstone had allowed his determination that his Lualaba should not be the Congo to make him clutch at every straw that made it seem probable that it was the Nile. Yet whatever his classical and

---

* President Lincoln had been assassinated in 1865.

biblical obsessions, Livingstone from August 1870 became convinced that before he could conclude his work, he would have to visit the sources which the two Arabs had described. After he had managed to examine the Lualaba near his present position, he would return to Ujiji and then travel south to approach the four fountains via Lake Bangweolo. But his immediate problem was how to get from Bambarre to the Lualaba.

In late January 1871, when Livingstone had all but abandoned any hope of ever leaving Bambarre, ten men arrived who had been sent from the coast to Ujiji and then directed on from there to join him in Manyuema. Livingstone realized that his letter to Kirk had reached its destination after all. The ten men were mutinous and almost at once demanded higher wages; the supplies they brought were less than a quarter of what Livingstone had asked for, but they had come, and he now had some quinine, some sugar, coffee, tea and a few fathoms of cloth. At first the men refused to go any further, but when Livingstone threatened to shoot their two leaders they changed their minds. Livingstone was very angry to learn that these rebellious porters sent by Kirk were not free men but slaves belonging to coastal Indian merchants (known as Banians). In his experience, not only were slaves far less dependable as servants and porters than free men, but it also struck him as grotesque that he, as one of the world's best known opponents of the slave trade, should have been sent slaves to serve him. Nevertheless, on 16 February 1871, after seven months' idleness, Livingstone and his party, now numbering thirteen, marched out of Bambarre, heading north-west.

In comparison with the bad health and other trials he had experienced during his previous attempts to reach the Lualaba, this last successful journey proved somewhat easier, although it was marred by the Banian slaves, who went off for ten days without permission and then returned, reporting that they had killed three Manyuema, in imitation of the slave traders they had been with. As if this was not bad enough, Livingstone's longest-serving followers had also been causing him serious problems. Smoking cannabis and employing prostitutes were not their worst sins. Some months earlier, Chuma, who aged ten had been rescued by Livingstone from a slave gang, had taken part in an Arab attack on local Manyuema villagers. Even Susi, his most reliable servant, had caused him great distress by manhandling him so alarmingly that he had felt obliged to fire a warning shot at him.[18] But recently both men had been behaving well.

By the end of March, after six weeks' travelling, Livingstone reached the Lualaba at a town called Nyangwe and gazed across its two miles of slowly moving water. Shortly after his arrival he once again started to hear disturbing reports that the Lualaba soon bent westwards and not

eastwards as he hoped. At Nyangwe itself the river's flow was due north.
Livingstone would obviously have to follow the river north to be sure of
its course, but at Nyangwe there was one important experiment he could
perform. His theory was that beyond Nyangwe the Lualaba flowed north-
eastwards and joined the Nile at Lake Albert or just above it. For this to
be possible, the altitude at Nyangwe would have to be substantially higher
than the altitude at Lake Albert. When Livingstone gauged the height of
Nyangwe with his boiling point thermometer, he was horrified to find
that it was only 2,000 feet, the same height Baker had given for Lake
Albert. This should have told Livingstone that it was most improbable
that the Lualaba had anything to do with the Nile, but by now he was too
far gone in his certainty to let a purely scientific fact change his mind.
There was another reason why he could not accept Baker's figures or his
own: Lake Tanganyika was 2,500 feet above sea level and, that being so,
the Lualaba, being lower, could not send a tributary into the western side
of Tanganyika. The easiest thing to do was to reject all the figures.
Nevertheless Livingstone was worried and acknowledged that if the
Lualaba joined the Nile it might very well be several hundred miles north
of Lake Albert, where the Nile's altitude would be lower.

The Africans and Arabs at Nyangwe generally believed that the Lualaba
did ultimately flow westwards, but Livingstone never listened. He might
have done had he not heard about a river called the Lomani a week after
his arrival in Nyangwe. The locals told him that six days north of Nyangwe,
the Lomani ran into the western side of the Lualaba, having flowed parallel
with it for several hundred miles. No African had any idea where the
Lomani's source was. Unfortunately, Livingstone thought he did: it was
south of Katanga and in the region of the four miraculous fountains with
their central mound. The existence of the Lomani seemed to confirm
everything the two Arabs had said. Obviously the Lomani was the river
that flowed from the twin sources northwards into the unvisited lake—
Lake Lincoln—and then joined the Lualaba several hundred miles north
of Lake Moero. Without pausing to think again, Livingstone made up his
mind once and for all: the Lualaba was the Nile because the Lomani's existence backed up the story the Arabs had told about the four sources. The
Arabs had been right, it will be remembered, because their information had
confirmed the report in Herodotus. The Lomani also fitted in with
Livingstone's earlier idea of the three lines of drainage.

The information about the Lomani once more diverted Livingstone
from the task he ought to have been contemplating. Before doing
anything else, he should have given all his energies to marching north to
see whether the Lualaba began to flow to the west. Instead, considering it
a foregone conclusion that the Lualaba was the Nile, he thought only of

tracing the Lomani south to reach the twin sources. But in fact what Livingstone wanted soon became academic. Local Africans refused to let him have canoes to cross the Lualaba, and he knew he would have to get to the western bank before being able to reach the Lomani. The riverside Wagenya people persisted in refusing help for several months to come, and at last Livingstone tried to get the slave traders in the town to help him, but his old friend Bogharib was not there and the Arabs in Nyangwe were the reverse of helpful. Some of them believed that Livingstone had come to spy on their slaving activities and that he might well be interested in starting a European ivory trade west of the Lualaba to rival their trade in Manyuema. Worst of all, the Banian slaves sent by Kirk had been in a semi-mutinous state since March, and by May had even been threatening to join Hassani, one of the local slave traders who had been inciting them to desert. They had no desire to embark with Livingstone on a dangerous journey in canoes on the Lualaba and were eager to return to Zanzibar via Ujiji as soon as possible. Livingstone wrote in his Field Diary that 'Muhamadans are unmitigated liars', and as proof of this added that his Banian slaves were currently saying: 'I don't want slaves nor ivory but I want to kill people.'[19] This was a deliberate strategy employed by them to make sure that no local person sold a canoe to him. The Banian slaves were so successful that in mid-July, after Livingstone had spent three months in Nyangwe, he was still desperate to buy canoes, and offered Dugumbe, the leading Arab in the town, £400 (an immense sum) and all his supplies at Ujiji if he would only get him and his men across the Lualaba. Dugumbe was still considering this proposition on 15 July: the day a terrible disaster occurred in Nyangwe.

Ever since his arrival in the town, Livingstone had found consolation for his failure to get canoes in going to the busy market place to watch the activity and bustle. Almost everything about the scene there pleased him—the women with their earthen pots on their heads, children carrying squawking hens, the disappointment on the faces of sellers who failed to convince potential customers of the value of a sheep or goat. On 15 July, Livingstone visited the market but could hear the distressing sound of firing on the opposite or west bank of the Lualaba. This alarmed him since Dugumbe had recently crossed the river; and Dugumbe was the man from whom Livingstone wanted to buy canoes, and with whom he had hoped to travel to the Lomani. This blood-letting on the west bank made Livingstone fear that by travelling with Dugumbe's men he would become 'a partaker in their blood guiltiness'. But on the east bank, in Nyangwe's market place, on this same day, Livingstone wandered among the 1,500 peaceful buyers and sellers without any sense that violence might be imminent here too. As the day was hot and sultry, and he was troubled by

6 The massacre at Nyangwe

events across the river, he did not choose to stay for long. On leaving, he was surprised to spot three of Dugumbe's armed henchmen, two of whom he knew by name. Weapons were forbidden in the market, so he assumed that they had brought guns with them only due to their ignorance of local customs. A moment later he knew better. He had walked about fifty yards from the armed men when suddenly two shots rang out behind him; a moment later screaming men and women were rushing past him. The three Arabs were now firing wildly into the backs of the fleeing crowd.

Many people had come to the market in canoes, which they had moored in a small creek just below the town. Hundreds now swarmed down into the creek at the same time and pandemonium broke out. Canoes were swamped without leaving the shore, and others cast off without paddles. Many people tried to swim out to an island in midstream. At the height of the chaos another group of Arabs just above the creek opened fire on the already terror-stricken people. Only three canoes got away and all these were capsized by the frenzied efforts of those in the water to pull themselves aboard. Soon Livingstone could see a long line of heads drifting away downstream; very few of those who took to the water survived. That evening Livingstone wrote despairingly: 'No one will ever know the exact loss of the bright sultry summer morning, it gave me the impression of being in hell.' The Arab estimate of four hundred dead was probably a couple of hundred too few.

When the shooting stopped, it was discovered that in the turmoil several hundred slaves had broken loose and had looted the market. On the other side of the river similar massacres were taking place and before long Livingstone could see plumes of smoke rising from burning villages. Though Dugumbe blamed the killings on an ill-judged alliance between Kimburu, the local Wagenya chief, and Manilla, one of Dugumbe's head slaves, Livingstone found this 'hardly credible'. Instead he believed that the Arabs' 'most potent motive . . . was to make an impression in the country as to the importance and greatness of the newcomers'. In other words, they wanted to cow the Wagenya and Manyuema into abject obedience to all their demands.

Livingstone recorded in his Field Diary that while the shooting had been going on, 'a worthless Moslem asserted that all was done by the people of the English. This will spread,' Livingstone added glumly, 'though the murderers are on the other side plundering and looting. It is awful—terrible, a dreadful world this is—as I write shot after shot falls on the fugitives . . .' Despite Livingstone's statement that the murderers were 'on the other side' (i.e. the Arab rather than the 'English' side), the group of British and American scholars and scientists who have recently used a sophisticated imaging process to decipher the brittle and faded 1871 Field Diary have suggested that he had, nevertheless, 'failed to foreclose the possibility that his slaves had taken part in the Nyangwe massacre'. Undoubtedly (through no fault of his own) Livingstone's Banian slaves were undisciplined and violent men, but there is no evidence that they were in the market place on 15 July, let alone killed anyone there. By then Livingstone mistrusted and detested his slaves, as they well knew; so it seems unlikely that they would have risked appearing in the market with guns in their hands when Livingstone was there. It may be wondered why the slaves would have cared whether Livingstone saw them commit crimes or not. In fact, by reporting them to the Sultan of Zanzibar, who wished to remain on good terms with Great Britain, Livingstone would have guaranteed that when they returned home they would receive a very severe punishment, possibly execution.

The (London) *Times*, under the heading 'Dr Livingstone not quite the saint we presumed', published on 2 November 2011 an edited version of the 'worthless Moslem' quote, omitting Livingstone's assertion that the murderers were 'on the other side', plainly leading readers to suppose that Livingstone's slaves had committed murders in the market. On the same day the quote appeared in the *Daily Telegraph*, also without Livingstone's qualifying comment. But this public caricaturing of these passages in the freshly transcribed 1871 Field Diary does not detract from the importance of this new primary source which gives a rawer and more immediate account of his life in this crucial year than emerges in his 1872 Unyanyembe Journal, which was his later amplification of the 1871 diary. Unlike the transatlantic team, I do not think that subsequent changes made in the later Unyanyembe Journal were dishonest in any fundamental way, at least as they affected the massacre. For instance, in his rage immediately after the massacre, he wrote in the Field Diary that he had told Dugumbe that he would like to see the murderers' heads placed 'on poles'. This he would change in the 1872 journal to 'my first impulse was to pistol the murderers'; similarly he removed a passage about wanting to send his men to flog a headman who had fraudulently tried to sell him a canoe that was not his property. This man had taken a large payment of cowries from Livingstone. But in other entries in the 1872 journal he admitted beating a man with a cane, and firing a shot at his servant, Susi. The 1871 diary shows Livingstone's problems in the stark and confusing light of actual experience before he had had time to reflect and rationalize. Thus the murderous behaviour of the Arabs, his own humiliating dependence on them, and the misbehaviour of the Banian slaves sent to him by Kirk, all come across with shocking clarity. But this misbehaviour would not disappear in the expanded 1872 journal. In this journal, after admitting that his men had claimed to have committed three murders during a ten-day period of desertion, Livingstone added: 'I would never trust them out of my sight again.' Though constant supervision would have been impossible, he would certainly have kept a sharp look-out for them in the market on the 15th as soon as the trouble had started.

The following day, many of the local chiefs, whose villages had been burned by Dugumbe and his chief lieutenant, Tagamoio, came to Livingstone and begged him 'to come back with them and appoint new localities for them to settle again'. Livingstone refused this invitation to become a kind of pre-colonial arbitrator. 'I told them that I was so ashamed of the company in which I found myself that I could scarcely look the Manyuema in the face.' In truth, with ten of his thirteen men totally unsuited to be peacemakers, he could have done nothing to help the chiefs. His survival—if he were to stay in Manyuema—would have depended on the very Arabs who had committed the murders. After what he had witnessed, Livingstone knew that he could never accept help from Dugumbe, even if the Arab offered a fleet of canoes for nothing. 'The open murder perpetrated on hundreds of unsuspecting women fills me with unspeakable horror—I cannot think of going anywhere with the Tagamoio crew.' The work of a morning had destroyed all Livingstone's hopes of reaching the river Lomani. If he left Nyangwe without either tracing the Lualaba north or following the Lomani south, the pain and suffering of the past two years would have been for nothing, yet only with Arab help could Livingstone hope to accomplish either of these tasks. His sense of outrage and disgust were too strong. Livingstone knew that he could never willingly depend on Arabs again. With no prospect of recruiting reliable porters at Nyangwe, only one course remained to him: the long return to Ujiji.[20]

On 23 October, after three gruelling months of travelling Livingstone reached Ujiji. A party of slave traders with several hundred slaves and thirty tons of ivory arrived just afterwards. 'All the traders were returning successful,' he wrote miserably. 'I alone had failed and experienced worry, thwarting, baffling, when almost in sight of the end towards which I strained.'[21] But Livingstone was sustained by the knowledge that he would have supplies in sufficient quantity to finance a return to the Lomani and the four fountains of Herodotus.

Within a couple of hours of landing Livingstone realized with a sinking heart that the events of 1869 had repeated themselves. The supplies Kirk had sent from the coast had been stolen and sold off by the man who had brought them to Ujiji and by other Arab traders in the town. There was virtually nothing left out of £600 worth of goods. To the east of Ujiji the war still went on, and there could be no immediate hope of getting goods from the coast to replace those stolen. If Livingstone had not left a few yards of calico with one of the few Arabs in Ujiji whom he could trust, he would have had nothing with which to buy food.

There seemed no hope at all now. Livingstone had fled from Nyangwe to escape having to rely on Arabs, and now at Ujiji, unless help of some sort arrived within weeks, he would have to ask for their charity. Livingstone's agony was all the more acute since he knew that Sherif Bosher, the man who had sold off all his goods, had invested the proceeds in ivory, which was still in Ujiji under lock and key. Bosher, however, had bribed the three principal men of the town, and all refused to let Livingstone have the key so that he could reclaim what was rightfully his.

All that Livingstone could do was write to Kirk explaining what had happened and asking for a further dispatch of stores. The loss meant that he would be heavily in debt, but without more supplies he would starve. Reliable reports of the fighting around Unyanyembe, to the east of Ujiji, suggested that it would be hopeless for Livingstone to attempt to get through to the coast with his handful of followers. The prospect ahead of him was at least ten months' waiting at Ujiji with no certainty that Kirk would manage to get a caravan through. During all that time, Livingstone knew he would have to exist on Arab credit. There was no other way he would be able to pay for the milch goats, wheaten flour, and fish needed for his recovery. He admitted in a letter to a friend: 'I was like the man who went from Jerusalem to Jericho, but no Good Samaritan would come the Ujijian way.'[22]

Two days after his arrival at Ujiji, Livingstone was amazed to hear that a white man had recently left Unyanyembe, two hundred miles east of

7 'Dr Livingstone, I presume?'

Ujiji. Who this white man was or where he was going, nobody had any idea. His nationality was as much a mystery as his name. Livingstone, in spite of himself, could not help hoping, praying, that this stranger, if he existed, would come to Ujiji. Without aid, Livingstone wondered whether he would live long enough for Kirk to get supplies to him.

Livingstone only had to endure three more days' suspense, and then at noon on what he reckoned to be 28 October, but was in fact a day in early or mid-November,* shots were heard outside the town, shots not fired in anger, but announcing the approach of a caravan. The rumour spread rapidly that the newcomer was an Englishman and soon crowds started to form outside Livingstone's house. In a few minutes the column of men had reached the centre of Ujiji and Livingstone could see that they were all dressed in long white robes and turbans, but, more remarkable still, they were carrying enough to sustain a traveller for many months: tin baths, tents, saddles, a folding boat, an impressive array of gigantic kettles. Whoever the leader of this party might be, Livingstone knew that he was 'no poor Lazarus like me'. Then out of the advancing crowd stepped the white man himself; a huge African preceded him carrying the Stars and Stripes. The stranger was immaculately dressed in a freshly pressed flannel suit; his boots glistened and his helmet was a dazzling white. Later the

---

* See Appendix concerning date of meeting.

visitor would write a book called *How I Found Livingstone* on the suggestion of his clever publisher. In it, the stranger would describe the crowd parting and Livingstone moving towards him as he lifted his hat and said, as formally as he could, in a voice that nonetheless trembled with excitement:

'Dr Livingstone, I presume?'[23]

In fact, for reasons which I will soon divulge, these words are very unlikely to have been spoken.

22

Stanley and the Livingstone Myth

⇒·◇·⇐

On 28 October 1869 Henry Morton Stanley, a twenty-eight-year-old journalist on the staff of the *New York Herald*, had been summoned to an important meeting by the owner and editor of that paper, James Gordon Bennett Jnr, who was currently staying at the Grand Hotel, Paris. Bennett was an autocratic newspaper proprietor who rarely spoke to any of his journalists, so Stanley was privileged to be given a face-to-face interview. He would later claim that Bennett had weighed in at once with a question about an astonishing assignment never discussed between them before:

'Where do you think Livingstone is?'
'I really do not know, sir!'
'Do you think he is alive?'
'He may be, and he may not be!' I answered.
'Well, I think he is alive, and that he can be found, and I am going to send you to find him.'
'What!' said I, 'do you really think I can find Dr Livingstone?'

And the answer of course was an emphatic *yes* from Bennett, who, according to Stanley, promised unlimited funding.

'Draw a thousand pounds now; and when you have gone through that, draw another thousand, and when that is spent draw another thousand, and when you have finished that draw another thousand, and so on; but, FIND LIVINGSTONE.'[1]

In fact Stanley's search for Livingstone had had a far more complicated genesis. Three years earlier, he himself had had the brilliantly original thought that if a journalist could find the long-absent Dr Livingstone in the wilds of central Africa and interview him there, it might come to be seen as the greatest scoop of the century.[2] But at the time that Stanley had had this wonderful idea, he had been a part-time journalist, making his living from odd jobs in America, ranging from working for a judge in New York to prospecting for gold in Colorado. Only after he had covered the Indian Wars in Nebraska for a Midwest newspaper and been sent on trial by the *New York Herald* to cover a British punitive expedition against the Emperor of Ethiopia, did James Gordon Bennett finally decide that the young journalist was worth funding for such an extraordinarily risky assignment. The likelihood was that Stanley would either fail to find his man or die in the attempt.

In fact Bennett's funding would be far less generous than Stanley later claimed. Repeat payments of £1,000 were never mentioned at their celebrated meeting, only two initial instalments of £500 each with an unspecified extra sum to come.[3] But when Stanley's ship had anchored in Zanzibar's harbour, he was horrified to find that Bennett had sent no money at all. This obliged him to beg the U.S. Consul in Zanzibar to pledge his personal credit. So Stanley was only able to spend £1,000 on his mission—half as much as Livingstone had spent in his and had thought scandalously inadequate. To save face, Stanley never admitted that Bennett had been so stingy with him and later claimed that his boss had spent £4,000 on his journey, enabling him to engage 192 porters, rather than the 100 he had actually hired.[4] It may therefore seem strange that Stanley would later attribute his life-changing Livingstone search idea to Bennett; but with his entire career seeming to depend upon his capricious employer's continuing patronage he needed to flatter him. And he had another reason for reticence. If he had let it be known that his prime motive for finding Livingstone had been his longing for fame and wealth, he would have been seen as a self-interested sensationalist rather than a brave and dedicated journalist acting partly from a humanitarian desire to succour the long-suffering explorer.

Stanley had a more general problem with the truth. He claimed to have been born in Missouri but was actually from Denbigh, north Wales, where his mother had been a promiscuous teenage barmaid, Elizabeth Parry, who had deserted her baby soon after his birth in 1841. The illegitimate boy's name was John Rowlands and his father had either been an alcoholic farm labourer of that name or an equally hard-drinking local solicitor.[5] John was brought up by his mother's father, until this kindly retired butcher died when his grandson was five. Soon afterwards, the boy's prosperous uncles deposited him in St Asaph workhouse where he endured its harsh routines until he was fifteen. This betrayal lived with him all his life. In the workhouse he and his fellow paupers had been led to think of themselves as the dregs of society, but instead of being destroyed by this knowledge it fired the young man with an overwhelming ambition to prove that he was not worthless. Two years after his discharge from the workhouse, John was working as a butcher's boy in Liverpool when he bravely decided to emigrate to America to improve his prospects in life.

On arriving in New Orleans in February 1859, he worked in a wholesale warehouse, supplying goods to Mississippi upriver stores, then as a cook on riverboats and finally as a shop boy in a store near Little Rock,

Arkansas. Here he started calling himself Henry Stanley, which was a name he had first seen printed on sacks of cotton in the store. Henry Hope Stanley owned most of the machinery used to compress raw cotton in New Orleans and it appealed to Rowlands to associate himself by name with this rich man. So in August 1860, when a census taker called at the store, nineteen-year-old John Rowlands gave his name as Henry Stanley.[6]

When the American Civil War started, rather than be called a coward, he enlisted for the Confederates under his brand new name and was captured during the bloody battle of Shiloh. In a Federal prison camp, where hundreds were dying of typhoid, he secured his release by agreeing to fight for the Union, but deserted soon afterwards. He worked his passage back to Britain and tried to persuade his mother to accept him at last. She refused and he returned to America where, after serving in the Federal Navy and deserting again, he wrote his first articles for newspapers in the Midwest. There followed a disastrous attempt to travel from Turkey to India and eventually China, but he was captured and robbed of everything by Turkish bandits and was lucky to escape with his life.[7] His hope had been to write a bestselling travel book on returning home.

In Wales, on his way back to America after this failure, he told his mother, who had grudgingly agreed to see him, that he had been adopted by a rich New Orleans cotton magnate and given his name. The date was 1869, and this was his first step on the way to denying his illegitimacy and his workhouse years. He had already decided that if he one day found Livingstone he would conceal his origins and appear as an American for the rest of his life. When Stanley had left James Gordon Bennett's Paris hotel room, he realized that if he found Livingstone he would be made for life, both financially and professionally. Socially, he knew, there would also be rewards, and for a man who had experienced an even harsher childhood than Livingstone's, this was an added spur.[8]

It is no mean tribute to Bennett's journalistic sense that, at the time he finally sanctioned Stanley's longstanding project to find the explorer, Livingstone, for the British public at least, was a forgotten figure. In December 1866 the Johanna men who had deserted Livingstone near Lake Nyassa had arrived in Zanzibar with a story that their master had been killed by tribesmen in the interior. Although this report of his death was generally believed, when obituaries appeared in the British press in early March 1867 they were brief and unemotionally factual. Only the Council of the Royal Geographical Society had reacted positively. Murchison had pressured a reluctant British Government into voting £1,200 for an expedition to prove or disprove the story of Livingstone's death. E.D. Young, who had served with Livingstone on the *Lady Nyassa*, had been appointed as leader of this search party. During the autumn of 1867 Young had reached the southern end of Lake Nyassa and had collected evidence which proved beyond doubt that Livingstone had passed through that area and had travelled far to the north without meeting his death. Young's discovery was made public in January 1868 and in the same month letters from Livingstone reached the British Consulate in Zanzibar. By the end of 1868 no further news had been heard of Livingstone and again rumours that he had died began to circulate, but, as in the early months of 1867, there was little public reaction in Britain. After the disasters of the Zambesi Expedition, Livingstone's reputation had fallen so low that he was not considered newsworthy. Bennett, however, had had the acumen to realize that Stanley was right to think that a face-to-face interview with this British explorer, who had not seen a white man for five or six years, could prove a story with such emotional and dramatic impact that the previous lack of interest in Livingstone would become entirely irrelevant. If Stanley managed to find Livingstone, Bennett now believed that the single incredible fact that a newspaper reporter had tracked down a man whom many supposed dead, in the heart of a vast and virtually unknown continent, would in itself create a sensation. It is important to stress at the outset that Bennett's decision to send Stanley would completely change the British estimate of Livingstone. Stanley's mission would turn a once adored but now forgotten explorer into the legendary figure the late Victorians enshrined.

Perhaps because a letter from Livingstone unexpectedly arrived in Zanzibar in the autumn of 1869—the one he had written to Kirk from Ujiji in May that year—Bennett decided against sending Stanley to Africa straight away. Instead he told Stanley that he should first send reports on other matters from Egypt, the Holy Land, Turkey, Persia and finally Bombay. This, Bennett knew, would occupy Stanley for a year by which time Livingstone would with luck be thoroughly lost again. In fact when Stanley eventually arrived at Zanzibar on 6 January 1871, no further news had been heard from Livingstone. Bennett's instinct had proved correct.

Three weeks before his thirtieth birthday, Stanley sighted the masts and rigging of the ships at anchor in Zanzibar's harbour and beyond them a jumble of white, flat-roofed houses, one of which was the American Consulate. Bennett had sent no money, and therefore Stanley had to beg a large enough dollar draft from Consul Webb to enable him to purchase supplies from local Indian traders and engage porters. Webb advised him to visit Dr John Kirk, then Acting British Consul on Zanzibar: because Kirk had been the medical officer and botanist on Livingstone's Zambesi Expedition and had corresponded with him during his current journey. Webb suggested that Kirk would know better than anyone where

Livingstone might be. But, wanting to get information about Livingstone without admitting that he hoped to meet him, Stanley learned nothing, after saying that he had come to explore the upper reaches of an unimportant river, the Rufiji. Stanley went back to see the canny Scottish doctor ten days later and very sensibly came clean. Consul Kirk rewarded Stanley with some straight speaking. 'Dr Livingstone', he said, 'is on the western side of Lake Tanganyika. He expects shortly to come to Ujiji [on Lake Tanganyika], which is about four months travel from here. I have sent him some fresh supplies & boatmen, and they are on the other side—that is on the coast at Bagamoyo, about 25 miles from here preparing to start for Ujiji.' Then Kirk issued a warning:

> Dr Livingstone is pretty well known to me, and I know that with all his modesty, he . . . appreciates more than any other man what he has done. If he hears of Baker in the neighbourhood he will go further away . . . If Burton & Speke were at Ujiji he would take himself to the west side of the Lake. He hates Burton like poison. He is a man of strong likings & dislikes. He is vain, and easily annoyed.[9]

Kirk added that Livingstone would definitely not want to be 'found' by an American newspaperman but Stanley made it obvious that he was not discouraged. So before the 'American' left, Kirk gave him a bundle of letters for the great man.[10]

From now on, Stanley was tormented by the thought that Livingstone would rush away into the bush as soon as he heard that a European was seeking him. And if his quest failed, Stanley feared that Bennett would not reimburse Consul Webb, obliging him (Stanley) to surrender his own modest life-savings to the Consul.[11] So Stanley *had* to succeed. He made this less likely by hiring two white colleagues, William L. Farquhar and John W. Shaw, who were both merchant seamen with some experience of navigation but none of African travel and with a liking for drink.[12] But two employees would prove competent: Selim Heshmy, a clever teenage Syrian Christian, who spoke Swahili and would communicate with the Arabs in the interior, and Sidi Mubarak Bombay, a veteran caravan leader and the captain of Stanley's twenty-strong escort of armed *askari* or soldiers. Stanley also came to admire the porters in his hundred-strong expedition. They were Swahili-speaking Zanzibar blacks, the Wangwana—mostly free men though some were the slaves of local merchants. He thought them 'far more intelligent than I could ever have believed . . .'[13]

At Bagamoyo on the mainland, Stanley found that the supplies, bought for Livingstone with half the sum voted by Parliament in May 1870, were still sitting in a hut in the town in February 1871.[14] He was staggered that John Kirk had not bothered to cross to Bagamoyo to check that these supplies were not long ago on their way to Unyanyembe.[15] His deep indignation would lead to a feud with Kirk that eventually sucked in Livingstone.

Stanley led the vanguard of his caravan out of Bagamoyo on 21 March 1871. After several blasts on a kudu horn, the column started on the road into the interior. Out in front, the *kirangozi* or guide carried the American flag sewn by the U.S. Consul's wife.[16] It was an extraordinary day for the former workhouse boy, resplendent in his sola topee and white flannels, as he rode ahead into the bush on his thoroughbred stallion.[17] For the first time he saw giraffe, hippopotami and antelope, as if he were 'an English nobleman' and the interior was his immense park.[18] Mercifully, for Stanley's peace of mind, he knew nothing of Livingstone's most recent geographical plans. He thought that the Doctor would return to Ujiji soon, although in March 1871 Livingstone himself had no intention of leaving the Lualaba.

Within days the realities of African travel hit Stanley. His two Arab horses were killed by the tsetse fly, and even some of his reputedly more hardy donkeys were sickening. Then the desertions began, as did Stanley's determined efforts to track down and punish the absconders. It took the expedition five days to march through the 'knee deep water and black mire' of the Makata swamp, and then Stanley, along with many of his porters, had contracted malaria.[19] Stanley's white colleagues, Shaw and Farquhar, were soon too ill to travel.[20] Farquhar was left behind with a chief and died not long afterwards.[21] Stanley detested Shaw for his addiction to prostitutes and Shaw hated him back.[22] On one occasion Shaw—half-crazed with fever—put a bullet through Stanley's tent when the journalist was sleeping within.[23]

Stanley arrived in the district of Unyanyembe—over two-thirds of the way to Ujiji—on 23 June, having marched 525 miles in eighty-four days[24] and having lost seventy-five of his hundred men to desertion despite his best efforts.[25] An Arab Swahili caravan had just arrived from Manyuema with news that Livingstone was dead. Another rumour was that he had shot himself in the thigh while hunting buffalo but would return to Ujiji when he had recovered.[26] According to an earlier report, he was marooned in Manyuema with only three of his porters remaining.[27]

Stanley was now in the land of the Nyamwezi, who were the greatest indigenous traders and travellers of central and East Africa. The European passion for ivory objects of all kinds had within the last two decades led the Arabs to enter the ivory trade, which had previously been monopolized by the Nyamwezi. The Arab Swahili traders in ivory and slaves were now squeezing out the Nyamwezi, whose chief, Mirambo, decided in 1871 to take control of the main trade route to the ivory regions of central Africa, which meant fighting the Arabs of Unyanyembe. This remarkable African ruler would make his first move against the Arabs just when Stanley was hoping to leave for Ujiji.[28]

The Governor of Unyanyembe told Stanley that war with Mirambo could not be avoided and invited him to join in on the Arabs' side. Since Mirambo was blocking the road out of Tabora to the west, Stanley knew that unless the African ruler was dislodged he (Stanley) would fail in his quest to find Livingstone. So clearing the road to Lake Tanganyika was a necessity. The Arabs' force was over two thousand strong, so the fifty men Stanley eventually managed to collect were not going to sway the balance.[29] But the Arabs persuaded him to participate by painting Mirambo as a murderous bandit who had usurped the Nyamwezi chiefship and was employing mercenaries—'ruga-ruga'—from neighbouring tribes.[30] When the fighting began, Stanley was still recovering from a bad attack of fever,[31] and would have been left behind and killed, after Mirambo defeated the Arabs, if his young translator, Selim, had not saddled his donkey and lifted his master on to the beast's back.[32]

When Mirambo sacked Tabora several days later, burning a quarter of the town, Stanley remained holed up with his fifty men.[33] If Mirambo winkled him out, he feared his body would be mutilated, as had been those of his Arab acquaintances, whose faces, genitals and stomachs were alleged to have been boiled and eaten by Mirambo's men.[34] But Mirambo unexpectedly held back. Still suspicious, Stanley decided not to try to reach Ujiji by the direct westerly route, but to avoid the war entirely, by marching south and south-west for ten days and only then starting to head north to Ujiji.

On the evening of 19 September, Stanley's fever left him, and he wrote by candle-light:

> I have taken a solemn, enduring oath, an oath to be kept while the least hope of life remains in me, not to be tempted to break the resolution I have formed, never to give up the search, until I find Livingstone alive, or find his dead body . . . No living man, or living men, shall stop me, only death can prevent me. But death—not even this; I shall not die, I will not die, I cannot die![35]

Stanley left Tabora on 21 September 1871 with only thirty-four men.[36] As the column headed south, seven *pagazi* refused to lift their loads. Stanley put several in chains and beat the rest. Naively, he admitted this in his book—as if unaware that other travellers kept quiet about such punishments.

By the end of the month, his colleague, John Shaw, was so ill that he had to be sent back to Tabora where he died. Stanley contracted malaria again and between bouts of delirium his moods swung from being 'ludicrously amiable' to wildly angry.[37] So at the Malagarazi river in late October, he was thrilled to hear that a white bewhiskered man had recently arrived at Ujiji.

Nearing Lake Tanganyika, the countryside became gentler, 'the green hills crowned by clusters of straw-thatched cones'.[38] Stanley ordered Selim 'to lay out my new flannel suit, to oil my boots, to chalk my helmet, and fold a new *puggaree* around it, that I may make as presentable an appearance as possible before the white man with the grey beard, and before the Arabs of Ujiji'.[39] Though Stanley was confident that Livingstone was at Ujiji, he still dreaded that Dr Kirk might have been right and Livingstone would leave when he heard that a white stranger was approaching. Even when he reached Ujiji on 10 November 1871,[40] Stanley still could not believe that some untoward event might not snatch everything from his grasp. Yet part of him was ecstatic: 'what would I not have given for a bit of friendly wilderness where, unseen, I might vent my joy in some mad freak, such as idiotically biting my hand, turning a somersault, or slashing at trees ... All around me was the immense crowd, hushed and expectant, and wondering how the scene would develop itself.'[41] Stanley was determined that 'his face should not betray emotion, lest it should detract from the dignity of a white man appearing under such extraordinary circumstances'.[42]

Stanley and his men pressed on to the centre of Ujiji with the Stars and Stripes held aloft. Volleys were fired—the age-old custom when a caravan entered a town—and a man stepped forward from the crowd 'dressed in a long white shirt, with a turban of American sheeting around his woolly head'. He said in English: 'How do you do, sir', and introduced himself as Susi, Livingstone's servant, before rushing away shouting: 'An Englishman coming.'[43] Stanley followed, seeing ahead of him a grey-bearded white man, in a navy cap, with a faded gold band round it. Spotting the Stars and Stripes, Livingstone imagined that the newcomer, who now held out his hand to him, was American.[44] As Stanley prepared to speak words of greeting, it was the most thrilling moment of his entire life.

This was when Stanley later claimed he asked the most famous question in the history of journalism: 'Dr Livingstone, I presume?' But at this crucial point in his diary three pages are torn out; and what motive could he have had for destroying these pages unless to change his account of the words actually spoken? Neither did Livingstone mention the famous question in *his* diary, nor in any letters which he wrote at this time. Stanley seems to have invented it because of his insecurity about his workhouse background and his longing to say something that a born gentleman might have uttered at a similarly momentous meeting.[45] Sadly, the very people he had attempted to impress later found his formal greeting a ludicrous parody. If ever there had been an excuse for effusive behaviour, surely this had been it. The invented words Stanley had hoped would lend dignity to his account of a most solemn occasion were later hailed with explosions of laughter and disbelief. They were used in music-hall burlesques; friends or strangers greeted each other substituting their own names for Livingstone's. 'Dr Livingstone, I presume?' one dummy asked another in a fashion plate in the October 1872 issue of *Tailor and Cutter*. A mass of advertisements came out using the phrase. Stanley himself was often met with 'Mr Stanley, I presume?' But he could never see the joke. The greatest irony of all was to be the fact that later generations would forget almost everything about the main achievements of the two men but would remember the joke phrase.

Stanley's fear that Livingstone might turn out to be 'a man who used an eye-glass, through which he would glare at me ferociously or icily'[46] turned out to be groundless the moment Livingstone ushered him into his *tembe*, and the local Arab and African onlookers withdrew. At first Stanley was too mesmerized by the man to make any written notes. 'The interest I take in him is too overpowering . . . my eyes rove over his face to speculate on every line & facial movement.'[47] There can be no doubt that Livingstone too had never been so pleased to see a white face as he was to see his visitor's. He was not exaggerating when he told Stanley: 'You have brought me new life.'[48] Stanley, who could not immediately have appreciated the absolute despair Livingstone had been in before his arrival, considered the Doctor's genuine and outspoken gratitude to be the first indication of a saintly character. Of course Livingstone would have been outrageously inhuman had he not responded emotionally to Stanley's arrival; for the journalist had brought not only food, medicines, supplies but also a package of letters that had been held up for months at Unyanyembe. Stanley was immensely impressed that Livingstone asked him to bring him up to date with world events without so much as a glance at his letters. 'He had acquired the art of being patient long ago, he said, and he had waited so long for letters that he could well afford to wait a few hours more.'[49] So Stanley regaled Livingstone with the first proper accounts of what had been happening in the outside world for the past five years. The doctor listened open-mouthed as Stanley told him about the Franco-Prussian War and the fall of Paris. Stanley filled him in on news items ranging from the inauguration of the transatlantic telegraph and the opening of the Suez Canal to the death of the British Foreign Secretary,

Lord Clarendon. But undoubtedly the information which Livingstone listened to with most attention was that, due to Sir Roderick Murchison's determined efforts, the Treasury had at last agreed to let him have more money for supplies. The sum voted had been £1,000.[50] The knowledge that he had not been entirely forgotten in England did not make him any the less grateful for what he called the 'disinterested kindness of Mr Bennett, so nobly carried into effect by Mr Stanley'.

Though Livingstone had at first alarmed Stanley by calling the *New York Herald* 'that despicable paper', the Doctor still found it gratifying to believe that Mr Bennett had acted only out of affection for him—an absurd idea which was given some credence by Stanley's kindness and consideration.[51] He divided everything he had brought into two piles and gave Livingstone one of them. He prepared food for the older man with his own hands and saw that he had four meals a day. In every way that he could think of he made life easier for the Doctor, whose health soon seemed to improve. Stanley did not minimize the dangers he had survived on his journey and Livingstone was duly appreciative of his 'truly noble braving of death & danger to serve me as a son might have done'.[52] In letter after letter Livingstone lavished praise on the newcomer. He told Agnes: 'He came with the true American characteristic generosity—the tears often started into my eyes on every fresh proof of kindness.'[53]

If Livingstone was grateful, so was Stanley. Each sight of Livingstone reminded him that he had succeeded. He lived from day to day dazed with pleasure, frequently enjoying little dialogues with himself: 'What was I sent for?—To find Livingstone—Have you found him?—Yes, of course; am I not in his house? Whose compass is that hanging on a peg there? Whose clothes, whose boots, are those? Who reads those newspapers, those "Saturday Reviews" and numbers of "Punch" lying on the floor?'[54]

Stanley would describe Livingstone as a book 'with a most unpretending binding' that 'gave no token of what element of power or talent lay within'.[55] Indeed this deceptive ordinariness was what made Livingstone unique among Victorian heroes. Stanley soon realized that he was Scottish, not English as he had at first thought, and that they were both Celts—not that Stanley admitted to being anything other than American—but he sensed at once that Livingstone was not the misanthropic loner Kirk had described. In his late fifties, Livingstone's character had softened from the self-obsessed man who had shown no pity for those who had died in the Shire Highlands. Stanley admired his understated faith: 'It is of the true, practical kind, never losing a chance to manifest itself in a quiet, practical way . . . It governs his conduct towards his servants, and towards the natives . . .'[56] When the Doctor declared that he had no intention of going home until he had finished his work, despite longing to see his family, the younger man was overwhelmed by such dedication.[57] Stanley saw in him not only 'Spartan heroism' but also 'something seer-like'.[58] Livingstone's conviction that he had been chosen to serve Africa made a lifelong impression on Stanley. When Livingstone admitted: 'I have lost a great deal of happiness I know by these wanderings. It is as if I had been born to exile', Stanley identified powerfully.[59]

Livingstone at nearly sixty seemed old to Stanley, who was then thirty, and though Livingstone's teeth 'showed indications of being worn out', his hazel eyes struck Stanley as 'remarkably bright, not dimmed in the least' and his hair merely 'streaked here and there with grey over the temples'.[60] Both men were keen tea drinkers, consuming numerous cups together over the weeks ahead,[61] and though Livingstone rarely drank alcohol, he did not refuse a glass when Stanley opened a bottle of Sillery champagne to celebrate their meeting. So from the beginning, Stanley found Livingstone easy to get on with, like 'an old friend'. 'There was a friendly or good-natured abandon about Livingstone ... He had not much to offer ... but what he had was mine and his.'[62] Livingstone often 'relapsed into his own inner world'; but Stanley knew *he* could be self-absorbed too. And since Livingstone seemed sure to guarantee him fame, no wonder the young journalist felt warmly towards him. Mutual gratitude is a good foundation for friendship, but there was more to it than that. Livingstone had always disliked all forms of pretentiousness and cant. Stanley was awkward, shy, defensive and given to bluster, but he was rarely pretentious or hypocritical. Livingstone almost certainly sensed his insecurity and perhaps suspected that Stanley, like himself, had had humble origins. Both men shared the same shyness and as a result were often thought brusque and rude. This could have led to violent misunderstanding but it did not, for they seemed to recognize the same traits in each other and to make allowances accordingly.

Livingstone was not, as Kirk had predicted he would be, offended when he discovered that Stanley was a journalist. He had always liked his work to be appreciated, and trusted Stanley to present his travels and efforts in a favourable light. It was highly gratifying to feel that Mr Bennett, thousands of miles away in America, had thought him important enough to spend £4,000 for an interview. This was the vastly exaggerated sum which Stanley casually mentioned to Livingstone in order to bolster, Stanley's, sense of self-importance. Livingstone had felt that the British Government and people had forgotten him and it therefore touched him all the more to think that a foreign nation had not done the same. Ever since he had tried to persuade his parents to emigrate there in the 1840s, he had thought highly of America, and now his affection naturally increased. He was not in any way offended when he heard that Kirk had been saying that Stanley would make his fortune out of him. Livingstone's reply was characteristic: 'He is heartily welcome, for it is a great deal more than I could ever make out of myself.'[63]

When Stanley dared ask Livingstone awkward questions about his missionary work it was a token of the strong rapport established between them that the Doctor did not lose his temper with his questioner. Stanley had realized that preaching to Africans, while travelling, was impossible. 'For at intervals of ten or twelve days' journey—Livingstone would enter on a new country which had a new language; and, of course, he would never stay long enough anywhere to learn it.'[64] So Stanley told Livingstone bluntly: 'I cannot see how one or two men can hope to make an impression on the minds of so many millions.' Livingstone replied without embarrassment that 'someone must begin the work. Christ was the beginner of the Christianity that is now spread over a large part of the world. I feel sometimes as if I was the beginner for attacking central Africa.'[65] Yet, after obliquely comparing himself with Christ, Livingstone was soon afterwards being humorously risqué, telling Stanley that the Duchess of Sutherland had asked John Speke whether African women really walked around naked. They do indeed, Speke had assured her. Livingstone then mimicked what was said by both parties:

'Oh, but surely they wear something,' the Duchess insisted.
      Whereat Speke replied: 'Maybe a string or so down here,' and suited the action to the word in a way that caused several ladies to cry, 'Oh! Captain Speke!' and the Duchess to hide her face with her fan.[66]

Livingstone did not place himself on a pedestal to impress Stanley. He never for instance made out that his servants and porters were always loyal, moral and obedient. In fact he admitted to Stanley that when he had reluctantly been travelling with the Arab slave and ivory trader, Muhammad bin Saleh, the trader had persuaded all but two of Livingstone's men to desert 'by selling the favours of his concubines to them'. This loss of men, Livingstone confided, had left him in his own words 'like a slave to every village chief I came across'.[67]

Livingstone wrote two letters to Mr Bennett within ten days of Stanley's arrival and both were of course for publication. If Stanley and Bennett stood to gain, so he felt did he. He was able to put his views on the slave trade before a vast audience and to give enormous publicity to the massacre he had witnessed at Nyangwe. Stanley's arrival could not have come at a better time from that point of view. In fact the publicity

given to these and other letters written by him, and the general furore
caused by Stanley's feat, were of crucial importance in the revival of public
indignation in Britain and America at the continuation of slavery in East
Africa. Graphic descriptions of a full-blown massacre, and not just a few
isolated deaths, were just what the missionary and philanthropic pressure
groups needed to spur the Government on to a policy of abolition rather
than restriction. Livingstone also used the *New York Herald* to put over his
arguments against notions of African racial inferiority.

> I have no prejudice against their colour; indeed, any one who lives long
> among them forgets that they are black and feels that they are just
> fellow-men . . . If a comparison were instituted, and Manyuema, taken
> at random, placed opposite say the members of the Anthropological
> Society of London, clad like them in kilts of grass cloth, I should like to
> take my place among the Manyuema, on the principle of preferring the
> company of my betters.[68]

Having said what he wanted to communicate, Livingstone was quite
prepared to please Stanley by writing a few whimsical passages about
Manyuema women and their beauty: 'their charming black eyes, beautiful
foreheads, nicely rounded limbs . . . But they must adorn themselves; and
this they do—oh, the hussies!—by filing their splendid teeth to points like
cat's teeth.'

Mr Bennett was prepared to pay £1,600—more than the original cost
of the expedition—to have Livingstone's two letters telegraphed to New
York in their entirety.[69] They were exactly what Stanley had had in mind
when he had asked the Doctor to write for Bennett.

Already Livingstone was becoming something of an honorary parent to
the young man who had never known his own father. 'His manner',
enthused Stanley, 'suits my nature better than that of any man I can
remember . . . I should best describe it as benevolently paternal . . . it
steals its influence on me without any effort on his part . . . [he] is
sincerely natural and converses with me as if I were of his own age or of
equal experience. The consequence is that I have come to entertain an
immense respect for myself, and begin to think myself somebody, though
I never suspected it before . . .'[70] When Stanley suffered a renewed bout
of fever, 'in an instant his [Livingstone's] tone changed and had he been
my own father, he could not have been kinder.'[71] The father and son
dimension was not confined to Stanley's imaginings. 'That good brave
fellow has acted as a son to me,' Livingstone would tell his daughter
Agnes.[72] He would even ask Stanley to find the grave of his son, Robert,
who had died in the battle of Gettysburg, and to erect a headstone.

Stanley, like Robert Livingstone, had fought in the Civil War, and this provided another emotional link. Normally unwilling to express personal feelings, Livingstone liked Stanley enough to speak of his wife's death to him. 'For some time I felt that I should never get over it.'[73]

Finding Livingstone kind and helpful, the young journalist was so grateful that he at once assumed that all the stories he had heard from Kirk and others about Livingstone's perverse antisocial behaviour had been malicious fabrications. Stanley made up his mind to remedy the situation once and for all; he knew that the despatches he would send back to the *New York Herald* would be published in other papers throughout the world. So Stanley set about canonizing Dr Livingstone: a figure 'without spleen or misanthropy', a man as near an angel 'as the nature of living man will allow'; not overtly or self-consciously pious either, but with quiet honesty. Nor was Livingstone gloomy or inward-looking, for he had a 'fund of quiet humour'.

> His gentleness never forsakes him; his hopefulness never deserts him. No harassing anxieties, distractions of mind, long separation from home and kindred, can make him complain . . . His is . . . the inflexibility of the Roman, the enduring resolution of the Anglo-Saxon—never to relinquish his work though his heart yearns for home.

This then was the picture of Livingstone which Stanley gave the world. He repeated it in speeches, articles, letters, and finally gave it more permanent form in his world-wide best-seller, *How I Found Livingstone*, published in England and America in 1872. But the lasting effect of Stanley's character study was its acceptance by almost all those who read or heard about it at the time, and by subsequent biographers until my biography was first published in 1973. Amazingly, Stanley's transformation of Livingstone's image was achieved less than a decade after the crushing failure of his Zambesi Expedition, when *The Times* had characterized that whole enterprise as a series of broken promises.

Then there had been the numerous avoidable deaths, but Stanley's talent as a journalist enabled him to persuade the public to forget five years of failure, during which 'saintly' and 'angelic' had definitely not been adjectives which Dr Livingstone's name had called to mind. Stanley cannot be accused of deliberate insincerity; the great personal meaning with which he had invested his meeting with Livingstone influenced him to some extent unconsciously, and Livingstone's unfeigned gratitude and genuine liking for him did the rest. Livingstone's patience with all Africans, even those who had deserted him, also justifiably impressed Stanley. But after a couple of months with Livingstone, Stanley wrote in his diary that Livingstone had spoken slightingly of the Universities' Mission, six of whose missionaries had gone to Africa at his behest and died, adding that: 'The more you do for people, the more ungrateful they are.' Then he complained about the R.G.S., saying that it had used his scientific observations without crediting him.[74]

On 3 March 1872, Stanley made an important admission in his diary:

> Livingstone reverted again to his grudges against the missionaries on the Zambezi and one of his officers (naval) on the Expedition . . . I have had some intrusive suspicions & thoughts that he was not of such an angelic temper as I believed him to be during my first month with him, but for the last month I have been driving them steadily from my mind . . . when however he reiterated his complaints against this man and the other—I felt the faintest fear that his strong nature was opposed to forgiveness & that he was not so perfect as at the first blush of friendship I thought him.

Casting around for reasons for ignoring the great man's vindictiveness, Stanley argued that it was not really 'a weakness to dwell on these bitter memories' because he [Stanley] had 'pestered him with questions'.[75] To be 'opposed to forgiveness' was hardly consistent with being as near an angel 'as the nature of living man will allow', but in subsequent despatches and articles Stanley made no qualification of his earlier rhapsodic praise for the saintly Doctor. Perhaps he disliked the idea of seeming to have been gullible, and he may also have realized that the story of the discovery of a forgotten saint made far better copy than any rather more truthful account would have done. Another reason for this whitewashing was Stanley's desire to point out to his neglectful family that he had at last been cherished as a son by a truly good man. Nor did he see Livingstone's attacks on others as being due to any fatal flaw in his character. Stanley shared Livingstone's pessimistic assumption that people were often in league against him, and so he tended to believe that the great man had in reality been wronged repeatedly. He certainly thought Livingstone justified in being enraged with John Kirk, whom Stanley had disliked ever since their first meeting. He was convinced that Kirk had neither taken sufficient care in the selection of members of the caravans despatched with goods for Livingstone, nor taken routine precautions to see that these caravans had set off from the coast at once. Before Stanley's arrival, Livingstone had already found fault with Kirk for sending him slaves rather than free men to Bambarre and thus causing him endless difficulties. Stanley's charges, apart from those already mentioned, were that Kirk had gone to

Sewji's—a firm notorious for its association with slave caravans—to get supplies, and had made no real effort to send mail to Livingstone. While Stanley had been with the Doctor, the U.S. Consul F.R. Webb had sent eleven packages to the journalist, but in the same period Livingstone had received nothing from Kirk.

But the rights and wrongs of the arguments Stanley used against Kirk are not really of cardinal importance. The row between the two men brought in Livingstone, but is far more revealing of Stanley's character than Livingstone's. I have therefore confined myself to a short summary. What mattered was that Livingstone—usually inclined to believe that former friends had let him down—was predictably furious when Stanley told him that he had found a consignment of goods for Livingstone, that had been sitting in Bagamoyo for a year, being plundered by the carriers employed by Kirk, while the unconcerned Consul had not troubled to come to the mainland from Zanzibar to check that the goods had been sent on their way to Ujiji. Livingstone was soon writing letters to most of his correspondents, telling them no longer to refer to Kirk, as Sir Roderick Murchison did, as 'companion of Livingstone'. One friend was told that Kirk was 'too lazy and indifferent to serve David Livingstone',[76] and another, that the Acting British Consul at Zanzibar had inflicted on him 'a loss of two years time, at least 1,800 miles of tramp, and what money I don't exactly know'.[77]

Stanley, who had merely intended to discredit Kirk, had had no idea that Livingstone might begin to see the whole matter as a monstrous conspiracy against him, in which Kirk, the British Government and the Council of the Royal Geographical Society were all in league. Livingstone soon suspected that Kirk had been acting on instructions from the Foreign Office to force him home. The extra £1,000 grant had merely been a blind to deceive him into believing that the Government still supported him. The Foreign Office was clearly ganging up with the members of the Council of the R.G.S. who wanted him home to get their hands on his precious notes.

So when Stanley, who had noticed that Livingstone had by no means made a thorough recovery, attempted to persuade the ailing traveller to come home to recuperate, get some artificial teeth, have an operation for his piles and build up his strength in England before returning to Africa for a final effort on the Lualaba, he was surprised and wounded that Livingstone refused even to consider the suggestion. This was despite the Doctor's longing to see his children—his youngest, Anna Mary, being only twelve. Ironically, Stanley remained unaware that his attack on Kirk had made Livingstone's refusal a foregone conclusion. Once Livingstone felt suspicious and persecuted there was no holding him and soon he was even suggesting that Kirk was trying to force him back to England so that he, Kirk, could 'finish up the sources'.[78] Livingstone had tried to persuade Kirk to come out to Africa in 1865, but since he could offer no salary, Kirk, who had then been contemplating marriage, had felt unable to accept. Livingstone now argued that Kirk had realized that he had made a sad mistake and was attempting, by unscrupulous means, to reverse it before it was too late.[79] In this state of mind Livingstone felt unable to trust anybody. In December 1871 he sent his daughter Agnes a rough map,* incorporating his latest conclusions on the Lualaba, and told her solemnly: 'Now I entrust it to you, and if you betray my confidence I shall never trust you again—if Sir Roderick asks, say that all your letter is private and confidential . . . He is not too easily put off but be firm.'[80]

Sir Roderick had been almost entirely responsible for getting Livingstone his extra £1,000 from the Government. Murchison had in fact blackmailed the Foreign Secretary, by telling him that he would publish the Foreign Office correspondence with Livingstone for 1864 and 1865. He had also told Clarendon that if no money were voted he would shame the Government by raising a public subscription fund.[81] Perhaps it was as well that Sir Roderick would never know that Livingstone had lost faith in him; he had been dead two months when Livingstone stopped trusting him.

Stanley had brought Livingstone new life and new hope and had saved him at a critical time, but the doubts he had raised in Livingstone's mind not only revived old traits such as vindictiveness and mistrust at a time when Livingstone seemed to have outgrown them, but also made sure Livingstone would never return to England to make a proper recovery before attempting to finish his work. Because the Government had been so stingy, Livingstone feared that unless he returned home having proved that he had found the Nile's source (which would make any book rights exceptionally valuable), he would be forced by poverty to accept some piffling Foreign Office overseas appointment. 'To return unsuccessful,' he told Agnes, would mean 'going abroad to an unhealthy consulate to which no public sympathy would ever be drawn'.[82] When the *Lady Nyassa* had finally been sold in Bombay, the money had been invested in a bank that failed. So now, unless he broke the trust fund he had set up for his children, Livingstone would have no money on his return. There would be no pension either. It would have to be death or success.

On the all-important subject of the Nile's source, Livingstone, who was normally so secretive, showed Stanley his sketch maps and confided to

---

* Reproduced as plate 30.

him all his ideas about the source. Then the older man invited him to come with him to the Lualaba to trace it downstream and prove it was the Nile. Stanley was tempted, but knowing James Gordon Bennett's unforgiving nature, felt he might never again work for the *New York Herald* unless he hurried to the coast with his news of the meeting.[83]

Eager not to lose a chance of travelling with Livingstone, Stanley suggested a shorter expedition. They could go together to the unvisited northern end of Lake Tanganyika. Since 1865, Stanley had known about Burton's claim that the river Rusizi flowed northwards out of Lake Tanganyika into the southern end of Baker's Lake Albert before continuing northwards as the White Nile. Livingstone shared this view, as Stanley knew from the R.G.S.'s publication of the Doctor's letter to John Kirk of 30 May 1869. In it Livingstone had said that he intended to 'go down' what he described as 'the [Nile's] eastern line of drainage'. He meant by this the northward-flowing river system originating in Lake Bangweolo, and then flowing north, via Lake Moero [Mweru], into the west side of Lake Tanganyika, and from that lake's northern tip via the Rusizi into Lake Albert.[84] But after realizing that the Lualaba flowed due north for four hundred miles from Bangweolo (and, he suspected, went on north for many more hundreds), Livingstone had dismissed Lake Tanganyika as almost an irrelevance. The Lualaba, he declared, was 'the central line of drainage [and] the most important line . . . [In comparison] the question whether there is a connection between the Tanganyika and the Albert N'yanza sinks into insignificance'.[85]

But Stanley reminded Livingstone that Sir Roderick Murchison and the R.G.S. wanted the Rusizi's direction of flow to be settled, and said he would pay all the expenses of their journey.[86] Recognizing an excellent offer, Livingstone was perfectly willing to attempt the same journey that had got the better of Burton and Speke due to the refusal of the local chief's oarsmen to obey them. Livingstone and Stanley accepted the loan of a large canoe from the Arab, Said bin Majid, and took with them none of the chief's men, only Stanley's cook, his translator, two guides and sixteen reliable Wangwana as rowers.

Stanley and Livingstone embarked on 16 November, six days after Stanley's arrival at Ujiji.[87] They kept close to the shore and Stanley was enchanted by 'a wealth of boscage of beautiful trees . . . exhaling an indescribably sweet fragrance'. He and the Doctor enjoyed seeing well-ordered fishing settlements, palm groves and cassava gardens.[88] Nothing worse happened than a few stones being flung at them. Stanley wanted to fire warning shots and later admitted: 'If Livingstone had not been in the boat, I would certainly have tried to teach them a lesson—for I have already begun to learn that the meeker one is the more natives of this temper encroach upon forbearance . . . The doctor said from his experience elsewhere the Arab slave traders must have been here & angered these people by their conduct. His explanations were so wise that I was glad we had not been driven to retaliate.'[89] Stanley was also impressed when Livingstone soothed two angry and drunken chiefs by showing them the white skin of his arm and inviting them to say whether anyone of his colour had ever injured them.

On 28 November they reached the head of the lake and saw that the Rusizi flowed into Tanganyika rather than out of it. So Burton was wrong and Lake Tanganyika could not be any kind of source or reservoir of the Nile. The Victoria Nyanza and the Lualaba's headwaters were now the only serious candidates for being the Nile's source. Livingstone suggested that while the height of two thousand feet which he had calculated for Nyangwe (the same as Baker's height for Lake Albert) made a direct link between the Lualaba and Lake Albert less likely, it remained perfectly possible for the Lualaba to pass Lake Albert to the west and join the Nile via the Bahr el-Ghazal further to the north. Stanley had been alarmed to notice on this journey to the Rusizi how prone Livingstone was to diarrhoea, especially when he was cold and wet. So Stanley was distressed when Livingstone told him he did not intend to go straight to Nyangwe to follow the river north, but meant to trek hundreds of miles south to swampy Lake Bangweolo first, to make sure he had not missed any more southerly sources of the Lualaba.[90]

On 13 December the two men returned to Ujiji after a journey of three hundred miles, and two weeks later set off for Tabora, Stanley on his way home, Livingstone to collect any supplies from Kirk's caravans that had not got through to Ujiji. En route Livingstone was stung by a swarm of bees. Although suffering terribly, that same evening he dined with Stanley, who had given his cook, Ferajji, orders to produce for dinner his best meatballs and custard dessert.[91] Tabora was reached on 18 February 1872, and once again Stanley vainly attempted to persuade Livingstone to change his mind about coming home. Then Stanley agreed instead to help Livingstone in any way he could. The two of them drew up a list of supplies which Livingstone would need for the long journey ahead of him, and Stanley promised to send everything with fifty porters as soon as he could after reaching the coast. These fifty men he swore would be free men and reliable too. As the time grew closer for parting, Livingstone tried to detain Stanley a little longer, until the rains ended, but Stanley, although in many ways reluctant to leave, was in others eager to get away: he had yet to telegraph his news to the world, and he knew that the longer he stayed with the Doctor, the longer Livingstone would have to wait for his fifty porters and the supplies.

On the evening of 13 March all Stanley's preparations for departure on the following day had been completed. Livingstone handed over to him the letters he had written while they had been together and, as a sign of his complete trust in Stanley, his journal. This was sealed with five seals and marked not to be opened until his own return to England or his death. In England it was to be entrusted to Agnes. Livingstone did not waste words on the parting. 'Mr Stanley leaves' was all he wrote. But there was no doubt at all that he felt considerably more. In letters to most of his friends he instructed them to treat Stanley with friendship and kindness, 'just as you would do to me'.[92]

'I shall see Livingstone no more unless he finishes his task,' Stanley confided to his diary.[93] 'At his age, drawing near his 60th year it appears to be a big task—from the cannibals on the Lualaba's banks, & the multitude of rivers he has mentioned.'[94] The Doctor filled the time by writing letters of introduction for Stanley to make use of in Britain.[95] On the evening of the 13th—their last together—the dividing door between their rooms was closed by Livingstone, 'and we both think our own thoughts,' wrote Staney in his diary. 'I bitterly regret the approach of the parting hour. I now forget the successive fevers, and their agonies, and the semi-madness to which they often plagued me. The regret I feel is greater than any pains I have endured . . .'[96] When Livingstone gave Stanley proper thanks, 'uttered with no mincing phrases, but poured out as it were at the last moment', Stanley reacted like 'a sensitive child of eight or so and yielded to such a burst of tears that only such a scene as this one could have forced'. In a rare admission of his own vulnerability Livingstone told Stanley that without his presence 'this house will look as if a death has taken place'.[97]

At dawn on the 14th, both men ate 'a sad breakfast'. Livingstone realized that Stanley might well prove his last link with the outside world; the job of tracing the Luapula and the Lomani on north from their adjacent sources and then going on along the Lualaba would have taxed his endurance to the utmost twenty years before. So Livingstone, to keep Stanley with him a little longer, accompanied him for the first few miles of his journey to the coast. As they walked side by side, Stanley 'took long looks at Livingstone to impress his features thoroughly on my memory'.[98] When they parted and Stanley went on alone, the journalist could barely keep back his tears, and when Chuma and Susi ran up to him to kiss his hands, it was too much for him. 'I betrayed myself, . . . "March! Why do you stop? Go on! Are you not going home?" And my people were driven before me. No more weakness. I shall show them such marching as will make them remember me.'[99]

Later, Stanley wrote a letter which he would never send. 'My dear Doctor, I have parted from you too soon. I feel it too deeply . . . The utter loneliness of myself, the void that has been created . . .'[100] Although Livingstone was inclined to be dismissive towards other explorers, he had treated Stanley as an equal. 'As if', marvelled Stanley, 'I were of his own age or of equal experience.'[101] With his workhouse background, Stanley had been utterly captivated by this lack of condescension. Livingstone's reward would be the picture of himself as a near saint, which Stanley painted in *How I Found Livingstone*.

Within a week of Stanley's landing in England on 1 August 1872, the story of his meeting with Livingstone had swept all other items off the main news pages of all the major papers in Britain. Whereas in March 1867, reports of Livingstone's death had been given barely half a column in most papers, now, throughout August and September 1872, it was not unusual to see two pages of ten full columns each, devoted exclusively to Livingstone. The main reason for this extraordinary volte-face was the realization by most editors of the fact that Mr Bennett had been aware of three years before, namely that a meeting between a journalist and a once-famous explorer, who had been seen by no member of his own race for five years, made an exceptionally good story. Stanley made it a much better one by turning up in Britain and claiming that Dr Livingstone was not only a great explorer, who had been forgotten by his own countrymen, but a near saint.

Just before Stanley had reached Britain, many papers had published articles insinuating, and some openly stating, that Stanley was a fraud and that he had not found Livingstone at all; all the information he claimed to possess could have been culled from despatches sent home by Livingstone in 1866 and 1867. On 2 August, the day after Stanley's arrival in Britain, the Foreign Secretary, in an open letter to *The Times*, had silenced all these critics by stating that all the despatches brought home by Stanley were without question genuine. Having previously cast doubt on Stanley, the press now attempted to make up for their previous errors by accepting, without reservation, his glowing picture of Dr Livingstone. The editor of the *Standard*'s description of Livingstone, as 'the brave, noble hearted and heavenly minded Dr Livingstone', became typical.[102] The Foreign Office released passages from Livingstone's despatches, and the story of his losses, his suffering and his continuing efforts was published in most papers in his own words. The reaction of the editor of the *Morning Post* was re-echoed in every other paper: 'To those who live at home at ease, it may well appear marvellous that any human being would voluntarily undergo the hardships suffered by Livingstone, or could undergo them and live to tell the tale.'[103] The idea of a lonely man, surrounded by cannibals and slave traders, floundering through swamps with ten-foot reeds, prostrated by fever, yet still forcing his way on through the 'Dark Continent', seemed so miraculous that most people never bothered to ask what he had been doing or whether he had achieved his objectives.

On the whole, when the press did touch on the value of Livingstone's discoveries they tended to accept that Speke and Baker had been wrong and that Livingstone had found the true source of the Nile. It would not be known positively that he had been deceived for another five years, and in the meantime the certainty of most geographers that the height Livingstone had given for Nyangwe meant that the Lualaba was the Congo was disparaged by many journalists as an 'armchair opinion'. So for the last years of his life and the first years after his death, Livingstone's reputation as a great geographer was built up sufficiently for the subsequent revelation of his crucial error to have a comparatively minor impact. Livingstone's reports on the massacre at Nyangwe also made a deep impression and it was often said that 'even the discovery of the Nile is secondary to that far greater object—namely putting an end to the slave trade'. Livingstone's former dependence on the Arabs received little attention.

There can be no doubt that Livingstone got a great deal more coverage than he would have done otherwise through the series of acrimonious rows Stanley became involved in during his months in Britain. The worst of these quarrels was over a British expedition sent out to relieve Dr Livingstone in early 1872. This party had been planned by the Council of the R.G.S. on the assumption that Stanley would never manage to get out of Unyanyembe owing to the war to the west of that town. The Relief Expedition, for which £4,000 was subscribed, arrived on the African mainland to find that Stanley had forestalled them. The officers resigned and the venture was abandoned. No contingency plan had been made for what they should do if Stanley succeeded; his failure had been considered a foregone conclusion. Stanley felt that the officers of the expedition had been carelessly chosen and that the whole business had been badly planned. When he got to Britain he said this, and so became embroiled in an unpleasant quarrel with the Council of the R.G.S. This was widely reported and sides were taken. Most of the papers took the view that the expedition should have gone on and done something, as opposed to returning to Britain, having wasted £2,300 of the money which had been publicly subscribed. The press in general made this row an excuse to attack the British Government for having abandoned Livingstone in the first place. Had they not done so, it was claimed, the Doctor would never have needed a Relief Expedition. Articles soon appeared castigating the Foreign Office for meanness and indifference to the fate of one of Britain's greatest men. The hypocrisy of these attacks went unnoticed. The press had, of course, been just as indifferent to Livingstone as the Government had been before Stanley had found him. It was a waste of time for the Foreign Office to issue statements saying that Livingstone, in addition to his £500 grant, had been voted £1,000, and that £1,200 of public money had been spent on the search party sent out in 1867. The press and public had made up their minds that a dedicated and godly man had been ignored by the people only because the Government had withheld information.

In 1864, after the Zambesi Expedition, Livingstone had been attacked in almost every national paper for having led innocent men to their death and having wasted a great deal of Treasury money on a venture which he ought to have known was doomed from the beginning. In 1872 Stanley wiped away the memory of Livingstone's earlier failures so effectively that today *his* picture of Dr Livingstone is still the accepted version.

There is one more important fact about Stanley's visit to Britain: he brought information about the slave trade, in the form of Livingstone's despatches, at a crucial time. During 1871 a House of Commons Select Committee had been set up to review the problem of the East African slave trade. The Committee had in the end come out in favour of total abolition of the seaborne trade. This conclusion was largely the result of evidence submitted by Kirk, Livingstone and Sir Bartle Frere—Livingstone's evidence, it should be added, dated back to the last despatches received in London prior to Stanley's visit: these had been written in 1867. Once the Select Committee had made its recommendations the Government was not bound to act on them, and, at the time of Stanley's arrival in Britain in August 1872, no final decision had been made. Livingstone's description of the massacre at Nyangwe, however, was an incredible piece of good fortune for the abolitionist lobby, and they used it most effectively. By the end of September 1872, Gladstone's Government had decided on the abolition of the sale of all slaves, whether for domestic use or for export. Sir Bartle Frere, the Governor of Bombay, was appointed to sign a treaty with the Sultan of Zanzibar to that effect. On 5 June 1873, after being threatened with a British naval blockade, the Sultan signed, and that day the slave market in Zanzibar was closed for ever. Frere himself was convinced that Livingstone's information had been crucial in provoking immediate government action, and he ought to have known.[104] So while there can be little doubt, in view of the Select Committee's findings, that abolition would have come in the end anyway, Livingstone's information ensured that the process was not delayed. It was tragic that Livingstone himself never lived to hear about Frere's treaty.

23

The Last Journey
1872–1873

⟫◆⟪

As Livingstone waited at Unyanyembe, throughout the spring and summer of 1872, he knew nothing about the fame Stanley had brought him, nor did he have any idea of the impact his anti-slavery despatches had had. All that came his way, as he waited six weary months for the men and supplies Stanley had promised to send from the coast, was news that a Relief Expedition had been sent and had broken up after Stanley's arrival at Zanzibar. Livingstone's son, Oswell, had been a member of the expedition, and like the others had decided not to press on. His father was shocked by this, and, even when he also knew that the others had resigned first, and that Oswell would therefore have had to go on alone, Livingstone did not forgive him. As he told Agnes, her brother should have had 'the sense to come with me and gain a little credit that may enable him to hold up his head among men and not be merely Dr Livingstone's son'.[1] And when, several weeks later, Livingstone received two letters from Oswell, telling him that his prime purpose in coming to Africa had been to persuade his father to come home, an enraged Livingstone not only accused Oswell of cowardice and duplicity but also described his letters as 'the most snobbish and impertinent I ever received or read'. Oswell, he continued, was 'as poor a specimen of a son as Africa ever produced': a young man who 'does not think of supporting himself by his own labour' but prefers 'to run away home calling loudly for more money'.[2] Livingstone's old sisters, who also wanted a cash handout, were additional targets for his scathing pen. 'I devoted all my money to these neer do weels [sic] and they forget the hand that fed, clothed & lodged them & say I forgot them.'[3] Livingstone's extreme irritation is not hard to understand. He felt that at the moment when he stood poised to begin the most important and arduous of all his journeys, his family— Agnes excepted—far from encouraging him, were doing everything in their power to discourage him so that he would consent to come home and write another best-seller for them to live off. That they might have been genuinely worried that unless he returned home, Africa would kill him, just as it had killed his wife, did not seem to have occurred to him.

During his six months at Tabora in Unyanyembe Livingstone had plenty of time to think not only of his ungrateful family, but also about his past and what he had so far achieved with his life. He recalled his failure to encourage traders and the Government's rejection of his colonial plans. For the first time in his life he could not help feeling that he had possibly been too ambitious. He thought back still further to his days in Bechuanaland and remembered the hopes he had once entertained of succeeding as an ordinary missionary. Now he wondered whether the conventional missionary approach might not have been the best. Missions could be established within a few hundred miles of the coast; that would be a beginning. Old ideas flooded back; had he really ever given 'native agency' a chance? Two missionaries in a place like Unyanyembe might be able to achieve something with the help of 'native teachers'.[4] Magomero had failed because the communications had been too bad; the same difficulties would not be experienced in the area midway between Lake Tanganyika and Zanzibar. But this idea only stayed with Livingstone for a week or two; soon he was off on a new theory, as wild and impracticable as any he had ever dreamed up. On the West African coast successful missions had converted large numbers of Africans. If these men, or a proportion of them, could be induced to join a voluntary emigration scheme from West to East Africa, their influence might prove to be enough to stop chiefs selling their people into slavery. Africans might be better for the job than whites: 'English people in a new country show themselves very often to be born fools.'[5] Soon Livingstone abandoned this idea too. But the real miracle is that, after all his previous rebuffs and disappointments, the man was still an optimist, still an idealist thinking of new ways of changing Africa. Livingstone had succumbed neither to fatalism nor to blind acceptance of the escapist dream that Providence alone would sort out everything.

During this time Livingstone also thought about his immediate aims. Although his itinerary would be completely dominated by the geographical task ahead, he could not help believing that this work was far less significant than action taken against the slave trade. 'What I have seen of this horrid system', he told a friend, 'makes me feel that its suppression would be of infinitely more importance than all the fountains [sources] together.'[6] Yet if he abandoned his Nile pilgrimage, there was no knowing whether he would be able to do any more to combat the slave trade in some other way. He would continue to write despatches, to keep up his journal and to hope that if he returned home the public would listen to him. If he could prove the Lualaba to be the Nile, he felt that his words would gain a prestige and authority which would otherwise be denied them. But later, as will be seen, when pain and illness once again began to destroy him, he reverted to his old obsession with the Nile as an end in itself: a compensation for every other failure. In his last weeks he would not be able to bear the memory of the deaths of Nyangwe, that 'come back unbidden, and make me start up at dead of night', without believing that his search for the source would in itself help end the slave trade.

Waiting for Stanley's men, Livingstone wrote the words that were to be cut into the stone that marks his grave in Westminster Abbey: 'All I can say in my loneliness* is, may heaven's rich blessing come down on every one—American, English, Turk—who will help to heal this open sore of the world.'[7]

Five days after Stanley had left, Livingstone had celebrated his fifty-ninth birthday with a reaffirmation of faith: '19th. March—Birthday. My Jesus, my King, my life, my all; I again dedicate my whole self to Thee. Accept me, and grant, O Gracious Father, that ere this year is gone I may finish my task. In Jesus' name I ask it. Amen, so let it be. David Livingstone.'[8]

And if he was to achieve anything like the task he had set himself within a year, Livingstone knew that he would have to be off soon, and so, as he waited and the days slipped by, he felt more and more impatient. The best months for travel were passing. But impatient though he was, Livingstone was once again excited and happy. The men would come with the needed supplies, and then he would redeem all past failures. In this mood he could write to friends jovially telling them 'that all past misdemeanors, faults, failings and nonsense are hereby condoned and obliterated ... I feel inclined to proclaim an amnesty to all the world'.[9] When the cold east wind and sudden showers gave him a touch of fever, his optimism was unchanged. He wrote asking Horace Waller, his friend from the Universities Mission, to make preparations for his return home when he had finished his work: 'Will you speak to a dentist about a speedy fitting of arteficial [sic] teeth? I beg your aid to secure lodgings for me say anywhere near Regent's Park—comfortable and decent, but not excessively dear.'[10]

Often in the past he had thought he would not survive, but now he had no such presentiments. In another letter to a friend he spoke of the same foreboding he had known in the past and went on: 'It is weakened now, as I seem to see the end to which I have been striving looming in the distance'.[11] In that distance were the four fountains of Herodotus, the source of the Lomani, the Lualaba and finally, somewhere two or three hundred miles north of Lake Albert, the Nile. First, in order to get to the sources of the Lomani river, Livingstone knew that he would have to skirt Bangweolo's southern shore. But this did not distress him, even though he must have realized that unless he could leave Unyanyembe by June, he

---

* On the stone 'solitude' replaced 'loneliness'.

would arrive at Bangweolo in the rains. In his own view there was no need for alarm; he had been there before and knew the shape of the lake, or thought he did.

As April, May and June passed, and the men still did not come, inactivity at last began to undermine Livingstone's good spirits. Doubts reappeared. Livingstone began a despatch to the Foreign Secretary outlining the route he intended to take: south-west to Bangweolo and then west along the southern shore of that lake. 'Being then in Lat 12° the course will be straight west to the fountains of Herodotus. But what if these fountains exist only in my imagination! Then we shall see.' He never finished the despatch for it ended: 'In battling down the central line of drainage: the Lualaba—the enormous amount of westing it made caused me at times to feel as if knocking my head against a stone wall. It might be the Congo and . . .'[12] In his journal over and over again he began to express the same doubt. 'I know too much to be positive'; and positive he desperately wanted to be.[13] To take such risks and suffer so much needlessly would be ironic beyond endurance, but there could be no turning back. He had already expressed himself with too much certainty to feel able to climb down; besides, Stanley's men would have left the coast weeks before. The case was beyond arguing now; only action remained, and he would go on, as he had always done. Two years before, in Manyuema, he had written to a friend: 'Had I known all the hunger, hardship, toil and time required, I might have preferred a strait-waistcoat to undertaking the task; but having taken it in hand, I could not bear to be beaten by it.'[14]

At last, on 9 August, an advance party of Stanley's men marched into Tabora; Livingstone could not contain his excitement. 'How thankful I am I cannot confess,' he wrote in his journal.[15] Stanley had sent fifty-six men in all. They had been extremely carefully chosen and twenty had served on Stanley's journey to Ujiji. Six were Nassick boys, who had been members of the abortive Relief Expedition, and the rest had been taken on at Bagamoyo on the coast. The men had all been engaged to serve for twenty-five to thirty dollars a year each for two years. Stanley had written into their contracts that if Livingstone's work should still be incomplete at the end of their term of service they should stay with him until he had reached a place where he could take on new porters. Stanley had equipped each man with a musket and had provided ten kegs of powder and three thousand bullets. Flour, sugar, coffee, tea, numerous varieties of tinned food, a new journal, a chronometer and a pile of Nautical Almanacs were included in the stores the men came with. In addition there were two riding donkeys, hundreds of yards of cloth and a slave chain, 'with which', Stanley told Livingstone in a letter carried by the men, 'you may imprison in iron collars any incorrigibles you may have'.[16] Livingstone, not surprisingly, never used the iron collars, but he was touched by Stanley's letter which reflected the sharp contrasts of the man himself, juxtaposing affection, exhortation and self-interest in a single paragraph.

My dear Doctor, very few amongst men have I found I so much got to love as yourself . . . England and America expect their people to do their duty. Do yours as persistently as heretofore & come back to your friends and country to be crowned with the laurel, and I will go forth to do mine . . . Do not forget the *Herald* please. The *Herald* will be grateful to me for securing you as a Correspondent . . .[17]

As Livingstone surveyed his new party, the best equipped that he had ever had, he thanked God Stanley had come and told Agnes: 'That good brave fellow has acted as a son to me'.[18] It was not an overestimate. Livingstone now had just over sixty men, including the five men who had stayed with him since 1866: James Chuma, Abdullah Susi, Hamoydah Amoda and two of the Nassick boys, Mabruki (Nathaniel Cumba) and Edward Gardner.

A start was made on 25 August. Livingstone's intention was to travel south-west until he hit Tanganyika, and then to follow the lake south to its foot. From there he would head south-west, skirt the southern shore of Bangweolo and then march due west to Katanga and the four fountains. The first weeks of the journey were smooth in comparison with his experiences in 1866 and 1869. Nevertheless, a series of minor misfortunes would together prove significant. First of all, a case of dried milk was left behind in Unyanyembe. Then his ten cows were allowed to stray into a belt of tsetse and died as a result. Milk was the only food which restored Livingstone's health when he had dysentery, so these two misfortunes coming together did not augur well for the future. The tsetse fly also accounted for the expedition's best riding donkey, which was a severe loss.

In the past, rain and mud had been the greatest hindrance to travelling. Now heat proved almost as bad. Throughout September and October, Livingstone's journal was full of complaints about how the relentless sun sapped his strength and slowed down the pace of his men. The heat was so intense that the porters' bare feet were blistered and burned by the soil. In these conditions it was a mistake to hug the shores of Tanganyika, since this meant constantly clambering up hills and out of valleys. But Livingstone was determined to map the southern part of the lake. He had suffered a minor attack of fever and severe dysentery before reaching the lake in early October, and the extra effort he forced on himself prevented a satisfactory recovery. It was a sadly typical error. By the middle of October he was admitting that he felt tired and ill, and that every effort was made only with the greatest difficulty. In his own words, he felt 'constrained to lie like a log'. The tiredness was due more to dysentery than heat, although he himself did not care to confess as much.

By the beginning of October they were nearing the southern end of the lake, and the hardships of climbing were over. The rains, however, were not far off and although the going was easier, the country was thinly populated and food was hard to come by. On 9 November, Livingstone's old problem of anal bleeding stopped them all for a few days. It was a clear indication that in spite of his recuperation during Stanley's visit, his recovery had been superficial at best. He knew the rains were coming and his previous journey to Bangweolo had told him that even if he managed to avoid the worst swamps, he would still have to ford a multitude of small rivers and marshes. But severe bleeding was not going to deter him. It never seemed to occur to him that he should turn back. The basis for such incredible optimism was his survival of previous hardships. It was impossible for him to believe that anything he would encounter in the future could be worse than conditions he had already mastered in the past.

As they pressed on south the food shortage increased and it was probably because of this that he temporarily abandoned his original idea of passing to the south of Lake Bangweolo. In fact his hand was forced on 3 December by a local guide who told him that if he continued south-west the food situation would get worse. Reluctantly he allowed the guide to take him to the north-western shore of Bangweolo. This journey of 170 miles was to take over a month, for by mid-December the full fury of the rains had once again transformed the country. For day after day the rain fell, sometimes in sheets, sometimes in a thin steady drizzle. Streams burst their banks, flat land became swamp and the party was held up for days on end trying to get canoes to cross the larger rivers. All this time, Livingstone was seldom dry. Often he slept on a wet bed.

Ironically, when he was at the north-western corner of the lake and the guide told him if he continued straight ahead he would be going west as he wished, he refused to believe him. He was convinced he was actually east of the lake proper. This conviction was directly due to the faulty longitudes he had taken on his first visit to the lake in 1868. Those observations had been forty miles too much to the west and so now he reckoned he was far to the east of the position the guide claimed to have brought him to. He wanted to get to the southern shore of the lake to make sure there were no sources south of it, before heading for Katanga as planned. Local Africans told him the best way to get round the lake was to head south-west. To Livingstone, who imagined himself north-east of the lake, a south-westerly course seemed madness. In his view, it would take him into the lake itself and not round it. Had the guide taken him a bit further he would have recognized where he was, for then he would have been almost at the point where he had reached the lake in 1868; but Livingstone was determined to take no further advice from local people. By trying to persuade him to go south-west, he was convinced that they had proved themselves eager to force him round the lake by the longest route. Instead he would head east and get round that way. It was to prove a disastrous decision.

Four years before, he had wrongly concluded that the lake was 150 miles long from east to west. He had been taken out in a canoe by locals who had turned back just too soon for him to see that Bangweolo was really only twenty-five miles of true lake and for the rest was marsh and bog. Most of this marshland was to the east of the true lake and this was the direction in which he was now heading. The longer he went on, the more confused he became. He expected water but found only endless reeds and mud. There was no high ground from which he might see into the distance. By mid-January 1873 he was well to the east of Bangweolo, just where he had thought himself weeks before. Now he believed himself safe to head south and thus skirt the lake. If he had then been as far to the east as he believed himself to be, this decision would have been fine. But south from where he now was led straight into the swamps, which stretched away almost a hundred miles to the south.

No landmarks that he had picked out on his previous journey were any use to him, for in the rains everything looked completely different. In early February the sky cleared enough for him to make new observations for latitude. Had he believed his new observations were accurate, all might have been well, for these new figures proved that the guide had not been lying and that he himself had been mistaken all along. This Livingstone would not accept. In his view the observations he had made in 1868, in far better conditions, were more likely to have been right. He concluded that water had wrecked the reflectors of his sextant and so ignored his new discoveries. From that time on he was doomed. For the next two months he would never again be sure where he was.[19]

By January of 1873 Livingstone's strength had reached a very low ebb. He was losing blood daily and with the constant cold and wet and the lack of milk and decent food there was no hope of his condition improving. The party rarely covered more than a mile and a half a day and even that was taxing their leader's powers to their limit. Hour after hour they all waded through oozing mud and overflowing streams. The wonder is that hardly any men deserted. All now seemed tied to the lonely man and felt unable to abandon him. Often Livingstone had to be carried across streams and rivers on the shoulders of his men, but they did not complain. These rivers were usually pitted with deep hollows and were sometimes half a mile wide. As Livingstone wrote on 24 January: 'Carrying me across one of the broad deep sedgy rivers is really a very difficult task . . . The first part, the main stream came up to Susi's mouth, and wetted my seat and legs. One held up my pistol behind, then one after another took a turn, and when he sank into a deep elephant's footprint, he required two to lift him.'[20]

As though the cold and the rain were not enough, they were also plagued by leeches, and when they did find dry ground, it was usually occupied by red ants. One night, as he lay in bed, Livingstone was attacked by an army of them. 'The first came on my foot quietly, then some began to bite between the toes, then the larger ones swarmed over the foot and bit furiously, and made the blood start out. I then went out of the tent and my whole person was instantly covered as close as small pox.'[21] Amazingly, Livingstone used this experience for scientific observation and described the shape and size of their mandibles and how they used their six legs to acquire leverage to bite. Nor was this an isolated example of his devoting time to minute observation. Whenever anything of interest occurred he noted it down, even something as apparently trivial as the appearance of a small frog. The following passage shows not only Livingstone's ability to forget himself in his appreciation of nature but also his complete lack of self-pity and complaining during these dreadful months.

Caught in a drenching rain, which made me fain to sit, exhausted as I was, under an umbrella for an hour trying to keep the trunk dry. As I sat

8 'The main stream came up to Susi's mouth'

in the rain a little tree-frog, about half an inch long, leaped on to a grassy leaf, and began a tune as loud as that of many birds, and very sweet; it was surprising to hear so much music out of so small a musician. I drank some rain water as I felt faint—in the paths it is now calf deep. I crossed a hundred yards of slush waist deep in mid channel, and full of holes made by elephant's feet, the path hedged in by reedy grass, often inter-twined and very tripping. I stripped off my clothes on reaching my hut in a village, and a fire during night nearly dried them. At the same time I rubbed my legs with palm oil, and in the morning had a delicious breakfast of sour goat's milk and porridge.[22]

But miraculously stoical though he was, the steady loss of blood and increasing weakness soon affected his thinking again. From now on he became more and more obsessive about the Nile and Herodotus' four foun-tains. Hopelessly lost, and by now bleeding slowly to death, Livingstone began writing despatches to the Foreign Secretary—despatches that would never be sent. Livingstone wrote as though he had already made his discovery; pathetically, only dates and geographical positions are omitted.

I have the pleasure of reporting to your Lordship that on the,   I succeeded at last in reaching your four remarkable fountains, each of which, at no great distance off, becomes a large river. They rise at the base of a swell of land or earthen mound, which can scarcely be called a hill, for it seems only about,   feet above the general level. Possibly these four gushing fountains may be the very same that were mentioned to Herodotus ... The geographical position of the mound or low earthen hill, may for the present be taken as latitude,   and longi-tude,   . The altitude above the sea,   .[23]

Then, as if waking from a dream, he remembers that the discovery is not yet made but still cannot admit it. Instead he will keep the fountains and confess as a postscript that the sources may lead to the Congo and not the Nile. That was the old doubt that still haunted him, while he listened to the falling rain and heard the screaming of the fish eagle. All around him stretched the flat deserted marshes and the unbroken lead-grey sky.

In late March he managed to get canoes to take his party on south-east through the marshy eastern stretches of the lake. In the end they would reach dry land; they would have to. Sitting in the canoes it was still harder to see where they were going and at this stage Livingstone probably passed one of the islands he had seen from a distance on his first visit in 1868. But reeds blotted out the view and on they went, punting six hours

at a time. The night was spent on a small treeless lump of land just above
the level of the water. 'No sooner did we land than a pitiless pelting rain
came on. We turned up a canoe to get shelter . . . The wind tore the tent
out of our hands and damaged it too. The loads are all soaked, and with
the cold it is bitterly uncomfortable. A man put my bed into the bilge, so
I was safe for a wet night.'[24]

The following morning, suffering the agonies of internal haemorrhage,
he wrote defiantly: 'Nothing earthly will make me give up my work in
despair. I encourage myself in the Lord my God and go forward.' But a
week more of punting in the constant rain, with no proper food and no
warmth, weakened him still further, and by 10 April he had to admit the
seriousness of his position. 'I am pale, bloodless and weak from bleeding
profusely ever since the 31st. of March last: an artery gives off a copious
stream and takes away my strength. Oh how I long to be permitted by the
Over Power to finish my work.'[25]

At this time the canoes were abandoned and the party went on again
on foot. Two hours' walking made Livingstone dizzy and weak. Soon he
was forced to lie down for long periods after any exertion. He fought
against being carried, but there seemed no alternative; in the past he had
only been helped across rivers, now he would be carried across drier
ground as well. But he still did not stop making observations, and went
on measuring rainfall in his portable gauge, and noted down any forms of
vegetation he had not seen before. After a long description of a species of
fish and its feeding habits, Livingstone went on to record with a beautiful
image how haunting he found the voice of the fish eagle. 'It is pitched in
a high falsetto key, very loud, and seems as if he were calling to some one
in the other world.' This was the only hint he gave until very near the end
that he knew how little time was left to him.

Now the party was moving south-west again, away from the worst
swamps, in a broad arc round the south of Bangweolo. It was what
Livingstone had initially hoped to do in November and December the
previous year. Now it was mid-April.

Even in the face of his rapidly increasing weakness he was inclined to
make light of the agonizing pain he was suffering: 'Very ill all night, but
remembered that the bleeding and most other ailments in this land are
forms of fever. Took two scruple doses of quinine and stopped it quite.'
The next day, 19 April, he wrote the greatest of all his many understate-
ments: 'It is not all pleasure this exploration.' The same day he confessed
himself almost too weak to hold a pencil. That Sunday, he managed to
read aloud some prayers to his men and to travel on a few hours, crossing
a small river in a canoe. 'The river', he wrote, with his old precision, 'is
about thirty yards broad, very deep, and flowing in marshes two knots

from S.S.E. to N.N.W. into Lake.'[26] This was the last detailed observation he made, although, while he could still write, he noted the number of hours marched each day.

On 21 April he knew that he was too weak to walk unassisted even a few steps, but he still tried to ride the surviving donkey. It was no use, as he soon discovered. After a few yards he fell to the ground, exhausted and faint. Susi at once lifted him, undid his belt and pistol and picked up his scarcely recognizable consul's cap, the insignia of office. His men then carried him back to his hut. Death was near now, but Livingstone wished to travel onwards while he still lived. Back in the village he sent men to ask the chief for guides to take him on further the following day.

Seeing that he would not walk again, but knowing that he would not rest in one place, Chuma and Susi constructed a litter or *kitanda* for the remaining miles. Next day they moved again as Livingstone recorded: '22nd. April—Carried on kitanda over Buga S.W. 2 ¼ [hours].'

For the next three days they carried the dying man on through the same flooded, treeless waste. On the 25th when they reached a village, Livingstone summoned a number of local men and with great difficulty asked them whether they knew about a hill and four adjacent fountains. All shook their heads. They were not travellers and all who used to go trading to the west were now dead. Unable to conceal his grief, Livingstone dismissed them, explaining that he was too ill to continue talking. If the fountains existed, surely they would have known. Perhaps he remembered his despatch to Lord Granville: 'But what if these fountains exist only in my imagination!—Then we shall see.'[27] To have come so far and to have suffered so much for yet another disappointment seemed intolerable.

On the 26th Livingstone gave his men the first clear indication that he expected to die soon. He instructed Susi to count over the bags of beads and to see to the purchase of two tusks to exchange for trade goods on the way back to Zanzibar. Despite this, Susi was uncertain whether the Doctor meant that he now thought of returning to the coast himself, or whether he was attempting to work out whether Susi and the others would have enough supplies to reach Zanzibar without him.

On 27 April Livingstone made the last entry in his journal: 'Knocked up quite and remain—recover—sent to buy milch goats. We are on the banks of R. Molilamo.'[28]

Milk was all-important, for when Livingstone was given mapira corn pounded up with ground-nuts, he was unable to eat it. By the next day no goats had been found and so no milk could be procured. Even so, Livingstone still wished to press on while life remained. Since by now he could not walk even to the door of his hut to reach his *kitanda* outside, he

9 The last entries in Livingstone's Journal. Incredibly, during the last week of his life, Livingstone was still making precise geographical observations: noting down thermometer readings for temperature, the width of rivers, their speed and exact direction of flow. From 22 April for four days he was too weak to write anything except the number of hours travelled: a total of 81/4 hours for the four days. In his pain and exhaustion he multiplied this figure by four to get 33 miles. But four miles an hour would be impossible in the circumstances. He was probably thinking back to the days when that had been his regular pace. The last entry on 27 April reads: 'Knocked up quite and remain—recover—sent to buy milch goats. We are on the banks of R. Molilamo.'

instructed the men to break down the wall of the hut and bring the litter up to his bed. Although his followers knew that all further progress was hopeless, they honoured his wishes. He would have few more demands to make. So on the 29th they pressed on.

After several hours a substantial river had to be crossed, and, since none of the canoes were wide enough to take the *kitanda*, he had to be lifted bodily. The pain, as he was carried the few feet into the canoe, was excruciating and the slightest pressure on his back was too great to be endured. As would be seen later, there was a clot of blood the size of a man's fist obstructing his lower intestine.

Once they had landed on the western bank they approached the village of Chitambo, a headman among the local Lala people. They were now seventy miles south-south-east of the southern shore of Lake Bangweolo. As they carried him towards the small village he often had to beg them to stop, for the slightest jolt was anguish to him. When his pain was less acute, Chuma and Susi noticed a deep drowsiness stealing over him. Some of the men had gone on to build a hut for him in the village and it was nearly completed when Livingstone's bearers arrived.

His followers did what they could to make his final resting place comfortable. The bed was raised from the floor by sticks and grass and his medicine chest was placed by the side of the bed on a packing case. It was agreed that somebody should keep constant watch with him night and day.

On 30 April Chief Chitambo came to pay a courtesy visit but Livingstone sent him away. He was too ill to speak. He dozed through the day, only occasionally troubling his people. On one occasion he asked Susi to hold his watch so that he could wind it, and on another, asked why some men outside were shouting. Then, in the evening, he asked Susi suddenly: 'Is this the Luapula?'* Susi told him gently that they were in Chitambo's village, near a small stream called the Lulimala. 'How many days is it to the Luapula?' he asked next. Susi told him three. A little later, as if utterly drained, he half sighed: 'Oh dear, dear!' and then fell asleep.

An hour later Susi was called to his bedside and was asked by his master to boil some water. Next Livingstone asked him to bring his medicine chest. Susi did this and opened it. He had to hold a candle very near to Livingstone's face, for his sight was failing. With a terrific effort the Doctor managed to select a little calomel. Then he asked Susi to pour some hot water into a cup and to bring another empty one. When Susi had done this Livingstone murmured: 'All right: you can go out now.'

Shortly after this, Majwara, the boy left to watch, fell asleep. He did not wake for three or four hours.

At 4 a.m. he burst into Susi's hut, in terrible distress, begging him to come at once. Susi roused Chuma and three others, and the six of them went to their master's hut. The sky was faintly tinged with the first light of dawn. A dim glow came from the entrance of the hut; a candle stuck with its own wax on to the top of a box was still burning. To their amazement, Livingstone was no longer in his bed. As he had felt death coming, with a final superhuman effort, he had somehow managed to raise himself into a kneeling position on his bed with his head on the pillow. For a

---

* The Luapula was the river linking Lake Bangweolo with Lake Moero and the Lualaba.

moment it seemed as though he was praying. Susi and the others did not go in at once but waited for some movement. When they saw none, one went in and touched the kneeling man's cheek. It was almost cold. David Livingstone had been dead for several hours.[29]

For the sixty Africans who had followed Livingstone's instructions without question since leaving Unyanyembe the previous August, the sudden loss of their leader, so far from their homes, could have proved catastrophic. Certainly, had the party broken up and the trade goods been thoughtlessly sold off and plundered, it is doubtful whether any could have reached the coast; but from the morning of Livingstone's death, Susi, Chowpereh and Manua Sera—Livingstone's appointed leaders—acted with a calm decisiveness that no European could have bettered. Jacob Wainwright wrote that Susi and the others knew that the easiest and safest course would have been to bury the body at the earliest opportunity and then to return to the coast. They were well aware of the powerful superstitions held by many tribes about corpses. At best, if they were discovered carrying a body through some villages, they would be fined heavily; at worst they might be attacked as witches. But a decision was made by the common consent of the entire party, arrived at after 'consultation', that the body should be preserved and, whatever the risks involved, carried to the coast and shipped to England for burial.[30] The majority, who had been engaged by Stanley, were of the same opinion in this matter as Livingstone's longest-serving men. It has recently been suggested that Livingstone's men may really have brought his body to Bagamoyo to protect themselves against possible charges of desertion or, worse still, murder. Of course their production of his eviscerated body would not have constituted proof that he had not been murdered. Since one of them—Jacob Wainwright—had written an inventory of all Livingstone's possessions including his diaries—all of which were to be brought to the coast—it seems most unlikely that they were unaware that Livingstone's diaries contained entries making clear just how ill he had been, and that these passages would have established their innocence. Jacob and several other former pupils of Nassick School could all read and write well in English.[31]

It will never be known how these Africans really saw Livingstone. He never discussed his aims with them, or asked their point of view, and yet without doubt they respected and admired him. Susi and the other leaders knew the names of the rivers he was seeking, as well as his keen interest in their relationship with the Lualaba, but even though these few would have had some knowledge of his immediate geographical aims, they certainly would not have appreciated why he had subjected himself to such suffering simply to find the source of a river and the direction in which it flowed. As one chief had once told Livingstone scornfully, when asked about a lake, 'It is only water—nothing to be seen'. Yet, despite their puzzlement, none of these men with Livingstone, during the last months of his life, left him. They too waded through the mud and the water, suffered rheumatism, sores, malaria and exhaustion. Susi, Chuma and Gardner had been with their leader every day since he had landed in Africa in 1866; they had stayed when all the others deserted, they had given up their own food so that Livingstone could eat, had carried him when he could not walk, had done their best to conceal his physical weakness from strangers. They had always known that Livingstone was not rich and could never make them adequate recompense for their service. The reason for their devotion was Livingstone's gentleness with all Africans. Most explorers kept their expeditions together by rigid discipline and frequent floggings, yet Livingstone had used a cane and other threats very reluctantly and only when exasperated beyond endurance or when encountering Africans involved in enslaving their own people. He had always worked on the principle that, since his men were not slaves, they should be allowed to leave him when they wished. It is a pathetic irony that, if Livingstone had shown his colleagues on the Zambesi a quarter of the tolerance and kindness that he reserved for Africans, he would have been a successful and popular leader of his fellow countrymen.

The day after Livingstone's death, Chuma went to see the local chief, Chitambo, and, hiding the fact that his master was dead, told him that the white man's followers wanted permission to build an enclosure outside the village, since they did not like living among the huts. The chief gave his consent, and work began the same day. A group of huts was built within a palisade. Slightly apart from the domestic buildings, a separate hut was constructed. This structure was open to the sky at the top and had especially strong walls to keep out wild animals. Inside, the corpse was prepared for the journey. An incision was made in the abdomen, and the intestines and internal organs were removed, placed in a tin box and buried. Jacob Wainwright, one of the Nassick boys sent out with Stanley's men, read the burial service as the box was lowered into the ground. When taking out the intestines, Chuma and Susi noticed a clot of blood several inches in diameter obstructing Livingstone's lower intestine. Such a large obstruction must have caused horrifying pain.

To preserve the body, the Africans first placed salt in the open trunk and next allowed the corpse to dry for fourteen days in the sun—the dry season was beginning. The body was moved a fraction once a day. Since the hut had no roof there was no need for this slightly macabre process to be observed.

When the prescribed period was completed, the face was bathed in brandy, as an extra preservative, and when the body had been wrapped in calico and encased in a cylinder of bark, it was sewn into a large piece of sailcloth. Susi added the finishing touch when he tarred the whole bundle to make doubly sure that it was watertight. The whole operation was efficient and quick.

Susi's abilities as a leader were confirmed by the speed with which he led his party to Unyanyembe—five months. During that time ten men died.[32] They suffered all the usual ravages of disease and on one occasion had to fight their way out of a hostile village. At Unyanyembe they met a group of Englishmen, who were leading out another Livingstone Relief party. This expedition was quite as unhappy as its immediate predecessor. Already one of its members, a grandson of Robert Moffat, had died of fever, and another, W.E. Dillon, would shortly blow his brains out. The leader was Lieutenant V. Lovett Cameron who had been sent by the R.G.S. to help Livingstone finish his work.

When Cameron had talked to the men he was satisfied that their master had died of natural causes and therefore urged Susi and the others to bury the body without delay to avoid being attacked as witches. If fear of becoming murder suspects had really motivated them, they would have done as Cameron advised the moment they thought themselves above suspicion. But they were acting out of respect to their dead master and, to their credit, politely refused to bury him and reiterated their determination to reach the coast.[33] Cameron then looked over the boxes and took Livingstone's geographical instruments for the use of his own party. Susi was reluctant to part with these but felt unable to resist. Perhaps Cameron's overbearing manner partly prepared Susi for what was to come when he reached Bagamoyo in February 1874.

Chuma was sent on to Zanzibar and there he discovered that Kirk was in England on leave and that Captain W.F. Prideaux was acting for him. Prideaux, on hearing that Livingstone's body was at Bagamoyo, despatched a warship, the disconcertingly named H.M.S. *Vulture*, to collect the corpse. Although Prideaux was aware that these sixty Africans had performed an amazing feat, he was completely at a loss to decide what should be done. He was only standing in for Kirk, and was too timid to risk sending any of Livingstone's men back to England with the body without first getting the consent of the Foreign Office. This, however, could never be achieved in time, so Prideaux decided that, rather than be blamed later for causing the Foreign Office unnecessary expense, he would pay the men—he had to do so out of his own pocket since Livingstone's last £1,000 had been spent—and send them to their homes. Prideaux would not recover his money from the Government until 1877. But the sixty Africans who had risked so much were not in a position to understand the acting Consul's financial dilemmas. At great personal risk they had brought the body of a man, whom they supposed to be famous in his own country, to the coast, and they were being sent away with their wages. For Chuma, Susi and Gardner it seemed a ludicrous ending to eight years' service. By the time the Royal Geographical Society struck commemorative medals for the fifty surviving men the following year, they had all dispersed and very few ever received this reward, which they would never have understood anyway; cloth, beads, rifles, cattle would have been fine—but a medal! Chuma and Susi in the end did gain by their association with Livingstone. A year later, James 'Paraffin' Young, who had given Livingstone such important financial aid, paid for his two best known servants to come to England to help edit the explorer's *Last Journals*, and fill in verbally any gaps in the narrative. After that they both returned to Zanzibar and became much sought-after caravan leaders.

One African attended Livingstone's funeral in Westminster Abbey and he, ironically, had only been with Livingstone since August 1872; but because Jacob Wainwright had been a pupil at the Church Missionary Society's Nassick School, the missionaries paid his passage to England as a fund-raising exercise. Chuma and Susi arrived too late to see Livingstone buried.

Had Livingstone known that his followers were never to receive any reward from the Government, he would not have been surprised; it would have been merely the last of many disappointments.

24

Livingstone and the British Empire

⟨⟩◆⟨⟩

The morning of 15 April 1874 was wet and windy, but shortly after dawn crowds started forming round the docks and quays of Southampton. By eight o'clock the Mayor and Aldermen of the town, dressed in their fur-trimmed robes, stood assembled on the quay. Behind them a military band was waiting, and not far away a company of the Royal Horse Artillery prepared to fire off a 21-gun salute at minute intervals. A long procession of black-draped carriages was being lined up just behind the main quay, but few eyes were concerned with preparations on land; the crowd and the reporters, the official artists and photographers were all looking out to sea.

A few minutes before nine, the silhouette of a battered and insignificant-looking steamer was sighted at the mouth of Southampton Water. The first of the salutes boomed out across the silent town, the band broke into the opening bars of the 'Dead March from Saul' and the telegraph operators started eagerly tapping out the news. Through binoculars it was soon possible to see on the deck a coffin draped with a Union Jack. Beside the Mayor and Aldermen a small black boy had now taken his place and lifted up a placard decorated with sable rosettes and streamers, bearing the inscription: 'To the memory of Dr Livingstone, friend of the African'.

The body was conveyed from Southampton to London by special train, and that evening was examined at the headquarters of the Royal Geographical Society so that a positive identification could be made. After eleven months the features were unrecognizable, but the lump in the bone of the left humerus, which had been shattered by a lion nearly thirty years before, was perfect proof.

For the next two days the body lay in state at the R.G.S. building in Savile Row, and crowds filed past the coffin. On 18 April burial took place in Westminster Abbey. The press acclaimed the hero and announced his virtues.

Westminster Abbey has opened her doors to men who have played larger and greater parts in the history of mankind; but the feeling amongst many this afternoon was, that seldom has been admitted one more worthy—one more unselfish in his devotion to duty—one whose ruling desire was stronger to benefit his kind and advance the sum of human knowledge and civilization—than the brave, modest, self-sacrificing, African explorer. The virtues which distinguished Livingstone are those which our country has always been ready to acknowledge, which our religion has taught us to revere, and seek to cultivate and conserve.[1]

Livingstone's bravery, endurance and self-sacrifice during his last years deserved tributes like this one. His dogged refusal to give up in the face of hopeless odds, his uncomplaining acceptance of agonizing pain and finally his lonely death, conjure up images so powerful that his contemporaries' adulation seems, in retrospect, the only possible response. That any man could voluntarily have undergone such hardship seemed, and still seems, so remarkable that to ask whether he achieved his aims or deceived himself appears in the end almost churlish. The fact that Livingstone in his last years had allowed himself to accept as true what he had wanted to believe, rather than what his scientific observations suggested, seems to call for sympathy rather than criticism. Those who wept in the streets on the day of his funeral did not know that the Lualaba was not the Nile— had they done so, it is doubtful whether they would have cared. Knowledge of Livingstone's mistake would only have deepened for them the pathos of his death. Very few found it necessary to examine his aims or to ask whether a search for the Nile's source had anything to do with missionary work or the spreading of Christianity.

In analysing the life of a great man—and Livingstone was undoubtedly great—there is always a basic problem: to be great is to be different, so ordinary criteria of judgement fall short. The point at which determination becomes obsession, and self sacrifice self-destruction, is very hard to estimate. Yet even if Livingstone's determination is called obsessive—and it was—it must be acknowledged that without this inflexibility he would never have left the mills, never have qualified as a doctor and never have ended his life in the swamps of Bangweolo; without it, too, he would have made a better husband and father, and a more approachable and likeable man. In the same way, had Livingstone been a precise and rational thinker rather than an idealist, he would never have attempted to cross Africa without backing or his own supplies, nor would he ever have managed to persuade the Government that he was the man to lead a full-scale expedition. Optimism enabled him to take on tasks which rational men would never have attempted; optimism also led to most of his disappointments and failures. Very often his best qualities were also his worst.

As a man, Livingstone had been marked for life by the harshness of his childhood. His efforts to leave the mills had been laughed at by other boys, and this had stiffened his determination rather than weakened it. Throughout his career, opposition and derision increased his efforts and strengthened his will. It is as true today as it was in the 1840s that between the ages of eighteen and twenty-five most young men learn, through close contact with other people, to accept that earlier ambitions and ideals may have been pitched too high. They come to realize that there are limits to their own abilities, and in marrying, or forming close attachments, are forced to recognize that compromise and concession are vital for the success of any close relationship. Until he was twenty-seven, Livingstone had studied medicine and theology so intensely that he had never had time to make these normal adjustments, and as a result he would never really understand people. On arriving in Africa the ordinary human weaknesses of his missionary colleagues had seemed far worse to him than they would have done to anybody who had not suffered Livingstone's severely limited youth and young manhood. In southern Africa there was no opportunity for Livingstone to gain that knowledge of other people which he had failed to acquire in Britain. He rowed with his colleagues, Ross and Edwards, because he could not make any allowances for their failings, which were not extreme; in the end he even quarrelled with the Moffats, whom he had admired. His marriage, which was in part one of convenience, brought no change. He saw his wife's position as that of an inferior rather than an equal partner and he rarely found time to play with his children. The closest relationships he formed were by letter—friendships at a distance.

In the long periods devoted to travel—he spent four and a half years alone on his trans-continental journey—his isolation deepened, and he returned still less aware of normal human motives and feelings. His thinking, too, started to suffer, since for years at a time he had nobody with whom to discuss his hopes and ideas. By crossing Africa he had performed an almost superhuman feat, but he seems not to have realized his own uniqueness, and he expected others to be able to reach similar attainments. When his colleagues on the Zambesi fell ill, and could not endure hardships which he considered routine, he despised them for it. This scorn became so pronounced that in the end he was able to shrug off the deaths of the missionaries, whom he had encouraged to come to the Zambesi and the Shire Highlands, as just another form of spinelessness and lack of guts. Horror of failure, which he never felt able to discuss with others, led him to lie deliberately and to blame innocent people for situations for which his own over-optimism was alone responsible. People were judged not as human beings but for their use, or lack of use, in carrying out his plans; and however important his objects, the callousness resulting from this attitude must rank as his major defect. His loyalty to Africans and his faith in their capacities were limitless, but he was easily swayed, on the scantiest of evidence, into believing the worst of fellow-countrymen who had previously served him well. As a leader of Europeans he was indecisive, unpredictable and unjust.

Livingstone's yearnings for praise and recognition were very human weaknesses, especially in view of his struggle to get out of the mills. Even his frequent denials of ambition, taken side by side with his determined efforts to prevent others gaining any credit for discoveries, were not serious flaws, although they dented his public reputation for modesty and selflessness. But Livingstone's love of fame never destroyed his real altruism. His frequent soul-searchings, about the purity of his motives and the ambiguity of his aims, are proof of that. He wanted to be thought well of, but, even if it led to self-deception, he had to be able to convince himself that his work had objectives beyond mere discovery.

The man's character and his aims can only be judged together, for his thinking was largely a product of his optimism and idealism. His whole life up to his arrival in Africa had been governed by his inflated hopes of missionary prospects there. When he saw the real situation, the shock was overwhelming, but, unlike most young missionaries, he had not accepted the inevitable limitations and compromises of conventional static missionary work. He needed definite hopes and aims and soon managed to supply new ones to replace those which circumstances had destroyed. Until his death, he had to convince himself that he was following a plan which would ultimately bring Christianity to vast new areas of Africa.

In the Zambesi he had seen a highway for traders and missionaries to use in a combined penetration of the interior. His thesis was that without commerce Christianity could not drive out the slave trade and could not persuade the Africans to abandon old customs. The argument that good trade drives out bad is fallacious, but Livingstone's main hope was that if formerly self-sufficient tribes traded with each other, their isolation would diminish and they would thus become less conservative and more receptive to new ideas. The introduction of currency might break down the power of petty chiefs and teach men to see themselves as individuals rather than members of a collective whole. Finally, if trade brought prosperity, the Africans might associate their new wealth with the Gospel. While Livingstone was well aware that those imagining that they might one day be able to build steam-engines—if they accepted Christ—were in for a shock, he was prepared to let them harbour plenty of lesser dreams for the sake of Christian expansion.

Soon the impracticality of the Zambesi as a highway, the climate and the harsh travelling conditions convinced Livingstone that private trade would be inadequate for the great task. Although in his early days in Africa he had felt that one race had no right to destroy the institutions and way of life of another, and had seen much to applaud in tribal society, from the late 1850s he correctly diagnosed the root cause for the rejection of Christianity: traditional African culture itself. Colonization, he next maintained, would not only give traders and missionaries security but would force social change on the Africans, destroying their customs and institutions and so leaving them psychologically prone to accepting a new set of beliefs. Colonization on the pattern of a minority of whites ruling, albeit philanthropically, a vast majority of blacks, became his main preoc-cupation. The failure of the Zambesi Expedition and the withdrawal of the Universities Mission made colonization less likely but, in Livingstone's view, no less indispensable. The Government thought otherwise and gave Livingstone repeated proof of their thinking.

Government rejection of his colonial plans, the extermination of the Makololo and the chaos in the Shire Highlands spelt the end of Livingstone's conception of his role as a divinely appointed guide for others to follow into the interior. By the mid-1860s all Livingstone's ideas seemed merely to have led him into a hopeless dead end. Throughout his life, Livingstone had conveniently jettisoned old plans and theories if they did not fit new circumstances—realistic perhaps, but a habit which too easily made former protestations seem insincere. In the end Livingstone could no longer persuade himself that he had a coherent set of aims. His search for the source of the Nile was a purely geographical task, and because often he could not believe that anything he might say or do could do much damage to the slave trade—incorrectly as it turned out—he had no real compensatory motive. The fact that he had once advanced radical ideas for 'progress' and change in Africa merely sharpened his sense of failure and defeat.

But he remained convinced that colonization was the answer, and in his attempt to convince people in Britain that they had a 'mission' in Africa, he had gone much further than he would have wished in endorsing the values of a British industrial society, which, in the past, he had acknowl-edged as leading to exploitation of the poor and to terrible social condi-tions. He also conveniently forgot that his previous experience of settlers, both English and Dutch, in southern Africa had convinced him that contact with Europeans often made Africans worse. Yet from the early 1860s Livingstone argued without reservation that the effects of new settlers in central Africa would be entirely beneficial. As usual, adverse circumstances had brought about this volte-face, and his arguments were not saved from severe contradictions by his unworkable qualification that settlers should be Christian.

Yet if Livingstone's colonial ideas were at variance with much of his earlier thinking, he cannot be accused of being motivated by a desire to exploit Africans. Colonization might mean the destruction of tribal society, but Livingstone was realistic enough to see possible advantages. He had admired African generosity and the responsibility which chiefs took for their people's welfare, but he had also been aware, since his arrival on the Zambesi in 1851, that Africans themselves were eager participants in the slave trade. The way the Makololo had treated their subject tribes had also told him that existing tribal culture did not in any way guarantee that members of indigenous small communities would lead idyllic lives. In fact Livingstone had still more substantial reasons for advocating European intervention. Pleasant though it might be to suppose that central and eastern Africa could have escaped all alien contact and thus have developed peacefully along traditional lines, it is scarcely realistic. In the early 1850s Livingstone had met Arabs and Portuguese Angolan traders in Barotseland. In the late 1860s he had seen the Arabs extend their trading operations well into what is now the Congo. As the search for slaves and ivory went on and the gun frontier expanded, so too did wars. The difficulties which Livingstone encountered in the Shire Highlands in 1863 seemed to him to constitute unanswerable proof that the Africans in that area would be better off under a British administration. In view of the slave raids, the famine and the Ngoni incursions, his point of view is not hard to understand.

Livingstone's appreciation of the seriousness of the conditions in the interior made his misery at the British Government's non-intervention all the more acute, and deepened his sense of failure. Of course, by ordinary standards his exploration made him unique, and placed him in a different category from all other nineteenth-century explorers with the possible exception of Stanley. For a start, he had spent not just a few years in Africa, like most of his rivals, but thirty, the first fifteen of them continuous. He had also operated in a far wider range of country than any other explorer: a vast area defined by places as far apart as Ujiji and the Cape from north to south, and Zanzibar and Loanda from east to west. His contributions to African ethnology, natural history, tropical medicine and linguistics were, at the time, unparalleled. He had also done more than any single man to break down Victorian stereotypes of the African, either as the humbly kneeling slave of abolitionist propaganda, or as the irredeemable 'savage' depicted by so many missionaries and travellers. But Livingstone's ambitions had been more extensive than all this; his object had been to bring sweeping social change to Africa, and in the year of his

death the chances for this seemed more remote than when he had first
come to the continent thirty-three years before.

As the Zambesi Expedition had drawn to its painful and humiliating
conclusion in 1863, and Livingstone had watched the bodies of some of
the thousands of Africans who had died of starvation floating down the
Shire, he had not abandoned his hopes for the Shire Highlands. The slave
raids, the famine, the Ngoni attacks and the deaths of four out of seven
missionaries had left him unmoved. Even when the expedition had been
recalled and the mission withdrawn, he had been able to write with
apparent conviction: 'Viewing calmly all the circumstances, I could not
conceive of a sphere in which the missionary prospects would be more
inviting than that which has now been abandoned . . . I have no doubt
that it will be done though I may not be alive to hear of it . . . the future
will justify my words & hopes.'[2]
      At the time, these sentiments seemed yet another example of
Livingstone's insane over-optimism. But, incredibly, after his death the
future *did* justify his words and hopes, and, more surprisingly still, in
many instances it did so through the efforts of some of the very people
whom Livingstone had quarrelled with and scorned. James Stewart, the
young Free Church of Scotland missionary, who had felt rejected by
Livingstone on the Zambesi, played a leading part; and the despised
Universities Mission and the London Missionary Society also contributed. Even Bedingfeld, as the commander of the British East African
Squadron, and Charles Livingstone, as the British Consul on the
West African island of Fernando Po, returned to the continent they
had hated.
      The eulogies and tributes that followed Livingstone's funeral did not
have any effect on the way politicians viewed Africa, but they did influence thousands of ordinary men and women to give money to any philanthropic or missionary society with African connections. The *Daily
Telegraph* expressed the sentiments of the average missionary subscriber in
its obituary article: 'The work of England for Africa must henceforth
begin where Livingstone left it off.'[3]
      James Stewart was one man whom any observer of the later stages of
the Zambesi Expedition might have thought would be violently opposed
to beginning anything where Livingstone had left off. Before leaving
Africa, Stewart had hurled his copy of *Missionary Travels* into the
Zambesi with the words: 'So perish all that is false in myself and others.'[4]
Yet, during Livingstone's funeral in Westminster Abbey, Stewart under-
went a sudden and, as it seemed to him, miraculous change of heart. He
shortly made up his mind to start a Free Church of Scotland Mission on

the shores of Lake Nyassa. The name he intended to give this settlement was Livingstonia. The Free Church of Scotland gave its blessing, and Scottish businessmen donated the necessary funds. Stewart chose E.D. Young, who had been with Livingstone on the *Lady Nyassa* and had led the first Livingstone Search Expedition, to take out the initial contingent. At this stage the Established Church of Scotland also decided to send a party. Soon their missionaries had started a mission in the Shire Highlands, named after Livingstone's birthplace, Blantyre. Today Blantyre is the most populous town in Malawi. In due course the Free Church had also set up Livingstonia. Young had made all this possible by doing what he and Livingstone had failed to do in 1863—namely getting a steamer overland past the Murchison Cataracts and on to the lake. Livingstonia and Blantyre were viable settlements by the early 1880s.

Missionaries were not the only men who came to Lake Nyassa in response to the appeals following Livingstone's death. In 1878, John and Frederick Moir, brothers who had previously been successful businessmen, founded the Livingstonia Central Africa Company—later to be called the African Lakes Company. The capital had been subscribed by James Stevenson and Sir William Mackinnon, like the Moirs both Scottish. These two shipping magnates would finally donate over £1 million to African projects. Amazingly, within ten years of Livingstone's death, what Livingstone himself had predicted twenty years before had come to pass. Two Scottish missions and one Scottish company were operating in the Shire Highlands and on the shores of Lake Nyassa. The area was not yet under British Protection, and in 1887 the missionaries and the members of the African Lakes Company were attacked by Arabs in a series of well-planned raids.

When the news of these armed onslaughts became known in England and Scotland early in 1888, a vigorous campaign began with the single aim of forcing the Prime Minister, Lord Salisbury, into declaring a protectorate. In February 1888 the Member for Glasgow raised the matter in the Commons; in April supporters of the Scottish Missions, the Universities Mission and the African Lakes Company sent a deputation to see Salisbury. This was followed by a petition from a number of Members of Parliament. August saw the formation by Scottish businessmen of a Nyassa Anti-Slavery and Defence Fund to buy arms for the missionaries. One petition the Prime Minister received had been signed by the majority of ministers in both the Established and Free Church of Scotland, asking incredulously how the Government could dare sign away David Livingstone's heritage. With this proof of public opinion in Livingstone's native land, Salisbury felt few qualms about ending his previous policy of non-involvement in the region. In 1891 he declared a protectorate over the whole area. Livingstone's colony had come into being. But important events were not confined to one area.

In his lifetime, Livingstone had been powerless to dissuade the London Missionary Society and the Universities Mission from abandoning south-central and eastern Africa. As a direct result of his death, they returned to it. The efforts in both cases were led by men who had been associated with the previous withdrawals. Bishop Steere, Tozer's successor, led the Universities Mission to a settlement on the eastern shore of Lake Nyassa, and Roger Price, the same Price whom Livingstone had so mercilessly lashed for cowardice at Linyanti, began the search for suitable sites for London Missionary Society settlements near Lake Tanganyika.

Livingstone's influence on the course of Stanley's life had by itself enormous consequences for Africa. After the death of his hero, Stanley resolved to sort out whether Lake Victoria or the headwaters of Livingstone's Lualaba could be said to be the source of the Nile. To find this out he needed to circumnavigate Lake Victoria and Lake Tanganyika and then trace the Lualaba north and finally finish Livingstone's work. (It was his habit to call the Lualaba the Livingstone river.) Backed by the *Daily Telegraph* and the *New York Herald*, he did just this, in a feat of exploration that ranks with Livingstone's trans-continental journey. The result was to prove that the Lualaba was the Congo and that Speke, in 1862, had been justified in claiming that Lake Victoria (and its tributaries) was the source of the Nile.

Stanley's journey had one other result of almost equal importance. During his circumnavigation of Lake Victoria Stanley stayed with Mutesa, the Kabaka of Buganda, on the northern shores of the lake. During this time Mutesa convinced Stanley that he wanted missionaries to come to his country. The Kabaka's real desire was to gain protection from the Khedive of Egypt's ambitions in Equatoria. Nevertheless Stanley took him at his word and in April 1875 wrote an appeal for missionaries, which was published in the *Daily Telegraph* later that year.

The consequences were momentous. The Anglican Church Missionary Society and the French Roman Catholic missionary order of White Fathers decided to make Uganda their African field. Before the arrival of these two parties, political intrigue was the order of the day in Mutesa's kingdom. A strong Arab faction had been established at his court for some years. Clearly the arrival of two rival groups of missionaries was going to bring quite unimaginable complications. Within a year both groups of missionaries realized just what they had let themselves in for: religious groupings were adopted by members of opposing political factions in the Kabaka's court. An alliance of one religious group *with* the Kabaka *against* the other formation could easily result in the massacre of the adherents of the isolated party. To guard against this, the rival missionaries armed their supporters and were soon able to put a thousand men into the field against all comers—whether the Kabaka, the Muslims or the opposing Christian party. Only a spark was needed to create an international incident. That spark came when Sir William Mackinnon's Imperial British East Africa Company entered Uganda with the primary object of forestalling a rival German company. The arrival of a British company in a country where the balance of power was almost equally divided between the armed supporters of French and British missionaries could only produce a crisis. The French, to protect their position, convinced the Kabaka that the British would depose him unless he was prepared to fight. An alliance was duly formed. This isolated the British missionaries and meant that if war broke out, the company would have to intervene on their countrymen's behalf. This was precisely what happened in January 1892.

During the next two years the Uganda issue almost split the Liberal Party wide open. Gladstone favoured a complete rejection of any further African advances; Rosebery, his Foreign Secretary, was determined that Uganda should become a protectorate. In April 1894 Rosebery got his way and Uganda became a British protectorate, but he could never have fought and won a battle to annex Uganda, had he not been able to utilize the public support whipped up by the missionary societies and individuals such as Livingstone's good friend, Henry Morton Stanley. So great was this support that a Liberal Government, committed to a policy of Home Rule for Ireland, was able paradoxically to create a new African colony. Afterwards Sir Edward Grey, justifying for the Government what appeared to be a Conservative and not a Liberal decision, said: 'If we had abandoned Uganda, we should have had month by month news of most sinister consequences reaching this country. The Government would have been assailed on all sides as being responsible.'[5] There could have been no clearer admission that the missionaries had made the annexation by Liberal politicians possible; and the missionaries, of course, had gone there in response to the appeals initiated by Stanley as a direct result of Livingstone's influence over him. The following year, to ensure that they had access to Uganda, the British Government negotiated with Germany to achieve control over the territory later known as Kenya. So, with the addition of Rhodesia—the area comprising modern Zimbabwe and Zambia—through the efforts of Cecil Rhodes, almost two-thirds of Britain's colonial empire in Africa had been secured.

The influence of Livingstone in Nyasaland and, through Stanley, in Uganda paved the way for still more colonial advances. The link is very clear, for had the missionaries not been inspired by Livingstone's death, and had the funds not poured in from Scottish philanthropists, there would have been no crisis on Lake Nyassa in 1887 and no war in Uganda in 1892. The presence of the missionaries and the operations of men like the Scot Sir William Mackinnon, had created the situations which gave rise to annexation.

But Livingstone's influence on Stanley's career, and thus on African history, went further than the British acquisition of Uganda and Kenya. Among Stanley's many admirers, after his completion of Livingstone's geographical work, was King Leopold II of Belgium, a minor European monarch. For twenty years Leopold had longed to carve out an African colony and exploit it. In ignorance of the Belgian king's secret plans, Stanley agreed to return to the Congo as his Chief Agent and set up for him (as Stanley believed) international trading stations on the river so the Congolese would be able to exchange their ivory, hardwoods and gums for European manufactured goods, brought upriver by international traders.[6] This was a project he was sure that Livingstone would have approved. Between 1879 and 1884 Stanley also built a road past the cataracts on the Lower Congo and launched steamers on the upper river. This work would lay the foundations for the future Congo Free State, eventually the Belgian Congo—a disaster in the making that Stanley had no means of foreseeing. At the time, while working for Leopold, he would not have realized that he was playing a major part in kick-starting the 'Scramble for Africa'.

In November 1880, while Stanley was road-building on the lower Congo, an Italian-born French naval officer, Lieutenant Pierre Savorgnan de Brazza, walked into his camp. Eager to add to their West African possessions, the French government had funded Brazza to pioneer a route from the Gabon coast to the river Congo. Since Stanley (unlike Leopold) wanted the river to be opened to the traders of all nations, Brazza's arrival did not worry him.[7] But unknown to Stanley, the Frenchman had recently signed a treaty with the most important African ruler on the northern shores of Stanley Pool—the lake created by the accumulating waters of the Congo just before it cascades over the lower rapids. Brazza intended to claim this chief's territory for France. But to the south of the Pool, and also on the upper Congo, Stanley made other treaties with different chiefs, effectively excluding the French from making trading agreements in the land to the south of the Congo. When Brazza crossed the Pool in person and attempted to seize Kinshasa by force, Stanley's resolute employees drove him off.[8]

These events occurred soon after a greater French humiliation had already left France eager to make compensatory colonial advances in Africa. Following the Khedive of Egypt's bankruptcy in 1867, Britain and

France—the owners of the fifteen-year-old Suez Canal—had taken control of the country. But fifteen years later, a group of Egyptian army officers seized power just when France was paralysed by internal politics. So Britain acted alone to inflict a crushing defeat on the nationalists. Victory made Britain the de facto ruler of Egypt. Brazza's defeat on the Congo, and the Egyptian debacle caused deep French resentment. From now onwards the dream became widespread in France that the nation might one day link her West African colonies with Sudan and the river Nile—creating 'a bridge across Africa' in compensation for Britain's 'misdeeds'.[9] But at the Berlin Conference in 1884, due to British and German pressure, the lion's share of the immense Congo state went to Leopold, with the French only receiving the smaller northern tranche of territory.

Unless Stanley had gone to Africa to complete Livingstone's work, he would never have been employed by the Belgian king, who would not have acquired the immense colony which he (Leopold) would pillage so mercilessly. The Berlin Conference was called into being principally to adjudicate on Leopold's demand to be accepted as the legally recognized colonial authority in the Congo basin. The consequent carve-up of West Africa, principally by France, Belgium and Britain, motivated Germany to claim Togoland, Kameroun and South West Africa. The 'Scramble for Africa' had begun in earnest. Germany's next move would be in East Africa, where the Sultan of Zanzibar's empire extended inland from the coast to the great lakes.[10] In 1885, Germany declared a protectorate over almost that entire territory. So the earlier informal and voluntary responses to Livingstone's life and work by groups of philanthropic and religious people were succeeded by armed expeditions, sent to Africa by European rulers, as if in response to humanitarian pressure, but often, as in the case of Leopold on the Congo and the Germans in South West Africa, to carry out rapacious, self-interested agendas in the lands recently revealed by the explorers.

Ten years after the Berlin Conference, Britain seized Uganda. The year in question—1894—marked an important shift in British colonial history. Gladstone resigned and Home Rule for Ireland went with him. He also failed to curb British naval expenditure, just as he failed to curb expansion in Africa. With Salisbury's return to power in 1895, mid-Victorian liberal policies of isolation and laissez-faire had finally given way to assertive imperialism. Joseph Chamberlain took over the Colonial Office, determined to continue advances in Africa. By 1898 Nigeria had been acquired and the French thwarted. In the same year French ambitions on the upper Nile and their dream of linking their West African Empire with the Red Sea ended with Kitchener's victory over the Mahdist forces at Omdurman and Commandant Marchand's retreat from Fashoda. The Sudan, like Egypt, had become British beyond dispute.

So, twenty years after Livingstone's death, those colonies which he had advocated to Palmerston and Russell as likely to be of mutual advantage to Britain and Africa had come into being. Livingstone's ideas had been expressed more than thirty years too soon. During his lifetime he had been defeated because most people thought of the Empire in terms of the white-settled territories such as Australia, Canada and New Zealand. Empire was generally understood to be the link between the mother country and the extended family of self-governing Britons overseas. Empire did not convey a picture of a small population of whites governing millions of Africans and Asians. In 1876 Disraeli's Royal Titles Bill had added the style of Empress of India to Queen Victoria's other titles. The move had not been popular. India was not a white-settled territory and was therefore considered alien; its singling out therefore seemed to many people to be a slight on the 'real' colonial empire.

Events in Africa between 1874 and 1894 forced a reassessment of what the Empire really was. The addition of new African colonies, peopled not by whites but by blacks, changed the whole balance of the Empire and inevitably altered the way people in Britain viewed it. This new view was significantly influenced by Livingstone's ideas and those of his missionary successors.

When Joseph Chamberlain, speaking after the annexation of Uganda in 1894, dilated on Britain's 'manifest destiny' to be a 'great civilizing power',[11] the sentiment echoed Livingstone's instructions to the members of the Zambesi Expedition: 'We come among them as members of a superior race and servants of a Government that desires to elevate the more degraded portions of the human family . . . to become harbingers of peace to a hitherto distracted and trodden down race.'[12] The coupling of moral fervour with the right to power was implicit in much of what Livingstone had written about Britain's special duty and mission as a colonizing nation. He had suggested without reservation that on people of British stock depended the 'hopes of the world for liberty and progress',[13] and had claimed that the presence of Englishmen in Africa would be 'an unmixed advantage' to the Africans themselves.[14] By the 1890s, after the discovery of gold on the Witwatersrand, 'imperialism'—once a pejorative term associated by the British with the Empire of Napoleon III of France—was a respectable portmanteau word used to describe the forcible acquisition of colonies. Its supporters—both Tory and Liberal imperialists—dressed up their big idea in the philanthropic and religious phrases which were used by missionaries to justify their own intrusion into far-flung parts of the world. Sometimes the idealism was genuine—the Arab Swahili slave trade was a great evil that required inter-vention—but philanthropy could mask less admirable motives for expan-sion: the carving out of new markets and the search for minerals.[15]

Among European explorers, Livingstone had not been unusually naive in seeing colonial advances as the way to usher in 'civilization'. In 1858, John Speke had written of the need for concerned and 'protecting [European] governments' to reach out into Africa to prevent the strong—whether African or Arab—from 'exploiting the weak.'[16] Such gentle atti-tudes would have sounded laughably idealistic to the hard-bitten civil servants in the British Colonial Office in the 1890s. But idealistic or not, such views were taken up and developed by the missionaries who went out to Africa, after and as a result of Livingstone's death. The concept of a national mission to elevate other races was convenient moral justification for governments interested in expansive colonial policies for other reasons.

When Livingstone had spoken of his nation's mission to 'civilize' the underdeveloped nations of the world, Britain's industrial and naval supremacy had seemed unchallengeable. After Livingstone's death it was soon clear that other potentially stronger nations were yearly cutting back the industrial lead. Livingstone's ideas for African development had been straightforward: commerce mattered primarily as the servant of Christianity; British rule only as the prelude to a Christian society. For later imperialists the philanthropic and religious slant given by missionaries to the idea of Empire could work as a convenient cover for the exploitation of diamonds, gold and copper. With Germany, America and Russia growing stronger, it was hoped that a cohesive and centrally dominated Empire would enable Britain to maintain her supremacy and counter the expanding powers of larger nations. This had never been part of Livingstone's plan. Mutual benefit, the spread of Christianity, and the 'diffusion of better principles' had been his concern when thinking of colonies, not the domination of vast areas for power and prestige.

The realities of the 1890s would have confronted Livingstone with the many paradoxes in his own thinking and would have forced him to a revi-sion of many ideas. He had advocated British rule and settlement but had never specified how the potential rulers and settlers should be chosen, nor had he given any thought to the problems that would have to be overcome before a just multiracial society could exist. With British rule, he had assumed that Christianity would come, and with Christianity in the ascendant there could be no injustice. It was the old optimism again, an optimism which all his previous experience of settlers should have led him to mistrust.

What Livingstone would have made of Africa today is a matter for speculation, but several facts are certain. He would have been grieved that

Britain's investment in the people of her African colonies was never generous, or even adequate, before the coming of independence, and that the industrial society which he extolled had not brought prosperity to Africa. He would have been appalled by the long war in southern Sudan and all other ethnic wars in Africa resulting from badly positioned colonial borders. He would have been astonished to learn that the decadent Portuguese had narrowly outstayed the British, and depressed that the descendants of the Boers, whom he had despised for what he called 'their stupid prejudice against colour',[17] had taken over the Government of South Africa and maintained the old racism until the mid-1990s. It seems certain that while Livingstone would have regretted the modest extent of the progress made in the former British colonies before independence, he would have applauded Britain's withdrawal from Africa in the middle of the twentieth century. In 1852 he had written with remarkable foresight:

> With colonies it is the same as with children—they receive protection for a time and obey from a feeling of weakness and attachment; but beyond the time at which they require a right to think for themselves, the attempt to perpetuate subordination necessarily engenders a hatred which effectually extinguishes the feeble gratitude that man in any condition is capable of cherishing.[18]

Undoubtedly Livingstone's greatest sorrow would have been that Africa is not yet the earthly paradise he had believed it might one day become.

The Date of the Stanley–Livingstone Meeting

I.C. Cunningham in Appendix 6 of the National Library of Scotland's publication *David Livingstone: A Catalogue of Documents* (Edinburgh 1985) attempted to examine all the evidence and establish a reliable date for the meeting. The problem is that Livingstone lost count of the days of the month long before they met, and Stanley thought he had briefly lost count too. (When attacks of fever could last several weeks and be accompanied by lapses into unconsciousness, this is entirely understandable.) According to Livingstone's journal (*David Livingstone: a Catalogue of Documents*, National Library of Scotland, 273 no. 11), he discovered, due to the arrival of the Muslim month of Ramadan on 14 February 1871, that his diary entries were twenty-one days ahead of the actual date. (Cunningham advances various reasons—which I will not go into here—for reducing this discrepancy to twenty days.) Livingstone had initially believed that Stanley had reached Ujiji on 16 November, so the change meant that Stanley had arrived on 26 or 27 October, if Livingstone was right about the twenty-one days, and if the Arabs in Ujiji could be relied upon to have started their Ramadan fasting on the correct date. (Stanley had brought with him a *Nautical Almanac* for 1871 which contained the information that Ramadan began on the 14th that year.)

Cunningham plumps for 27 October 1871 as the correct date, and in doing so is much influenced, not only by Livingstone, but by François Bontinck's argument put forward in 'La date de la rencontre Stanley–Livingstone (*Africa, Rivista trimestrale di studi documentazione dell'Istituto Italo-Africano*, xxiv 3 September 1979, 225–45). However, Bontinck was ignorant of much of Livingstone's evidence, and relied heavily on Stanley's despatch to the *New York Herald* dated by the explorer 10 November 1871, in which he stated that, having reflected on the matter, he thought he had arrived at Ujiji on 3 November 1872, rather than the 10th. In *How I found Livingstone* (hereafter H.I.F.L.), pages 274–5, Stanley stated that he had recovered from a prolonged bout of fever and delirium on the real date of 14 July 1871, and on coming round had been told that the date was in fact 21 July. Stanley claimed that he had there and then altered his diary to the new date, thus ensuring that he would think the famous meeting happened a week later than it did. So when Stanley wrote in H.I.F.L. that the meeting took place on 10 November, Bontinck concluded (since Stanley really thought 3 November was the correct date, according to his almost contemporary 10 November despatch to the *New York Herald*) that the explorer had mistakenly added rather than subtracted a week. (By subtracting a week from 3 November he would indeed have arrived at 27 October, the date Bontinck proclaimed to be correct.) But Stanley's date of 3 November for the meeting is clearly itself the result of a subtraction—being a week earlier than Stanley's diary date for the meeting of 10 November, given in his most reliable and earliest diary notebook. To confuse matters further, the claims advanced about dates in Stanley's despatch, supposedly of 10 November, must be considered suspect. He and Livingstone did not discuss their muddle over dates until 14 November (the start of Ramadan).

In H.I.F.L., Stanley claimed he altered his diary, changing 14 July into 21 July. In fact no such alteration was made by him in his notebook diary. (He related on 14 July that he recovered his senses on that day, and remained convalescent in bed till the 25th, when he got up). So what are we to make of this fact, and the fact that he retained the 10 November date both in H.I.F.L., and in the fair copy diary that he wrote up after completing his book? It seems to me that when Livingstone expounded his views about the true date to Stanley after Ramadan started, the younger man, who hero-worshipped the Doctor, felt briefly uncertain of his own ideas about the date. Because Livingstone continued to believe that the meeting had taken place two weeks earlier than 10 November, Stanley seems to have defensively concocted the story of being misinformed by Shaw about the date after coming round from delirium in mid-July. He used this fiction about Shaw to *seem* to move his date closer to Livingstone's, but when it came to fixing the date permanently, both in H.I.F.L. and his copy diary, he reverted to his original notebook diary date, presumably because he believed that it was right. For instance, the date he gives for his final departure from Ujiji with Livingstone is the same in his notebook diary (27 December), in H.I.F.L., page 566, and in his fair copy diary. In all three the meeting is stated to have occurred on 10 November. In L.J.(2) 157 the date of departure for the northern tip of Lake Tanganyika is set by Livingstone as 16 November. Stanley sets the date slightly less exactly as 'about a week or so after my entrance into Ujiji' (H.I.F.L., p. 476). A week after 10 November would have been 16 or 17 November. It could be argued that Stanley stuck to his original date of the 10th because he hated being wrong, but it could also be argued that he stuck to it because he knew it was right and that he had only ever pretended otherwise out of deference to Livingstone.

As to whether Livingstone's calculations were right, I do not believe it will ever be possible to be sure. At intervals between July 1870 and February 1871, while in Manyuema, Livingstone was seriously ill, and he did indeed lose touch with the date. For instance, he mentions Muslim months beginning on 11 June and 10 July 1871 that ought to have begun on 21 May and 20 June, apparently being about twenty days out. (See Cunningham p. 40 note 6.) But Livingstone's confusion about the date on which he arrived at Ujiji, and Stanley's confusion springing from it (Cunningham p. 40 note 4), should alert one to the strong possibility that the twenty- or twenty-one-day discrepancy is by no means a proven quantity. Livingstone in his Field Diary 39 said that he reached Ujiji on 23 October, whereas Stanley gained the impression presumably from Livingstone that he had arrived on 16 October (Stanley to *New York Herald*, 10 November Bennett *Despatches*, p. 59). Stanley in this same despatch said that the meeting took place eighteen days later. Yet on 11 November in Stanley's large copy diary he says that he reached Ujiji 14 (corrected from 10) days after Livingstone had reached it.

In short, in my opinion it is entirely safe to say that Stanley met Livingstone either on a day in late October or during the first half of November 1871. I incline much more strongly towards Stanley's chosen date of 10 November than to Livingstone's late October date—and not only for the reasons given above. I also believe that because Stanley's natural inclination, as Livingstone's honorary son, would have been to support the older man's date, his ultimately preferring his own date is significant.

Sources

⟫◦⟪

MANUSCRIPT

1. BODLEIAN LIBRARY, OXFORD. The Clarendon Papers Dep C So. Letters from David Livingstone and Sir Roderick Murchison to Lord Clarendon concerning the Zambesi Expedition.

2. THE BRITISH LIBRARY, LONDON. Ad. MS. 50184—Eighty-five letters from David Livingstone to members of his family. Also several rough drafts of Foreign Office despatches. Ad. MS. 37410—Letters written to Edmund Gabriel 1854-5. Ad. MS. 38991—Layard Papers. Several letters from Lord John Russell to A. Layard concerning Livingstone's finances in 1865.

3. LIVINGSTONE MEMORIAL, BLANTYRE. (Now the DAVID LIVINGSTONE CENTRE.) Miscellaneous Journals, Diaries and Notebooks, including the originals of the *Last Journals* and a manuscript copy of *Missionary Travels*. Most of the letters formerly at Blantyre have now been deposited in the National Library of Scotland.

4. LIVINGSTONE MUSEUM, ZAMBIA. Miscellaneous letters to friends: James Young, W.C. Oswell, A. Sedgwick, etc. Charles Livingstone's letters to his wife: 1857 to his death.

5. LIVINGSTONE ONLINE. This website displays many Livingstone letters and a spectrally imaged version of the previously indecipherable 1871 Field Diary. The Anglo-American imaging project is the brainchild of academics from U.C.L., U.C.L.A., Birkbeck and other British and American universities.

6. SCHOOL OF ORIENTAL AND AFRICAN STUDIES (LONDON MISSIONARY SOCIETY COLLECTION), LONDON. David Livingstone's Missionary Correspondence 1837–58. (Most of this has been published in *Livingstone's Missionary Correspondence 1841–1816*, ed. I. Schapera, London 1961.) Letters from Livingstone to the L.M.S. concerning the Makololo Mission 1860–2. Miscellaneous letters to friends: D.G. Watt, M. Prentice, H. Drummond. Letters from Mrs Livingstone to the L.M.S. 1852–5. Neil Livingstone's letters to the L.M.S. 1838 and 1853. R. Moffat's letters to the L.M.S. Helmore Papers concerning the Makololo Mission. Lane Papers: letters to E. Gabriel. Moir Papers: miscellaneous.

7. NATIONAL ARCHIVES OF ZIMBABWE, HARARE. The most important letters in this large collection are those written by Livingstone to Sir Thomas Maclear and Sir Roderick Murchison 1855–68. Also miscellaneous letters to Kirk, the Foreign Office, etc. Charles Livingstone: letters to F. Fitch. James Stewart: correspondence. J.T. Baines: private correspondence. R. Thornton: family letters.

8. NATIONAL LIBRARY OF SCOTLAND, EDINBURGH. Wilson Collection: letters from Livingstone to his family. Miscellaneous letters to friends: including Sir Thomas Maclear, Sir Bartle Frere, B. Pyne, Dr Tweedie, H. Dickson, G. Drummond, M.J. Dyke, etc. Various maps, notebooks, journals, including an unpublished private diary for the years 1861–3. Harryhausen Collection of Stanley letters, including several to Livingstone.

9. PRIVATE COLLECTIONS. Harryhausen Collection: family letters, mainly 1860–7. Pyne Collection: letters written by Livingstone from Bechuanaland to B. Pyne.

10. PUBLIC RECORD OFFICE, LONDON. Livingstone's Government Correspondence: F.O. series 2/49B, 63/842, 63/871, 63/894, 84/1249, 84/1265, 97/322, etc. Many of Livingstone's later despatches from 1866 can be found in the *Proceedings of the Royal Geographical Society*; originals of most of these are in the P.R.O.
11. RHODES HOUSE, OXFORD. Waller Papers: eighty-five letters to H. Waller 1862–72. Various letters to John Kirk and miscellaneous letters.
12. ROYAL MUSEUM OF CENTRAL AFRICA, BRUSSELS. Stanley's personal papers, including official and private letters, exploration diaries, notebooks, maps, books, memoranda, etc., etc.
13. WELLCOME MEDICAL LIBRARY, LONDON. Miscellaneous letters.

PUBLISHED WORKS

1. LIVINGSTONE'S BOOKS, JOURNALS, LECTURES AND LETTERS

CHAMBERLIN, D., (ED.), *Some Letters from Livingstone 1840–1872*, London 1940.
FOSKETT, R., *The Zambesi Doctors: David Livingstone's Letters to John Kirk 1858–1872*, Edinburgh 1964.
LIVINGSTONE, D., *Missionary Travels and Researches in South Africa*, London 1857.
LIVINGSTONE, D. and C., *Narrative of an Expedition to the Zambesi and its Tributaries*, London 1865.
MONK, W. (ED.), *Dr Livingstone's Cambridge Lectures*, Cambridge 1858.
SCHAPERA, I. (ED.), *Livingstone's African Journal, 1853–1856*, London 1963, 2 vols.
SCHAPERA, I. (ED.), *Livingstone's Missionary Correspondence 1841–1856*, London 1961.
SCHAPERA, I. (ED.), *Livingstone's Private Journals 1851–1853*, London 1960.
SCHAPERA, I. (ED.), *David Livingstone: Family Letters, 1841–1876*, London 1959, 2 vols.
WALLER, H. (ED.), *The Last Journals of David Livingstone in Central Africa*, London 1874, 2 vols.
WALLIS, J.P.R. (ED.), *The Matabele Mission: A Selection from the Correspondence of John and Emily Moffat, David Livingstone, and Others 1858–1878*, London 1945.
WALLIS, J.P.R. (ED.), *The Zambesi Expedition of David Livingstone 1858–1863*, London 1956, 2 vols.
I have also quoted from letters appearing in: *The Proceedings of the Royal Geographical Society*, vols xii, xiv, xvii, xviii; *The Atlantic Monthly*, July 1922; *The Christian World*, February 1933; *The Congregationalist*, October 1925; *The Cape Town Mail* 26 April 1853.

2. BIOGRAPHIES AND OTHER WORKS

[I have only added to this bibliography books published after 1973 when I have used them directly in the text of this new edition, and when they have provided new and relevant biographical information.]

ADAMSON, W., *Life of Fergus Ferguson*, London 1900.
ANSTRUTHER, I., *I Presume: Stanley's Triumph and Disaster*, London 1956.
BENNETT, N.R. and YLVISAKER M. (EDS), *The Central African Journal of Lovell J. Procter 1860–64*, Boston 1971.
BLAIKIE, W.G., *The Personal Life of David Livingstone*, London 1880.
BRIDGES, ROY *Four Travel Journals* Hakluyt Society Series iii Vol 18 Part Four London 2007.
CAMPBELL, J.R., *Livingstone*, London 1929.
CHADWICK, O., *Mackenzie's Grave*, London 1959.
CHAPMAN, J., *Travels in the Interior of South Africa*, London 1868, 2 vols.
COOLEY, W.D., *Dr Livingstone and the Royal Geographical Society*, London 1874.
COUPLAND, R., *Livingstone's Last Journey*, London 1945.
COUPLAND, R., *Kirk on the Zambesi*, Oxford 1928.

CUMMING, R.G., *Five Years of a Hunter's Life in the Far Interior of South Africa*, London 1850, 2 vols.

DEBENHAM, F., *The Way to Ilala: David Livingstone's Pilgrimage*, London 1955.

DEVEREUX, W.C., *A Cruise in the Gorgon*, London 1869.

DICK, T., *The Christian Philosopher or The Connexion of Science and Philosophy with Religion*, London 1842.

DOLMAN, A., *In the Footsteps of Livingstone*, London 1924.

FLETCHER, R.S., *A History of Oberlin College*, Oberlin 1943.

FORSTER, MARGARET, *Good Wives?*, London 2001.

FOSKETT, R. (ED.), *The Zambesi Journal and Letters of Dr John Kirk 1858–1863* London 1965, 2 vols.

FRAZER, A.Z., *Livingstone and Newstead*, London 1913.

FREEMAN, J.J., *A Tour in South Africa*, London 1851.

GELFAND, M., *Livingstone the Doctor*, Oxford 1957.

GOODWIN, H., *Memoir of Bishop Mackenzie*, Cambridge 1865.

HEALEY, EDNA, *Wives of Fame*, London 1986.

HELLY, DOROTHY O., *Livingstone's Legacy: Horace Waller and Victorian Mythmaking*. Athens, OH, 1987.

HEWART, G., *Curiosities of Glasgow Citizenship*, Glasgow 1881.

JEAL, TIM, *Explorers of the Nile: The Triumph & Tragedy of a Great Victorian Adventure*, London and New Haven, CT, 2011.

JEAL, TIM, *Stanley: The Impossible Life of Africa's Greatest Explorer*, London and New Haven 2007.

JOHNSTON, H.H., *The Story of My Life*, London 1923.

JOHNSTON, H.H., *Livingstone and the Exploration of Central Africa*, London 1891.

LEWIS, E., *Trader Horn*, New York 1927.

LEYLAND, J., *Adventures in the Far Interior of South Africa*, London 1866.

MACKENZIE, J., *Ten Years North of the Orange River*, Edinburgh 1871.

MACNAIR, J.I., *Livingstone the Liberator*, London 1940.

MARTELLI, G., *Livingstone's River*, London 1970.

METHUEN, H.H., *Life in the Wilderness: or, Wanderings in South Africa*, London 1846.

NORTHCOTT, C., *Robert Moffat: Pioneer in Africa 1817–1870*, London 1961.

OSWELL, W.E., *William Cotton Oswell*, London 1900, 2 vols.

PETTITT, C., *Dr Livingstone, I Presume?*, London 2007.

RANSFORD, O.N., *Livingstone's Lake*, London 1966.

ROWLEY, H., *The Story of the Universities' Mission to Central Africa*, London 1866.

SCHAPERA, I. (ED.), *Apprenticeship at Kuruman: Being the Journals and Letters of Robert and Mary Moffat, 1820–1828*, London 1951.

SEAVER, G., *David Livingstone: His Life and Letters*, London 1957.

SHEPPERSON, G., *David Livingstone and the Rovuma*, Edinburgh 1965.

SILLERY, A., *Sechele: The Story of an African Chief*, Oxford 1954.

SIMMONS, J., *Livingstone and Africa*, London 1955.

SLATER, M.I., *Isabella Price, Pioneer*, London 1931.

SMITH, E.W., *Great Lion of Bechuanaland*, London 1951.

SPEKE, J.H., *What Led to the Discovery of the Source of the Nile*, Edinburgh 1863.

STANLEY, D. (ED.), *The Autobiography of Sir Henry Morton Stanley*, London 1909.

STANLEY, H.M., *How I Found Livingstone*, London 1872.

TABLER, E.C. (ED.), *The Zambesi Papers of Richard Thornton*, London 1963, 2 vols.

WADDINGTON, J., *Congregational History*, London 1869–80, 5 vols.

WALLIS, J.P.R. (ED.), *The Matabele Journals of Robert Moffat 1829–1860*, London 1945, 2 vols.

WALLIS, J.P.R. (ED.), *The Zambesi Journal of James Stewart 1862–1863*, London 1952.

WALLIS, J.P.R., *Thomas Baines of King's Lynn*, London 1941.

WRIGHT, S., *Annals of Blantyre*, Glasgow 1885.

YOUNG, E.D., *The Search After Livingstone*, London 1868.

3. GENERAL BACKGROUND

AGAR-HAMILTON, J.A.I., *The Native Policy of the Voortrekkers*, Cape Town 1928.

CAIRNS, H.A.C, *Prelude to Imperialism*, London 1965.

COUPLAND, R., *The British Anti-Slavery Movement*, London 1933.

COUPLAND, R., *East Africa and its Invaders*, Oxford 1956.

COUPLAND, R., *The Exploitation of East Africa 1856–90*, London 1939.

CUST, R.N., *Notes on Missionary Subjects*, London 1889.

DUFFY, J., *Portuguese Africa*, Harvard 1959.

ESCOTT, H., *A History of Scottish Congregationalism*, London 1960.

FAULKNER, H.U., *Chartism and the Churches*, Columbia 1916.

GANN, L.H. and DUIGNAN, P., *Burden of Empire*, London 1968.

GIFFORD, P. and LOUIS, W.R., *Britain and Germany in Africa: Imperial Rivalry and Colonial Rule*, New Haven, CT, 1967.

GLUCKMAN, H.M., 'As Men are Everywhere Else', *The Listener* 22 Sept. 1955.

GLUCKMAN, H.M., *Politics, Law and Ritual in Tribal Society*, Oxford 1965.

GLUCKMAN, H.M. and COLSON, E., *Seven Tribes of British Central Africa*, London 1951.

GROVES, C.P., *The Planting of Christianity in Africa*, London 1948–58, 4 vols.

HAIGHT, M.V.J., *European Powers and South East Africa*, London 1967.

HARRIES, L.P., *Islam in East Africa*, London 1954.

KOEBNER, R. and SCHMIDT, H.D., *Imperialism; The Story and Significance of a Political Word, 1840–1960*, Cambridge 1964.

LOVETT, R., *The History of the London Missionary Society*, London 1899, 2 vols.

LUCAS, W.V. and JAMES, E.O., *Christianity and Native Rites*, London 1950.

OLIVER, R., *The Missionary Factor in East Africa*, London 1952.

OLIVER, R. and MATHEW, G. (EDS), *History of East Africa*, Oxford 1963.

PERHAM, M., *Lugard: The Years of Adventure, 1858–1898*, London 1956.

ROBINSON, R., GALLAGHER, J. and DENNY, A., *Africa and the Victorians*, London 1961.

ROSS, J., *A History of Congregational Independency in Scotland*, London 1900.

SCHAPERA, I., *The Tswana*, London 1953.

THEAL, G. MCC., *History of South Africa*, London 1926–7, vols v–vii (new edn).

WALKER, E.A., *A History of Southern Africa*, London 1957 (3rd edn).

Notes

The principal evidence for the reconstruction of Map 5b is as follows:

(a) A rough sketch map sent by Livingstone to his daughter Agnes with a letter dated 12.12.71 (see plate 23), in B.M. Ad. Ms. 50184.

(b) The map facing page 448 of H.M. Stanley's *How I Found Livingstone*, London 1872. (Livingstone discussed the watershed in detail with Stanley, whose map is based on those conversations.)

(c) Two letters from Livingstone to Kirk, dated 30.5.69 and 14.5.71, respectively (both are published in *The Zambesi Doctors: David Livingstone's Letters to John Kirk 1858–1872*, ed. R. Foskett, Edinburgh 1964).

(d) *The Last Journals of David Livingstone in Central Africa*, ed. H. Waller, London 1874, Vol. 2, 49–50. Also two maps published with the *Last Journals*.

(e) Letter from Livingstone to B. Frere, dated 27.11.70, published in *Proceedings of the Royal Geographical Society*, vol. xviii, 265–6.

ABREVIATIONS USED IN THE NOTES

A.J.	(1) & (2) *Livingstone's African Journal 1853-1856*, ed. I. Schapera, London 1963, 2 vols.
Auto	*The Autobiography of Sir Henry Morton Stanley*, ed. Dorothy Stanley, 1909.
Bennett	*Stanley's Despatches to the New York Herald 1871–77*, ed. Norman R. Bennettt, 2007.
B.L.	Ad. MS British Library Additional Manuscripts.
Blaikie	*The Personal Life of David Livingstone*, W.G. Blaikie, London 1880.
Blantyre/ D.L.C	The Livingstone Memorial, Blantyre, Scotland. Now David Livingstone Centre.
C.D.	Stanley's Congo Diaries, R.M.C.A., Brussels.
Chamberlin	*Some Letters from Livingstone 1840–1872*, ed. D. Chamberlin, London 1940.
D.L.	David Livingstone. I have similarly abbreviated all members of the Livingstone family: e.g. Charles L., Agnes L., etc.
F.L.(1) & (2)	*David Livingstone: Family Letters 1841–1856*, ed. I. Schapera, London 1959, 2 vols.
F.O.	Foreign Office. Livingstone's official government correspondence in the Public Record Office F.O. series.
H.I.F.L.	*How I Found Livingstone*, H.M. Stanley, London 1872.
Kirk	*The Zambesi Journal and Letters of Dr John Kirk 1858-1863*, ed. R. Foskett, London 1965, 2 vols.
L.J.(1) & (2)	*The Last Journals of David Livingstone in Central Africa*, ed. H. Waller, London 1874, 2 vols.
L.M. Zambia	Livingstone Museum, Zambia.
L.M.S./ S.O.A.S.	The London Missionary Society Archive now at S.O.A.S.
L.O.	Livingstone Online Website

M.C.   *Livingstone's Missionary Correspondence 1841–1856*, ed. I. Schapera, London 1961.

M.M.   *The Matabele Mission: A Selection from the Correspondence of John and Emily Moffat, David Livingstone, and others 1818–1878*, ed. J.P.R. Wallis, London 1945.

M.T.   *Missionary Travels and Researches in South Africa*, D. Livingstone, London 1857.

              Narrative Narrative of an Expedition to the Zambesi and its Tributaries, D. and C. Livingstone, London 1865.

N.A.Z.   National Archives of Zimbabwe.

N.L.S.   National Library of Scotland.

P.J.   *Livingstone's Private Journals 1851-1853*, ed. I. Schapera, London 1960.

P.R.G.S.   Proceedings of the Royal Geographical Society.

R.M.C.A.   Royal Museum of Central Africa, Brussels.

S.D.   Stanley's Diaries in R.M.C.A., Brussels.

Seaver   *David Livingstone: His Life and Letters*, G. Seaver, London 1957.

S.J.   *The Zambesi Journal of James Stewart 1862–1863*, ed. J.P.R. Wallis, London 1952.

U.P.J.   Unpublished Private Journal of David Livingstone 1861–3 in National Library of Scotland.

Z.J.(1) & (2) *The Zambesi Expedition of David Livingstone 1858–1863*, ed. J.P.R. Wallis, London 1956, 2 vols.

U.S.J.   Unpublished sections of James Stewart's Journal in the National Archives of Rhodesia.

INTRODUCTION

1. Blaikie 386.

PART ONE: ASPIRATION

I. FACTORY BOY, 1813–1836

1. Notes written by Janet Livingstone *c.* 1880 for Dr Blaikie, N.L.S.
2. *Curiosities of Glasgow Citizenship*, G. Hewart (Glasgow 1881), 112–13.
3. *Parliamentary Papers*. Report of the Minutes of Evidence on the state of Children employed in Manufactories of the United Kingdom. 1816 vol. 3 397.
4. Neil Livingstone's letters, L.M.S./S.O.A.S. Janet Livingstone's notes for Dr Blaikie, N.L.S.
5. *Livingstone and the Exploration of Central Africa*, H.H. Johnston (London 1891), 57.
6. M.M. 42.
7. D.L. to L.M.S. 5.9.37, L.M.S./S.O.A.S.
8. 'Dr Thomas Dick and Dr Livingstone', A.W. Ferguson, *Broughty Ferry Guide*, Feb. 1913; *People's Journal* (Dundee) 7.6.1952.

9. D.L.'s *Essay on the Holy Spirit*, L.M.S./S.O.A.S.

2. MEDICAL STUDIES AND MISSIONARY TRAINING, 1836–1840

1. Neil L. to L.M.S. 26.4.38, L.M.S./S.O.A.S.
2. *Livingstone the Doctor*, M. Gelfand (Oxford 1957), Intro.
3. Answers to Questions, L.M.S./S.O.A.S.
4. Neil L. to L.M.S. 26.4.38, L.M.S./S.O.A.S.
5. R. Cecil to L.M.S. 26.1.39, L.M.S./S.O.A.S.
6. R. Cecil to L.M.S. 25.2.39, L.M.S./S.O.A.S.
7. Blaikie 22.
8. Seaver 27.
9. Blaikie 21.
10. Chamberlin 12.
11. D.L. to Janet L. 5.5.39, N.L.S.
12. D.L. to Janet L. 8.12.41, N.L.S.
13. D.L. to Thomas L. 24.9.69, N.L.S.
14. D.L. to L.M.S. 2.7.39, L.M.S./S.O.A.S.
15. Mrs Moffat to R. Moffat 27.6.40, N.A.Z.

16. Chamberlin 8.
17. D.L. to G. Drummond 25.7.40, N.L.S.
18. Precise definition given by Miss I. Fletcher, former Archivist L.M.S./ S.O.A.S.
19. D.L. to Mrs Neil L. (undated), N.L.S.
20. D.L. to Mrs Neil L. 51.10.54, N.L.S.
21. 'The Niger Expedition', Charles Dickens, *Household Words* 19.8.48.
22. D.L. to T. Prentice 5.3.41, L.M.S./ S.O.A.S.
23. A.J.(2).356.

3. AFRICA AND SOUTH AFRICA, 1841

This general chapter was based on material from:
A History of Southern Africa, E.A. Walker (London 1957), 3rd edn.
Portuguese Africa, J. Duffy (Harvard University Press 1959).
The Planting of Christianity in Africa, C.P. Groves (London 1948–58), 4 vols.
The History of the London Missionary Society, R. Lovett (1899), 2 vols.
History of South Africa, G. McC. Theal (London 1926–7), vols V–VII new edn.
Cambridge History of the British Empire vol. II (1940).

4. EARLY DISAPPOINTMENT: KURUMAN, 1841–1843

1. D.L. to D.G. Watt 7.7.41, L.M.S./ S.O.A.S.
2. D.L. to R. Cecil 13.5.41, *The Congregationalist* Oct. 1925.
3. Ibid.
4. D.L. to D.G. Watt 14.4.42, L.M.S./ S.O.A.S.
5. D.L. to L.M.S. 23.9.41, M.C. 2.
6. D.L. to Mrs McRobert 2.12.41, L.M.S./S.O.A.S.
7. D.L. to D.G. Watt 14.4.42, L.M.S./ S.O.A.S.
8. D.L. to Janet and Agnes L. 30.3.41, F.L.(1).31.
9. D.L. to D.G. Watt 7.2.41, L.M.S./ S.O.A.S.
10. D.L. to Janet L. 8.12.41, F.L.(1).44.
11. D.L. to B. Pyne 22.12.41, Rhodes House.
12. D.L. to Janet L. 8.12.41, F.L.(1).46.

13. D.L. to B. Pyne 22.12.41, Rhodes House.
14. Ibid.
15. D.L. to M. Prentice 8.4.42, L.M.S./ S.O.A.S.
16. D.L. to D.G. Watt 14.4.42, L.M.S./ S.O.A.S.
17. D.L. to Mr and Mrs Neil L. 29.9.41, F.L.(1).40.
18. Blaikie 39.
19. D.L. to L.M.S. 24.6.43, M.C. 36.
20. Ibid.
21. D.L. to D.G. Watt 14.4.42, L.M.S./ S.O.A.S.
22. Ibid.
23. D.L. to G. Drummond 20.6.43, N.L.S.
24. D.L. to Janet L. 21.8.43, F.L.(1).80.
25. D.L. to L.M.S. 30.10.43, M.C. 49.
26. D.L. to D.G. Watt 14.4.42, L.M.S./ S.O.A.S.

5. A FALSE START: MABOTSA, 1844–1845

1. *A Tour in South Africa*, J.J. Freeman (London 1851), 279–80. D.L. to L.M.S. 24.6.43, M.C. 42–3.
2. *The Matabele Journals of Robert Moffat 1829–60*, ed. J.P.R. Wallis (London 1945), 2 vols: (1).29–30.
3. D.L. to L.M.S. 3.7.42, M.C. 18.
4. D.L. to Mr and Mrs Neil L. 14.5.45, F.L.(1).122.
5. D.L. to G. Drummond 21.11.44, N.L.S.
6. D.L. to J.H. Parker 11.5.44, Wellcome Medical Library.
7. Ibid.
8. D.L. to Janet L. 21.5.44, F.L.(1) 101.
9. D.L. to F. Ferguson 23.7.43, N.L.S.
10. D.L. to J. McRobert 24.7.43, L.M.S./S.O.A.S.
11. M.T. 158–9.
12. M.T. 20.
13. P.J. 244.
14. D.L. to Agnes L. 4.4.42, F.L.(1).56–7.
15. D.L. to H. Dickson 8.5.40, N.L.S.
16. D.L. to G. Drummond 20.6.43, N.L.S.
17. A.B. Pyne Private Collection.
18. D.L. to D.G. Watt 27.9.43, L.M.S./ S.O.A.S.
19. D.L. to B. Pyne 22.12.41, Rhodes House.

20. D.L. to B. Pyne 22.6.43, Rhodes House.
21. *Congregational History*, J. Waddington, 4 (London 1880), 89–90.
22. R. Moffat to L.M.S. 24.2.44, L.M.S./S.O.A.S.
23. D.L. to B. Pyne 22.6.43, Rhodes House.
24. D.L. to R. Moffat 15.2.44, F.L.(1).90.
25. D.L. to L.M.S. 2.12.44, M.C. 59.
26. D.L. to D.G. Watt 2.4.45, L.M.S./S.O.A.S.
27. A.B. Pyne Private Collection.
28. D.L. to Mrs Neil L. 14.5.45, F.L.(1).121.
29. D.L. to J.S. Moffat 2.10.58, M.M. 44.
30. D.L. to M.L. Dyke 20.5.47, N.L.S.
31. *Trader Horn*, Ethelreda Lewis (New York 1927), 150.
32. D.L. to D.G. Watt 15.8.45, L.M.S./S.O.A.S.
33. D.L. to D.G. Watt 8.6.46, L.M.S./S.O.A.S.
34. D.L. to D.G. Watt 18.6.43, L.M.S./S.O.A.S.
35. *The Missionary Magazine and Chronicle* vii 50.
36. D.L. to B. Pyne 28.1.45, N.L.S.
37. D.L. to D.G. Watt 15.8.45, L.M.S./S.O.A.S.
38. D.L. to J. Moore 9.8.47, F.L.(1).198n.
39. L.M.S. to D.L. 14.7.52, M.C. 208.
40. D.L. to Miss M. Moffat 12.9.44, F.L.(1).105.
41. D.L. to R. Moffat 1.7.46, F.L.(1).176.
42. D.L. to D.G. Watt 23.5.45, L.M.S./S.O.A.S.
43. Blaikie 62, Macnair, J.I. *Livingstone the Liberator* (London 1940), 91–2.

6. LIVINGSTONE AND THE BOERS: CHONUANE, 1845–1847

1. Blaikie 64.
2. D.L. to A. Murray 10.6.47, Union Archives, Pretoria (copy L.M.S./S.O.A.S.).
3. *Life in the Wilderness: or, Wanderings in South Africa*, H.H. Methuen (London 1846), 198.
4. *Travels in the Interior of South Africa*, J. Chapman (London 1868), 2 vols: (I).113.
5. *Ten Years North of the Orange River*, J. Mackenzie (Edinburgh 1871), 105.

6. D.L. to Mrs McRobert 18.1.46, Wellcome Medical Library.
7. D.L. to R. Moffat 5.9.45, F.L.(1).143.
8. D.L. to R. Moffat 29.9.47, F.L.(1).219.
9. D.L. to Agnes L. 11.11.45, F.L.(1).157.
10. M.T. 9.
11. D.L. to R. Moffat 12.5.45, F.L.(1).118.
12. D.L. to L.M.S. 10.4.46, M.C. 91.
13. D.L. to Neil L. 17.1.46, F.L.(1).161.
14. Ibid.
15. L.M.S. to D.L. 30.12.45, M.C. 85.
16. D.L. to R. Moffat 11.2.46, F.L.(1).165.
17. M.T. 37.
18. *The Native Policy of the Voortrekkers*, J.A.I. Agar-Hamilton (Cape Town 1928), 181.
19. *Cape Town Mail* 26.4.53 (quoted F.L.(1)(2).
20. D.L. to R. Moffat 11.2.46, F.L.(1).170.
21. D.L. to R. Moffat 11.3.46, F.L.(1).171.
22. D.L. to R. Moffat Nov. 1848, F.L.(1).261.
23. Chamberlin 268.
24. D.L. to L.M.S. 17.3.47, M.C. 108.
25. L.M.S. to D.L. 23.12.48, M.C. 124.

7. THE ONLY CONVERT: KOLOBENG, 1847–1849

1. *William Cotton Oswell*, W.E. Oswell (London 1900).
2. D.L. to J.J. Freeman 24.8.50, M.C. 152.
3. Blaikie 71.
4. D.L. to Mr and Mrs Neil L. 5.7.48, F.L.(1).160.
5. D.L. to Neil L. 17.1.46, F.L.(1).160.
6. D.L. to Mrs Neil L. 4.5.47, F.L.(1).199.
7. D.L. to Janet L. 31.1.49, F.L.(2).18.
8. D.L. to Mr and Mrs Neil L. 9.2.51, F.L.(2).122.
9. D.L. to Janet L. 20.4.49, F.L.(2).32.
10. D.L. to L.M.S. 24.6.43, M.C.38.
11. *Robert Moffat: A Pioneer in Africa 1817–1870*, C. Northcott (Lutterworth 1961), 83.
12. D.L. to Mr and Mrs Neil L. 5.7.48, F.L.(1).246.

13. D.L. to R. Moffat 1.7.46, F.L.(1).177.
14. Chamberlin 25.
15. M.T. 21.
16. A.J.(I).57–8.
17. D.L. to R. Moffat 29.9.47, F.L.(1).219.
18. D.L. to D.G. Watt 13.2.48, L.M.S./S.O.A.S.
19. M.T. 18.
20. Fragments of Kolobeng Journal, P.J. 298.
21. Ibid. 299.
22. D.L. to H. Drummond 21.11.48, L.M.S./S.O.A.S.
23. D.L. to R. Moffat Nov. 1848, F.L.(1).261.
24. D.L. to Janet L. 31.1.49, F.L.(2).19.
25. P.J. 304.
26. D.L. to R. Moffat 11.4.49, F.L.(2).30.
27. D.L. to R. Moffat 4.5.49, F.L.(2).43.
28. D.L. to L.M.S. 26.5.49, M.C. 130.
29. M.T. 5.
30. A.J.(1).61.
31. Ibid. 157.
32. Ibid.
33. D.L. to L.M.S. 17.3–47, M.C. 108.

PART TWO: ACHIEVEMENT

8. NORTH TO THE ZAMBESI, 1849–1851

1. D.L. to L.M.S. 3.9.49, M.C. 134.
2. Ibid. 133.
3. D.L. to R. Moffat 8.7.50, F.L.(2).83–5.
4. Ibid.
5. Ibid.
6. Ibid.
7. Seaver 129.
8. D.L. to R. Moffat 24.8.50, F.L.(2). 101–2.
9. P.J. 70–1.
10. D.L. to L.M.S. 3.6.51, M.C. 151.
11. M.T. 79.
12. P.J. 13.
13. Ibid. 16.
14. D.L. to Charles L. 8.10.51, *Atlantic Monthly* 1922 (July).
15. A.J.(2).320–1.
16. P.J. 210.
17. A.J.(1).157.
18. A.J.(2).432–43.
19. P.J. 167–8.
20. A.J.(1).234.
21. P.J. 282.

22. D.L. to L.M.S. 17.10.51, M.C. 190.
23. D.L. to W. Thompson 27.9.55, M.C. 286.
24. D.L. to L.M.S. 17.10.51, M.C. 190.
25. D.L. to R. Moffat 8.7.50, F.L.(2).85.
26. D.L. to J.J. Freeman 9.1.50, M.C. 42.
27. D.L. to L.M.S. 17.10.51, M.C. 189.
28. D.L. to Mr and Mrs Neil L. 30.9.53, F.L.(2).228.
29. M.C. xxii.

9. RETURN TO LINYANTI, 1852–1853

1. D.L. to W. Thompson 6.9.52, M.C. 215.
2. D.L. to Children Feb 1853, F.L.(2).206; D.L. to Charles L. 8.10.51, *Atlantic Monthly* 1922 (July); D.L. to Mary L. 5.5.52 FL (2).
3. D.L. to R. Moffat 2.4.52, F.L.(2).172.
4. Neil L. to L.M.S. 25.6.53, L.M.S./S.O.A.S.
5. Mary L. to L.M.S. 19.10.53, L.M.S./S.O.A.S.
6. D.L. to Mary L. 14.1.53, F.L.(2).202.
7. D.L. to Mary L. 27.11.56, F.L.(2).294.
8. D.L. to Children 2.10.53, F.L.(2).230.
9. D.L. to Children Feb 1853, F.L.(2).206.
10. D.L. to Charles L. 29.5.52, *Atlantic Monthly* 1922 (July).
11. Ibid.
12. D.L. to L.M.S. 26.5.52, M.C. 203.
13. P.J. 90–1.
14. D.L. to Mrs Moffat 26.9.55, F.L.(2).271.
15. M.T. 121; & D.L. to Charles L. 6.2.53, F.L.(2).211.
16. *Matabele Journals of Robert Moffat* (I), 378–9.
17. P.J. 104.
18. Ibid.
19. D.L. to Charles L. 2.6.53, F.L.(2).213.
20. M.T. 10.
21. P.J. 108.
22. Kolobeng Notebook 1850–3, Blantyre.
23. P.J. 119.
24. D.L. to W. Thompson 17.9.53, M.C. 241.

10. FROM COAST TO COAST, 1853–1856

1. D.L. to R. Gray 28.11.60, Wellcome Medical Library.

2. M.C. 194, 247, 281.
3. *Travels in the Interior of South Africa*, J. Chapman (London 1868), 1, 171, 289.
4. P.J. 169.
5. Ibid.
6. Ibid. 146.
7. Ibid. 206.
8. Ibid. 223.
9. D.L. to Thompson 17.9.53, M.C. 243.
10. P.J. 228.
11. Ibid. 163.
12. Ibid. 176.
13. D.L. to L.M.S. 24.9.53, M.C. 250.
14. Ibid. 252.
15. P.J. 220.
16. D.L. to L.M.S. 24.9.53, M.C. 250.
17. Ibid. 250–1.
18. *Dr Livingstone and the Royal Geographical Society*, W.D. Cooley (London 1874), 7–8.
19. M.T. 229.
20. Ibid. 230.
21. A.J.(1).4.
22. M.T. 243–4.
23. Ibid. 250–1.
24. A.J.(1). 7.
25. M.T. 212.
26. A.J.(1).5.
27. Ibid. 51.
28. M.T. 279.
29. Ibid. 281–2.
30. A.J.(1).51–2.
31. Ibid. 52.
32. M.T. 301.
33. A.J.(1).56.
34. M.T. 298.
35. A.J.(1).81.
36. M.T. 239–42.
37. A.J.(1).114.
38. D.L. to L.M.S. 14.1.55, M.C. 270.
39. D.L. to Thompson 13.9.55, M.C. 279, 281.
40. M.T. 392.
41. D.L. to Charles L. 8.11.54, F.L.(2).256.
42. A.J.(1).151.
43. A.J.(1).225–6.
44. M.T. 357.
45. A.J.(2).304.
46. M.T. 441.
47. Ibid.
48. A.J.(2).243.
49. See note 3 above.
50. M.T. 492.
51. A.J.(2).331.
52. D.L. to L.M.S. 12.10.55, M.C. 294.
53. A.J.(2).326.
54. Ibid. 346.
55. M.T. 551–2.
56. A.J.(2).373.
57. Ibid.
58. Ibid. 374.
59. D.L. to Mr and Mrs Neil L. 30.9.53, F.L.(2).228.
60. M.T. 604.
61. *The Way to Ilala: David Livingstone's Pilgrimage*, F. Debenham (London 1957), 120–1.
62. D.L. to L.M.S. 2.3.56, M.C. 302–3.
63. L.M.S. to D.L. 24.8.55, M.C. 277.
64. *The Times* 8.8.54.

PART THREE: FAME

11. NATIONAL HERO: THE FIRST VISIT HOME, 1856–1858

1. Blaikie 178–9.
2. *London Journal* Dec 1856.
3. Ibid.
4. Blaikie 189.
5. D.L. to G. Adderley 19.5.65, N.L.S.
6. Charles L.: Letters to his wife, L.M. Zambia.
7. Ibid.
8. D.L. to Mary L. 28.8.57, B.L. Ad. MS. 50184.
9. D.L. to Robert L. 31.5.59, L.M.S.; *Good Wives* Margaret Forster 60–1; *Wives of Fame* Edna Healey 50–1.
10. D.L. to E. Gabriel 4.4.56, Lane Papers L.M.S./S.O.A.S.
11. D.L. to Mr and Mrs Neil L. 30.9.53, F.L.(2).228.
12. D.L. to R. Murchison 5.8.56, Z.J.(1). xviii.
13. R. Murchison to Lord Clarendon 5.1.57, Clarendon Papers Bodleian Dep C 80.
14. Charles L.: Letters to his wife, L.M, Zambia.
15. D.L. to J.S. Moffat 15.10.59, M.M. 85.
16. L.M.S. Board Minutes.
17. Ibid.
18. *Great Lion of Bechuanaland*, E. Smith (London 1957), 24, 28.

19. L.M.S. Board Minutes (quoted M.C. xxiii).
20. D.L. to R. Murchison 22.12.56, Z.J.(1).xxii.
21. D.L. to R. Murchison 15.4.57, Z.J.(1) xxiii–iv.
22. D.L. to R. Murchison 26.1.57, Clarendon Papers Bodleian Dep C 80 224ff.
23. D.L. to T. Maclear 13.5.57, Z.J.(1). xxiv.
24. Charles L. to wife 5.5.57, L.M. Zambia.
25. D.L. to Lord Clarendon 14.3.57, Clarendon Papers Bodleian Dep C 80.
26. L.M.S. to R. Moffat 4.4.57, L.M.S./ S.O.A.S.
27. Board Minutes L.M.S. (quoted M.C. xxv).
28. D.L. to L.M.S. 22.2.58, L.M.S./ S.O.A.S.
29. D.L. to L.M.S. 6.3.58, L.M.S./ S.O.A.S.

12. THE PRICE OF OPTIMISM: THE MAKOLOLO MISSION, 1857–1860

1. D.L. to L.M.S. 12.10.55, M.C. 293–4.
2. D.L. to L.M.S. 24.9.53, M.C. 253.
3. D.L. to L.M.S. 12.10.55, M.C. 302.
4. R. Moffat to L.M.S. 19.4.58, L.M.S./S.O.A.S.
5. Ibid.
6. Ten Years North of the Orange River, J. Mackenzie (Edinburgh 1871), 39.
7. D.L. to L.M.S. 6.3.58, L.M.S./ S.O.A.S.
8. Mrs Helmore to O. Helmore 24.11.59, Helmore Papers L.M.S./ S.O.A.S.
9. D.L. to L.M.S. 10.11.60, L.M.S./ S.O.A.S.
10. D.L. to L.M.S. 25.2.62, L.M.S./ S.O.A.S.
11. D.L. to J.S. Moffat 24.11.61, M.M. 160.
12. D.L. to Janet L. 1.1.62, N.L.S.
13. Narrative 300.
14. D.L. to Agnes L. 30.11.60, N.L.S.
15. J. Mackenzie to L.M.S. 3.10.59, L.M.S./S.O.A.S.
16. Charles L. to F. Fitch 8.8.62, N.A.Z.

13. HER MAJESTY'S CONSUL

1. R. Murchison to Lord Clarendon 15.5.57, Clarendon Papers Bodleian Dep C 80.
2. The Way to Ilala, 129–30.
3. Z.J.(2).416.
4. Narrative 8.
5. M.T. 679.
6. D.L. to Lord Clarendon 19.3.57, Clarendon Papers Bodleian Dep C 80.
7. D.L. to Lord Clarendon 1.12.57, F.O. 63/842.
8. See note 2 above.
9. Livingstone's River, G. Martelli (London 1970), 37.
10. Kirk on the Zambesi, R. Coupland (London 1928), 92–3.
11. Ibid. 90–1.

PART FOUR: REVERSAL

14. THE ZAMBESI EXPEDITION SETS SAIL

1. Copy of Indenture dated 19.12.57, N.A.Z.
2. Z.J.(1).3.
3. Seaver 303.
4. Charles L.: Letters to his wife. L.M. Zambia.
5. Kirk on the Zambesi 105.
6. Ibid. 106.
7. D.L. to M. Elwin 22.3.58, Wellcome Medical Library.

15. THE ROCKS IN GOD'S HIGHWAY, 1858

1. Z.J.(1).6.
2. Z.J.(1).12.
3. N. Bedingfeld to D.L. 11.6.58, Z.J.(1).13.
4. D.L. to N. Bedingfeld 28.6.58, Z.J.(1).18.
5. N. Bedingfeld to D.L. 30.6.5 8, Z.J.(1).22–4.
6. D.L. to F. Fitch 28.10.59, N.A.Z.
7. Z.J.(1).37.
8. D.L. to T. Maclear 31.7.59, N.A.Z.
9. Kirk 47.
10. Ibid.
11. Ibid. 115.
12. Ibid. 121.
13. Z.J.(1).61.
14. Ibid. 63.

15. Ibid.
16. D.L. to J.S. Moffat 2.10.58, M.M. 43.
17. Kirk 128–32.
18. Z.J.(1).68.
19. Kirk 133.
20. *Kirk on the Zambesi* 136.
21. D.L. to T. Maclear 19.12.58, N.A.Z.
22. A.J.(2).409.

16. COLONIAL DREAMS : THE SHIRE AND LAKE NYASSA, 1859–1860

1. Z.J.(1).88.
2. D.L. to Agnes L. 1.6.59, B.L. Ad. MS. 50184.
3. Z.J.(1).125.
4. A.J.(2).409.
5. O.N. Ransford supported Candido's claim in his book *Livingstone's Lake* (London 1966), 52–6.
6. Kirk 153.
7. U.P.J. 87, N.L.S.
8. D.L. to E. Gabriel, Lane Papers L.M.S./S.O.A.S.
9. D.L. to W.C. Oswell 1.11.59, Rhodes House.
10. Kirk 209.
11. Ibid. 408.
12. D.L. to F.O. 15.10.59, Z.J.(2).332–7.
13. F.O. 63/871.
14. Lord John Russell to D.L. 17.4.60, N.A.Z.
15. D.L. to R. Murchison 15.2.59, N.A.Z.
16. D.L. to R. Murchison 8.8.59, N.A.Z.
17. D.L. to Thomas L. 7.1.62, N.L.S.
18. A.J.(2).446.
19. D.L. to R. Murchison 6.11.54, N.A.Z.
20. Seaver 444.
21. Blaikie 190; R. Gray to D.L. 31.3.59, N.A.Z.
22. D.L. to R. Gray 31.10.59, N.A.Z.
23. Kirk 156.
24. *Narrative* 74.
25. Kirk 156.
26. Z.J.(1).84.
27. D.L. to Robert L. 31.5.59, N.L.S.
28. Z.J.(1).85.
29. Z.J.(1).136.
30. Kirk 115, 128.
31. Charles L. to his wife 15.11.58, L.M. Zambia.
32. *Thomas Baines of King's Lynn*, J.P.R. Wallis (London 1941), 161–2.

33. Charles L. to his wife 5.2.59, L.M. Zambia.
34. Z.J.(1).xi.
35. Kirk 210.
36. Z.J.(1).59.
37. Charles L. to his wife 30.7.59, L.M. Zambia.
38. D.L. to T. Maclear 31.7.59, N.A.Z.
39. O. Thornton to R. Thornton 1.12.59, N.A.Z.; H. Thornton to R. Thornton 1.12.59, N.A.Z.
40. Charles L. to his wife 28.11.59, L.M. Zambia.
41. Kirk 264.
42. Seaver 355–6.
43. D.L. to W.C. Oswell 1.11.59, Rhodes House.
44. Z.J.(1).134.
45. Kirk 220.
46. Charles L. to F. Fitch 4.12,60, N.A.Z.
47. Z.J.(1).163–4.
48. Z.J.(1).169.
49. Kirk 307.
50. Ibid.
51. Ibid. 310.
52. Z.J.(2).252.
53. D.L. to Secretaries of *U.M.C.A.* 29.11.60, N.A.Z.
54. D.L. to Bishop of Oxford Nov 1860, *Congregational History*, J. Waddington, vol. 4, 449.
55. *Mackenzie's Grave*, O. Chadwick (London 1959), 20.

17. DEATH OF A FIGHTING BISHOP

1. *The Universities' Mission to Central Africa* (hereafter *U.M.C.A.*), H. Rowley (London 1866), 5.
2. F.O. 63/894.
3. *Congregational History*, vol. 4, 451.
4. F.O. 63/871.
5. *U.M.C.A.*, 42.
6. *Kirk on the Zambesi* 191.
7. Charles L. to his wife 11.2.61, L.M. Zambia.
8. *Congregational History*, vol. 4, 451.
9. *Mackenzie's Grave* 48.
10. Ibid. 49; *Narrative* 36; Z.J.(1).184; Kirk 358.
11. *Mackenzie's Grave* 51.
12. D.L. to Agnes L. 25.11.61, B.L. Ad. MS. 50184.

13. U.P.J. 6, N.L.S.
14. Ibid.
15. N. R. Bennett and M. Ylvisaker (eds.), *The Central African Journal of Lovell J. Procter 1860–64* (Boston 1971).
16. D.L. to J.S. Moffat 23.2.62, M.M. 164.
17. *U.M.C.A.*, 193.
18. *Kirk on the Zambesi* 217.
19. *Congregational History*, vol. 4, 460.
20. *Mackenzie's Grave* 104.
21. *U.M.C.A.*, 316.
22. U.P.J. 23, N.L.S.
23. Kirk 419.
24. Mary L. to Mrs F. Fitch 13.7.61, N.A.Z.
25. *U.M.C.A.*, 322.
26. *A Cruise in the Gorgon*, W. C. Devereux (London 1869), 166–7.
27. Ibid. 164–5.
28. Ibid, 219.
29. Kirk 415.
30. J. Kirk to A. Kirk 25.7.62.
31. U.S.J. 1.12.61 N.A.Z.
32. Ibid. Jan. 1861.
33. Charles L. to F. Fitch 16.3.62, N.A.Z.
34. Charles L. to Mrs Fitch 9.1.62, N.A.Z.
35. Charles L. to his wife 28.2.62, L.M. Zambia.
36. U.P.J. 41, N.L.S.
37. *Mackenzie's Grave* 123.
38. S.J. 12.
39. Kirk 419.
40. Blaikie 248.
41. D.L. to J.S. Moffat 3.3.62, M.M. 170.
42. S.J. 208.
43. *Congregational History*, vol. 4, 459.
44. D.L. to Rowley 15.3.62, *Christian World* 2.2.1933.
45. D.L. to H. Waller 12.2.63, Blantyre.

18. DISASTER AND COLLAPSE:
THE END OF THE ZAMBESI EXPEDITION,
1862–1864

1. D.L. to Agnes L. 28.4.62, Harryhausen Private Collection.
2. Kirk 439.
3. Blaikie 251–2.
4. D.L. to Mrs Neil L. 29.4.62, Harryhausen Private Collection.
5. U.P.J. 42, N.L.S.
6. Ibid. 45.

7. D.L. to Mrs Neil L. 29.4.62, Harryhausen Private Collection.
8. U.P.J. 45, N.L.S.
9. D.L. to Oswell L. 28.4.62, L.M.S./S.O.A.S.
10. U.P.J. 43.
11. S.J. 62.
12. D.L. to Mrs Neil L. 29.4.62, Harryhausen Private Collection.
13. S.J. 59.
14. U.P.J. 48, N.L.S.
15. L.M.S. to D.L. 9.10.62, L.M.S./S.O.A.S.
16. Kirk 463.
17. Ibid. 475.
18. D.L. to R. Moffat 25.10.62, B.L. Ad. MS 50184.
19. *Scottish Historical Review* xxxix (1960), 121.
20. Kirk 482.
21. U.P.J. 10.1.63, N.L.S.
22. Ibid. 2.11.62.
23. Charles L. to F. Fitch 27.1.63, N.A.Z.
24. S.J. 321.
25. Ibid. 220.
26. U.P.J. 172, N.L.S.
27. *U.M.C.A.*, 286.
28. D.L. to Agnes L. Sept 1869, B.L. Ad. MS 50184.
29. Kirk 482.
30. U.P.J. 168, N.L.S.
31. S.J. 228.
32. U.P.J. 178, N.L.S.
33. D.L. to Lord John Russell 28.4.63, U.P.J. 189, N.L.S.
34. D.L. to H. Waller 24.4.63, Rhodes House.
35. D.L. to Agnes L. 8.7.63, B.L. Ad. MS 50184.
36. D.L. to T. Maclear 5.11.63, N.A.Z.
37. D.L. to R. Moffat 10.8.63, B.L. Ad. MS 50184.
38. *Dr Livingstone's Cambridge Lectures*, W. Monk (Cambridge 1860), 352.
39. D.L. to J.S. Moffat 12.12.63, M.M. 225–6.
40. *Mackenzie's Grave* 221.
41. D.L. to Bishop Tozer 19.12.63, N.A.Z.
42. D.L. to J.S. Moffat 12.12.63, M.M. 226.
43. *Narrative* 579.
44. D.L. to F.O. 12.12.63, U.P.J. 231 N.L.S.
45. D.L. to Agnes L. 10.8.63, B.L. Ad. MS 50184.

46. S.J. 227.
47. D.L. to F.O. 22.2.62, N.A.Z.
48. Blaikie 279.
49. D.L. to Maclear 26.2.64, N.A.Z.
50. Seaver 442.
51. Blaikie 264.
52. Charles L. to his wife 2.11.63, L.M. Zambia.

PART FIVE: REJECTION

19. THE LAST VISIT HOME, 1864–1865

1. F.O. 97/322.
2. D.L. to Agnes L. 25.7.64, B.L. Ad. MS 50184.
3. S.J. 231.
4. D.L. to Agnes L. 25.7.64, B.L. Ad. MS 50184.
5. D.L. to J. Kirk 8.8.63 (copy of letter supplied by G.L. Guy Esq., Dullstroom, South Africa).
6. D.L. to Thomas L. June 1864, Moir Papers L.M.S./S.O.A.S.
7. D.L. to T. Maclear 5.11.63, N.A.Z.
8. Robert L. to D.L. undated, N.A.Z. (quoted Seaver 454).
9. D.L. to Thomas L. June 1864, Moir Papers L.M.S./S.O.A.S.
10. *Livingstone the Liberator*, J.I. Macnair (London 1940), 282.
11. D.L. to Agnes L. Sept. 1869, B.L. Ad. MS 50184.
12. Ibid.
13. *City Island and Coast*, R. Burton (London 1872), (2), 101–3.
14. *Prelude to Imperialism*, H.A.C. Cairns (London 1965), 206.
15. D.L. to L.M.S. 25.5.65, L.M.S./ S.O.A.S.
16. D.L. to R. Murchison 29.11.65, N.A.Z.
17. *The. Way to Ilala* 293–4.
18. D.L. to Agnes L. Sept. 1869, B.L. Ad. MS 50184.
19. D.L. to B. Braithwaite Nov 1870, L.M.S./S.O.A.S.
20. Lord John Russell to D.L. 28.3.65, F.O. 84/1249.
21. Omitted by H. Waller from L.J.(2).72.
22. D.L. to B. Braithwaite Nov 1870, L.M.S./S.O.A.S.
23. Lord John Russell to A. Layard 25.3.65, B.L. Ad. MS 38991.
24. Lord John Russell to Murray 26.4.65, F.O. 84/1249.

25. D.L. to Lord John Russell 23.5.65, F.O. 84/1249.
26. D.L. to B. Braithwaite Nov 1870, L.M.S./S.O.A.S.

PART SIX: ATONEMENT

20. NYASSA TO TANGANYIKA, 1866–1869

1. *Livingstone's Last Journey*, R. Coupland (London 1947), 15.
2. Seaver 470.
3. *The Zambesi Doctors*, R. Foskett (Edinburgh 1964), 109.
4. L.J.(1).13–14.
5. This information about Susi supplied by D.H. Simpson Esq., Librarian, Royal Commonwealth Society.
6. *East Africa and its Invaders*, R. Coupland (Oxford 1956), 325.
7. D.L. to Agnes L. 29.1.66, Harryhausen Private Collection.
8. L.J.(1).7.
9. D.L. to R. Murchison 27.11.65, N.A.Z.
10. L.J.(1).23.
11. Ibid. 29.
12. D.L. to Agnes L. 18.5.66, B.L. Ad. MS 50184.
13. L.J.(1).70.
14. Ibid. 58.
15. Ibid. 56.
16. Ibid. 62–3.
17. D.L. to Lord Clarendon 20.8.66, F.O. 84/1265.
18. D.L. to Lord Clarendon 11.6.66, F.O. 84/1265.
19. D.L. to Thomas L. 28.8.66, N.L.S.
20. D.L. to R. Murchison 18.12.67, N.A.Z.
21. D.L. to Thomas L. 28.8.66, N.L.S.
22. Seaver 493.
23. L.J.(1).15.
24. Ibid. 141.
25. Ibid. 168.
26. Ibid. 170.
27. *The Way to Ilala* 235.
28. L.J.(1).173–6.
29. *Livingstone's Last Journey* 55.
30. D.L. to Seward 1.2.67, P.R.G.S. xii 180.
31. L.J.(1).205.
32. *The Way to Ilala* 243.
33. D.L. to R. Murchison 18.12.67, N.A.Z.
34. L.J.(1).287.

35. D.L. to R. Murchison 18.12.67, N.A.Z.
36. L.J.(1).288.
37. D.L. to Lord Clarendon 8.7.68, P.R.G.S. xiv 8–9.
38. D.L. to J. Kirk 8.7.68, P.R.G.S. xiv 8.
39. L.J.(1).309.
40. *The Way to Ilala* 256.
41. L.J.(I).346.
42. L.J.(2).2.
43. D.L. to Agnes L. 4.7.68, B.L. Ad. MS 50184.
44. D.L. to A. Sedgwick 24.8.66, Rhodes House.

21. FANTASY IN MANYUEMA, 1869–1871

1. L.J.(2).11.
2. Ibid. 14.
3. *Zambesi Doctors* 138.
4. L.J.(2).47–8.
5. D.L. to Agnes L. 5.2.71, B.L. Ad. MS 50184.
6. D.L. to Thomas L. 24.9.69, N.L.S.
7. D.L. to Agnes L. 5.2.71, B.L. Ad. MS 50184.
8. Blaikie 334; L.J.(2).93.
9. Ibid. 59.
10. Ibid. 72.
11. U.P.J. 11, N.L.S.
12. D.L. to Agnes L. 5.2.71, B.L. Ad. MS. 50184.
13. Herodotus *History* Book 2.
14. L.J.(2).49–50.
15. D.L. to T. Maclear Nov 1870, P.R.G.S. xvii 68.
16. D.L. to B. Frere 27.11.70, P.R.G.S. xviii 265–6.
17. D.L. to Agnes L. Sept 1869, B.L. Ad. MS 50184.
18. Unyanyembe Journal 11.02.11, 11.03.71 Blantyre/D.L.C.; Helly 172–3; Unyanyembe Journal 13.06.70; L.J.(2).99, 124.
19. 1871 Field Diary 28 March, 16, 17 May L.O.; Unyanyembe Diary 30 May 1871; Field Diary 1 July 1871 L.O.
20. 1871 Field Diary 13 June, 15–17 July L.O.; Unyanyembe Journal 11 March, 4, 15–17 July 1871 Blantyre/D.L.C.; L.J.(2).133–6.
21. L.J. (2).154.

22. L.J. (2).155; D.L. to T. Maclear & Mr Mann P.R.G.S. Vol. XVII 17 Nov 1871, 172–3, 67–73.
23. H.I.F.L. 405–12.

22. STANLEY AND THE LIVINGSTONE MYTH

1. H.I.F.L. xvii–xviii (intro).
2. Jeal *Stanley* 65–6; Bennett 51; viz *The Times* 17.12.66, report for *New York Herald* 28.08.72; Finley Anderson to Stanley 3.01.67 R.M.C.A.; *Stanley* Richard Hall (1974) 148.
3. Jeal *Stanley* 85–7; Stanley to Bennett 17.01.71 R.M.C.A.; S.D. 28.10.71 R.M.C.A.; H.I.F.L. xviii; Levien to Stanley 29.11.69 R.M.C.A.
4. Jeal *Stanley* 91–3; H.I.F.L. 68; Stanley to Bennett 17.01.1871. R.M.C.A.; S.D. 21, 25.02.1871 R.M.C.A.
5. 'Stanley: The Mystery of the Three Fathers' Emyr Wyn Jones 127–51 *National Library of Wales Journal* 1993 Vol. 28 127–51; 'Stanley's Father I Presume?' Bob Owen *Hel Achau* 1985 No. 15 23–7.
6. William Henry Stanley Compiled Service Record card no. 46045291 26 July 1861 National Archives USA; Jeal *Stanley* 40.
7. Jeal *Stanley* Chapters Three and Four.
8. Jeal *Stanley* 63–6 and associated notes; Stanley to Noe 25.12.66 R.M.C.A.; *South Wales Daily News* 12.05.1904 'Morien' Morgan's notes of interview with Elizabeth Parry 1886 Cardiff Public Library; Bennett 415; Noe to ed. *New York Sun* 16.05.72.
9. Jeal *Stanley* 96–7.
10. P.R.G.S. vol. xvi 1871–2 415.
11. S.D. 31.12.71 R.M.C.A.
12. H.I.F.L. 27; S.D. 21.11.70.
13. Jeal *Stanley* 98.
14. Ibid. 98–9.
15. H.I.F.L. 697; Stanley to ed. *Times* 13.11.72.
16. Bennett 14–15.
17. H.I.F.L. 73.
18. Ibid. 262.
19. Bennett 19.
20. H.I.F.L. 157.
21. T. Griffiths-Jones, 'W.L. Farquhar's Grave', *Tanganyika Notes & Records* no. 5 1948 28–33.
22. H.I.F.L. 66–7.

23. Ibid. 160.
24. Bennett 20–1.
25. H.I.F.L. 264.
26. S.D. 20 June, 18 May 71.
27. Bennett 22.
28. Jeal *Stanley* see note 27 503.
29. H.I.F.L. 268; S.D. 23.08.71.
30. S.D. 28.07.71; H.I.F.L. 279.
31. Auto 257.
32. Bennett 45–7.
33. H.I.F.L. 303, 313; S.D. 22.08.71.
34. S.D. 23, 24 Aug 71.
35. H.I.F.L. 411.
36. S.D. 20.09.71.
37. H.I.F.L. 325–7.
38. Ibid. 403–4.
39. Ibid. 405.
40. See Appendix: The Date of the Stanley-Livingstone Meeting.
41. Stanley *The Autobiography of Sir Henry Morton Stanley*, ed. D. Stanley (London 1909), 264 (Auto).
42. H.I.F.L. 411.
43. Bennett 89; H.I.F.L. 409–10.
44. Ibid. 410–12; S.D. 3.11.71.
45. H.I.F.L. 411.
46. Ibid. 560–1.
47. S.D. 11.11.71.
48. H.I.F.L. 416.
49. Bennett 95–6.
50. L.J.(2).156.
51. S.D. 11.11.71; H.I.F.L. 424.
52. D.L. to W. Thompson Nov 72 L.M.S./S.O.A.S.
53. D.L. to Agnes L. 18.11.71 B.L.
54. H.I.F.L. 416.
55. Bennett 95.
56. Ibid. 97.
57. H.I.F.L. 234.
58. Ibid. 432; S.D. 16.11.71.
59. S.D. 4.03.72, 5.01.70.
60. Bennett 95.
61. H.I.F.L. 416.
62. Bennett 96.
63. *Livingstone's Last Journey* 213 n.
64. 'A Memorial to Livingstone' lecture by Stanley 21.04.94 R.M.C.A.
65. S.D. 4.03.72.
66. S.D. 14.02.72.
67. Ibid. 12.11.71.
68. *Livingstone's Last Journey* 171.
69. H.I.F.L. 619.
70. S.D. 16.11.71.
71. Ibid. 28.11.71.
72. DL to Agnes L 23.08.72 B.L.

73. S.D. 8.01.72.
74. S.D. 6, 9.01.72.
75. Ibid. 3.03.72.
76. D.L. to B. Braithwaite 8.01.72 L.M.S./S.O.A.S.
77. D.L. to Dr Wilson 24.01.72 L.M.S./S.O.A.S.
78. D.L. to Agnes L. Feb 72 B.L.
79. Ibid. 16.11.71.
80. Ibid. 12.12.71.
81. R.Murchison to Lord Clarendon 1.04.70 FO2/42B.
82. D.L. to Agnes L. 1.07.72 B.L.
83. S.D. 8.01.72.
84. D.L. to Kirk 30.05.69 *The Zambesi Doctors* 138–9.
85. H.I.F.L. 427.
86. L.J.(2). 157.
87. H.I.F.L. 476, 479; L.J.(2). 157.
88. H.I.F.L. 478–81.
89. S.D. 22.11.71.
90. S.D. 5.03.72.
91. S.D. 27.01.72.
92. D.L. to Bates 20.02.72 N.L.S.
93. S.D. 7.03.72.
94. S.D. 24.02.72.
95. S.D. 6.03.72.
96. S.D. 13.11.71.
97. S.D. 13.03.72.
98. S.D. 14.03.72.
99. Auto 279–80.
100. Stanley to DL 15.03.72 N.L.S.
101. S.D. 16.11.71.
102. *Standard* 6.08.72.
103. *Morning Post* 7.08.72.
104. Blaikie 384–5.

23. THE LAST JOURNEY, 1872–1873

1. D.L. to Agnes L. 1.7.72, B.L. Ad. MS 50184.
2. D.L. to John Livingstone Dec 1872, Private Collection of the late Mr Quentin Keynes.
3. D.L. to Agnes L. 2.6.72, B.L. Ad. MS 50184.
4. L.J.(2).211–12.
5. D.L. to B. Braithwaite 8.1.72, L.M.S./S.O.A.S.
6. D.L. to Dr Wilson 24.1.72, N.L.S.
7. L.J.(2).182.
8. Ibid. 174.
9. D.L. to H. Waller 19.2.72, Rhodes House.
10. D.L. to H. Waller 2.9.72, Rhodes House.

11. Seaver 620.
12. D.L. to Earl Granville 1872 (otherwise undated), B.L. Ad. MS 50184.
13. L.J.(2).188, 193–4.
14. D.L. to B. Braithwaite Dec. 1870, P.R.G.S. xviii 278.
15. L.J.(2).229.
16. H.M. Stanley to D.L. 23.5.72, N.L.S.
17. H.M. Stanley to D.L. 27.5.72, N.L.S.
18. D.L. to Agnes L. 23.8.72, B.L. Ad. MS 50184.
19. *The Way to Ilala* 197–517.
20. L.J.(2).269.
21. Ibid. 277.
22. Ibid. 42.
23. *The Way to Ilala* 272.
24. L.J.(2).288.
25. Ibid. 294.
26. Ibid. 298.
27. D.L. to Earl Granville 20.2.72, B.L. Ad. MS 50184.
28. L.J.(2).303.
29. Ibid. 299–308; *Four Travel Journals*: 'Jacob Wainwright's Diary of the Transportation of Dr Livingstone's Body to the Coast 4 May 1877–18 February 1874' ed. Roy Bridges Hakluyt Society (2007) n 2 p. 361.
30. Ibid. n 6 p. 361, also n 2 p 363 'After the burial we sat down and cried.' Wainwright to Moore Acc 12444 N.L.S.
31. Ibid. 335 where Bridges argues that bringing D.L.'s body to the coast was motivated partly by devotion and partly by prudence—their logic being that unless they arrived at the coast with the body they might be accused of having deserted their employer.
32. J. Wainwright to O.L. Oct 1873, L.M.S./S.O.A.S.
33. *Dr Livingstone, I Presume?*, Clare Pettitt (2007) 125.

24. LIVINGSTONE AND THE BRITISH EMPIRE

1. *Glasgow Herald* 20.4.74.
2. D.L. to T. Maclear 26.2.64, N.A.Z.
3. Quoted H.I.F.L. Intro. xxviii, 2nd edn
4. S.J. 190.
5. *The Missionary Factor in East Africa*, R. Oliver (1952) 157.
6. Jeal *Stanley* 238; Stanley to Strauch 8.01.80 R.M.C.A.; *Scottish Geographical Society Magazine* Jan–March 1884; Stanley to Sanford 27.02.79 Sanford Museum.
7. C.D. 9.11.80, 27 no month 80 R.M.C.A.; *Brazza of the Congo*, Richard West (1972) 102–3.
8. *Explorers of the Nile* 355 & n 3–5 487.
9. *Africa and the Victorians*, R. Robinson, J. Gallagher & A. Denny (1961) for the thesis that French resentment of the British assumption of sole power in Egypt led them to seek compensation elsewhere and was an essential driver of the 'Scramble for Africa'.
10. *Britain and Germany in Africa*, P. Gifford and W.R. Louis, see chapter by Jean Stengers 'King Leopold and Anglo-French Rivalry 1882–84'; also in same vol. R. O. Collins, 'Origins of the Nile Struggle . . .'.
11. *Lugard*, M. Perham 461.
12. Z.J.(2).416.
13. M.T. 679.
14. Seaver 444.
15. *Explorers of the Nile* 386.
16. Ibid. 100–1; *What Led to the Discovery of the Source of the Nile*, J. H. Speke (1863) 367–8.
17. M.T. 29–30.
18. Kolobeng Notebook 1850–3 David Livingstone Centre.

Index

Tabora, 348–9, 360, 366

Tagamoio (Dugumbe's aide), 338

Tanganyika, Lake: undiscovered by Europeans, 90; Burton and Speke discover, 191, 284, 359; as possible source of Nile, 285, 301–2; on Arab slave route, 309, 322; DL reaches, 314, 323; connection with Lake Moero, 315; and lines of drainage, 325–6, 328; altitude, 334; DL and Stanley travel to northern end, 359–60; and DL's final journey, 369–70

Tete: fort established, 26; exploration, 90; on Zambesi, 101; DL aims for, 152, 192; Portuguese settle, 153–5, 315; DL reaches, 154–5, 186; DL denied consular powers in, 194; Zambesi Expedition at, 209–10, 232

Thornton, Helen, 229

Thornton, Octavia, 229

Thornton, Richard: on Zambesi Expedition, 200; recuperates at Tete, 211; visits Kebrabasa, 212; dismissed, 227, 229; poor relations with Charles Livingstone, 227, 232; accused of laziness, 229; death, 266; notes undeciphered, 272n

Tidman, Arthur: and DL's expedition to Ngami, 93–4; and LMS's policy of expansion in Africa, 114, 166–8; and DL's proposals for Makololo mission, 166–7, 172–4, 179; appeal for LMS funds, 172–4; and Makololo Mission tragedy, 180–1, 184; DL writes to condemning Burton, 187; on death of Mary Livingstone, 262

Times, The, 144, 155, 159, 271, 337, 355, 362

Tippu Tip, 315–16

Tozer, William George, Bishop of Nyasaland, 269–70, 281

Transvaal: established, 31; DL aims to missionize in, 71; Boers in, 114

tsetse fly, 95, 222, 369

Uganda: annexed by British, 3, 391, 393–4; missionaries and conflict in, 390–2; war (1892), 392

Ujiji: DL reaches on final expedition, 300, 313, 316–17, 322–3; DL's stores pillaged at, 322, 324, 339; DL in, 324–5; as Arab trading centre, 324; DL returns to from Nyangwe, 339; Stanley meets DL in, 340, 349–51, 397–9

United States of America: religious revival, 13; missionaries in southern Africa, 33; *see also* North America

Universities Mission: arrival in Africa, 225, 231, 234–8; formed, 225; members, 238; travel to interior, 240; first encounters slaving party, 241–2; at Magomero, 243–4; conflict with Ajawa, 243–5; Devereux criticises, 252; and death of Mackenzie and Burrup, 256; threatened withdrawal from Africa, 257; deaths, 265; DL disparages, 356; withdrawn, 386; achievements, 388; returns to east and central Africa, 390

Unyanyembe: DL's corpse reaches, 279; fighting, 339; Kirk sends supplies to, 347; Stanley reaches, 347; DL in, 365–7

Vaal river, 31

Vanderkamp, J., 30

Victoria, Queen, 279, 394

Victoria Falls (Mosioatunya), 148–9

Victoria Nyanza, Lake, 284–6, 360, 390

Vulture, HMS, 380

Wagenya people, 334, 337

Wainwright, Jacob, 378, 380

Waller, Horace, 238, 241–2, 244, 257, 265, 275, 367

Walweitch, Dr, 143

Wangwana people, 346–7, 359

Wardlaw, Dr Ralph, 13, 17

Washington, Captain (*later* Admiral) John, RN, 192–3, 200, 257

Webb, Ethel, 283

Webb, F.R. (US consul in Zanzibar), 343, 345–6, 357

Webb, William, 283

White Fathers (religious order), 390

Wikatani, 298, 310

Wilberforce, Samuel, Bishop of Oxford, 235, 239

Wilberforce, William, 27, 31

Wilkes, Henry, 12

Wilson, Captain (of *Gorgon*), 254

Wilson, J.H., 43, 91, 99

Witwatersrand, 394

Xhosa people, 30

Young, Lieutenant E.D., 267, 271, 345, 389

Young, James ('Paraffin'), 17, 292, 332, 381

LIVINGSTONE

TIM JEAL is also the biographer of Henry Morton Stanley (National Book Critics' Circle Award in Biography and *Sunday Times* Biography of the Year 2007), and Robert Baden-Powell, which (like *Livingstone*) was chosen as a Notable Book of the Year by the *New York Times* and the *Washington Post*. In 2011 his *Explorers of the Nile* was a *New York Times* Editor's Choice and a BBC Radio 4 Book of the Week.

⟹∙◆∙⟸

'Well researched and written, both analytical and intuitive ... An excellent biography.'—Richard West *Sunday Times*

'Jeal's rich telling of this tale seems certain to be the standard biography of both man and myth; it is hard to imagine why anyone need write the story again.'—*Smithsonian*

'Tim Jeal's book draws on a far wider range of published and manuscript material than was available to earlier biographers; it is detailed, painstaking, and mostly detached and should become a standard work.'
—*Times Literary Supplement*

'A big impressive attempt to find the man behind the icon ... It is exciting, complex, sometimes appalling, but very convincing.'
—Edmund Fuller *Wall Street Journal*

'Mr Jeal has succeeded in making Livingstone a more estimable man than ever emerged from the myth ... In cutting one hero down to size, he builds up another – a hero of Conradian stamp and stature.'
—Paul Scott (Booker prize winner)

'An unhaloed portrait of a very great man ... Jeal's biography is first rate, informative, judicious, scholarly.'—Alden Whitman *New York Times*

'Brilliant ... Without detracting from Livingstone's incredible achievements, Mr Jeal describes too his faults and failings in such a way that the myth is destroyed but the man himself is vividly revealed.'
—Graham Lord *Sunday Express*

'A major biography of both the man and the legend he ill-fitted ... An achievement of historical insight and tempered judgment – it should become the standard biography for a long time to come.' —Virginia Kirkus

'There truly has been nothing as riveting on the subject as this book by Tim Jeal. In this hypnotic account of his career, Mr Jeal is particularly good in his description of the clash of cultures ... At last we have the real truth about Dr Livingstone.' —Dillibe Onyeama *Books & Bookmen*

'Writers under thirty so seldom tackle a major work of historical study that it would tax the memory of the oldest observer to think of a parallel case to Jeal's spectacular feat of precocity'—*Newsday*

'A biography the thoroughness of which comes right up to present day high academic standards.'—C.P. Snow *Financial Times*

'Neither advocate nor debunker, using sources made available in the last decade, Jeal has written a fascinating story of the essential man ... one that suggests that celebrity is only one measure, and often a distorting one.'
—Robert Kirsch *Los Angeles Times*

'Jeal is a writer to watch ... and this is a full-scale portrait, superbly and solidly readable.'—John Braine *Daily Express*

'The balance Jeal provides is long overdue. He does what biography should do: brings to life a vivid character without perpetuating the myths that obscure reality.'—Daniel Webster *Philadelphia Inquirer*

'A truly shattering exposure of the hagiographical picture of Livingstone as the great African missionary which Victorian piety left to us.'
—Christopher Hollis *Tablet*

'A superb biography, not to be missed either by armchair explorers or students of human nature. Jeal reveals the famed missionary and explorer as he really was.'—*Cleveland Plain Dealer*

'Tim Jeal brings out Livingstone's deep absorption with Africa and with Africans as people.'—Peter Macdonald *Scotsman*

'Likely to be a standard work.' David Paton *Church Times*

'This brilliant and original biography.'
—Peter Cadogan *Times Educational Supplement*

'A thrilling and in the end moving work ... The Livingstone who emerges is a man of terrifying dimensions.'—*Irish Press*

'It is a leading merit of Tim Jeal's biography, that while fudging none of his faults, he nevertheless leaves us in no doubt of his greatness.'
—C.P. Ravilious *Tribune*

'Brilliantly done; it will be the standard life.'—Michael Hennell *Churchman*

'The central role that Livingstone played in the process of colonization is brought out for the first time in this excellent new biography by Tim Jeal.'
—Philip Whitehead *Listener*

'Mr Jeal has done well with his provocative biography: Livingstone is less of a saint, but more of a man.'—Richard Hall *Observer*